Lecture Notes in Computer Science 6352

Commenced Publication in 1973
Founding and Former Series Editors:
Gerhard Goos, Juris Hartmanis, and Jan van Leeuwen

Konstantinos Diamantaras   Wlodek Duch
Lazaros S. Iliadis (Eds.)

Artificial Neural Networks – ICANN 2010

20th International Conference
Thessaloniki, Greece, September 15-18, 2010
Proceedings, Part I

 Springer

Volume Editors

Konstantinos Diamantaras
TEI of Thessaloniki, Department of Informatics
57400 Sindos, Greece
E-mail: kdiamant@it.teithe.gr

Wlodek Duch
Nicolaus Copernicus University
School of Physics, Astronomy, and Informatics
Department of Informatics
ul. Grudziadzka 5, 87-100 Torun, Poland
E-mail: duch@phys.uni.torun.pl

Lazaros S. Iliadis
Democritus University of Thrace, Department of Forestry
and Management of the Environment and Natural Resources
Pantazidou 193, 68200 Orestiada Thrace, Greece
E-mail: liliadis@fmenr.duth.gr

Library of Congress Control Number: 2010933964

CR Subject Classification (1998): I.2, F.1, I.4, I.5, J.3, H.3

LNCS Sublibrary: SL 1 – Theoretical Computer Science and General Issues

ISSN   0302-9743
ISBN-10   3-642-15818-8 Springer Berlin Heidelberg New York
ISBN-13   978-3-642-15818-6 Springer Berlin Heidelberg New York

springer.com

© Springer-Verlag Berlin Heidelberg 2010
Printed in Germany

Typesetting: Camera-ready by author, data conversion by Scientific Publishing Services, Chennai, India
Printed on acid-free paper   06/3180

Preface

This volume is part of the three-volume proceedings of the 20th International Conference on Artificial Neural Networks (ICANN 2010) that was held in Thessaloniki, Greece during September 15–18, 2010.

ICANN is an annual meeting sponsored by the European Neural Network Society (ENNS) in cooperation with the International Neural Network Society (INNS) and the Japanese Neural Network Society (JNNS). This series of conferences has been held annually since 1991 in Europe, covering the field of neurocomputing, learning systems and other related areas.

As in the past 19 events, ICANN 2010 provided a distinguished, lively and interdisciplinary discussion forum for researches and scientists from around the globe. It offered a good chance to discuss the latest advances of research and also all the developments and applications in the area of Artificial Neural Networks (ANNs). ANNs provide an information processing structure inspired by biological nervous systems and they consist of a large number of highly interconnected processing elements (neurons). Each neuron is a simple processor with a limited computing capacity typically restricted to a rule for combining input signals (utilizing an activation function) in order to calculate the output one. Output signals may be sent to other units along connections known as weights that excite or inhibit the signal being communicated. ANNs have the ability "to learn" by example (a large volume of cases) through several iterations without requiring a priori fixed knowledge of the relationships between process parameters.

The rapid evolution of ANNs during the last decades has resulted in their expansion in various diverse scientific fields, like engineering, computer science, mathematics, artificial intelligence, biology, environmental science, operations research and neuroscience. ANNs perform tasks like pattern recognition, image and signal processing, control, classification and many others.

In 2010 ICANN was organized by the following institutions: Aristotle University of Thessaloniki, University of Macedonia at Thessaloniki, Technological Educational Institute of Thessaloniki, Hellenic International University and Democritus University of Thrace.

The conference was held in the Kapsis Hotel and conference center in Thessaloniki, Greece. The participants were able to enjoy the atmosphere and the cultural heritage of Thessaloniki, which is built by the seaside and has a glorious history of 2300 years.

As a matter of fact, a total of 241 research papers were submitted to the conference for consideration. All of the submissions were peer reviewed by at least two academic referees. The international Program Committee of ICANN 2010 carefully selected 102 submissions (42%) to be accepted as full papers. Additionally 68 papers were selected for short presentation and 29 as posters.

The full papers have up to 10 pages, short ones have up to 6 pages and posters have up to 4 pages in the proceedings.

In addition to the regular papers, the technical program featured four keynote plenary lectures by the following worldwide renowned scholars:

- Prof. Alessandro E.P. Villa: NeuroHeuristic Research Group, Information Science Institute, University of Lausanne, Switzerland and Institut des Neurosciences, Université Joseph Fourier, Grenoble, France. Subject: "Spatiotemporal Firing Patterns and Dynamical Systems in Neural Networks";
- Prof. Stephen Grossberg: Department of Cognitive and Neural Systems, Center for Adaptive Systems, and Center of Excellence for Learning in Education, Science, and Technology, Boston University. Subject: "The Predictive Brain: Autonomous Search, Learning, Recognition, and Navigation in a Changing World";
- Prof. Sergios Theodoridis: Department of Informatics and Telecommunications, National and Kapodistrian University of Athens. Subject: "Adaptive Learning in a World of Projections";
- Prof. Nikola Kasabov: Knowledge Engineering and Discovery Research Institute (KEDRI), Auckland University of Technology. Subject: "Evolving Integrative Spiking Neural Networks: A Computational Intelligence Approach".

Also two tutorials were organized on the following topics:

- Prof. J.G. Taylor: Department of Mathematics, King's College London. Subject: "Attention versus Consciousness: Independent or Conjoined?";
- Dr. Kostas Karpouzis: Image, Video and Multimedia Systems Lab, Institute of Communication and Computer Systems (ICCS/NTUA). Subject: "User Modelling and Machine Learning for Affective and Assistive Computing".

Finally three workshops were organized namely:

- The First Consciousness Versus Attention Workshop (CVA);
- The Intelligent Environmental Monitoring, Modelling and Management Systems for Better QoL Workshop (IEM3);
- The First Self-Organizing Incremental Neural Network Workshop (SOINN).

The ENNS offered 12 travel grants to students who participated actively in the conference by presenting a research paper, and a competition was held between students for the best paper award.

The three-volume proceedings contain research papers covering the following topics: adaptive algorithms and systems, ANN applications, Bayesian ANNs, bio inspired-spiking ANNs, biomedical ANNs, data analysis and pattern recognition, clustering, computational intelligence, computational neuroscience, cryptography algorithms, feature selection/parameter identification and dimensionality reduction, filtering, genetic-evolutionary algorithms, image, video and audio processing, kernel algorithms and support vector machines, learning algorithms and systems, natural language processing, optimization, recurrent ANNs, reinforcement learning, robotics, and self organizing ANNs.

As General Co-chairs and PC Co-chair and in the name of all members of the Steering Committee, we would like to thank all the keynote invited speakers and the tutorial-workshops' organizers as well. Also, thanks are due to all the reviewers and the authors of submitted papers. Moreover, we would like to thank the members of the Organizing Committee headed by Prof. Yannis Manolopoulos and Prof. Ioannis Vlahavas. In particular, we wish to thank Dr. Maria Kontaki for her assistance and support towards the organization of this conference.

Additionally, we would like to thank the members of the Board of the European Neural Network Society for entrusting us with the organization of the conference as well as for their assistance. We wish to give our special thanks to Prof. Wlodzislaw Duch, President of the ENNS, for his invaluable guidance and help all the way.

Finally, we would like to thank Springer for their cooperation in publishing the proceedings in the prestigious series of Lecture Notes in Computer Science. We hope that all of the attendees enjoyed ICANN 2010 and also the conference site in Thessaloniki, both scientifically and socially. We expect that the ideas that have emerged here will result in the production of further innovations for the benefit of science and society.

September 2010

Wlodzislaw Duch
Kostandinos Diamandaras
Lazaros Iliadis

Organization

Executive Committee

General Chairs	Konstantinos Diamantaras
	(Alexander TEI of Thessaloniki)
	Wlodek Duch
	(Nikolaus Copernicus University, Torun)
Program Chair	Lazaros Iliadis (Democritus University of Thrace)
Workshop Chairs	Nikola Kasabov (Auckland University of Technology)
	Kostas Goulianas (Alexander TEI of Thessaloniki)
Organizing Chairs	Yannis Manolopoulos (Aristotle University)
	Ioannis Vlahavas (Aristotle University)
Members	Maria Kontaki (Aristotle University)
	Alexis Papadimitriou (Aristotle University)
	Stavros Stavroulakis (Aristotle University)

Referees

Luis Alexandre
Cesare Alippi
Plamen Angelov
Bruno Apolloni
Amir Atiya
Monica Bianchini
Dominic Palmer Brown
Ivo Bukovsky
F.F. Cai
Gustavo Camps-Valls
Ke Chen
Theo Damoulas
Tharam Dillon
Christina Draganova
Gerard Dreyfus
Peter Erdi
Deniz Erdogmus
Pablo Estevez
Mauro Gaggero
Christophe Garcia
Erol Gelenbe
Christos Georgiadis
Mark Girolami

T. Glezakos
Giorgio Gnecco
G. Gravanis
Barbara Hammer
Ioannis Hatzilygeroudis
Tom Heskes
Timo Honkela
Amir Hussain
Sylvain Jaume
Yaochu Jin
D. Kalles
Achilles Kameas
Hassan Kazemian
Stefanos Kollias
D. Kosmopoulos
Costas Kotropoulos
Jan Koutnik
Konstantinos Koutroumbas
Vera Kurkova
Diego Liberati
Aristidis Likas
I. Maglogiannhs
Danilo Mandic

Francesco Marcelloni
Konstantinos Margaritis
Thomas Martinetz
Matteo Matteucci
Ali Minai
Nikolaos Mitianoudis
Roman Neruda
Erkki Oja
Mihaela Oprea
Karim Ouazzane
Theofilos Papadimitriou
Charis Papadopoulos
Constantinos Pattichis
Barak Pearlmutter
Elias Pimenidis
Vincenzo Piuri
Mark Plumbley
Manuel Roveri
Leszek Rutkowski
Marcello Sanguineti
Mike Schuster
Hiroshi Shimodaira
A. Sideridis
Olli Simula

Athanassios Skodras
S. Spartalis
Alessandro Sperduti
Soundararajan Srinivasan
Andreas Stafylopatis
Johan Suykens
Johannes Sveinsson
Anastasios Tefas
Athanasios Tsadiras
Ioannis Tsamardinos
T. Tsiligkiridis
Marc Van Hulle
Marley Vellasco
Michel Verleysen
Vassilios Verykios
Alessandro E.P. Villa
Jun Wang
Aaron Weifeng
Yong Xue
K. Yialouris
Hujun Yin
Xiaodong Zhang
Rodolfo Zunino

Sponsoring Institutions

European Neural Network Society (ENNS)
Aristotle University of Thessaloniki
Alexander TEI of Thessaloniki
University of Macedonia
Democritus University of Thrace
International Hellenic University

Table of Contents – Part I

ANN Applications

Bayesian ANN

Bio Inspired – Spiking ANN

Biomedical ANN

Computational Neuroscience

Feature Selection/Parameter Identification and Dimensionality Reduction

Filtering

Genetic – Evolutionary Algorithms

Image – Video and Audio Processing

Table of Contents – Part II

Kernel Algorithms – Support Vector Machines

Knowledge Engineering and Decision Making

Recurrent ANN

Reinforcement Learning

Robotics

Self Organizing ANN

Adaptive Algorithms – Systems

Optimization

Table of Contents – Part III

Classification – Pattern Recognition

Learning Algorithms and Systems

Computational Intelligence

IEM3 Workshop

CVA Workshop

SOINN Workshop

IF-Inference Systems Design for Prediction of Ozone Time Series: The Case of Pardubice Micro-region

Vladimír Olej and Petr Hájek

Institute of System Engineering and Informatics
Faculty of Economics and Administration, University of Pardubice, Studentská 84
532 10 Pardubice, Czech Republic
vladimir.olej@upce.cz, petr.hajek@upce.cz

Abstract. The paper presents basic notions of fuzzy inference systems based on the Takagi-Sugeno fuzzy model. On the basis of this fuzzy inference system and IF-sets introduced by K.T. Atanassov, novel IF-inference systems can be designed. Thus, an IF-inference system is developed for time series prediction. In the next part of the paper we describe ozone prediction by IF-inference systems and the analysis of the results.

Keywords: Fuzzy inference systems, IF-sets, IF-inference systems, time series, ozone prediction.

1 Introduction

Classification and prediction [1], [2] can be realized by fuzzy inference systems (FISs). Based on general FIS structure, we can design two basic types - Mamdani type and Takagi-Sugeno type [1], [2]. Both types of FISs differ in the way of obtaining the output. Different output formulation results in different if-then rules construction. These rules can be designed by user (based on their experience), or the user can obtain them through extraction from historical data. Fuzzification of input variables and application of operators in if-then rules are the same in both types of FISs.

At this time, there are several generalizations of the fuzzy set theory for various objectives [3], [4]. The intuitionistic fuzzy sets (IF-sets) theory represents one of the generalizations, the notion introduced by K.T. Atanassov [5], [6]. The concept of IF-sets can be viewed as an alternative approach to define a fuzzy set in cases where available information is not sufficient for the definition of an imprecise concept by means of a conventional fuzzy set. In this paper we will present IF-sets as a tool for reasoning in the presence of imperfect facts and imprecise knowledge. The IF-sets are for example suitable for the ozone prediction as they provide a good description of object attributes by means of membership functions μ and non-membership functions ν. They also present a strong possibility to express uncertainty.

In the paper we present basic notions of Takagi-Sugeno type FIS for time series prediction. Based on the FIS defined in this way and the basic notions of IF-sets, we define a novel IF-inference system. Further, the paper includes a comparison of the prediction results obtained by the FIS characterized by membership functions μ, by

K. Diamantaras, W. Duch, and L.S. Iliadis (Eds.): ICANN 2010, Part I, LNCS 6352, pp. 1–11, 2010.

the FIS characterized by non-membership functions ν, and by the IF-inference system. The comparison is realized for the example of ozone prediction in the Pardubice micro region, the Czech Republic.

2 IF-Inference System Design

General structure of FIS is defined in [2], [7]. It contains a fuzzification process of input variables by membership functions μ, the design of the base of if-then rules or automatic extraction of if-then rules from input data, application of operators (AND,OR,NOT) in if-then rules, implication and aggregation within these rules, and the process of defuzzification of gained values to crisp values. In the process of defuzzification, standardization of inputs and their transformation to the domain of the values of membership functions μ takes place. The input to fuzzification process is a crisp value given on the universum (reference set). The output of the fuzzification process is the membership function μ value. The design of the base of if-then rules can be realized by extraction of if-then rules from historical data, provided that they are available. In [2], [7] there are mentioned optimization methods of the number of if-then rules. Operator AND between elements of two fuzzy sets can be generalized by t-norm [8] and operator OR between elements of two fuzzy sets can be generalized by s-norm [8].

The Takagi-Sugeno type FIS was designed in order to achieve higher computational effectiveness. This is possible as the defuzzification of outputs is not necessary. Its advantage lies also in involving the functional dependencies of output variable on input variables. The output level y_k of each of the k-th if-then rule R_k is weighted by $w_k = \mu(x_1)$ AND $\mu(x_2)$ AND ... AND $\mu(x_m)$. The final output y of the Takagi-Sugeno type FIS is the weighted average of all N if-then rule R_k outputs y_k, k=1,2, ... ,N, computed as follows

$$y = \frac{\sum_{k=1}^{N} y_k \times w_k}{\sum_{k=1}^{N} w_k}. \tag{1}$$

The concept of IF-sets is the generalization of the concept of fuzzy sets, the notion introduced by L.A. Zadeh [8]. The theory of IF-sets is well suited to deal with vagueness. Recently, in this context, IF-sets have been used for intuitionistic classification [9] and prediction models which can accommodate imprecise information.

Let a set X be a non-empty fixed set. An IF-set A in X is an object having the form [5], [6]

$$A = \{ \langle x, \mu_A(x), \nu_A(x) \rangle \mid x \in X \}, \tag{2}$$

where the function $\mu_A : X \to [0,1]$ defines the degree of membership function $\mu_A(x)$ and the function $\nu_A : X \to [0,1]$ defines the degree of non-membership function $\nu_A(x)$, respectively, of the element $x \in X$ to the set A, which is a subset of X, and $A \subset X$, respectively; moreover for every $x \in X$, $0 \le \mu_A(x) + \nu_A(x) \le 1$, $\forall x \in X$ must hold. The amount

$$\pi_A(x) = 1 - (\mu_A(x) + \nu_A(x)) \tag{3}$$

is called the hesitation part, which may cater to either membership value or non-membership value, or both. For each IF-set in X, we will call $\pi_A(x) = 1 - (\mu_A(x) + \nu_A(x))$ as the intuitionistic fuzzy index (IF-index) of the element x in set A. It is a hesitancy degree of x to A. It is obvious that $0 \le \pi_A(x) \le 1$ for each $x \in X$. The value denotes a measure of non-determinancy. The IF-indices $\pi_A(x)$ are such that the larger $\pi_A(x)$ the higher a hesitation margin of the decision maker. The IF-indices allow us to calculate the best final results (and the worst one) we can expect in a process leading to a final optimal decision.

Next we define an accuracy function H to evaluate the degree of accuracy of IF-set by the form $H(A) = \mu_A(x) + \nu_A(x)$, where $H(A) \in [0,1]$. From the definition H, it can be also expressed as follows $H(A) = \mu_A(x) + \nu_A(x) = 1 - \pi_A(x)$. The larger value of $H(A)$, the more the degree of accuracy of the IF-set A. If A and B are two IF-sets of the set X, then

- $A \cap B = \{\langle x, \min(\mu_A(x), \mu_B(x)), \max(\nu_A(x), \nu_B(x)) \rangle \mid x \in X\}$,
- $A \cup B = \{\langle x, \max(\mu_A(x), \mu_B(x)), \min(\nu_A(x), \nu_B(x)) \rangle \mid x \in X\}$,
- $A \subset B$ iff $\forall x \in X$, $(\mu_A(x) \le \mu_B(x))$ and $(\nu_A(x) \ge \nu_B(x))$,
- $A \supset B$ iff $B \subset A$,
- $A = B$ iff $\forall x \in X$, $(\mu_A(x) = \mu_B(x)$ and $\nu_A(x) = \nu_B(x))$,
- $\overline{A} = \{\langle x, \nu_A(x), \mu_A(x) \rangle \mid x \in X\}$.

Let there exist a general IF-system defined in [10]. Then it is possible to define its output y^η as

$$y^\eta = (1 - \pi_A(x)) \times y^\mu + \pi_A(x) \times y^\nu, \tag{4}$$

where y^μ is the output of the FIS$^\mu$ using the membership function $\mu_A(x)$, y^ν is the output of the FIS$^\nu$ using the non-membership function $\nu_A(x)$. Then, based on equation (4), it is possible to design the IF-inference system of Takagi-Sugeno type presented in Fig. 1. For the IF-inference system designed in this way, the following facts hold. If IF-index:

- $\pi_A(x) = 0$, then the output of IF-inference system $y^\eta = (1 - \pi_A(x)) \times y^\mu$ (Takagi-Sugeno type FIS is characterized by membership function μ).
- $\pi_A(x) = 1$, then the output of IF-inference system $y^\eta = \pi_A(x) \times y^\nu$ (Takagi-Sugeno type FIS is characterized by non-membership function ν).
- $0 < \pi_A(x) < 1$, then the output of IF-inference system $y^\eta = (1 - \pi_A(x)) \times y^\mu + \pi_A(x) \times y^\nu$ (Takagi-Sugeno type FIS is characterized by membership function μ and non-membership function ν).

Let $x_1, x_2, \dots, x_j, \dots, x_m$ be input variables FIS$^\eta$ defined on reference sets $X_1, X_2, \dots, X_j, \dots, X_m$ and let y^η be an output variable defined on reference set Y. Then FIS$^\eta$ has m

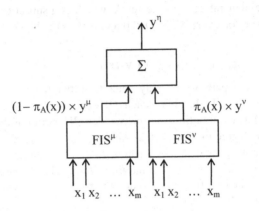

Fig. 1. IF-inference systems

input variables $x_1, x_2, \ldots, x_j, \ldots, x_m$ and one output variable y^η, where $\eta = \mu$ are membership functions ($\eta = \nu$ are non-membership functions).

Further, each set X_j, $j = 1, 2, \ldots, m$, can be divided into $i = 1, 2, \ldots, n$ fuzzy sets which are represented by following way

$$\eta_{j,1}(x), \eta_{j,2}(x), \ldots, \eta_{j,i}(x), \ldots, \eta_{j,n}(x). \tag{5}$$

Individual fuzzy sets, where $\eta = \mu$ are membership functions ($\eta = \nu$ are non-membership functions) represent a mapping of linguistic variables values which are related to sets X_j. Then the k-th if-then rule R_k in FIS^η can be defined as follows

$$R_k: \text{if } x_1 \text{ is } A_{1,i(1,k)}{}^\eta \text{ AND } x_2 \text{ is } A_{2,i(2,k)}{}^\eta \text{ AND } \ldots \text{ AND } x_j \text{ is}$$
$$A_{j,i(j,k)}{}^\eta \text{ AND } \ldots \text{ AND } x_m \text{ is } A_{m,i(m,k)}{}^\eta \text{ then } y^\eta = h,$$
$$\text{or } y^\eta = f(x_1, x_2, \ldots, x_m), j = 1, 2, \ldots, m; i = 1, 2, \ldots, n, \tag{6}$$

where $A_{1,i(1,k)}{}^\eta, A_{2,i(2,k)}{}^\eta, \ldots, A_{j,i(j,k)}{}^\eta, \ldots, A_{m,i(m,k)}{}^\eta$ represent the values of linguistic variable for FIS^μ and FIS^ν, h is constant, $f(x_1, x_2, \ldots, x_m)$ is a linear or polynomial function. The output y^μ of FIS^μ (the output y^ν of FIS^ν) is defined in the same way as presented in equation (1).

3 Inference Mechanism of IF-Inference Systems

The results of the designed IF-inference system of Takagi-Sugeno type can be interpreted by means of the following rationale. Fuzzy sets, the notion introduced by L.A. Zadeh, are represented by membership function $\mu_A(x)$ degree, that is

$$A = \{\langle x, \mu_A(x) \rangle |\ x \in X\}. \tag{7}$$

Fuzzy sets have associated a non-membership function $\nu_A(x)$ degree

$$A = \{\langle x, \mu_A(x), \nu_A(x) \rangle |\ x \in X\} = \{\langle x, \mu_A(x), 1 - \mu_A(x) \rangle |\ x \in X\}. \tag{8}$$

Since $\mu_A(x) + \nu_A(x) = \mu_A(x) + 1 - \mu_A(x) = 1$, fuzzy sets are considered as a particular case IF-sets. Let be given an automorphism [11] of the unit interval, i.e. every function $\psi: [0,1] \rightarrow [0,1]$, that is continuous and strictly increasing such that $\psi(0)=0$ and $\psi(1)=1$. Further, let be given a function n: $[0,1] \rightarrow [0,1]$ in such a way that it holds $n(0)=1$ and $n(1)=0$. It is called a strong negation and it is always strictly decreasing, continuous and involutive. Then, as proved by [11], n: $[0,1] \rightarrow [0,1]$ is a strong negation if and only if there exists an automorphism ψ of the unit interval such that $n(x) = \psi^{-1}(1 - \psi(x))$. Let L^* be a set for which

$$L^* = \{(x,y)|(x,y) \in [0,1] \times [0,1] \text{ and } x+y \leq 1\} \quad (9)$$

and the elements $0_{L*}=(0,1)$ and $1_{L*}=(1,0)$. Then $\forall((x,y),(z,t)) \in L^*$ it holds:

- $(x,y) \leq_{L*} (z,t)$ iff $x \leq z$ and $y \geq t$. This relation is transitive, reflexive and antisymmetric.
- $(x,y) = (z,t)$ iff $(x,y) \leq_{L*} (z,t)$ and $(z,t) \leq_{L*} (x,y)$.
- $(x,y) \lessdot (z,t)$ iff $x \leq z$ and $y \leq t$.

The designed IF-inference system of Takagi-Sugeno type works with the inference mechanism, based on Atanassov's intuitionistic fuzzy t-norm and t-conorm, by means of t-norm and t-conorm [12] on interval $[0,1]$. A function $\mathbf{T}: (L^*)^2 \rightarrow L^*$ is called Atanassov's intuitionistic fuzzy t-norm if it is commutative, associative, and increasing in both arguments with respect to the order $\leq_{L*}$ and with neutral element 1_{L*}. Similarly, a function $\mathbf{S}: (L^*)^2 \rightarrow L^*$ is called Atanassov's intuitionistic fuzzy t-conorm if it is commutative, associative, and increasing with neutral element 0_{L*}. Atanassov's intuitionistic fuzzy t-norm $\mathbf{T}$ is called t-representable if and only if there exists a t-norm T and t-conorm S on interval $[0,1]$ such that $\forall(x,y),(z,t) \in L^*$ it holds

$$\mathbf{T}((x,y),(z,t)) = (T(x,z),S(y,t)) \in L^*. \quad (10)$$

If T=min on interval $[0,1]$ then $\mathbf{min}((x,y),(z,t)) = (\min(x,z),\max(y,t))$. Accordingly, Atanassov's intuitionistic fuzzy t-conorm $\mathbf{S}$ can be defined, and it is called t-representable if and only if there exist a t-norm T and t-conorm S on interval $[0,1]$ such that $\forall(x,y),(z,t) \in L^*$ it holds

$$\mathbf{S}((x,y),(z,t)) = (S(x,z),T(y,t)) \in L^*. \quad (11)$$

If S=max on interval $[0,1]$ then $\mathbf{max}((x,y),(z,t)) = (\max(x,z),\min(y,t))$. An Atanassov's intuitionistic fuzzy negation [12] is a function $\mathbf{n}: L^* \rightarrow L^*$ such that it is decreasing with respect to the $\leq_{L*}$ and $\mathbf{n}(0_{L*})= 1_{L*}$ and $\mathbf{n}(1_{L*})= 0_{L*}$. Then if $\forall((x,y),(z,t)) \in L^*$ $\mathbf{n}(\mathbf{n}((x,y))) = (x,y)$, it is said that $\mathbf{n}$ is involutive. Function $\mathbf{n}: L^* \rightarrow L^*$ is an involutive Atanassov's intuitionistic fuzzy negation if there exists an involutive fuzzy negation n such that

$$\mathbf{n}((x,y)) = (n(1-y), 1-n(x)). \quad (12)$$

Based on presented facts a generalized Atanassov's IF-index can be defined as a function $\pi_G: L^* \rightarrow [0,1]$ associated with the strong negation n if it satisfies the following conditions:

- $\pi_G(x,y)= 1$ iff x=0 and y=0.
- $\pi_G(x,y)= 0$ iff x+y=1.

- If $(z,t) \preccurlyeq (x,y)$, then $\pi_G(x,y) \leq \pi_G(z,t)$.
- $\pi_G(x,y) = \pi_G(\mathbf{n}((x,y))) \ \forall (x,y) \in L^*$ such that $\mathbf{n}$ is generated from an involutive negation n.

4   Modelling and Analysis of the Results

It is known that ozone (O_3) is an effective anti-greenhouse gas particularly in the upper troposphere, thus playing a direct role in climate change. In addition to its potential human health hazard, ozone adversely impacts the yields of agricultural crops and causes noticeable foliage damage. Therefore, the development of effective prediction models [13], [14], [15], [16], [17], [18] of ozone concentrations in urban areas is important. Development of these models is difficult because the meteorological parameters and photochemical reactions involved in ozone formation are complex [19], [20].

The data for our investigations was obtained from the Czech Hydro-meteorological Institute. This data contains the average daily ozone measurements and the average daily meteorological variables (such as temperature, wind speed, wind direction, humidity, air pressure and solar radiation), vehicle emission variables (nitrogen dioxide NO_2, carbon monoxide CO, nitric oxide NO, and nitrogen oxides NO_x, sulphur dioxide SO_2, particulate matter PM_{10} and $PM_{2.5}$), and other dummy variables (working day, month). All the measured variables used in this study are actual same day values. The genetic algorithm [21] was used to reduce the original set of input variables and thus to select only significant variables. It was shown that oxides of nitrogen NO_x, nitric oxide NO, nitrogen dioxide NO_2, month of measurement, humidity, solar radiation, and the ozone level at day ahead were important to predict daily average ozone levels. The general formulation of the model is as follows $y = f(x_1^t, x_2^t, \ldots, x_m^t)$, m=7, where y is daily average ozone level at time t+1, x_1^t is oxide of nitrogen, x_2^t is nitric oxide, x_3^t is nitrogen dioxide, x_4^t is dummy variable (month), x_5^t is humidity, x_6^t is solar radiation, x_7^t is daily average ozone level at time t. Samples of time series x_1^t and x_2^t are presented in Fig. 2 and Fig. 3.

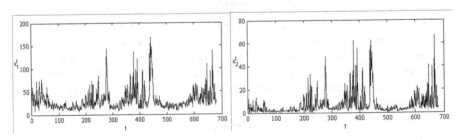

Fig. 2. Time series x_1^t **Fig. 3.** Time series x_2^t

The data for years 2005-2007 was selected from the city of Pardubice, the Czech Republic. The data for 2005-2006 was used as training set O_{train}, and the data for 2007 was used as testing set O_{test} to test the prediction ability of the models. The basic statistics on the used data are shown in Table 1.

Table 1. Basic statistics of ozone data

Parameter	Mean	Standard deviation	Min	Max
x_1^t	31.14	22.26	7	168.8
x_2^t	6.89	8.94	0.5	66.4
x_3^t	20.09	9.45	4.8	69.8
x_4^t	7.27	3.36	1	12
x_5^t	76.51	11.55	35	99
x_6^t	4.72	4.09	0	12.6
x_7^t	50.53	24.00	3.6	125.4
y	50.41	23.69	3.6	125.4

Based on the given facts (chapter 2), such FIS^μ is designed which is characterized by means of membership function μ, and FIS^ν characterized by non-membership function ν (with input variables $x_1^t, x_2^t, \ldots, x_m^t$, m=7). Input variable x_1^t in time t is represented by two membership functions μ for FIS^μ and two membership functions ν for FIS^ν. Membership functions μ and non-membership functions ν, for IF-index π=0.2, are shown in Fig. 4 and Fig. 5.

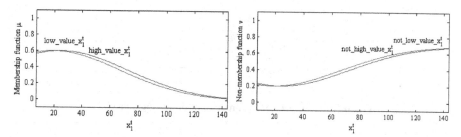

Fig. 4. Input membership function μ for x_1^t of FIS^μ **Fig. 5.** Input non-membership functions ν for x_1^t of FIS^ν

The other input variables are represented in a similar manner. Membership function μ and non-membership function ν, and if-then rules were designed using subtractive clustering algorithm [22]. The idea behind fuzzy clustering is to divide the data space into fuzzy clusters. After projecting the clusters onto the input space, the antecedent parts of the fuzzy if-then rules can be found. The consequent parts of the if-then rules are represented by functions $y^n = f(x_1, x_2, \ldots, x_m)$. In this way, one cluster corresponds to one if-then rule.

To be specific, two if-then rules are designed for FIS^μ and FIS^ν respectively. The output level y_k of each of the k-th if-then rule R_k is weighted (see chapter 2). The final outputs y^μ and y^ν of the FIS^μ and FIS^ν are the weighted averages of all the if-then rule R_k outputs y_k, k=1,2, ... ,N. The output of IF-inference system is represented by the predicted value y^n in time t+1. The results of the ozone prediction on testing data O_{test} for μ_{max}=0.6 for IF-index π=0.2 are presented in Fig. 6, where μ_{max} represents the maximum value of input membership functions μ and Fig. 7 include the daily average ozone level at time t+1 and output variable y^n.

Appendix shows the quality of ozone prediction represented by Root Mean Squared Error (RMSE) for different values of μ_{max} and different values of IF-index π. A higher value of IF-index π shows on a higher indeterminacy or uncertainty. For

IF-index $\pi=1$ we are not able to say if the value of input variable belongs or not belongs to an IF-set. The results show that the RMSE$^\mu$ is for FIS$^\mu$ constant. The size of μ_{max} does not affect the resulting error of FIS$^\mu$. This results from the fact that the output y^μ is a weighted average of outputs y_k from the single if-then rules R_k. Relative weights w_k remain the same for different values of μ_{max}. Maximum RMSE is obtained for the FIS$^\nu$ and the FIS$^\eta$, for which $\nu_{min}=0$ holds, i.e. $\mu_{max}+\pi=1$. Therefore, non-membership functions ν limited in this way are not suitable for the used data. The RMSE for FIS$^\nu$ and FIS$^\eta$ increases with a higher IF-index π, i.e. with a higher uncertainty and a lower accuracy function H(A). Extreme situations of the IF-inference system are to be found when IF-index $\pi=0$, then $\mu + \nu = 1$ (fuzzy sets are considered as a particular case IF-sets) and if IF-index $\pi=1$, then $\mu = 0$ and $\nu = 0$ (complete ignorance of the problem).

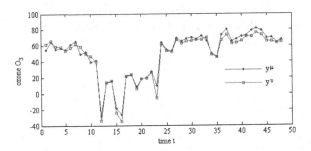

Fig. 6. The results of ozone prediction for testing data O_{test}

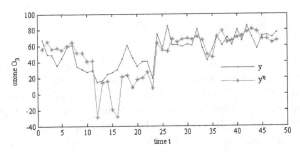

Fig. 7. The daily average ozone level y at time t+1 and output variable y^η

The results, however, show that it is possible to achieve a relatively low level of RMSE (on training and testing data) even in the cases where it is not possible to determine the membership functions μ and non-membership functions ν unambiguously (i.e. for a high IF-index π).

5 Conclusion

The model based on IF-sets is designed in the paper as it allows processing uncertainty and the expert knowledge. IF-sets can be viewed in the context as a proper tool for representing hesitancy concerning both membership and non-membership of an element to a set. The IF-inference system FIS^η defined this way works more effectively than the standard of Takagi-Sugeno type FIS^μ as it provides stronger possibility to accommodate imprecise information and to better model imperfect fact and imprecise knowledge.

In this study we present a novel approach to times series prediction based on the extension of Takagi-Sugeno type FIS^μ which is characterized by membership function μ with Takagi-Sugeno type FIS^ν which is characterized by non-membership function ν. The central point in the design of IF-inference system lies in the IF-index π expressing the level of uncertainty. The model design was carried out in Matlab in MS Windows XP operation system.

Acknowledgments. This work was supported by the scientific research project of the Ministry of Environment, the Czech Republic under Grant No: SP/4i2/60/07 with title Indicators for Valuation and Modelling of Interactions among Environment, Economics and Social Relations.

References

[1] Bandemer, H., Gottwald, S.: Fuzzy Sets, Fuzzy Logic, Fuzzy Methods. John Wiley and Sons Inc., New York (1995)

[2] Kuncheva, L.I.: Fuzzy Classifier Design. Springer, Germany (2000)

[3] Dubois, D., Gottwald, S., Hajek, P., Kacprzyk, J., Prade, H.: Terminological Difficulties in Fuzzy Set Theory-The case of Intuitionistic Fuzzy Sets. Fuzzy Sets and Systems 156, 485–491 (2005)

[4] Atanassov, K.T.: Answer to D. Dubois, S. Gottwald, P. Hajek, J. Kacprzyk, H. Prade's Terminological Difficulties in Fuzzy Set Theory-The case of Intuitionistic Fuzzy Sets. Fuzzy Sets and Systems 156, 496–499 (2005)

[5] Atanassov, K.T.: Intuitionistic Fuzzy Sets. Fuzzy Sets and Systems 20, 87–96 (1986)

[6] Atanassov, K.T.: Intuitionistic Fuzzy Sets. Springer, Heidelberg (1999)

[7] Pedrycz, W.: Fuzzy Control and Fuzzy Systems. John Wiley and Sons, New York (1993)

[8] Zadeh, L.A.: Fuzzy Sets. Inform. and Control 8, 338–353 (1965)

[9] Olej, V., Hájek, P.: Air Quality Modelling by Kohonen's Self-organizing Feature Maps and Intuitionistic Fuzzy Sets. In: Pobil, A.P. (ed.), pp. 22–27. ACTA Press, Canada (2008)

[10] Montiel, O., Castillo, O., Melin, P., Sepúlveda, R.: Mediative Fuzzy Logic: A new Approach for Contradictory Knowledge Management. Soft Computing 20, 251–256 (2008)

[11] Barrenechea, E.: Generalized Atanassov's Intuitionistic Fuzzy Index. Construction Method. In: IFSA-EUSFLAT, Lisbon, pp. 478–482 (2009)

[12] Deschrijver, G., Cornelis, C., Kerre, E.: On the Representation of Intuitionistic Fuzzy t-norm and t-conorm. IEEE Transactions on Fuzzy Systems 12, 45–61 (2004)

[13] Yi, J., Prybutok, V.R.: A Neural Network Model Forecasting for Prediction of Daily Maximum Ozone Concentration in an Industrialized Urban Area. Environmental Pollution 92, 349–357 (1996)

[14] Hubbard, M.C., Cobourn, W.G.: Development of a Regression Model to Forecast Ground-level Ozone Concentration in Louisville. Atmospheric Environment 32, 2637–2647 (1998)

[15] Wang, W., Lu, W., Wang, X., Leung, Y.T.: Prediction of Maximum Daily Ozone Level using Combined Neural Network and Statistical Characteristics. Environment International 29, 555–562 (2003)

[16] Agirre-Basurko, E., Ibarra-Berastegi, G., Madariaga, I.: Regression and Multilayer Perceptron-based Models to Forecast Hourly O3 and NO2 Levels in the Bilbao Area. Environmental Modelling Software 21, 430–446 (2006)

[17] Sousa, S.I.V., Martins, F.G., Alvim-Ferraz, M.C.M., Pereira, M.C.: Multi Linear Regression and Artificial Neural Network based on Principal Components to Predict Ozone Concentrations. Environmental Modelling Software 22, 97–103 (2007)

[18] Brunelli, U., Piazza, V., Pignato, L., Sorbello, F., Vitabile, S.: Two Days ahead Prediction of Daily Maximum Concentrations of SO2, O3, PM10, NO2, CO in the Urban Area of Palermo, Italy. Atmospheric Environment 41, 2967–2995 (2007)

[19] Iliadis, L.S., Papaleonidas, A.: Intelligent Agents Networks Employing Hybrid Reasoning: Application in Air Quality Monitoring and Improvement. Communications in Computer and Information Science 43, 1–16 (2009)

[20] Paschalidou, A.K., Iliadis, L.S., Kassomenos, P., Bezirtzoglou, C.: Neural Modelling of the Tropospheric Ozone Concentrations in an Urban Site. In: 10th International Conference on Engineering Applications of Neural Network, Thessaloniki, pp. 29–31 (2007)

[21] Olej, V.: Modelling of Economics Processes by Computational Intelligence. M and V Press, Hradec Králové (2003) (in Slovak)

[22] Chiu, S.: Fuzzy Model Identification Based on Cluster Estimation. Journal of Intelligent snd Fuzzy Systems 2, 267–278 (1994)

Appendix: RMSE on testing data O_{test} for different values of μ_{max} and IF-index π

μ_{max}	0.1	0.2	0.3	0.4	0.5	0.6	0.7	0.8	0.9
$\pi=0.1$									
$RMSE^{\mu}$	12.47	12.47	12.47	12.47	12.47	12.47	12.47	12.47	12.47
$RMSE^{v}$	14.87	14.94	15.02	15.13	15.28	15.51	15.88	16.60	23.03
$RMSE^{\eta}$	12.61	12.62	12.63	12.64	12.65	12.67	12.70	12.76	13.18
$\pi=0.2$									
$RMSE^{\mu}$	12.47	12.47	12.47	12.47	12.47	12.47	12.47	12.47	
$RMSE^{v}$	14.88	14.95	15.06	15.20	15.42	15.77	16.47	23.03	
$RMSE^{\eta}$	12.78	12.80	12.81	12.84	12.88	12.94	13.06	14.00	
$\pi=0.3$									
$RMSE^{\mu}$	12.47	12.47	12.47	12.47	12.47	12.47	12.47		
$RMSE^{v}$	14.89	14.98	15.11	15.31	15.65	16.33	23.03		
$RMSE^{\eta}$	12.97	13.00	13.04	13.09	13.18	13.36	14.93		
...									
$\pi=0.6$									
$RMSE^{\mu}$	12.47	12.47	12.47	12.47					
$RMSE^{v}$	14.95	15.20	15.77	23.03					
$RMSE^{\eta}$	13.72	13.86	14.19	18.13					
$\pi=0.7$									
$RMSE^{\mu}$	12.47	12.47	12.47						
$RMSE^{v}$	15.02	15.51	23.03						
$RMSE^{\eta}$	14.05	14.38	19.30						
$\pi=0.8$									
$RMSE^{\mu}$	12.47	12.47							
$RMSE^{v}$	15.20	23.03							
$RMSE^{\eta}$	14.50	20.51							
$\pi=0.9$									
$RMSE^{\mu}$	12.47								
$RMSE^{v}$	23.03								
$RMSE^{\eta}$	21.76								

Superior-Order Curvature-Corrected Voltage Reference Using a Current Generator

Cosmin Popa

Faculty of Electronics, Telecommunications and Information Technology,
Iuliu Maniu 1-3, Bucharest, Romania
cosmin_popa@yahoo.com

Abstract. A CMOS voltage reference with a logarithmic curvature-correction will be presented. The first-order compensation is realized using an original *OVF* (Offset Voltage Follower) block as *PTAT* voltage generator, with the advantages of reducing the silicon area and of increasing accuracy. The new logarithmic curvature-correction technique will be implemented using an *ADA* (Asymmetric Differential Amplifier) block for compensating the logarithmic temperature dependent term from the first-order compensated voltage reference. In order to increase the circuit accuracy, an original temperature dependent current generator will be designed for computing the exact type of the implemented curvature-correction. The SPICE simulations confirm the theoretical estimated results, showing very small values of the temperature coefficient. The circuit is implemented in $0.35\mu m$ CMOS technology and consumes only $9\mu A$ for $t = 25^{o}C$, being supplied at the minimal supply voltage $V_{DD} = 1.7V$. The temperature coefficient of the reference voltage is $8.5\,ppm/^{o}C$, while the line sensitivity is $0.7mV/V$ for a supply voltage between $1.7V$ and $7V$.

Keywords: Temperature dependence, superior-order curvature-correction technique, voltage reference circuit.

1 Introduction

Very important stages in applications such as A/D and D/A converters, data acquisition systems, memories or smart sensors, voltage reference circuits and theirs temperature behavior are intensively studied in the last decade and many researches have been developed for improving them.

Because of the superior performance of bipolar voltage references with respect to the circuits using MOS transistors, the first approaches of high-performance voltage reference were implemented in bipolar technology. However, because of the nonlinear temperature dependence of the base-emitter voltage [1], there exists a theoretical limit for improving the temperature stability of a simple BGR. Basic

K. Diamantaras, W. Duch, L.S. Iliadis (Eds.): ICANN 2010, Part I, LNCS 6352, pp. 12–21, 2010.

bandgap references, with a temperature coefficient of about hundred ppm/K, useful only for applications that do not require a very good accuracy of the reference voltage, have been presented in literature [2]. In order to improve the temperature behavior of the bipolar bandgap reference, correction techniques [3] have been developed. In CMOS bandgap references that are still using bipolar transistors, the required bipolar devices are realized as parasitic vertical or lateral transistors, available in CMOS technology. The result will be a small degradation of the temperature behavior of the circuit because of the poorer match of MOS devices' parameters with respect to those of bipolar transistors.

Another approaches of CMOS references [4]-[8], using exclusively MOS devices and (or without) resistors implements the $CTAT$ voltage reference using a threshold voltage extractor circuit, which generates the MOS device threshold voltage, with negative linear temperature dependence. The disadvantage of this class of CMOS references is that the exact temperature dependence of V_T is not so simple to estimate, so a curvature correction technique for improving the thermal behavior of the voltage reference is relatively difficult to design.

The new proposed realization of a CMOS voltage reference uses a gate-source voltage of a MOS transistor working in weak inversion as $CTAT$ voltage generator. The idea is that the negative linear dependent term from $V_{GS}(T)$ expression to be compensated by a complementary term implemented using an OVF (Offset Voltage Follower) block. The new curvature-correction technique proposes the compensation of the nonlinear temperature dependence of the gate-source voltage using an original block, ADA (Asymmetric Differential Amplifier), biased at drain currents with different temperature dependencies ($PTAT$ and $PTAT^{\alpha}$, respectively).

In order to improve the circuit accuracy, a digitally selected curvature-correction technique will be implemented, based on an original implementation of a temperature-dependent current generator circuit.

2 Theoretical Analysis

The block diagram of the voltage reference is presented in Fig. 1.

Fig. 1. The block diagram of the voltage reference

The $CTAT$ voltage generator is designed using the gate-source voltage for a subthreshold operated MOS transistor. The OVF block implements the first-order compensation of the gate-source voltage, while *ADA* block compensates the logarithmic temperature dependence of $V_{GS}(T)$.

2.1 The Superior-Order Curvature-Corrected Voltage Reference

The temperature dependence of the gate-source voltage. The gate-source voltage of a MOS transistor working in weak inversion represents the simplest implementation in CMOS technology of a voltage generator with a negative linear temperature dependence (*CTAT*). Considering a $PTAT^{\alpha}$ dependence of the drain current, where α is a constant parameter, it results the following expression for the gate-source voltage temperature dependence:

$$V_{GS}(T) = V_{FB} + E_{G0} + \frac{V_{GS}(T_0) - V_{FB} - E_{G0}}{T_0} T + \frac{nkT}{q}(\alpha + \gamma - 2)ln\frac{T}{T_0}, \quad (1)$$

T_0 being the reference temperature and γ - a technology dependent parameter. The first term is a constant term, the second one is a linear term, which will be compensated by a complementary linear dependent on temperature voltage and the last term models the nonlinearity of the gate-source voltage temperature dependence. This term will be compensated by a suitable logarithmic dependent on temperature voltage, also added with $V_{GS}(T)$.

The Offset Voltage Follower block. The main temperature dependence of V_{GS} from (1) is given by the linear dependent on temperature term. The new technique [4] for obtaining a *PTAT* voltage is based on an O̱ffset V̱oltage F̱ollower (*OVF*) block, presenting an improved accuracy and a much smaller silicon area consumption with respect to the classical *PTAT* voltage generator because matched transistors replace matched resistors. The first-order curvature-corrected reference voltage will have the following expression:

$$V_{REF}^{(1)}(T) = V_{FB} + E_G + \frac{nkT}{q}(\gamma - 1)ln\frac{T}{T_0}. \quad (2)$$

The superior-order curvature-correction technique using an Asymmetric Differential Amplifier. After the first-order compensation, the last logarithmic temperature dependent term from (2) represents the main temperature dependence of the reference voltage. The new superior-order curvature correction technique proposed for minimized this undesired behavior uses an A̱symmetrical Ḏifferential Amplifier (*ADA*) for compensating the logarithmical term from (3). The *ADA* block presented in Fig. 2 is a PMOS differential amplifier whose drain currents have different temperature dependencies: I_1 is linear increasing with temperature (*PTAT*) and I_α is $PTAT^{\alpha}$ current.

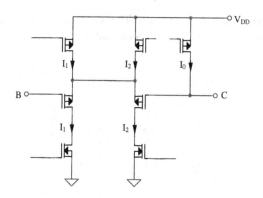

Fig. 2. The *ADA* for logarithmic curvature-correction

Taking into account the expression (1) of $V_{GS}(T)$, for a weak inversion operation of all transistors from Fig. 2, the $V_{CB}(T)$ voltage expression will be:

$$V_{CB}(T) = V_{GS}(\,PTAT\,) - V_{GS}(\,PTAT^{\alpha}\,) = (\,1 - \alpha\,)\frac{nkT}{q}\ln\frac{T}{T_0}. \qquad (3)$$

The curvature-corrected reference voltage is:

$$V_{REF}^{(sup)}(T) = V_{REF}^{(1)}(T) + V_{CB}(T) = V_{FB} + E_G + \frac{nkT}{q}(\gamma - \alpha)\ln\frac{T}{T_0}. \qquad (4)$$

In order to remove the temperature dependence (4) of V_{REF}, it is necessary to bias the transistor from the *CTAT* generator at a $PTAT^{\alpha}$ drain current, with $\alpha = \gamma$.

2.2 The Temperature-Dependent Current Generator Circuit

The necessity of designing this circuit is derived from the difficulty of an exact estimation of technological dependent parameter γ, having usual values is included in the (2,3) range. The original method for obtaining (with improved accuracy) the desired value of γ is to obtain a circuit having an output current with the following temperature dependence:

$$I_{OUT}(T) = ct.T^{\gamma} = ct.T^{2}T^{\gamma - 2}. \qquad (5)$$

It is possible to obtain I_{OUT} current in two steps:

- The implementation of a $PTAT^2$ current
- The implementation of a $PTAT^{2-\gamma}$

The set of the desired value of γ will be digitally made by setting the temperature dependence of $PTAT^{2-\gamma}$ current.

The current-mode square-root circuit. The core of the temperature dependent current generator circuit is represented by a current-mode square-root circuit (Fig. 3).

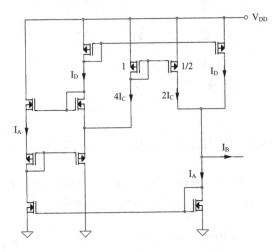

Fig. 3. The current-mode square-root circuit

In order to improve the circuit frequency response, only MOS transistors working in saturation will be used. The silicon occupied area is strongly reduced by replacing classical MOS devices by a FGMOS (Floating Gate MOS) transistor. The symbolic representation of the square-root circuit is shown in Fig. 4.

Fig. 4. The symbolic representation of the square-root circuit

After some computations, the output current of the circuit from Fig. 3 could be expressed as $I_C = \sqrt{I_A I_B}$.

The current multiplier circuit. Another circuit required for obtaining the desired temperature dependence of the output current is the current multiplier circuit from Fig. 5. In order to increase the circuit modularity, two square-root circuits from Fig. 3 and a current mirror have been used.

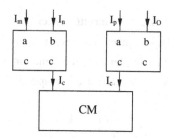

Fig. 5. The current multiplier circuit

The symbolic representation of the current multiplier circuit is shown in Fig. 6. The implementing relation between the currents is: $I_p = I_m I_n / I_O$.

Fig. 6. The symbolic representation of the current multiplier circuit

The current squaring circuit. The next block used for obtaining the exact value of parameter γ is the current squaring circuit (Fig. 7). This block is derived from the current square-root circuit from Fig. 3. The implementing relation between the currents is $I_a = I_c^2 / I_b$.

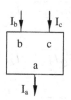

Fig. 7. The current squaring circuit

The current selection circuit. In order to select the active currents from the output current expression, a selection circuit (Fig. 8) will be used.

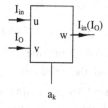

Fig. 8. The current selection circuit

The implementation of $PTAT^2$ **current generator.** The main part of the temperature dependence of I_{OUT} current is represented by its $PTAT^2$ variation. The block diagram of the circuit that implements this function is shown in Fig. 9. I_O is, in a first-order approximation, independent on temperature, while I_1 current has a $PTAT$ variation.

Fig. 9. The $PTAT^2$ current generator

The implementation of the $PTAT^{2-\gamma}$ **current generator.** The precision of computing the exact value of he parameter γ is associated to the possibility of a very accurated modifying of $PTAT^{2-\gamma}$ temperature dependence. In order to increase the circuit accuracy, a digitally-selected current generator will be implemented in Fig. 10. A digital word $a_1 - a_4$ will be used for selecting the desired value of the output current temperature dependence. The expression of the currents from Fig. 10 will be:

$$I_{1/2} = \sqrt{I_O I_1} = I_O^{1-\frac{1}{2}} I_1^{\frac{1}{2}}, \tag{6}$$

$$I_{1/4} = \sqrt{I_O I_{1/2}} = I_O^{1-\frac{1}{4}} I_1^{\frac{1}{4}}, \tag{7}$$

$$I_{1/8} = \sqrt{I_O I_{1/4}} = I_O^{1-\frac{1}{8}} I_1^{\frac{1}{8}}, \tag{8}$$

$$I_{1/16} = \sqrt{I_O I_{1/8}} = I_O^{1-\frac{1}{16}} I_1^{\frac{1}{16}} \tag{9}$$

and:

$$I_{OUT2} = I_O^{1-\sum_{k=1}^{4}\frac{a_k}{2^k}} I_1^{\sum_{k=1}^{4}\frac{a_k}{2^k}}. \tag{10}$$

So, the temperature dependence of I_{OUT2} current could be modified by changing the digital word $a_1 - a_4$. The maximal error (the error is considered equal to the difference between the desired and the impleented values of the T exponent) is $T^{1/16}$. This error could be reduced by increasing the number of the square-root blocks from Fig. 10. The result will be a compromise between complexity and circuit accuracy. In conclusion, the exact value of parameter γ could be digitally-selected with an error equal to $T^{1/16}$ for $n = 4$ current squaring circuits.

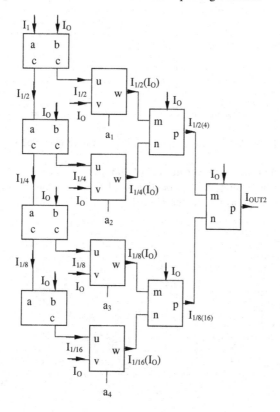

Fig. 10. The $PTAT^{2-\gamma}$ current generator

3 Simulated Results

The current consumption of the proposed voltage reference is maintained under $9\mu A$, making the proposed voltage reference circuit valuable for low-power low-voltage applications. The SPICE simulation of the temperature dependence for the reference voltage is shown in Fig. 11. The SPICE software was used as it gives very accurate results in CMOS VLSI designs. The temperature coefficient of the reference voltage is $8.5\,ppm/°C$, for the maximal variation range of the temperature $-30°C - 100°C$, mainly caused by the technological errors and by the mismatches of devices' parameters. The circuit consumes only $9\mu A$ for $t = 25°C$, being supplied at $V_{DD} = 1.7V$.

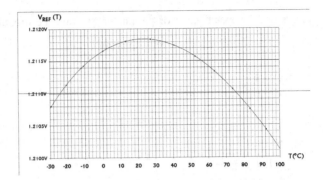

Fig. 11. The SPICE simulation for the superior-order curvature-corrected voltage reference

In order to evaluate the line sensitivity of the superior-order curvature-corrected voltage reference, the temperature dependence of the reference voltage is simulate having the supply voltage as parameter (Fig. 12).

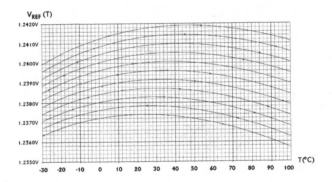

Fig. 12. The SPICE simulation $V_{REF}(T)$ with V_{DD} as parameter

The line sensitivity of the proposed circuit is $0.7mV/V$ for a supply voltage between $1.7V$ and $7V$. A comparison between the proposed circuit and the previous reported voltage references is presented in Table 1.

Table 1. Comparison between the proposed circuit and the previous reported voltage references

	Techn (μm)	V_{DD} (V) (min)	I_{DD} (μA)	TC (ppm/°C)	Line sens. (mV/V)	V_{REF} (mV)
This work	0.35	1.7	9	8.5	0.7	1220
[4]	0.6	1.5		15	4.4	603
[5]	0.4	4.4		117	1.1	515
[6]	1.2	1.2	500	100	2.5	1000
[7]	0.6	3	9.7	36.9	0.83	309
[8]	0.8	0.95	92	19		536
[9]	0.7	3	30	15		1210

For the minimal value of the supply voltage, $V_{DD} = 1.7V$, the low-power operation of the proposed circuit is achieved by a very small value of the supply current, $I_{DD} = 9\mu A$ comparing with other circuits. The voltage reference presented in this paper has better values for temperature coefficient, $8.5\,ppm/^{o}C$ and for line sensitivity, $0.7mV/V$ with respect to the results reported by previous similar works.

4 Conclusions

A CMOS voltage reference with a logarithmic curvature-correction was presented. In order to increase the circuit accuracy, an original temperature dependent current generator has been designed for computing the exact type of the implemented curvature-correction. The circuit was implemented in $0.35\mu m$ CMOS technology and consumes only $9\mu A$ for $t = 25^{o}C$, being supplied at the minimal value of the supply voltage, $V_{DD} = 1.7V$. The temperature coefficient of the reference voltage is $8.5\,ppm/^{o}C$, while the line sensitivity is $0.7mV/V$ for a supply voltage between $1.7V$ and $7V$. The voltage reference has many applications in VLSI designs, such as data acquisition systems or analog signal processing designs.

Aknowledgments

This work was supported by POSDRU/89/1.5/S/62557 project.

References

1. Filanovsky, I.M., et al.: BiCMOS Cascaded Bandgap Voltage Reference. In: IEEE 39th Midwest Symposium on Circuits and Systems, pp. 943–946 (1996)
2. Popa, C.: Curvature-Compensated Bandgap Reference. In: The 13th International Conference on Control System and Computer Science. University "Politehnica" of Bucharest, pp. 540–543 (2001)
3. Ferroand, M., Salerno, F.: A Floating CMOS Bandgap Voltage Reference for Differential Applications. IEEE Journal of Solid-State Circuits, 690–697 (1989)
4. Leung, K.N., Mok, P.K.T.: A CMOS Voltage Reference Based on Weighted VGS for CMOS Low-Dropout Linear Regulators. IEEE Journal of Solid State Circuits, 146–150 (2003)
5. Banba, H., et al.: A CMOS Bandgap Reference Circuit with Sub-1V Operation. IEEE Journal of Solid State Circuits, 670–674 (1999)
6. Jiang, Y., Lee, E.K.F.: Design of Low-Voltage Bandgap Reference Using Transimpedance Amplifier. IEEE Trans. Circuits Syst. II, 552–555 (2000)
7. Leung, K., Mok, P.: A CMOS Voltage Reference Based on Weighted VGS for CMOS Low-Dropout Linear Regulators. IEEE Journal of Solid-State Circuits, 146–150 (2003)
8. Malcovati, P., Maloberti, F., Pruzzi, M., Fiocchi, C.: Curvature Compensated BiCMOS Bandgap with 1-V Supply Voltage. In: Proc. ESSCIRC, pp. 52–55 (2000)

A Neural Network-Based Method for Affine 3D Registration of FMRI Time Series Using Fourier Space Subsets

Luis C. Freire[1,2], Ana R. Gouveia[3], and Fernando M. Godinho[4]

[1] Escola Superior de Tecnologia da Saúde de Lisboa, Instituto Politécnico de Lisboa,
1990-096, Lisboa, Portugal
luis.freire@estesl.ipl.pt
[2] Instituto de Biofísica e Engenharia Biomédica da Faculdade de Ciências da
Universidade de Lisboa, 1749-016 Lisboa, Portugal
[3] Faculdade de Ciências da Saúde da Universidade da Beira-Interior,
6200-506 Covilhã, Portugal
[4] Atomedical, Laboratório de Medicina Nuclear, 1600-028 Lisboa, Portugal

Abstract. In this work, we present a neural network (NN)-based method for 3D affine registration of FMRI time series, which relies on a limited number of Fourier coefficients of the images to be aligned. These coefficients are comprised in a small cubic neighborhood located at the first octant of a 3D Fourier space (including the DC component). Since the affine transformation model comprises twelve parameters, the Fourier coefficients are fed into twelve NN during the learning stage, so that each NN yields the estimates of one of the registration parameters. Different sizes of subsets of Fourier coefficients were tested. The construction of the training set and the learning stage are fast requiring, respectively, 90 s and 2 to 24 s, depending on the number of input and hidden units of the NN. The mean absolute registration errors are of approximately 0.03 mm in translations and 0.05 deg in rotations (except for pitch), for the typical motion amplitudes encountered in FMRI studies. Results with an actual time series suggest that the proposed method is suited to the problem of prospective (in frame) FMRI registration, although brain activation must be simulated, and learned, by the NN.

1 Introduction

Registration aims at determining the spatial transformation between images of the same or different subjects, acquired with the same or different imaging modalities, and also to align images with the coordinate system of a treatment device or tracked localizer [7]. Registration is an important concept in medical image processing, specially when accurately relating information of different images for diagnosis or treatment.

According to [11], the registration methods proposed in the literature can be broadly classified into three categories: feature-based, data-reductive and voxel similarity-based (VSB). The latter are widely accepted as the best registration methods since they are fully automatic and reproducible.

K. Diamantaras, W. Duch, L.S. Iliadis (Eds.): ICANN 2010, Part I, LNCS 6352, pp. 22–31, 2010.
© Springer-Verlag Berlin Heidelberg 2010

VSB methods often rely on a trial-and-error optimization scheme during which a similarity measure is maximized or minimized. It is generally accepted that VSB methods that rely on similarity measures that assume a functional [15,12] or a statistical [2] relation between the values of corresponding voxels in the two images, yield the best results. However, the computation time of VSB methods is often long, which is due not only to the trial-and-error nature of the optimization scheme, but also to the necessity of re-interpolating the floating image, at the lattice points of the reference image, every time the d-dimensional search space - in which d defines the number of registration parameters - is sampled. For these reasons, VSB methods have traditionally been employed in retrospective registration, *i.e.*, the motion estimates are determined after the acquisition of the image is concluded.

However, prospective registration is an equally interesting, and challenging, issue. For instance, suppose one wants to use the registration parameters to influence certain acquisition-related parameters, such as in FMRI studies, in which motion estimates could be used to modify the acquisition parameters in order to minimize motion-related artifacts. This would, however, require an extremely fast registration method, preferably based on a limited dataset of the K-space rather than on the full data from direct space. In this work, we propose a NN-based registration method, which relies on small data subsets extracted from the images' Fourier spaces.

NN have been used in different registration problems. Elhanany and co-workers performed affine registration of 2D non-medical images using a Multiple-Layer Perceptron (MLP), whose inputs are sub-samples of the original images' DCT coefficients [3]. Other authors also performed affine registration of 2D non-medical images using a MLP, but using a 2D PCA scheme to extract features to feed the NN [16]. These approaches seem to be accurate, being both remarkably robust to noise. The authors that use NN for surface-based rigid-body registration emphasize the celerity improvement of this approach, with a sub-voxel accuracy comparable to the conventional methods [17]. On the other way, Liu and co-workers registered 3D ear models with PCA extraction and concluded that this method is faster and more robust than the traditional ones [10]. Another rigid application (not surface-based) used 2D MR and CT brain images [14]. The authors performed a registration based on PCA using a NN to compute the first principal directions and centroids of the images. We too have once proposed a NN-based method for multimodality image registration [4]. However, this method was limited to 2D (affine) registration and was based on geometric features' extraction. A NN-based method which relies on Fourier coefficients has also been proposed by Abche and co-workers for 2D registration of MRI images [1].

The NN-based method proposed in this work is tested using simulated and real data, considering a 3D affine geometric model. We emphasize that, contrary to other learning-based approaches, which learn the optimal similarity measures [9,5,13,8], the proposed method learns the translation, rotation, scaling and shearing parameters, making use of the interpolation properties of the MLP.

2   Materials and Methods

2.1   The Neural Network

In this work, the determination of the registration parameters is done using *one NN per registration parameter*. Abche indicates that the simultaneous determination of the registration parameters may lead to a better-optimized set of estimates [1]. However, our preliminary results on this issue do not support that strategy (results not presented here).

Each NN comprises an input layer, a hidden layer and an output layer. The different layers are fully connected. The determination of the coefficients between consecutive layers is done through the Generalized Delta Learning Rule, using a sigmoidal activation function of the form $sgm(x) = 1/(1 + e^{-x})$.

During the supervised training, the weighting coefficients between consecutive layers are updated by minimizing the squared error between the optimal (known) solution - represented through "vector" y_k - and the observed soution - "vector" O_k. The W_{kj} and w_{ji} coefficients are updated following the relations:

$$W_{kj} = W_{kj} + \eta\delta_k h_j \tag{1}$$

$$w_{ij} = w_{ij} + \eta\delta_k W_{kj}h_j(1 - h_j)x_i, \tag{2}$$

where $\delta_k = (y_k - O_k)O_k(1 - O_k)$ and x_i is the value in the ith input unit. w_{ji} represents the weighting coefficient between the ith input unit and the jth hidden unit and W_{kj} the weighting coefficient between the jth hidden unit and the kth output unit. In the proposed method, each of the twelve NN contains only one output unit (*i.e.*, $k=1$), which is used as an interpolator of the corresponding registration parameter. The sigmoid function is applied to O and y values in order to render them between 0 and 1. In Figure 1, one may see a schematic representation of each NN used to estimate a registration parameter.

2.2   Simulations

The training of the NN is done using one learning dataset which comprises one thousand Fourier subsets, obtained from images created by applying the same number of random affine transformations to an actual FMRI 3D image. This image had dimensions $64 \times 80 \times 18$, $3.75 \times 3.75 \times 6.00$ mm, but it was reduced to a $64 \times 64 \times 16$ geometry by eliminating the 8 most anterior and posterior coronal slices and the 2 bottom axial slices (see Figure 2). This reduction in image dimensions allowed the application of a IFFT algorithm.

The affine geometric model is characterized by 12 degrees of freedom: 3 translations (t_x, t_y and t_z), 3 rotations (r_x, r_y and $r : z$), 3 scalings (s_x, s_y and s_z), and 3 shearings (sh_x, sh_y and sh_z). The geometric parameters of the simulated misregistrations follow uniform distributions between -1.0 and 1.0 mm for translations, between -1.0 and 1.0 degrees for rotations, and between -1.0 and 1.0 % for scaling and shearing. These values were chosen considering that larger amplitudes are not expected in a typical FMRI study. All simulated data were

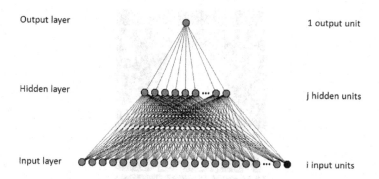

Fig. 1. Basic architecture of each of the twelve NN. The different layers of the NN are fully connected. The number of input units ranges from 129 to 1459; the number of hidden units, from 18 to 60 (see text below). The output unit yields the estimate of the corresponding registration parameter (of t_x, t_y, t_z, r_x, r_y, r_z, s_x, s_y, s_z, sh_x, sh_y and sh_z).

corrupted with rician noise obtained considering Gaussian distributions with FWHM of 1% of mean brain value.

However, in order to assess the influence of the range of the simulated mis-registrations on the final accuracy, the experiment was repeated considering movements between -2.0 and 2.0 mm for translations, between -2.0 and 2.0 degrees for rotations, and between -2.0 and 2.0 % in both scaling and shearing. In both experiments, the mean absolute registration errors were compared to the ones provided by a custom VSB (Mutual Information) registration method (characterized by a Powell optimization scheme and a cubic-spline interpolation method).

For each 3D image in the data set, the corresponding Fourier space was calculated by IFFT. The learning dataset of the NN is constructed by selecting a cubic subset of the Fourier space (in both real and imaginary spaces), with dimensions $n \times n \times n$. In both experiments, we have tested subsets with $n =$ 4, 5, 6, 7, 8, and 9, yielding, respectively, 128, 250, 432, 686, 1024 and 1458 coefficients (*i.e.*, $2n^3$). The number of input units is increased by 1 in order to accommodate for bias, which has always the value 1.

In each case, the number of hidden units in each NN was adjusted to the number of input units. Using a pure heuristic formula, we have decided to set the number of hidden units to 18, 25, 33, 41, 51 and 60, respectively. No exploratory work aimed at optimizing these values was conducted.

2.3   Evaluation of the Training Process

The evolution of the training process was assessed using an evaluation dataset, which comprises 100 simulated examples - generated in the same way the learning datasets were. The accuracy of the NN-based motion correction method was assessed by calculating the mean absolute error, in each registration parameter,

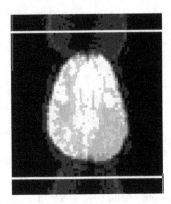

Fig. 2. Axial slice of the original image, before resizing it to a $64 \times 64 \times 16$ geometry. Horizontal bars indicate image limits after resizing.

between the simulated (known) misregistration value and the experimental (motion correction) value yielded by the corresponding NN. The method was finally applied on an actual FMRI time series.

3   Results and Discussion

The results for both experiments mentioned above are presented in Tables 1 and 2, respectively. These results refer to the mean absolute errors for the 12 registration parameters, which are expressed in mm, degrees, or percentage. The bottom row presents the mean absolute errors for the custom VSB(MI) method, for comparison purposes.

We may see from Tables 1 and 2 that the mean absolute errors are in the order of hundredths or tenths of mm, degrees or %. We may also see that an increase in the size of the Fourier subset leads to a decrease in registration accuracy, which may be due to the augmented complexity of the NN and to the *curse of dimensionality* associated to the increasing number of inputunits. This is observed for all transformation parameters except for r_x, which may be due a confounding influence between pitch and shearing. In fact, the Fourier coefficients containing spectrum power associated to these small rotations/shearing effects may be contained inside the smaller neighborhoods. Besides, it is known that the r_x parameter is difficult to estimate due to simmetry of the head around the x axis (left-right).

In Table 1, it is also possible to see that the proposed method yields results similar to the VSB (MI) custom method mentioned above, except for r_x, in which the latter yields better results, and for s_z, in which one observes the opposite. Surprisingly, for larger displacements, the VSB(MI) method yields the worst results than the NN($5 \times 5 \times 5$) method.

Table 1. Mean absolute registration error, for each registration parameter and Fourier-space subset, for experiment 1 (random transformation parameters uniformely distributed between ±1 mm, deg and %). Translation and rotation errors are expressed in mm and degrees, respectively; scaling an shearing errors in %. Botton lines refers to the custom VSB(MI) method.

Fourier subset $(n \times n \times n)$	δt_x [mm]	δt_y [mm]	δt_z [mm]	δr_x [deg]	δr_y [deg]	δr_z [deg]	δs_x [%]	δs_y [%]	δs_z [%]	δsh_x [%]	δsh_y [%]	δsh_z [%]
$4 \times 4 \times 4$	0.029	0.032	0.028	0.155	0.051	0.068	0.025	0.026	0.023	0.008	0.005	0.005
$5 \times 5 \times 5$	0.026	0.031	0.032	0.122	0.043	0.047	0.031	0.028	0.030	0.007	0.005	0.004
$6 \times 6 \times 6$	0.025	0.031	0.030	0.100	0.043	0.049	0.037	0.036	0.037	0.006	0.007	0.006
$7 \times 7 \times 7$	0.036	0.028	0.036	0.084	0.038	0.042	0.049	0.055	0.050	0.007	0.006	0.007
$8 \times 8 \times 8$	0.031	0.037	0.034	0.069	0.046	0.041	0.056	0.056	0.054	0.009	0.008	0.009
$9 \times 9 \times 9$	0.038	0.042	0.042	0.070	0.049	0.053	0.066	0.068	0.067	0.018	0.011	0.010
VSB(MI)	0.021	0.026	0.048	0.059	0.055	0.034	0.015	0.024	0.119	0.042	0.032	0.092

Table 2. Mean absolute registration error, for each registration parameter and Fourier-space subset, for experiment 2 (random transformation parameters uniformely distributed between ±2 mm, deg and %). Translation and rotation errors are expressed in mm and degrees, respectively; scaling an shearing errors in %. Botton lines refers to the custom VSB(MI) method.

Fourier subset $(n \times n \times n)$	δt_x [mm]	δt_y [mm]	δt_z [mm]	δr_x [deg]	δr_y [deg]	δr_z [deg]	δs_x [%]	δs_y [%]	δs_z [%]	δsh_x [%]	δsh_y [%]	δsh_z [%]
$4 \times 4 \times 4$	0.079	0.081	0.073	0.242	0.085	0.124	0.024	0.024	0.022	0.013	0.009	0.009
$5 \times 5 \times 5$	0.026	0.031	0.032	0.122	0.043	0.047	0.031	0.028	0.030	0.007	0.005	0.004
$6 \times 6 \times 6$	0.025	0.031	0.030	0.100	0.043	0.049	0.037	0.036	0.037	0.006	0.007	0.006
$7 \times 7 \times 7$	0.036	0.028	0.036	0.084	0.038	0.042	0.049	0.055	0.050	0.007	0.006	0.007
$8 \times 8 \times 8$	0.031	0.037	0.034	0.069	0.046	0.041	0.056	0.056	0.054	0.009	0.008	0.009
$9 \times 9 \times 9$	0.038	0.042	0.042	0.070	0.049	0.053	0.066	0.068	0.067	0.018	0.011	0.010
VSB(MI)	0.017	0.021	0.068	0.103	0.070	0.030	0.018	0.035	0.231	0.095	0.058	0.167

We note that these errors correspond to the motion correction estimates yielded by the 12 NN after having learned the one thousand simulated examples. Figure 3 represents, for the first evaluation dataset, the evolution of the mean absolute error as the number of learning examples increases. These error curves follow a negative exponential-like curve starting at approximately 0.7 mm or 0.7 degrees, which corresponds to the RMS of the simulated misregistration values. This indicates that the one thousand images may not be entirely necessary for the NN to learn. Besides, these error curves do not decrease monotonically (mainly for translations and rotations), which stresses the necessity of a robust stopping criterion for the learning process, which is currently being developed. For scaling and specially for shearing, the curves decrease monotonically.

The learning stage requires computation times ranging from 2 s to 24 s, on an ordinary computer, depending on the size of the Fourier space subset. The calculation of the registration parameters for the 100 examples comprised in the

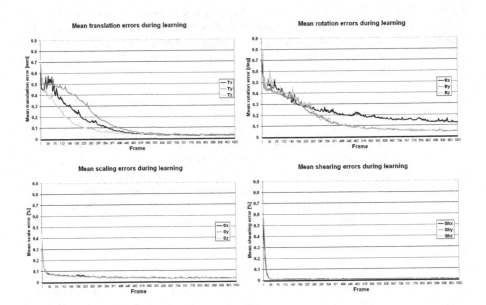

Fig. 3. Evolution of the mean absolute error for the first evaluation dataset, as the number of learning images increases: *top*: for translations and rotations; *bottom*: for scaling and shearing

evaluation dataset, takes less than 0.1 s. Our custom VSB(MI) method takes approximately 2 hours.

The construction of the learning dataset (Fourier subsets of the one thousand images) requires approximately 90 seconds, which is possible due to the fact that one reduced the image dimensions to powers of 2 in order to allow the use of a IFFT algorithm.

The application of the proposed method to an actual time series (the one from which the 3D frame used for simulations was extracted) yielded encouraging results, such as the ones presented in Figure 4, which shows the translation and rotation estimates obtained using the proposed method (with 5 × 5 × 5 Fourier coefficients) and the custom VSB(MI) registration method, considering the affine transformation model.

We may see that for the different motion estimates, the proposed method yields results that follow the general tendency of VSB(MI) estimates. However, it is also possible to see that in almost all registration parameters, NN motion estimates are biased by the presence of functional activation (the functional paradigm of the actual time series comprises 10 on-of periods). This suggests that brain activation must be simulated, and learned, by the NN.

It is also important to emphasize that the direct comparison between motion estimates obtained by the proposed method and by the custom VSB(MI) may not be the most adequate criterion since both methods seem affected by the increasing number of transformation parameters. This can be seen in Figure 5,

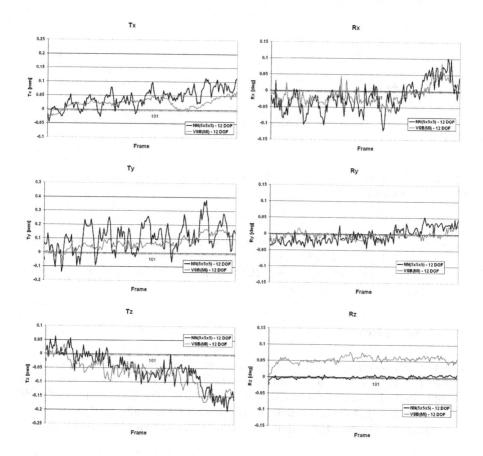

Fig. 4. Translation and rotation estimates for the 180 frames of the actual time series

in which we present the rotation estimates for VSB(MI), considering the affine (12 DOF) and a rigid-body (6 DOF) geometric models. We may see that for the latest frames, the VSB(MI) consistently diverge from each other.

The NN motion estimates also present a general behavior that is more irregular than VSB(MI) estimates, which stresses the necessity of improving the general robustness of the method. This may be due to the increased number of motion parameters, which is known to reduce the smoothness of the energetic landscape of any registration method.

Nevertheless, the proposed work indicates that for each single actual FMRI time series, comprised by one reference image followed by typically hundreds of test images, one may establish the following acquisition protocol:

1. acquire one reference image after the scanner reached the steady-state (which typically occurs after acquiring 10 to 20 images);
2. construct the training set of 1000 images from this reference image (elapsed time of 90 s, or less, if less training images are generated);

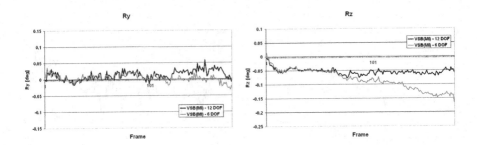

Fig. 5. Rotation parameters for the 180 frames of the actual time series using the VSB(MI) registration method

3. train the NN (elapsed time comprised between 2 and 24 s, depending on the number of input and hidden units);
4. start acquiring (and registering) the test images (after a total elapsed time of approximately 110 s, or less).

4   Conclusion

This work shows that the proposed method seems suitable for fast 3D affine motion correction of images using data from the corresponding Fourier space. The use of a limited (small) subset of data extracted from the Fourier space of each image indicates that the presented method may be eventually used for prospective registration during the acquisition of 3D frames, possibly from navigation echoes.

The registration is treated as a regression problem, which is possible since NN have the ability of modeling complex (non-linear) functions and are considered universal estimators [6]. Based on a training set of simulated images, the NN learn how to relate a subset of the Fourier space to the registration parameters, which are the output of the twelve NN. After the learning stage, the NN is able to compute the transformation parameters almost instantly. In fact, as mentioned in other works (*e.g.* [18]), the main advantage of NN modeling is that once trained, the computational effort needed to compute the function is extremely small.

Further work involves improving the robustness of the proposed method against activation presence, which shall be taken into consideration during the learning stage.

References

1. Abche, A., Yaacoub, F., Maalouf, A., Karam, E.: Image registration based on neural network and fourier transform. In: Proceedings of the 28th IEEE EMBS Annual International Conference, pp. 4803–4806 (2006)

2. Collignon, A., Maes, F., Delaere, D., Vandermeulen, D., Suetens, P., Marchal, G.: Automated multi-modality image registration based on information theory. In: IPMI 1995, pp. 263–274. Kluwer Academic Press, Dordrecht (1995)
3. Elhanany, I., Sheinfeld, M., Beck, A., Kadmon, Y., Tal, N., Tirosh, D.: Robust image registration based on feedforward neural networks. In: Proceedings of the IEEE International Conference on Systems, Man, and Cybernetics, vol. 1502, pp. 1507–1511 (2000)
4. Freire, L., Godinho, F.: Multimodality image registration using a neural-network-based method. Proceedings of the EANM Congress, European Journal of Nuclear Medicine 32(1), S76–S77 (2005)
5. Guetter, C., Xu, C., Sauer, F., Hornegger, J.: Learning based non-rigid multi-modal image registration using kullback-leibler divergence. In: Duncan, J.S., Gerig, G. (eds.) MICCAI 2005. LNCS, vol. 3750, pp. 255–262. Springer, Heidelberg (2005)
6. Haykin, S.: Neural Networks, A Comprehensive Foundation (1999)
7. Hill, D.L., Batchelor, P.G., Holden, M., Hawkes, D.J.: Medical image registration. Physics in Medicine and Biology 46(3), R1–R45 (2001)
8. Lee, D., Hofmann, M., Steinke, F., Altun, Y., Cahill, N., Schlkopf, B.: Learning similarity measure for multi-modal 3D image registration. In: CVPR - IEEE Conference on Computer Vision and Pattern Recognition, pp. 186–193 (2009) (abstract)
9. Leventon, M., Grimson, E.: Multi-modal volume registration using joint intensity distributions. In: Wells, W.M., Colchester, A.C.F., Delp, S.L. (eds.) MICCAI 1998. LNCS, vol. 1496, pp. 1057–1066. Springer, Heidelberg (1998)
10. Liu, H., Yan, J., Zhang, D.: Three-dimensional surface registration: A neural network strategy. Neurocomputing 70, 597–602 (2006)
11. Maintz, J.B.A., Viergever, M.A.: A survey of medical image registration. Medical Image Analysis 2(1), 1–36 (1998)
12. Roche, A., Malandain, G., Pennec, X., Ayache, N.: The correlation ratio as a new similarity measure for multimodal image registration. In: Wells, W.M., Colchester, A.C.F., Delp, S.L. (eds.) MICCAI 1998. LNCS, vol. 1496, pp. 1115–1124. Springer, Heidelberg (1998)
13. Sabuncu, M., Ramadge, P.: Using spanning graphs for efficient image registration. IEEE Transactions on Image Processing 17(5) (2008)
14. Shang, L., Cheng Lv, J., Yi, Z.: Rigid medical image registration using PCA neural network. Neurocomputing 69, 1717–1722 (2006)
15. Woods, R.P., Mazziotta, J.C., Cherry, S.R.: MRI-PET registration with automated algorithm. Journal of Computer Assisted Tomography 17(4), 536–546 (1993)
16. Xu, A., Jin, X., Guo, P.: Two-dimensional PCA combined with PCA for neural network based image registration. In: Jiao, L., Wang, L., Gao, X.-b., Liu, J., Wu, F. (eds.) ICNC 2006. LNCS, vol. 4222, pp. 696–705. Springer, Heidelberg (2006)
17. Yan, C., Ong, S., Ge, Y., Zhang, J., Teoh, S., Okker, B.: A neural network approach for 3d surface modeling and registration. In: Proceedings of the 2004 IEEE International Workshop on Biomedical Circuits and Systems, S3.2-17–20 (2004)
18. Zhang, J., Ge, Y., Ong, S., Chui, C., Teoh, S., Yan, C.: Rapid surface registration of 3d volumes using a neural network approach. Image and Vision Computing 26, 201–210 (2008)

Neural Networks Regression Inductive Conformal Predictor and Its Application to Total Electron Content Prediction

Harris Papadopoulos and Haris Haralambous

Computer Science and Engineering Department, Frederick University,
7 Y. Frederickou St., Palouriotisa, Nicosia 1036, Cyprus
{h.papadopoulos,h.haralambous}@frederick.ac.cy

Abstract. In this paper we extend regression Neural Networks (NNs) based on the Conformal Prediction (CP) framework for accompanying predictions with reliable measures of confidence. We follow a modification of the original CP approach, called Inductive Conformal Prediction (ICP), which enables us to overcome the computational inefficiency problem of CP. Unlike the point predictions produced by conventional regression NNs the proposed approach produces predictive intervals that satisfy a given confidence level. We apply it to the problem of predicting Total Electron Content (TEC), which is an important parameter in trans-ionospheric links. Our experimental results on a dataset collected over a period of 11 years show that the resulting predictive intervals are both well-calibrated and tight enough to be useful in practice.

Keywords: Conformal Prediction, Confidence Measures, Predictive Intervals, Regression, Neural Networks, Total Electron Content.

1 Introduction

Conformal Prediction (CP) is a novel framework for complementing the predictions of traditional machine learning algorithms with valid measures of their confidence. Confidence measures indicate the likelihood of each prediction being correct and therefore provide the ability of making much more informed decisions. This makes them a highly desirable feature of the techniques developed for many real-world applications.

CP was initially proposed in [1] and later greatly improved in [2]. In these papers CP was applied to Support Vector Machines for classification. Soon it started being applied to other popular algorithms, such as k-Nearest Neighbours for classification [3], Neural Networks for classification [4], Ridge Regression [5] and k-Nearest Neighbours Regression [6]. The results reported in these papers show that the generated algorithms, called Conformal Predictors (CPs), produce confidence measures that are both reliable and useful in practice. Furthermore, to date CPs have been applied to a variety of problems, such as the early detection of ovarian cancer [7], the classification of leukaemia subtypes [8], the prediction of plant promoters [9] and the diagnosis of acute abdominal pain [10].

K. Diamantaras, W. Duch, L.S. Iliadis (Eds.): ICANN 2010, Part I, LNCS 6352, pp. 32–41, 2010.
© Springer-Verlag Berlin Heidelberg 2010

In this paper we develop a regression CP based on Neural Networks (NNs), which is one of the most popular machine learning techniques. Some indicative fields in which NNs have been used with success are medicine, image processing, environmental modelling, robotics and the industry; see e.g. [11,12,13,14]. In order to apply CP to NNs we follow a modified version of the original CP approach, called Inductive Conformal Prediction (ICP). ICP was proposed in [15] for regression and in [16] for classification, in an effort to overcome the computational inefficiency problem of CP. As demonstrated in [4], which describes ICP and its application to classification NNs, this computational inefficiency problem renders the original CP approach highly unsuitable for being coupled with NNs; and in general any method that requires long training times.

In the case of regression, instead of the point predictions produced by conventional techniques, CPs produce predictive intervals that satisfy a given level of confidence. The important property of these intervals is that they are well-calibrated, meaning that in the long run the intervals produced for some confidence level $1 - \delta$ will not contain the true label of an example with a relative frequency of at most δ. Moreover, this is achieved without assuming anything more than that the data are independent and identically distributed (i.i.d.), which is the typical assumption of most machine learning methods.

We apply the proposed method to the problem of predicting Total Electron Content (TEC) which is an important parameter that represents a quantitative measure of the detrimental effect of the ionosphere (an ionised region in the upper atmosphere) on electromagnetic signals from space-based systems propagating through it. Prediction of TEC enables mitigation techniques to be applied in order to reduce these undesirable ionospheric effects on communication, surveillance and navigation systems. For this reason, the use of NNs for TEC prediction was addressed in many studies such as [17,18,19]. In this work we make one step further and provide predictive intervals, which make mitigation techniques more effective as they allow taking into account the highest possible TEC value at a desired confidence level.

2 Inductive Conformal Prediction

This section gives a brief description of the CP framework and its inductive version which is followed in this paper, for a more detailed description the interested reader is referred to [20]. We are interested in making a prediction for the label of an example x_{l+g}, based on a set of training examples $\{(x_1, y_1), \ldots, (x_l, y_l)\}$, where each $x_i \in \mathbb{R}^d$ is the vector of attributes for example i and $y_i \in \mathbb{R}$ is the label of that example. Our only assumption is that all (x_i, y_i), $i = 1, 2, \ldots$, are independent and identically distributed.

The idea behind CP is to assume every possible label $\tilde{y}$ of the example x_{l+g} and check how likely it is that the extended set of examples

$$\{(x_1, y_1), \ldots, (x_l, y_l), (x_{l+g}, \tilde{y})\} \tag{1}$$

is i.i.d. This in effect will correspond to the likelihood of $\tilde{y}$ being the true label of the example x_{l+g} since this is the only unknown value in (1).

To do this we first assign a value $\alpha_i^{\tilde{y}}$ to each pair (x_i, y_i) in (1) which indicates how strange, or nonconforming, this pair is for the rest of the examples in the same set. This value, called the *nonconformity score* of the pair (x_i, y_i), is calculated using a traditional machine learning algorithm, called the *underlying algorithm* of the corresponding CP. More specifically, the nonconformity score of a pair (x_i, y_i) is the degree of disagreement between the actual label y_i and the prediction $\hat{y}_i$ of the underlying algorithm, after being trained on (1); note that in the case of the pair $(x_{l+g}, \tilde{y})$ the actual label is replaced by the assumed label $\tilde{y}$. The function used for measuring this degree of disagreement is called the *nonconformity measure* of the CP.

The nonconformity score $\alpha_{l+g}^{\tilde{y}}$ is then compared to the nonconformity scores of all other examples to find out how unusual $(x_{l+g}, \tilde{y})$ is according to the nonconformity measure used. This comparison is performed with the function

$$p((x_1, y_1), \ldots, (x_l, y_l), (x_{l+g}, \tilde{y})) = \frac{\#\{i = 1, \ldots, l, l + g : \alpha_i^{\tilde{y}} \geq \alpha_{l+g}^{\tilde{y}}\}}{l + 1}, \qquad (2)$$

the output of which is called the p-value of $\tilde{y}$, also denoted as $p(\tilde{y})$. An important property of (2) is that $\forall \delta \in [0, 1]$ and for all probability distributions P on Z,

$$P^{l+1}\{((x_1, y_1), \ldots, (x_l, y_l), (x_{l+g}, y_{l+g})) : p(y_{l+g}) \leq \delta\} \leq \delta; \qquad (3)$$

a proof can be found in [20]. This makes it a valid test of randomness with respect to the i.i.d. model. According to this property, if $p(\tilde{y})$ is under some very low threshold, say 0.05, this means that $\tilde{y}$ is highly unlikely as the probability of such an event is at most 5% if (1) is i.i.d.

Assuming it were possible to calculate the p-value of every possible label following the above procedure, we could then exclude all labels with a p-value under some very low threshold, or *significance level*, δ and have at most δ chance of being wrong. Consequently, given a confidence level $1 - \delta$ a regression CP outputs the set

$$\{\tilde{y} : p(\tilde{y}) > \delta\}, \qquad (4)$$

in other words the interval containing all labels that have a p-value greater than δ. Of course it is impossible to explicitly consider every possible label $\tilde{y} \in \mathbb{R}$, so regression CPs follow a different approach which makes it possible to compute the predictive interval (4). This approach is described in [5] for Ridge Regression and in [6] for k-Nearest Neighbours Regression.

The only drawback of the original CP approach is that due to its transductive nature all its computations, including training the underlying algorithm, have to be repeated for every test example. This makes it very computationally inefficient especially for algorithms that require long training times such as NNs. ICP is based on the same theoretical foundations described above, but performs inductive rather than transductive inference. As a result ICP is almost as efficient as its underlying algorithm [4].

ICP splits the training set (of size l) into two smaller sets, the *proper training set* with $m < l$ examples and the *calibration set* with $q := l - m$ examples.

It then uses the proper training set for training its underlying algorithm and the calibration set for calculating the p-value of each possible label $\tilde{y}$. More specifically, it trains the underlying algorithm on $(x_1, y_1), \ldots, (x_m, y_m)$ and uses it to compute the nonconformity score α_{m+i} of each example in the calibration set $x_{m+i}, i = 1, \ldots, q$. This needs to be done only once as now x_{l+g} is not included in the training set of the underlying algorithm. From this point on, it only needs to compute the nonconformity score $a_{l+g}^{\tilde{y}}$ of each new example x_{l+g} being assigned each possible label $\tilde{y}$ and calculate the p-value of $\tilde{y}$ as

$$p(\tilde{y}) = \frac{\#\{i = m+1, \ldots, m+q, l+g : \alpha_i \geq \alpha_{l+g}^{\tilde{y}}\}}{q+1}. \tag{5}$$

Again it is impossible to explicitly go through every possible label $\tilde{y} \in \mathbb{R}$ to calculate its p-value, but it is possible to compute the predictive interval (4) as we show in the next section.

3   Neural Networks Regression ICP

In order to use ICP in conjunction with some traditional algorithm we first have to define a nonconformity measure. Recall that a nonconformity measure is a function that measures the disagreement between the actual label y_i and the prediction $\hat{y}_i$ for the example x_i. In the case of regression this can be easily defined as the absolute difference between the two

$$\alpha_i = |y_i - \hat{y}_i|. \tag{6}$$

We first describe the Neural Networks Regression ICP (NNR ICP) algorithm with this measure and then define a *normalized nonconformity measure*, which has the effect of producing tighter predictive intervals by taking into account the expected accuracy of the underlying NN on each example.

The first steps of the NNR ICP algorithm follow exactly the general scheme given in Section 2:

- Split the training set $\{(x_1, y_1), \ldots, (x_l, y_l)\}$ into two subsets:
  - the proper training set: $\{(x_1, y_1), \ldots, (x_m, y_m)\}$, and
  - the calibration set: $\{(x_{m+1}, y_{m+1}), \ldots, (x_{m+q}, y_{m+q})\}$.
- Use the proper training set to train the NN.
- For each pair $(x_{m+i}, y_{m+i}), i = 1, \ldots, q$ in the calibration set:
  - supply the input pattern x_{m+i} to the trained NN to obtain $\hat{y}_{m+i}$ and
  - calculate the nonconformity score α_{m+i} with (6).

At this point however, it becomes impossible to follow the general ICP scheme as there is no way of trying out all possible labels $\tilde{y} \in \mathbb{R}$ in order to calculate their nonconformity score and p-value. Notice though that both the nonconformity scores of the calibration set examples $\alpha_{m+1}, \ldots, \alpha_{m+q}$ and the prediction of the trained NN $\hat{y}_{l+g}$ for the new example x_{l+g} will remain fixed as we change the assumed label $\tilde{y}$. The only value that will change is the nonconformity score

$\alpha_{l+g}^{\tilde{y}} = |\tilde{y} - \hat{y}_{l+g}|$. Thus $p(\tilde{y})$ will only change at the points where $\alpha_{l+g}^{\tilde{y}} = \alpha_{m+i}$ for some $i = 1, \ldots, q$. As a result, for a given confidence level $1 - \delta$ we only need to find the biggest α_{m+i} such that when $\alpha_{l+g}^{\tilde{y}} = \alpha_{m+i}$ then $p(\tilde{y}) > \delta$, which will give us the maximum and minimum $\tilde{y}$ that have a p-value greater than δ and consequently the beginning and end of the corresponding predictive region. More specifically, after calculating the nonconformity scores of all calibration examples the NNR ICP algorithm continues as follows:

- Sort the nonconformity scores of the calibration examples in descending order obtaining the sequence $\alpha_{(m+1)}, \ldots, \alpha_{(m+q)}$.
- For each new test example x_{l+g}:
  - supply the input pattern x_{l+g} to the trained NN to obtain $\hat{y}_{l+g}$ and
  - output the predictive interval

$$(\hat{y}_{l+g} - \alpha_{(m+s)}, \hat{y}_{l+g} + \alpha_{(m+s)}), \tag{7}$$

where $s = \lfloor \delta(q + 1) \rfloor$.

3.1   A Normalized Nonconformity Measure

We extend nonconformity measure definition (6) by normalizing it with the predicted accuracy of the underlying NN on the given example. This leads to predictive intervals that are larger for the "difficult" examples and smaller for the "easy" ones. As a result the ICP can satisfy the required confidence level with intervals that are on average tighter. This measure is defined as

$$\alpha_i = \frac{|y_i - \hat{y}_i|}{\exp(\mu_i)}, \tag{8}$$

where μ_i is the prediction of the value $\ln(|y_i - \hat{y}_i|)$ produced by a linear NN trained on the proper training patterns with the corresponding labels (and exp is the exponential function). We use the logarithmic instead of the direct scale to ensure that the estimate is always positive. When using (8) as nonconformity measure the predictive interval produced by the ICP for each new pattern x_{l+g} becomes

$$(\hat{y}_{l+g} - \alpha_{(m+s)} \exp(\mu_{l+g}), \hat{y}_{l+g} + \alpha_{(m+s)} \exp(\mu_{l+g})), \tag{9}$$

where again $s = \lfloor \delta(q + 1) \rfloor$.

4   Total Electron Content Prediction

TEC is defined as the total amount of electrons along a particular line of sight and is measured in total electron content units (1 TECu $= 10^{16}$ el/m^2). It is an important parameter in trans-ionospheric links since when multiplied by a factor which is a function of the signal frequency, it yields an estimate of the delay imposed on the signal by the ionosphere (an ionized region ranging in height above the surface of the earth from approximately 50 to 1000 km) due

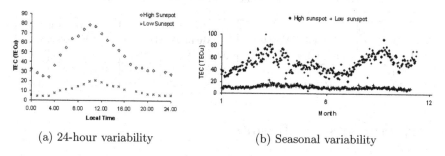

(a) 24-hour variability   (b) Seasonal variability

Fig. 1. 24-hour and seasonal variability of TEC for low and high solar activity

to its dispersive nature [21]. Consequently, accurate prediction of TEC can be used in the application of mitigation techniques for the reduction of ionospheric imposed errors on communication, surveillance and navigation systems.

The density of free electrons within the ionosphere and therefore TEC depend upon the strength of the solar ionizing radiation which is a function of time of day, season, geographical location and solar activity [22]. Figure 1a shows two examples of the 24-hour variability of TEC during low and high solar activity, which is expressed by an index called sunspot number. Examples of its seasonal variability are shown in Figure 1b, which plots the noon values of TEC again for low and high sunspot. As can be observed from these figures solar activity has an important effect on both the 24-hour and seasonal variability of TEC.

The TEC measurements used in this work consist of a bit more than 60000 values recorded between 1998 and 2009. The parameters used as inputs for modelling TEC are the hour, day and monthly mean sunspot number. The first two were converted into their quadrature components in order to avoid their unrealistic discontinuity at the midnight and change of year boundaries. Therefore the following four values were used in their place:

$$sinhour = \sin(2\pi\frac{hour}{24}), \tag{10}$$

$$coshour = \cos(2\pi\frac{hour}{24}), \tag{11}$$

$$sinday = \sin(2\pi\frac{day}{24}), \tag{12}$$

$$cosday = \cos(2\pi\frac{day}{24}). \tag{13}$$

It is worth to note that in ionospheric work solar activity is usually represented by the 12-month smoothed sunspot number, which however has the disadvantage that the most recent value available corresponds to TEC measurements made six months ago. In our case in order to enable TEC data to be modeled as soon as they are measured, and for future predictions of TEC to be made, the monthly mean sunspot number values were modeled using a smooth curve defined by a summation of sinusoids.

Table 1. Tightness and empirical reliability results

Nonconformity Measure	Median Width			Interdecile Mean Width			Percentage of Errors (%)		
	90%	95%	99%	90%	95%	99%	90%	95%	99%
(6)	16.15	21.88	38.17	16.32	22.02	38.67	10.12	5.02	1.01
(8)	13.04	16.24	25.91	14.20	17.69	28.27	9.73	4.92	1.00

5   Experiments and Results

The experiments were performed following a 2-fold cross-validation process. The 60421 examples of the dataset were split randomly in two parts of almost equal size (one with 30211 and one with 30210 examples) and our tests were repeated twice, each time using one of the two parts as training set and the other as test set. This was done in order to evaluate the proposed method on the whole range of possible sunspot values (which exhibit an 11 year cycle), since solar activity has a strong effect on the variability of TEC. The choice of two rather than more folds was made due to the large size of the dataset.

The underlying NN had a fully connected two-layer structure, with 5 input, 13 hidden and 1 output neurons. The hidden layer consisted of neurons with hyperbolic tangent activation functions, while the output neuron had a linear activation function. The number of hidden neurons was determined by trial and error on the original NN. The training algorithm used was the Levenberg-Marquardt backpropagation algorithm with early stopping based on a validation set created from 10% of the proper training examples. In an effort to avoid local minima ten NNs were trained with different random initialisations and the one that performed best on the validation set was selected for being applied to the calibration and test examples. The calibration set consisted of 999 examples which were selected randomly from the training set; this resulted in $q + 1$ in (5) being 1000. The inputs of the network were normalized setting their minimum value to -1 and their maximum value to 1. Finaly, in order to ensure that the results reported here do not depend on the particular split of the dataset in the two folds or in the particular choice of calibration examples, our experiments were repeated 10 times with different permutations of the examples.

In terms of point predictions both our method and the original NN perform quite well with a RMSE of 5.5 TECu and a correlation coefficient between the predicted and the actual values of 0.94. However since the advantage of our method is that it outputs predictive intervals, the aim of our experiments was to check their tightness and therefore usefulness, and their empirical reliability. To this end the first and second parts of Table 1 report the median and interdecile mean widths of the obtained predictive intervals with the two nonconformity measures, while the third and last part reports the percentage of errors, which is in fact the percentage of intervals that did not contain the true label of the example. We chose to report the median and interdecile mean values instead of the mean for evaluating predictive interval tightness so as to avoid the strong impact of a few extremely large or extremely small intervals.

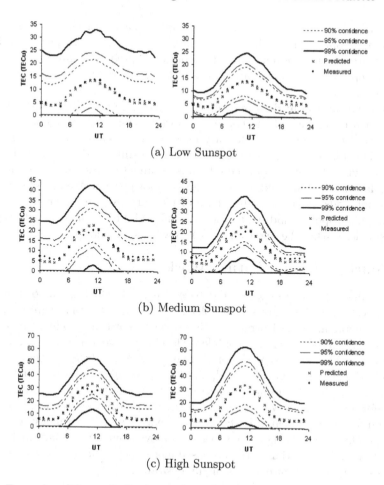

(a) Low Sunspot

(b) Medium Sunspot

(c) High Sunspot

Fig. 2. Examples of the predictive intervals produced by nonconformity measure (6) on the left and (8) on the right for typical days in low, medium and high sunspot periods

The values in the first two parts of Table 1 do not really give us much information on their own, in order to evaluate them we should consider the range of the measured values in our dataset, which are between 0 and 110 TECu. If we now transform the values in the table to the percentage of this range that they represent we see that the predictive intervals of the proposed method are quite impressive. For example, the median width obtained with nonconformity measure (8) for a confidence as high as 99% covers 23.5% of the range, while for the 95% confidence it only covers 14.8%. It is also worth to mention that, since the produced intervals are generated based on the size of the absolute error that the underlying algorithm can have on each example, a few of the intervals start from values below zero, which are impossible for the particular application. So we could in fact make these intervals start at zero without making any additional errors and this would result in slightly smaller values than those reported in this table. We chose not to do so here in order to evaluate the actual intervals as output by our method without any intervention. The third part of Table 1 demonstrates clearly the reliability of the obtained predictive intervals. The percentages reported in this part are almost equal to the required significance level in all cases.

By comparing the median and interdecile mean values of the intervals produced when using each of the two nonconformity measures we see that, as expected, our normalized nonconformity measure (8) gives on average tighter intervals. The difference between the two measures is further demonstrated graphically in Figure 2, which plots the intervals obtained by each measure for three typical days in the low, medium and high sunspot periods. We can see that unlike the intervals of measure (6), those of measure (8) are larger at noon and in the high sunspot period, when the variability of TEC is higher, but they are much smaller during the night and in the low sunspot period.

6   Conclusions and Future Work

We have developed a regression ICP based on NNs, which is one of the most popular techniques for regression problems. Unlike conventional regression NNs, and in general machine learning methods, our algorithm produces predictive intervals that satisfy a required confidence level. Our experimental results on the prediction of TEC show that the predictive intervals produced by the proposed method are not only well-calibrated, and therefore highly reliable, but they are also tight enough to be useful in practice. Furthermore, we defined a normalized nonconformity measure, which results in tighter predictive intervals. Our main direction for future research is the development of more such measures, which will hopefully give even tighter intervals. Moreover, our future plans include the application and evaluation of the proposed method on other problems for which provision of predictive intervals is highly desirable.

References

1. Gammerman, A., Vapnik, V., Vovk, V.: Learning by transduction. In: Proceedings of the Fourteenth Conference on Uncertainty in Artificial Intelligence, pp. 148–156. Morgan Kaufmann, San Francisco (1998)
2. Saunders, C., Gammerman, A., Vovk, V.: Transduction with confidence and credibility. In: Proceedings of the 16th International Joint Conference on Artificial Intelligence, Los Altos, CA, vol. 2, pp. 722–726. Morgan Kaufmann, San Francisco (1999)
3. Proedrou, K., Nouretdinov, I., Vovk, V., Gammerman, A.: Transductive confidence machines for pattern recognition. In: Elomaa, T., Mannila, H., Toivonen, H. (eds.) ECML 2002. LNCS (LNAI), vol. 2430, pp. 381–390. Springer, Heidelberg (2002)
4. Papadopoulos, H.: Inductive conformal prediction: Theory and application to neural networks. In: Fritzsche, P. (ed.) Tools in Artificial Intelligence, I-Tech, Vienna, Austria, pp. 315–330 (2008), http://intechweb.org/downloadpdf.php?id=5294
5. Nouretdinov, I., Melluish, T., Vovk, V.: Ridge regression confidence machine. In: Proceedings of the 18th International Conference on Machine Learning (ICML 2001), pp. 385–392. Morgan Kaufmann, San Francisco (2001)

6. Papadopoulos, H., Gammerman, A., Vovk, V.: Normalized nonconformity measures for regression conformal prediction. In: Proceedings of the IASTED International Conference on Artificial Intelligence and Applications (AIA 2008), pp. 64–69. ACTA Press (2008)
7. Gammerman, A., Vovk, V., Burford, B., Nouretdinov, I., Luo, Z., Chervonenkis, A., Waterfield, M., Cramer, R., Tempst, P., Villanueva, J., Kabir, M., Camuzeaux, S., Timms, J., Menon, U., Jacobs, I.: Serum proteomic abnormality predating screen detection of ovarian cancer. The Computer Journal (2008)
8. Bellotti, T., Luo, Z., Gammerman, A., Delft, F.W.V., Saha, V.: Qualified predictions for microarray and proteomics pattern diagnostics with confidence machines. International Journal of Neural Systems 15(4), 247–258 (2005)
9. Shahmuradov, I.A., Solovyev, V.V., Gammerman, A.J.: Plant promoter prediction with confidence estimation. Nucleic Acids Research 33(3), 1069–1076 (2005)
10. Papadopoulos, H., Gammerman, A., Vovk, V.: Confidence predictions for the diagnosis of acute abdominal pain. In: Artificial Intelligence Applications & Innovations III. IFIP, vol. 296, pp. 175–184. Springer, Heidelberg (2009)
11. Mantzaris, D., Anastassopoulos, G., Adamopoulos, A., Gardikis, S.: A non-symbolic implementation of abdominal pain estimation in childhood. Information Sciences 178(20), 3860–3866 (2008)
12. Iliadis, L.S., Maris, F.: An artificial neural network model for mountainous water-resources management: The case of cyprus mountainous watersheds. Environmental Modelling and Software 22(7), 1066–1072 (2007)
13. Yang, S., Wang, M., Jiao, L.: Radar target recognition using contourlet packet transform and neural network approach. Signal Processing 89(4), 394–409 (2009)
14. Iliadis, L.S., Spartalis, S., Tachos, S.: Application of fuzzy t-norms towards a new artificial neural networks' evaluation framework: A case from wood industry. Information Sciences 178(20), 3828–3839 (2008)
15. Papadopoulos, H., Proedrou, K., Vovk, V., Gammerman, A.: Inductive confidence machines for regression. In: Elomaa, T., Mannila, H., Toivonen, H. (eds.) ECML 2002. LNCS (LNAI), vol. 2430, pp. 345–356. Springer, Heidelberg (2002)
16. Papadopoulos, H., Vovk, V., Gammerman, A.: Qualified predictions for large data sets in the case of pattern recognition. In: Proceedings of the 2002 International Conference on Machine Learning and Applications, pp. 159–163. CSREA Press (2002)
17. Cander, L.R., Milosavljevic, M.M., Stankovic, S.S., Tomasevic, S.: Ionospheric forecasting technique by artificial neural network. Electronics Letters 34(16), 1573–1574 (1998)
18. Maruyama, T.: Regional reference total electron content model over japan based on neural network mapping techniques. Ann. Geophys. 25, 2609–2614 (2007)
19. Haralambous, H., Vrionides, P., Economou, L., Papadopoulos, H.: A local total electron content neural network model over Cyprus. In: Proceedings of the 4th International Symposium on Communications, Control and Signal Processing (IS-CCSP). IEEE, Los Alamitos (2010)
20. Vovk, V., Gammerman, A., Shafer, G.: Algorithmic Learning in a Random World. Springer, New York (2005)
21. Kersley, L., Malan, D., Pryse, S.E., Cander, L.R., Bamford, R.A., Belehaki, A., Leitinger, R., Radicella, S.M., Mitchell, C.N., Spencer, P.S.J.: Total electron content - a key parameter in propagation: measurement and use in ionospheric imaging. Annals of Geophysics 47(2-3), 1067–1091 (2004)
22. Goodman, J.: HF Communications, Science and Technology. Van Nostrand Reinhold, New York (1992)

Prediction of Compaction Characteristics of Granular Soils by Neural Networks

Marzena Kłos and Zenon Waszczyszyn

Rzeszów University of Technology, Chair of Structural Mechanics,
ul. W. Pola 2, 35-959 Rzeszów, Poland
{marklos,zewasz}@prz.edu.pl

Abstract. New experimental data discussed in [5] are used in the present paper. Application of the penalized error function, Principle Data Analysis and Bayesian criterion of Maximum Marginal Likelihood enabled design and training of numerically efficient small neural networks. They were applied for identification of two compaction characteristics, i.e. Optimum Water Content and Maximum Dry Density of granular soils.

Keywords: Compaction characteristics, granular soils, neural networks.

1 Introduction

Engineering structures which involve earthworks such as roadway embankment, earth dams and soil liners often require compaction to improve soil conditions. In case of granular soils, Optimum Water Content (OWC) and Maximum Dry Density (MDD) are essential characteristics for the design of compacted earthwork. These characteristics can be found experimentally by means of Proctor's Standard laboratory Test ASTM D558-57, cf. [1].

Proctor's Test is laborious and time consuming. That is why Artificial Neural Networks (ANNs) have been used to predict compaction characteristics, cf. [2], [3], [4], [5]. The application of standard ANNs was discussed in [3], [4] in case of synthetic soils composed of four different components. In book [2] it was proved that granular soils can be analyzed only by means of grain size distribution $\{D_x\}$. New measurement of these data discussed in [5] is an experimental base of the present paper.

The application of network error measure with penalty terms and application of the Principle Component Analysis (PCA) enabled obtaining satisfactory results for efficient networks without losing the approximation accuracy.

2 Adopted Data

According to [2] input and output vectors are composed of variables corresponding to grain size distribution and compaction characteristics:

$$\mathbf{x}_{(10\times1)} = \{C_U, D_x \,|\, x = 10\%, \cdots, 90\%\}, \quad \mathbf{y}_{(2\times1)} = \{OWC, MDD\}, \tag{1}$$

K. Diamantaras, W. Duch, L.S. Iliadis (Eds.): ICANN 2010, Part I, LNCS 6352, pp. 42–45, 2010.
© Springer-Verlag Berlin Heidelberg 2010

where x [%] is the percentage of grain diameters D [mm] below which soil mass is placed. The uniformity coefficient $C_U = D_{60} / D_{10}$ is also introduced as an input variable.

The total number of patterns $P = 121$ was randomly split into the learning (training) and testing sets of pattern numbers L and T, respectively. Basic computations were carried out for 30% of training patterns, i.e. $T = 0.3\,P$. In [1], [5] the total set of patterns was split into the learning, validation and testing sets composed of $L = 0.5\,P$, $V = T = 0.25\,P$ patterns, respectively.

3 Neural Network Analysis

The following network error was applied:

$$E_i \equiv E_{\mathcal{D}i} + E_{Wi} = \frac{\beta}{2} \sum_{p=1}^{P} \left\{ t_{pi} - y(\mathbf{x}_{pi}; \mathbf{w}) \right\}^2 + \frac{\alpha}{2} \sum_{j}^{W} w_j^2, \qquad (2)$$

where the first term $E_{\mathcal{D}i}$ is the standard Least Square Error function and E_{Wi} corresponds to a penalized, regularization function. Both terms are weighted by hyperparameters α and β.

The MATLAB neural toolbox [6] was used applying a single hidden layer composed of H sigmoid neurons and linear output. The networks were trained by means of the Levenberg-Marquardt learning method. In Table 1, values of the Root Mean Square Errors $RMSE_i^S$ and determination $(R_i^S)^2$ have been listed.

The computations carried out in [5] were based on the application of the network standard error restricted to remaining only the term $E_{\mathcal{D}}$ in (2). The conclusions from papers [3] and [4] that the ANN of single outputs should be applied for prediction of compaction was confirmed in [5]. The errors obtained for the best networks 5-4-1 for prediction of OWC and network 10-4-1 for MDD, are shown in Table 1.

Table 1. Network learning and testing errors

ANN No.	ANN architecture	Outputs	$RMSE_i^S$		$(R_i^S)^2$	
			L	T	L	T
1*	5-4-1	OWC	0.121	0.159	0.75	0.65
2*	10-4-1	MDD	0.077	0.085	0.91	0.89
3	10-4-2	OWC	0.098	0.112	0.89	0.79
	PCA	MDD	0.055	0.065	0.96	0.90
4	4-5-2	OWC	0.110	0.139	0.78	0.60
	PCA	MDD	0.070	0.081	0.87	0.80

* $T = 0.25\,P$.

The neural analysis is based on the error measure (2) with the penalized term. In (2) hyperparameters α and β are introduced. In the computations performed in the present paper, the fixed values $\alpha = 0.01$ and $\beta = 50.0$ were adopted, taken from [7] as initial values in the Bayesian Evidence procedure

In the present paper the PCA (Principle Component Analysis) was applied, cf. [8]. The (10×10) covariance matrix, computed for the input data set of $P = 121$ patterns, was formulated. The first four eigenvalues proved to be significantly higher than others. The errors corresponding to the original number of ten inputs, i.e. ANN No3 and network ANN No4 with the compressed inputs, are shown in Table 1.

For the prediction purposes the relative error $Re_i = (y_i / t_i - 1) \times 100\%$ is introduced, where coordinates y_i, t_i determine points on the planes $i = OWC, MCC$. In Figs 1a the lines $Re = \pm C \%$ bound the area in which prediction points with the relative errors $|Re| \leq C$ are placed. The bounded area corresponds to the cumulative parameter SR [%], called Success Ratio. SR is defined by the formula $SR = (SRe / S) \times 100\%$, where: SRe – number of prediction points in the Re area, S – total number of points of data sets $S = L, T$.

In Figs 1b the cumulative curves $SR_i^S (Re_i^S)$ are shown for the learning and testing sets computed by the networks 10-4-2, PCA and 4-5-2, PCA.

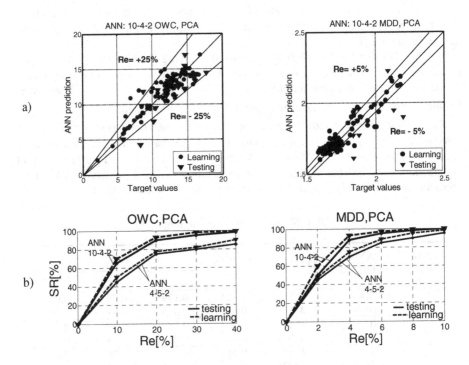

Fig. 1. a) Areas of $SR = 90\%$ with error bounds Re shown for network ANN: 10-4-2, PCA, **b)** Cumulative curves of Success Ratios $SR (Re)$ for the Re percent of correctly predicted compaction characteristics OWC and MDD and networks ANN: 10-4-2. 4-5-2, PCA

4   Final Remarks

1. The application of the penalized network error function (2) enables formulation of efficient networks with two outputs for the compaction characteristics OWC (Optimum Water Content) and MDD (Maximum Dry Density) prediction.

2. The application of the Bayesian criterion MML (Maximum Marginal Likelihood) makes it possible to design ANN with the use of only training set of patterns and compute optimal values of hyperparameters in the error function (2).

3. PCA transformation improves the accuracy of neural approximation. The network ANN: 10-4-2, PCA gives the best results from among all the networks presented in Table 1. This concerns especially the testing determination $(R_i^T)^2$. The network ANN: 4-5-2 PCA with compressed inputs gives slightly higher values of errors than network 10-4-2, PCA.

4. The Success Ratio curves $SC(Re)$ shown in Figs 1b, are close to each other for the above discussed networks for both the training and testing results. If we assume that about 80% of testing patterns are correctly predicted with $SR \approx 90\%$, the error area bounds are $|Re| \approx 25\%$ and $|Re| \approx 5\%$ for the compaction characteristics OWC and MDD, respectively.

Acknowledgments. The authors would like to acknowledge financial support from the Polish Ministry of Science and Higher Education, Grant No. N N506 4326 36, "Joining of artificial neural networks and Bayesian reasoning for the analysis of identification problems in structural dynamics and geotechnics".

References

1. Proctor, R.R.: Description of Field and Laboratory Methods. Eng. News Records 111, 286–289 (1993)
2. Sulewska, M.: Artificial Neural Networks for Evaluation of Compaction Parameters of Cohesionless Soils (in Polish). Committee Civil Eng. of the Polish Acad. Sci., Warsaw – Białystok (2009)
3. Najjar, Y.M.: On the Identification of Compaction Characteristics by Neuronets. Computers and Geotechnics 18, 167–187 (1996)
4. Sinha, S.K., Wang, M.C.: Artificial Neural Network Prediction Models for Soil Compaction and Permeability. Geotech. Geol. Eng. 26, 47–64 (2008)
5. Sulewska, M.: Neural Modeling of Compatibility Characteristics of Cohesionless Soil. Comp. Aided Mech. Eng. Sci. (submitted for publication)
6. Demuth, H., Beale, M.: Neural Network Toolbox: For Use with MATLAB, User's Guide, Version 3. The Mathworks Inc. (1998)
7. Nabney, I.T.: Netlab: Algorithms for Pattern Recognition. Springer, London (2004)
8. Waszczyszyn, Z., Słoński, M.: Selected Problems of Artificial Neural Network Development. In: Waszczyszyn, Z. (ed.) Advances of Soft Computing in Engineering. CISM Courses and Lectures, ch. 5, vol. 512, pp. 237–316. Springer, Wien (2010)

Modelling Power Output at Nuclear Power Plant by Neural Networks

Jaakko Talonen, Miki Sirola, and Eimontas Augilius

Aalto University, School of Science and Technology,
P.O. Box 15400 FI-00076 Aalto, Finland
{talonen,miki,eimontas}cis.hut.fi
http://www.cis.hut.fi/talonen

Abstract. In this paper, we propose two different neural network (NN) approaches for industrial process signal forecasting. Real data is available for this research from boiling water reactor type nuclear power reactors. NNs are widely used for time series prediction, but it isn't utilized for Olkiluoto nuclear power plant (NPP), Finland. Preprocessing, suitable input signals and delay analysis are important phases in modelling. Optimized number of delayed input signals and neurons in hidden-layer are found to make possible prediction of idle power process signal. It is mainly concentrated on algorithms on input signal selection and finding the optimal model for one-step ahead prediction.

Keywords: Nuclear Power Plant, Neural Networks, One-step Ahead Prediction, Model Input Selection, Evaluation Methods.

1   Introduction

In this paper, Feed-Forward back-propagation [1] (FF) and Elman Neural Network [2] (ENN) with different parameters are used for modelling the system. The main goal in our group is to develop monitoring and forecasting methods by given data, not the analysis of the recorded events [3,4].

Conventional way for time series modelling by NNs is using numerical data of delayed signals as inputs. The first temporal event is represented by the first element in the input vector, and so on. Therefore the number of inputs in prediction model is high, though a rather small group of process signals are selected for model. At Olkiluoto thousands of signals are measured, and only few signals help on modelling output. The high dimensionality of the system makes input signal selection hard. A subset of signals are selected automatically when there exists a large amount of process signals [4]. It is possible to decrease number of inputs by paying attention to model signal selection or with use of ENN, because it has an additional units in hidden-layer. Recurrent connections are used to associate a static pattern with a serially ordered output pattern. With these connections it is possible to have its own previous output, so NN has its own memory. FF is selected, because it is used frequently in time series forecasting. Prediction was performed by selecting one stored data set for deeper analysis.

K. Diamantaras, W. Duch, L.S. Iliadis (Eds.): ICANN 2010, Part I, LNCS 6352, pp. 46–49, 2010.

2   Description of Used Methods

2.1   Signal Selection for Modelling

The complexity of delays is the most common reason, why it is usually expected that there are no delays between variables. In practice, the unwanted effect of delay can be decreased by filtering, for example by Moving Average (MA) with larger size of time window [3].

Time series prediction is estimation of future values based on its and other signals past samples. A signal, which is responding latest, can be predicted by its delayed signal measurements and other process signals. Delays and linear correlation are examined before modelling. Observations on signals are made at the same unit time intervals over the same time period. Delays are detected by cross-correlation function. It is standardized cross-covariance function and for two signals T and P it is defined as

$$r_{TP}(\tau) = \frac{E[(T(t) - \mu_T)(P_i(t + \tau) - \mu_{P_i})]}{\sigma_T \sigma_{P_i}}, \tag{1}$$

where τ is the time lag, σ denotes the standard deviation, T is the idle power measurements and P_i is one of the potential inputs with delayed measurements.

2.2   Elman Recurrent and Feed-Forward Neural Networks

In an ENN all neurons are in one hidden-layer [2] and there are connections to a context layer from each node, so previous hidden-layer output values are saved. Delayed values are re-connected to all nodes in hidden-layer, see Fig. 1.

Comparative method in our experiments is a FF with one hidden-layer. It is similar as shown in Fig. 1, but without the context layer. Major problem is that it can learn only static input-output mapping [1]. The training mode begins in our experiments with randomly selected weights and those are optimized in training.

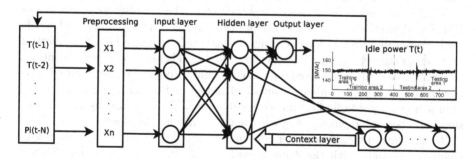

Fig. 1. In ENN re-connections to hidden-layer are simplified by one arrow. Input signals are delayed idle power values and other process signal values P_i, which rely with output $T(t)$. The number of delayed input signals N is depending on the cross-correlation analysis.

In each epoch the NN adjusts the weights in the direction that reduces the error. The weights gradually converge to the locally optimal set of values. Many epochs are usually required before training is completed, but then probability of over-training is higher.

2.3 Model Evaluation Methods

Most of the existing literature [5] on time series prediction frequently employ only one performance criterion for prediction evaluation. Mean Squared Error (MSE) is also a default criterion in Matlab, when training NNs. In industry, process signals can have unexpected large changes. Quality of model cannot be evaluated just using MSE,because information of error distribution is not given.

The Normalized Mean Square Error (NMSE) is an estimator of the overall deviations between predicted X_i and measured values divided by sample size and variance of the real measured signal outputs T. Median of Absolute Error (MAE) is the absolute value of the difference between the model and the measurement. This can be expressed as a percentage error by dividing absolute error by measurement value. It describes the common error of predictions.

3 Experiments

In our experiments all input signals are scaled from -1 to 1. Predicted output signal is rescaled and examined in the original scale. Data was divided for training and testing parts. Training part was used for input signal selection and for optimizing weight values in the NN. The most effective training method was Levenberg-Marquardt back-propagation method.

Data set was divided to two different training and testing sets, see output in Fig. 1. In set 2 there is unexpected large changes in data (t=235,546). Based on practical experience it is useful to detect these abnormalities, therefore results in this paper are performed using training and testing area 2. It is divided to training $t =]max(delayed input)..400]$ and testing $t =]400..800]$ areas.

Number of epochs is selected by minimizing the training and test errors. NMSE and MAE are used as criteria for evaluation. With large number of epochs net is over-trained. Six hidden neurons and 10 epochs seems to be better selection than 50 epochs, when other parameters are fixed. These parameters are optimal only on the case of four delayed input signals and three delayed steps for effective power and generator voltage. Number of hidden-units and number of delayed inputs are changed to find optimized results. Each NN is trained by using rather small number of hidden neurons with sigmoid transfer functions.

Results with different parameter values are listed on Table 1. NNs cannot be compared straight with the same parameter values. FF is faster, but ENN is better when comparing the best evaluation results.The parameter combination, which gives the best result on testing area is not the best on training area. It is recommended to examine MAE, when interest is on normal operation states.

Table 1. Results for the idle power prediction using training and testing area 2. Parameter I is the number of delayed inputs: idle power + effective power + generator voltage. Parameter N is the number of nodes in the hidden-layer. The best evaluation results are underlined.

NN	I	N	Train MSE	NMSE	MAE	Test MSE	NMSE	MAE
ENN	4 + 2	5	0.0470	0.0124	0.1384	0.2949	0.1798	0.1412
ENN	6 + 6 + 6	4	0.0433	0.0114	<u>0.1326</u>	0.1536	0.0936	0.1410
ENN	3 + 2 + 2	4	0.0477	0.0126	0.1377	0.0868	0.0529	0.1437
ENN	3 + 2 + 2	8	<u>0.0424</u>	<u>0.0112</u>	0.1339	0.5177	0.3157	<u>0.1406</u>
ENN	4 + 2 + 2	5	0.0474	0.0125	0.1378	<u>0.0524</u>	<u>0.0138</u>	0.1440
FF	4 + 2	5	0.0486	0.0128	0.1385	0.0860	0.0524	0.1414
FF	4 + 2 + 2	5	0.0572	0.0151	0.1413	0.1392	0.0593	0.1439
FF	3 + 2 + 2	8	0.0502	0.0133	0.1438	0.1855	0.1131	0.1465

4 Conclusions

Two different approaches for idle power forecasting was presented in this paper. Cross-correlation method gives valuable information of possible input signals. Both, FF and ENN gave good prediction results. ENN with five hidden-neurons and input signals $N_T = 4$ and $N_{P_i} = 2$ gave the best results for the test set.

Possible limitation for the NN is the slowness of the method. In the real world application the selection of parameters and modelling will be problematic, if frequency of time series is high. Before implementation NN to NPP, research work on nonstationary processes has to be done. NN should be re-trained on larger process state changes.

References

1. Haykin, S.: Neural networks: a comprehensive foundation. Prentice Hall PTR, Upper Saddle River (1994)
2. Ding, S., Jia, W., Su, C., Xu, X., Zhang, L.: PCA-Based Elman Neural Network Algorithm. Advances in Computation and Intelligence, 315–321 (2008)
3. Talonen, J., Sirola, M.: Abnormal Process State Detection by Cluster Center Point Monitoring in BWR Nuclear Power Plant. In: Proceedings of the International Conference on Data Mining, DMIN, pp. 247–252 (2009)
4. Sirola, M., Talonen, J., Lampi, G.: SOM based methods in early fault detection of nuclear industry. In: Proceedings of the 17th European Symposium On Artificial Neural Networks, ESANN (2009)
5. Hu, Q., Xie, M., Ng, S., Levitin, G.: Robust recurrent neural network modeling for software fault detection and correction prediction. Reliability Engineering & System Safety 92(3), 332–340 (2007)

Time Series Forecasting by Evolving Artificial Neural Networks Using *"Shuffle"*, Cross-Validation and Ensembles

Juan Peralta, German Gutierrez, and Araceli Sanchis

Computer Science Department, University Carlos III of Madrid
Avenida de la Universidad 30 28911 Leganes, Spain
{jperalta,ggutierr,masm}@inf.uc3m.es

Abstract. Accurate time series forecasting are important for several business, research, and application of engineering systems. Evolutionary Neural Networks are particularly appealing because of their ability to design, in an automatic way, a model (an Artificial Neural Network) for an unspecified non-linear relationship for time series values. This paper evaluates two methods to obtain the pattern sets that will be used by the artificial neural network in the evolutionary process, one called "shuffle" and another one carried out with cross-validation and ensembles. A study using these two methods will be shown with the aim to evaluate the effect of both methods in the accurateness of the final forecasting.

Keywords: Evolutionary Computation, Genetic Algorithms, Artificial Neural Networks, Time Series, Forecasting, Ensembles.

1 Introduction

Time series forecasting is an essential research field due to its applications in several research, commercial and industry areas, and can be performed by Statistical methods or Artificial Neural Networks (ANN) [1]. The ANN have the capability, without any information but the data, of extracting the nonlinear relationship between the inputs and outputs of a process. There are, in the literature some "state of art" by Abraham [2] and Yao [3] about automatic methods to design ANN based on Evolutionary Computation (EC).

In order to deal with model unction $x_t = f(x_{t-1}, x_{t-2}, ..., x_{t-k})$, time series known values will be transformed into a patterns set, depending on the k inputs nodes of a particular ANN. If the number of input nodes are different their pattern set are different and will be used to train and validate each ANN generated in the GA. The fitness value for each individual will be then the minimum validation error along the training of ANN topology. Once that GA reaches the last generation, the best individual (i.e. ANN) is used to forecast the future (and unknown) time series values (a_t) one by one using the k previous known values ($a_{t-1}, ..., a_{t-k}$). Value k is the number of input nodes of the best individual.

K. Diamantaras, W. Duch, L.S. Iliadis (Eds.): ICANN 2010, Part I, LNCS 6352, pp. 50–53, 2010.

This contribution reports two methods, *"Shuffle"* and cross-validation, to obtain the pattern sets used for ANN learning algorithm in a previous approach [4] based on Genetic Algorithms (GA). *"Shuffle"* refers to the way the whole pattern set will be split between train pattern set and validation pattern set. Cross-validation will be used for time series with few elements, so that cross-validation will be used to obtain several pattern subsets which will help to evaluate more accurately every specific ANN obtained in the GA.

2 *"Shuffle"*, Cross-Validation and Ensembles

In previous work, train and validation sets are obtained in a sequentially manner (train first 70%, validation last 30%). But, in this new approach, "shuffle", the process of splitting the patterns set will consist of obtaining train and validation sets in a random way from time series data, see (Fig. 1). So it will let different parts of the time series to train the ANN and also different parts of the time series to validate the ANN, in order to obtain better generalization ability.

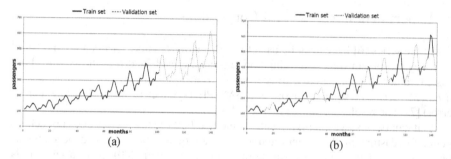

Fig. 1. Passengers: train and validation patterns sequentially (a) and randomly (b) obtained

Cross-validation has been used to forecast time series. In this study, the total pattern set will be split into n complementary pattern subsets (n from 2 to 8). Fig.2 shows an example of cross-validation with three pattern subsets. So that a individual in GA is an ANN topology, applying cross-validation to this individual gives n different ANN architectures (i.e. topology plus connection weights) and it n different fitness values depending on which patterns are used to train and validate the topology. So, applying cross-validation, the final fitness value for an individual will be the average of all its fitness values from each of its architectures.

When last generation of the GA is reached and its best individual have to be used to forecast, what of the its n architecture from cross-validation should be used? To solve this new problem Ensembles similar to Yao in [5] will be used to obtain only one model to carry out the final forecasting send to any competition or any company that need just a forecast (not several). In [5] the ensemble takes the different architectures obtained in last generation of the evolving cross-validation process, rather than an individual, to form the final result. But in our work, the different architectures (the same input and hidden nodes but different weight values) from the best individual in the last generation using cross-validation are linearly combined as an ensemble. And this ensemble will be used to give only one forecast. The weight for each model of the linear combination is given by the eq. 1 (a), and the ensemble output is given by eq. 1 (b). (n is the number of models into the ensemble and β is a scaling factor).

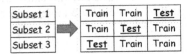

Fig. 2. Example of cross validation with 3 patterns subsets

$$(a) \quad w_i = \frac{\exp(\beta(n+1-i))}{\sum_{j=1}^{n} \exp(\beta_j)} ; (b) \quad O = \sum_{j=1}^{n} w_j o_j \tag{1}$$

3 Experimental Results and Conclusions

Five time series [6] have been be used to evaluate our methods. Sequential and *"Shuffle"* ways to obtain train and validation subsets are evaluated into the system. Forecasted values are compared with real values (i.e. test set) and two error values are used: MSE (mean squared error) and SMAPE (symmetric mean absolute percent error) [7]. The results are shown in Table 1.

As it can be observed applying shuffle method to these time series does not achieve better forecasting in Passengers and Dow-Jones time series. It could be explained because of the few elements of those time series (less than 200). If train and validation pattern subsets obtained are split in a random way, then all the patterns used to adjust the connection's weights does not correspond to consecutives time series values. So the relationship between inputs and output could be harder to learn if there are few patterns for learning and they are not consecutive (i.e. mixing up the training and validation patterns). On the other hand, the same experiment was also carried out with Quebec and Mackey-Glass time series, larger than previous ones (about 730 elements) Applying shuffle to these time series gets better results, specially for Mackey-Glass.

Our approach does not seem to achieve an improvement using *"Shuffle"* with short time series (i.e. Passengers, Temperature and Dow-Jones), so cross-validation, usually used when not too many data are given, have been tried for these time series. The number of subsets in which the total pattern set has been split goes from two to eight. All forecasted values, obtained from the ensemble of the ANN architectures are compared with real values and SMAPE error is shown. Results are shown in Table 2. We can observe that applying cross-validation to these time series obtain different results depending on the time series and the number of subsets the total pattern set has been split. The problem now arise in which is the optimum number of subsets which should be used to forecast a time series using cross-validation.

Table 1. SMAPE and MSE error for the best individual in the last generations

	Sequentially		Shuffle	
	MSE	%SMAPE	MSE	%SMAPE
Passengers (120 values)	0.00039	**3.065**	0.00521	8.999
Temperature (206 values)	0.00406	4.845	0.00384	**4.441**
Dow-Jones (129 values)	0.01437	**5.512**	0.02065	6.689
Quebec (735 values)	0.02149	12.121	0.01312	**9.218**
Mackey-Glass (731 values)	0.00363	8.672	0.00016	**1.818**

Table 2. SMAPE error using Cross-validation and Ensembles

	0 Sub	2 Sub	3 Sub	4 Sub	5 Sub	6 Sub	7 Sub	8 Sub
Passengers	3.065	*16.227*	11.104	6.774	4.519	9.136	4.198	**2.790**
Temperature	*4.845*	**3.385**	3.413	3.625	3.730	3.952	3.842	3.817
Dow-Jones	5.512	6.194	6.728	*7.581*	7.112	**5.093**	6.962	6.125

The results disclose that shuffle only improves forecasting for not short time series. An issue arises at this point: how the positive/negative effect of shuffle depends on the number of time series elements (i.e. size of training/validation subsets). On the other hand, cross-validation let us improve the result for short time series, but another issue arise, the optimum number of subsets to split the total pattern set. As it is a totally automatic method, it will not be necessary any previous knowledge from the user. The user just have to give the time series he wants to forecast and the number of future elements he wants to be forecasted to the system; and this method will give these forecasted values as result to the user. This approach got 6th position in NN5 Forecasting Competition [7].

Acknowledgments. The research reported here has been supported by the Spanish Ministry of Science and Innovation under project TRA2007-67374-C02- 02.

References

1. Zhang, G., Eddy Patuwo, B., Hu, M.Y.: Forecasting with artificial neural networks: The state of the art. International Journal of Forecasting 14(1), 35–62 (1998)
2. Abraham, A.: Meta learning evolutionary artificial neural networks. In: 3rd Int. Conf. on Neural, Parallel and Scientific Computations, Atlanta, USA (2006)
3. Yao, X.: Evolving artificial neural networks. Proceedings of the IEEE 87(9), 1423–1447 (1999)
4. Peralta, J., Gutierrez, G., Sanchis, A.: Shuffle design to improve time series forecasting accuracy. In: CEC 2009: Proceedings of the 11thConference on Evolutionary Computation, pp. 741–748. IEEE Press, Los Alamitos (2009)
5. Yao, X.: Evolving artificial neural network ensembles. In: Studies in Computational Intelligence, pp. 851–880 (1993)
6. Hyndman, R.J. (n.d.): Time Series Data Library,
   http://www.robjhyndman.com/TSDL (accessed on June 2010)
7. ANN & CI Time Series Forecasting,
   http://www.neural-forecasting-competition.com (accessed on June 2010)

Prediction of Power Consumption for Small Power Region Using Indexing Approach and Neural Network

Krzysztof Siwek[1], Stanisław Osowski[1,2], Bartosz Swiderski[3], and Lukasz Mycka[2]

[1] Warsaw University of Technology
[2] Military University of Technology, Warsaw, Poland
{sto,ksiwek}@iem.pw.edu.pl
[3] Warsaw University of Life Sciences
swidersb@iem.pw.edu.pl

Abstract. The problem of prediction of 24-hour ahead power consumption in a small power region is a very important practical problem in power engineering. The most characteristic feature of the small region is large diversity of power consumption in the succeeding hours of the day making the prediction problem very hard. On the other side the accurate forecast of the power need for each of 24 hours of the next day enables to achieve significant saving on power delivery. The paper proposes the novel neural based method of forecasting the power consumption, taking into account the trend of its change associated with the particular hour of the day, type of the day as well as season of the year

Keywords: Load forecasting, 24-hour ahead power consumption prediction, detrending operation.

1 Introduction

Electricity-supply planning requires the optimization of the decisions concerning the short-term demand for each of 24 hours of the next day. Accurate forecast allows to minimize the cost of delivery of electrical energy for customers and thus is very important to economize the power engineering.

Most papers devoted to load forecasting consider the large power systems, usually concerning the whole country [1],[5],[6]. The prediction problem for such systems is relatively easy, since the constant part of the total load is usually very large with respect to its peak values. Much more difficult is small power region, where the variability of load is very large and hence more difficult to predict.

If we look for example at the hourly consumption of the electrical energy of the small power region of Lodz in Poland (Fig. 1) we can see the trends concerning these dependencies. The upper figure represents the period of 2 years and in the bottom one we have limited this period to one week only. The upper figure shows clearly the yearly seasonal changes and the bottom one - the daily changes associated with different days of the week (from Monday to Sunday).

It is well known that reducing the variability of the predicted time series leads to the increase of prediction accuracy [2],[4]. The most straightforward approach to reduce the variation of the predicted time series is to remove the trends due to the

K. Diamantaras, W. Duch, L.S. Iliadis (Eds.): ICANN 2010, Part I, LNCS 6352, pp. 54–59, 2010.

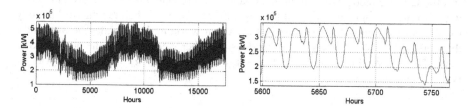

Fig. 1. The hourly consumption of the electrical energy in a small power region: a) of the whole 2 years, b) of one chosen week

daily, weekly and seasonal cycles of the power demand. The paper develops this direction of the time series processing. We propose the indexation of the time series aimed in elimination of the trends due to the type of the day, daily hour cycle and the season of the year. The transformed time series after removing these trends are subject to prediction by applying the neural network models, either the multilayer perceptron (MLP) or Support Vector Machine (SVR).

2 The Proposed Approach

Our main task is to predict the power demand $P(d,h)$ for dth day and hth hour of the power region by considering its past history and the predicted temperature of the day under prediction. To reduce the variability of the predicted time series we index the time series, eliminating the trends due to the type of the day, daily hour cycle and the season of the year. We apply the multiplicative model of this indexation.

2.1 Elimination of Trends

The elimination of the trends is performed in few phases. The first step is to determine the index corresponding to jth day of the weak ($j = 1, 2, ..., 7$). To estimate this index we calculate the mean value of the load for each jth day of the year, divide it by the mean of the year and average by the years. Denoting it by α_{dw} we can use the following formula

$$\alpha_{dw}(j) = \underset{years}{mean}\left(\frac{P_m(y,j)}{P_m(y)}\right) \qquad (1)$$

In this expression $P_m(y,j)$ denotes the average power consumption of jth day of the week corresponding to yth year, and $P_m(y)$ is the mean power for all days of yth year. The final value of this index is averaged over all years under consideration. After calculating this index we can remove the daily trend by dividing the real time series $\mathbf{P}(w,j)=[P_1(w,j), P_2(w,j),..., P_{24}(w,j)]$ of each jth day of wth week by the value of daily index $\alpha_{dw}(j)$, i.e.,

$$\mathbf{P}_1(w,j) = \frac{\mathbf{P}(w,j)}{\alpha_{dw}(j)} \qquad (2)$$

Additionally we recognize also the load patterns corresponding to workdays and holidays. We will recognize 5 types of the days: the workday just before non-working day (holiday or weekend), the workday just after non-working day (holiday or weekend), the workday between two non-working days, all other working days, the non-working days. To remove this trend we define the day type index α_{dt} in the same way as before.

$$\alpha_{dt}(t) = \underset{years}{mean}\left(\frac{P_{1m}(y,t)}{P_{1m}(y)}\right) \tag{3}$$

where $P_{1m}(y,t)$ denotes the average power consumption $\mathbf{P}_1$ of the days of the same type t (workdays or holidays) corresponding to yth year, and $P_m(y)$ is the mean power for all days of yth year. The final value of this index is averaged over all years under consideration. Removing this trend corresponds to the division of the real time series $\mathbf{P}_1$ by the value of $\alpha_{dt}(t)$, i.e.,

$$\mathbf{P}_2(w,t) = \frac{\mathbf{P}_1(w,t)}{\alpha_{dt}(t)} \tag{4}$$

The next step is removing the trend corresponding to the particular hour h of the day ($h=1, 2, \ldots, 24$). The procedure is identical to the previous ones. The hourly index $\alpha_h(h)$, is then defined as

$$\alpha_h(h) = \underset{years}{mean}\left(\frac{P_{2m}(y,h)}{P_{2m}(y)}\right) \tag{5}$$

To remove the trend corresponding to the particular hour of each dth day we perform the detrending operation

$$\mathbf{P}_3(d,h) = \frac{\mathbf{P}_2(d,h)}{\alpha_h(h)} \tag{6}$$

The last operation is to remove the seasonality trend characterizing the succeeding day of the year ($d=1, 2, \ldots, 365$). If we denote the seasonality index by α_s we can define it in the form

$$\alpha_s(d) = \underset{years}{mean}\left(\frac{P_{3m}(y,d)}{P_{3m}(y)}\right) \tag{7}$$

where $P_{3m}(y,d)$ denotes the average power consumption $\mathbf{P}_3$ of all 24 hours of the day d corresponding to yth year, and $P_{3m}(y)$ is the mean power for all days of yth year. In this way we define the transformed load pattern $P_4(d,h)$ of each hour of the days under consideration as

$$\mathbf{P}_4(d,h) = \frac{\mathbf{P}_3(d,h)}{\alpha_s(d)} \tag{8}$$

As a result of all these steps we get the final detrended time series $\mathbf{P}_4(d)=[P_4,(d,1)$, $P_4(d,2),\ldots, P_4(d,24)]$ corresponding to all days under consideration ($d=1$, 2, ..., p). This time series is of much lower variance than the original one. The ratio std/mean for the whole data has been reduced from 0.289 (original data) to 0.128 (after detrending operation).

The prediction task is now moved to the time series represented by $P_4(d,h)$ of much smaller variability. Smaller variance of this time series means easier prediction task for the neural network and higher probability of achieving better accuracy.

After predicting the time series $P_4(d,h)$ we can return to the original values. Taking into account the cumulation of all indexing operations the real load pattern corresponding to hth hour of dth day can be presented as follows

$$P(d,h) = P_4(d,h)\alpha_{dw}(j)\alpha_{dt}(t)\alpha_h(h)\alpha_s(d) \tag{9}$$

The index j corresponds here to proper day of the week ($j = 1$, 2, ...,7) and t denotes the actual type of the working or nonworking day. For each day d and hour h the proper values of indices should be applied. Knowing them in advance the prediction task is simplified to prediction of the detrended values $P_4(d,h)$. This task will be done by applying the neural network predictor.

2.2 Neural Network Predictors

The prediction of the detrended time series $P_4(d,h)$ will be done by applying two types of supervised neural networks: the MLP and SVR. The predictive model is built for each hour independently. In building this model for dth day and hth hour we assume that all previous values of $P_4(i,j)$ are available for $i= d-1$, $d-2$, ... and $j= 24$, 23 ,...1. The assumed model of prediction takes into account the predicted value of minimal $T_{min}(d)$ and maximal $T_{max}(d)$ temperatures of the next dth day, the values of the load in the last 2 hours of two previous day, as well as the load of hth and $(h-1)$ hours of the same type of day (the same day a week ago). This model may be generally written in the following form

$$\hat{P}_4(d,h) = f(P_4(d-1,h), P_4(d-1,h-1), P_4(d-2,h), P_4(d-2,h-1),$$
$$P_4(d-7,h), P_4(d-7,h-1), T_{min}(d), T_{max}(d)) \tag{10}$$

The values denoted by hat mean the predicted and without hat – the real power consumption. The expression $f()$ represents here the approximation function implemented by the neural network. As the neural approximator we have tried two very efficient solutions of neural networks: the multilayer perceptron [3] and Support Vector Machine working in the regression mode [7].

The expression (10) defines explicitly the input signals to the neural predictors. They are equal to the variables appearing in the brackets on the right side of the equation. Irrespective of the applied neural network they are composed of 8 signals: six correspond to the previous (detrended) load and two to the predicted minimal (night) and maximal (day) temperatures of the day.

3 The Numerical Results of Prediction

In the numerical experiments we have used the analysed data of the small power region of Lodz. All experiments have been performed using Matlab platform [8]. In the first phase the detrending process of the whole data was done and all four indexing coefficients determined. As a result of it the detrended time series $P_4(d,h)$ corresponding to all data set has been determined. This data set has been normalized column wise by dividing all entries by the maximum value of each hour.

In the next phase the neural predictors of different forms have been applied to provide the estimation of the normalized $\hat{P}_4(d,h)$. The whole set of data has been split into two parts. Two third of it was used for learning the predictor and one third left for testing the network. We have applied two neural networks: the MLP and SVR. Both used the same structure of input data defined by expression (10). There were 8 inputs: 6 corresponded to the power consumption of the previous hours and days and two others to the maximum and minimum temperatures predicted for the day under prediction. Irrespective of the network solution there was single output neuron, responsible for predition of the normalized power of the particular hour h. 24 neural predictors corresponding to each hour of the day were trained.

In the case of MLP the number of hidden neurons was adjusted by using the cross validation approach. This task was performed for each hour independently. As a resulst the number of hidden neurons of MLP was changing from 5 to 8 neurons of sigmoidal nonlinearity.

In the case of Gaussian kernel SVR we have applied similar strategy. The tolerance ε was fixed to 0.005, while the optimal values of C, and σ have been determined in a similar fashion as in the case of MLP by trying the predefined values of them and using the validation data set. As a result of such introductory experiments we have fixed the regularization constant for all 24 SVR networks on $C=100$ and the Gaussian width $\sigma=10$. These hyperparameters have been used in real learning procedure of all SVRs.

After learning procedure the parameters of the neural predictors have been fixed and the networks tested using the testing data set. In this way we got the forecasted values of $\hat{P}_4(d,h)$, on the basis of which we were able to recover the real predicted values $P(d,h)$ for the days used in testing, by applying the equation (9). The quality of prediction system has been assessed on the basis of mean absolute percentage errors (MAPE), maximum percentage error (MAXPE) and root mean squared error (RMSE).

Table 2 presents the total results of testing in the form of MAPE, MAXPE and RMSE. We have compared them with the results of prediction by using crude data, without detrending procedure (the direct application of SVM and MLP).

Table 2. The comparison of the results of prediction by using different solutions of forecasting systems

Prediction method	MAPE [%]	MAXPE [%]	RMS [kW]
Indexation+SVM	3.4855	49.1397	1.4531e4
Indexation+MLP	3.5352	50.0892	1.5162e4
Direct SVM	3.5824	81.0938	1.5782e4
Direct MLP	3.6559	94.7229	1.5836e4

Direct application of neural predictors (without detrending) was evidently less effi-cient. All measures of quality were the worst, irrespective of the applied type of pre-dictor. The best results of forecasting correspond to the application of indexation combined with neural predictors. Both SVM and MLP predictors were of comparable accuracy, although the SVM was slightly better. Especially high improvement was observed for maximum percentage error. Application of detrending procedure has reduced this error in a very significant way. For example at direct application of SVM the MAXPE=81.09%. After detrending the data this error was reduced to 49.14% (39.5% of relative improvement). The explanation for this may be the fact, that the detrending procedure reduces significantly the abrupt changes of the time series com-ponents corresponding to the specific types and certain hours of the day. Hence their accurate prediction is much easier.

4   Conclusions

The paper has presented the new approach to the forecasting problem of the power consumption in the small power region. The most important point in this approach is application of the indexation of the data in order to remove different trends related to the type of the date, hour of the day and season of the year. Combination of this in-dexation approach with the neural type predictors has resulted in a great reduction of the forecasting error and improving the accuracy of forecasting. The numerical results have shown significant improvement of accuracy with respect to the direct approach (prediction of the crude data without detrending).

Acknowledgments. This research activity was financed by MNiSzW from the fund intended for science development.

References

1. Fan, S.F., Chen, L.: Short-term load forecasting based on adaptive hybrid method. IEEE Trans. Power Syst. 21, 392–401 (2006)
2. Gonzalez-Romera, E., Jaramillo-Moran, M.A., Carmona-Fernandez, D.: Monthly electric energy demand forecasting based on trend extraction. IEEE Tr. P.S. 21, 1946–1953 (2006)
3. Haykin, S.: Neural networks, a comprehensive foundation. Macmillan, N. Y. (2002)
4. Koehler, A., Snyder, R., Ord, J.K.: Forecasting models and prediction intervals fort he multiplicative Holt-Winters method. Int. J. Forecasting 17, 269–286 (2001)
5. Mandal, P., Senjyu, T., Urasaki, N., Funabashi, T.: A neural network based several hours ahead electric load forecasting using similar days approach. Electrical Power and Energy Systems 28, 367–373 (2006)
6. Osowski, S., Siwek, K., Szupiluk, R.: Ensemble Neural Network Approach for Accurate Load Forecasting in the Power System. AMCS 19(2), 303–315 (2009)
7. Schölkopf, B., Smola, A.: Learning with Kernels. MIT Press, Cambridge (2002)
8. Matlab user manual, MathWorks, Natick (2008)

Fault Prognosis of Mechanical Components Using On-Line Learning Neural Networks

David Martínez-Rego, Óscar Fontenla-Romero,
Beatriz Pérez-Sánchez, and Amparo Alonso-Betanzos

Laboratory for Research and Development in Artificial Intelligence (LIDIA),
Department of Computer Science, Faculty of Informatics,
University of A Coruña, A Coruña, Spain
dmartinez@udc.es, ofontenla@udc.es, bperezs@udc.es, ciamparo@udc.es

Abstract. Predictive maintenance of industrial machinery has steadily emerge as an important topic of research. Due to an accurate automatic diagnosis and prognosis of faults, savings of the current expenses devoted to maintenance can be obtained. The aim of this work is to develop an automatic prognosis system based on vibration data. An on-line version of the Sensitivity-based Linear Learning Model algorithm for neural networks is applied over real vibrational data in order to assess its forecasting capabilities. Moreover, the behavior of the method is compared with that of an efficient and fast method, the On-line Sequential Extreme Learning Machine. The accurate predictions of the proposed method pave the way for future development of a complete prognosis system.

1 Introduction

Common maintenance strategies in industry nowadays are reactive maintenance (repairing a fault when it appears), which is being abandoned progressively because of its high costs; and preventive maintenance (based on physical inspections at scheduled intervals of time). Predictive maintenance is one of the main areas of research nowadays for industrial engines and also for aerospace, automotive, and marine vehicles, because it results in a significant reduction of the overall operating costs. It is based on the fact that a mechanical component breakdown is usually preceded by a period in which a smooth and crescent degradation of behavior and performance can be detected. If suitable on-line monitoring is used, these incipient faults can be identified and action can be taken before causing major problems or damage to other parts of the equipment. In case of mechanical components of a windmill, the monitoring of security relevant components and signals is the state of the art and is required by certification guidelines. The existence of a fault detection system in this setting is of prime importance because it has a number of potential benefits, such as the avoidance of premature breakdown, reduction of maintenance costs avoiding the replacement of intact parts of the preventive maintenance, possibility of remote diagnosis (very important because windmill are usually placed at remote sites), and prognosis and adaptation of the repairing actions to the time which is more

K. Diamantaras, W. Duch, L.S. Iliadis (Eds.): ICANN 2010, Part I, LNCS 6352, pp. 60–66, 2010.

convenient for the wind plant (i.e. when low wind speed), improving the production factor of the plant. In the case of rotating machines, such as the mechanical parts of the windmills (bearings, gearboxes, etc.), vibration monitoring is used and fault detection systems evaluate spectral analysis data, such as FFT, Cepstrum, envelope curve analysis, etc. to yield diagnosis and also estimations of remaining lifetime of the piece. The rationale for this is that almost any fault can be detected through the vibrations that are present along all the components of a mechanical machine. The vibration analysis is based on the alterations that appear in the vibrational behavior of a machine when a latent defect appears in any of its components. Currently, predictive maintenance in windmills is done manually or in a semi-automatic way by qualified experts, thus making maintenance a high cost service. Several models have been used for automatic diagnosis and prognosis [1,2], among which some of them use Artificial Intelligence techniques [3,4]. Specifically in the case of prognosis, very few papers can be found [5,11]. In this paper, a prognostic model based on a supervised feedforward on-line learning algorithm [9] for two-layer feedforward neural networks based on sensitivity analysis, called on-line SBLLM (Sensitivity-Based Linear Learning Method) is described. The algorithm offers a very appealing combination of speed, reliability and simplicity, very adequate for real-time prediction.

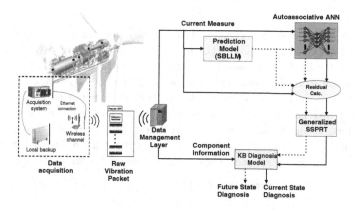

Fig. 1. System architecture

2   The Overall System for Diagnosis and Prognosis

The final aim of our work is the development of an automatic predictive maintenance system based on Machine Learning and Knowledge-based systems techniques. Figure 1 depicts the main architecture of $GIDAS^©$ system. In the first stage, raw vibrational data is acquired directly from the machine using a set of accelerometers and acquisition systems specifically programmed for this task. Subsequently these measures are transmitted via a TCP/IP connection (mainly wireless connections due to the target application environments) to a central node which treats these data to obtain informational parameters. The most used parameters in vibration-based diagnosis are Root Mean Square (RMS) of the signal and Fast Fourier Transform (FFT). The present fault diagnosis subsystem uses a combination of (a) an Artificial Neural Network (ANN), (b) a sequential statistical test and (c) a rule based system which reflects the possible diagnostics for each component. Although vibration-based fault diagnosis has been treated in recent years, few papers studying fault prognosis can be found in the literature [5,8]. Our aim is to extend the analysis capabilities of the system introducing a forecaster of future machine state. This subsystem will forecast the state of diagnosis parameters extracted from raw vibration measurements of a component and hence predict future possible faults. Although some other works used neural networks for this task [11], the capability of incremental online adaptation owing to changes in the latent state of the physical component was not taken into account and will be needed in the model used. An adaptive system based on state of the art concept drift forecasters and an on-line version of the SBLLM learning algorithm [9] can give us a accurate forecaster able to adapt to latent changes.

3   The Machine Learning Model Used for Prediction

The on-line SBLLM learning method was developed for a two-layer feedforward neural network. It considers the network as composed of two subnetworks and the novelty is that the weights of layers 1 and 2 are calculated independently by minimizing for each layer l a loss function, $Q^{(l)}$. The method considers Q as the sum of squared errors *before* the nonlinear activation functions (g_k and f_j) instead of *after* them as is the standard case in learning algorithms. Thus, being S the size of the training data set, with I inputs (x_{is}) and J desired outputs (d_{js}), z_{ks} is the desired output for hidden neuron z and $\bar{z}_{ks} = g_k^{-1}(z_{ks})$, the alternative loss functions used for solving subnetwork 1 and subnetwork 2 can be written as $Q^{(1)} = \sum_{s=1}^{S} \sum_{k=1}^{K} \left(\sum_{i=0}^{I} w_{ki}^{(1)} x_{is} - \bar{z}_{ks} \right)^2$

$Q^{(2)} = \sum_{s=1}^{S} \sum_{j=1}^{J} \left(\sum_{k=0}^{K} w_{jk}^{(2)} z_{ks} - \bar{d}_{js} \right)^2$ where $\bar{d}_{js} = f_j^{-1}(d_{js})$, d_{js} is the desired output for output neuron j. This loss function, that measures the error before the nonlinearity, was proposed in [10]. In this previous work it was shown that the optimum of this alternative loss function, up to first order of a Taylor series, is the same as that of the loss function that is obtained when the sum of squared errors *after* the nonlinear activation functions is employed. The advantage of the presented loss function is that the optimum set of weights, for each layer, can be easily calculated by solving a system of linear equations that are obtained deriving $Q^{(1)}$ and $Q^{(2)}$ with respect to the weights and equating to zero. Considering these ideas the proposed learning method is described.

Step 0: Initialization. Initialize the outputs of the intermediate layer (z_{ks}) as the outputs associated with some random weights.

For the current sample (index s) performs the following steps.

Step 1: Subproblem solution. The weights of layers 1 and 2 are calculated independently by solving the system of linear equations that are obtained deriving $Q^{(1)}$ and $Q^{(2)}$ with respect to the weights and equating to zero:

$$\sum_{i=0}^{I} \left(\hat{A}_{pi}^{(1)} + x_{is} x_{ps} \right) w_{ki}^{(1)} = \hat{b}_{pk}^{(1)} + \bar{z}_{ks} x_{ps}; \quad p = 0, 1, \ldots, I; \quad k = 1, \ldots, K$$

$$\sum_{k=0}^{K} \left(\hat{A}_{qk}^{(2)} + z_{ks} z_{qs} \right) w_{jk}^{(2)} = \hat{b}_{qj}^{(2)} + \bar{d}_{js} z_{qs}; \quad q = 0, \ldots, K; \quad j = 1, \ldots, J,$$

where $\hat{A}^{(l)}$ and $\hat{b}^{(l)} (l = 1, 2)$, are a matrix and a vector that store the coefficients obtained in previous epochs to calculate the values of the weights. They handle the knowledge previously acquired and use it to progressively approach the optimum value of the weights. The on-line learning algorithm is updating its knowledge depending on the information that is acquired over time. In the initial epoch the matrix $\hat{A}^{(l)}$ and vector $\hat{b}^{(l)}$ contain values equal to zero.

Step 2: Calculate the sensitivities. Obtain the sensitivities of the cost function Q with respect to the output $\mathbf{z}$ of the hidden layer,

$$\frac{\partial Q}{\partial z_{ks}} = \frac{-2 \left(\sum_{i=0}^{I} w_{ki}^{(1)} x_{is} - g_k^{-1}(z_{ks}) \right)}{g_{k'}(z_{ks})} + 2 \sum_{j=1}^{J} \left(\sum_{r=0}^{K} w_{jr}^{(2)} z_{rs} - f_j^{-1}(d_{js}) \right) w_{jk}^{(2)}$$

being $\bar{z}_{ks} = g_k^{-1}(z_{ks})$, $\bar{d}_{js} = f^{-1}(d_{js})$, $k = 1, ..., K; j = 1, ..., J$ and $z_{0s} = 1, \forall s$.

Step 3: Update intermediate outputs. Using the Taylor series approximation over the cost function, $Q(\mathbf{z} + \Delta \mathbf{z}) = Q(\mathbf{z}) + \sum_{k=0}^{K} \sum_{s=1}^{S} \frac{\partial Q(\mathbf{z})}{\partial z_{ks}} \Delta z_{ks} \approx 0$, the following increments are calculated to update the desired outputs of the hidden neurons $\Delta \mathbf{z} = -\rho \frac{Q(\mathbf{z})}{||\nabla Q||^2} \nabla Q$, where ρ is a relaxation factor or step size. This procedure continues from Step 1 using the next available sample.

4   The Experimental Settings

In order to show the adequacy of the proposed algorithm for prognosis of faults in mechanical components, the bearing dataset provided by the Center for Intelligent Maintenance Systems (IMS), University of Cincinnati was used [6]. For obtaining the data, four bearings were installed in one shaft. All bearings are forced lubricated and accelerometers were installed in each of them. The rotation speed was kept constant at 2000 rpm, and a 6000lb radial load was placed onto the shaft and bearing by a spring mechanism (Figure 2). Two of the three datasets containing acceleration measurements corresponding to the 8

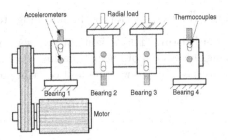

Fig. 2. The bearing test rig and sensor placement for obtaining the bearing dataset used in the experiment

accelerometers installed were employed in this paper. Set 2 contains vibration data collected every 10 minutes by a NI DAQ Card 6062E with a sampling rate of 20Khz during 7 days. At the end of the test-to-failure experiment an outer race failure occurred on bearing 1. Set 3 contains vibration data collected as in set 2, during 30 days. At the end of the test-to-failure experiment, an outer race failure occurred on bearing 3. The on-line SBLLM was applied over the two data sets in order to check its forecasting ability. In machine vibration monitoring, the common practice is to extract from the raw acceleration signal the root mean square (RMS), that is to be used as a global parameter to assess the state of the machine component. The normal functioning of the forecasting system will be on-line and sequentially, as the samples are obtained in a real environment, so the algorithm was applied directly over the RMS signal (without filtering), and several trials with different number of hidden neurons were carried out. So as to complete the experiment, the algorithm was also applied over a filtered RMS signal. Finally, the results of the SBLLM are compared with those obtained by the OSELM (On-line Sequential Extreme Learning Machine)[7], an state of the art algorithm due to its generalization performance and its fast learning speed.

5   Results

Figures 3(a) and 3(b) show the results obtained after applying the on-line SBLLM and the OSELM algorithms, respectively to the Set 2 of the IMS bearing data and predicting the t+15 sample using the samples t and t-1. There are two different situations explored: without filtering the RMS signal (left column), trying to reproduce the real monitoring scenario of a fault monitoring system, and filtering the RMS signal (right columm). In both cases, the number of hidden neurons is varied for a more complete study of behavior. The original RMS signal is displayed with a discontinuous line, while the prediction is displayed on a continuous line. As it can be seen, the behavior of our proposed algorithm is very stable, obtaining very low errors for any number of hidden neurons in both cases, filtered and raw RMS. The OSELM algorithm shows an adequate behavior when the number of hidden neurons is similar to the number of inputs (2 in this case) when using filtered and non filtered RMS signals. However, it is very unstable when the number of hidden neurons is different from the number of inputs, specially in the case of non filtered RMS. Figures 4(a) and 4(b) display the results of applying on-line SBLLM and OSELM to the vibration data of Set 3, that is for forecasting the outer race failure on bearing 3. The results obtained are of the same type as in the case above.

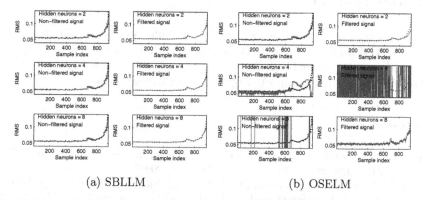

(a) SBLLM   (b) OSELM

Fig. 3. Results obtained using SBLLM and OSELM as forecasters in Set 2

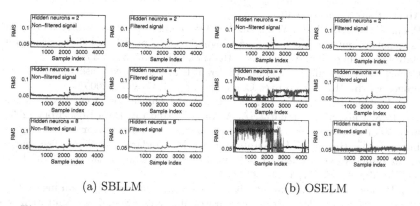

(a) SBLLM   (b) OSELM

Fig. 4. Results obtained using SBLLM and OSELM as forecasters in Set 3

6   Conclusions

An algorithm called on-line SBLLM has been applied to the prediction of faults in mechanical components using vibration monitoring. To prove its adequacy, an experimental analysis was carried out over real data sets in which bearing failures occurred under different circumstances. The algorithm was applied directly to the raw RMS signal, trying to emulate the normal conditions in which a real-time on-line monitoring system will work. However, and for the sake of completeness it was also tried over a filtered RMS signal. In both cases, the algorithm showed stability and robustness. The results were compared to OSELM, one of the on-line algorithm with better generalization power and fast learning speed. As it was shown in the experiments carried out, on-line SBLLM showed a more stable behavior, specially in the most interesting case of non-filtered signals.

Acknowledgements

The authors wish to acknowledge support of (a) Xunta de Galicia under project codes 08DPI145E and 2007/134 and (b) Spanish Ministerio de Ciencia e Innovación under project code TIN2009-10748, and FPU grant of D. Martínez-Rego. All projects are partially supported by European Union ERDF.

References

1. Wegerich, S.: Similarity-based modeling of vibration features for fault detection and identification. Sensor Review 25(2), 114–122 (2005)
2. Ericsson, S., Gripp, N., Jihansson, E., Persson, L., Sjøberg, R., Strømberg, J.: Towards automatic detection of local bearing defects in rotating machines. Mechanical Systemas and Signal Processing 19, 509–535 (2005)
3. Sakthivel, N.R., Sugumaran, V., Babudevasenapati, S.: Vibration based fault diagnosis of monoblock centrifugal pump using decision tree. Expert Systems with Applications 37, 4040–4049 (2010)
4. Pham, H.T., Tran, V.T., Yang, B.: A hybrid nonlinear autoregressive model with exogenous input and autoregressive moving average model for long-term machine state forecasting. Expert Systems with Applications 37, 3310–3317 (2010)
5. Goebel, K., Bonanni, P., Eklund, N.: Towards an integrated reasoner for bearings pronostics. In: IEEE Aerospace Conference, pp. 3647–3657 (2005)
6. Lee, J., Qiu, H., Yu, G., Lin, J.: Rexnord Technical Services: Bearing Data Set, IMS, Univ. of Cincinnati. NASA Ames Prognostics Data Repository (2007), http://ti.arc.nasa.gov/project/prognostic-data-repository
7. Liang, N.-Y., Huang, G.-B., Saratchandran, P., Sundararajan, N.: A fast and accurate online sequential learning algorithm for feedforward networks. IEEE Trans. on Neural Networks 17, 1411–1423 (2006)
8. Qiu, H., Lee, J., Lin, J.: Wavelet filter-based weak signature detection method and its application on roller bearing prognostics. Journal of Sound and Vibration 289, 1066–1090 (2006)
9. Pérez-Sánchez, B., Fontenla-Romero, O., Guijarro-Berdiñas, B.: An Incremental Learning Method for Neural Networks Based on Sensitivity Analysis. In: Proc. of the XIII Conferencia de la Asociación Española para la Inteligencia Artificial, Sevilla, Spain, pp. 529–537 (2009)
10. Castillo, E., Fontenla-Romero, O., Alonso-Betanzos, A., Guijarro-Berdiñas, B.: A Global Optimum Approach for One-Layer Neural Networks. Neural Computation 14, 1429–1449 (2002)
11. Tse, P.W., Atherton, D.P.: Prediction of machine deterioration using vibration based fault trends and recurrent neural networks. Journal of Vibration and Acoustics 121, 355–362 (1999)

Discovery of Exogenous Variables in Data with More Variables Than Observations

Yasuhiro Sogawa[1], Shohei Shimizu[1], Aapo Hyvärinen[2], Takashi Washio[1],
Teppei Shimamura[3], and Seiya Imoto[3]

[1] The Institute of Scientific and Industrial Research, Osaka University, Japan
[2] Dept. Comp. Sci. Dept. Math. and Stat., University of Helsinki, Finland
[3] Human Genome Center, Institute of Medical Science, University of Tokyo, Japan

Abstract. Many statistical methods have been proposed to estimate causal models in classical situations with fewer variables than observations. However, modern datasets including gene expression data increase the needs of high-dimensional causal modeling in challenging situations with orders of magnitude more variables than observations. In this paper, we propose a method to find exogenous variables in a linear non-Gaussian causal model, which requires much smaller sample sizes than conventional methods and works even when orders of magnitude more variables than observations. Exogenous variables work as triggers that activate causal chains in the model, and their identification leads to more efficient experimental designs and better understanding of the causal mechanism. We present experiments with artificial data and real-world gene expression data to evaluate the method.

Keywords: Bayesian networks, independent component analysis, non-Gaussianity, data with more variables than observations.

1   Introduction

Many empirical sciences aim to discover and understand causal mechanisms underlying their objective systems such as natural phenomena and human social behavior. An effective way to study causal relationships is to conduct a controlled experiment. However, performing controlled experiments is often ethically impossible or too expensive in many fields including bioinformatics [1] and neuroinformatics [2]. Thus, it is necessary and important to develop methods for causal inference based on the data that do not come from such controlled experiments.

Many methods have been proposed to estimate causal models in classical situations with fewer variables than observations ($p<n$, p: the number of variables and n: the number of observations). A linear acyclic model that is a special case of Bayesian networks is typically used to analyze causal effects between continuous variables [3,4]. Estimation of the model commonly uses covariance structure of data only and in most cases cannot identify the full structure (edge directions and connection strengths) of the model with no prior knowledge on the

K. Diamantaras, W. Duch, L.S. Iliadis (Eds.): ICANN 2010, Part I, LNCS 6352, pp. 67–76, 2010.

structure [3,4]. In [5], the authors proposed a non-Gaussian variant of Bayesian networks called LiNGAM and showed that the full structure of a linear acyclic model is identifiable based on non-Gaussianity without pre-specifying any edge directions between the variables, which is a significant advantage over the conventional methods [4,3].

However, most works in statistical causal inference including Bayesian networks have discussed classical situations with fewer variables than observations ($p<n$), whereas modern datasets including microarray gene expression data increase the needs of high-dimensional causal modeling in challenging situations with orders of magnitude more variables than observations ($p \gg n$)[1,2]. Here we consider situations in which p is on the order of 1,000 or more, while n is around 50 to 100. For such high-dimensional data, the previous methods are often computationally intractable or statistically unreliable.

In this paper, we propose a method to find exogenous variables in a linear non-Gaussian causal model, which requires much smaller sample sizes than conventional methods and works even when $p \gg n$. The key idea is to identify which variables are exogenous instead of estimating the entire structure of the model. The simpler task of finding exogenous variables than that of the entire model structure would require fewer observations to work reliably. The new method is closely related to a fairly recent statistical technique called independent component analysis (ICA).

Exogenous variables work as triggers that activate a causal chain in the model, and their identification leads to more efficient experimental designs of practical interventions and better understanding of the causal mechanism. A promising application of Bayesian networks for gene expression data is detection of drug-target genes [1]. The new method proposed in this paper can be used to find which genes a drug first affects and how it triggers the gene network.

The paper is structured as follows. We first review ICA and linear causal models in Section 2. We then define a non-Gaussian causal model and propose a new algorithm to find exogenous variables in Section 3. The performance of the algorithm is evaluated by experiments on artificial data and real-world gene expression data in Sections 4 and 5. Section 6 concludes the paper.

2   Background Principles

2.1   Independent Component Analysis

Independent component analysis (ICA) [6] is a statistical technique originally developed in signal processing. ICA model for a p-dimensional observed continuous random vector x is defined as

$$x = As, \tag{1}$$

where s is a p-dimensional continuous random vector whose components s_i are mutually independent and non-Gaussian and are called independent components, and A is a constant $p \times p$ invertible matrix. Without loss of generality, we assume s_i to be of zero mean and unit variance. Let $\widetilde{\mathbf{W}}=\mathbf{A}^{-1}$. Then we have $\boldsymbol{s}=\widetilde{\mathbf{W}}\boldsymbol{x}$. It is known that the matrix $\widetilde{\mathbf{W}}$ are identifiable up to permutation of the rows [7].

Let $\widehat{\boldsymbol{s}}=\mathbf{W}\boldsymbol{x}$. A major estimation principle for $\widetilde{\mathbf{W}}$ is to find such $\mathbf{W}$ that maximizes the sum of non-Gaussianity of estimated independent components $\widehat{s}_i$, which is known to be equivalent to maximize independence between the estimates when the estimates are constrained to be uncorrelated [6]. In [8], the author proposed a class of non-Gaussianity measures:

$$J(\widehat{s}_i) = J_G(\boldsymbol{w}_i) = [E\{G(\boldsymbol{w}_i^T\boldsymbol{x})\} - E\{G(z)\}]^2, \tag{2}$$

where $\boldsymbol{w}_i^T$ is the i-th row of $\mathbf{W}$ and is constrained so that $E(\widehat{s}_i^2)=E\{(\boldsymbol{w}_i^T\boldsymbol{x})^2\}=1$ due to the aforementioned assumption on unit variance of s_i, G is a nonlinear and non-quadratic function and z is a Gaussian variable with zero mean and unit variance. In practice, the expectations in Eq. (2) are replaced by their sample means. In the rest of the paper, *we say that a variable u is more non-Gaussian than a variable v if $J(u)>J(v)$*. The author of [8] further proposed an estimation method based on maximization of non-Gaussianity and proved a theorem to show its (local) consistency:

Theorem 1. *Assume that the input data $\boldsymbol{x}$ follows the ICA model in Eq. (1). Assume that G is a sufficiently smooth even function. Then the set of local maxima of $J_G(\boldsymbol{w}_i)$ under the constraint $E\{(\boldsymbol{w}_i^T\boldsymbol{x})^2\}=1$ includes the rows of $\widetilde{\mathbf{W}}$ for which the corresponding independent components s_i satisfy the following condition $E\{s_ig(s_i)-g'(s_i)\}[E\{G(s_i)\}-E\{G(z)\}]>0$, where $g(\cdot)$ is the derivative of $G(\cdot)$, and $g'(\cdot)$ is the derivative of $g(\cdot)$.* □

Note that any independent component s_i satisfying the condition in Theorem 1 is a *local* maximum of $J_G(\boldsymbol{w})$ but may not correspond to the *global* maximum. Two conjectures are widely made [6], **Conjecture 1:** the assumption in Theorem 1 is true for most reasonable choices of G and distributions of the s_i; **Conjecture 2:** the global maximum of $J_G(\boldsymbol{w})$ is one of s_i for most reasonable choices of G and the distributions of s_i. In particular, if $G(s)=s^4$, Conjecture 1 is true for any continuous random variable whose moments exist and kurtosis is non-zero [8], and it can also be proven that there are no spurious optima [9]. Then the global maximum should be one of s_i, *i.e.*, Conjecture 2 is true as well. However, kurtosis often suffers from sensitivity to outliers. Therefore, more robust functions such as $G(s)=-\exp(-s^2/2)$ are widely used [6].

2.2 Linear Acyclic Causal Models

Causal relationships between continuous observed variables x_i ($i = 1, \cdots, p$) are typically assumed to be (i) *linear* and (ii) *acyclic* [3,4]. For simplicity, we assume that the variables x_i are of zero mean. Let $k(i)$ denote such a causal order of x_i that no later variable causes any earlier variable. Then, the linear causal relationship can be expressed as

$$x_i := \sum_{k(j)<k(i)} b_{ij}x_j + e_i, \tag{3}$$

where e_i is an external influence associated with x_i and is of zero mean. (iii) The *faithfulness* [4] is typically assumed. In this context, the faithfulness implies that correlations and partial correlations between variables x_i are entailed by the graph structure, *i.e.*, the zero/non-zero status of b_{ij}, not by special parameter values of b_{ij}. (iv) The external influences e_i are assumed to be independent, which implies there are *no unobserved confounders* [4].

We emphasize that x_i is equal to e_i if it is not influenced by any other observed variable x_j $(j \neq i)$ inside the model, *i.e.*, all the b_{ij} $(j \neq i)$ are zeros. That is, an external influence e_i is *observed* as x_i. Then the x_i is called an *exogenous observed variable*. Otherwise, e_i is called an *error*. For example, consider the model defined by

$$x_1 = e_1$$
$$x_2 = 1.5x_1 + e_2$$
$$x_3 = 0.8x_1 - 1.3x_2 + e_3.$$

x_1 is equal to e_1 since it is not influenced by either x_2 or x_3. x_1 is an exogenous observed variable, and e_2 and e_3 are errors. Note that it is obvious that there *exists at least one exogenous observed variable* $x_i(=e_i)$ due to the acyclicity and no unobserved confounder assumptions.

3 A New Method to Identify Exogenous Variables

3.1 A New Non-gaussian Linear Acyclic Causal Model

We make two additional assumptions on the distributions of e_i to the model (3) and define a new non-Gaussian linear causal model. Let the observed variables x_i in a p-dimensional vector be $\boldsymbol{x}$ and external influences e_i in a p-dimensional vector $\boldsymbol{e}$. Let a $p \times p$ matrix $\mathbf{B}$ consist of the causal effects b_{ij} where the diagonal elements b_{ii} are all zeros. Then the model (3) is written in a matrix form as:

$$\boldsymbol{x} = \mathbf{B}\boldsymbol{x} + \boldsymbol{e}. \tag{4}$$

Recall that the set of the external influences e_i consist of both exogenous observed variables and errors. To distinguish the exogenous variables and errors, we make the following additional assumptions, **Assumption 1:** External influences that correspond to exogenous observed variables are non-Gaussian; **Assumption 2:** External influences that correspond to errors are non-Gaussian but less non-Gaussian than the exogenous observed variables. That is, *the model (4)=the model (3)+Assumptions 1 and 2*. The first assumption is made to explain why observed data are often considerably non-Gaussian in many fields [6]. The second assumption reflects two facts: i) in statistics, errors have been typically considered to arise as sums of a number of unobserved (non-Gaussian) independent variables, which is why classical methods assume that errors are Gaussian resorting to the central limit theorem; ii) the distinction between Gaussian and non-Gaussian variables is artificial in practice, though. In reality, many variables are not exactly Gaussian. Therefore, we allow the errors to be strongly non-Gaussian as long as they are less non-Gaussian than exogenous variables.[1]

The distinction between exogenous variables and errors leads to a very simple estimation of exogenous variables proposed in the next subsections.

3.2 Identification of Exogenous Variables Based on Non-gaussianity and Uncorrelatedness

We relate the linear non-Gaussian causal model (4) with ICA similarly to [5]. Let us solve the model (4) for x and then we have an ICA model represented by Eq. (1) as follows

$$x = (\mathbf{I} - \mathbf{B})^{-1}e = \mathbf{A}'e. \tag{5}$$

Note that $\mathbf{I}-\mathbf{B}$ is invertible since it can be permuted to be lower triangular due to the acyclicity assumption if one knew causal orders $k(i)$ [5] and its diagonal elements are all non-zero (unity). In the next section we propose a new algorithm to find exogenous variables $x_i(=e_i)$ using the relation (5). In this section we present two lemmas that ensures the validity of the algorithm.

Lemma 1. *Assume that the input data x follows the model (4) and that Conjecture 2 (Section 2.1) is true. Let us denote by V_x the set of all the observed variables x_i. Then, the most non-Gaussian observed variable in V_x is exogenous: $J(x_i)$ is maximum in $V_x \Rightarrow x_i=e_i$.* □

Proof. Eq. (5) shows that the model (4) is an ICA model, where external influences e_i are independent components (ICs). The set of the external influences consist of exogenous observed variables and errors. Due to the model assumption (Assumption 2 in Section 3.1), exogenous observed variables are more non-Gaussian than errors. Therefore, the most non-Gaussian *exogenous* observed variable is the most non-Gaussian IC. Next, according to Conjecture 2 that is here assumed to be true, the most non-Gaussian IC, *i.e.*, the most non-Gaussian *exogenous* observed variable, is the global maximum of the non-Gaussianity measure $J(w^T x)=J_G(w)$ among such linear combinations of observed variables $w^T x$ with the constraint $E\{(w^T x)^2\}=1$, which include all the observed variables x_i in V_x. Therefore, the most non-Gaussian observed variable is the most non-Gaussian *exogenous* variable. ∎

Lemma 2. *Assume the assumptions of Lemma 1. Let us denote by E a strict subset of exogenous observed variables so that it does not contain at least one exogenous variable. Let us denote by U_E the set of observed variables uncorrelated with any variable in E. Then the most non-Gaussian observed variable in U_E is exogenous: $J(x_i)$ is maximum in $U_E \Rightarrow x_i=e_i$.* □

---

[1] It would be rather easy to show that our algorithm in Section 3.3 allows Gaussian errors as well.

Proof. First, the set V_x is the union of three disjoint sets: E, U_E and C_E, where C_E is the set of observed variables in $V_x \backslash E$ correlated with a variable in E. By definition, any variable in U_E are not correlated with any variable in E. Since the faithfulness is assumed, the zero correlations are only due to the graph structure. Therefore, there is no directed path from any variable in E to any variable in U_E. Similarly, there is a directed path from each (exogenous) variable in E to a variable in C_E. Next, there can be no directed path from any variable in C_E to any variable in U_E. Otherwise, there would be a directed path from such a variable in E from which there is a directed path to a variable in C_E to a variable in U_E through the variable in C_E. Then, due to the faithfulness, the variable in E must correlate with the variable in U_E, which contradicts the definition of U_E.

To sum up, there is no directed path from any variable in $E \cup C_E$ to any variable in U_E. Since any directed path from the external influence e_i associated with any variable x_i in V_x must go through x_i, there is no directed path from the external influence associated with any variable in $E \cup C_E$ to any variable in U_E. In other words, there can be directed paths from *only* the external influences associated with any variables in U_E to some variables in U_E. Then, we again have an ICA model: $\widetilde{x} = \widetilde{A}' \widetilde{e}$, where $\widetilde{x}$ and $\widetilde{e}$ are vectors whose elements are the variables in U_E and corresponding external influences in e in Eq. (5), and $\widetilde{A}'$ is the corresponding submatrix of A' in Eq. (5). Recursively applying Lemma 1 shows that the most non-Gaussian variable in U_E is exogenous. ∎

To find uncorrelated variables, we simply use the ordinary Gaussianity-based testing method [10] and control the false discovery rate [11] to 5% for multiplicity of tests. Though non-parametric methods [10] is desirable for more rigorous testing in the non-Gaussian setting, we used the Gaussian method that is more computationally efficient and seems to work relatively well in our simulations. Future work would address what is the better testing procedure taking non-Gaussianity into account.

3.3   Exogenous Generating Variable Finder: EggFinder

Based on the discussions in the previous subsection, we propose an algorithm to find exogenous variables one by one, which we call EggFinder (ExoGenous Generating variable Finder):

1. Given V_x, initialize $E = \emptyset$, $U_E^{(1)} = V_x$, and $m := 1$.
2. Repeat until no variables x_i are uncorrelated with exogenous variable candidates, *i.e.*, $U_E^{(m)} = \emptyset$:
   (a) Find the most non-Gaussian variable x_m in $U_E^{(m)}$:

$$x_m = \arg \max_{x \in U_E^{(m)}} J(x), \tag{6}$$

where J is the non-Gaussianity measure in Eq. (2) with

$$G(x) = -\exp(-x^2/2). \tag{7}$$

(b) Add the most non-Gaussian variable x_m to E, that is, $E=E\cup\{x_m\}$.

(c) Let $U_E^{(m+1)}$ to be the set of variables x_i uncorrelated with any variable in E, and $m:=m+1$.

In Step 2c, we use the Gaussianity-based testing method and control the false discovery rate to 5%.

4   Experiments on Artificial Data

We studied the performance of EggFinder when $p\gg n$ under a linear non-Gaussian acyclic model having a sparse graph structure and various degrees of error non-Gaussianity. Many real-world networks such as gene networks are often considered to have scale-free graph structures. However, as far as we know, there is no standard way to create a *directed* scale-free graph. Therefore, we first randomly created a (conventional) sparse directed acyclic graph with $p=1,000$ variables using a standard software Tetrad (http://www.phil.cmu.edu/projects/tetrad/). The resulting graph contained 1,000 edges and $\ell=171$ exogenous variables. We randomly determined each element of the matrix **B** in the model (4) to follow this graph structure and make the standard deviations of x_i owing to parent observed variables ranged in the interval $[0.5, 1.5]$.

We generated non-Gaussian exogenous variables and errors as follows. We randomly generated a non-Gaussian exogenous observed variable $x_i(=e_i)$ that was sub- or super-Gaussian with probability 50%. We first generated a Gaussian variable z_i with zero mean and unit variance and subsequently transformed it to a non-Gaussian variable by $s_i = \mathrm{sign}(z_i)|z_i|^{q_i}$. The nonlinear exponent q_i was randomly selected to lie in $[0.5, 0.8]$ or $[1.2, 2.0]$ with probability 50%. The former gave a sub-Gaussian symmetric variable, and the latter a super-Gaussian symmetric variable. Finally, the transformed variable s_i was scaled to the standard deviation randomly selected in the interval $[0.5, 1.5]$ and was taken as an exogenous variable. Next, for each error e_i, we randomly generated h ($h=1$, 3, 5 and 50) non-Gaussian variables having unit variance in the same manner as for exogenous variables and subsequently took the sum of them. We then scaled the sum to the standard deviation selected similarly to the cases of exogenous variables and finally took it as an error e_i. A larger h (the number of non-Gaussian variables summed) would generate a less non-Gaussian error due to the central limit theorem.

Finally, we randomly generated 1,000 datasets under each combination of h and n ($n=30$, 60, 100 and 200) and fed the datasets to EggFinder. For each combination, we computed percentages of datasets where all the top m estimated variables were actually exogenous. In Fig. 1, the relations between the percentage and m are plotted for some representative conditions due to the limited space. First, in all the conditions the percentages monotonically decrease when m increases. Second, the percentages generally increase when the sample size n increases. Similar changes of the percentages are observed when the errors are less non-Gaussian. This is reasonable since a larger n enables more accurate

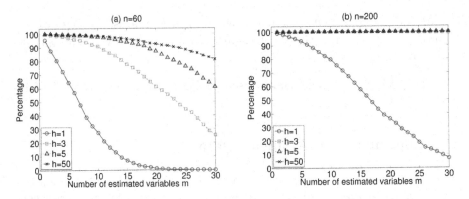

Fig. 1. Percentages of datasets where all the top m estimated variables were actually exogenous under (a) $n{=}60$; (b) $n{=}200$

estimation of non-Gaussianity and correlation, and a larger h generates data more consistent with the assumptions of the model (4). In summary, EggFinder successfully finds a set of exogenous variables up to more than $m{=}10$ in many practical conditions. However, EggFinder may not find all the exogenous variables when $p{\gg}n$, although it asymptotically finds all the exogenous variables if all the assumptions made in Lemmas 1 and 2 hold.

Interestingly, EggFinder did not fail completely and identified a couple of exogenous variables even for the $h{=}1$ condition where the distributional assumption on errors was most likely to be violated. This is presumably because the endogenous variables are sums of non-Gaussian errors and exogenous variables, so due to the central limit theorem they are likely to be less non-Gaussian than the exogenous variables, even if the errors and exogenous variables have the same degree of non-Gaussianity.

5   Application to Microarray Gene Expression Data

To evaluate the practicality of EggFinder, we analyzed a real-world dataset of DNA microarray collected in experiments on human breast cancer cells [12], where epidermal growth factor EGF was dosed to the breast cancer cells, and their gene expression levels were measured. The experiment was conducted with completely random sampling of the cells under every combination of two factors. The first factor was the concentration of EGF (0.1, 0.5, 1.0, and 10.0 nmol/ℓ), and the second factor was the elapsed time after its dose (5, 10, 15, 30, 45, 60 and 90 minutes). The total number of experimental conditions was 27. No experiment under the condition of the concentration of EGF 10.0 nmol/ℓ at 45 minutes elapsed time was conducted. For each condition, gene expression levels of 22,277 genes of were measured using Affymetrix GeneChip microarrays.

As a standard preprocessing, we first conducted t-tests for the differences of means of the gene expression levels between the lowest and highest concentration

Table 1. Candidates of exogenous genes found by EggFinder

The genes likely to be exogenous	The others
ACBD3	CAPRIN2
ARPC2	CDC2L6
EIF3M	FKBP15
GULP1	IFT52
MED13	KDM6B
MUT	LOC100134401
NCOA2	LOC202181
NOLC1	PHF20L1
PPIB	PMS2L2
RBMS1	PPDPF
RRM1	PPIH
RSRC1	PPPDE1
SET	RAB14
SKAP2	SH3YL1
UBE2D2	

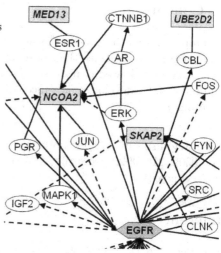

Fig. 2. A part of the pathway network from EGFR to candidates found by EggFinder. The genes boxed and indicated in italic type are the candidates.

conditions of EGF under 5, 10, 15 and 30 minutes elapsed time. We then selected 1,000 genes that expressed the most significance of the differences since such genes were likely to relevant to EGF dosing. Thus, we obtained a data matrix with the number of variables $p=1,000$ and the sample size $n=27$.

Subsequently, we applied EggFinder to the data matrix. Table 1 shows 29 candidates of exogenous genes found by EggFinder. To evaluate the candidates, we obtained gene pathways from EGF receptor EGFR to the candidates by Ingenuity Pathways Database (http://www.ingenuity.com/) which is a literature-based biological pathway database. A part of the gene pathways are shown in Fig. 2 where both a dashed line and a solid line stand for a direct influence from a gene to another gene. A dashed line goes through some intermediate factor such as enzymes, while a solid line does not. In the obtained gene pathway network, 15 of the 29 candidates listed in the left column in Table 1 are reached from EGFR within two edges. These 15 candidates are likely to be exogenous under the biological knowledge. However, it dose not mean that the other 14 candidates listed in the right column in Table 1 are not exogenous at all since the biological knowledge on the exogeneity of genes has not been sufficiently accumulated in the database. We merely obtained no strong evidence that the 14 candidates are exogenous by Ingenuity Pathways Database. For instance, among the 14 candidates, CAPRIN2 might be also expected to be exogenous since it is known to be induced by FGF (Fibroblast Growth Factor) similar to EGF [13]. In biological aspects, the relation between EGFR and these 14 candidates are worth to be examined. By using EggFinder, we can narrow down to the genes worth for examining.

6 Conclusion

We proposed a method to find exogenous variables from data having orders of magnitude more variables than observations. Experiments on microarray gene expression data showed that our method is promising. This would be an important first step for developing advanced causal analysis methods in the challenging situations $p \gg n$.

Acknowledgments. This work was supported in part by the Grant-in-Aid (21700302, 21650029) from the Ministry of Education, Culture, Sports, Science and Technology.

References

1. di Bernardo, D., Thompson, M., Gardner, T., Chobot, S., Eastwood, E., Wojtovich, A., Elliot, S., Schaus, S., Collins, J.: Chemogenomic profiling on a genome-wide scale using reverse-engineered gene networks. Nature Biotech. 23, 377–383 (2005)
2. Londei, A., D'Ausilio, A., Basso, D., Belardinelli, M.O.: A new method for detecting causality in fMRI data of cognitive processing. Cog. Proc. 7, 42–52 (2006)
3. Pearl, J.: Causality: Models, Reasoning, and Inference. Camb. Univ. Press, Cambridge (2000)
4. Spirtes, P., Glymour, C., Scheines, R.: Causation, Prediction, and Search. Springer, Heidelberg (1993)
5. Shimizu, S., Hoyer, P.O., Hyvärinen, A., Kerminen, A.: A linear non-gaussian acyclic model for causal discovery. J. Mach. Learn. Res. 7, 2003–2030 (2006)
6. Hyvärinen, A., Karhunen, J., Oja, E.: Independent component analysis. Wiley, New York (2001)
7. Comon, P.: Independent component analysis, a new concept? Signal Processing 36, 62–83 (1994)
8. Hyvärinen, A.: Fast and robust fixed-point algorithms for independent component analysis. IEEE Trans. on Neural Networks 10, 626–634 (1999)
9. Delfosse, N., Loubaton, P.: Adaptive blind separation of independent sources: a deflation approach. Signal Processing 45, 59–83 (1995)
10. Lehmann, E., Romano, J.: Testing Statistical Hypotheses. Springer, Heidelberg (2005)
11. Benjamini, Y., Hochberg, Y.: Controlling the false discovery rate: a practical and powerful approach to multiple testing. J. Roy. Stat. Soc. B 57, 289–300 (1995)
12. Ivshina, A.V., George, J., Senko, O., Mow, B., Putti, T.C., Smeds, J., Lindahl, T., Pawitan, Y., Hall, P., Nordgren, H., Wong, J.E.L., Liu, E.T., Bergh, J., Kuznetsov, V.A., Miller, L.D.: Genetic reclassification of histologic grade delineates new clinical subtypes of breast cancer. Cancer Res. 66, 10292–10301 (2006)
13. Lorén, C., Schrader, J., Ahlgren, U., Gunhaga, L.: FGF signals induce Caprin2 expression in the vertebrate lens. Differentiation 77, 386–394 (2009)

Bayesian Joint Optimization for Topic Model and Clustering

Tikara Hosino

Nihon Unisys, Ltd.

Abstract. Statistical clustering is the method for dividing the given samples by assumed distributions. In high dimensional problems, such as document or image clustering, the direct method is suffered from over-fitting and the curse of the dimensionality. In many cases, we firstly reduce the dimensionality, then apply the clustering algorithm. However these methods neglect the interaction among two processes. In this report, we propose the hierarchical joint distribution of Latent Dirichlet Allocation and Polya Mixture and give the parameter estimation algorithm by Gibbs sampling method. Some benchmarks show the effectiveness of the proposed method.

1 Introduction

We often face the situation which we acquire the large collection of samples that is not well structured. Then, we firstly divide the given samples into the category which shares some characteristics of the samples. Statistical clustering is the method for dividing the set of given samples by using the user assuming distributions which is called the generative models. For example, the generative models such as the mixture of Gaussian and the mixture of the multinomial are widely used and shows their effectiveness.

In the case of clustering for image or document data, the main obstacle lies in their high dimensional feature vectors. For example, in the image clustering, if we directly use the pixels as the feature vector, even the small black-white 16 pixel's image has 256 dimension. Moreover, the case of document clustering, the words are commonly used feature vector, has the dimension whose order is higher than ten thousands.

In high dimensional clustering, if we apply the algorithm directly, then we are suffered from the scarcity of the number of samples against the dimension, or the curse of the dimensionality which is cause by the concentration on the sphere. In an ordinary case, we preprocess the data by the dimensionality reduction or the feature selection. For dimensionality reduction, we usually chose the principal component analysis (PCA) for continuous data and the latent Dirichlet allocation (LDA) for the discrete data [1,2]. After the dimensionality reduction, we apply the clustering algorithm to the compressed samples. However, the problem of these methods are neglecting the interaction among the dimensionality reduction and clustering processes. Therefore, for example, they cannot project the samples to the subspace which facilitates the clustering.

K. Diamantaras, W. Duch, L.S. Iliadis (Eds.): ICANN 2010, Part I, LNCS 6352, pp. 77–86, 2010.
© Springer-Verlag Berlin Heidelberg 2010

Recently, to tackle the problem, the joint optimization approaches are proposed [4,5]. These methods naturally synthesize the dimensionality reduction and the clustering via the generative joint model which has hierarchical structure. In this paper, we give the joint hierarchical distribution of LDA and Polya mixture (PM) for the discrete data clustering. Additionally, we propose the efficient parameter estimation algorithm by Gibbs sampling (which is a kind of Markov Chain Monte Carlo (MCMC) method). Some benchmark experiments show the effectiveness of our proposed method.

2   Hierarchical Joint Model

In this chapter, we firstly introduce LDA as the compressed model and PM as the clustering model. Then, we propose the hierarchical joint distribution of them. In the following explanation, we use the document generation process as examples.

2.1   LDA

Generative Model. We assume the document is generated from K topics and each topic has M words. Moreover, we assume the document D (length L) is generated from the following processes.

- $\theta \sim Dir(\alpha)$ Sampling topic parameters θ from Dirichlet distribution with parameter α
- $\eta_k \sim Dir(\beta_k)$ Sampling each topic's word parameters η_k from Dirichlet distribution with parameter β_k
  Then, each word w_l is generated from
- $z_l \sim Mul(1; \theta)$ Sampling topic z_l from multinomial with parameter θ
- $w_l \sim Mul(1; \eta_{z_l})$ Sampling word w_l from multinomial with parameter η_{z_l} which is conditional on the topic z_l

Another point of view, LDA is considered as the matrix factorization whose elements is restricted to non-negative and has some normalizing constraints. The $N \times M$ document word matrix whose row represents the document and whose column represents the word, LDA factorizes the matrix to $N \times K$ and $K \times M$ matrices. In general, we chose the number of the topics K in $K << N$, therefore the number of parameter satisfies $NM << (N + M)K$ which shows the approximation of the matrix with the smaller number of parameters.

Definition. We define the LDA model. Let the observed word sequence as $w = (w_1, \ldots, w_L)$ and the hidden topic sequence as $Z = (z_1 \ldots, z_L)$. Moreover, let the model parameters $\theta, \eta, \alpha, \beta$ as introduced above. Then, the probability distribution of LDA is written by

$$p(w, z, \theta, \eta | \alpha, \beta) = p(\theta | \alpha) \prod_{k=1}^{K} p(\eta_k | \beta_k) \prod_{l=1}^{L} p(w_l | \eta, z_l) p(z_l | \theta).$$

where $p(w_l|\eta_{z_l}), p(z_l|\theta)$ are multinomial distributions which are given by

$$Mul(\theta|l;p) \equiv \begin{pmatrix} l \\ \theta_1 \cdots \theta_k \end{pmatrix} p_1^{\theta_1} \cdots p_k^{\theta_k}, \sum_{j=1}^{k} p_j = 1, \tag{1}$$

and $p(\theta|\alpha), p(\eta_k|\beta_k)$ are Dirichlet distributions which are given by

$$Dir(\theta|\alpha) \equiv \frac{\Gamma(\alpha_1 + \cdots + \alpha_k)}{\Gamma(\alpha_1) \cdots \Gamma(\alpha_k)} \theta_1^{\alpha_1-1} \cdots \theta_k^{\alpha_k-1} \tag{2}$$

Then, we can integrate out the parameters θ, η and the complete likelihood is written by

$$p(w, z|\alpha, \beta) = \int p(w, z, \theta, \eta|\alpha, \beta)d\theta d\eta$$

$$= \frac{\Gamma(\sum_k \alpha_k) \prod_k \Gamma(n_k + \alpha_k)}{\prod_k \Gamma(\alpha_k) \; \Gamma(L + \sum_k \alpha_k)} \prod_{k=1}^{K} \frac{\Gamma(\sum_m \beta_m) \prod_m \Gamma(n_{km} + \beta_m)}{\prod_m \Gamma(\beta_m) \; \Gamma(n_k + \sum_m \beta_m)}, \tag{3}$$

where n_k is the number of the topic k and the n_{km} is the number of topic k and word m. Remarkably, n_k and n_{km} are the count of hidden variables.

2.2   PM

Generative Model. The generative processes of PM are as follows. The document D which has length L is sampling from

- $z \sim Mul(1;\theta)$ Sampling the component z from multinomial with parameter θ
- $q \sim Dir(\alpha_z)$ Sampling the parameter q from the Dirichlet which is conditioned on component z.
  Then L length words are sampled from multinomial with parameter q
- $w_l \sim Mul(L;q)$.

Definition. Let the observed bag of words as $w = (w_1, \ldots, w_L)$ and let the model parameters z, q, α as described above. Then, the complete likelihood is written by

$$p(w, z, q|\alpha) = p(w|q)p(q|\alpha, z)p(z|\theta). \tag{4}$$

Following the same argument of LDA, we can integrate out the distribution by q.

$$p(w, z|\alpha) = \prod_k (\theta_k \frac{\Gamma(\sum_m \alpha_{km})}{\Gamma(\sum_m n_m + \alpha_{km})} \prod_m \frac{\Gamma(n_m + \alpha_{km})}{\Gamma(\alpha_{km})})^{z_k}, \tag{5}$$

where, n_m is count of w_m. Additionally, in the case of PM, we can sum over the hidden variable z_k.

$$p(w|\alpha) = \sum_k \theta_k \frac{\Gamma(\sum_m \alpha_{km})}{\Gamma(\sum_m n_m + \alpha_{km})} \prod_m \frac{\Gamma(n_m + \alpha_{km})}{\Gamma(\alpha_{km})} \tag{6}$$

2.3 Joint Model

In this paper, we propose the method for binding these models by the hierarchical joint distribution. Concretely, we set the prior probability of LDA to PM. Then, the generative model of the document is as follows.

- Sampling the document cluster z_0 from multinomial with parameter θ_0
- Sampling the topic parameter θ_1 from Dirichlet with parameter α_0 which condition on z_0.
- Sampling the topic z_1 from multinomial with parameter θ_1
- Sampling the word w from multinomial with parameter θ_2 which condition on z_1

The proposed model assumes the clustering process is generated on low dimensional topic space. Additionally, we assume the number of cluster is K and the number of topics is J, and we choose the prior distributions are conjugate form of the likelihoods. Then, the joint probability distribution of the proposed model is defined by

$$
p(w, \theta_0, \theta_1, \theta_2, \alpha_0, \alpha_1, z_0, z_1 | a_0, b_0, a_1, b_1, \alpha_2)
$$

$$
= \prod_{k=1}^{K} \prod_{j=1}^{J} Mul(w|\theta_{2j})^{z_{1j}} Dir(\theta_{2j}|\alpha_1) Ga(\alpha_1|a_1, b_1) Mul(z_1|\theta_1) Dir(\theta_1|\alpha_{0k})^{z_{0k}}
$$

$$
Ga(\alpha_{0k}|a_0, b_0) Mul(z_0|\theta_0) Dir(\theta_0|\alpha_2) \tag{7}
$$

where $Ga(\alpha|a, b)$ is gamma distribution which is given by

$$
Ga(\alpha|a, b) = \frac{b^a}{\Gamma(a)} \alpha^{a-1} e^{-b\alpha}. \tag{8}
$$

The graphical model of the proposed distribution is represented as figure (1).

3 Learning Algorithm

In this chapter, we introduce the Gibbs sampling algorithm for the proposed distribution. Since the learning algorithm is repeating Gibbs sampling of LDA and PM models, we introduce the each method respectively.

3.1 Learning of LDA

Collapsed Gibbs Sampling is known as the efficient LDA learning method[6]. By the discussion of the previous chapter, the core of the algorithm is the estimation of the hidden variable sequence $Z = (z_1, \ldots, z_L)$. The predictive distribution of

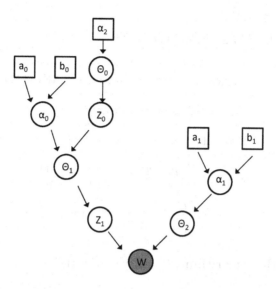

Fig. 1. The graphical model of the proposed method. The same parameter symbols belong to the same distributions

the model given all hidden variables except for z_l is written by,

$$p(z_l = t_{k'}, w_l = v_{m'} | W, Z, \alpha, \beta)$$

$$= \frac{\frac{\Gamma(\sum_k \alpha_k)}{\prod_k \Gamma(\alpha_k)} \frac{\prod_k \Gamma(n_k+\alpha_k+\delta_{kk'})}{\Gamma(L+\sum_k \alpha_k+1)}}{\frac{\Gamma(\sum_k \alpha_k)}{\prod_k \Gamma(\alpha_k)} \frac{\prod_k \Gamma(n_k+\alpha_k)}{\Gamma(L+\sum_k \alpha_k)}} \prod_{k=1}^{K} \frac{\frac{\Gamma(\sum_m \beta_m)}{\prod_m \Gamma(\beta_m)} \frac{\prod_m \Gamma(n_{km}+\beta_m+\delta_{mm'}\delta_{kk'})}{\Gamma(n_k+\sum_m \beta_m+\delta_{kk'})}}{\prod_{k=1}^{K} \frac{\Gamma(\sum_m \beta_m)}{\prod_m \Gamma(\beta_m)} \frac{\prod_m \Gamma(n_{km}+\beta_m)}{\Gamma(n_k+\sum_m \beta_m)}}$$

$$= \frac{n_k + \alpha_k}{L + \sum_k \alpha_k} \frac{n_{km} + \beta_m}{n_k + \sum_m \beta_m}. \tag{9}$$

Here, we use the characteristic of the Gamma function and Kronecker δ_{ij} which are defined by

$$\frac{\Gamma(x+1)}{\Gamma(x)} = x, \quad \delta_{ij} = \begin{cases} 1 & i = j \\ 0 & i \neq j \end{cases} \tag{10}$$

Therefore, if hidden variables are given, the update algorithm is given by which subtract the z_l from the predictive distribution(9),

$$\frac{n_k + \alpha_k - \delta_{kk'}}{L + \sum_k \alpha_k - 1} \frac{n_{km} + \beta_{km} - \delta_{mm'}\delta_{kk'}}{n_k + \sum_m \beta_{km} - 1} \tag{11}$$

We sample the hidden variable z_l from the predictive distribution (9). We estimate all $Z = (z_1, \ldots, z_L)$ by repeating the these processes. If we use the given Z, the estimation of hyper parameters α, β comes down to the learning of Polya distribution. From the description of the algorithm, the computational cost and the memory requirements is the number of elements of samples $O(N \times L)$.

3.2   Learning of PM

Gibbs Sampling for PM is already known [3].

Preparation. Subsequently, we use the characteristics of the Gamma Function,

$$\Gamma(x+1) = x\Gamma(x) \tag{12}$$

and the definition of Beta integral.

$$B(p,q) = \frac{\Gamma(p)\Gamma(q)}{\Gamma(p+q)} = \frac{(p-1)!(q-1)!}{(p+q-1)!}$$

$$= \int_0^1 x^{p-1}(1-x)^{q-1}dx \tag{13}$$

Derivation of the Algorithm. Firstly, we derive the estimation algorithm for α_k.

The second term of the formula (6), by using the definition of the Beta integral(13), is written by

$$\int_0^1 x^{\alpha_1 + \cdots + \alpha_K - 1}(1-x)^{n_i - 1}dx. \tag{14}$$

Therefore, we introduce the auxiliary variable x_i which is given by the sample from the Beta distribution.

$$x_i \sim \text{Beta}(\alpha_1 + \cdots + \alpha_K, n_i) \tag{15}$$

From the characteristics of the Gamma function, the third term of the equation (6) is rewritten as

$$\frac{\Gamma(n_{ik} + \alpha_k)}{\Gamma(\alpha_k)} = \prod_{j=0}^{n_{ik}-1} (\alpha + j) = \prod_{j=0}^{n_{ik}-1} \sum_{y_j=0,1} \alpha_k^{y_j} j^{1-y_j} \tag{16}$$

Therefore, we introduce the auxiliary variable y_i from the sample of the Bernoulli distribution.

$$y_j \sim \text{Bernoulli}(\frac{\alpha_k}{\alpha_k + j}) \tag{17}$$

Using these auxiliary variables x_i, y_i the posterior distribution of α is given by Bayes theorem.

$$p(\alpha_k|D) \propto p(\alpha_k) \prod_{i=1}^{N} x_i^{\alpha_k} \prod_{j=0}^{n_{ik}-1} \alpha_k^{y_j} \tag{18}$$

Then, if the prior of $p(\alpha_k)$ is the Gamma distribution $Ga(\alpha_k|a,b)$. The posterior distribution is given by

$$p(\alpha_k|D) \propto \alpha^{-1+a+\sum_{i=1}^{N}\sum_{j=0}^{n_{ik}-1} y_j} e^{-\alpha_k(b-\sum_{i=1}^{N}\log(x_i))}. \qquad (19)$$

Therefore, the estimation of α_k is given by the sample from the following Gamma distribution.

$$\alpha_k \sim Ga(a + \sum_{i=1}^{N}\sum_{j=0}^{n_{ik}-1} y_j, b - \sum_{i=1}^{N}\log(x_i)) \qquad (20)$$

Secondly, we derive Gibbs sampling for pm. The hidden variables of the pm is sampled from

$$p(k|w,\alpha) \propto \theta_k \frac{\Gamma(\sum_m \alpha_{km})}{\Gamma(\sum_m n_m + \alpha_{km})} \prod_m \frac{\Gamma(n_m + \alpha_{km})}{\Gamma(\alpha_{km})} \qquad (21)$$

Then, using these hidden variables, the parameters θ are sampled from

$$\theta \sim Dir(n_{km} + \alpha_{2k}) \qquad (22)$$

and the parameter α_k is sampled from equation (20). The computational cost and the memory requirement are $O(N \times L)$.

3.3 Estimation of Proposed method

As shown by the Graphical model of figure (1), the conditional probability of the LDA and PM is separated with the hidden topic vectors z_1. Therefore, Gibbs sampler of the proposed method is achieved by iterating the following steps. Firstly, estimate LDA by Collapsed Gibbs sampling. Secondly, estimate PM by auxiliary sampling using the estimated topic vector of LDA. Then, we set the prior distribution of LDA to the estimated PM parameter. The detailed inference process is given at algorithm (1). The computational cost and the memory requirements are the addition of LDA and PM algorithm, $O(N \times L)$.

Algorithm 1. Gibbs Sampling for Proposed Method

---

   while convergence **do**
      for $n = 0$ to N **do**
         For each document, Gibbs Sampling LDA using equation (11) and get Z_n
      end for
      for $n = 0$ to N **do**
         For given Z_n Gibbs Sampling PM using equation (20) and equation (21)
      end for
      Set the prior of LDA α_K to estimated PM parameter.
   end while

---

4   Experiment

We execute the numerical experiments for testing the performance of the proposed method. For comparison, we chose Maximum Margin Clustering (MMC) [8,9] which has high accuracy rate in the clustering algorithm. Moreover, to investigate the effect of joint estimation, we chose the pipelined estimation through LDA to PM.

4.1   Correct Rate

In the experiments, we set the number of clusters equal to the true number of classes k for all the clustering algorithm. To assess clustering accuracy, we firstly take a set of labeled data, remove the labels for all data samples and run the clustering algorithm, then we label each of the resulting clusters with the majority class according to the original training labels, and finally measure the number of correct classifications made by each clustering.

4.2   Datasets

We use 4 data sets in experiments, which are image and documents datasets. Digits from the UCI repository[1] and MNIST Hand Written Digits[2] are image datasets. 20 newsgroup[3] and RCVI [11] are documents datasets. For the 20 newsgroup dataset, we chose the label which contains autos, motorcycles, baseball, hockey from the version 20-news-18829. For RCVI, we use the data samples with the four topic codes (CCAT, ECAT, GCAT, and MCAT) from the "Topic Codes" in the sample set. Number of samples, classes, dimension for each dataset are shown by table 1.

Table 1. Datasets for Experiments

Dataset	Samples	Classes	Dimension
UCI Digit 1279	2256	4	64
MNIST 1-7	13007	2	784
MNIST 3-8	11982	2	784
News20	3977	4	22275
RCV1	20371	4	28068

4.3   Result

The results are summarized on table 2. Topics represents the number of topics in LDA. The results of MMC are quoted from [8,9].

---

[1] http://archive.ics.uci.edu/ml/datasets/

[2] http://yann.lecum.com/exdb/mnist

[3] http://people.csail.mit.edu/jrennie/20newsgroups/

Table 2. Correct Rate

Dataset	Topics	MMC	Pipelined	Proposed
UCI Digit 1279	16	**94.0**	82.8	89.5
MNIST 1-7	32	97.3	98.5	**98.7**
MNIST 3-8	32	81.9	**83.6**	82.7
News20	8	70.6	89.7	**94.4**
RCV1	8	62.0	62.9	**70.1**

4.4 Discussion

Firstly, in the experiments, the proposed method shows that the digit data is competitive or slightly worse and the document data is outperform to the ordinary methods. For explaining the reason, we investigate the estimated topics and clusters from their posterior distributions. Then, we observed that the document cluster shares the topics, for example at the News20 data, the topic which has high probability words 'the", "to" and "and" is shared by all clusters, which is implicitly assumed in our proposed method. However, the digit data has no topic sharing among the clusters. In our primary experiments, the mixture of LDA models which has no shared topic assumption improves the performance of the digit data.

Secondly, the proposed joint method consistently outperforms the pipelined one. This result suggests that the feedback from the clustering facilitates the finding the well structured subspace.

5   Conclusion

We propose the clustering model for discrete data which jointly estimate the dimensionally reduction and the clustering. Then, we give the efficient parameter estimation algorithm by Gibbs sampling. In numerical experiments, the proposed method outperform previous method on some datasets which have high dimensionality and shares the topics among clusters. Model selection for the number of topics and clusters using WAIC [10] are future works.

Acknowledgments. This research is supported by Promotion program for Reducing global Environmental loaD through ICT innovation (PREDICT), Ministry of Internal Affairs and Communications of Japan.

References

1. Bishop, C.M.: Bayesian PCA. Advances in Neural Information Processing Systems 11, 382–388 (1999)
2. Blei, D.M., Ng, A.Y., Jordan, M.I.: Latent dirichlet allocation. Journal of Machine Learning Research 3, 993–1022 (2003)

3. Teh, Y.W., Jordan, M.I., Beak, M.J., Blei, D.M.: Hierarchical Dirichlet processes. Journal of the American Statistical Association 101(476), 1566–1581 (2006)
4. Watanabe, K., Akaho, S., Okada, M.: Clustering on a subspace of exponential family using variational Bayes method. In: Proceedings of International Conference on Information Theory and Statistical Learning (2008)
5. Katahira, K., Matsumoto, N., Sugase-Miyamoto, Y., Okanoya, K., Okada, M.: Doubly Sparse Factor Models for Unifying Feature Transformation and Feature Selection. Journal of Physics: Conference Series (in press)
6. Griffiths, T., Steyvers, M.: Finding scientific topics. Proceedings of the National Academy of Sciences 101 (2004)
7. Sadamitsu, K., Mishina, T., Yamamoto, M.: Topic-based language models using Dirichlet mixtures. IEICE-D-II J88-D-II(9), 1771–1779 (2005)
8. Zhao, B., Wang, F., Zhang, C.: Efficient multiclass maximum margin clustering. In: ICML 2008: Proceedings of the 25th International Conference on Machine Learning (2008)
9. Li, Y.-F., Tsang, I.W., Kwok, J., Zhou, Z.-H.: Tighter and Convex Maximum Margin Clustering. JMLR W&CP 5, 344–351 (2009)
10. Watanabe, S.: Equations of states in singular statistical estimation. Neural Networks 23(1) (2010)
11. Lewis, D.D., Yang, Y., Rose, T., Li, F.: Rcv1: A new benchmark collection for text categorization research. JMLR 5, 361–397

An Incremental Bayesian Approach for Training Multilayer Perceptrons

Dimitris Tzikas[1,2] and Aristidis Likas[1,2]

[1] Biomedical Research Institute — FORTH
University Campus of Ioannina GR 45110, Ioannina, Greece
[2] Department of Computer Science
University of Ioannina, GR 45110, Ioannina, Greece

Abstract. The multilayer perceptron (MLP) is a well established neural network model for supervised learning problems. Furthermore, it is
well known that its performance for a given problem depends crucially on
appropriately selecting the MLP architecture, which is typically achieved
using cross-validation. In this work, we propose an incremental Bayesian
methodology to address the important problem of automatic determination of the number of hidden units in MLPs with one hidden layer.
The proposed methodology treats the one-hidden layer MLP as a linear
model consisting of a weighted combination of basis functions (hidden
units). Then an incremental method for sparse Bayesian learning of linear models is employed that effectively adjusts not only the combination
weights, but also the parameters of the hidden units. Experimental results for several well-known classification data sets demonstrate that the
proposed methodology successfully identifies optimal MLP architectures
in terms of generalization error.

1 Introduction

The *multilayer perceptron* (MLP) is a very popular neural network model for
supervised learning problems. Assuming a *training set* $\{x_n, t_n\}_{n=1}^N$, we can model
the data generation process using a function y so that $t_n = y(x_n) + \epsilon_n$, where
ϵ_n is an error term. The MLP is a parametric form that is commonly used for
the underlying function y. We are interested in the two-layer MLP which has
one hidden layer with M hidden units and an output layer with a single unit.
The output of such an MLP can be considered as a weighted linear model with
respect to the hidden units:

$$y(x) = w^T h(x) + b = \sum_{j=1}^{M} w_j h_j(x) + b, \qquad (1)$$

where b is the output bias, $w = (w_1, \ldots, w_M)^T$ are the weights, $h(x) = (h_1(x), \ldots, h_M(x))^T$ and the functions $h_j(x)$ are the outputs of the hidden units. Each hidden
unit computes a weighted sum of the input $x = (x_1, \ldots, x_d)^T$, which is then passed
through an activation function. Here, the hyperbolic tangent function $tanh(z) =$

K. Diamantaras, W. Duch, L.S. Iliadis (Eds.): ICANN 2010, Part I, LNCS 6352, pp. 87–96, 2010.
© Springer-Verlag Berlin Heidelberg 2010

$\frac{e^{2z}-1}{e^{2z}+1}$ is used, whose output ranges from -1 to $+1$. It must be noted that the sigmoid logistic function could also have been used. The weights of the j-hidden unit are denoted with $\boldsymbol{u}_j = (u_{j1}, \ldots, u_{jd})^T$ and we also assume a bias a_j:

$$h_j(\boldsymbol{x}) = \tanh\left(\boldsymbol{u}_j^T \boldsymbol{x} + a_j\right) = \tanh\left(\sum_{i=1}^{d} u_{ji}x_i + a_j\right). \tag{2}$$

Once the number M of hidden units is given, training of an MLP, i.e. estimating the parameters (weights $\boldsymbol{w}$, $\boldsymbol{u}$ and the biases a, b) of the network is relatively simple, because the derivatives of the MLP can be easily computed and general–purpose optimization algorithms, (e.g. quasi-Newton methods such as BFGS) can be effectively employed.

Multilayer perceptrons (with one hidden layer) have the property that they can approximate any function with arbitrary accuracy if a sufficient number of hidden units is used. Although this result is important, it must be noted that training MLPs with large numbers of hidden units usually leads to poor generalization performance. Therefore, in practice, best results are obtained when using the smallest number of hidden units that are sufficient to model the unknown function. Although some sampling-based Bayesian methods based on Markov Chain Monte Carlo have been proposed for tackling the MLP model selection problem [6], such methods have not achieved widespread use due to high computational complexity and the difficulty in deciding when to terminate the sampling procedure. For this reason the cross-validation approach is considered as the typical method used to estimate the number of MLP hidden units by considering several MLP architectures with different number of hidden units and selecting the network that exhibits the best cross-validation performance.

In this paper, we propose a training methodology for the MLP with one hidden layer, that automatically estimates the appropriate number of hidden units and also learns the network parameters. The methodology is based on the sparse Bayesian linear model [1] and the underlying automatic relevance determination (ARD) principle that automatically determines the number of basis functions in linear models. We follow an incremental approach that starts with only one hidden unit and iteratively adds hidden units to the model. For each added hidden unit, optimal values for the weights and bias are estimated. In order to stop adding units when a sufficient number has been added to the model, we assume a sparse distribution for the weights of the output unit. This sparse prior distribution enforces the removal of hidden units that do not sufficiently contribute to the model, by setting the corresponding hidden to output connection weights equal to zero.

In the next section we describe the main idea of our method where the MLP is treated as a weighted linear combination of basis functions (hidden units), thus the incremental sparse Bayesian learning framework can be applied to estimate both the combination weights and the parameters of the hidden units. The sparsity enforcing prior imposed on the combination weights enforces many of them to become zero, thus the corresponding hidden units are removed from the network. Section 3 summarizes sparse Bayesian learning for linear models, while Section 4 presents the proposed method for incremental Bayesian MLP training. Experimental results are presented in Section 5, while the last section provides conclusions and some directions for future work.

2 Automatic Model Selection for the Multilayer Perceptron

The multilayer perceptron of eq. (1) can be considered as a linear model, where the hidden units $h_j(\boldsymbol{x})$ play the role of basis functions. Linear models are very popular models, possibly because the weights $\boldsymbol{w}$ of the linear model can be computed very efficiently. Recent advances in sparse Bayesian modeling [1] allow for the automated estimation of the number of basis functions as follows: initially a model with many basis functions is assumed and then by imposing a sparse prior on the weights and ii) performing Bayesian inference of the weight values, we achieve pruning of basis functions that are not supported by the training data, i.e. the corresponding weights are found to be zero. This is very important, because by pruning irrelevant basis functions, an appropriate model is automatically selected. Following this aproach, we can use very flexible models with many basis functions, even if we have a small training set; irrelevant basis functions will be pruned and overfitting will be avoided.

A major shortcoming of the typical sparse Bayesian linear model is that basis functions are fixed and they have to be selected a priori. On the other hand, the hidden units of the MLP, which we treat as basis functions, contain parameters u_{ji}, a_j that are essential to be estimated. In this work, we employ an incremental Bayesian methodology [2], that simultaneously estimates the weights of the sparse linear model and parameters of its basis functions. This methodology, allows to treat a two-layer MLP as a sparse Bayesian linear model with adjustable basis function parameters. The weights of the connections from the hidden to the output layer correspond to the weights of the linear model and can be efficiently computed. Furthermore, imposing a sparse prior on these weights we could estimate the appropriate number of hidden units. The weights of the connections from input to the hidden layer of the MLP, correspond to parameters of the basis functions and could estimated simultaneously to the linear model weights using the methodology proposed in [2].

3 Sparse Bayesian Learning

3.1 Sparse Bayesian Linear Regression

In this section we briefly describe learning of sparse Bayesian linear models [1], which have the form of (1). We assume that the observations of the training set $\{\boldsymbol{x}_n, t_n\}_{n=1}^N$ have been corrupted with additive Gaussian noise with precision (i.e. inverse variance) β_n:

$$p(t_n|\boldsymbol{B}) = N(t_n|y(\boldsymbol{x}_n), \beta_n^{-1}). \tag{3}$$

where B is a diagonal matrix with elements $\beta_1, \ldots, \beta_N$. Assuming that the basis functions $h_j(x)$ are fixed, and defining the fixed 'design' matrix $\Phi = (h(x_1), \ldots, h(x_N))^T$, with $h(x) = (h_1(x), \ldots, h_M(x))^T$, the likelihood of the observations can be written as:

$$p(t|w, B) = N(t|\Phi w, B). \tag{4}$$

In order to achieve sparse solutions, i.e. prune irrelevant basis functions, a Gaussian prior distribution with separate variance α_i^{-1} is assumed for each weight w_i:

$$p(w|\alpha) = \prod_{i=1}^{M} N(w_i|0, \alpha_i^{-1}), \tag{5}$$

where $\alpha = (\alpha_1, \ldots, \alpha_M)^T$. Moreover, we assume that each α_i is drawn from a Gamma distribution whose parameters are set to near zero values so as to be uninformative.

The posterior distribution of the weights given the observations can be computed using Bayes's law:

$$p(w|t, \alpha, B) = \frac{p(t|w, B)p(w|\alpha)}{p(t|\alpha, B)}, \tag{6}$$

where $p(w|a)$ is given by (5). It can be shown that the weight posterior distribution follows a Gaussian distribution [1]:

$$p(w|t, \alpha, B) = N(w|\mu, \Sigma), \tag{7}$$

with

$$\mu = \Sigma \Phi^T B t, \tag{8}$$
$$\Sigma = (\Phi^T B \Phi + A)^{-1}, \tag{9}$$

and $A = \text{diag}(\alpha)$.

When the basis functions contain adjustable parameters the linear model is very flexible and a stronger prior on α is needed. Such a prior has been proposed in [3] and penalizes models with large number of 'effective' parameters. The prior depends on the trace of a so called 'smoothing matrix' $S = \Phi \Sigma \Phi^T B$ as follows:

$$p(\alpha) \propto \exp(-c\,\text{trace}(S)), \tag{10}$$

where the sparsity parameter c provides a mechanism to control the amount of desired sparsity. When using specific values of the sparsity parameter c, some known model selection criteria are obtained [4]:

$$c = \begin{cases} 0 & \text{None,} \\ 1 & \text{AIC (Akaike information criterion),} \\ \log(N)/2 & \text{BIC (Bayesian information criterion),} \\ \log(N) & \text{RIC (Risk inflation criterion).} \end{cases} \tag{11}$$

When using this prior, the following update formulas for the weight precisions α can be obtained [2]:

$$\alpha_i = \frac{\gamma_i}{\mu_i^2 - 2c\gamma_i \Sigma_{ii}}, \tag{12}$$

where μ and Σ are given from equations (8) and (9) respectively and $\gamma_i = 1 - \alpha_i \Sigma_{ii}$.

The learning algorithm iteratively applies the updates of α, μ and Σ until convergence. During those iterations, due to the sparse prior on the weights, some parameters α_i take very large values, thus the corresponding weights w_i are set to zero and the corresponding basis functions $h_i(x)$ are removed from the model. In this way automatic model selection is achieved.

3.2 Sparse Bayesian Classification

In this work for simplicity we only consider binary classification problems and assume that the outputs are coded so that $t_n \in \{0, 1\}$ [1]. Then, the likelihood of the training set is given by:

$$p(t|w) = \prod_{n=1}^{N} y_n^{t_n} (1 - y_n)^{1-t_n}, \tag{13}$$

where $y_n = \sigma(y(x_n|w))$ with $\sigma(z)$ being the logistic sigmoid function. Using the Laplacian approximation, the classification problem can be mapped to a regression problem [1] with heteroscedastic noise $p(\epsilon_n) = N(\epsilon_n|0, \beta_n)$. The noise precision is given by:

$$\beta_n = y_n(1 - y_n), \tag{14}$$

and the regression targets $\hat{t} = (\hat{t}_1, \ldots, \hat{t}_N)^T$ are:

$$\hat{t} = \Phi w + B^{-1}(t - y), \tag{15}$$

where $y = (y_1, \ldots, y_N)^T$ and $B = \text{diag}(\beta_1, \ldots, \beta_N)$.

3.3 Incremental Sparse Bayesian Learning

Notice that the computational cost of the sparse Bayesian learning algorithm is high for large datasets, because the computation of Σ in (9) requires $O(N^3)$ operations. A more computationally efficient incremental algorithm has been proposed in [5]. It initially assumes that $\alpha_i = \infty$, for all $i = 1, \ldots, M$, which corresponds to assuming that all basis functions have been pruned because of the sparsity constraint. Then, at each iteration one basis function may be either added to the model or re-estimated or removed from the current model. When adding a basis function to the model, the corresponding parameter α_i is set to the value that maximizes the likelihood.

---

[1] Multiclass problems can be solved using the one-vs-all approach, which builds only two class models.

More specifically, the method is based on the remark that the terms of the likelihood that depend on a single parameter α_i are [5]:

$$l_i = \frac{1}{2}\left(\log \alpha_i - \log(\alpha_i + s_i) + \frac{q_i^2}{\alpha_i + s_i}\right),\tag{16}$$

where

$$s_i = \boldsymbol{h}_i^T \boldsymbol{C}_{-i}^{-1} \boldsymbol{h}_i, \qquad\qquad q_i = \boldsymbol{h}_i^T \boldsymbol{C}_{-i}^{-1} \hat{\boldsymbol{t}},\tag{17}$$

$\boldsymbol{h}_i = (h_i(\boldsymbol{x}_1), \ldots, h_i(\boldsymbol{x}_N))^T$ and $\boldsymbol{C}_{-i} = \boldsymbol{B} + \sum_{j\neq i} \alpha_j \boldsymbol{h}_j \boldsymbol{h}_j^T$. In regression we have $\hat{\boldsymbol{t}} = \boldsymbol{t}$ and usually $\boldsymbol{B} = \beta \boldsymbol{I}$, while in classification $\boldsymbol{B}$ and $\hat{\boldsymbol{t}}$ are given by (14) and (15) respectively.

Based on the above likelihood decomposition, in [2] the following update equation for α_i has been derived when the the sparsity prior $p(\boldsymbol{\alpha})$ of equation (10) is assumed:

$$\alpha_i = \frac{s_i^2}{q_i^2 - (2c+1)s_i} \qquad\qquad \text{if } q_i^2 > (2c+1)s_i,$$

$$\alpha_i = \infty \qquad\qquad\qquad\qquad \text{if } q_i^2 \leq (2c+1)s_i.\tag{18}$$

The incremental training algorithm proceeds iteratively, by selecting at each iteration a basis function h_i (from a fixed pool of basis functions) and adding this basis function to the model if $q_i^2 > (2c+1)s_i$ or removing it otherwise. An important question that arises in the incremental algorithm is which basis function to select at each iteration. There are several possibilities, for example we could choose a basis function at random or with some additional computational cost, we could test several and select the one whose addition will cause the largest increase to the marginal likelihood. However in the above description we have made the assumption that the basis functions contain no adjustable parameters which is not convenient for the MLP case where the hidden units contain parameters to be learnt from the data. Such an approach is described next.

4   Incremental Bayesian MLP Learning

The proposed algorithm for incremental Bayesian MLP training is based on an extension [2] of the incremental method described above. This extension also allows for learning the parameters of the basis functions. In the MLP case, basis functions correspond to hidden units and we will use this term in the description that follows. More specifically, at each iteration we select the most appropriate hidden unit to add to the model as measured by the increment in the likelihood l_i. Therefore, in order to select a hidden unit for addition to the model we perform an optimization of the marginal likelihood with respect to the parameters of the hidden unit. Since we assume continuous parameters for the hidden units, continuous optimization methods should be employed, which exploit the derivatives of the likelihood l_i with respect to the parameters of the hidden unit.

The incremental algorithm performs three operations at each iteration; it first attempts to add a hidden unit to the model and adjusts its parameters, then updates all parameters of the current model and finally removes any hidden units that no longer contribute to the model. The algorithm is summarized in by following steps:

1) Select a Hidden Unit to Add to the Model. In order to add a hidden unit i, we maximize the likelihood l_i with respect to its parameters θ_{ik} (weights and bias). We can perform this maximization using a continuous numerical optimization method. The required derivatives are computed as [2]:

$$\frac{\partial l_i}{\partial \theta_{ik}} = -\left(\frac{1}{\alpha_i + s_i} + \frac{q_i^2 + c\alpha_i}{(\alpha_i + s_i)^2}\right) r_i + \frac{q_i}{\alpha_i + s_i} \omega_i, \tag{19}$$

where

$$r_i \equiv \frac{1}{2}\frac{\partial s_i}{\partial \theta_{ik}} = \boldsymbol{h}_i^T \boldsymbol{C}_{-i}^{-1}\frac{\partial \boldsymbol{h}_i}{\partial \theta_{ik}}, \qquad \omega_i \equiv \frac{\partial q_i}{\partial \theta_{ik}} = \boldsymbol{t}^T \boldsymbol{C}_{-i}^{-1}\frac{\partial \boldsymbol{h}_i}{\partial \theta_{ik}}. \tag{20}$$

Notice that since we use a local optimization method (in our case the quasi-Newton BFGS), we can only attain a local maximum of the marginal likelihood, which depends on the initialization. For this reason, in order to add a hidden unit we perform this maximization several times, each time with different initialization and then we keep the parameters that correspond to the best solution. Note that this optimization is not computationally demanding, since it involves only the parameters related to a hidden unit and not all the parameters of the current network model.

2) Optimize Current Model. Although we optimize the parameters of each hidden unit at the time that we add it to the model, it is possible that the optimal values for the already existing network parameters will change, because of the addition of the new hidden unit. For this reason, after the addition of a hidden unit, we further optimize the parameters α_i and $\boldsymbol{\theta}_i$ of all hidden units of the current model. Again, this optimization is performed using a continuous numerical optimization method (BFGS), and it is usually very efficient because the starting values are usually very close to the optimal.

4) Remove Hidden Units. After updating the hyperparameters $\boldsymbol{\alpha}$ of the current model, it is possible that some of the existing hidden units will no longer contribute to the model. This happens because of the sparsity prior, which allows only few of the basis functions (i.e. hidden units) to be used in the estimated model. For this reason, we remove from the model those hidden units that no longer contribute to the model, specifically those with $\alpha_i > 10^{12}$. Note that α_i is the inverse variance of the weight w_i which follows a zero mean Gaussian distribution. Thus a large α_i value implies an almost zero variance, thus the weight w_i is equal to its mean which is zero and the corresponding unit is removed from the model. The removal of hidden units is important, not only because we avoid the additional computational cost of updating their parameters, but also because we avoid possible singularities of the covariance matrices due to numerical errors in the updates.

5) Repeat Until Convergence. We assume that the algorithm has converged when the increment of the likelihood is negligible ($\Delta L < 10^{-6}$) for ten successive iterations.

5   Numerical Experiments

In this section we provide numerical experiments that demonstrate the effectiveness of the proposed method. We have considered several commonly used benchmark data sets[2] that are summarized in Table 1. The purpose of these experiments is to compare the performance of the proposed methodology against the typical approach where the number of hidden units is selected through cross-validation, and to demonstrate the ability of the proposed method to automatically determine the appropriate model complexity.

Table 1. Dataset Description

Dataset	patterns (N)	features (d)
wdbc	569	30
bupa	345	6
sonar	208	60
pima-diabetes	768	8
ionosphere	351	34

For each dataset, we use the Levenberg-Marquardt optimization method to train multilayer perceptrons with one hidden layer and number of hidden units M in the range from 1 to 10. We then apply the proposed methodology that automatically estimates the appropriate number of hidden units, using $c = log(N/2)$ that corresponds to the BIC (Bayesian information criterion). In order to evaluate the methods, we use 10-fold cross validation. Moreover, in order to account for the dependence of the typical MLP training algorithm on the initial values of its parameters, we train each MLP ten times, starting from different initial values. Then, the solution with the minimum error (on the training set) is evaluated on the test set.

---

[2] These datasets can be obtained from the UCI Machine Learning Repository, at `http://archive.ics.uci.edu/ml/`

The average error values (using 10-fold cross validation) for all datasets are reported in Table 2 and Table 3. In Table 2 bold values indicate the best result for each data set using the typical training approach. It is clear that for every data set the proposed method provides an estimate of M (Table 3) that is nearly equal to the best performance result of Table 2. This indicates that our method successfully estimates the number M of hidden units that define the MLP architecture with the minimum cross-validation error. Furthermore, the error rates obtained using the proposed method are comparable and in some cases superior to the error rates of the best MLP in Table 2.

Table 2. Average classification error rates using MLP with M hidden units

M	wdbc	bupa	sonar	pima-diabetes	ionosphere
1	**3.34**	35.68	22.57	23.18	12.83
2	4.05	31.62	24.45	23.56	14.24
3	3.87	32.19	**19.69**	**23.04**	**11.69**
4	3.87	**30.73**	19.74	25.25	16.51
5	3.87	32.46	26.88	24.35	15.35
6	4.22	32.77	23.48	25.25	12.23
7	3.16	35.10	25.40	25.51	18.52
8	4.75	35.06	22.12	27.08	17.97
9	3.87	36.23	20.60	24.74	15.67
10	4.22	32.71	21.67	26.29	18.82

Table 3. Average classification error rates and estimated number of hidden units M using the proposed method

	wdbc	bupa	sonar	pima-diabetes	ionosphere
M	1.40	3.10	3.00	1.00	3.30
Error	2.81	29.32	19.24	23.18	11.97

6 Conclusions

We have proposed a methodology to automatically obtain an effective estimation of the number of hidden units of the multilayer perceptron. The methodology is based on treating the MLP as a linear model, whose basis functions are the hidden units. Then, we use a sparse Bayesian prior on the weights of the linear model that enforces irrelevant basis functions (equivalently unnecessary hidden units) to be pruned from the model. In order to train the proposed model, we use an incremental training algorithm which at each iteration attempts to add a hidden unit to the network and adjusts its parameters assuming a sparse Bayesian learning framework. Numerical experiments using well-known classification data sets demonstrate the effectiveness of the proposed method in providing low complexity networks exhibiting low generalization error.

We consider that the proposed method provides a viable solution to the well-studied problem of estimating the number of hidden units in MLPs. Therefore, is our aim to perform more extensive experiments with this method considering not only classification, but also regression data sets. In addition we plan to compare the method against other classification or regression models like SVM, RVM and Gaussian Processes. Finally, it would be interesting to extend the method in order to be used for training MLPs with two hidden layers.

Acknowledgments

This work was part funded by the European Commission (Project ARTREAT: Multi-level patient-specific artery and atherogenesis model for outcome prediction, decision support, treatment, and virtual hand-on training, FP7-224297 - Large-scale Integrating Project).

References

1. Tipping, M.E.: Sparse Bayesian learning and the relevance vector machine. Journal of Machine Learning Research 1, 211–244 (2001)
2. Tzikas, D., Likas, A., Galatsanos, N.: Sparse bayesian modeling with adaptive kernel learning. IEEE Transactions on Neural Networks 20(6), 926–937 (2009)
3. Schmolck, A., Everson, R.: Smooth relevance vector machine: a smoothness prior extension of the RVM. Machine Learning 68(2), 107–135 (2007)
4. Holmes, C.C., Denison, D.G.T.: Bayesian wavelet analysis with a model complexity prior. In: Bernardo, J.M., Berger, J.O., Dawid, A.P., Smith, A.F.M. (eds.) Bayesian Statistics 6: Proceedings of the Sixth Valencia International Meeting. Oxford University Press, Oxford (1999)
5. Tipping, M.E., Faul, A.: Fast marginal likelihood maximisation for sparse Bayesian models. In: Proceedings of the Ninth International Workshop on Artificial Intelligence and Statistics (2003)
6. Neal, R.M.: Bayesian Learning for Neural Networks. Lecture Notes in Statistics, vol. 118. Springer, Heidelberg (1996)

Application of Semi-Bayesian Neural Networks in the Identification of Load Causing Beam Yielding

Bartosz Miller

Rzeszow University of Technology
ul. W. Pola 2, 35-959 Rzeszow, Poland
bartosz.miller@prz.edu.pl
http://www.prz.edu.pl

Abstract. Possible yielding of the cross-section of a structure might significantly decrease the safety margin of the investigated structure. The cross-section yielding causes a change of structure stiffness and, further, dynamic characteristics. The measurement of the changes of the dynamic parameters may provide information necessary to identify the load causing yielding of the cross-section, and further the yielding index (calculated when the load causing yielding is known) enables evaluation of structure safety margin. In the paper the semi-Bayesian neural networks are utilized to solve the identification problem.

Keywords: Identification, inverse problems, Bayesian neural networks, finite element method, dynamics.

1 Introduction

Plastic deformation of a structure may arise as a result of external actions and/or as a result of section defects (microdefects) [3]. Determination of the section yielding index (possible when the load applied to the structure is known) enables evaluation of the safety margin of the structure [6]. When the load parameters are unknown, they may be identified e.g. by the modal analysis of dynamic responses and estimation of dynamic characteristics (eigenfrequencies and eigenvectors). By measuring the dynamic response changes, the structure state might be assessed, and the load causing the partial yielding (herein called *main load*) may be identified. In the paper the dynamic responses are measured for the *current* state of the structure (with cross-section yielding) and for the current state disturbed by a known, small in comparison with the load to be identified, external load (*control load*). The changes of the characteristics between the current and the disturbed state of the structure (loaded with both the main and the control loads) are taken into account.

The investigated structure is a simply supported beam (see Fig. 1a), the cross-section (see Fig. 1b) refers to standard I-beam I340 and the material model applied is shown in Fig. 1c, the values of $E = 205\,GPa$, $\nu = 0.3$ and $\sigma_0 = 345\,MPa$ correspond to the properties of high-strength steel 18G2A.

K. Diamantaras, W. Duch, L.S. Iliadis (Eds.): ICANN 2010, Part I, LNCS 6352, pp. 97–100, 2010.

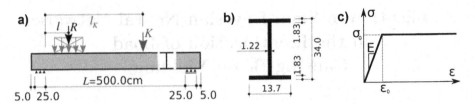

Fig. 1. a) Investigated beam with the load to be identified (left: resultant value R, location l) and control load (right: resultant value K, location l_K), b) cross-section, c) material model: elastic–perfect plastic

The measurable quantities adopted herein are formulated as pseudo-experimental data simulated by the FE commercial code ADINA [1]. As a tool to solve the inverse problem, namely the identification of load parameters, Semi-Bayesian Neural Networks (SBNNs) [2,8,4] are used. In the commonly used BNN package [7] the recommended procedure of network training is Scaled Conjugate Gradient (SCG) optimization. This method is compared to the Levenberg-Marquardt (LM) optimization also applied in the present paper.

The number of considered eigenfrequencies (possible values of j) and eigenvectors elements (possible values of P) was widely discussed in [5], finally the following input vector was adopted: $\mathbf{x} = \{l_K, \Delta f_j, v_{jP} | j = 1, 2, 3; P = A, B, C, D\}^T$, where l_K is the location of the control load (see Fig. 1), Δf_j is the relative change of the jth eigenfrequency caused by the application of the control load, v_{jP} is j^{th} eigenvector element measured in point P (points A, B, C and D are located to the right of the left support, at a distanfe of 50cm, 150cm, 250cm and 475cm, respectively, see [5]).

The output vector is composed of location l of the load resultant and the resultant R: $\mathbf{y} = \{l, R\}^T$.

2   Application of SBNN

In Fig. 2a and Fig. 2b results obtained from SBNN, trained by SCG algorithm, are presented. The horizontal axis corresponds to the errors in percent, while the vertical axis shows the percentage of testing patterns with a particular relative error of identification.

The SCG training algorithm needs an enormous number of training epochs to obtain networks working with satisfactory accuracy. In order to avoid a very long training the LM algorithm was adopted also for the SBNN training. The application of LM algorithm gives significant improvement in the obtained accuracy, see Fig. 2c and Fig. 2d. The ratio of correct identification of load parameters increases about 20% after the application of LM algorithm.

As shown in Fig. 2e and Fig. 2f, further improvement of the results can be obtained by the application of two separate one output networks instead of a single two output network. The application of two one output networks increases the prediction of correct identified load parameters up to almost 80% of all the

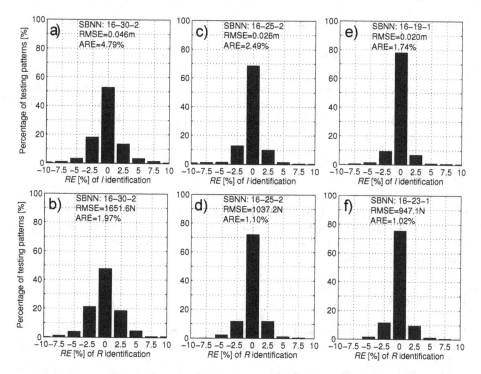

Fig. 2. Relative errors of identification obtained by: two-output SBNN trained by SCG algorithm for a) load location, b) load resultant, two-output SBNN trained by LM algorithm for c) load location, d) load resultant and by two single-output SBNN trained by LM algorithm for e) load location, f) load resultant

considered patterns. Fig. 2 presents also numerical values of the Average Relative Error (ARE) and Root Mean Square Error (RMSE).

3 Final Remarks

The paper presents identification of the load causing the cross-section partial yielding. The main novelties are the application of SBNN and the identification performed without the knowledge of an initial state of the investigated structure and the application of LM algorithm in the SBNN training.

In the identification procedure, the dynamic characteristics are used as the source of data describing the current state of the structure. The additional data are obtained after loading the structure with an additional, known load. No data describing the initial state of the structure are used.

Semi-Bayesian neural networks, used as a tool to solve the identification problem, seem to be very efficient and give a possibility to use the Maximum of Marginal Likelihood criterion [9] for design of the optimal network architecture.

Moreover, this enables the use of all the patterns for learning since the testing set is not required.

The accuracy of the obtained results is high. Numerically simulated measurements, involved in the identification procedure, are obtained by three accelerometers. The measurement set-up is therefore, using present-day equipment, rather easy to implement. However, in practical cases it can be necessary to use the data obtained from one accelerometer as a datum point, so the number of accelerometers may be enlarged by one.

Acknowledgements

Financial support by the Polish Ministry of Science and High Education, grant No. **N N506 432636** *Connection of neural networks and Bayesian inference in the identification analysis of structural dynamics and geomechanics problems*, is gratefully acknowledged.

References

1. ADINA R&D Inc. Theory and Modeling Guide. Watertown, MS, USA (2009)
2. Bishop, C.M.: Pattern Recognition and Machine Learning. Springer, Heidelberg (2006)
3. Chen, W.F., Han, D.J.: Plasticity for structural engineers. Springer, Heidelberg (1988)
4. Kłos, M., Waszczyszyn, Z.: Modal analysis and modified cascade Neural networks in identification of geometrical parameters of circular arches. Paper Submitted for Publication in the Journal Computers&Structures
5. Miller, B., Waszczyszyn, Z., Ziemiański, L.: Identification of Load Parameters for an Elastic-Plastic Beam Basing on Dynamic Characteristics Changes. In: Rutkowski, L., et al. (eds.) ICAISC 2010. LNCS, vol. 6114, pp. 590–597. Springer, Heidelberg (2010)
6. Moran, M.M.: Change of dynamic characteristics due to plastification. In: Computational Plasticity. Fundamentals and Applications 1995, Pineridge Press-CIMNE, Swansea-Barcelona (1967-1997)
7. Nabney, I.T.: NETLAB Algorithms for Pattern Recognition. Springer, Heidelberg (2004)
8. Waszczyszyn, Z., Ziemiański, L.: Parameter Identification of Materials and Structures. In: Mróz, Z., Stavroulakis, G.E. (eds.) Neural Networks in the Identification Analysis of Structural Mechanics Problems. CISM Lecture Notes, Springer, Wien (2004)
9. Waszczyszyn, Z., Słoński, M.: Maximum of marginal likelihood criterion instead of cross-validation for designing. In: Rutkowski, L., et al. (eds.) ICAISC 2008. LNCS (LNAI), vol. 5097, pp. 186–194. Springer, Heidelberg (2008)

Globally Optimal Structure Learning of Bayesian Networks from Data

Kobra Etminani[1], Mahmoud Naghibzadeh[1], and Amir Reza Razavi[2]

[1] Dept. of Computer Engineering, Ferdowsi University of Mashhad, Iran
[2] Dept. of Medical Informatics, Medical University of Mashhad, Iran
etminani@wali.um.ac.ir, naghibzadeh@um.ac.ir,
razaviar@mums.ac.ir

Abstract. The problem of finding a Bayesian network structure which maximizes a score function is known as Bayesian network structure learning from data. We study this problem in this paper with respect to a decomposable score function. Solving this problem is known to be NP-hard. Several algorithms are proposed to overcome this problem such as hill-climbing, dynamic programming, branch and bound, and so on. We propose a new branch and bound algorithm that tries to find the globally optimal network structure with respect to the score function. It is an any-time algorithm, i.e., if stopped, it gives the best solution found. Some pruning strategies are applied to the proposed algorithm and drastically reduce the search space. The performance of the proposed algorithm is compared with the latest algorithm which showed better performance to the others, within several data sets. We showed that the new algorithm outperforms the previously best one.

Keywords: Bayesian networks, structure learning, discrete variables.

1 Introduction

A Bayesian network or Belief Network (BN) is a directed acyclic graph (DAG) where nodes stand for random variables and edges stand for conditional dependencies. The random variables can be discrete or continuous. In this paper, learning Bayesian network structure for discrete variables is studied.

Bayesian network structure learning from data has attracted a great deal of research in recent years. Finding the best structure for Bayesian network is known to be NP-Hard [1, 2]. Consequently, much of the research has focused on methods that find suboptimal solutions. Generally, there are several approaches to learn a structure. Some methods are based on scoring functions that depend on the data and some approaches are based on statistical similarities among variables. We focus on those methods that are based on scoring functions and try to find the optimal solution according to this function.

Buntine in [3] proposes a hill-climbing method that performs a stochastic local search. However, this algorithm may get stuck in a local maximum. Although the approach is simple and applicable to small networks, since it is an exhaustive method

K. Diamantaras, W. Duch, L.S. Iliadis (Eds.): ICANN 2010, Part I, LNCS 6352, pp. 101–106, 2010.
© Springer-Verlag Berlin Heidelberg 2010

it cannot be applied to networks with large number of variables due to large number of possible edge modifications. Most exact methods that guarantee to find the optimal structure according to a scoring function, are based on dynamic programming [4, 5, 6], and branch and bound [7, 8] techniques. The time and/or space complexities of the methods that use dynamic programming approach forbid the application of those approaches to networks with large number of variables ($n > 30$). Campos et al. in [7] propose a branch and bound algorithm that extremely reduces the search space of possible structures, while guaranteeing to obtain the optimal solution. The procedure runs at most $\prod_i |C(i)|$ steps, where $C(i)$ is the size of the cache for variable i, which is the needed space to store the required local scores for variable i. Memory requirement for storing this cache is $\sum_i C(i)$ (in the worst case it is $O(n 2^n)$). It is an anytime algorithm and gives the current best solution whenever stopped.

We present a new branch and bound (B&B) algorithm that guarantees to find the global optimal Bayesian network structure in less time and memory requirements comparing to the best exact previous methods. It uses a decomposable scoring function and drastically reduces the search space for possible structures.

The rest of the paper is organized as follows: In Section 2, the Bayesian networks and scoring functions (i.e. problem description) are introduced. The proposed algorithm is explained in Section 3. The performance of the new method through experiments is showed in Section 4 and the paper ends with new ideas for future work in Section 5.

2 Problem Description

A BN is a DAG, composed of n random variables, that represents joint probability densities over these variables. Usually, a BN can be defined as a triple $(\mathcal{G}, \mathcal{V}, \mathcal{P})$, where $\mathcal{G}$ denotes the DAG, $\mathcal{V}$ denotes the set of random variables $\{V_1,...,V_n\}$ (nodes in $\mathcal{G}$) and $\mathcal{P}$ is a set of conditional probability densities $p(V_i | \pi_i)$ where π_i denotes the parents of V_i in the graph. Each discrete variable V_i has a finite number of values, r_i and the number of configurations of the parent set, q_i, that is $q_i = \prod_{V_j \in \pi_i} r_i$.

The goal of Bayesian network structure learning is to find the globally optimal structure from data. We assume data is complete with no missing values and consisted of discrete variables. If not, the data is cleaned by removing rows with missing values and discretizing the continuous variables. Given the complete discrete data D with N instances, we want to find a network structure that maximizes a scoring function:

$$\max_G score(G) . \tag{1}$$

In this study, we assume a scoring function that is decomposable, i.e.:

$$score(G) = \sum_i localScore(V_i | \pi_i) . \tag{2}$$

where $localScore(V_i | \pi_i)$ is the local score for node V_i given its parents π_i . Many common scores such as BDeu [3], BIC [8], BD [9], BDe [10] and AIC [11] are decomposable.

3 The Proposed Branch and Bound Algorithm

In this section, the proposed branch & bound algorithm used to find global optimum structure of the Bayesian networks and its complexity is explained.

We define each node of the branch & bound tree, as follows:

Definition 1. A tree node *tn* of the branch & bound tree is defined by *tn(NS, s)*, where *NS* is the network structure that this node stores and *s* is the score of this network structure.

The main idea of our proposed method is:

1. calculate the needed local scores of each node considering Lemmas in [7]
2. create the root of the branch & bound tree by considering the best local score for each node in the network structure
3. if the network structure store in the node is a DAG then algorithm is finished and global best network structure is found, otherwise let $d = 1$
4. create the children of this node by replacing the parent set of variable V_d (node in the network) with its 1th, 2nd, ... best parent configurations (the parent sets that provide 1th, 2nd, ... best local score for V_d)
5. while creating a child, if a DAG is found, update the best network found. In addition, check the new child and create the other children if needed
6. choose the next leaf node (if existed) and assign d with the depth of this node
7. if the next node is null the algorithm is finished, otherwise go to step 3.

The proved Lemmas in [7] are used here in the first step to reduce the cache size. Therefore, the size of cache memory (required to keep local scores for the next step) is equal to [7]. In the proposed algorithm, it is supposed to replace the parent set of each node V_d with its all possible parent configurations (which are sequentially chosen based on the computed local scores sorted in a descending order) in the *d*th depth of the tree with a pre-set order. We consider a fixed ordering of variables when the algorithm begins and we keep it to the end of the algorithm. Therefore, node V_i always denotes the *i*th variable in the ordering. However, we try not to create all the tree nodes. We prune this tree using the criteria explained later according to Bayesian networks properties. The pruning, in practice, extremely decreases the number of nodes to be created to find the global best network structure, in comparison with [7].

The bounding rules considered are as follows:

1. If *NS* is a DAG, the best net score found for the DAG until that point is updated (if NS leads to a better score). Here, there is no need to add further nodes to the tree, otherwise:
2. If the new node obtains worse score than the best score found for a DAG until that point, then this node cannot lead to a better result. We do not add this node to the tree.
3. Suppose we are at *d*th depth of the tree (i.e. we want to replace the parent set of V_d with its 1th, 2nd, ... best parent configuration). If there is a cycle that contains only $\{V_1,...,V_{d-1}\}$, this cycle cannot be removed. The reason is that

the parent sets of $V_d, V_{d+1}, ..., V_n$ are replaced with their other best parent sets from depth d to the maximum depth (depth n). However, the cycle contains the nodes ($\{V_1, ..., V_{d-1}\}$) that never change from depth d to the maximum depth n and no DAG can be found from this new node in the tree.

4. If the new node is in the depth n, there is no need to add it to the tree because it cannot lead to a result since the network nodes are finished and it is not a DAG.

The new child (if one of the above criteria is satisfied we put null in new child) is added to the parent node.

Fig. 1 shows the new branch & bound algorithm. The input to this algorithm is the local scores that are computed and stored in a file, previously and the output is the global best network structure. After creating all possible children nodes for *parentNode*, the next node to be expanded is selected. We select a leaf with the maximum score to be the *parentNode* next time.

Algorithm 1. *EtminaniB&B(localScores)*

---

  rootNode(NS_r, s_r) = create a node by considering the best parent config for each node

parentNode = rootNode
d = 1   // *d* shows depth of tree
while *(parentNode)* **do**
/* expand nodes for each kth maximum local score for node V_d (if needed)*/

   for each *k* ∈ | *localScore(V_d)* |

      childNode = CreateNode(k)
      if *(NotNeeded(childNode))*
         exit for
   end for
      parentNode = MaxPossibleLeafNode() //continue from the next maximum leaf(if existed)
end while
return best network found

Fig. 1. The proposed branch & bound algorithm

The required memory for the proposed algorithm for storing the needed local scores is the same as [7] and it is data dependent. In the worst case, all tree nodes should be created and none of the criteria satisfies to prune the tree and reduces the search space (this case practically never happens but we consider it as the worst case), so the maximum number of nodes is $\sum_{i=1}^{n} \prod_{j=1}^{i} | C(j) |$.

4   Experiments

In this study, datasets available at the UCI repository were used [12], to demonstrate the capability of our method. Some of these datasets contain missing data which were removed. The properties of the datasets, the size of the generated cache (the reduced cached based on proven Lemmas in [7]) and the size of the cache if all local scores were computed for the BIC scoring function are presented in Table 1.

Table 2 presents the results of two distinct algorithms: the proposed branch & bound algorithm described in Section 4 (EtminaniB&B), and the branch & bound algorithm presented in [7] (CassioB&B)[1] . Number of nodes in the branch & bound tree are shown to facilitate a better comparison between the two algorithms. The time column represents only the time of running the algorithms. The time required to compute the needed local scores is not included, because it is similar for both algorithms.

Table 1. Dataset properties and cache size for B&B algorithm and total cache size without reduction

name	n	N	Reduced Cache size	Total cache size ($n2^n$)
Abalone	9	4177	65	$2^{11.2}$
Tic-tac-toe	10	958	28	$2^{13.3}$
Bc-wisconsin	11	669	97	$2^{14.5}$
Wine	14	178	98	$2^{17.8}$
Heart-hungerian	14	294	8246	$2^{17.8}$
Heart-cleveland	14	303	45	$2^{17.8}$
Mushroom	22	5644	260	$2^{26.4}$
Spect-heart data	23	80	275	$2^{26.5}$
King rock	36	3196	524	$2^{41.2}$

Table 2. Comparison of BIC scores, number of created tree nodes and running time among EtminaniB&B and CassioB&B

Name	EtminaniB&B			CassioB&B		
	Score	No. tree nodes	Time (s)	Score	No. tree nodes	Time (s)
Abalone	-16571.7	76	< 1	-16571.7	1205	< 1
Tic-tac-toe	-9656.2	33	< 1	-9656.2	65	< 1
Bc-wisconsin	-3359.6	43	< 1	-3359.6	3909	9
Wine	-1889.8	155	< 1	-1889.8	259	1.2
Heart-hungerian	-2368.0	18	< 1	-2368.0	170	< 1
Heart-cleveland	-3410.8	21	< 1	-3410.8	18	< 1
Mushroom	-691.0	1	< 1	-691.0	1	< 1
Spect-heart data	-761.0	343	4.5	-761.0	288	2.8
King rock	-290.5	1	< 1	-290.5	1	< 1

In mushroom and king rock datasets, both of them create only one node. The reason is that the root of the B&B tree was already a DAG in this data set (best parent set for each node leads to DAG) and no additional node is created.

Our method (EtminaniB&B) most of the time creates smaller number of nodes in the branch & bound tree and leads to the global optimal result in less running time than the previous B&B (CassioB&B).

The new algorithm can result into the same result in almost less running time and smaller number of nodes in the B&B tree. In [7], Cassio et al. show the superiority of

---

[1] We have run the dynamic programming idea of [4], (which is worse than the two branch & bound algorithm in time and space). We omit it because of lack of space.

their algorithm compared to the previous methods [4, 5]. Now, we show the advantages and the performance of our new method to [7].

5 Conclusion and Future Work

In this study, learning the Bayesian network structure from data for discrete variables is studied. A new branch and bound algorithm is presented that guarantees global optimality with respect to a decomposable scoring function. It is an any-time method, i.e. if stopped it provides the best solution found so far. We made use of two previously proven lemmas to reduce the search space and the required memory.

Several common datasets are used to demonstrate the benefits of the proposed method. The experiments show that the proposed approach provides better results, i.e. resulting in smaller number of nodes and less running time, most of the cases.

Several aspects remain for the future work such as applying other criteria to forbid unnecessary computing for local scores and creating unneeded B&B tree nodes which can reduce the search space and the required memory.

References

1. Chickering, D.M., Meek, C., Heckerman, D.: Large-sample learning of Bayesian networks is NP-Hard. In: Proceedings of the 19th Annual Conference on Uncertainty in Artificial Intelligence, pp. 124–133. Morgan Kaufmann Publishers, San Francisco (2003)
2. Chickering, D.M.: Learning Bayesian networks is NP-complete. Learning from Data: Artificial Intelligence and Statistics V, 121–130 (1996)
3. Buntine, W.: Theory refinement on Bayesian Networks. In: Proceedings of the Seventh Conference on Uncertainty in Artificial intelligence, Los Angeles, pp. 52–60 (1991)
4. Silander, T., Myllymaki, P.: A Simple Approach for Finding the Globally Optimal Bayesian Network Structure. In: Proceedings of the 22nd Annual Conference on Uncertainty in Artificial Intelligence, pp. 445–452 (2006)
5. Singh, A.P., Moore, A.W.: Finding Optimal Bayesian Networks by Dynamic Programming. Technical Report, Carnegie Mellon University CALD-05-106 (2005)
6. Koivisto, M., Sood, K., Chickering, D.M.: Exact Bayesian structure discovery in Bayesian networks. Journal of Machine Learning Research 5, 549–573 (2004)
7. Campos, C.P., Zeng, Z., Ji, Q.: Structure Learning of Bayesian Networks using Constraints. In: Proceedings of the 26th International Conference on Machine Learning, Canada (2009)
8. Schwartz, G.: Estimating the dimensions of a model. Annals of Statistics 6, 461–464 (1978)
9. Cooper, G., Herskovits, E.: A Bayesian method for the induction of probabilistic networks from data. Machine Learning 9, 309–347 (1992)
10. Hecherman, D., Geiger, D., Chickering, D.M.: Learning Bayesian networks: The combination of knowledge and statistical data. Machine Learning 20, 197–243 (1995)
11. Akaike, H.: A new look at the statistical model identification. IEEE Transactions on Automatic Control 19, 716–723 (1974)
12. Asuncion, A., Newman, D.: UCI machine learning repository,
    http://archive.ics.uci.edu/ml/datasets.html

Action Potential Bursts Modulate the NMDA-R Mediated Spike Timing Dependent Plasticity in a Biophysical Model

Vassilis Cutsuridis

Center for Memory and Brain, Boston University, Boston, MA, USA
vcut@bu.edu

Abstract. Spike timing dependent plasticity (STDP) requires the temporal association of presynaptic and postsynaptic action potentials (APs). However, some synapses in the CA1 region of the hippocampus are suprisingle unreliable at signaling the arrival of single spikes to the postsynaptic neuron [4]. In such unreliable synapses pairing of excitatory postsynaptic potentials (EPSPs) and single APs at low frequencies is ineffective at generating plasticity [2], [3]. A recent computational study [7] has shown that the shape of the STDP curve strongly depends on the burst interspike interval in the presence/absence of inhibition when a presynaptic dendritic burst and a postsynaptic somatic spike were paired together. In this study, we investigate via computer simulations the conditions under which STDP is affected when now a high frequency somatic burst instead of a single spike is paired with another dendritic spike. We show that during such pairing conditions in the absence of inhibition a symmetric STDP profile with a distinct positive LTP region is evident at 10-30ms interstimulus interval and flat LTD tails at all other interstimulus intervals. The symmetry is preserved at all burst interspike intervals. When inhibition is present, the STDP profile shape into a Mexican hat shaped one or an inverted symmetrical one with flat LTP tails.

Keywords. Computer model, bursts, STDP, GABA inhibition, LTP, LTD, calcium.

1 Introduction

Experimental studies in pyramidal neurons in the hippocampus have shown that the magnitude and sign of changes in synaptic strength depend critically on the precise timing of pre- and postsynaptic action potentials (APs), with postsynaptic APs preceding EPSPs typically leading to long-term depression (LTD), while APs evoked just after EPSP onset typically lead to long-term potentiation (LTP) [5]. Spike-timing-dependent plasticity (STDP) is an extension of Hebb's law, which states that neurons that simultaneously fire together, they wire together [1]. While the cellular mechanisms underlying STDP are not well understood, most studies agree NMDA receptors play an important role because they are able to detect coincident pre- and postsynaptic activity via relief of voltage-dependent magnesium block [5]. During STDP the voltage driving the unblockage of NMDA receptors is supplied by postsynaptic APs, which actively

K. Diamantaras, W. Duch, L.S. Iliadis (Eds.): ICANN 2010, Part I, LNCS 6352, pp. 107–116, 2010.

propagate back into the dendrites of many neuronal types . However, under certain experimental conditions single APs attenuate and can fail to backpropagate into some dendrites of pyramidal neurons [13]. This failure of AP backpropagation can be rescued during high-frequency AP bursts due to boosting of AP backpropagation following AP summation and the generation of dendritic calcium spikes [3]. Consistent with the potential role of AP burst-evoked dendritic calcium spikes in synaptic plasticity, a number of studies indicate a role of AP burst firing in STDP[3]. These findings prompted me to investigate how STDP is affected when a somatic burst is paired with a dendritic spike in the presence of a high frequency inhibition (GABA). Previous work from my group [6], [7], [8] has shown that the experimentally observed asymmetric STDP curve in the hippocampus undergoes an asymmetry-to-symmetry transition [10], [11], [12], which depends on the frequency of inhibition (theta vs. gamma), the conductance value of GABA inhibition, the relative timing between the GABAergic spike train and the excitatory pre-postsynaptic interstimulus interval, and on the burst interspike interval.

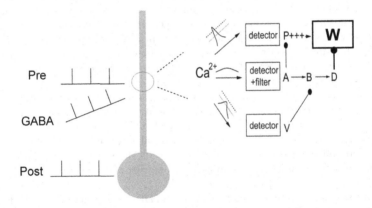

Fig. 1. Model CA1 neuron with its three transient inputs to the soma and dendrite. Synaptic plasticity at the dendritic synapses (circled region) is governed by a model calcium detector system [9]. P detector: potentiation detector; D detector: depression detector; V detector: veto detector; W: synaptic weight.

2   The Model

The CA1 pyramidal cell model with its three calcium detectors used herein has been described in detail in [6], [7], [8]. Briefly, the model pyramidal cell consists of two compartments: a soma and a dendrite. The generation of action potentials is due to the interplay of a wealth of ionic currents such as Na^+, K^+, Ca^{2+}-activated K^+ and Ca^{2+} currents as well as synaptic currents (AMPA, NMDA and $GABA_A$). Hodgkin-Huxley mathematical formalism was used to describe the ionic and synaptic mechanisms of the modelled pyramidal cell. The model used calcium as the postsynaptic signaling agent for STDP and it has been shown to be consistent with classical long-term potentiation (LTP) and long-term depression (LTD) induced by several doublet stimulation paradigms in the absence and presence of inhibition [6], [7], [8].

In the model, calcium enters the neuron through: (1) voltage-gated calcium channels (VGCCs), and (2) NMDA channels located at the dendrite. VGCCs are activated by the arrival of backpropagating action potentials (BPAPs) initiated in the soma by excitatory postsynaptic spikes. The NMDA channels are activated by the synergistic action of excitatory and inhibitory postsynaptic potentials and sufficient membrane potential depolarization due to the BPAP, which removes the magnesium block and allows calcium to enter the cell. In the model, calcium influx from neither channels alone elicits plasticity. Plasticity results only from the synergistic action of the two calcium sources (NMDA and VGCC).

The mechanism for plasticity has a modular structure consisting of three biochemical detectors, which respond to the instantaneous calcium level and its time course in the dendrite. The detection system consists of: (1) a potentiation (P) detector which detects calcium levels above a high-threshold ($4\mu M$) and triggers LTP, (2) a depression (D) detector which detects calcium levels exceeding a low threshold level ($0.6\mu M$), remains above it for a minimum time period and triggers LTD, and (3) a veto (V) detector which detects levels exceeding a mid-level threshold ($2\mu M$) and triggers a veto to the D response. A graphical schematic of the model neuron and its calcium detectors for spike timing dependent plasticity (STDP) is shown in Figure 1.

In this study we investigate how the pairing of an excitatory spike applied to the dendrite and an excitatory burst of action potentials applied to the soma both repeated every 300ms (every theta cycle) affect the STDP in the dendrite in the presence and/or absence of high frequency inhibition applied to the dendrite.

3   Experiments

To investigate how the STDP profile is affected by the pairing of excitatory bursts and excitatory single spikes in the presence/absence of GABAergic inhibition,we designed the following experimental protocol: Excitatory burst of spikes with variable burst interspike interval and single spikes, which were repeatedly applied to the soma and dendrite, respectively, for 2 s (7 times at about 3 Hz) were paired in the absence and presence of an 100 Hz GABAergic inhibitory spike train applied between the excitatory pair interval $\Delta\tau$. Based on this protocol, we designed the following four physiological experiments (see figure 2), where the burst interspike interval, ISI, was allowed to vary:

- ISI = 1.6 ms
- ISI = 5 ms
- ISI = 10 ms
- ISI = 20 ms

During all experimental paradigms, we varied the conductance of GABA inhibition and observed its effects on the amplitude of the dendritic Ca^{2+} spike and the STDP curve. These results are reported in the next section.

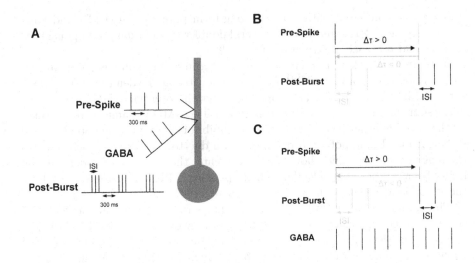

Fig. 2. (A) Model CA1 neuron with its three transient inputs to the soma and dendrite. Inputs: an excitatory burst to the soma, an excitatory spike to the dendrite and an inhibitory spike to the dendrite. Each input repeats every 300 ms for about 2 sec. (B) Pairing of a dendritic spike with a somatic burst in the absence of inhibition (GABA). (C) Pairing of a dendritic spike with a somatic burst in the presence of GABA inhibition.

4   Results

4.1   Pairing of a Somatic Burst and a Dendritic Spike in the Absence of GABA Inhibition as a Function of Burst Interspike Interval

In this section we investigate the effects of the burst ISI on the STDP profile in the absence of GABA inhibition. A presynaptic (dendritic) spike is paired with a postsynaptic (somatic) burst. The interstimulus interval $\Delta\tau$ is the interval between the presynaptic spike and the first spike ofthe postsynaptic burst (see Figure 2). The simulated STDP profile as a function of the interstimulus interval $\Delta\tau$ for different ISIs in the absence of GABA is depicted in Figure 3. A symmetric STDP profile centered at +10 ms is evident for all ISIs. Interestingly the LTP value when the ISI is 5 ms and 10 ms is greater than when ISI is 1.6 ms, but lower when ISI is 20 ms.

In the preSpike10postBurst stimulation paradigm (see Figures 4A-L), where a presynaptic (dendritic) spike preceeds by 10ms a postsynaptic (somatic) burst, calcium influx results from two sources: (1) through NMDA channels activated by the presynaptic spike, and (2) through VGCCs activated by the postsynaptic burst. This results in more than two calcium spikes depending on the ISI (see Figure 4C). The first calcium spike, which is the result of the presynaptic spike

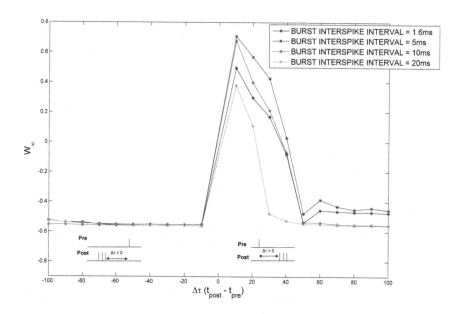

Fig. 3. Simulated asymmetric STDP profile as a function of burst interspike intervals in the absence of GABA inhibition. $\Delta\tau$ (tpost - tpre) is the interstimulus interval between the dendritic spike and the first spike of the somatic burst. $\Delta\tau$ ranges from -100 to 100 in increments of 10 ms. (Inset-left) PostBurst - PreSpike scenario, where the dendritic spike follows by $\Delta\tau$ the somatic burst, comprised of three spikes. $\Delta\tau$ takes values from -10 ms to -100 ms. The pairing repeats every 300 ms. (Inset-right) PreSpike - PostBurst scenario, where a dendritic spike precedes the somatic burst by $\Delta\tau$. $\Delta\tau$ takes values from +10 ms to +100 ms. The pairing repeats every 300 ms.

activated NMDA channels, is always above $4\mu M$ regardless of the burst ISI. This high peak calcium spike on its own trigger all calcium detectors (P, D and V). Increases in P response assisted by the inhibition of the D response due to the activated V response will lead to the growth of W (see Figure 4D). In the case where burst ISI is either 5 ms, 10 ms or 20 ms additional calcium spikes will be generated (see blue, red and green traces in Figure 4C). When the ISI is 5 ms or 10 ms, the second peak calcium values are above $4\mu M$ and the weight (W) will be extra boosted (see Figure 4C). When the ISI is 20 ms, the peak values of the third and fourth calcium peaks are all below the $4\mu M$ threshold, but still above the $2\mu M$ threshold. This means that the 3rd and 4th calcium spike will result from a reduced P response. But because they are above the $2\mu M$ threshold, the veto response will be activated, which will prevent the intermediate agents A and B from activating the depression (D) detector. Hence at ISI = 20 ms, W will plateau at lower value than when ISI is 1.6 ms, 5 ms and 10 ms (see Figure 4D - L).

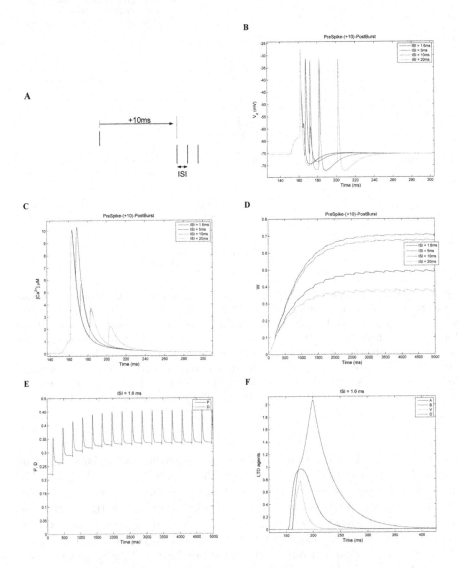

Fig. 4. (A) PreSpike-10-PostBurst stimulation paradigm used. The interstimulus interval between the dendritic spike (pre) and somatic burst (post) is set to +10ms. (B-L) Direct comparison of V_d, $[Ca^{2+}]$, W, P and D, and LTD agents at various burst ISIs in the absence of GABA inhibition.

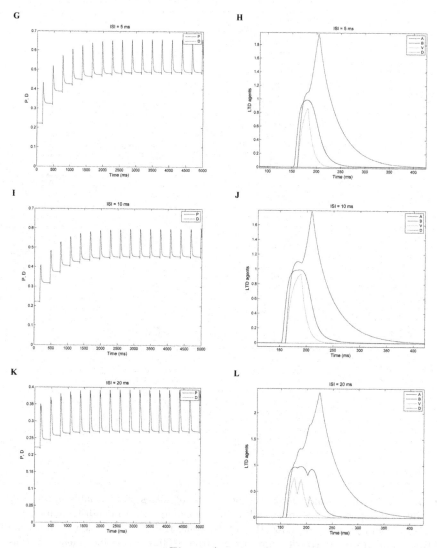

Fig. 4. (*continued*)

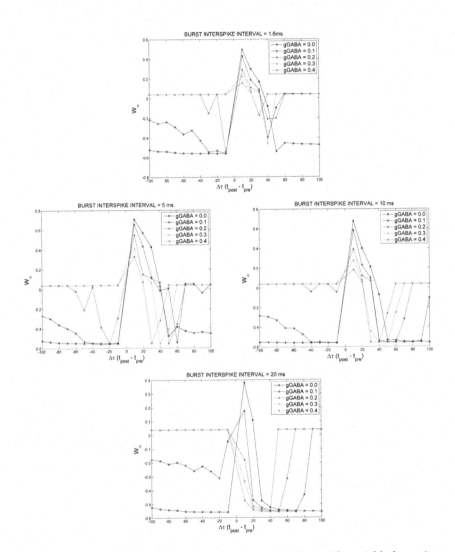

Fig. 5. STDP profiles from the pairing of a burst of spikes with variable burst inter-spike interval applied to the soma and a single spike applied to dendritic synapses in the absence and presence of a 100 Hz GABA spike train as a function of increasing GABA conductance. $\Delta\tau$ (tpost - tpre) ranges from -100 to 100 in increments of 10ms. (Top-left) Burst interspike interval is 1.6 ms. (Top-right) Burst interspike interval is 5 ms. (Bottom-left) Burst interspike interval is 10 ms. (Bottom-right) Burst interspike interval is 20 ms.

4.2 Pairing of a Somatic Burst and a Dendritic Spike in the Presence of an 100Hz GABA Spike Train as a Function of Increasing GABA Conductance

Figure 5 is a composite figure of four graphs of W_∞ vs $\Delta\tau$ as a function of burst ISI and GABA conductance. The effect of GABA on the STDP profile is different for each ISI. When ISI is 1.6 ms, 5 ms and 10 ms, the gaussian shaped STDP curve centered at +10 ms, is transforms to a Mexican hat one when gGABA = 0.1-0.2 mS/cm^2 to an asymmetric one at g_{GABA} = 0.3-0.4 mS/cm^2. When ISI is 20 ms, the gaussian shaped STDP curve switches to an a Mexican hat one with asymmetric LTD tails when gGABA is 0.1 mS/cm^2 and to an inverted gaussian one when gGABA is greater than 0.1 mS/cm^2 with the largest LTD value at +30-40 ms.

5 Conclusion

A Ca^{2+} dynamics model of the CA1 pyramidal neuron with three calcium amplitude detectors was used to study the pairing effects of somatic AP bursts and dendritic single spikes on the spike timing dependent plasticity in the dendrite in the presence/absence of inhibition. In contrast to previous computational work [6], [7], [8], where an asymmetrical-to-symmetrical STDP curve is evident when somatic spikes are paired with dendritic bursts, in this study the STDP profile is symmetrical for all burst ISI and GABA conductance values. In the future, I intend to investigate whether this STDP symmetry is present when a dendritic burst is paired with a somatic one in the presence of different GABA gamma frequency sub-bands and conductance values.

Acknowledgement. This work was funded by the EPSRC project grant EP/D04281X/1 and the NSF Science of Learning Center CELEST grant 0835976.

References

[1] Hebb, D.O.: The organization of behavior. John Wiley, New York (1949)

[2] Kampa, B.M., Letzkus, J.J., Stuart, G.J.: Requirement of dendritic calcium spikes for induction of spike-timing-dependent synaptic plasticity. J. Physiol. 574(1), 283–290 (2006)

[3] Letzkus, J.J., Kampa, B.M., Stuart, G.J.: Learning rules for spike timing-dependent plasticity depend on dendritic synapse location. J. Neurosci. 26(41), 10420–10429 (2006)

[4] Allen, C., Stevens, C.F.: An evaluation of causes for unreliability of synaptic transmission. Proc. Natl. Acad. Sci. U.S.A. 91(22), 10380–10383 (1994)

[5] Bi, G.Q., Poo, M.M.: Synaptic modifications in cultured hippocampal neurons: dependence on spike timing, synaptic strength and postsynaptic cell type. J. Neurosci. 18, 10464–10472 (1998)

[6] Cutsuridis, V., Cobb, S., Graham, B.P.: A Ca^{2+}dynamics model of the STDP symmetry-to-asymmetry transition in the CA1 pyramidal cell of the hippocampus. In: Kůrková, V., Neruda, R., Koutník, J. (eds.) ICANN 2008,, Part II. LNCS, vol. 5164, pp. 627–635. Springer, Heidelberg (2008)

[7] Cutsuridis, V., Cobb, S., Graham, B.P.: How Bursts Shape the STDP Curve in the Presence/Absence of GABA Inhibition. In: Alippi, C., et al. (eds.) ICANN 2009. LNCS, vol. 5768, pp. 229–238. Springer, Heidelberg (2009)

[8] Cutsuridis, V., Cobb, S., Graham, B.P.: Modelling the STDP Symmetry-to-Asymmetry Transition in the Presence of GABAergic Inhibition. Neural Network World 19(5), 471–481

[9] Rubin, J.E., Gerkin, R.C., Bi, G.Q., Chow, C.C.: Calcium time course as signal for spike-timing-dependent plasticity. J. Neurophysiol. 93, 2600–2613 (2005)

[10] Aihara, T., Abiru, Y., Yamazaki, Y., Watanabe, H., Fukushima, Y., Tsukada, M.: The relation between spike-timing dependent plasticity and Ca^{2+} dynamics in the hippocampal CA1 network. Neuroscience 145(1), 80–87 (2007)

[11] Tsukada, M., Aihara, T., Kobayashi, Y., Shimazaki, H.: Spatial analysis of spike-timing-dependent LTP and LTD in the CA1 area of hippocampal slices using optical imaging. Hippocampus 15(1), 104–109 (2005)

[12] Nishiyama, M., Hong, K., Mikoshiba, K., Poo, M., Kato, K.: Calcium stores regulate the polarity and input specificity of synaptic modification. Nature 408, 584–589 (2000)

[13] Jarsky, T., Roxin, A., Kath, W.L., Spruston, N.: Conditional dendritic spike propagation following distal synaptic activation of hippocampal CA1 pyramidal neurons. Nat. Neurosci. 8(12), 1667–1676 (2005)

Cell Microscopic Segmentation with Spiking Neuron Networks

Boudjelal Meftah[1,2], Olivier Lezoray[2],
Michel Lecluse[3], and Abdelkader Benyettou[4]

[1] Equipe EDTEC, Université de Mascara, Mascara, Algérie
[2] Université de Caen Basse-Normandie, GREYC UMR CNRS 6072,
6 Bd. Maréchal Juin, F-14050, Caen, France
[3] Service d'anatomie et de cytologie pathologiques, Centre Hospitalier Public du
Cotentin, Rue du Val de Saire, F-50130 Cherbourg-Octeville, France
[4] Laboratoire Signal Image et Parole, Université Mohamed Boudiaf, Oran, Algérie

Abstract. Spiking Neuron Networks (SNNs) overcome the computational power of neural networks made of thresholds or sigmoidal units. Indeed, SNNs add a new dimension, the temporal axis, to the representation capacity and the processing abilities of neural networks. In this paper, we present how SNN can be applied with efficacy for cell microscopic image segmentation. Results obtained confirm the validity of the approach. The strategy is performed on cytological color images. Quantitative measures are used to evaluate the resulting segmentations.

Keywords: Cell microscopic images, Hebbian learning, Segmentation, Spiking Neuron Networks.

1 Introduction

Image analysis in the field of cancer screening is a significant tool for cytopathology [1],[2]. Two principal reasons can be highlighted. First, the quantitative analysis of shape and structure of nuclei coming from microscopic color images brings to the pathologist valuable information for diagnosis assistance. Second, the quantity of information that the pathologist must deal with is large, in particular when the number of cancer screening increases. That is why, a segmentation scheme for microscopic cellular imaging must be efficient for reliable analysis.

Many cellular segmentation methods have been presented so far [3],[4]. They include watershed [5],[6],[7], region-based [8] and threshold-based methods [9]. Application of active contour has been widely investigated for cell segmentation [10],[11]. Cells stained with Papanicolaou international staining make it possible to classify the color pixels among three classes [12]: background, cytoplasm or nucleus. However, this classification cannot be perfect. Indeed, a fraction on nuclei pixels have the same color then cytoplasm pixels because of the variability of the nuclei according to the type of the cells and to the chromatin distribution. Moreover, for some cytopathologies, the mucus present in the background has the same color than some cells (cytoplasm and nucleus).

K. Diamantaras, W. Duch, L.S. Iliadis (Eds.): ICANN 2010, Part I, LNCS 6352, pp. 117–126, 2010.
© Springer-Verlag Berlin Heidelberg 2010

Another problem for the design of cellular segmentation schemes is on how to evaluate the segmentation quality. Indeed, almost all the segmentation schemes have some parameters. Human observation highlights that the values chosen for these parameters are significant for the quality of the segmentation. However, for an automatic selection of the optimal parameter values, the quality of segmentation must be also automatically evaluated. In literature, there are several quality segmentation criteria: Lui and Borsotti [13], classification rates and other statistical measures [14].

Spiking Neuron Networks (SNNs) are often referred to as the 3rd generation of neural networks [15]. Highly inspired from natural computing in the brain and recent advances in neuroscience, they derive their strength and interest from an accurate modeling of synaptic interactions between neurons, taking into account the time of spike firing. SNNs overcome the computational power of neural networks made of thresholds or sigmoidal units [16]. The use of spiking neurons promises high relevance for biological systems and, furthermore, might be more flexible for computer vision applications [17].

In this paper, a spiking neural network is used to segment cellular microscopic images with two approaches : unsupervised and supervised training with Hebbian based winner-take-all learning. This learning modifies the weights of the pre-synaptic neurons with the winning output [18]. This observation is in agreement with the fact that, in biological neural networks, different axonal connections will have different signal transmission delays [19]. In this article, we seek, through a series of experiments, the best parameters of the SNN network to have a good segmentation.

The paper is organized as follows : in the first Section, related works are presented within the literature of spiking neural network (SNNs). Second Section is the central part of the paper and is devoted to the description of the architecture of a spiking neural network with multiple delay connections, the encoding mechanism for converting the real valued inputs into time vectors and the learning rule. Results and discussions of the experiments are reported in the third Section. Last Section concludes.

2   Spiking Neuron Networks

Spiking neural networks (SNNs) are a class of ANNs that are increasingly receiving the attention as both a computationally powerful and biologically plausible mode of computation [20],[21]. SNNs model the precise time of the spikes fired by a neuron, as opposed to the conventional neural networks which model only the average firing rate of the neurons. It is proved that the neurons that convey information by individual spike times are computationally more powerful than the neurons with sigmoidal activation functions [22].

A network architecture consists in a feedforward network of spiking neurons with multiple delayed synaptic terminals (Fig.1(a)). Neurons in the network generate action potentials, or spikes, when the internal neuron state variable, called "membrane potential", crosses a threshold ϑ. The relationship between input spikes and the internal state variable is described by the spike response model (SRM), as introduced by Gerstner [23]. Depending on the choice of suitable spike-response functions, one can adapt this model to reflect the dynamics of a large variety of different spiking neurons. Formally, a neuron j, having a set

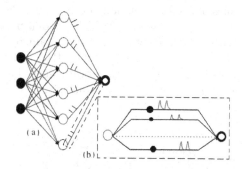

Fig. 1. (a) Spiking neural network architecture; (b) Multiple synapses transmitting multiple spikes

Γ_j of immediate predecessors ("pre-synaptic neurons"), receives a set of spikes with firing times t_i, $i \in \Gamma_j$. Any neuron generates at most one spike during the simulation interval, and fires when the internal state variable reaches a threshold ϑ. The dynamics of the internal state variable $x_j(t)$ are determined by the impinging spikes, whose impact is described by the spike-response function $\varepsilon(t)$ modeling a simple α-function weighted by the synaptic efficacy w_{ij}:

$$x_j(t) = \sum_{i \in \Gamma_j} \sum_{k=1}^{m} w_{ij}^k \varepsilon(t - t_i - d^k) \tag{1}$$

In the network as introduced in [24], an individual connection consists in a fixed number of m synaptic terminals, where each terminal serves as a sub-connection that is associated with a different delay and weight (Fig.1(b)). The delay d^k of a synaptic terminal k is defined by the difference between the firing time of the pre-synaptic neuron, and the time the post-synaptic potential starts rising.

3   Network Architecture, Learning and Encoding

However, before building a SNN, we have to explore three important issues: network architecture, information encoding and learning method. Then, we will use a SNN to segment cellular images.

3.1   Network Architecture

The network architecture consists in a fully connected feedforward network of spiking neurons with connections implemented as multiple delayed synaptic terminals. We consider two different topologies for unsupervised and supervised learning. For unsupervised learning, the SNN performs its learning directly on the pixels of the image to classify. For unsupervised learning, a reference data set of pixels from different images is used for learning.

In both topologies depicted in Figure 2(a) and Figure 2(b), the network consists in an input layer, a hidden layer, and an output layer. The first layer is composed of RGB values of pixels. Each node in the hidden layer has a localized activation $\Phi^n = \Phi(\|X - C_n\|, \sigma_n)$ where $\Phi^n(.)$ is a radial basis function (RBF) localized around C_n with the degree of localization parameterized by σ_n. Choosing $\Phi(Z, \sigma) = exp - (Z^2/2\sigma^2)$ gives the Gaussian RBF. This layer transforms the RGB values of pixels in first layer to temporal values. Third layer consist in class outputs (cell background, cytoplasm and nuclei).

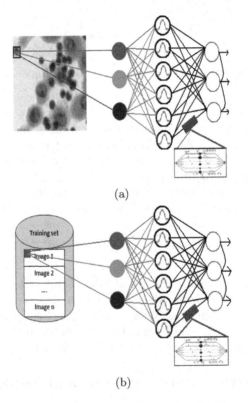

(a)

(b)

Fig. 2. (a) Network topology for unsupervised training; (b) Network topology for supervised training

Instead of a single synapse, with its specific delay and weight, this synapse model consists in many sub-synapses, each one with its own weight and delay d^k, as shown in Figure 1.b. The total contribution of all presynaptic neurons is given by equation (1). The neuron model implemented is the SRM_0 [23]. The delays d^k are fixed for all sub-synapses k, varying from zero in 1ms fixed intervals.

3.2   Information Encoding

Bohte et al. [25], presented a method for encoding the input data to enhance the precision. Each neuron of entry is modeled by a local receiving field (RF). For a variable with range of $[Max..Min]$, a set of m Gaussian receptive RF neurons are used. The center C_i and the width σ_i of each RF neuron i are determined by the following equations:

$$C_i = I_{min} + \left(\frac{2i-3}{2}\right)\left(\frac{I_{max} - I_{min}}{m-2}\right) \tag{2}$$

$$\sigma_i = \frac{1}{\gamma}\frac{I_{max} - I_{min}}{m-2} \tag{3}$$

where m is number of receptive fields in each population and a value of 1.5 is used for the variable γ. For each n-dimensional input pattern, the encoding scheme results in a matrix $n \times m$ of values between 0 and 1. These values are then converted to delay times. While converting the activation values of RFs into firing times, a threshold has been imposed on the activation value. A receptive field that gives an activation value less than this threshold will be marked as not-firing and the corresponding input neuron will not contribute to the post-synaptic potential.

3.3   Learning Method

The approach presented here implements the Hebbian reinforcement learning method through a winner-take-all algorithm [26],[27]. For unsupervised learning, a Winner-Takes-All learning rule modifies the weights between the input neurons and the neuron first to fire in the output layer using a time-variant of Hebbian learning. The synaptic weights should be randomly initialized. When an input pattern is presented to the network, neurons are expected to fire. The first neuron to fire is called the winner of the competitive process. Only the weights of the winner neuron are updated using a Hebbian learning rule $L(\Delta t)$. This learning function controls the learning process by updating the weight. It increases the weights of the connections that received spikes immediately before the fire of j and decrease remaining weights. For a weight with delay d^k from neuron i to neuron j we use [28]:

$$\Delta w_{ij}^k = \eta L(\Delta t_{ij}) \tag{4}$$

And

$$L(\Delta t) = (1+b)e^{\frac{(\Delta t - c)^2}{2(k-1)}} - b \tag{5}$$

with

$$k = 1 - \frac{\nu^2}{2ln\frac{b}{1+b}}$$

where: L(.) is the learning function; η is the learning rate; ν determines the width of the learning window; Δt is the difference between the arriving of the spike and the fire of neuron j; b determines the negative update given to a neuron; c fixes the peak of the learning function; w_{ij}^k is the increase of the kth connection between neurons i and j. The weights are limited to the range 0 to w_{max}, the maximum value that a weight can take.

4   Experimental Results and Discussion

4.1   Microscopic Cells Database

For the considered class of microscopic images, a microscopy expert has to choose judicious images that well describe the whole segmentation problem (a ground truth). This ground truth database can be used for the learning step and also as a reference segmentation to evaluate the relevance of an automatic segmentation. In the sequel, we will consider a publicly available database[1] [29] of 8 microscopic images of bronchial tumors (752 x 574 pixels). The pixels of these images have to be classified into one of the three following classes background, cell cytoplasm and cell nucleus. Figure 3(a)-(b) shows a microscopic color image and its ground truth. Pixel dataset has been split to produce training, validation and test sets.

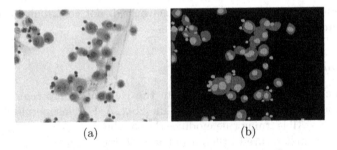
(a)   (b)

Fig. 3. (a) Original image; (b) Ground truth

4.2   Segmentation Results

Several experiments are carried out by changing the number of synapses, the number of receptive fields and the size of training corpus to select the best network parameters. Table 1 show these parameters.

Table 1. Best parameter of the SNN

Receptive field	Subsynapse	Threshold	Training set	η	τ	υ	b	c
8	12	9	10%	0.0025	3	5	-0.007	-2.3

---

[1] http://users.info.unicaen.fr/~lezoray/database.php

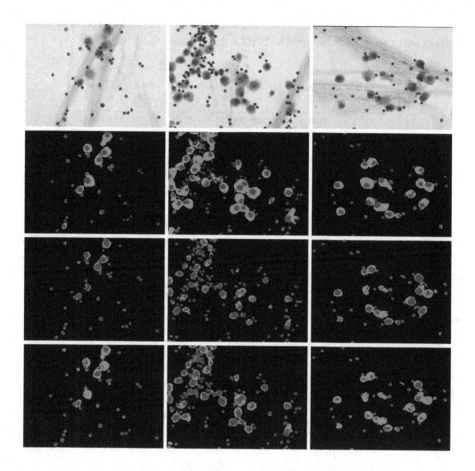

Fig. 4. Cell microscopic images (First row); expert segmentation (Second row); segmentation produced by unsupervised training (Third row) and segmentation produced by supervised training (Fourth row)

Images in Figure 4 show segmentation results with our segmentation scheme in comparison with the expert segmentation. It is worth to note that the mucus present in all images is correctly identified as background.

4.3 Evaluation Methods

To evaluate our approach, we use several classification rates. These classifications rates are expressed as follows:

$$
\begin{aligned}
R_0 &= \frac{Number\ of\ pixels\ well\ classified}{Number\ of\ pixels\ of\ the\ image} \\
R_1 &= \frac{Number\ of\ nuclei\ pixels\ well\ classified}{Number\ of\ nuclei\ pixels\ of\ the\ image} \\
R_2 &= \frac{Number\ of\ background\ pixels\ well\ classified}{Number\ of\ background\ pixels\ of\ the\ image} \\
R_3 &= \frac{R_1+R_2}{2}
\end{aligned}
\tag{6}
$$

Results in Table 2 show that SNN with supervised training has the best classification accuracies as compared to SNN with unsupervised training.

Table 2. Classification rates (best rates bold faced)

	SNN with unsupervised training	SNN with supervised training
R_0	89.07%	**94.27%**
R_1	69.57%	**80.37%**
R_2	94.55%	**99.06%**
R_3	82.06%	**89.71%**

Table 3 presents a comparison of the the classification accuracies obtained
by Meurie et al. [29] for different classifiers as well as with our SNN supervised
training. Our approach clearly outperforms all these state-of-the-art methods.

Table 3. Segmentation rates and comparison with Meurie et al. approaches [29], with
best rates bold faced

Classifier	R_1
SVM	74.2%
Bayes	74.6%
K-means	74.4%
MLP	73%
Fisher 1	72.3%
KNN	70%
Supervised SNN	**80.37%**

5   Conclusion

An automated approach for the segmentation of cells has been presented. Segmentation is based on spiking neural networks with unsupervised training and
supervised training. At first, the network is build, a subset of the images pixels
is taken to be learned by the network and finally the SNN processes the rest of
the images to have as a result a number of classes quantizing the cell image.

References

1. Knesek Jr., E.A.: Roche Image Analysis System. Acta Cytologica 40(1), 60–66
   (1996)
2. Patten Jr., S.F., Lee, S.S.J., Nelson, A.C.: Neopath Autopap 300 Automatic pap
   Screener System. Acta Cytologica 40(1), 45–52 (1996)

3. Di Rubeto, C., Dempster, A., Khan, S., Jarra, B.: Segmentation of Blood Image using Morphological Operators. In: Proc. of the 15th Int. Conference on Pattern Recognition, Barcelona, Spain, September 3-8, vol. 3, pp. 397–400 (2000)
4. Anoraganingrum, D.: Cell Segmentation with Median Filter and Mathematical Morphology Operation. In: Proc. of the International Conference on Image Analysis and Processing, Venice, Italy, September 27-29, pp. 1043–1046 (1999)
5. Lezoray, O., Cardot, H.: Cooperation of Pixel Classification Schemes and Color Watershed: a Study for Microscopical Images. IEEE Transactions on Images Processing 11(7), 738–789 (2002)
6. Lin, G., Adiga, U., Olson, K., Guzowski, J.F., Barnes, C.A., Roysam, B.: A hybrid 3D Watershed Algorithm Incorporating Gradient Cues and Object Models for Automatic Segmentation of Nuclei in Confocal Image Stacks. Cytometry A 56(1), 23–36 (2003)
7. Adiga, U.P.S., Chaudhuri, B.B.: An Efficient Method based on Watershed and Rulebased Merging for Segmentation of 3-D Histopathological Images. Pattern Recognition 34(7), 1449–1458 (2001)
8. Mouroutis, T., Roberts, S.J., Bharath, A.A.: Robust Cell Nuclei Segmentation Using Statistical Modeling. BioImaging 6, 79–91 (1998)
9. Wu, H.S., Barba, J., Gil, J.: Iterative Thresholding for Segmentation of Cells from Noisy Images. J. Microsc. 197, 296–304 (2000)
10. Karlosson, A., Strahlen, K., Heyden, A.: Segmentation of Histological Section using Snakes. In: Bigun, J., Gustavsson, T. (eds.) SCIA 2003. LNCS, vol. 2749, pp. 595–602. Springer, Heidelberg (2003)
11. Murashov, D.: Two-Level Method for Segmentation of Cytological Images using Active Contour Model. In: Proc. of the 7th Int. Conference on Pattern Recognition and Image Analysis, PRIA-7, St. Petersburg, Russian Federation, October 18-23, vol. III, pp. 814–817 (2004)
12. Papanicolaou, G.N.: A new procedure for staining vaginal smears. Science 95, 432 (1942)
13. Borsotti, M., Campadelli, P., Schettini, R.: Quantitative Evaluation of Color Image Segmentation Results. Pattern Recognition Letters 19, 741–747 (1998)
14. Glory, E., Meas-Yedid, V., Pinset, C., Olivo-Marin, J.C., Stamon, G.: A Quantitative Criterion to Evaluate Color Segmentation Application to Cytological Imges. In: Blanc-Talon, J., Philips, W., Popescu, D.C., Scheunders, P. (eds.) ACIVS 2005. LNCS, vol. 3708, pp. 227–234. Springer, Heidelberg (2005)
15. Maass, W.: Networks of spiking neurons: The third generation of neural network models. Neural Networks 10(9), 1659–1671 (1997)
16. Paugam-Moisy, H., Bohte, S.M.: Computing with Spiking Neuron Networks. In: Kok, J., Heskes, T. (eds.) Handbook of Natural Computing, 40p. Springer, Heidelberg (2009) (to appear)
17. Thorpe, S.J., Delorme, A., VanRullen, R.: Spike-based strategies for rapid processing. Neural Networks 14(6-7), 715–726 (2001)
18. Gupta, A., Long, L.N.: Hebbian learning with winner take all for spiking neural networks. In: IEEE International Joint Conference on Neural Networks (IJCNN), Atlanta, Gerogia, pp. 1189–1195 (2009)
19. Wu, B.J.: Introduction to neural dynamics and signal transmission delay. Walther de Gruyter, Berlin (2001)
20. Maass, W.: On the relevance neural networks. MIT-Press, London (2001)
21. Gerstner, W., Kistler, W.M.: Spiking neuron models, 1st edn. Cambridge University Press, Cambridge (2002)

22. Maass, W.: Fast sigmoidal networks via spiking neurons. Neural Computation 9, 279–304 (1997)
23. Gerstner, W.: Time structure of the activity in neural network models. Phys. Rev. E 51, 738–758 (1995)
24. NatschlNager, T., Ruf, B.: Spatial and Temporal Pattern Analysis via Spiking Neurons Network. Comp. Neural Systems 9(3), 319–332 (1998)
25. Bohte, S.M., La Poutre, H., Kok, J.N.: Unsupervised clustering with spiking neurons by sparse temporal coding and Multi-Layer RBF Networks. IEEE Transactions on Neural Networks 13(2), 426–435 (2002)
26. Ludemir, B.T.B., De Carvalho, C.P.: Artificial neural networks - theory and applications, 1st edn. LTC Editora, Rio de Janeiro (2000)
27. Oster, M., Liu, S.C.: A winner-take-all spiking network with spiking inputs. In: Proceedings of the 11th IEEE International Conference on Electronics, Circuits and Systems (ICECS 2004), vol. 11, pp. 203–206 (2004)
28. De Berredo, R.C.: A review of spiking neuron models and applications. M. Sc. Dissertation, University of Minas Gerais (2005)
29. Meurie, C., Lezoray, O., Carrier, C., Elmoataz, A.: Combination of Multiple Pixel Classifiers for Microscopic Image Segmentation. International Jornal of Robotic and Automation, Special Issue on Color Image and Analysis for Machine Vision 20(2), 63–69 (2005)

Investigation of Brain-Computer Interfaces That Apply Sound-Evoked Event-Related Potentials

Masumi Kogure, Shuichi Matsuzaki, and Yasuhiro Wada

Nagaoka University of Technology,
1603-1 Kamitomioka, Nagaoka, Niigata 940-2188, Japan
mkogure@stn.nagaokaut.ac.jp

Abstract. Assessing brain wave functions that are evoked by auditory stimuli is an important area of study that may lead to the development of brain computer interface (BCI) systems that incorporate natural features of auditory perception such as tone, pitch, and sound-source locations (e.g. direction). We analyzed event-related potentials (ERPs) evoked by auditory stimuli that are applicable to BCI systems. In recent studies, sound localization systems have been intensively studied in order to enhance BCI system development in a way that reproduces a virtual 3D auditory environment, applicable to human-machine communications. We conducted experiment using a sound localization system in which subjects were instructed to listen to a sound cue and answering the relative direction (i.e. the direction to which the sound cue is emitted from an observer) of the sound source. For each trial, a target direction was indicated by the experimenter, although the direction of the sound cue emitted during the trials was not necessarily the target direction. Changes in brain activity were measured using an electroencephalogram (EEG) . Experimental results showed that prominent excitations in EEG signals were observed during a trial where the target direction corresponded to the sound source direction, by subtracting the mean EEG signal of the non-target trials from that of the target trials.

1 Introduction

Recently, brain computer interfaces (BCIs),which are systems that stablish a direct pathway connecting an external device (e.g. computer, robot) and the human brain, have increasingly been a topic of research. If further development of BCI systems that are capable of manipulating machines that are controlled by a user's brain activity is attained, then those machines or robots are expected to become a powerful communication tool, especially for disabled people such as patients with amyotrophic lateral sclerosis (ALS).

There are two ways to assess human brain activity; one way uses invasive equipment that involves injecting electrodes directly into the brain, while the other uses noninvasive equipment such as electrodes attached to the scalp. In this study, we used the noninvasive electroencephalogram (EEG), with focus placed on assessing event related potentials (ERPs). ERPs are thought to contain

K. Diamantaras, W. Duch, L.S. Iliadis (Eds.): ICANN 2010, Part I, LNCS 6352, pp. 127–134, 2010.

patterns that make it possible to discriminate external events. These ERPs are thought to be generated at the area around the median line of the parietal region. BCI systems that apply ERPs have an advantage in that users only have to focus attention on the stimulus. In this study, we measured ERPs that can be evoked in response to auditory stimuli and then evaluated whether the methods are applicable to BCI systems.

2 Audio Stimulus BCI

To develop a BCI system capable of performing a variety of tasks, it is necessary to design control rules in which a particular brain activity pattern corresponds to a control command to the machine. In this study we employed an auditory stimulus as a component to develop a novel BCI system with high flexibility involving auditory-related parameters such as sound-source direction and the auditory tone. We designed a task using sound cues that required subjects to discriminate the cue parameters. Interestingly, those parameters can be evaluated in parallel. For example, a task that requires discrimination of four directions and two tones at the same time results in a flexibility rating of eight for that task. Thus, the flexibility increases exponentially in response to an increase in the number of combined tasks. In addition, if we employ a sound localization [1,2] system that simulates the placement of auditory cues in virtual 3D space, it is not necessary to use speakers placed in a real space, and we can expect to develop a simple BCI that requires only an earphone (Fig. 1).

In this study, we conducted an experiment in which the subject had to discriminate a target and non-target using two directions of sound-source locations in two patterns, "right or left" or "front or rear," and the count the number of sound cues heard from the target direction.

3 Experiment

3.1 Subject

Five healthy men aged 22-24 years old participated in the experiments. Informed consent was obtained from each subject and approved by the ethics committee of Nagaoka University of Technology.

3.2 Experimental Environment

Fig. 2 shows the positional relationship of the subject and the loudspeakers during the experiments. We measured two auditory tasks: to discriminate right (R) from left (L) directions, and to discriminate front (Fr) from rear (Re) directions. Two computers were used for this experiment. One was connected to an electroencephalograph to record the EEG, and the other one controlled the sound emitted from the speakers. The computer controlling the sound was connected to the electroencephalograph with a parallel cable, and trigger signal was sent to the electroencephalograph for each trial from this computer. This trigger signal was used to mark task onset on EEG data.

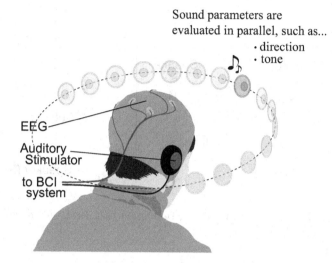

Sound parameters are
evaluated in parallel, such as...
· direction
· tone

EEG

Auditory
Stimulator

to BCI
system

Fig. 1. Image of BCI system: The development of a simple and flexible BCI that requires only an earphone with the use of sound localization is anticipated

3.3 Measurement Instrument

We used a digital electroencephalograph (Biosemi, ActiveTwo AD-box ADC-12) to measure the EEGs. Fig. 3 shows the measurement configuration. EEG electrodes were arranged according to the international standardized 10-20 system. The reference electrode was applied to the right ear and is identified as CMS.

3.4 Experiment Task

Fig. 4 shows the time sequence of one trial. After a pre-rest of 1500 milliseconds, a sound was presented from the L or R speaker, as in Fig. 2(a), or was presented from the Fr or Re speaker as in Fig. 2(b). We employed pure sound of 440 [Hz] for the sound, and the duration was 500 milliseconds. The next trial was started after a post-auditory rest of 3500 [ms]. Subjects were told the target direction that for each session, and were instructed to count the number of times they heard sound cues from the target direction. Target trials were presented at the rate of 13-20 % per session. One session was composed of 30 trials, and we measured five sessions for each discrimination task. We instructed subjects to close their eyes to avoid the influence of visual stimuli or blinks during tasks.

4 Data Analysis

4.1 Preprocessing

In EEG measurements, we used a bandpass filter (3-pole Butterworth 1-5 [Hz]) to filter out alpha rhythms causing the eyes to close (blinking) and because

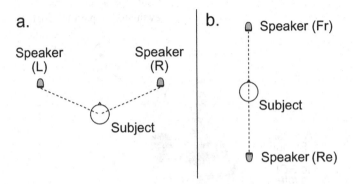

Fig. 2. Experimental environment: discrimination task for right or left direction (a) and front or rear direction (b)

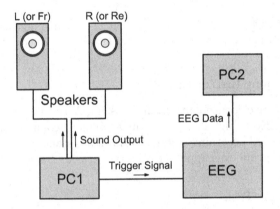

Fig. 3. Measurement configration: PC1 controls stimulus sounds and trigger signal to mark task onset on EEG data. PC2 was used to record EEG data

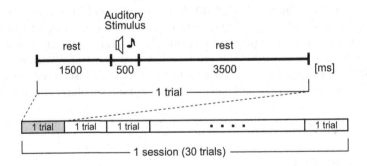

Fig. 4. Time sequence

the ERPs were composed of low-frequency components. The trigger signal input time was set to be 0, and the data were extracted from -200 [ms] to 1000 [ms] at each trial. The baseline correction was determined as the average value from -100 [ms] to 0 [s].

4.2 Target and Non-target Discrimination

It is necessary to discriminate ERPs from one trial EEG wave to attain BCI -applied ERPs. Therefore, we checked whether ERPs were discriminated from our measured data, and the discriminating rate.

  To discriminate between target and non-target trials from the EEG data, we focused on the gradient of the wave when ERPs were evoked. In the target trials, the amplitude of the wave tended to be larger than in the non-target trials, and the gradient of the wave was larger too.

  We measured peak-to-peak amplitude for each unit time window (A_{pp}) and compared A_{pp} to the threshold amplitude (A_{th}). If A_{pp} exceeded A_{th}, we counted how many A_{pp}s exceeded A_{th} consecutively. We defined the number of times as C, and compared C to a minimum threshold (C_{thmin}) and maximum threshold (C_{thmax}). If C fitted between C_{thmin} and C_{thmax}, that trial was discriminated as a target; anything else was discriminated as a non-target; C_{thmax} was set to reject abnormal amplitude levels due to noise. Fig. 5 is a pattern diagram that shows the sequence of discrimination. We checked the optimal value of the three thresholds, A_{th}, C_{thmin}, and C_{thmax}, for each electrode.

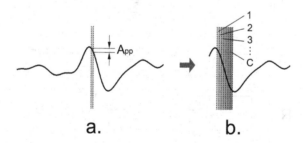

a.   **b.**

Fig. 5. Discrimination method: (a) we compared peak-to-peak amplitude for each time window (A_{pp}) to threshold amplitude (A_{th}). If A_{pp} was larger than A_{th}, we counted the number of A_{pp}s where the magnitude was larger than the magnitude of A_{th} for each trial, with the number referred to as C. (b) We counted C until A_{pp} continued to exceed A_{th}, and compared C to the minimum threshold of C (C_{thmin}) and maximum threshold of C (C_{thmax}). If C was between C_{thmin} and C_{thmax}, that trial was discriminated as a target direction corresponding to the sound source direction.

5   Result

We calculated the average EEG of the target and non-target trials for each direction. Additionally, we subtracted the averaged non-target trials from the averaged target trials so that it removes fluctuations uncorrelated to the event-related potentials evoked by target selection. Fig. 6 shows the subtracted EEG signals for the electrodes Fz, Cz, and Pz for each direction. The five narrow waves indicate the subtracted EEG signals for each of the five subjects, and the bold wave is the average of the five waves.

Thus, those fluctuations indicate endogenous potentials evoked in response to the perceived direction. The electrode that showed the largest amplitude was Pz, and prominent negative electrical potentials were observed for each direction. These results suggest that ERPs were evoked by discriminating the sound-source direction. This suggests it is possible to develop a BCI that estimates auditory stimuli while providing the ability to detect the direction subjects are currently paying attention to.

Table 1 lists the results of the discrimination rates of the target and non-target trials for each subject. In the target and non-target trials, the respective discrimination rates were 65.4 - 76.3 % and 66.4 - 70.5 % on average. Fig. 7 shows selected electrodes indicated in Table 1. These were mainly distributed at the right rear scalp, and in particular, P2, P6, PO8 were selected more than once.

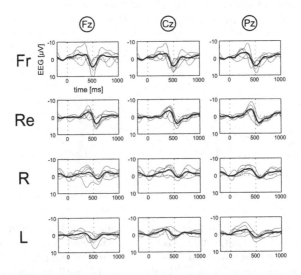

Fig. 6. Subtracted EEG at Fz, Cz, and Pz: the mean non-target trials were subtracted from those of the target trials to remove external components. The five narrow waves indicate the subtracted EEG signals for each of the five subjects, and the bold wave is the average of the five waves.

Table 1. Discrimination rate, threshold values, and selected electorodes on each target directions: threshold values were:
A_{th}: 0.1-4.0 [μV](0.1 μV intervals), C_{thmin}: 1-10 (1 interval), C_{thmax}: 3-12 (1 interval)

	Subject	Cthmin	Cthmax	Ath [µV]	electrode	Target [%]	Nontarget [%]
Target Fr	M.M	10	12	0.8	CP5	65.4	75
	T.I	8	11	0.7	CP4	76.9	66.1
	T.S	3	5	2.7	FC3	92.3	66.9
	T.Y	5	7	1.7	T8	65.4	66.9
	Y.S	1	3	3.1	P2	81.5	67.5
	Average					76.3	68.5

	Subject	Cthmin	Cthmax	Ath [µV]	electrode	Target [%]	Nontarget [%]
Target Re	M.M	5	7	1.7	P6	69.2	66.9
	T.I	6	8	1	O2	69.2	68.5
	T.S	5	7	1.6	P2	69.2	68.5
	T.Y	3	5	2.8	Pz	57.7	65.3
	Y.S	4	6	1.9	PO8	61.5	62.9
	Average					65.4	66.4

	Subject	Cthmin	Cthmax	Ath [µV]	electrode	Target [%]	Nontarget [%]
Target L	M.M	3	5	2	T8	69.2	74.2
	T.I	8	10	0.5	P6	76.9	66.9
	T.S	7	9	0.9	F7	73.1	61.3
	T.Y	10	12	0.5	P6	73.1	67.7
	Y.S	7	9	0.9	F7	84.6	73.4
	Average					75.4	68.7

	Subject	Cthmin	Cthmax	Ath [µV]	electrode	Target [%]	Nontarget [%]
Target R	M.M	4	6	1.9	Oz	69.2	70.2
	T.I	8	10	0.9	F1	57.7	69.4
	T.S	5	7	3.8	Fp1	73.1	70.2
	T.Y	4	6	1.8	P1	84.6	66.1
	Y.S	9	12	0.8	PO8	52.4	76.8
	Average					67.4	70.5

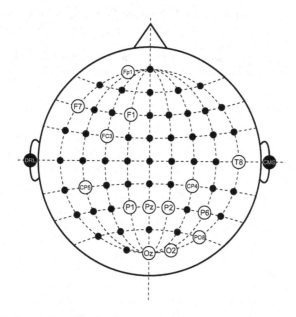

Fig. 7. Selected electrodes: the distribution of selected electrodes indicated in Table 1. These were distributed mainly at the right rear scalp, and in particular, P2, P6, and PO8 were selected more than once.

6   Conclusion

We analyzed ERPs involving discrimination of external events, and assessed the applicability of incorporating the ERPs evoked by auditory stimuli into BCI systems. A task to discriminate the sound source direction of auditory stimuli was carried out to investigate the possibility of applying it to develop a BCI.

We conducted an experimental in which subjects counted the number of sound cues emitted from a target direction (there were two patterns; either "Left or Right" or "Front or Rear"). We observed that ERPs were shown that reflected a target selection, which was calculated by subtracting the average of non-target trials from the average of target trials. Thus, it may be possible to develop a BCI that is capable of estimating the direction of a sound source.

To detect ERPs from EEG data from one trial, we calculated the discrimination rate using the difference in the EEG amplitude and gradient. As a result, the discrimination rate in the target trials was 65.4 - 76.3 %, while that in the non-target trials was 66.4 - 70.5 %.

In a future study, we plan to investigate the development of BCI systems with greater flexibility by conducting experiments using more patterns of sound-source directions in discrimination tasks, and to assess ERP patterns evoked by auditory tones.

References

1. Yano, S., Hokari, H., Shimada, S.: A Study on Personal Difference in the Transfer Functions of Sound Localization Using Stereo Earphones. IEICE Trans. Fundamentals E83-A(5), 877–887 (2000)
2. Aoki, J., Hokari, H., Shimada, S.: Sound localization with multi-loudspeakers by usage of a coincident microphone array. Acoust. Sci. & Tech. 24(5), 250–258 (2003)

Functional Connectivity Driven by External Stimuli in a Network of Hierarchically Organized Neural Modules

Vladyslav Shaposhnyk[1,2], Pierre Dutoit[1,3],
Stephen Perrig[3], and Alessandro E.P. Villa[1,3,4]

[1] Neuroheuristic Research Group, Grenoble Institute of Neuroscience,
Université Joseph Fourier, Grenoble, France
[2] Non-linear Analysis Department, Institute for Applied System Analysis,
State Techical University "Kyivskyy Politechnichnyy Instytut", Kiev, Ukraine
[3] Sleep Research Laboratory, Dept. of Psychiatry Belle-Idée,
Hôpitaux Universitaires de Genève, Switzerland
[4] Neuroheuristic Research Group, Information Science Institute,
University of Lausanne, Switzerland
http://www.neuroheuristic.org/

Abstract. Complex neural modules with embedded neural development and synaptic plasticity features have been connected to form a hierarchical recurrent circuit. Virtual electrodes have been used to record a "neural" generated signal, called electrochipogram EChG, from each module. The EChG are processed by frequency domain methods to determine the modifications in functional connectivity by assessing quadratic phase coupling. The experimental paradigm is aimed to describe what happened prior to, at the beginning, towards the end, and after repeating an external input at fixed frequency. The results are discussed by comparing with the same signal processing methods applied to a human study.

Keywords: Spiking neural networks, hierarchical neural networks, distributed computing, computational neuroscience, EEG.

1 Introduction

At mesoscopic level, the recording of brain activity by means of electroencephalography (EEG), electrocorticography (ECoG) and local field potentials (LFP) collects the signals generated by multiple cell assemblies. The neurophysiological processes underlying those signals are determined by highly non-linear dynamical systems [1]. Because of these nonlinearities the functional interactions between brain areas that are simultaneously sampled by electrophysiological techniques generate signals that can be better analyzed by third order polyspectral methods that retain phase relationships [2]. This analysis was applied to EEG by pioneers as early as the 1970s [3]. Phase coupling frequencies can be

K. Diamantaras, W. Duch, L.S. Iliadis (Eds.): ICANN 2010, Part I, LNCS 6352, pp. 135–144, 2010.
© Springer-Verlag Berlin Heidelberg 2010

interpreted as frequencies of resonance of standing waves whose wavelength is associated to the average distance between interacting cell assemblies [4,5].

In the present study we simulate the activity of interconnected neural networks undergoing neural developmental phases. The implementation of such complex models requires high performance of the simulation that can be achieved thanks to a powerful hardware platform, its bio-inspired capabilities, its dynamical topology, and generic flexibility of artificial neuronal models presented elsewhere [6,7]. The outcome is the implementation of each neural network into a *Ubidule* and a network of *Ubidules* as a *Ubinet*. Within each *Ubidule* the emergence of functional connectivity driven by neural development, cell and synaptic pruning, and selective external stimuli was assessed by recording Electrochipograms (EChG) which are analog signals similar to EEG generated by virtual electrodes located into each *Ubidule* [8].

The experimental paradigm is aimed to describe what happened prior to, at the beginning, towards the end, and after repeating an external input at fixed frequency. The rationale is that the spike timing dependent plasticity (STDP) embedded in the neural network models would drive the build-up of auto-associative network links, within each *Ubidule*, such to generate an areal activity, detected by EChG, that would reflect the changes in the corresponding functional connectivity within and between *Ubidules*. This experiment is compared to a small set of recordings performed in patients suffering of primary insomnia whose EEG recordings were analyzed during several sleep phases, before and after a clinical treatment.

2   Hybrid System Implementation

The *Ubidule* is a custom reconfigurable electronic device allowing an implementation of several bio-inspired mechanisms such as growth, learning, and neural processing [9]. The common *Ubidule* platform is an hybrid system with an XScale-class processor that manages the software components of the system, such as ontogenetic processes, communications with other *Ubidules*, monitoring and recording of the activity. This processor is equipped with an open hardware subsystem which allows connecting any sort of USB device (sensors, actuators, Wifi / Bluetooth dongles, mass storage, etc.). The processor runs an embedded Linux operating system which facilitates *Ubidule* programming and management while ensuring portability at the same time.

Both hardware and software platforms are based upon modular architecture that offers interoperability among the hardware and the software parts of the system and simplifies the usage of bio-inspired features of the hardware. The neural system simulator consists of multiple computational modules, each one corresponding to a neural network, exchanging their neural activity and/or receiving input data from hardware sensors (camera, photodiode, radars, etc.) and/or providing output to hardware actuators (motor, diode array, etc.). The characteristics of the implementation naturally geared the modeling framework towards agent oriented programming. An evaluation of the available platforms of this kind led us to select JADE [10] for the development and runtime execution of peer-to-peer applications which are based on the agent oriented paradigm [11]. It is a JAVA-based multi-agent development system that fulfils the FIPA specifications [12].

In this study each network is a 2D lattice of 20 x 20 units that includes 80% of excitatory units and 20% of inhibitory units. Our framework implements several features of brain maturation, including apoptosis active during the very initial 700 time units and STDP active from the end of apoptosis until the end of simulation. This framework was extensively described elsewhere [13,6,7]. Synaptic pruning occured when the activation level of a synapse reached a value of zero, so that besides cell death and axonal pruning of dead cells provoked by apoptosis, the units whose all synaptic connections were characterized by a zero level of activation were definitely eliminated from the network. All units were simulated by leaky integrate-and-fire neuromimes with background activity used to simulate the effect of afferences that were not explicitly simulated within a network. The background activity to each neuron was set to 900 *spikes/s* with a low amplitude (1 *mV*) generated by uncorrelated Poisson distributed inputs. In each *Ubidule* two sets of 20 excitatory units were randomly selected among the excitatory units corresponding to the "input" and "output" layers of the *Ubidule*. The neurons of these layers send and receive connections from the other units of both types (excitatory and inhibitory) within the network in addition to the connections with other *Ubidules*.

Our circuit topology remained fixed during all simulations and the *Ubidules* were characterized by their role in the network, *i.e.*, *sensory*, *processing*, or *motor* (Fig. 1). In our network, the *u1Sensory Ubidule* has a pure sensory role. *Ubidules* labeled *u3Process, u4Process, u5Process, u6Process* have a pure information processing role and are characterized by having neither external inputs nor afferences from the motor *Ubidule*. They are all reciprocally interconnected and send efferent projections to *u2Motor*.

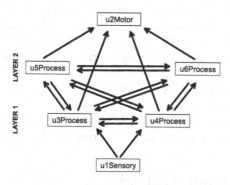

Fig. 1. The *Ubinet* hierarchical circuit used in all simulations. Solid arrows depict connections and directions of information flow between the *Ubidules*

3   Electrochipograms

Our design of the bio-inspired artificial neural networks allowed us to implement realistic virtual electrodes to record neuro-mimetic signals, called *Electrochipograms* (EChG), characterized by dynamics and features similar to those recorded in living brain structures. In our implementation the virtual electrode measures the potentials over a certain 'area' of the 2D lattice neuronal network according to an appropriate weighted sum [8]. The main parameters of the electode are its position over the neural network and its sensibility function. The tip of the virtual electrode was located in the middle of the 2D lattice of each *Ubidule* neural network. The sensibility function depends only on the distance between a given point of the lattice and the centre of the electrode field. According to this model, all neurons located at the same radial distance from the center of the electrode field make an equivalent contribution to the final electrode output and thus form an equi-potential layer [8]. In this study, the sensibility radius was set equal to 9 with a linear decaying function.

The EChG was recorded with a 6 channels virtual electrode system with one channel per *Ubidule* during 350 trials. Each trial had a fixed duration and included two intervals: a stimulation interval followed by an inter-stimulus interval. The stimulation was generated by spatio-temporal external stimuli applied only to the input layer of *u1Sensory* lasting 128 (*Type A*) and 512 (*Type B*) time steps. The group of simulations with higher stimulation frequency ($0.89\ Hz$) was called "Simulations A" and the group with lower stimulation frequency ($0.67\ Hz$) was called "Simulations B". The extensive use of Fast Fourier Transform in our signal analysis imposed, for improved efficiency, sampling frequencies which are powers of two. In practice the time-steps of the simulator were selected for convenient time units, *i.e.*, 1024 *time steps* corresponding to 1000 *ms*. The inter-stimulus interval was always equal to 1000 *ms*. The recording time was divided into four periods defined following the amount of time the *Ubinet* was exposed to the stimulation: *(i) PRE-learning* beginning at time zero and lasting 27 trials characterized by the absence of any external stimulation (*i.e.*, only the background activity was present during the stimulation interval); *(ii) EARLY-learning* lasting 50 trials, between trials #28 and #77; *(iii) LATE-learning* lasting 50 trials, between trials #228 and #277; and *(iv) POST-learning* lasting 50 trials, between trials #278 and #327 again characterized by the absence of any external stimulation.

The signals recorded *during the stimulation interval* were averaged across several trials in order to compute evoked potentials (*e.g.*, Fig. 2). The signals recorded *during the inter-stimulus interval* were used for frequency domain analyses that included power spectrum, bispectrum and bicoherence analyses.

4   Power Spectrum Analysis

Figure 3 shows the averaged evoked potentials for the "first" (*u3P,u4P*) and the "second" (*u5P,u6P*) processing layers and their corresponding Power Spectrum

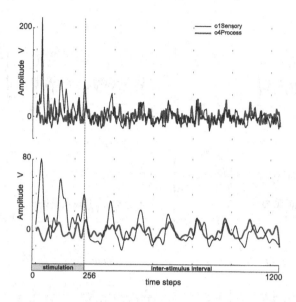

Fig. 2. Evoked potentials averaged over 50 trials obtained from *u1Sensory* (blue solid trace) and from *u4Process* (green dotted trace) *Ubidules* during the *EARLY-learning* stage. The stimulus was applied during 256 time steps. The upper panel displays the raw evoked potentials and the lower panel shows the signals smoothed by a Blackmann smoothing window in order to emphasize the low frequency components.

Densities (PSD). In the PSD several peaks could be observed around 10 Hz, 15 Hz and 25 Hz. The results obtained during the *EARLY-learning* stage were not significantly different from the *PRE* recording condition. This suggests that PSD is little affected by the stimulus structure and by the subsequent functional connectivity at the begin of the stimulation. This is probably due to the fact that stimulus-driven selective cell and synaptic pruning were not yet producing any effect. During the *LATE* period the PSDs were characterized by a generalized decrease in the power and the preservation of the peak near 10 Hz with a noticeable decrease of the other peaks. It is interesting to notice that in the *POST-learning* stage the multiple peaks tended to appear again, thus suggesting that they are mainly driven by the combined effect of background activity and internal features of the model. Another general observation is that in mature networks, *i.e.* during the *LATE*- and *POST-learning* phases in comparison with *EARLY*- and *PRE-learning* phases, PSD is getting lower, which means the total amount of energy transferred by the neural networks is decreasing. The *POST-learning* phase was characterized by 3.5 dB/Hz lower values of power than appropriate values during PRE-learning phases. This decrease is likely to be associated to the pruning of synpatic links and cell death.

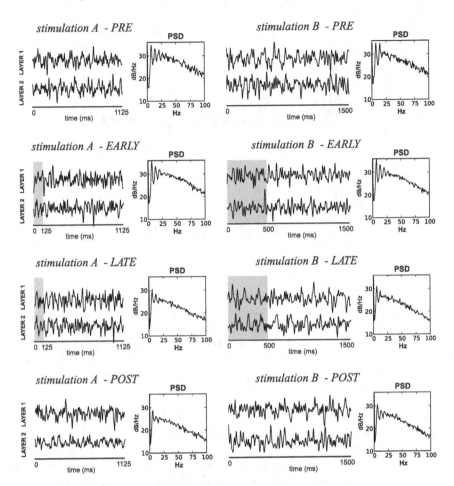

Fig. 3. Evoked Potentials and Power Spectrum Densities for the averaged recordings of the pair of Ubidules in Layer 1 and in Layer 2. The left panels correspond to stimulus Type A and the right panels to stimulus Type B. The gray stripes correspond to the periods of stimulation. From top to bottom the results referred to the *PRE-learning*, *EARLY-learning*, *LATE-learning* and *POST-learning* periods.

5 Quadratic Phase Coupling

The bispectral analysis was performed for all channels separatedly and the values of phase-coupled frequencies (*i.e.*, the frequencies of resonance f_3) were determined. Let us consider the distribution of all phase-coupled frequencies f_3 observed in single-channel and cross-channel analyses. Let us consider the frequency band $]1-24]$ Hz for EChG and LF the relative number of f_3 falling into this low frequency range. Let us consider the frequency band $]60-84]$ Hz and HF the relative number of f_3 falling into this high frequency range. The *index of resonant frequencies IRF* is defined in the range 0–100 as follows:

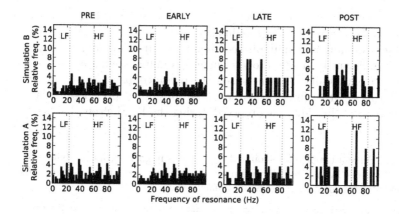

Fig. 4. Relative distribution of the frequencies of resonance for each period for Simulations A and B. Bin size corresponds to 2 Hz intervals. The dotted lines delineate the limits of LF and HF bands.

$IRF = \frac{1}{2} \times \left(100 + \left(\frac{HF-LF}{HF+LF} \times 100\right)\right)$. A value of IRF close to 100 corresponds to a shift of f_3 towards higher frequencies and value of IRF close to 0 corresponds to a shift of f_3 towards lower frequencies. IRF values close to 50 indicates the phase-coupling was equally distributed in low- and high-frequency bands. The raw frequency ratio is simply defined by $RFR = \frac{LF}{HF}$. This means a large value of RFR corresponds to a shift of phase-coupling towards higher frequencies and a low value of RFR corresponds to a shift towards lower frequencies.

Figure 4 shows the distribution of f_3 in the range 1 to 100 Hz during all recording periods and for the two types of stimulus used in the *Ubinet* simulation. These histograms show a shift towards an increase in low-frequencies resonances during the *LATE-learning* phase, especially when compared with the distribution during the *POST-learning*, when the input stimulus was absent. The quantitative assessment of this analysis presented in Table 1 emphasizes the change in the value of IRF between *EARLY-* and *LATE-learning* phases. $IRF \approx 60$ decreased to $IRF \approx 14$ followed by an increase to the range 26–29 during the *POST-learning* phase suggests that the shift towards low frequencies of phase-coupling was provoked by the learning protocol and not only due to the maturation of the network. The analysis of IRF and RFR shows also that in the *POST-learning* stage the resonant features remained affected by the functional connectivity that developed during the trials with external stimulation and the values were intermediate between *PRE/EARLY-learning* and *LATE-learning* phase.

Table 2 shows the relative count of phase-coupling in the frequency bands of interest and the values of indexes IRF and RFR for all recording periods in controls and patients suffering primary insomnia before and after treatment [14]. The frequency ranges of the bands refer to those generally used for human studies and are different from those used for studying the *Ubinet* activity. However, there is a linear correspondence between the two sets of frequency bands. The general pattern was a high level of high frequency coupling in the group of patients before treatment. The main effect of the treatment was to reduce high-frequency coupling and shift phase-coupling towards low frequencies, somehow with a significant increase of low frequency coupling compared to the controls. The treatment significantly increased the phase-coupling in the low frequency band during all other intervals, either re-establishing a level close to the controls or even beyond that level, as observed during the REM sleep phases.

Table 1. Percentage of phase-coupled frequencies in each frequency bands of interest for the stimulus Type A and B within neural network development stages. *IRF*: index of resonant frequencies. *RFR*: raw frequency ratio.

Learning Phase	Percentage of phase-coupled frequencies			Indexes	
	LF:] 1-24] Hz	]24-60] Hz	HF:]60-84] Hz	IRF	RFR
Stimulus Type A					
PRE	27	53	20	43	1.34
EARLY	20	50	30	60	0.66
LATE	38	56	6	13	6.67
POST	38	49	13	26	2.83
Stimulus Type B					
PRE	20	48	32	62	0.62
EARLY	21	47	31	60	0.68
LATE	49	43	8	14	6.00
POST	44	38	18	29	2.43

Table 2. Percentage of phase-coupled frequencies in each frequency bands of interest for the the control group and for the group of patients before and after treatment. *REM*: rapid eye movement sleep. *NREM*: rapid eye movement sleep.

Subject Group	Percentage of phase-coupled frequencies			Indexes	
	LF:] 1-13] Hz	]13-33] Hz	HF:]33-48] Hz	IRF	RFR
Eyes Closed					
Control	12	74	14	54	1.17
Patient before	2	77	21	91	10.50
after treatment	8	88	4	33	0.50
NREM					
Control	57	30	13	19	0.23
Patient before	27	60	13	33	0.48
after treatment	42	57	1	2	0.02
REM					
Control	4	90	5	56	1.25
Patient before	4	85	12	75	3.00
after treatment	19	79	2	10	0.11

6   Discussion

This paper described the implementation of a neuronal system simulator on a hybrid scalable multi-agent hardware platform based on the *Ubidules* framework [9] and its application to the study of information processing in hierarchically organized neural networks circuits. We have explored one simple *Ubinet* network circuit characterized by a sensory network processing the external input that projects to a hierarchically organized multilayered (in our case formed by only two layers) recurrent network of processing areas which eventually project on a motor network that generates an activity keen to be encoded into actuators. The experimental approach to the *Ubinet* activity by recording the EChG was aimed to assess the effect of a repeated stimulation on the functional connectivity established between the *Ubidules*. Our *PRE-learning* stage could represent a control situation driven exclusively by the background activity of the subject's brain. The subject is naive to the coming stimulus so that a learning process can occur. During the *EARLY-learning* stage the repetition of the stimuli at regular intervals might initiate an unsupervised recognition process that eventually shaped the functional connectivity of feature detecting cell assemblies after selective synaptic and cell pruning.

The third order spectral analysis of EChG and EEG allows to determine the frequency range of quadratic phase coupling (resonant frequency) across cortical areas [4,5]. According to the usual interpretation based on standing waves theory, high resonant frequencies mean that information processing is transmitted at short distance (*i.e.*, the distance between two nodes of the wave). A coupling that occurs at high frequencies may be interpreted as a sign of focal cortical interactions. Conversely, a coupling at low frequencies suggests an increased cross-areal involvement in neural processing.

A remarkable result is the finding that in the *Ubinet* simulations the *LATE-learning* stages were characterized by $IRF \approx 14$ compared with *PRE-* and *EARLY-learning* stages ($IRF \approx 43 - 62$). In the study with human Subjects we observed that controls and patients after treatment were characterized, during all sleep phases by values of IRF lower than insomniac patients before treatment. It is also worth reporting that the only condition that let appear a difference of resonant frequencies in the range $]13\text{-}33]$ Hz was during NREM sleep irrespective of the treatment. This last result suggests that despite an overall shift of resonant frequencies towards recovery, focal cortical interactions tended to persist in patients during NREM sleep periods. Both an appropriate stimulation of the *Ubinet* and the cognitive brain therapy appear to modify the ratio of resonant frequencies provoking a shift of the indexes towards low frequencies at all brain states. Our findings suggest that new tools provided by modular and scalable neural network simulators offer new opportunities to neurophysiologists and clinicians to test hypotheses based on the analysis of neural signals at mesoscopic levels.

Acknowledgments. The authors ackowledge the support by the European Union FP6 grant #034632 (PERPLEXUS) and the contributions of J. Iglesias,

Victor Contreras-Lámus for the simulations of O. Brousse, Th. Gil, G. Sassatelli, F. Grize for the JADE integration and of K. Espa-Cervena for the analysis of the clinical data.

References

1. Nunez, P.L., Srinivasan, R.: Electric Fields of the Brain. Oxford University Press, New York (2006)
2. Brillinger, D.R.: An introduction to polyspectra. Ann. Math. Stat. 36, 1351–1374 (1965)
3. Dumermuth, G., Huber, P.J., Kleiner, B., Gasser, T.: Analysis of the interrelations between frequency bands of the EEG by means of the bispectrum. A preliminary study. Electroencephalogr. Clin Neurophysiol. 31, 137–148 (1971)
4. Villa, A.E.P., Tetko, I.V., Dutoit, P., De Ribaupierre, Y., De Ribaupierre, F.: Corticofugal modulation of functional connectivity within the auditory thalamus of rat. J. Neurosci. Meth. 86, 161–178 (1999)
5. Villa, A.E.P., Tetko, I.V., Dutoit, P., Vantini, G.: Non-linear cortico-cortical interactions modulated by cholinergic afferences from the rat basal forebrain. BioSystems 58, 219–228 (2000)
6. Iglesias, J., Villa, A.E.P.: Effect of stimulus-driven pruning on the detection of spatiotemporal patterns of activity in large neural networks. BioSystems 89, 287–293 (2007)
7. Iglesias, J., Villa, A.E.P.: Emergence of preferred firing sequences in large spiking neural networks during simulated neuronal development. Int. J. Neural Syst. 18(4), 267–277 (2008)
8. Shaposhnyk, V.V., Dutoit, P., Contreras-Lámus, V., Perrig, S., Villa, A.E.P.: A framework for simulation and analysis of dynamically organized distributed neural networks. In: Alippi, C., Polycarpou, M., Panayiotou, C., Ellinas, G. (eds.) ICANN 2009. LNCS, vol. 5768, pp. 277–286. Springer, Heidelberg (2009)
9. Sanchez, E., Perez-Uribe, A., Upegui, A., Thoma, Y., Moreno, J.M., Villa, A., Volken, H., Napieralski, A., Sassatelli, G., Lavarec, E.: Perplexus: Pervasive computing framework for modeling complex virtually-unbounded systems. In: AHS 2007: Proceedings of the Second NASA/ESA Conference on Adaptive Hardware and Systems, Washington, DC, USA, pp. 587–591. IEEE Computer Society, Los Alamitos (2007)
10. Bellifemine, F.L., Caire, G., Greenwood, D.: Developing Multi-Agent Systems With Jade. Wiley, Wiltshire (2007)
11. Brousse, O., Guillot, J., Sassatelli, G., Gil, T., Robert, M., Moreno, J.M., Villa, A., Sanchez, E.: A bio-inspired agent framework for hardware accelerated distributed pervasive applications. In: 2009 NASA/ESA Conference on Adaptive Hardware and Systems, Washington, DC, USA, pp. 415–422. IEEE Computer Society, Los Alamitos (2009)
12. Fipa, D.T.: Fipa communicative act library specification (2001)
13. Iglesias, J., Eriksson, J., Grize, F., Tomassini, M., Villa, A.E.: Dynamics of pruning in simulated large-scale spiking neural networks. BioSystems 79(1), 11–20 (2005)
14. Perrig, S., Dutoit, P., Espa-Cervena, K., Shaposhnyk, V., Pelletier, L., Berger, F., Villa, A.E.P.: Changes in quadratic phase coupling of eeg signals during wake and sleep in two chronic insomnia patients, before and after cognitive behavioral therapy. Frontiers in Artificial Intelligence and Applications 204, 217–228 (2009)

Transmission of Distributed Deterministic Temporal Information through a Diverging/Converging Three-Layers Neural Network

Yoshiyuki Asai[1,2,3] and Alessandro E.P. Villa[2,3]

[1] The Center for Advanced Medical Engineering and Informatics,
Osaka University, Osaka, Japan
asai@bpe.es.osaka-u.ac.jp
[2] INSERM U836; Grenoble Inst. of Neuroscience; Université Joseph Fourier, Neuro
Heuristic Research Group, Eq. 7 - Nanomédecine et Cerveau, Grenoble, France
alessandro.villa@ujf-grenoble.fr
[3] Neuro Heuristic Research Group, Information Science Institute,
University of Lausanne, Lausanne, Switzerland
http://www.neuroheuristic.org/

Abstract. This study investigates the ability of a diverging/converging neural network to transmit and integrate a complex temporally organized activity embedded in afferent spike trains. The temporal information is originally generated by a deterministic nonlinear dynamical system whose parameters determine a chaotic attractor. We present the simulations obtained with a network formed by simple spiking neurons (SSN) and a network formed by a multiple-timescale adaptive threshold neurons (MAT). The assessment of the temporal structure embedded in the spike trains is carried out by sorting the preferred firing sequences detected by the pattern grouping algorithm (PGA). The results suggest that adaptive threshold neurons are much more efficient in maintaining a specific temporal structure distributed across multiple spike trains throughout the layers of a feed-forward network.

Keywords: Spiking neural networks, synfire chains, adaptive threshold neurons, computational neuroscience, preferred firing sequences.

1   Introduction

A neuronal network can be considered as a highly complex nonlinear dynamical system able to exhibit deterministic chaotic behavior, as suggested by the experimental observations of single unit spike trains, which are sequences of the exact timing of the occurrences of action potentials [1,2]. Previous studies [3,4] showed that deterministic nonlinear dynamics in noisy time series could be detected by applying algorithms aimed at finding preferred firing sequences with millisecond order time precision from simultaneously recorded neural activities. A neural network is also characterized by the presence of background activity of unspecified or unknown origin that is often represented by stochastic inputs to

K. Diamantaras, W. Duch, L.S. Iliadis (Eds.): ICANN 2010, Part I, LNCS 6352, pp. 145–154, 2010.
© Springer-Verlag Berlin Heidelberg 2010

each cell of the network. Then, a neuron belonging to a cell assembly, somehow associated to a deterministic nonlinear system, within the network is expected to receive inputs characterized by an embedded temporal structure as well as inputs corresponding to the stochastic background activity. It has been shown that the characteristic transfer function of a neuronal model and the statistical feature of the the background activity may affect the transmission of temporal information through synaptic links [5].

In the current paper we extend our previous analysis to diverging/converging feed-forward neuronal networks–synfire chains–which are supposed to represent the most appropriate circuits able to transmit information with the best temporal accuracy [6]. Moreover the temporally organized activity was fed to the network in a distributed way across the input spike trains [7]. We suggest that adaptive threshold neurons are much more efficient in maintaining a specific temporal structure throughout the layers of a synfire chain.

2   Methods

2.1   Spiking Neuron Model

We investigated two neuron models aimed to reproduce the dynamics of regular spiking neurons. The first is a simple spiking neuron (SSN) [8] described as:

$$\frac{dv}{dt} = 0.04v^2 + 5v + 140 - u + I_{ext}(t) \ , \tag{1}$$

$$\frac{du}{dt} = a(bv - u) \ ,$$

with the auxiliary after-spike resetting, $v \leftarrow c$ and $u \leftarrow u+d$ when $v \geq +30 \ mV$. v represents the membrane potential $[mV]$, u is a membrane recovery variable, a and b control the time scale of the recovery variable and its sensitivity to the subthreshold fluctuation of the membrane potential. This model generates an action potential with a continuous dynamics followed by a hyperpolarization modeled as a discontinuous resetting. Parameters were set as $a = 0.02$, $b = 0.2$, $c = -65$, $d = 8$ so to mimic the behavior of a regular spiking neuron [8].

The second model is a multiple-timescale adaptive threshold (MAT) model [9] derived from [10]. In this model, the dynamics of the membrane potential is described as a non-resetting leaky integrator,

$$\tau_m \frac{dV}{dt} = -V + R \ A \ I_{ext}(t) \ , \tag{2}$$

where τ_m, V, R and A are the membrane time constant, membrane potential, membrane resistance, and scaling factor, respectively. A spike is generated when the membrane potential V reaches the adaptive spike threshold $\theta(t)$,

$$\theta(t) = \omega + H_1(t) + H_2(t) \ ,$$

$$\frac{dH_1}{dt} = -H_1/\tau_1 \ , \tag{3}$$

$$\frac{dH_2}{dt} = -H_2/\tau_2 \ ,$$

where ω is the resting value, H_1 and H_2 are components of the fast and slow threshold dynamics (characterized by decaying time constants τ_1 and τ_2, respectively) which has a discrete jump when $V(t) \geq \theta(t)$,

$$H_1 = H_1 + \alpha_1 , \quad H_2 = H_2 + \alpha_2 . \tag{4}$$

Parameters were set to values $\tau_m = 5$ ms, $R = 50$ MΩ, $A = 0.106$, $\omega = 19$ mV, $\tau_1 = 10$ ms, $\tau_2 = 200$ ms, $\alpha_1 = 37$ mV, $\alpha_2 = 2$ mV. The model with the above parameter values reproduces the activity of a regular spiking neuron [9].

Let us denote I_{ext} the input synaptic current, defined as

$$I_{ext} = -A_{ext} \sum_k g_{syn}(t - t_k) , \tag{5}$$

where A_{ext} is an intensity of the synaptic transmission of the spike received as an external input ($A_{ext} = 1$ was used here for all simulations), t_k represents time when the k-th spike arrives to the neuron model, and g_{syn} is the post synaptic conductance represented by

$$g_{syn}(t) = C_0 \frac{e^{-t/\tilde{\tau}_1} - e^{-t/\tilde{\tau}_2}}{\tilde{\tau}_1 - \tilde{\tau}_2} , \tag{6}$$

where $\tilde{\tau}_1$ and $\tilde{\tau}_2$ are rise and decay time constants given by 0.17 and 4 ms, respectively, and C_0 is a coefficient used to normalize the maximum amplitude of $g_{syn}(t)$ to 1. Notice that a single synaptic current given to a neuron is not strong enough to evoke post-synaptic neuronal discharges. Hence, it is necessary for a post-synaptic neuron to integrate several arriving synaptic currents for a spike generation.

2.2   Input Spike Train

We consider the deterministic dynamical system described by Zaslavskii [11]:

$$\begin{cases} x_{n+1} = x_n + v(1 + \mu y_n) + \varepsilon v \mu \cos x_n , & (mod. \ 2\pi) \\ y_{n+1} = e^{-\gamma}(y_n + \varepsilon \cos x_n) , \end{cases} \tag{7}$$

where $x, y, \mu, v \in \mathbf{R}$, the parameters are $\mu = \frac{1-e^{-\gamma}}{\gamma}$, $v = \frac{400}{3}$ and initial conditions set to $x_0 = y_0 = 0.3$. With this parameter set the system exhibits a chaotic behavior. Time series $\{x_n\}$ are generated by iterative calculation. A new time series $\{w_n\}$ corresponding to the sequence of the inter-spike-intervals is derived by $w_n = x_{n+1} - x_n + C$, where $C = \min\{(x_{n+1} - x_n)\} + 0.1$ is a constant to make sure $w_n > 0$. The dynamics was rescaled in milliseconds time units with an average rate of 5 $events/s$ ($i.e.$, 5 $spikes/s$) in order to let the mean rate of the $Zaslavskii$ spike train be comparable to neurophysiological experimental data. We calculated $N = 10000$ points of time series $\{w_n\}$ which corresponds to a spike train lasting $L = 2000$ $seconds$.

Given a dynamical information ratio D, where $0 \leq D \leq 1$, a percentage of spikes corresponding to $(1 - D) \times 100$ % are selected at random (uniformly

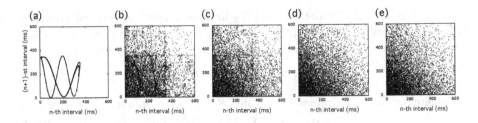

Fig. 1. Return maps of input spike trains with an average rate of 5 *spikes/s* as a function of the dynamical information ratio (D). The $(n+1)$-st inter-spike-interval are plotted against the n-th inter-spike-interval. The axes are scaled in *ms* time units. (a) $D = 1$, (b) $D = 0.7$, (c) $D = 0.5$, (d) $D = 0.3$, (e) $D = 0$.

distributed) and deleted from the initial Zaslavskii spike train, thus yielding a *sparse Zaslavskii spike train*. Then, the sparse Zaslavskii spike train is merged with a Poissonian spike train with mean firing rate $N(1 - D)/L$ *spikes/s*, thus yielding an *input spike train* with an average rate close to 5 *spikes/s* and a duration of 2000 *s*. In case of overlapping spikes only one event is kept in the input spike train. Notice that if $D = 1$ all input spike trains are identical to the original Zaslavskii spike train and if $D = 0$ all input spike trains are independent Poissonian spike trains. For a given dynamical information ratio D this procedure is repeated 20 times such to provide 20 different input spike trains. In the current simulations the dynamical information ratio ranged from 0 to 1.0 with 0.1 steps. Return maps of input spike trains are shown in Fig. 1.

2.3   Neuronal Network

We consider a diverging/converging neural network composed of three layers (Fig. 2). Each layer includes 20 neurons characterized by the same neuronal model with identical parameter values. Each neuron belonging to the first layer receives fifteen input spike trains randomly selected out of the twenty that were generated for a given dynamical information ratio D. Hence, a neuron in the first layer receives afferences from 15 input spike trains (each one firing on average at $= 5$ *spikes/s*) and an independent Poissonian spike train with a mean firing rate of 425 *spikes/s* as background activity. This means a neuron of the first layer integrates about 500 *spikes* in 1000 *millisecond* by the fourth order Runge-Kutta numerical integration method with 0.01 *ms* time steps. Each neuron of the next layer receives afferences from 15 neurons randomly selected in the previous layer. In addition, each neuron receives an independent Poissonian spike train with a mean firing rate of 425 *spikes/s* as background activity. We observed that those neurons integrated between 490 and 540 *spikes* in 1000 *ms* The explicit synaptic transmission delay is not considered here. All connections were hardwired, and no synaptic plasticity was taken into account. Each simulation run lasted 2000 *s*.

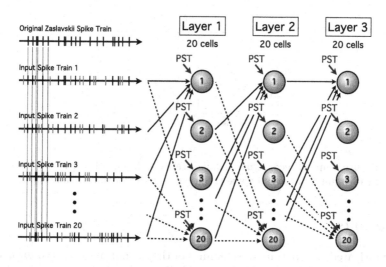

Fig. 2. Convergent/divergent feed-forward circuit formed by three neuron layers. Each cell receives 15 afferent spike trains randomly selected out of 20 and a PST (independent Poissonian spike train).

2.4 Pattern Detection and Reconstruction of Time Series

Subsets of spike trains were obtained by using the Pattern Grouping Algorithm (PGA) [12,13,14] as follows. Firing sequences repeating at least 5 times and above the chance level ($p = 0.05$) are detected by PGA. The interval between the first and the last spike of the firing sequence defines the duration of the pattern that was set to $\leq 600\ ms$. Given a maximum allowed jitter in spike timing accuracy ($\pm 3\ ms$) clusters of firing sequences are represented by a template pattern. For example, if there are 9 triplets (*i.e.*, firing sequences formed by 3 spikes) belonging to the same cluster, a subset of the original spike train that includes 27 spikes ($= 9 \times 3$) can be determined by a template pattern. Then, the subset of the original spike train referred to as "reconstructed spike train" is obtained by pooling all spikes belonging to all template pattern clusters [4]. The reconstructed spike train from the original Zaslavskii series included 92.3% of the original spikes and its return map is shown in Fig. 3a. In a case of a Poissonian spike train with an average rate of 5 *spikes/s* the reconstructed spike train included only 0.4% spikes of the original series (Fig. 3b).

Moreover, we have measured the dispersion of spike distribution by the Fano factor [15], which is $F = 1$ for a Poissonian spike train, and the similarity ratio S between two spike trains defined as follows. Suppose that spike trains A and B contain N_A and N_B spikes and M spikes occur in A and B at the same time. The similarity ratio is defined by $S = 2M/(N_A + N_B)$, which is $S = 1$ for two identical spike trains. If we allow the coincidence to occur within a given jitter ($\Delta = 5\ ms$ here), then the condition $t_B^n - \Delta \leq t_A^k \leq t_B^n + \Delta$ satisfies the coincidence of the n-th spike in train B with the k-th spike in train A.

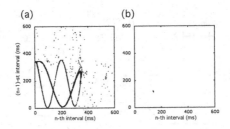

Fig. 3. Return maps of reconstructed spike trains with mean firing rate at 5 *spikes/s*. (a) from the original Zaslavskii spike train; (b) from a Poissonian spike train.

3   Results

We investigated the continuous dynamics of the membrane potential for neurons characterized by the models SSN and MAT and analyzed their output spike trains at all layers. Table 1 summarizes the mean firing rates as a function of the layer and of dynamical information ratio D. The rates increased with an increase of D and for the same D they increased with the order of the layer.

In the 1st layer we analyzed the effect of the model by comparing cells that received the same inputs. Figure 4 shows the example of two different neurons (cells no. 114 and 115) located in the 1st layer. In the bottom panel the input spike trains with dynamical information ratio $D = 0.5$ and the Poissonian background are sorted in order to emphasize the spikes belonging to Zaslavskii. Zaslavskii spikes increase the chance to overlap and to produce a stronger postsynaptic current by temporal summation with an increase in D. In this example, eight spikes belonging to the original Zaslavskii spike train arrive simultaneously at $t = 2150 \ ms$ (see the upward arrow in the last panel of Fig. 4) and evoke a suprathreshold current that generates a spike.

The return maps of the raw output spike trains of one representative neuron of each layer and for each neuronal model are shown in Fig. 5a as a function of D. As D decreased, the attractor contour become blurred. Notice that for exclusive Poissonian input spike trains ($D = 0$) the return maps of the SSN model (Fig. 5a (rightmost column) show a bias in the distribution of points, with empty bands

Table 1. Mean firing rate (spikes/s) of a neuron of SSN and MAT models as a function of the order of the layer (1st-2nd-3rd) and of the dynamical information ratio D. SD ranged between 0.02 and 0.03 spikes/s.

		SSN model							MAT model					
D	1	0.7	0.5	0.4	0.3	0.2	0	1	0.7	0.5	0.4	0.3	0.2	0
1st	6.4	6.1	5.9	5.7	5.4	5.1	4.8	6.6	6.4	6.1	5.7	5.3	4.9	4.5
2nd	6.8	6.6	6.4	6.2	5.8	5.4	5.0	7.7	7.1	6.7	6.4	5.8	5.2	4.5
3rd	7.0	6.9	6.7	6.5	6.1	5.7	5.2	8.9	7.9	7.3	6.9	6.3	5.6	4.7

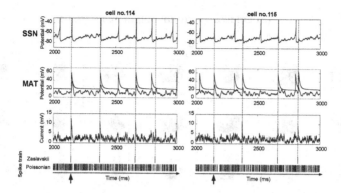

Fig. 4. Left and right panels shows data from two neurons belonging to the 1st layer. Dynamics of the membrane potentials for model SSN (first row) and for model MAT (second row), and the total post-synaptic input current (third row) are shown as a function of the input spike trains (bottom panels) where Zaslavskii and Poissonian spike trains are sorted out. The dynamical information ratio was set to $D = 0.5$.

near the axis, due to an internal temporal structure embedded within the model dynamics. In the MAT model it is interesting to observe that with an increase in the order of the layer the attractor contour become clearer even for D as low as $D = 0.3$. The "reconstructed spike trains" statistics are summarized in Table 2 and the return maps illustrated by Fig. 5b clearly show the noise filtering effect obtained by applying PGA, thus revealing the underlying attractor contour.

Table 2. Firing rate statistics of the reconstructed spike trains of SSN and MAT neurons shown in Fig. 5b as a function of the order of the layer (1st-2nd-3rd) and of the dynamical information ratio D

	SSN model							MAT model						
D	1	0.7	0.5	0.4	0.3	0.2	0	1	0.7	0.5	0.4	0.3	0.2	0
					Firing rate (spikes/s)									
1st	5.2	3.9	2.7	2.1	1.6	1.2	1.1	5.0	5.1	3.4	1.8	1.1	0.3	0.2
2nd	5.0	4.1	3.3	2.7	2.4	1.8	1.3	5.2	5.2	4.6	3.4	1.4	0.3	0.2
3rd	4.8	4.1	3.0	2.9	2.0	1.7	1.5	5.2	5.2	4.8	3.7	1.8	0.8	0.1
					Fano factor									
1st	0.55	0.64	0.97	1.21	1.53	1.86	1.79	0.67	0.64	0.84	1.36	1.84	2.74	2.68
2nd	0.56	0.64	0.81	1.00	1.08	1.37	1.90	0.71	0.73	0.69	0.83	1.71	2.72	2.56
3rd	0.58	0.66	0.91	0.95	1.34	1.50	1.64	0.67	0.70	0.69	0.79	1.48	2.39	3.26
					Similarity ratio (%)									
1st	79.9	58.8	31.9	18.8	9.8	4.6	2.0	89.1	86.7	64.2	38.7	20.0	2.9	0.4
2nd	25.5	8.0	5.1	4.6	4.3	2.7	2.0	86.6	85.2	74.8	57.3	24.4	3.8	0.4
3rd	5.5	5.7	4.8	4.4	3.6	2.8	2.0	87.4	82.0	67.9	49.3	22.1	5.8	0.1

152   Y. Asai and A.E.P. Villa

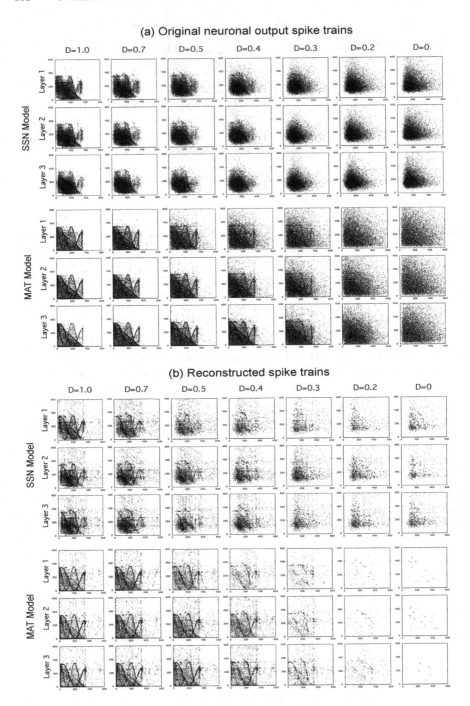

Fig. 5. Return maps of neuronal output spike trains and spike trains reconstructed from them. One neuron from each layer was selected as an example for several dynamical information ratio D and for both of the SSN and MAT models.

With a decrease of D, the number of spikes detected by PGA decreased (*i.e.* the firing rate of the reconstructed spike trains decreased). In the case of SSN significant amount of spikes were detected by PGA even for $D \leq 0.3$, but the return maps don't show the contour of the Zaslavskii attractor and the preferred firing sequences detected by PGA can be attributed to the intrinsic dynamics of the model. On the opposite, the MAT model seldom introduced a temporal structure in the output spike train due to intrinsic model dynamics. With the MAT model notice that the similarity ratio and the firing rate of the reconstructed spike train increased from the 1st to the higher order layers with $D = 0.4$. In both models, the Fano factor was larger for small values of D and became less than 1 at the third layer for both models with $D \geq 0.4$. Looking at the similarity ratio the two models behaved very differently. Furthermore, for the MAT model only the similarity ratio tended to be preserved across the layers for $D \geq 0.5$ and was even near 0.5 in the 3rd layer with $d = 0.4$.

4   Discussion

The deterministic sequence of spikes generated by a chaotic attractor was distributed and embedded in the input spike trains fed to a partially convergent/divergent feed-forward layered network. We have provided evidence that a multiple-timescale adaptive threshold (MAT) neuronal model [9] was able to retain and transmit a sizable amount of the initial temporal information up to the 3rd layer with dynamical information ratio as low as $D = 0.4$. Conversely, a simple spiking neuron (SSN) model [8] introduced a bias in the temporal pattern of the output spike train associated to its model dynamics which interfered with the input temporally organized information. It is interesting to notice that by passing through the successive layers, the similarity ratio of the SSN neurons decreased drastically despite the fact the reconstructed spike train and the Fano factor were kept rather high.

The current study does not pretend to exclude SSN models from being able to preserve and transmit temporal information through complex neural network circuits because we did not carry out a parameter search of that class of models in order to optimize the performance. The MAT model is interesting because in presence of a pure stochastic input very few spikes were detected by the PGA filtering procedure, thus indicating that this model did not introduce a bias. We consider that this work may be viewed as seminal addressing the novel problem because it suggests that MAT class of models might represent a good candidate for integrating a distributed deterministic temporal information and preserve its dynamics through networks of cell assemblies. Our further work is aimed to determine the limits of this performance by increasing the number of layers, designing inhomogeneous and diverging/converging networks with recurrent connections and with the introduction of explicit synaptic delays and spike timing dependent plasticity.

Acknowledgments

This study was partially funded by the bi-national JSPS/INSERM grant SYR-NAN and Japan-France Research Cooperative Program.

References

1. Mpitsos, G.J.: Chaos in brain function and the problem of nonstationarity: a commentary. In: Basar, E., Bullock, T.H. (eds.) Dynamics of Sensory and Cognitive Processing by the Brain, pp. 521–535. Springer, Heidelberg (1989)
2. Celletti, A., Villa, A.E.P.: Determination of chaotic attractors in the rat brain. J. Stat. Physics 84, 1379–1385 (1996)
3. Tetko, I.V., Villa, A.E.: A comparative study of pattern detection algorithm and dynamical system approach using simulated spike trains. In: Gerstner, W., Hasler, M., Germond, A., Nicoud, J.-D. (eds.) ICANN 1997. LNCS, vol. 1327, pp. 37–42. Springer, Heidelberg (1997)
4. Asai, Y., Yokoi, T., Villa, A.E.P.: Detection of a dynamical system attractor from spike train analysis. In: Kollias, S.D., Stafylopatis, A., Duch, W., Oja, E. (eds.) ICANN 2006. LNCS, vol. 4131, pp. 623–631. Springer, Heidelberg (2006)
5. Asai, Y., Guha, A., Villa, A.E.P.: Deterministic neural dynamics transmitted through neural networks. Neural Networks 21, 799–809 (2008)
6. Abeles, M.: Local Cortical Circuits. Springer, Heidelberg (1982)
7. Asai, Y., Villa, A.E.: Spatio temporal filtering of the distributed spike train with deterministic structure by ensemble of spiking neurons. In: The 8th Intenational Neural Coding Workshop Proceedings, Tainan, Taiwan, pp. 81–83 (2009)
8. Izhikevich, E.M.: Which model to use for cortical spiking neurons? IEEE Transactions on Neural Networks 15, 1063–1070 (2004)
9. Kobayashi, R., Tsubo, Y., Shinomoto, S.: Made-to-order spiking neuron model equipped with a multi-timescale adaptive threshold. Front Comput. Neurosci. 3 (2009), doi:10.3389/neuro.10.009.2009
10. Brette, R., Gerstner, W.: Adaptive exponential integrate-and-fire model as an effective description of neuronal activity. J. Neurophysiol. 94, 3637–3642 (2005)
11. Zaslavskii, G.M.: The simplest case of a strange attractor. Phys. Let. 69A, 145–147 (1978)
12. Villa, A.E.P., Tetko, I.V.: Spatiotemporal activity patterns detected from single cell measurements from behaving animals. In: Proceedings SPIE, vol. 3728, pp. 20–34 (1999)
13. Tetko, I.V., Villa, A.E.P.: A pattern grouping algorithm for analysis of spatiotemporal patterns in neuronal spike trains. 1. detection of repeated patterns. J. Neurosci. Meth. 105, 1–14 (2001)
14. Abeles, M., Gat, I.: Detecting precise firing sequences in experimental data. Journal of Neuroscience Methods 107, 141–154 (2001)
15. Sacerdote, L., Villa, A.E., Zucca, C.: On the classification of experimental data modeled via a stochastic leaky integrate and fire model through boundary values. Bull. Math. Biol. 68, 1257–1274 (2006)

Noise-Induced Collective Migration
for Neural Crest Cells

Masataka Yamao[1], Honda Naoki[2], and Shin Ishii[2,3]

[1] Graduate school of information science, Nara Institute of Science and Technology,
8916-5 Takayama, Ikoma, Nara 630-0192 Japan
masataka-y@is.naist.jp
[2] Graduate school of informatics, Kyoto University, Gokasho, Uji,
Kyoto 611-0011, Japan,
n-honda@sys.i.kyoto-u.ac.jp, ishii@i.kyoto-u.ac.jp
[3] RIKEN, 2-1, Hirosawa, Wako, Saitama 351-0198 Japan

Abstract. Formations of neuronal networks and body tissues are controlled by multi-cellular collective migration during embryonic development. Despite the fact that individually migratory cells show stochastic
behaviors, the development is precisely regulated. Although such a property of single cell migration has been investigated, relationship between
microscopic property of individual cell migration and macroscopic multi-
cellular migration remains largely unknown. To explore this, we focused
on migration of neural crest cells, during which cells collectively migrate
accompanied with autonomous formation of stream. Computer simulations of our multi-cellular model suggested that the stochastic migration
in the level of single cells works to efficiently achieve collective migration.

1   Introduction

During embryonic development, cell migration plays an essential role of many biological functions, such as axon guidance for wiring neuronal networks and tissue
formations. Such cell migration is directed by extra-cellular cue molecules as a
chemo-attractant or repellant. The migrating behaviors at the level of individual
cells are often not deterministic but instead innately stochastic, as they perform
a biased random walk up toward gradient of chemo-attractants [1,2]. Although
such a stochastic nature of single cells may seem disadvantageous for precise
control, the embryonic development is a reproducible phenomenon. There must
be homeostatic mechanism by which cellular stochastic nature is absorbed at
the level of multi-cellular systems, although developmental processes should be
unstable enough to break the symmetry for forming biological patterns, whereas
being stable to maintain the reproducibility of the patterns.

Multi-cellular migration shows various types of migration mode, depending
on cell types and time scales of their development. These modes are classified
into two main categoriess, individual and collective migrations [3]. Individual
one is very dispersive allowing cells to cover local area, for example, as immune cell trafficking [4]. Collective migration consists of cohesive multi-cellular

K. Diamantaras, W. Duch, L.S. Iliadis (Eds.): ICANN 2010, Part I, LNCS 6352, pp. 155–163, 2010.
© Springer-Verlag Berlin Heidelberg 2010

units, which function for building complex tissues and axonal projection of developing neurons. It has been recently shown that the migration modes can be experimentally interconverted between individual and collective migrations by manipulating the expression level of proteins underling cell properties [5]; up-regulation of cell adhesion molecule (CAM) in individually migratory cells leads to collective migration [6], whereas down-regulation of CAM in collectively migrating cohort results in individual migration [7,8]. The migrating mode could be transited through alternation of many physical parameters of cell migration, such as driving force, stiffness of the cell and randomness of the migration.

In this study, we examine how these parameters contribute the transition between migration modes. To this end, we focus on "neural crest migration" as a model biological system, because even without extra-cellular signals, neural crest cells collectively migrate to branchial arches from rhombomeres accompanied with forming stream. We constructed a bio-physical model of multi-cellular migration and performed a computer simulation, which led us to hypothesize that migratory cells exploit the stochasticity within the multi-cellular system to efficiently achieve collective migration with autonomous stream.

2   Model

Although the cellular migration is a complicated process, during which a cell receives extracellular signals and processes those through intracellular signal transduction, which controls the cell shape by regulating the reorganization of

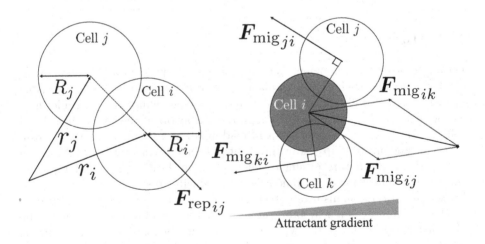

Fig. 1. Model for simulation. If cells indicated by white circles are overlapped, repulsive force F_{rep} is induced (left panel). A migrating cell indicated by a black circle generates driving forces $F_{\mathrm{mig}_{ij}}$, $F_{\mathrm{mig}_{ik}}$ and their reaction forces $F_{\mathrm{mig}_{ji}}$, $F_{\mathrm{mig}_{ki}}$ are also applied to both contacted cells.

cytoskeleton and motor proteins, a minimum of cellular characteristics was extracted in our model, as follows. The model multi-cellular system consists of a number of mechanically interacting cells (Fig. 1). These cells were, for simplicity, regarded as two-dimensional disks whose radiuses are slightly variant, and packed in the two-dimensional rectangular space. In this model, when cells contact, repulsive forces are generated, because deformation of their morphologies is assumed to produce elastic force (Fig. 1, left). To address cell migration, we consider two types of cell, actively migrating and non-migratory cells. The migratory cells are assumed to have chemotactic ability and be attracted by extra-cellular signals toward the same direction with certain randomness. The non-migratory cells are adhered by migratory cells and utilized as ground surface for generating the driving force of migration, satisfying principle of action and reaction (Fig. 1, right). Also, the non-migratory cells are assumed to spontaneously yield random movement. Thus, the dynamics of cellular positions are described as:

$$\eta d\mathbf{r}_i = \left\{ \sum_{j \in \mathcal{N}_i} \mathbf{F}_{\mathrm{rep}_{ij}} + \sum_{j \in \mathcal{M}_i} \mathbf{F}_{\mathrm{mig}_{ij}} \right\} dt + \sigma_i d\mathbf{W}_i \tag{1}$$

$$\mathbf{F}_{\mathrm{rep}_{ij}} = k\left((R_i + R_j) - \|\mathbf{r}_i - \mathbf{r}_j\| \right) \frac{\mathbf{r}_i - \mathbf{r}_j}{\|\mathbf{r}_i - \mathbf{r}_j\|} \tag{2}$$

$$\mathbf{F}_{\mathrm{mig}_{ij}} = \begin{pmatrix} F_{\mathrm{mig}x} \\ F_{\mathrm{mig}y} \end{pmatrix} = s(i) \begin{pmatrix} \frac{\|\Delta y\|}{\|\mathbf{r}_i - \mathbf{r}_j\|} \\ -\frac{\|\Delta y\|}{\Delta y} \frac{\Delta x}{\|\mathbf{r}_i - \mathbf{r}_j\|} \end{pmatrix} \tag{3}$$

$$s(i) = \begin{cases} 1 & \text{cell } i \text{ is migratory} \\ -1 & \text{cell } i \text{ is not migratory} \end{cases} \tag{4}$$

where k: Young modulus, R_i: radius of cell i, $\mathbf{r}_i$: position of cell i, σ_i: fluctuation intensity of cell i, $d\mathrm{W}_i$: independent random variable sampled by Gaussian distribution with variance of $(dt)^2$, $\mathcal{N}_i$: set of indices of all cells contacting with cell i, $\mathcal{M}_i$: index set of another type of cells contacting with i, and η: viscous modulus. In this formulation, acceleration was not addressed under the assumption that viscosity of cellular environment is enough high. In this model, driving forces for rightward migration of a migrating cell depend on the number of contacts with non-migratory cells because action-reaction forces are generated at constant intensity for each contact. Then, a simple geometrical constraint is satisfied, $\mathbf{F}_{\mathrm{mig}} \cdot (\mathbf{r}_i - \mathbf{r}_j) = 0$, $\|\mathbf{F}_{\mathrm{mig}}\| = 1$ and $(\mathbf{F}_{\mathrm{mig}})_x > 0$, leading to equation (3). To avoid the effect from the boundary of the two-dimensional space, torus condition was employed. Parameters used are listed as follows, $k = 10$, $\eta = 1$, R_i is sampled from Gaussian distribution with mean 1 and variance 0.16, and σ_i depend on the simulation, because noise effects are our interest in this study.

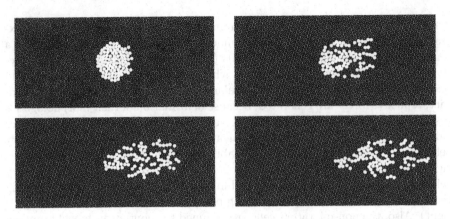

Fig. 2. Snapshots in a single series of simulation. White and black disks indicate migratory and non-migratory cells, respectively. The migratory cells are initially distributed as a cluster at $t = 0$ (upper left panel), then migrate rightward progressively at $t = 16, 32, 48$ (the other three panels). Fluctuation intensities are set to $\sigma_\mathrm{mig} = 0$, $\sigma_\mathrm{n} = 0$.

3 Result

3.1 Noise-Induced Collective Migration

In our simulation, migratory cells were initially distributed in the center of the space and migrated rightward (Fig. 2). Through many simulation runs with changing parameter values, we found there are three specific migration patterns depending on the stochasticity of single cells (Fig. 3). First, when cells are not fluctuated by themselves, the migrating cells form chain-like structure, but this structure is not stably maintained and frequently divided to a couple of small clusters. Second, when migratory cells are strongly fluctuated and non-migratory cells are weakly fluctuated, migratory cells actively move forming one large cellular stream. Third, when migratory cells are weakly fluctuated and non-migratory cells are strongly fluctuated, migratory cells are rapidly dispersed. These simulation results suggest that even though streams of migratory cells are not routed by extra-cellular signals, multi-cellular system has a potential to show such patterns, and that the modes of multi-cellular migration are regulated by both intrinsic noise and environmental noise.

To quantitatively evaluate such an aggregation of migratory cells, we defined an order parameter which is a mean number of migratory cells around themselves:

$$\phi = \frac{1}{\#\mathcal{C}} \sum_{i,j \in \mathcal{C}} H(\bar{R} - \|\boldsymbol{r}_i - \boldsymbol{r}_j\|), \tag{5}$$

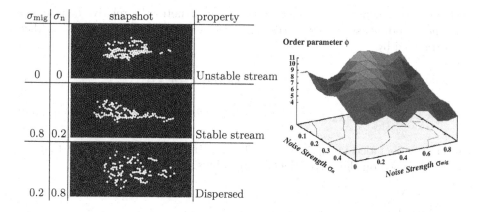

σ_{mig}	σ_{n}	snapshot	property
0	0		Unstable stream
0.8	0.2		Stable stream
0.2	0.8		Dispersed

Fig. 3. Effect of cellular stochastic property on migrating modes. Left table summarizes specific migrating patterns depending on the parameters, where σ_{mig} and σ_{n} indicate fluctuation intensities of migratory and non-migratory cells. Right figure shows the order parameter indicated by equation (5), against various pairs of noise strengths of migratory and non-migratory cells.

where $\mathcal{C}$ is the index set of chemotactic cells, $\bar{R}$ is a constant set to 5 here, and $H(x)$ is the Heaviside step function. Fig. 3 (right) shows how this order parameter depends on the strength of stochasticity in migrating and non-migratory cells. Even though fluctuation intuitively facilitates mixing the migratory cells, an optimal stochasticity exists for achieving collective migration as Fig. 3 (right) shows.

3.2 Long-Distant Interaction between the Migratory Cells

Although each cell has solely repulsive force with adjacent cells, in our model, the migratory cells seem to be attractive each other for the collective mode, so that their interaction could be complex and long-distant. To examine the effective interaction between migratory cells, we reconstruct effective potential field between the cells, assuming that cellular movement is determined by

$$\frac{\mathrm{d}\boldsymbol{r}}{\mathrm{d}t} = -\frac{\partial U}{\partial \boldsymbol{r}} + \begin{pmatrix} v \\ 0 \end{pmatrix}, \tag{6}$$

where v indicates average velocity due to driving force for migration. To reconstruct the potential, we simulated the system including only two migratory cells, and then obtained vector field of velocity as a function of relative coordinates between the two cells. Although the potential is usually obtained by directly integrating vector field with respective to $\boldsymbol{r}$, we took a different approach; potential was described by a parametric polynomial function;

$$U(x,y) = a_{00} + a_{10}x + a_{01}y + a_{20}x^2 + a_{11}xy + a_{02}y^2 + \cdots, \tag{7}$$

where a_{ij} is coefficient of $x^i y^j$ and $\boldsymbol{x} = (x, y)$ denotes the relative coordinates on the two-dimensional space. Relative velocity of the migrating cell is then re-expressed by

$$v_x = \frac{\partial U}{\partial x} = a_{10} + 2a_{20}x + a_{11}y + \cdots, \tag{8}$$

$$v_y = \frac{\partial U}{\partial y} = a_{01} + a_{11}x + 2a_{02}y + \cdots, \tag{9}$$

where v is included in a_{10}. These coefficients are estimated by the least square method, based on the vector field sampled by simulations:

$$
\begin{pmatrix} a_{10} \\ a_{01} \\ a_{20} \\ a_{11} \\ a_{02} \\ a_{30} \\ a_{21} \\ a_{12} \\ a_{03} \\ \vdots \end{pmatrix} = -
\begin{pmatrix}
1 & 0 & 2x_1 & y_1 & 0 & 3x_1^2 & 2x_1y_1 & y_1^2 & 0 & \cdots \\
0 & 1 & 0 & x_1 & 2y_1 & 0 & x_1^2 & 2x_1y_1 & 3y_1^2 & \cdots \\
1 & 0 & 2x_2 & y_2 & 0 & 3x_2^2 & 2x_2y_2 & y_2^2 & 0 & \cdots \\
0 & 1 & 0 & x_2 & 2y_2 & 0 & x_2^2 & 2x_2y_2 & 3y_2^2 & \cdots \\
1 & 0 & 2x_3 & y_3 & 0 & 3x_3^2 & 2x_3y_3 & y_3^2 & 0 & \cdots \\
0 & 1 & 0 & x_3 & 2y_3 & 0 & x_3^2 & 2x_3y_3 & 3y_3^2 & \cdots \\
\vdots & \vdots & \vdots & \vdots & \vdots & \vdots & \vdots & \vdots & \vdots & \ddots
\end{pmatrix}^{\dagger}
\begin{pmatrix} v_{x1} \\ v_{y1} \\ v_{x2} \\ v_{y2} \\ v_{x3} \\ v_{y3} \\ \vdots \end{pmatrix}, \tag{10}
$$

where $\dagger$ denotes Moore-Penrose pseudoinverse.

Potential landscapes were determined for two cases that the cluster of the migratory cells was and was not stably maintained (Fig. 4). In the first case, the potential landscape shapes as saddle-node, which indicates that the migratory cells in parallel are attracting each other and then tandemly arrayed in, leading

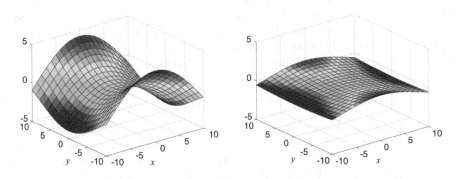

Fig. 4. Potential landscape representing interaction between the two migratory cells.The cell migrates according to the slope of the potential due to the effect of the other cell at the original point, which is migrating along a line $y = 0$. Left and right panels indicate the cases where the collective migration was and was not stably maintained which correspond to stable stream and dispersed as shown in Fig. 3.

to the collective migration. In the latter case, the potential becomes almost flat (slightly saddle-node), suggesting no attractive interaction between the migratory cells. These results also support our hypothesis of noise-induced collective migration

3.3 The Speed of Collective Migration

Next, we investigated the effect of population size of migrating cells. We found that increase in the population allows the collective migration to emerge more stably and to speed up in a saturating manner (Fig. 5, green line), which is consistent with experiments [9]. We additionally examined the relationship between the speed and stiffness which is another important property of cells (Fig. 5, red and blue lines). When all the cells are soft, the speed of the collective migrating becomes independent of the population size, because the driving force of migration is enough to overcome the potential field produced by surrounding cells. When they are hard, on the other hand, the collective migration slows down due to strong potential barrier produced by hard surrounding cells.

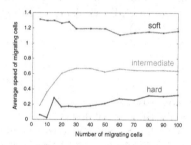

Fig. 5. The average speed profile of migratory cells depending on their population size and stiffness. Soft, intermediate and hard cells are represented by $k = 5, 10, 15$, respectively. Other parameters are set as follows, $\sigma_{mig} = 0.8$, $\sigma_n = 0.2$.

4 Disccusion

By simulating multi-cellular migration by simple mechanistic cells, we have found such a system can emerge collective migration typically seen in neural crest cell systems. In our model, the cellular migration is modeled as just applying driving force to the cell toward a specific direction with randomness, while reaction forces are applied to neighboring cells. However, an in vivo mechanism of cellular migration must be more complicated than we have assumed here. In reality, a chemotactic cell extends special structures called filopodia and lamellipodia, with which cytoskeletal network regulates cell motility. Although we ignored a complex rheological property of such structures [10], the minimum model that we adopted was still informative in understanding the system property of multi-cellular migration.

Our model can explain neural crest migration with formation of stream. This collective migration was hypothetically thought to be extra-cellularly regulated by repulsive cue molecule [11]. Recently, however, it has been reported that down-regulation of repulsive cue, neurophilin-1, does not affect the collective migration of neural crest cells [12]. Our model indicates that a combination of physical interplay between the cells and stochastic nature of migration leads to the collective migration with autonomous formation of stream.

How chemotactic cells manage to suppress intrinsic stochasticity of signal transduction has been previously discussed [1], whereas multi-cellular functions that are actively organized by stochastic migration of individual cells have not been examined. Therefore, our work is first presenting a possible model for emerging collective motion of multi-cellular systems.

Acknowledgments

This study was partially supported by the Global COE Program (M.Y.) and a research fellowship from the Japan Society for the Promotion of Science (19-11235 to H.N.) both from the MEXT (Ministry of Education, Culture, Sports, Science, and Technology of Japan).

References

1. Ueda, M., Shibata, T.: Stochastic signal processing and transduction in chemotactic response of eukaryotic cells. Biophysical Journal 93, 11–20 (2007)
2. Naoki, H., Sakumura, Y., Ishii, S.: Stochastic control of spontaneous signal generation for gradient sensing in chemotaxis. Journal of Theoretical Biology 255, 259–266 (2008)
3. Friedl, P., Wolf, K.: Plasticity of cell migration: a multiscale tuning model. Journal of Cell Biology 188, 11–19 (2009)
4. Arrieumerlou, C., Meyer, T.: A local coupling model and compass parameter for eukaryotic chemotaxis. Developmental Cell 8, 215–227 (2005)
5. Friedl, P., Gilmour, D.: Collective cell migration in morphogenesis, regeneration and cancer. Nature Reviews Molecular Cell Biology 10, 445–457 (2009)
6. Thiery, J.: Epithelial–mesenchymal transitions in tumour progression. Nature Reviews Cancer 2, 442–454 (2002)
7. Hegerfeldt, Y., Tusch, M., Brocker, E., Friedl, P.: Collective Cell Movement in Primary Melanoma Explants: Plasticity of Cell-Cell Interaction,{beta} 1-Integrin Function, and Migration Strategies. Cancer Research 62, 2125–2130 (2002)
8. Wolf, K., Wu, Y., Liu, Y., Geiger, J., Tam, E., Overall, C., Stack, M., Friedl, P.: Multi-step pericellular proteolysis controls the transition from individual to collective cancer cell invasion. Nature Cell Biology 9, 893–904 (2007)
9. Young, H., Bergner, A., Anderson, R., Enomoto, H., Milbrandt, J., Newgreen, D., Whitington, P.: Dynamics of neural crest-derived cell migration in the embryonic mouse gut. Developmental Biology 270, 455–473 (2004)

10. Lim, C., Zhou, E., Quek, S.: Mechanical models for living cells–a review. Journal of Biomechanics 39, 195–216 (2006)
11. Eickholt, B., Mackenzie, S., Graham, A., Walsh, F., Doherty, P.: Evidence for collapsin-1 functioning in the control of neural crest migration in both trunk and hindbrain regions. Development 126, 2181–2189 (1999)
12. McLennan, R., Kulesa, P.: In vivo analysis reveals a critical role for neuropilin-1 in cranial neural crest cell migration in chick. Developmental Biology 301, 227–239 (2007)

Unsupervised Learning of Relations

Matthew Cook[1,*], Florian Jug[2], Christoph Krautz[2,**], and Angelika Steger[2]

[1] Institute of Neuroinformatics,
University of Zurich and ETH Zurich, Switzerland
cook@ini.phys.ethz.ch
[2] Institute of Theoretical Computer Science,
ETH Zurich, Switzerland
{fjug,ckrautz,asteger}@inf.ethz.ch

Abstract. Learning processes allow the central nervous system to learn relationships between stimuli. Even stimuli from different modalities can easily be associated, and these associations can include the learning of mappings between observable parameters of the stimuli. The data structures and processing methods of the brain, however, remain very poorly understood. We investigate the ability of simple, biologically plausible processing mechanisms to learn such relationships when the data is represented using population codes, a coding scheme that has been found in a variety of cortical areas. We require that the relationships are learned not just from the point of view of an omniscient observer, but rather the network itself must be able to make effective use of the learned relationship, within the population code representations. Using a form of Hebbian learning, local winner-take-all, and homeostatic activity regulation away from the periphery, we obtain a learning framework which is able to learn relationships from examples and then use the learned relationships for a variety of routine nervous system tasks such as inference, de-noising, cue-integration, and decision making.

1 Introduction

One of the key properties of the brain is the ability to notice and learn the relations between inputs in an unsupervised manner [1, 2, 3, 4]. It is believed that this is achieved by modifying the structure [5, 6, 7] and the dynamics [8, 9, 10] of biological neural networks, for example through the plasticity of synapses or other neural processes [11, 12, 13].

Phenomenologically, the ability of brains to discover relationships between otherwise independent events has been known since the pioneering work by Pavlov [2]. His work on dogs showed that a neutral stimulus (the ringing of a bell) can be induced to elicit an associated reaction (production of saliva) by ringing a bell every time the dog gets food. After training, the association between the bell and salivation may be due to the food representation being activated by the bell representation.

* Supported by EU Project Grant FET-IP-216593.
** Supported by ETH Research Grant ETH-23 08-1.

In the following decades, it became clear that the ability to learn relations between different sensory inputs is in fact omnipresent in our brains. As an example of an inference task, when we hear a sound, we can use the audio input to estimate (*inference*) the visual location of the corresponding visual input. This process is continually maintained by learning mechanisms: if we wear prism glasses that shift the visual input, it is possible to re-learn the correspondence. Or, given uncertain visual and audio cues about the location of a stimulus, we can combine these cues (*cue-integration*) to get a better estimate of the location. If visual and audio cues differ so much as to be inconsistent, for example due to light or sound being reflected so as to appear to have a different source, then we simply base our position estimate on the stronger of the two competing inputs (*decision*).

Biological data shows that neural populations, regions and areas encode specific sensory, motor, and cognitive modalities (see e.g. [14, 15] and contained references). Connected regions exchange signals and thus influence their mutual activity [14], and simulations have also exhibited such interactions in networks with hand-crafted connectivity [9, 15, 16]. Simulations such as these have shown how inference, de-noising, cue-integration, or decision tasks can be performed on input received from different visual, motor, or other sources, for complex problems like coordinate transformations. However, exhibiting these abilities in networks that learn the relationships, rather than using hand-crafted weights, has remained a challenge.

Given the presence of such abilities in the brain, the question that immediately arises is *how* the brain implements them. A major step in this regard was achieved by Zipser and Andersen [17], who trained an artificial neural network with simulated biological data using the backpropagation algorithm [18]. In their network, hidden nodes developed gain field properties [17]. While their result shows that neural networks are able to learn such tasks in principle, the learning strategy they used seems unlikely to be the one used in our brains: the back-propagation algorithm is a supervised learning scheme, using an externally generated error signal, and it is generally considered to be biologically implausible [19, 20].

Our goal is to exhibit the ability to learn arbitrary relationships using biologically plausible learning. We present a model that can learn the relationships between inputs in an *unsupervised* way (that is, without externally supplied error signals). In fact, our model is purely based on biologically motivated building blocks like population coding, Hebbian learning, and homeostatic activity regulation. After learning the relationship, our model can use the learned relation to improve its population code representations: the network will produce population codes for missing inputs based on supplied inputs (*inference*), will smooth noisy population codes (*de-noising*), will adjust population codes to be more consistent with each other (*cue-integration*), and will choose between alternative population code representations when faced with inconsistent data (*decision*).

A key feature of our network is that its dynamics do not have to be modified from outside in order to switch between these tasks, or even to re-learn a relationship when it changes.

2   The Network and Its Dynamics

In this paper we consider the following network (see Figure 1) to demonstrate how relations between two sets of parameters X and Y can be learned. The network consists of two populations, A and B, consisting of n rate coded units each.

2.1   The Network

The units in A get input from an external source X by point-to-point connections, i.e., each unit in A receives input from exactly one unit in X and each unit in X sends input to exactly one unit in A. Similarly, a second input Y, is connected to B by point-to-point connections. X and Y are supposed to encode one single scalar value each. To realize this encoding we use what is known as population coding, see e.g. [21]. Intuitively, this means that each unit in X has one preferred value and that its firing rate depends on how close its preferred value is to the actual value. In Figure 1 we illustrated this encoding by representing X and Y by two (noisy) population codes.

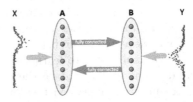

Fig. 1. Projection diagram of the sample network discussed in the text: two populations with bidirectional connectivity. Labeled ellipses represent populations of neural nodes. Dark gray arrows depict directed, full connectivity, light gray arrows indicate point to point connections used to feed population coded input into the network. Blue dots show one possible input of this kind.

The units within each of the populations A and B are laterally interconnected such that each population is effectively a soft winner-take-all circuit [22]. The connection weight $w_{i,j}$ between units i and j is defined as:

$$w_{i,j} = \gamma \cdot e^{-\frac{1}{2}(d(i,j)/\sigma)^2} - \delta. \tag{1}$$

The distance d between i and j is $d(i,j) = \min\{|i - j|, n - |i - j|\}$. In order to avoid boundary effects we let the distance measure wrap around. (Note that this implies that we identify the smallest value $v_{\min}$ and the largest value $v_{\max}$ encoded by the population code. In the case $v_{\min} = 0$ this means that we perform calculations modulo $v_{\max}$.)

Besides being laterally connected, the units in A and B are also interconnected. Effectively we connect each unit $i \in A$ to all units $j \in B$ and vice versa. The initial connection weights $w_{i,j}$ are set to values chosen randomly in $[0, 1]$.

Learning the relations between the inputs X and Y is done by adapting the connections between the populations A and B using a Hebbian learning rule [23].

2.2   The Dynamics

We simulate our network over discrete time steps. At time t the rate-coded units in A and B each have a real-valued activity level a, which we denote with a superscript as a^t. At each time step t each unit j updates its activity level a_j^t. This update is influenced by (*i*) the activities of the neurons in the same populations (via the lateral connections), (*ii*) the activities of the units in the other population (via the connections between A and B), and (*iii*) a homeostatic activity regulation term h_j^t (used to keep the activity level of each unit roughly constant over time).

We explain the details of the update below. Here we just outline the interplay between the main ingredients. The lateral connections implement soft winner-take-all dynamics (WTA) [22]. Essentially, they are used to "clean-up" noisy input. The weights $w_{i,j}^t$ between the populations A and B are updated by a Hebbian learning (HL) scheme, eventually encoding the learned relationship. The homeostatic activity regulation (HAR) [24] forces units to regulate themselves so that each unit is active roughly a given proportion of the time. This makes sure that every unit is used, and that each unit is used in moderation.

It is worth noting that the presented components work on quite different time scales. The WTA dynamics operate on a short time scale, allowing the network to converge quickly. HAR and HL operate on a much longer time scale, averaging over a much larger sample of inputs. A sketch of how Hebbian learning (HL), soft winner-take-all (WTA) and homeostatic activity regulation (HAR) play together is illustrated in Figure 2.

Hebbian Learning. The update of the weights $w_{i,j}^t$ depends on (*i*) the activities a_i^t and a_j^t of units i and j at time t, and (*ii*) two global parameters α_l and α_d. The Hebbian learning rate α_l regulates the speed at which connections get learned and is usually set to the same value as α_d, the Hebbian decay rate. The weights are updated according to:

$$w_{i,j}^{t+1} = (1 - \alpha_d) \cdot w_{i,j}^t + \alpha_l \cdot a_i^t \cdot a_j^t . \tag{2}$$

To speed up the running time of simulations it suffices to do these updates only after the WTA converged.

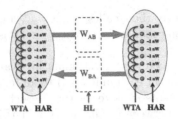

Fig. 2. The presented mechanism is a combination of three strategies. Synaptic connections between areas are controlled by Hebbian learning (HL). Local connections within an area support soft winner-take-all (WTA) dynamics, so nearby units within an area exhibit similar activity patterns. Homeostatic activity regulation (HAR) within each unit modulates the Hebbian learning so that a unit does not become permanently active or inactive, but maintains a desired average activity level.

Homeostatic Activity Regulation. We use the following update formula for the homeostatic activity terms:

$$h_j^t = -c \cdot \left(\bar{a}_j^t - a_{\text{target}} \right), \tag{3}$$

where a_{target} is a parameter and

$$\bar{a}_j^t = (1 - \omega)\bar{a}_j^{t-1} + \omega a_j^t \tag{4}$$

for some additional parameter ω defining the decay rate of the averaging.

Neural Units and Update Dynamics. At each discrete time step t each unit j updates its activity level a_j^t. To compute it we first take the weighted sum over the activity levels of all units connected to unit j. This includes both the lateral connectivity within the population as well as the connections coming from other populations. This sum is corrected by the homeostatic activity regulation term h_j^t. Finally we apply a non-linear function θ that restricts the activity level to the range $[0, 1]$. Formally the update rule is defined as

$$a_j^{t+1} = \theta\!\left(h_j^t + \sum_{i \in \Gamma_j^{\text{in}}} w_{i,j}^t \cdot a_i^t \right), \tag{5}$$

where Γ_j^{in} is the set of units connected to unit j, and

$$\theta(x) = \frac{1}{1 + e^{-m(x-s)}} \tag{6}$$

and m and s are parameters that determine the slope and the shift of $\theta(x)$.

3   Results

In the following we present our experimental results. Note that the network dynamics introduced in the previous chapter remains unchanged throughout all experiments that we present. In order to switch from one task to another we only change the input fed to the network.

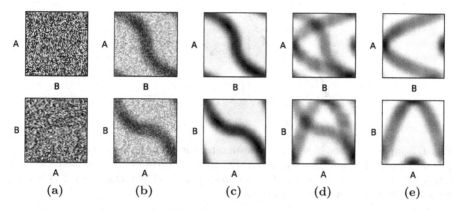

Fig. 3. The time course of learning and relearning in the sample network. Each plotted subfigure shows a snapshot of the connection weights W_{AB} (top row) and W_{BA} (bottom row) for different times during learning and relearning. The weights are color coded (black for strong, white for weak connections). **(a)** Initial random weights. **(b)** Weights captured during learning. **(c)** Weights after the relation $y = x^3$ was learned. **(d)** Weights captured during relearning. **(e)** Weights after the relation $y = x^2$ was learned.

3.1 Learning and Relearning

In order to feed interpretable input we have set a preferred stimulus p_i for each node i in A and B. To encode the value v in X (or Y) we set the input x_i (y_i) for node i in A (B) according to:

$$x_i(v) = C \cdot e^{-(v-p_i)^2/(2\sigma^2)} . \tag{7}$$

This enables us to feed arbitrary scalar values to populations A and B. If these values satisfy any functional relation, the network will learn the relationship hidden in a sequence of input pairs. Note that the weights between populations A and B are constantly changing over time. If after a certain relationship was learned the input changes and a different relation is presented the weights will change to reflect the new relation. Figure 3 shows how the weight matrices W_{AB} and W_{BA} change in the course of learning and relearning.

3.2 Inference Tasks

After the network has learned a relation we can then also omit one of the inputs and infer the other value. This is done as follows. We only feed input in X (or in Y) and let the network converge. After convergence one can use the activities in A and B to compute the population vector [25] giving us the values v_A and v_B encoded by A and B.

Figure 6 shows the result of such inference tasks. We tested the inference accuracy by encoding all values $v_i \in \{p_i | i \in A\}$ in X (respectively all values $v_j \in \{p_j | j \in B\}$ in Y) and observing the values v_B (respectively v_A) computed by the network.

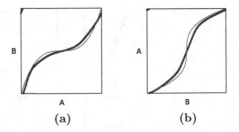

Fig. 4. Simple inference in sample network after the network has learned the relation $y = x^3$ (green thin line in both plots). **(a)** shows the results of the inference tasks (thick blue line) for a set of population codes fed to A (horizontal axis). **(b)** like (a) but for the opposite inference direction.

3.3   De-noising and Cue-Integration Tasks

In all of the following examples we add some noise on top of the activations computed with Equation (7). Figure 5(a) shows how the network performs inference with noisy input.

In addition to such noisy input signals our network can also cope with noisy values v_X and v_Y. Figure 5(b) is an example for the case when the inputs in X and Y are not in line with the learned relation R. The network settles in a state where the computed values v_A and v_B are again consistent with R. Figure 5(c) shows the same experiment but with different input strength set in X and Y. Note that the population receiving the stronger input gets significantly less shifted towards a place consistent with R than the other one.

Note that the soft winner-take-all implemented in our populations A and B is the reason for the described phenomena to work.

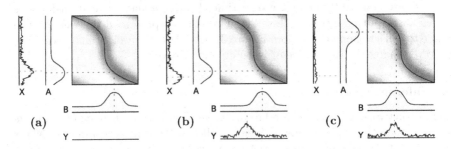

Fig. 5. Inference and de-noising: **(a)** An example of inference from X to B which shows also the de-noising properties of the network with respect to noise in the firing rates of the units, **(b)** when two inputs are presented which are inconsistent with the learned relation the network shifts both peaks until their positions are in accordance with the relation, **(c)** same as (b) but with unequal reliability of the inputs (unequal input strength); note that the larger (more reliable) peak is much less shifted than in (b).

Clearly, such a de-noising task gets more and more difficult (and unreliable) depending on "how much" the value fed into Y differs from the "true" value that is consistent with the input in X. Eventually, if this difference gets too large, then the system will stop to find a compromise between these two values and instead will start to neglect one of the inputs. That, is the network will decide between the two values.

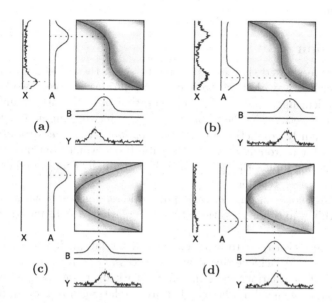

Fig. 6. Decision tasks. **(a)** when the peaks of the inputs are not close to the learned relationship the network uses one of the inputs and infers the other one, **(b)** when in X there are two contradicting inputs present, while one is being supported by the input in Y, the network decides for that combination of peaks., **(c)** in the case of a non-invertible function like $y = x^2$ there exist two possible peak positions and the system decides for one of the two, **(d)** same as (c) but the network's decision is biased by a very small input fed to X.

3.4 Decision Tasks

As indicated at the end of the previous section, the network can be forced to decide whether to follow input X or input Y. Figure 6 shows the input and the settled state for four decisions being performed by the network.

Given inputs of similar strength the variance in the noise determines how the network will decide. If the inputs are of equal strength the network will essentially decide on one of them "randomly", meaning that small artifacts from the learning history will be responsible for the decision.

Figure 6(b) illustrates another, more complicated decision task. In this example the input in X actually contains two peaks. If the second input relates to one of these two peaks (with respect to R), the network will reinforce this peak and settle in a state consistent with R.

If the learned relation R corresponds to a non-invertible function (like $y = x^2$ for x in $[-1, 1]$) then, clearly, an input in Y may be in correspondence with more than one consistent X-value. The network will then have to pick one of the possible solutions. This example is illustrated in Figure 6(c). In addition, Figure 6(d) illustrates that already a seemingly small "noise" in the input in X suffices to move the generated value to the one that has a higher consistency with the input.

4 Discussion

In this paper we showed that it is possible to setup the dynamics of a simple network in such a way that it can learn the relations between two inputs X and Y. After learning, that is, after presentation of sufficiently many related input pairs, the network is then able to (*i*) *infer* missing input, (*ii*) to mediate between slightly conflicting inputs (*de-noising*), (*iii*) *cue-integration*, and (*iv*) *decide* between strongly conflicting inputs. If one would continue to present strongly conflicting inputs the system will then gradually change and eventually have learned the new relation.

The building blocks of our network, population coding, soft winner-take-all, Hebbian learning, and homeostatic activity regulation, are all biologically well motivated.

The next step, clearly, is to learn higher order relations between more than two input signals. To achieve this it will be necessary to replace the effectively one-dimensional populations used in our network by more complex recurrent networks capable of encoding these higher order relationships. Indeed, the internal connectivity of the areas, reflecting the topology of the input space, would ideally be learned based on the observed inputs themselves. This would allow both higher dimensional transformations (such as those related to gain fields [9]) and more abstract relationships to be learned with the same mechanisms.

References

[1] Carew, T.J., Hawkins, R.D., Kandel, E.: Differential classical conditioning of a defensive withdrawal reflex in aplysia californica. Science 219(4583), 397–400 (1983)
[2] Pavlov, I.: Conditioned Reflexes: An Investigation of the Physiological Activity of the Cerebral Cortex. Oxford University Press, London (1927)
[3] Rescorla, R., Wagner, A.: Variations in the Effectiveness of Reinforcement and Nonreinforcement. In: Classical Conditioning II: Current Research and Theory, pp. 64–99. Appleton-Century-Crofts, New York (1972)
[4] Wagner, A.R., Logan, F.A., Haberlandt, K., Price, T.: Stimulus selection in animal discrimination learning. J. Exp. Psychol. 76(2), 171–180 (1968)
[5] Bailey, C., Kandel, E.: Structural changes accompanying memory storage. Annu. Rev. Physiol. 55, 397–426 (1993)
[6] Bailey, C., Chen, M.: Morphological basis of long-term habituation and sensitization in aplysia. Science 220(4592), 91–93 (1983)
[7] Bailey, C., Chen, M.: Morphological basis of short-term habituation in aplysia. J. Neurosci. 8(7), 2452–2459 (1988)

[8] Kandel, E., Spencer, W.A.: Electrophysiology of hippocampal neurons. ii. after-potentials and repetitive firing. J. Neurophysiol. 24, 243–259 (1961)

[9] Salinas, E., Sejnowski, T.: Gain modulation in the central nervous system: where behavior, neurophysiology, and computation meet. Neuroscientist, 430–440 (2001)

[10] Rutishauser, U., Ross, I., Mamelak, A., Schuman, E.: Human memory strength is predicted by theta-frequency phase-locking of single neurons. Nature (2010) (online first)

[11] Barco, A., Bailey, C.H., Kandel, E.: Common molecular mechanisms in explicit and implicit memory. J. Neurochem. 97(6), 1520–1533 (2006)

[12] Kandel, E.: Cellular mechanisms of learning and the biological basis of individuality. In: Principles of Neural Science, 4th edn., McGraw-Hill, New York (1991)

[13] Martin, S.J., Grimwood, P.D., Morris, R.G.: Synaptic plasticity and memory: an evaluation of the hypothesis. Annu. Rev. Neurosci. 23, 649–711 (2000)

[14] Felleman, D., Essen, D.V.: Distributed hierarchical processing in the primate cerebral cortex. Cereb. Cortex 1(1), 1–47 (1991)

[15] Salinas, E., Abbott, L.F.: Coordinate transformations in the visual system: how to generate gain fields and what to compute with them. Prog. Brain Res. 130, 175–190 (2001)

[16] Pouget, A., Sejnowski, T.: Spatial transformations in the parietal cortex using basis functions. J. Cognitive Neurosci. 9(2), 222–237 (1997)

[17] Zipser, D., Andersen, R.A.: A back-propagation programmed network that simulates response properties of a subset of posterior parietal neurons. Nature 331(6158), 679–684 (1988)

[18] Rumelhart, D.E., Hinton, G., Williams, R.J.: Learning representations by back-propagating errors. Nature 323, 533–536 (1986)

[19] Crick, F.: The recent excitement about neural networks. Nature 337, 129–132 (1989)

[20] Zipser, D., Rumelhart, D.: The neurobiological significance of the new learning models. In: Computational Neuroscience. MIT Press, Cambridge (1993)

[21] Deneve, S., Latham, P., Pouget, A.: Efficient computation and cue integration with noisy population codes. Nat. Neurosci. 4(8), 826–831 (2001)

[22] Douglas, R., Martin, K.: Recurrent neuronal circuits in the neocortex. Curr. Biol. 17(13), 496–500 (2007)

[23] Hebb, D.: The Organization of Behavior: A Neuropsychological Theory. Wiley, New York (1949)

[24] Turrigiano, G., Nelson, S.: Homeostatic plasticity in the developing nervous system. Nat. Rev. Neurosci. 5, 97–107 (2004)

[25] Georgopoulos, A.P., Kalaska, J.F., Caminiti, R., Massey, J.T.: On the relations between the direction of two-dimensional arm movements and cell discharge in primate motor cortex. J. Neurosci. 2(11), 1527–1537 (1982)

Learning Internal Representation of Visual Context in a Neural Coding Network

Jun Miao[1], Baixian Zou[2], Laiyun Qing[3], Lijuan Duan[4], and Yu Fu[5]

[1] Key Laboratory of Intelligent Information Processing, Institute of Computing Technology,
Chinese Academy of Sciences, Beijing 100190, China
[2] Department of Information Science and Technology, College of Arts and Science of Beijing
Union University, Beijing 100083, China
[3] School of Information Science and Engineering,
Graduate University of the Chinese Academy of Sciences, Beijing 100049, China
[4] College of Computer Science and Technology, Beijing University of Technology,
Beijing 100124, China
[5] Department of Computing, University of Surrey, Guildford, Surrey, UK GU2 7XH
jmiao@ict.ac.cn, zoubx@ygi.edu.cn, lyqing@gucas.ac.cn,
ljduan@bjut.edu.cn, y.fu@surrey.ac.uk

Abstract. Visual context plays a significant role in humans' gaze movement for target searching. How to transform the visual context into the internal representation of a brain-like neural network is an interesting issue. Population cell coding is a neural representation mechanism which was widely discovered in primates' visual neural system. This paper presents a biologically inspired neural network model which uses a population cell coding mechanism for visual context representation and target searching. Experimental results show that the population-cell-coding generally performs better than the single-cell-coding system.

Keywords: Visual context, Neural Coding, object search.

1 Introduction

Contextual cues play an important role in target searching in human vision system, which are proved by psychological experiments [1]. Only a small number of research work [2-5] utilized global or local context for object locating. Miao and et al. [5] proposed a visual perceiving and eyeball-motion controlling neural network to search target by reasoning with visual context that is encoded with a singe cell coding mechanism. This representation mechanism led to a relatively large encoding quantity for memorizing the prior knowledge about the target's spatial relationship contained in the visual context. The single-cell-coding means using one cell or one response to represent one object or control the movement. In contrast to it, the population-cell-coding uses an ensemble of cells or responses to represent an object or synthesize a movement [6]. Single and population cell coding mechanisms have been an argumentative issue in understanding human brain and vision functions, which was discussed and debated in the special issue for binding problem [7]. Wang [8] addressed that the

K. Diamantaras, W. Duch, L.S. Iliadis (Eds.): ICANN 2010, Part I, LNCS 6352, pp. 174–183, 2010.
© Springer-Verlag Berlin Heidelberg 2010

main problem of the single-cell-coding is that it would not allow perceiving novel objects, which is an ability of the perceptual system. In this paper, we propose a visual neural network system that encodes the top-down knowledge of visual context and reasoning the location of the target using population cell coding mechanism.

2 Visual Context Encoding Architecture and Algorithms

Visual context is related to two types of features: low-level features for global or local image representation and the high-level features for representing spatial relationship in terms of horizontal and the vertical distances (Δx, Δy) between two object centers or between the center of a target and the center of global or local image.

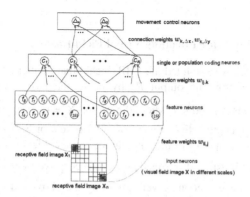

Fig. 1. Single or population cell coding structure for visual field image representation and gaze movement controlling

A unified neural coding structure is designed for learning the internal representation of the visual context, which can implement single and population cell coding mechanisms, as illustrated in Fig. 1. The coding structure consists of two parts. The first part is visual field image encoding, which includes the first three layers: the first layer - input neurons, the second layer - feature neurons, and the third layer - single or population cell coding neurons. This coding system inputs a local image from a group of visual fields in different resolutions. Then it extracts features and encodes the current visual field image in terms of connection weights between the second layer and the third layer. The second part is the spatial relationship encoding and decoding, which includes the last two layers: the third layer - single or population coding neurons and the fourth layer- movement control neurons. It encodes the spatial relationship either between two object centers or between the center of the target and the center of the current visual field image in the connection weights between the third layer and the fourth layer, which correspond to the horizontal and vertical shift distances (Δx, Δy) from the center position (x, y) of the current visual field to the center of the target.

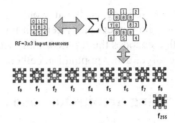

Fig. 2. Extend LBP features extracted by 256 feature neurons, each of which is computed by a sum of eight pairs of differences between surrounding pixels (labels=0~7) and the central pixel (label=8) in its receptive field (RF) =3×3 input neurons (pixels). They are illustrated in the 256 feature templates above, in which the gray box represents weight 1 while the black box represents weight −1.

2.1 Features Employed for Encoding Visual Field Image

As illustrated in Fig. 2, we extended the LBP (local binary patterns) [9] features to the new features with continuous output R_{ij} by using the basis functions { $f_j(\mathbf{X}_i)$ } ($0 \leq j \leq 255$) in Equations (1) and (2), where the vector $\mathbf{X}_i = (x_{i0}\ x_{i2}...x_{i8})^T$ represents the i-th image block or receptive field image of 3×3 pixels or 3×3 input neurons. The term R_{ij} represents the response of the j-th feature extracted from the i-th image block.

In our coding system illustrated in Fig. 1, for each receptive field image $\mathbf{x}_i$, there are 256 feature neurons in the second layer extracting the above extended LBP features { $R_{ij} = f_j(\mathbf{X}_i)$ }(j=0~255) and only the first m ($1 \leq m \leq 256$) neurons having the largest responses { $R_{ij'} = f_{j'}(\mathbf{X}_i)$ }($R_{ij'} \in \{R_{ij}\}$, j'=1~m, j=0~255) win through the competition. To maximally decrease the coding quantity, m may be set to 1 for enough sparsity.

$$\begin{cases} R_{ij} = f_j(\mathbf{X}_i) = \mathbf{W}_j^T \mathbf{X}_i^E = \sum_{l=0}^{7} w_{il,j}(x_{il} - x_{i8}) \\ w_{il,j} = (-1)^{b_l} \end{cases} \quad (1) \qquad b_l = \begin{cases} 0 & \text{if } (x_{il} - x_{i8}) < 0\ , \ (l\text{=}0\text{~}7) \\ 1 & \text{otherwise} \end{cases} \quad (2)$$

2.2 Visual Context Encoding

In our paper, the visual context refers to the visual field image and the spatial relationship (Δx, Δy) from the centers of the visual field to the center of the target. Thus encoding such context need to calculate and store the representation coefficients of the spatial relationship and the visual field images which are centered at all the possible positions surrounding the target center and are in all the possible scales. The algorithm is described as follows:

BEGIN LOOP1 Select a scale s from the set $\{s_l\}$ for the current visual field;
    BEGIN LOOP2 Select a starting gaze point (x_J, y_J) as the center of the visual field from an initial point set $\{(x_J, y_J)\}$ distributed in the context area of the target;
      1. Input an image from the current visual field, and output a relative position prediction for the real relative position of target center $(\Delta x, \Delta y)$ in terms of gaze movement distances $(\Delta \hat{x}, \Delta \hat{y})$;

      2. If the prediction error $ER = \sqrt{(\Delta \hat{x} - \Delta x)^2 + (\Delta \hat{y} - \Delta y)^2}$ is larger than the maximum error limit $ER(s)$ for the scale s of the current visual field, move the center of the visual field to the new gaze point position $(x + \Delta \hat{x}, y + \Delta \hat{y})$; go to 1 until $ER \leq ER(s)$ or the iteration number is larger than a maximum limit;

      3. If $ER > ER(s)$, generate a new coding neuron (let its response $R_k=1$); encode the visual context by computing and storing the connection weights $\{w_{ij,k}\}$(initialized to zeros) between the new coding neuron and the feature neurons (their responses $R_{ij} = f_j(\mathbf{X}_i)$) and the connection weights $(w_{k,\Delta x}, w_{k,\Delta y})$ (initialized to zeros) between the new coding neuron and two movement control neurons (let their responses $R_{\Delta x} = \Delta x$ and $R_{\Delta y} = \Delta y$) respectively using the Hebbian rule $\Delta w_{a,b} = \alpha R_a R_b$;
    END LOOP2
END LOOP1

2.2.1 Encoding of Visual Field Images

The k-th coding neuron in layer 3 represents or encodes a visual field image pattern $\mathbf{X}^{(k)}$ with a group of connection weights $\{w_{ij,k}\}$ between the feature neurons in the second layer and the k-th coding neuron. The ij-th feature neuron extract the j-th feature $\{R_{ij} = f_j(\mathbf{X}_i^{(k)})\}$ ($0 \leq j \leq 255$) from the i-th receptive field image $\mathbf{X}_i^{(k)}$ ($1 \leq i \leq n$). All the receptive field images $\{\mathbf{X}_i^{(k)}\}$ compose the visual field image $\mathbf{X}^{(k)}$. The connection weights $\{w_{ij,k}\}$ are computed with Hebbian rule in Equation (3), where α is the learning rate; t is the iteration number; R_a and R_b are responses of two neurons which are connected by a synapse with a connection weight $w_{a,b}$. Thus each weight $w_{ij,k}$ between the ij-th feature neuron and the k-th coding neuron is formularized in Equation (4), where α and R_k are the learning rate and the response of the k-th coding neuron respectively. Both they are set to be 1 for simplifying computation, and then Equation (4) is changed to Equation (5). The lengths of all the weights $\{w_{ij,k}\}$ are finally normalized to one for unified similarity computation and comparison.

$$\begin{cases} \Delta w_{a,b}(t) = \alpha R_a R_b \\ w_{a,b}(t+1) = w_{a,b}(t) + \Delta w_{a,b}(t) \end{cases} (3) \quad \begin{cases} w_{ij,k}(0) = 0, \quad \Delta w_{ij,k}(0) = \alpha R_{ij} R_k = \alpha f_j(\mathbf{X}_i^{(k)}) R_k \\ w_{ij,k}(1) = w_{ij,k}(0) + \Delta w_{ij,k}(0) = \alpha f_j(\mathbf{X}_i^{(k)}) R_k \end{cases} (4) \quad w_{ij,k}(1) = f_j(\mathbf{X}_i^{(k)}) (5)$$

2.2.2 Encoding of Spatial Relationship

The spatial relationship $(\Delta x_k, \Delta y_k)$ between the center of the visual field and the center of the target is encoded in terms of two connection weights $(w_{k,\Delta x}, w_{k,\Delta y})$ between the k-th coding neuron and the two movement control neurons with Hebbian rule in Equations (6) and (7), where β and R_k are the learning rate and the response of the k-th coding neuron respectively. Similarly, both of them are set to 1 for simplifying computation, and then Equations (6) and (7) are simplified to Equations (8).

$$\begin{cases} w_{k,\Delta x}(0)=0, \quad \Delta w_{k,\Delta x}(0)=\beta R_k R_{\Delta x}=\beta R_k \Delta x_k \\ w_{k,\Delta x}(1)=w_{k,\Delta x}(0)+\Delta w_{k,\Delta x}(0)=\beta R_k \Delta x_k \end{cases} \quad (6) \quad \begin{cases} w_{k,\Delta y}(0)=0, \quad \Delta w_{k,\Delta y}(0)=\beta R_k R_{\Delta y}=\beta R_k \Delta y_k \\ w_{k,\Delta y}(1)=w_{k,\Delta y}(0)+\Delta w_{k,\Delta y}(0)=\beta R_k \Delta y_k \end{cases} \quad (7) \quad \begin{cases} w_{k,\Delta x}(1)=\Delta x_k \\ w_{k,\Delta y}(1)=\Delta y_k \end{cases} \quad (8)$$

2.3 Visual Context Decoding for Gaze Movement Control

Visual context decoding includes the responding of a single or population coding neuron(s) and the decoding of spatial relationship.

2.3.1 Response of a Single or Population Coding Neuron(s)

When the coding system inputs a visual field image $\mathbf{Y}$ for test, a single cell or population cells in the third layer may respond(s) through competition among the total N coding neurons to represent a visual field image pattern. With reference to Fig. 1, for the i-th receptive field image $\mathbf{Y}_i$, the k-th coding neuron inputs m responses $\{ R_{ij'} \}$ ($1 \leq j' \leq m \leq 256$) weighted by $\{w_{ij',k}\}$ from m feature neurons which extract features $\{ R_{ij'} = f_{j'}(\mathbf{Y}_i) \}$ from $\mathbf{Y}_i$. Therefore for the visual field image $\mathbf{Y}$ which is composed of the receptive field images $\{ \mathbf{Y}_i \}$ ($1 \leq i \leq n$), the response of the k-th coding neuron in the third layer is:

$$R_k = C_k(\mathbf{Y}) = C_k(\mathbf{Y}_1 \ \mathbf{Y}_2...\mathbf{Y}_n) = \sum_{i=1}^{n}\sum_{j'=1}^{m} w_{ij',k} R_{ij'} = \sum_{i=1}^{n}\sum_{j'=1}^{m} w_{ij',k} f_{j'}(\mathbf{Y}_i) \quad (9)$$

where $w_{k,ij'} \in \{w_{k,ij}\}$, $R_{ij'} \in \{R_{ij}\}$, $f_{j'}(\mathbf{Y}_i) \in \{f_j(\mathbf{Y}_i)\}$, $j'=1 \sim m$ and $j=0 \sim 255$. The weights $\{w_{k,ij'}\}$ are obtained at the encoding or training stage discussed in Section 2.2.1. The $R_{ij'}$ is the response of the j'-th feature neuron for the receptive field image $\mathbf{Y}_i$, belonging to the first m largest responses among the total feature responses $\{R_{ij}\}$. Substituting Equation (5) into (9), we get Equation (9a).

$$R_k = C_k(\mathbf{Y}) = \sum_{i=1}^{n}\sum_{j'=1}^{m} w_{ij',k} f_{j'}(\mathbf{Y}_i) = \sum_{i=1}^{n}\sum_{j'=1}^{m} f_{j'}(\mathbf{X}_i^{(k)}) f_{j'}(\mathbf{Y}_i) \quad (9a) \qquad R_k = \mathbf{W}_{\mathbf{X}^{(k)}}^{\mathrm{T}} \mathbf{f}_{\mathbf{Y}} = \mathbf{f}_{\mathbf{Y}}^{\mathrm{T}} \mathbf{f}_{\mathbf{X}^{(k)}} \quad (9b)$$

Let $\mathbf{W}_{\mathbf{X}^{(k)}} = (w_{i=1,j'=1,k} w_{i=1,j'=2,k}...w_{i=n,j'=m,k})^{\mathrm{T}}$, $\mathbf{f}_{\mathbf{X}^{(k)}} = (f_{j'=1}(\mathbf{X}_{i=1}^{(k)}) f_{j'=2}(\mathbf{X}_{i=1}^{(k)})...f_{j'=m}(\mathbf{X}_{i=n}^{(k)}))^{\mathrm{T}}$, and $\mathbf{f}_{\mathbf{Y}} = (f_{j'=1}(\mathbf{Y}_{i=1}) f_{j'=2}(\mathbf{Y}_{i=1})...f_{j'=m}(\mathbf{Y}_{i=n}))^{\mathrm{T}}$, then Equation (9a) is changed to its inner product form between two groups of features shown in Equation (9b). Equation (9) indicates that the response of the k-th coding neuron in the third layer is a similarity measure between the new image $\mathbf{Y}$ and the k-th visual field image pattern $\mathbf{X}^{(k)}$ memorized in the coding system.

2.3.2 Decoding of Spatial Relationship for Gaze Movement Control

Gaze movement control is directly responsible for visual object research. This has been implemented in a structure that consists of the two layers of neurons: single or population cell coding neurons and movement control neurons (see Fig. 1). The movement control neurons, divided into Δx and Δy neurons, whose responses ($R_{\Delta x}$, $R_{\Delta y}$) represent the relative position (Δx, Δy) of the target to the current gaze point (x, y) or the center of the current visual field image. For the current visual field image input, the first M coding neurons which have the largest responses play the main role in activating the movement control neurons. If $M=1$, it is the single-cell-coding controlling mechanism, otherwise it is the population-cell-coding mechanism. The responses of gaze movement control neurons can be formulated as Equation (10), where $R_{k'}$ is the k'-th largest response of a coding neuron among the total N coding neurons; $R^{*}_{k'}$ is the percentage form of the $R_{k'}$ and is used for the synthesis of gaze movement; $w_{k',\Delta x}$ and $w_{k',\Delta y}$ are the connection weights from the k'-th coding neuron to the movement control neurons in x and y directions respectively. At learning or encoding stage, both of $w_{k',\Delta x}$ and $w_{k',\Delta y}$ are calculated using Equations (6) ~ (8). Substituting Equation (8) into Equation (10), the synthesis of movement is represented by Equation (11).

$$\begin{cases} R_{\Delta x} = \sum_{k'=1}^{M} w_{k',\Delta x} R^{*}_{k'}, \quad R_{\Delta y} = \sum_{k'=1}^{M} w_{k',\Delta y} R^{*}_{k'} \quad (10) \\ R^{*}_{k'} = \dfrac{R_{k'}}{\sum_{k'=1}^{M} R_{k'}} \end{cases} \qquad \begin{cases} R_{\Delta x} = \sum_{k'=1}^{M} R^{*}_{k} \cdot \Delta x_{k}. \quad (11) \\ R_{\Delta y} = \sum_{k'=1}^{M} R^{*}_{k} \cdot \Delta y_{k}. \end{cases} \qquad \begin{cases} R_{\Delta x} = \Delta x_{k'=1} \quad (12) \\ R_{\Delta y} = \Delta y_{k'=1} \end{cases}$$

Formula (11) means that the gaze movement distances (decoded at the perception or test stage) is the weighted sum of the spatial relationship (encoded at the learning or training stage, which are weighted by the first M largest responses of coding neurons). Especially, when $M=1$ (single cell coding), the responses $(R_{\Delta x}, R_{\Delta y})$ of two movement control neurons are activated by a single neuron who has encoded a historical spatial relationship $(\Delta x_{k'}=1, \Delta y_{k'}=1)$ in connection weights $w_{k'=1,\Delta x}$ and $w_{k'=1,\Delta y}$ respectively. In this case, Equation (11) is simplified to Equation (12).

An entire algorithm for gaze movement control for target search is given as follows:

BEGIN LOOP1 Select a starting gaze point (x_J, y_J) as the center of the visual field from a random initial point set $\{(x_J, y_J)\}$ distributed in the image area;
  BEGIN LOOP2 Select a scale s from the set $\{s_l\}$ for the current visual field in the order of from the maximum to the minimum;
    Input an image from the current visual field, and output a relative position prediction in terms of gaze movement $(\Delta \hat{x}_I, \Delta \hat{y}_I)$ for the real relative position of the target center $(\Delta x, \Delta y)$;
  END LOOP2
  The position of the target center (x, y) starting from the initial gaze point (x_J, y_J) is predicted by
$$\hat{x}_J = x_J + \sum_I \Delta \hat{x}_I \quad \text{and} \quad \hat{y}_J = y_J + \sum_I \Delta \hat{y}_I$$
END LOOP1
Computing the density $D(x, y)$ of the gaze point distribution $\{(\hat{x}_J, \hat{y}_J)\}$
Select the position with the largest density as the finally predicted target position:
$$(\hat{x}, \hat{y}) = \arg\max\{D(x, y)\}.$$

The algorithm uses a gradual search strategy that move an initial gaze point to the center of target from the largest visual field to the smallest visual field by decoding global and local context.

3   Learning Properties of Single and Population Coding

A learning problem can be proposed as: Given a group of visual context patterns{ $(\mathbf{X}^{(k)}, (\Delta x_k, \Delta y_k))$ } $(1 \le k \le N)$ and a visual field image $\mathbf{Y}$, how to estimate the relative position $(\Delta x, \Delta y)$ of the target? One solution is letting the half-unknown visual context $(\mathbf{Y}, (\Delta x, \Delta y))$ be represented or synthesized by the known visual context patterns { $(\mathbf{X}^{(k)}, (\Delta x_k, \Delta y_k))$ } $(1 \le k \le N)$, i.e. Equation (13). Then the leaning problem becomes a problem of how to determine the values of the coefficients { c_k }. To compute the coefficients { c_k }, dividing Equation (13) into Equation (14).

$$(\mathbf{Y}, (\Delta x, \Delta y)) = \sum_{k=1}^{N} c_k \cdot (\mathbf{X}^{(k)}, (\Delta x_k, \Delta y_k)) \tag{13}$$

$$\begin{cases} \mathbf{Y} = \sum_{k=1}^{N} c_k \mathbf{X}^{(k)} \\ (\Delta x, \Delta y) = \sum_{k=1}^{N} c_k \cdot (\Delta x_k, \Delta y_k) \end{cases} \tag{14}$$

$$\begin{cases} \mathbf{Y} \approx \hat{\mathbf{Y}} = \sum_{k'=1}^{M} c_{k'} \mathbf{X}^{(k')} \\ (\Delta x, \Delta y) \approx (\Delta \hat{x}, \Delta \hat{y}) = \sum_{k'=1}^{M} c_{k'} \cdot (\Delta x_{k'}, \Delta y_{k'}) \end{cases} \tag{15}$$

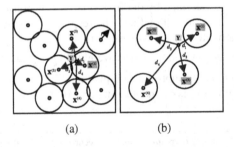

(a)   (b)

Fig. 3. Illustration of encoded visual field image patterns { $\mathbf{X}^{(k)}$ } with their neighbor areas (radius r), the test visual field image $\mathbf{Y}$ and their distances $\{d_i\}$ or the similarity measurement (e.g. $1/(1+d_i)$) in data space. (a) Densely encoded samples suitable for single cell decoding for a new sample (e.g. using $\mathbf{X}^{(k'=1)}$ to represent $\mathbf{Y}$ for distances $d_1 < r \ll d_2 < d_3 < d_4$); (b) Sparsely encoded samples suitable for population cell decoding (e.g. using { $\mathbf{X}^{(k')}$ } $(k'=1\sim3)$ to represent $\mathbf{Y}$ for distances $r < d_1 < d_2 < d_3 \ll d_4$).

The coefficients { c_k } could be obtained by decomposing $\mathbf{Y}$ based on the basis functions { $\mathbf{X}^{(k)}$ }, and then are used to synthesize the unknown relative position (Δx, Δy) by known spatial relationships { $(\Delta x_k, \Delta y_k)$ }. Usually the exact decomposition coefficients { c_k } for the basis functions { $\mathbf{X}^{(k)}$ } can not be obtained in a simple and easy way. We use an estimated visual context $(\hat{\mathbf{Y}}, (\Delta \hat{x}, \Delta \hat{y}))$ to approximate the real visual context $(\mathbf{Y}, (\Delta x, \Delta y))$ instead. Then Equation (14) is transformed to Equation (15), where $c_{k'} \in \{c_k\}$, $\mathbf{X}^{(k')} \in \{\mathbf{X}^{(k)}\}$, $(\Delta x_{k'}, \Delta y_{k'}) \in \{(\Delta x_k, \Delta y_k)\}$, $k'=1\sim M$, $k=1\sim N$, and $M = 1 \sim N$. Substituting the equation (9b) into equation (11), we get the responses of two movement control neurons as the estimation of $(\Delta x, \Delta y)$ in Equation (16). Thus, encoding the visual context and decoding the spatial relationship with $(R_{\Delta x}, R_{\Delta y})$ to produce a gaze movement for target locating can be modeled with a regression function shown in Equation (17), where the coefficient $c_{k'}$ is the percentage form of the similarity between the new visual field image $\mathbf{Y}$ and the k'-th encoded visual field image pattern $\mathbf{X}^{(k')}$. Particularly, when using the single coding mechanism ($M=1$), the equation (17) is simplified to Equation (18).

$$ (16) \quad R_{\Delta x} = \Delta \hat{x} = \frac{\sum_{k=1}^{M} \mathbf{f}_{\mathbf{Y}}{}^T \mathbf{f}_{\mathbf{X}^{(k)}} \Delta x_k}{\sum_{k=1}^{M} \mathbf{f}_{\mathbf{Y}}{}^T \mathbf{f}_{\mathbf{X}^{(k)}}}, \quad R_{\Delta y} = \Delta \hat{y} = \frac{\sum_{k=1}^{M} \mathbf{f}_{\mathbf{Y}}{}^T \mathbf{f}_{\mathbf{X}^{(k)}} \Delta y_k}{\sum_{k=1}^{M} \mathbf{f}_{\mathbf{Y}}{}^T \mathbf{f}_{\mathbf{X}^{(k)}}} $$

$$ (17) \quad (\Delta x, \Delta y) \approx (\Delta \hat{x}, \Delta \hat{y}) = F_{rg}(\Delta x_{k'}, \Delta y_{k'}) = \sum_{k'=1}^{M} c_{k'} \cdot (\Delta x_{k'}, \Delta y_{k'}) $$

$$ c_{k'} = \frac{\mathbf{f}_{\mathbf{Y}}{}^T \mathbf{f}_{\mathbf{X}^{(k')}}}{\sum_{k'=1}^{M} \mathbf{f}_{\mathbf{Y}}{}^T \mathbf{f}_{\mathbf{X}^{(k')}}} $$

$$ (18) \quad (\Delta x, \Delta y) \approx (\Delta \hat{x}, \Delta \hat{y}) = (\Delta x_{k'=1}, \Delta y_{k'=1}) $$

From the equation (18), it can be learned that for the case of single cell coding, the system produces a movement associated to the memorized visual field image pattern to which the new visual field image is most similar. If the coding system encoded enough visual field image patterns $\{\mathbf{X}^{(k)}\}$ ($1 \leq k \leq N$) and associated spatial relationship $\{(\Delta x_k, \Delta y_k)\}$ ($1 \leq k \leq N$), a new visual field image $\mathbf{Y}$ can be easily located in the neighbor area of an encoded $\mathbf{X}^{(k)}$ in the data space, as illustrated in Fig. 3(a). In this case, the single cell coding is suitable and the associated prediction $(\Delta x_k, \Delta y_k)$ is exact enough. However, the encoding quantity for coding system to memorize such visual context could be very large. From the equation (17), for the case of population cell coding, the system produces a movement according to a group of encoded visual field image patterns to which the new visual field image is similar. If the sparse visual field image patterns are stored in the coding system, the possibility of a new visual field image located in the neighbor area of an encoded image pattern is very small, as illustrated in Fig. 3(b). In this case, the single cell coding can not provide exact representation and prediction. Thus, the prediction should be compensated by other cells that are also similar to the new input. Therefore population cell coding is suitable here and the gaze movement is synthesized by a group of movements $\{(\Delta x_k, \Delta y_k)\}$ ($1 \leq k \leq M$) associated to the similar encoded image patterns $\{\mathbf{X}^{(k')}\}$ ($1 \leq k \leq M$). By transforming the distance measurement into the similarity measurement, e.g., $s_{k'} = 1/(1+d_{k'})$, Fig. 3(b) shows that there are M encoded visual field images $\{\mathbf{X}^{(k')}\}$ ($k'=1 \sim M$, here $M=3$) are most similar to the new visual field image $\mathbf{Y}$, i.e., $s_1 > s_2 > ... > s_M \gg s_{M+1} > ... > s_N$. Our experimental results showed that M is not a stable parameter to be selected directly for the system's best generalization performance. Instead, we use a similarity factor $P = s_M / s_1$ to control M. The parameter P can be obtained by the following algorithm:

182   J. Miao et al.

BEGIN LOOP P_i=1 to p ($0 \leq p < 1$) with a step $\Delta p (\Delta p < 0)$, where P_i is the factor determining M_i, i.e., the number of first M_i largest response coding neuron;

1. Train the coding system with the given maximum error limit and the value of M which is controlled by the factor P_i, then get the system complexity N_i after training, where N_i is the number of layer-3 coding neurons generated in the system;

2. Sort all the N_i coding neurons' responses in a sequence from the maximum response $MaxR$ to the minimum response; if the (M_i+1)-th ($1 \leq M_i \leq N_i$) neuron's response is the first one smaller than or equaling to P_i*MaxR, then P_i and N_i are recoded as candidates;

END LOOP

Get P among $\{P_i\}$, where P corresponds to the smallest N_i.

Please note that the result of M will be 1 and N when $P = 1$ and $P = 0$ respectively.

4 Experiments

We constructed two visual context coding systems respectively using single-cell-coding and population-cell-coding mechanisms for target search experiments. The head-shoulder image database from the University of Bern has been used. In this database, totally there are 300 images with 30 people in ten different poses (ten images each person). The image size is 320×214 pixels. The average radius of the eyeballs of these 30 persons is 4.02 pixels. The two coding systems are compared by applying them to search the left eye centers. Visual context was encoded or learned with a group of initial gaze points placed in a uniform distribution, while decoded or tested with a group of initial gaze points in a random distribution. For each target searching, two experiments were designed to compare the systems' performances. The first experiment (Exp.1) used 30 images (30 people, one image in frontal pose each person) for training and the rest for testing. The second experiment (Exp.2) used 90 images (9 people, 10 images each person) for training and the rest for testing.

We compare the population cell coding and the single cell coding on the database. Table 1 listed the details of the number of total feature neurons in layer 2, the number of total coding neurons in layer 3, the number of connections between feature neurons and coding neurons, the mean and standard deviation of locating errors and the comprehensive test error, where P=0.9 and P=0.8 make the two systems for Exp.1 and Exp.2 have the smallest complexities respectively; P=1.0 means a single cell is responsible for context coding.

Table 1. Performance comparison between two coding systems

| experiment | coding system | #1* | #2* | locating error (unit: pixel) | | |
				mean (*mn*)	standard deviation (*sd*)	comprehensive error $\sqrt{mn^2 + sd^2}$
Exp.1 (30 vs. 270)	Single cell (P=1.0)	2314	0.43	2.15	4.33	4.83
	Population cell (P=0.9)	1906	0.35	1.93	2.44	3.11
Exp.2 (90 vs. 210)	Single cell (P=1.0)	7340	5.02	1.64	1.47	2.20
	Population cell (P=0.8)	5405	1.02	1.89	1.22	2.25

* #1 : number of coding neurons in layer 3 ; #2 : number of connections between feature neurons and coding neurons (unit: million).

From Table 1, it can be learned: (1)With large samples, i.e., the case of Exp. 2, the locating accuracy of the population coding system is almost same to the accuracy of the single cell coding system, but it required the lest coding information. The ratios of the average coding quantity required by the population coding to the coding required by the single cell coding system are about 77%. (2) With small samples, i.e., the case of Exp. 1, the locating accuracy of the population coding system is 35.6% higher than the accuracy of the single cell coding system. Meanwhile, the coding quantity required by the population coding is 12% smaller than the single cell coding systems.

5 Conclusion

In this paper, an internal presentation model of visual context in form of neural coding network is presented. Experimental results indicated that population-cell-coding is generally more efficient than the single-cell-coding system in representing the context as well as controlling the gaze motion for target search.

Acknowledgments. This research is supported in part by NSFC (60673091, 60702031 and 60970087), Hi-Tech R&D Program of China (2006AA01Z122), BJNSF (4072023 and 4102013), BMEC (No.KM200610005012), BMF for Excellent Talents (No.20061D0501500211) and National Basic Research Program of China (2009CB320902).

References

1. Chun, M., Jiang, Y.: Contextual Cueing: Implicit Learning and Memory of Visual Context Guides Spatial Attention. Cognitive Psychology 36, 28–71 (1998)
2. Torralba, A.: Contextual Priming for Object Detection. IJCV 53(2), 169–191 (2003)
3. Kruppa, H., Santana, M., Schiele, B.: Fast and Robust Face Finding via Local Context. In: Proc. Joint IEEE International Workshop on Visual Surveillance and Performance Evaluation of Tracking and Surveillance (2003)
4. Bergboer, N., Postma, E., van den Herik, H.: Context-based object detection in still images. Image and Vision Computing 24, 987–1000 (2006)
5. Miao, J., Chen, X., Gao, W., Chen, Y.: A Visual Perceiving and Eyeball-Motion Controlling Neural Network for Object Searching and Locating. In: Proc. IJCNN, pp. 4395–4400 (2006)
6. Bear, M., Connors, B., Paradiso, M.: Neuroscience: Exploring the Brain, 2nd edn. Lippincott Williams & Wilkins (2001)
7. Special issue on binding problem. Neuron 24(1) (1999)
8. Wang, D.: The Time Dimension for Scene Analysis. IEEE-TNN 16(6), 1401–1426 (2005)
9. Ahonen, T., Hadid, A., Pietikainen, M.: Face Recognition with Local Binary Patterns. In: Pajdla, T., Matas, J. (eds.) ECCV 2004. LNCS, vol. 3021, pp. 469–481. Springer, Heidelberg (2004)

Simulating Biological-Inspired Spiking Neural Networks with OpenCL

Jörn Hoffmann, Karim El-Laithy, Frank Güttler, and Martin Bogdan

Universität Leipzig, Department of Computer Science,
Johannisgasse 26, 04103 Leipzig, Germany
{jhoffmann,kellaithy,guettler,bogdan}@informatik.uni-leipzig.de
http://www.informatik.uni-leipzig.de/ti

Abstract. The algorithms used for simulating biologically-inspired spiking neural networks (BIANN) often utilize functions which are computationally complex and have to model a large number of neurons - or even a much larger number of synapses in parallel. To use all available computing resources provided by a standard desktop PC is an opportunity to shorten the simulation time and extend the number of simulated neurons and their interconnections. OpenCL offers an open platform for heterogeneous computing to employ CPUs, GPUs, DSP or FPGAs in an uniform way. This paper introduces a handy simulation framework being sufficient to accelerate different kinds of neural networks with off-the-shelf hardware. To illustrate this, different large networks comprising a complex synaptic model in combination with a leaky Integrate-and-Fire neuron model are implemented as standard Matlab code and with OpenCL separately. In comparison to the Matlab model, OpenCL reaches a speedup of $\smile$ 83 on a quad-core processor and of $\smile$ 1500 on a GPU.

Keywords: Neural networks, OpenCL, Data parallelism, GPGPU.

1   Introduction

A crucial point of the detailed models representing the anatomic facts in neurobiology is the corresponding needed computational power. Supercomputers have been used to simulate neurons and synapses into depth to ion channels. Unfortunately, high performance computing clusters are not always accessible for a wide range of researchers simulating even simplified bioanalogical models. Thus, simulating complex biological inspired neural models on standard hardware is highly desired. Recent computer architectures tend to increase the computing performance by adding more and more distinct computing units. Based on the computing history, an observable trend tells that the number of transistors will be doubled approximately every two years.

To unveil the potential an off-the-shelf platform provides, one has to make use of both the parallel and the specialized compute units. Multipurpose neuro-simulators have been written in the past, mainly exploiting one special hardware, see e.g. the simulators described in [1–4]. The major part of the simulators just mentioned are targeting to computational-efficient neurons, e.g. Izhikevich Spiking Neuron [5]. These models describe the underlying dynamics of both neuronal and synaptic activities within the

K. Diamantaras, W. Duch, L.S. Iliadis (Eds.): ICANN 2010, Part I, LNCS 6352, pp. 184–187, 2010.

neural system. They are useful to build large networks and fit for different applications, e.g. real-time use for robots and pattern matching. However, the precise description of neural activity involves a large number of synergistic and cooperative variables, that may prevent the understanding of the underlying dynamics.

OpenCL is an open standard for parallel programming a heterogeneous collection of discrete computing devices within a single system. The framework, includes a C-like language, an API, libraries and a runtime system at once. It provides a low-level hardware abstraction formulated in a hierarchy of models which made OpenCL feasible for different hardware architectures like CPUs, GPUs, DSPs and others. Primarily it allows to write portable and data-parallel executed code which can be used on different computing devices at once.

In this paper an approach towards the efficient use of standard hardware, especially the graphical processor unit (GPU), in order to boost up simulation time of complex biological inspired neural networks is presented. The objective is to show the possibility to use OpenCL as a generalized platform for more models than presented in this paper.

2   Neural Representations

The neurons in our simulations are Leaky-Integrate-and-Fire (LIF) units. The synaptic representation uses a recently proposed synaptic model for both fast and short-term spike-time dependent potentiation (STDP) whereas the synaptic model is computationally complex [6]. Since the models are not the simplest available representation they are chosen in order to exhibit a real processing load for the proposed implementation techniques.

Each synaptic connection is modeled as a stochastic activity-dependent connections using the modified synaptic stochastic model (MSSM) [6]. In this model, the transmission probability of an arriving action potential, i.e. spike, from a presynaptic neuron via a synapse to a postsynaptic neuron is estimated. The probability-of-release involved is governed by two counteracting mechanisms: facilitation and depression. Facilitation reflects the Ca^{2+} concentration in the presynaptic neuron, while depression represents the effect of the concentration of ready-to-release vesicles in the pre-synaptic neuron. For details and description of the model, please review [6].

3   Simulation

We have implemented a generic, object-oriented simulation framework called LpzNeuro in C++. Within the framework, OpenCL is used since it offers a data parallel programming and execution model which fits well for neural networks due to their inherently concurrent nature. Network entities, i.e. neurons and synapses, functionally correlate to OpenCL kernels which operate on all neural structures at the same time. From the user point of view, mainly OpenCL kernels, thus "functions" have to be provided to the framework. To represent conditions of a network entity, variables can be described, transferred and assigned to kernels in a generic way. If a simulation doesn't fit this frame, simulation base classes can be derived and altered by means of the object oriented nature.

For the mentioned neural model, we've realize a concrete simulator which realizes a time discrete, straightforward process. Within each step, all kernels manipulating network entities are sequentially issued. A typical kernel sequence could be the following: Kernel_Neuron, Kernel_Synapse and Kernel_Reduce to compute action potentials, to adjust the synaptic values and to summarize the post-synaptic-potential induced to the affected neurons in the next step.

For this simulator, the neuron data is completely transferred to a device at the beginning of the simulation. Thereafter no further host-to-device transfers are necessary. While this is true for neurons, a large connection matrix has to be piecewise up- and downloaded to the device in every step if the device memory capacity isn't sufficient large enough. As a consequence, the synapse kernel invocation also has to be done in consecutive manner relating to the fraction (rows) of the matrix which can be stored on the device. To minimize the static time OpenCL needs to issue kernels or to enqueue memory transfers, LpzNeuro copies as much rows as possible to a defined I/O-buffer on the device. Regarding a concrete connection scheme, within this simulator almost a full connected network is assumed. This implies not to use an event based approach. Instead the current implementation follows a static approach, which better fits to our synapse-centric view. Within the simulation process, every possible synapse is processed but only the actually present synapses are allowed to store their states.

4 Measurements

Matlab simulation was tested on a Sun Fire X4440 Server with four quad-core AMD Opteron, while LpzNeuro was executed on a desktop PC equipped with an Intel Core i7-950 quad-core processor at 3.06 GHz and with 12 GB RAM. For the GPU test a NVidia 9800GT (G92 architecture) with 512 MB RAM was used. The Matlab neuron and synapse source code has been used for transcription as kernels under LpzNeuro. Due to the C-alike Syntax of Matlab, transcriptions are easy to perform. Only nested conditional clauses and variable access had to be adapted to the data parallel programming model of a kernel.

For this setup, Matlab and LpzNeuro simulation trails are compared, confer figure 1. The y-axis shows the mean time of 1,000 simulation steps and uses a logarithmic scale. On the x-axis the number of synaptic connection is drawn. In both cases the network was connected in exactly the same manner. To mimic an ordinary use case, LpzNeuro was configured such that after every step all values of interest were transferred back to the host, for example the count of the neurotransmitters or the action potentials of all neurons. Additionally, the simulator transferred the connection matrix to the device in ever step. This isn't necessary for small networks but for large ones which won't fit to the device global storage. As depicted, the simulation on the GPU is clearly superior to the Matlab implementation: the Matlab solution needs roughly 3 days (236912 seconds) to process 223437 synapses whereas the proposed solution using OpenCL needs only 158 seconds. This leads to a speedup of approx. 1500 times. For comparison, the quad-core needs 2850 seconds resulting in a speedup of 83 times (not shown in the figure).

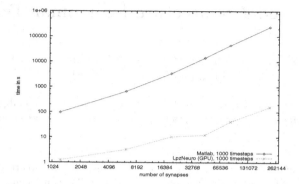

Fig. 1. Comparison between Matlab and LpzNeuro based simulation of a pre-connected network

5 Conclusion and Future Work

In this paper LpzNeuro for accelerating simulation time for biological inspired neural networks using OpenCL was presented. This approach shows that even complex models can profit from standard hardware used in desktop PC. Using LpzNeuro a complex biological inspired neural model obtained a speed up of ∽ 1500. Remark, the neural model used here can be easily replaced by other models already implemented e.g. in Matlab or C/C++. Although our simulation results are promising, the approach can still be improved in future. E.g. using a sparse representation for the connection matrix on the processing device leads to a more efficient memory usage. Besides, our approach can be easily expanded to several processing devices with reference to piecewise computation of the connection matrix. Moreover, the often unnecessary and thus inefficient computation for not connected or not affected synapses is to be considered. Results for not existing connections are thrown away at the end that waste some of the available computing power. Thus, algorithms to avoid this case to improve the usage available resources are to be considered in future.

References

1. Blas, A.D., Jagota, A., Hughey, R.: Optimizing neural networks on simd parallel computers. Parallel Computing 31(1), 97–115 (2005)
2. Bernhard, F., Keriven, R.: Spiking Neurons on GPUs, pp. 236–243. Springer, Heidelberg (2006)
3. Khan, M.M., Lester, D.R., Plana, L.A., Rast, A.D., Jin, X., Painkras, E., Furber, S.B.: Spinnaker: Mapping neural networks onto a massively-parallel chip multiprocessor. In: IJCNN, pp. 2849–2856 (2008)
4. Guzhva, A., Dolenko, S., Persiantsev, I.: Multifold acceleration of neural network computations using gpu. In: Alippi, C., Polycarpou, M., Panayiotou, C., Ellinas, G. (eds.) ICANN 2009. LNCS, vol. 5768, pp. 373–380. Springer, Heidelberg (2009)
5. Izhikevich, E.M.: Simple model of spiking neurons. IEEE Trans. Neural Networks, 1569–1572 (2003)
6. El-Laithy, K., Bogdan, M.: Synchrony state generation in artificial neural networks with stochastic synapses. In: Alippi, C., Polycarpou, M., Panayiotou, C., Ellinas, G. (eds.) ICANN 2009. LNCS, vol. 5768, pp. 181–190. Springer, Heidelberg (2009)

Bio-inspired Architecture for Human Detection

Daniel Alejandro González Bandala, Pedro Luis Sánchez Orellana,
and Claudio Castellanos Sánchez

Laboratory of Information Technology, LTI at Cinvestav - Tamaulipas, México
{dgonzalez,psanchez,castellanos}@tamps.cinvestav.mx

Abstract. In this paper we propose a bio-inspired architecture to detect, describe and distinguish objects in motion. By using neuronal and physiological mechanisms in primary visual cortex (V1), middle temporal (MT) and inferotemporal (IT) areas we can start isolating the objects from their environment; then, track, label and distinguish the humans from non-human figures in motion and finally, represent the person's silhouette to get a better understanding of the body structure.

Keywords: Bio-inspired architecture; complex and simple neurons.

1 Introduction

The visual recognition systems have become very important in our daily lives. Despite many obstacles, the recognition task has drawn attention of many researchers who created applications to recognize human figures in motion. Some applications have focused on tasks like video surveillance for security [1] and control applications usually involving human-machine interaction. These applications can be summarized into three main categories:

- First, the *model-free approaches*, that identify the subject by matching the hypotheses of pose structure from the observation and choose the most similar hypothesis from a DB [5] without using explicit information of the body.
- Second, the *3D model-based approaches*. Some of them use probabilistic information to construct a 3D model from 2D views [4].
- Third, the *partial-model-based approaches*. Some researchers use an a priori knowledge of the human body which is usually represented as a reference model [2].
- Fourth, the *bio-inspiration*. This approach mainly mimics the brain capabilities of the primates. It generalizes the shape detection of objects in the environment without the presence of background motion nor uniformity of the illumination conditions [6].

In this paper, we focus on a mix of the bio-inspired and partial-model-based approaches in order to achieve the task of recognizing humans in motion. In the following sections we will mention the biological motivations and foundations of our work, our proposed architecture, some of our results and finally, the conclusions achieved so far.

K. Diamantaras, W. Duch, L.S. Iliadis (Eds.): ICANN 2010, Part I, LNCS 6352, pp. 188–192, 2010.

2   Proposed Architecture

The proposed architecture to detect, describe and distinguish the moving objects is an extension of our previous work to detect articulated or non-articulated objects in motion [9,7]. This architecture is basically divided into four stages (see part (a) of figure 1). This work also includes some ideas of partial-model-based approaches as the ratios (pre-calculated empirically) to improve the localization of the legs and the head.

The first stage is the spatial treatment, a convolution with our Gabor-like oriented filters with two phases. Next, the V1 complex cells modelled with a temporal treatment to integrate the information from both phases of the Gabor-like filter. Then we use a neural model, based on the SOM neural network, to simulate the retinotopical map of MT [10] to track the figures in motion [3]. These figures produce different activation patterns in the neurons which are used to define the type of object in motion (for example, to determine whether or not the figure is a human). Finally, the location of the objects is mapped into the IT module. It processes the information to decompose the object into more basic elements: polygon and lines-like [8]. The obtained lines are used to describe the motion in the upper and lower extremities of the body (for example, head and legs).

2.1   First Stage (A): Spatial Treatment

Our architecture begins by applying our Gabor-like oriented filters that model the responses of the simple cells in V1. This filtering ensures the capacity to detect the local motion in a simple and local way as defined by Castellanos [7].

2.2   Second Stage (B): Integrated Information

There are biological clues [12] about the integration of several phases of simple cells in V1 by complex cells in the same area. These complex cells respond selectively to lines or edges at particular orientations. This property can be modelled by the so called Gabor energy function which is related to the behaviour of complex cells in V1 [13] and defined by Sanchez [9]. The result is a new non-linear filter bank of 8 channels, each one represents a different orientation.

2.3   Third Stage (C): Tracking

We simulate a retinotopical neural map in MT by using a SOM architecture to determine the motion direction and object type in the scene. This neural map is used to learn the upper part motion of the body (the head) since this part remains unchanged during the motion. Then, we manipulate the SOM learning rule as follows:

$$Wv(t+1) = Wv(t) + \theta(v,t)\alpha(t)(D(t) - Wv(t)) \tag{1}$$

In the above equation D is the euclidean distance function, α is the learning function. These weights are used to initialize the following net to track the head in the whole image sequence $(T_{1,...,n})$. The final location of the neurons is averaged to determine a centroid, then we calculate the angle θ of the slant between the images T_i and T_{i+1}.

2.4 Fourth Stage (D): Extraction of Basic Elements

Once located the top and lower part of the motion object (head and legs in our case), these parts are described by simpler elements as polygon or lines (in out case, lines). We manipulate again the learning rule of Kohonen model to allow a map construction to simulate lines in certain orientations between the neurons in the following way:

$$Wv(t+1) = Wv(t) + \theta(v,t)\alpha(t)(L_\theta(i,j) - Wv(t)) \tag{2}$$

where L is a function of line construction that uses two neurons initialised in the position of the pattern activation of the complex cells. The L function is described as follows:

$$L_\theta(x,y) = \sum_{i,j}^{n}(C_\theta(i), C_{360-\theta}(j)) \tag{3}$$

where C is the response of complex cells, θ is the proposed orientation for the neuron communication. To evaluate the lines, they must fulfill $L_\theta < (D_{i,j}) * (C(i) + C(j))/2$, where D is the euclidean distance of the two involved complex cells. This ratio allows us to discriminate the lines that do not cover a certain portion of active complex neurons C.

3   Results and Conclusions

Our bio-inspired architecture describes human figures in motion into real and uncontrolled scenarios. Also, this architecture helps us to understand the mechanisms that have a key role in the generation of important information for shape reconstruction in motion into our brain. We tested our model using a set of 56 natural image sequences of a walking person in different angles (from 0 to 315 degrees) and distances (between 10 and 15 meters) with the camera standing still in uncontrolled outdoor conditions (see part (b) of figure 1).

We combine our previous technique of detection and refinement of human shapes into video sequences to isolate and refine them by reconstruction of multiple orientations from V1 complex cells. Besides,the pattern representation allows to describe the object shape. Another advantage of our architecture is the angle measure between lines that could work for applications like face or gait recognition.

However, our architecture doesn't infer the missing information. Seeing the part (b) of figure 1, there are some images where the occlusion between the

Fig. 1. (a) Our proposed architecture is composed by 2 phases and 8 oriented simple cells bank, a non-linear integration complex cell model, a MT and IT model to represent the motion objects. (b) Results projected onto the original sequence of images. Our architecture allows to detect and reconstruct a human body even from different perspectives.

moving parts of the body hinders the representations of them. This could be solved by adding extra information in the process of locating the limbs following the partial-model-based approaches.

References

1. Xu, H., Jiwei, L., Lei, L., Zhiliang, W.: Gait recognition considering directions of walking. IEEE Cybernetics and Intelligent Systems, 1–5 (2006)
2. Starck, J., Hilton, A.: Spherical Matching for Temporal Correspondence of Non-Rigid Surfaces. In: ICCV 2005: Proceedings of the Tenth IEEE International Conference on Computer Vision, pp. 1387–1394 (2005) ISBN:0-7695-2334-X-02
3. Nichols, M.J., Newsome, W.T.: Middle Temporal Visual Area Microstimulation Influences Veridical Judgments of Motion Direction. J. Neurosci. 22(21), 9530–9540 (2002)
4. Chen, H., Bhanu, B.: 3d free-form object recognition in range images using local surface patches. Pattern Recogn. Lett. 28(10), 1252–1262 (2007)
5. Mokhber, A., Achard, C., Milgram, M.: Recognition of human behavior by space-time silhouette characterization. Pattern Recogn. Lett. 29(1), 81–89 (2008)
6. Lerner, Y., Epshtein, B., Ullman, S., Malach, R.: Class information predicts activation by object fragments in human object areas. J. Cognitive Neuroscience 20(7), 1189–1206 (2008)
7. Castellanos Sánchez, C.: Neuromimetic indicators for visual perception of motion. In: 2nd International Symposium on Brain, Vision and Artificial Inteligence, vol. 103, pp. 134–143 (2007)
8. Kobatake, E., Tanaka, K.: Neuronal selectivities to complex object features in the ventral visual pathway of the macaque cerebral cortex. J. Neurophysiol. 71(3), 856–867 (1994)
9. Sánchez Orellana, P.L., Castellanos Sánchez, C.: Bio-inspired Connectionist Architecture for Visual Detection and Refinement of Shapes. In: ICANN, pp. 745–754 (2009)

10. Silva, S., Madeira, J., Santos, B.S.: There is More to Color Scales than Meets the Eye: A Review on the Use of Color in Visualization. In: IV 2007: Proceedings of the 11th International Conference Information Visualization, pp. 943–950 (2007) ISBN 0-7695-2900-3
11. Sunaert, S., van Hecke, P., Marchal, G., Orban, G.A.: Motion-responsive regions of the human brain. Exp. Brain Res. 127(4), 355–370 (1999)
12. Ersoy, B., Kagan, I., Rucci, M., Snodderly, M.: Modeling the responses of v1 complex cells to natural temporal inputs. J. Vis. 4(8), 278 (2004)
13. Petkov, N., Kruizinga, P.: Computational models of visual neurons specialised in the detection of periodic and aperiodic oriented visual stimuli: bar and grating cells. Biological Cybernetics 76(2), 83–96 (1997)

Multilayer and Multipathway Simulation on Retina

Hui Wei, Xudong Guan, and Qingsong Zuo

Department of Computer Science, Fudan University, Shanghai 200433, P.R. China

Abstract. In many fields including digital image processing and artificial retina design, they always confront a balance issue among real-time, accuracy, computing load, power consumption and other factors. It is difficult to achieve an optimal balance among these conflicting requirements. However, human retina can balance these conflicting requirements very well. It can efficiently and economically accomplish almost all the visual tasks. This paper presents a bio-inspired model of the retina, which simulates various types of retina cells and complex structure of retina. The Model can be used in bionic chip design, physiological assumptions verification, image processing, and a variety of goals.

Keywords: Retina, Bio-inspired Neural Computing, Simulation, Balance.

1 Introduction

In recent decades, computer vision has been widely applied to target tracking, object detection, position estimation, even missile guidance, and many other fields. However, many computer vision applications are still far from meeting all the requirements especially in real-time and accuracy balance, but our visual system not only can meet the real-time processing, but also can ensure high precision, not only can satisfy the various computing load requirements, but also can keep low power consumption. It might be an effective way to model retina's structure to try to solve the problem above.

This paper presents a realistic simulation retina model. With the help of this model, we can study retina internal representation of outside world and corresponding information processing pathways, and further, the model can guide the design of artificial retina chips.

2 Designs and Implementation of Retina Model

2.1 Overall Structure of Retina Model

Generally, retina includes photoreceptor cells, horizontal cells, bipolar cells, amacrine cells and ganglion cells, each of which includes a number of subtypes. The synaptic connections among cells constitute a very complex structure. There are a variety of synapses such as feed-forward synapse, feedback synapse, and horizontal connections synapse. Figure 1 is the overall structure of retina model which is abstracted from physiology and is used as a basis of our computing model. Based on this information processing diagram of retina, the paper presents a simulation retina model.

K. Diamantaras, W. Duch, L.S. Iliadis (Eds.): ICANN 2010, Part I, LNCS 6352, pp. 193–198, 2010.

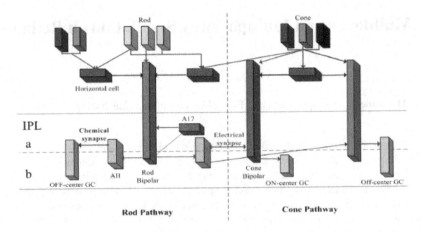

Fig. 1. Main information processing pathways model of retina

2.2 Photoreceptor Layer Simulation

Photoreceptor layer samples external optical signals and converts the external information into electronic signals. Fig.2 is a flow chart of photoreceptor layer simulation.

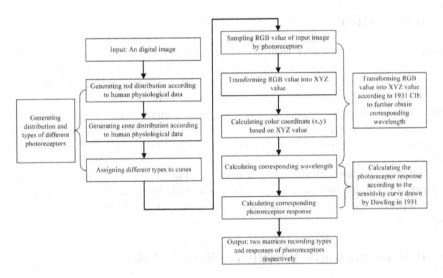

Fig. 2. Flow chart of photoreceptors layer simulation

Actually, photoreceptor layer simulation is a complex process. Generally, there are three steps. First, different types and distributions of photoreceptors are generated. Secondly, the corresponding wavelength is calculated according to the input RGB image information. Wavelength is the only factor to trigger photoreceptors to fire. Finally, calculating the strength of photoreceptors response based on the photoreceptor-wavelength sensitivity curve. (For detailed information, please refer to <<Realistic Emulation on Retina Photoreceptor Layer>> [10]).

2.3 Horizontal Cells and Bipolar Cells Simulation

Horizontal cell layer and bipolar cell layer are highly related to each other so they are put together to simulate. A new weight assignment method based on traditional DOG function is presented here to simulate horizontal and bipolar layer. This method solves some problems caused by DOG function in discrete situation. If there are n cells in central area of a bipolar cell's receptive field, the weight of ith cell is as Formula 1:

$$CWi = 1/(\sqrt{2\pi} \cdot \sigma_{center}) \cdot e^{-((x_i-x_0)^2+(y_i-y_0)^2)/2\cdot\sigma_{center}^2} / (\sum_{i=1}^{n} 1/(\sqrt{2\pi} \cdot \sigma_{center}) \cdot e^{-((x_i-x_0)^2+(y_i-y_0)^2)/2\cdot\sigma_{center}^2}) \quad (1)$$

Then the overall reaction of central area is as Formula 2:

$$Center_{exc}(x_0, y_0) = \sum_{i=1}^{n} P(x_i, y_i) * CWi \quad (2)$$

If there are m cells in surrounding area, the weight of jth cell is as Formula 3:

$$SWj = 1/(\sqrt{2\pi} \cdot \sigma_{surround}) \cdot e^{-((x_j-x_0)^2+(y_j-y_0)^2)/2\cdot\sigma_{surround}^2} / (\sum_{j=1}^{m} 1/(\sqrt{2\pi} \cdot \sigma_{surround}) \cdot e^{-((x_j-x_0)^2+(y_j-y_0)^2)/2\cdot\sigma_{surround}^2}) \quad (3)$$

Then overall reaction of surrounding area is as Formula 4:

$$Surround_{inh}(x_0, y_0) = \sum_{j=1}^{m} P(x_j, y_j) * SWj \quad (4)$$

Now the final output of the bipolar cell is as Formula 5:

$$BipolarR (x_0, y_0) = Center_{exc}(x_0, y_0) - Surround_{inh}(x_0, y_0) \quad (5)$$

2.4 Amacrine Cells Simulation

Amacrine cells play a significant role in visual signals integration and modulation. Dark vision, motion detection, non-classical receptive field formation, and time-domain information encoding are all relevant to amacrine cells. AII amacrine is simulated because AII has largest number and is regarded as the most important amacrine types. The information AII received from off-rod bipolar is as Formula 6:

$$AamcrineR (x_0, y_0) = \sum_{i=1}^{n} (RodBR(x_i, y_i) * 1/(\sqrt{2\pi} \cdot \sigma_{center}) \cdot e^{-((x_i-x_0)^2+(y_i-y_0)^2)/2\cdot\sigma_{center}^2}) \quad (6)$$

The information AII exchanged with on-cone bipolar cells:

$$Temp = C * AamcrineR (x_0, y_0) \quad (7)$$

$$AamcrineR (x_0, y_0) = (1-C) * AamcrineR (x_0, y_0) + C * ConeBR(x_0, y_0) \quad (8)$$

$$ConeBR (x_0, y_0) = (1-C) * ConeBR (x_0, y_0) + Temp \quad (9)$$

The C represents exchange rate. According to physiological data, C is set to 20%.

2.5 Ganglion Cells Simulation

As the final layer in retina, ganglion cell is responsible for collecting all information and transmitting information to brain. There are four types of ganglion cells considering P and M taxonomy and on and off taxonomy. The specific input proportion and relationships among different cells are shown in Figure 3:

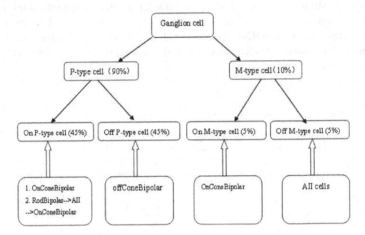

Fig. 3. Input proportion and relationships among different cells

On-center P type cells and on-center M type cell's reaction function is as Formula 10:

$$GanlionR\ (x_0,y_0)=\sum_{i=1}^{n}(OnBipolarR(x_i,y_i)*1/(\sqrt{2\pi}\cdot\sigma_{center})\cdot e^{-((x_i-x_0)^2+(y_i-y_0)^2)/2\cdot\sigma_{center}^2})\ (10)$$

The off-center P type cells receive off-center bipolar cell input. Its response function is shown as Formula 11:

$$GanlionR\ (x_0,y_0)=\sum_{i=1}^{n}(OffBipolarR(x_i,y_i)*1/(\sqrt{2\pi}\cdot\sigma_{center})\cdot e^{-((x_i-x_0)^2+(y_i-y_0)^2)/2\cdot\sigma_{center}^2})\ (11)$$

The off-center M type cells receive AII input. Its response function is as Formula 12:

$$GanlionR\ (x_0,y_0)=\sum_{i=1}^{n}(AResponse\ (x_i,y_i)*1/(\sqrt{2\pi}\cdot\sigma_{center})\cdot e^{-((x_i-x_0)^2+(y_i-y_0)^2)/2\cdot\sigma_{center}^2})\ (12)$$

3 Experiment Design and Results Analysis

3.1 Perception Efficiency of Retina for Different Stimulus Size in Different Position of Retina

It is known that the photoreceptors are in non-uniform distribution. The experiment is designed to test what size of an object can be fully perceived in different position of retina. We divided retina photoreceptors into 10 rings according to distribution data. In each ring, different size objects were used to test whether this part of retina can perceive the stimulus. The object size changed from smallest to bigger, if a certain size can always cause action potential, that means the size can be fully 100%

perceived in this ring of retina. This size stimulation is called "threshold stimulation". If an object is smaller than this size, it can not always cause response.

The experimental result is as shown in Fig.4 and Fig.5. In Fig.4, XYZ axes represent ring number, object size and perception percentage respectively. If all threshold stimulation sizes were recorded, they can be drawn into a curve as Fig5.

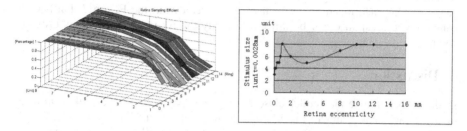

Fig. 4. Perception efficiency of different size in different position

Fig. 5. The threshold stimulation size stimulus in different position of retina

Physiology shows that density of ganglion cells decreases with the increase of eccentricity, which indicates that the perceive ability of retina may be weaker and weaker with increase of eccentricity. But it is not always true from the Fig.5, the reason is that we can not just consider ganglion cells density, but also need to take the photoreceptor cells density into account. For example, in the central area, although ganglion cells density is very high but the final response depends on the collected signals within all its receptive field, so how large the receptive field is and how many photoreceptors located within receptive field are the key to activate ganglion cells.

3.2 Ganglion Cells Representation of the Object

In ganglion cell layer, the final response may be quite different from original input image because the signals are classified and processed by different pathway, but the important information such as boundary, brightness and complexity will still be shown in the ganglion cells output. Figure 6 is an input image, Figure 7 is the corresponding ganglion cells output.

Fig. 6. Input image: Chinese chess

Fig. 7. Vertical view of ganglion cell layer response

As seen from Figure 7, the central area responses were much stronger than the peripheral area, which is consistent with the human eye characteristics that there are very high density and resolution in central area to distinguish detailed and fine information, and also more information in central area is transmitted into higher cortex. In addition, the edge information, as one of the most factors to understand the world, is well demonstrated in the ganglion cells layer. Meanwhile distribution characteristic of ganglion cells mentioned above is also can be seen from the Figure 7. Further, the ganglion cells response can be utilized to study the meaning of neural information coding.

4 Discussion

In this paper, the retina model closely integrated physiology data with simulation model, which makes model much closer to the real retina. But the model does not simulate dynamic visual information processing. That will be the next step to do. Retina's functions and structures are complex and diverse, there are still a lot of secrets waiting for us to explore.

Acknowledgments. Supported by 973 Program (Project No.2010CB327900) and Shanghai Science and Technology Development Funds (Project No.08511501703).

References

1. Shah, S., Martin, D.: Visual information processing in primate cone pathways. I.A model. IEEE Transactions On Systems, Man, And Cybernetics-Part B: Cybernetics 26(2), 259–274 (1996)
2. Publio, R., Oliveira, R.F., Roque, A.C.: A realistic model of rod photoreceptor for use in a retina network model. Neurocomputing 69, 1020–1024 (2006)
3. Niu, W.-Q., Yuan, J.-Q.: A multi-subunit spatiotemporal model of local edge detector cells in the cat retina. Neurocomputing (2008)
4. Tang, Q., Sang, N., Zhang, T.: A Neural Network Model for Extraction of Salient Contours. In: Wang, J., Liao, X.-F., Yi, Z. (eds.) ISNN 2005. LNCS, vol. 3497, pp. 316–320. Springer, Heidelberg (2005)
5. Cucurachi, G., Tascini, G., Piazza, F.: Neural Network for Region Detection. In: Proceedings of the 9th International Conference on Image Analysis and Processing, Vol. II, pp. 228–237
6. Reddick, W.E., Glass, J.O., Cook, E.N., Elkin, T.D., Deaton, R.J.: Automated segmentation and classification of multispectral magnetic resonance images of brain using artificial neural networks. IEEE Transactions on Medical Imaging 16(6), 911–918 (1997)
7. Risinger, L., Kaikhah, K.: Motion detection and object tracking with discrete leaky integrate-and-fire neurons. Appl. Intell. (2007)
8. Behrend, M.R., Ahuja, A.K., Humayun, M.S., Weiland, J.D., Chow, R.H.: Selective Labeling of Retinal Ganglion Cells with Calcium Indicators by Retrograde Loading In Vitro. Journal of Neuroscience Methods 179(2), 166–172 (2009)
9. Caspi, A., Dorn, J.D., McClure, K.H., Humayun, M.S., Greenberg, R.J., McMahon, M.J.: Feasibility Study of a Retinal Prosthesis: Spatial Vision with a 16-Electrode Implant. Archives of Ophthalmology 127(4), 398–401 (2009)
10. Guan, X., Wei, H.: Realistic Simulation on Retina Photoreceptor Layer. In: 2009 International Joint Conference on Artificial Intelligence, IJCAI 2009, pp. 179–184 (2009)

Analysis of Astrophysical Ice Analogs Using Regularized Alternating Least Squares

Raul Llinares, Jorge Igual, Julio Miro-Borras, and Andres Camacho

Universidad Politecnica de Valencia, Camino de Vera s/n
46022 Valencia, Spain
rllinares@dcom.upv.es

Abstract. The determination of the compounds that are present in molecular clouds is carried out from the study of the infrared spectrum of astrophysical ices. This analysis plays a fundamental role in the prediction of the future evolution of the cloud under study. The process is simulated in the laboratory under similar conditions of thermal and energetic processing, recording the infrared absorption spectrum of the resultant ice. The spectrum of each ice can be modeled as the linear instantaneous superposition of the spectrum of the different compounds, so a Source Separation approach is proper. We propose the use of Alternating Least Squares (ALS) and a Regularized version (RALS) to identify the molecules that are present in the ice mixtures. Since the spectra and abundances are non-negative, a non-negativity constraint can be applied to obtain solutions with physical meaning. We perform several simulations of synthetic mixtures of ices in order to compare both solutions and to show the usefulness of the approach.

1 Introduction

The knowledge of the chemistry of the ice clouds of the Interstellar Medium leads to the study of the determination of the necessary conditions for biogenic materials to appear [1]. The study is based on the analysis of the infrared spectrum of the different ices found in the cloud in order to identify their components. This study is usually carried out in the laboratory where the experiment can be controlled and the influence of variables such as the temperature or irradiation can be evaluated. Finally, the purpose is to simulate real environments in the laboratory to predict the future evolution of the cloud [2].

Different Blind Source Separation (BSS) techniques have been applied to identify the compounds present in astrophysical ice mixtures. The main advantage of these signal processing tools over spectral libraries is the possibility of identifying new unexpected compounds. The application of the simple linear instantaneous mixture model has been firstly addressed in [3]. An ensemble learning solution and a detailed explanation of the Independent Component Analysis model can be found in [4]. A Non-negative Matrix Factorization approach including a sparseness restriction is applied in [5]. All these BSS algorithms were revealed as powerful techniques to analyze large databases in order to determine the compounds present in every ice.

K. Diamantaras, W. Duch, L.S. Iliadis (Eds.): ICANN 2010, Part I, LNCS 6352, pp. 199–204, 2010.

Alternating Least Squares (ALS) is a classical algorithm for decomposing a data matrix into the product of two matrices under certain constraints. It is widely used as optimization technique in Self-Modeling Curve Resolution (SMCR) [6]. SMCR is a technique for separating pure spectra and concentration profiles from a matrix of spectra obtained from mixtures of components with varying concentrations [7]. Like the BSS methods, the SMCR methods attempt to determine the composition of the mixtures without, or with incomplete prior knowledge of the pure components or of the mixture procedure. An overview of the application of SMCR optimized by ALS to spectroscopic data acquired by monitoring chemical reactions and other processes is presented in [8].

In this study, we investigate the application of ALS in the analysis of astrophysical ices as a new application. We propose the use of a regularized ALS version exploiting the prior information about the sources (sparseness) to improve the quality of the analysis. Finally, we show that ALS and RALS are useful tools for the task of identifying the compounds in laboratory simulations of astrophysical ice mixtures.

2   Methods and Materials

2.1   Observation Model

We state the formulation of the problem as follows: the infrared absorption spectrum of the ices, $\mathbf{x}$, is the linear superposition of the absorption spectra of the molecules present in each ice, $\mathbf{s}$. The relative abundance of every molecule in the ices is modeled by the mixing matrix $\mathbf{A}$. In matrix form, the model is expressed in the following way:

$$\mathbf{X} = \mathbf{AS} + \mathbf{V} \tag{1}$$

where $\mathbf{X}(M, N)$ is the matrix of experimental data of dimensions M ices (mixtures) by N wavenumbers (observations); $\mathbf{A}(M, K)$ is the matrix of relative abundances profiles (mixing matrix) of the K different molecules (sources) present in the mixtures; $\mathbf{S}(K, N)$ is the matrix of the molecule spectra, whose K rows contain the pure spectra associated with the K molecules present in the mixtures and $\mathbf{V}(M, N)$ is the additive noise term that must be considered in real measurements.

The review of some physical considerations about the absorption spectra and the molecules to justify the conditions of suitability of the BSS model (2) for the problem is carried out in [4].

2.2   Regularized Alternating Least Squares

ALS is a signal processing technique for estimating the matrices $\mathbf{A}$ and $\mathbf{S}$ of the model (2) from the observation data matrix $\mathbf{X}$. The algorithm consists of two alternating steps:

$$\mathbf{S} = \left(\mathbf{A}^T \mathbf{A}\right)^{-1} \mathbf{A}^T \mathbf{X} \tag{2}$$

$$\mathbf{A} = \mathbf{X}\mathbf{S}^T \left(\mathbf{S}\mathbf{S}^T\right)^{-1} \tag{3}$$

Equations (3) and (4) can be derived by first estimating the gradients of the squared Euclidean distance, $D_F(\mathbf{X}\,\|\,\mathbf{AS}) = \frac{1}{2}\,\|\mathbf{X} - \mathbf{AS}\|_F^2$ with respect to $\mathbf{A}$ and $\mathbf{S}$ and then, equating them to zero.

We can exploit an interesting property of the sources to adapt the ALS algorithm to the application. Considering the histogram of the spectra of the molecules, most of them correspond to supergaussian signals, due to the fact that there is no absorption in most wavelengths. This constraint can be introduced adding a new term to the corresponding cost function enforcing the sparseness. Hence, the cost function of the regularized version (RALS) reads:

$$D_F(\mathbf{X}\,\|\,\mathbf{AS}) = \frac{1}{2}\,\|\mathbf{X} - \mathbf{AS}\|_F^2 + \alpha_S J_S(\mathbf{S}) \tag{4}$$

where $\alpha_S \geq 0$ is the regularization parameter and the function $J_S(\mathbf{S}) = \sum_{jk} s_{jk}$ is used to enforce the sparse representation of the solution. In this case, the corresponding alternating least squares estimation is given by the following two equations:

$$\mathbf{S} = \left(\mathbf{A}^T \mathbf{A} + \alpha_S\right)^{-1} \mathbf{A}^T \mathbf{X} \tag{5}$$

$$\mathbf{A} = \mathbf{X}\mathbf{S}^T \left(\mathbf{S}\mathbf{S}^T\right)^{-1} \tag{6}$$

The parameter α_S of RALS is given by the exponential rule $\alpha_S = \alpha_0 e^{(-k/\tau)}$ where α_0 and τ are constant values and k is the iteration number. This choice avoids getting stuck in local minima [9].

Two constraints must to be applied to the algorithm. The first one is the non-negativity: the solutions are obtained by projecting (3), (4) and (6), (7) onto $\mathbb{R}_+$, i.e., $\mathbf{S} \leftarrow max\{\varepsilon, \mathbf{S}\}$ and $\mathbf{A} \leftarrow max\{\varepsilon, \mathbf{A}\}$. The second constraint refers to the normalization: the k-column of the matrix $\mathbf{A}$ must accomplish $\|a_k\| = 1$, $\forall k$.

2.3   Database

The data corresponds to the public ice analogs database of the University of Leiden [10]. This database contains the infrared spectra of laboratory analogs of interstellar ices. Different mixtures of molecules (from one up to three components selected from H_2, H_2O, NH_3, CH_4, CO, H_2CO, CH_3OH, $HCOOH$, O_2, N_2 and CO_2) at different temperatures and UV radiation exposures were produced, the final spectrum being calculated ratioing the measured and the background spectrum. The units of the data are absorbance and cm^{-1}. Fig. 1 shows the spectra of the pure ices (molecules) used in the experiments.

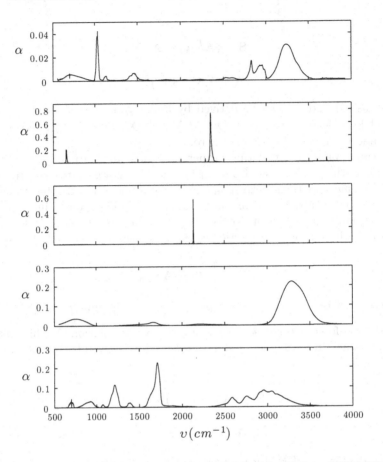

Fig. 1. Spectrum of the pure ices: CH_3OH, CO, CO_2, H_2O and $HCOOH$

3   Simulation Results

The algorithms ALS (defined by equations (3) and (4)) and RALS (defined by equations (6) and (7)) were tested with synthetic mixtures of ices. In addition, we compared the perfomance of ALS and RALS with the regularized version of the NMF algorithm based on Frobenius norm (RNMF) [5] (the MATLAB implementation of the three algorithms can be found in [11]). The optimal values corresponding to the regularization parameters were calculated experimentally for this dataset according to the SIR of the estimated sources. The obtained values were $\alpha_0 = 100$ and $\tau = 100$ for RALS and $\alpha_S = 0.06$ for RNMF.

We mixed the five pure molecule spectra shown in Fig. 1 with a uniformly distributed randomly generated mixing matrix $\mathbf{A} \in \mathbb{R}^{10 \times 5}$. For the three algorithms, we choose an initial $\mathbf{A}$ and $\mathbf{S}$ with the following procedure: the algorithm was run 10 times for a number of 200 iterations; then we calculated the SIR and chose the best out of the ten trials as the initialization point. Fig. 2 shows a box and whisker plot of the results of the mean-SIR obtained by a Montecarlo analysis performed for 100 runs. RALS outperforms RNMF and ALS in terms of SIR. The SIR obtained by RALS was $29.08 \pm 1.41 \cdot 10^{-13}$ dB confirming that the choice of the exponential rule for the regularization terms avoids getting stuck in local minima. Comparing the results of the non-regularized version (ALS) with those of both regularized versions (RALS and RNMF), it can be seen that the sparsness constraint fits the algorithms better to the application.

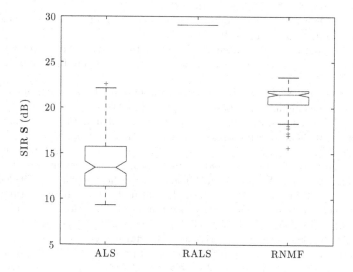

Fig. 2. Box and whisker plot of the SIR for **S** obtained by the different methods

4   Conclusions

In this paper we have proposed a new application of ALS in Astrophysics. We have addressed how ALS can be adapted to the applicaton improving the results. The supergaussian statistical behaviour of the ice spectra can be taken into account as a sparseness constraint added to the ALS cost function. The use of a self-compensate regularization term generally leads to a convergence to the global desired solution. The performance of RALS is compared with the non-modified version of the algorithm, ALS, and with the modified version of the classical NMF algorithm imposing sparseness, RNMF. RALS is shown to be superior in terms of performance with synthetic mixtures of ices. The proposed RALS method is a promising tool for the identificacion of compounds in astrophysical ices.

Acknowledgements. This work has been funded by the Valencia Regional Government (Generalitat Valenciana) through project GV/2010/002 (Conselleria d'Educacio) and by the Universidad Politecnica de Valencia under grant no. PAID-06-09-003-382.

References

1. Allamandola, L.J., Bernstein, M.P., Sandford, S.A., Walker, R.L.: Evollution of Interestellar Ices. Space Science Reviews 90, 219–232 (1999)
2. Baratta, G.A., Palumbo, M.E., Strazzulla, G.: Laboratory and astronomical IR spectra: an experimental clue for their comparison. Astronomy and Astrophysics 357, 1045–1050 (1997)
3. Igual, J., Llinares, R., Salazar, A.: Source Separation of Astrophysical Ice Mixtures. In: Rosca, J.P., Erdogmus, D., Príncipe, J.C., Haykin, S. (eds.) ICA 2006. LNCS, vol. 3889, pp. 368–375. Springer, Heidelberg (2006)
4. Igual, J., Llinares, R.: An informed source separation of astrophysical ice analogs. Digital Signal Processing 17, 947–964 (2007)
5. Igual, J., Llinares, R.: Nonnegative Matrix Factorization of Laboratory Astrophysical Ice Mixtures. IEEE Journal of Selected Topics in Signal Processing 2, 697–706 (2008)
6. Jiang, J., Liang, Y., Ozaki, Y.: Principles and methodologies in self-modeling curve resolution. Chemom. Intell. Lab. Syst. 71, 1–12 (2004)
7. de Juan, A., Cassasas, E., Tauler, R.: Sot-Modeling of analytical data. Encyclopedia of analytical chemistry: instrumentation and applications (2000)
8. Garrido, M., Rius, F.X., Larrechi, M.S.: Multivariate curve resolution–alternating least squares (MCR-ALS) applied to spectroscopic data from monitoring chemical reactions processes. Analytical and Bioanalytical Chemistry 390, 2059–2066 (2008)
9. Cichocki, A., Zdunek, R.: Regularized alternating least squares algorithms for non-negative matrix/tensor factorization. In: Liu, D., Fei, S., Hou, Z., Zhang, H., Sun, C. (eds.) ISNN 2007. LNCS, vol. 4493, pp. 793–802. Springer, Heidelberg (2007)
10. http://www.strw.leidenuniv.nl/~schutte/database.html
11. Cichocki, A., Zdunek, R.: NMFLAB for signal processing. Technical report, Laboratory for Advanced Brain Signal Processing, BSI RIKEN, Saitama, Japan (2006)

A BCI System Based on Orthogonalized EEG Data and Multiple Multilayer Neural Networks in Parallel Form

Kenji Nakayama, Hiroki Horita, and Akihiro Hirano

Graduate School of Natural Science and Technology, Kanazawa University
Kanazawa, 920-1192, Japan
nakayama@t.kanazawa-u.ac.jp
http://leo.ec.t.kanazawa-u.ac.jp/~nakayama

Abstract. A BCI system, using orthogonalized EEG data sets and multiple multilayer neural networks (MLNNs) in a parallel form, is proposed. In order to emphasize feature of multi-channel EEG data, Gram-Schmidt orthogonalization has been applied. Since there are many channel orders to be orthogonalized, many kinds of orthogonalized data sets can be generated for the same EEG data set by changing the channel order. These data sets have different features. In the proposed method, different channel orders are assigned to the multiple MLNNs in a training phase and in a classification process. A good solution can be searched for by changing the channel orders within a small number of trials. By using EEG data for five mental tasks, a correct classification rate is increased from 88% to 92%, and an error classification rate is decreased from 4% to 0%.

Keywords: BCI, EEG, Brain waves, Neural network, Mental task, Orthogonal components, Gram-Schmidt.

1 Introduction

Approaches to BCI systems include nonlinear classification by using spectrum power, adaptive auto-regressive model and linear classification, space patterns and linear classification, hidden Markov models, and so on [1]. Furthermore, neural networks have been also applied [2]. In our previous works, FFT of EEG data and a multilayer neural network (MLNN) have been applied to the BCI. Efficient pre-processing techniques to extract features have been also employed [5]. Furthermore, the generalization learning methods have been applied [4],[6]. Effects of sensor locations has been analyzed for BCI using MEG data [7].

Methods to extract essential features of the multi-channel EEG data have been proposed. In our previous work, Gram-Schmidt orthogonalization has been applied to generate the orthogonal components [8]. The orthogonalized data sets have different features for the different channel order to be orthogonalized, resulting in different classification performances. For this reason, the optimum channel order should be searched for [8].

K. Diamantaras, W. Duch, L.S. Iliadis (Eds.): ICANN 2010, Part I, LNCS 6352, pp. 205–210, 2010.

2   BCI System Based on Multiple MLNNs

2.1   Gram-Schmidt Orthogonalization

The vectors $\{x_1, x_2, \cdots, x_M\}$, which express the brain waves at M-channels, are usually linearly independent. This set can be transferred into the orthogonal vector set $\{v_1, v_2, \cdots, v_M\}$ by Gram-Schmidt orthogonalization [9]. $\{v_i\}$ are Fourier transformed and their amplitude are pre-processed [5], and are used as the MLNN input data [8].

2.2   Proposed BCI System Using Orthogonalized EEG and Multiple MLNNs in Parallel Form

In order to overcome the above channel order problem, a BCI system using multiple MLNNs in a parallel form, shown in Fig.1, is proposed in this paper.

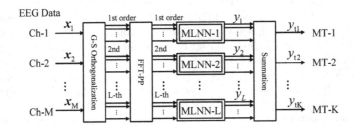

Fig. 1. A BCI system using orthogonalized EEG data and multiple MLNNs in parallel form. L kinds of channel orders are used for MLNN-1~MLNN-L.

Let v_{ij} be the i-th orthogonalized input data set generated by using the i-th channel order. L input data sets, $v_{ij}, i = 1 \sim L, j = 1 \sim M$, are generated from the same EEG data set, and are applied to MLNN-i, $i = 1 \sim L$ individually. They are trained independently so as to output the desired response. In the classification process, letting the output of MLNN-i be $y_i = [y_{i1}, y_{i2}, \cdots, y_{iK}]^T, i = 1 \sim L$, the total output y_{tk} is given by Eq.(1). The mental task is classified based on the maximum element in $y_t = [y_{t1}, y_{t2}, \cdots, y_{tK}]^T$ [5].

$$y_{tk} = \frac{1}{L} \sum_{i=1}^{L} y_{ik}, \qquad k = 1 \sim K \tag{1}$$

2.3   Conventional Multiple MLNNs in Parallel Form

A similar structure has been proposed as shown in Fig.2 [10], denoted 'Method-I' in this paper. MLNN-i, $i = 1 \sim L$ receive the same input data, that is $x_1, x_2, \cdots, x_M$, and provide the outputs, $y_i = [y_{i1}, y_{i2}, \cdots, y_{iK}]^T, i = 1 \sim L$, which represent the corresponding mental task. In order to realize high generalization performances, different initial connection weights are assigned to MLNN-1 $\sim$MLNN-L. Each MLNN is trained so as to output the desired targets. The final outputs are also given by Eq.(1)

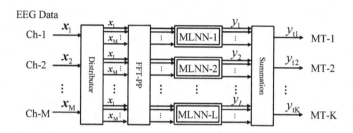

Fig. 2. Conventional Method-I: EEG data are not orthogonalized. Initial connection weights of MLNN-1 $\sim$ MLNN-L are different.

Another conventional approach using multiple MLNNs is 'Bagging Method' [11], called 'Method-II' in this paper. MLNN-1 $\sim$MLNN-L are trained by using different EEG data for the same mental task. Each MLNN is trained to output the desired targets, and the final outputs are given by Eq.(1). In the classification process, a single EEG data set is applied to all MLNNs.

In the proposed method (Fig.1), the EEG data are orthogonalized. On the other hand, the conventional methods, that is Method-I and Method-II, use the original EEG data. As described in Sec.2.1, the Gram-Schmidt orthogonalization process can generate different orthogonalized data sets by changing the channel order. This means that feature of each channel can be emphasized, at the same time, different kinds of feature sets can be generated, which can be effectively applied to MLNNs. These two points of the proposed method can improve the mental task classification performance.

3   Simulations and Discussions

In this paper, EEG data, available from the web site of Colorado State University [3], are used. The following five kinds of mental tasks are employed. (1)Baseline-relaxed situation, (2)Multiplication, (3)Letter composing, (4)Rotation of a 3-D object, (5)Counting numbers.

3.1   Simulation Setup

The EEG data with a 10 sec length for five mental tasks were measured 10 times. Therefore, 10 data sets are available. Among them, 8 data sets are used for training and the remaining 2 data sets are used for testing. Five different combinations of 2 data sets are used for the testing. Thus, five independent trials are carried out. Classification accuracy is evaluated based on the average over five trials [1].

Mental task classification is evaluated based on a correct classification rate (P_c), an error classification rate (P_e) and a rate of correct and error classification (R_c) as follows:

$$P_c = \frac{N_c}{N_t} \times 100\%, \quad P_e = \frac{N_e}{N_t} \times 100\% \tag{2}$$

$$R_c = \frac{N_c}{N_c + N_e}, \quad N_t = N_c + N_e + N_r \tag{3}$$

N_c, N_e and N_r are the numbers of correct and error classifications and rejections, respectively. When the MLNN outputs are smaller than the threshold, no estimation is provided, that is 'Rejected'. N_t is the total number of the testing data. R_c is used to evaluate a correct classification rate except for 'Rejection'.

The number of hidden units is 20. The threshold for rejection is set to be 0.7. The MLNNs are trained by the error back propagation learning algorithm.

3.2 Classification Performances

Table 1 shows classification performances of the proposed BCI system shown in Fig.1. In the learning process, small random numbers, uniformly distributed in $[-0.05, 0.05]$, are added to the MLNN input in 'Generalization' and not added in 'No Generalization'. The channel orders, with which good classification performances are obtained in the BCI system using a single MLNN shown in Fig.1, are used. 'L' is the number of the MLNNs in a parallel form. For example, in the case of '$L = 5$', five kinds of the above channel orders are used for MLNN-1~MLNN-5. 'Average' means average values of P_c, P_e and R_c of the BCI system for all channel orders. In this table, P_e is always zero. P_c can be improved by the generalization method.

Table 1. Classification performance of proposed method

L	No Generalization			Generalization		
	$P_c[\%]$	$P_e[\%]$	R_c	$P_c[\%]$	$P_e[\%]$	R_c
Average	71.5	12.2	0.855	82.3	8.1	0.911
5	76	0	0.947	80	0	0.957
10	80	0	0.929	78	0	0.978
20	78	0	1.0	84	0	1.0
30	76	0	1.0	84	0	1.0

Table 2 shows classification performance of Method-I. Even though P_c can be improved from the proposed method, P_e stil remains $4 \sim 6\%$. Table 3 shows classification performances of Method-II. Compared to the previous two methods, the classification accuracy is not so good.

Table 2. Classification performance of Conventional Method-I

	No Generalization			Generalization		
L	$P_c[\%]$	$P_e[\%]$	R_c	$P_c[\%]$	$P_e[\%]$	R_c
Average	76.1	7.3	0.912	86.8	5.4	0.942
5	76	6	0.927	88	4	0.957
10	76	6	0.927	88	4	0.957
20	76	6	0.927	88	4	0.957
30	76	6	0.927	88	4	0.957

Table 3. Classification performance of Conventional Method-II (Bagging Method)

	No Generalization			Genaralization		
L	$P_c[\%]$	$P_e[\%]$	R_c	$P_c[\%]$	$P_e[\%]$	R_c
Average	65.5	13.9	0.825	75.9	11.5	0.867
5	60	8	0.882	76	0	1.0
10	66	6	0.917	76	0	1.0
20	66	6	0.917	76	2	0.974
30	68	6	0.919	76	2	0.974

3.3 Searching for Good Solution in Proposed BCI System

The following searching method is proposed in this paper. In one trial, the combination of the channel orders, which are randomly determined and are used in the BCI system shown in Fig.1, is changed 10 times. 10 kinds of solutions for the BCI system can be obtained. Among them, the best solution is selected. This kind of the trial is repeated 5 times (Trial: 1st, 2nd, 3rd, 4th, 5th), in order to confirm general efficiency. The simulation results are shown in Table 4. Good solutions with the highest R_c are selected in each trial, and are listed in this table. As shown in this table, very high P_c, that is more than 90%, and very low P_e, that is zero, can be obtained for $L = 10$. These results are very superior to the results of the conventional methods.

This result means (1) the channel orders assigned to multiple MLNNs can be determined randomly, and (2) the good solution can be searched for by changing the combination of the channel orders only 10 times. The same results were obtained for another subjects.

Table 4. Classification performance of proposed method. Best solution is searched for.

Trial	$L = 5$			$L = 10$		
	$P_c[\%]$	$P_e[\%]$	R_c	$P_c[\%]$	$P_e[\%]$	R_c
1st	88	0	1.0	92	0	1.0
2nd	88	0	1.0	92	0	1.0
3rd	88	2	0.978	92	0	1.0
4th	92	0	1.0	92	0	1.0
5th	88	0	1.0	92	0	1.0

4 Conclusion

A BCI system, which uses multiple MLNNs in a parallel form with the orthogonalized EEG data sets, is proposed. Different channel orders are assigned to the
multiple MLNNs. By searching for good solutions for different combinations of
the channel orders, the correct classification of $P_c = 92\%$ and the error classification of $P_e = 0\%$ can be obtained. These results are very superior to those of
the conventional methods.

References

1. Anderson, C., Sijercic, Z.: Classification of EEG signals from four subjects during
   five mental tasks. In: Bulsari, A.B., Kallio, S., Tsaptsinos, D. (eds.) EANN 1996,
   Systems Engineering Association, PL34, FIN-20111, Finland, pp. 407–414 (1996)
2. Muller, K.R., Anderson, C.W., Birch, G.E.: Linear and non-linear methods for
   brain-computer interfaces. IEEE Trans. Neural Sys. Rehab. Eng. 11(2), 165–169
   (2003)
3. Colorado State University, http://www.cs.colostate.edu/eeg/
4. Robert, J., Burton, M., Mpitsos, G.J.: Event-dependent control of noise enhances
   learning in neurla networks. Neural Networks 5(4), 627–637 (1992)
5. Nakayama, K., Inagaki, K.: A brain computer interface based on neural network
   with efficient pre-processing. In: Proc. IEEE, ISPACS 2006, Yonago, Japan, pp.
   673–676 (December 2006)
6. Nakayama, K., Kaneda, Y., Hirano, A.: A brain computer interface based on FFT
   and multilayer neural network-Feature extraction and generalization. In: Proc.
   IEEE, ISPACS 2007, Xiamen, China, pp. 101–104 (December 2007)
7. Nakayama, K., Kaneda, Y., Hirano, A., Haruta, Y.: A BCI using MEG vision
   and multilayer neural network - Channel optimization and main lobe contribution
   analysis. In: Proc., IEEE ISPACS 2008, Bangkok, Thailand, pp. 316–319 (February
   2009)
8. Nakayama, K., Horita, H., Hirano, A.: Neural network based BCI by using orthogonal components of multi-channel brain waves and generalization. In: Kůrková, V.,
   Neruda, R., Koutník, J. (eds.) ICANN 2008, Part II. LNCS, vol. 5164, pp. 879–888.
   Springer, Heidelberg (2008)
9. Strang, G.: Linear Algebra and its Applications. Academic Press, Inc., N.Y. (1976)
10. Caruana, R.: Multitask learning. Machine Learning 28(1), 41–75 (1997)
11. Bauer, E., Kohavi, R.: An empirical comparison of voting classification algorithms:
    Bagging, Boosting, and Variants. Machine Learning 36, 105–142 (1999)

Using an Artificial Neural Network to Determine Electrical Properties of Epithelia

Thomas Schmid[1], Dorothee Günzel[2], and Martin Bogdan[1]

[1] Dept. of Computer Engineering, Faculty of Mathematics and Informatics,
University of Leipzig, Johannisgasse 26, 04103 Leipzig, Germany
[2] Institute of Clinical Physiology, Charité,
Campus Benjamin Franklin, 12200 Berlin, Germany

Abstract. The present study introduces a new approach for modeling electrical properties of epithelia. Artificial neural networks (ANNs) are used to estimate key parameters that otherwise can only be measured directly by applying complex and time-consuming laboratory methods. Assuming an electrical model equivalent to an epithelial layer, an ANN can be trained to learn the relation between these parameters and experimentally obtained impedance spectra. We demonstrate that even with a naive ANN our approach reduces the error rate of parameter estimation to less than 20 per cent. Successful test runs provide a proof of concept.

Keywords: Artificial neural network, epithelia, electrical circuit, impedance spectroscopy, FlexNet.

1 Introduction

Epithelia form barriers between external and internal compartments of an organism. Dysfunctions of epithelial layers can lead to diseases, e.g. to severe diarrhea in inflamed or infected gut. Another major task is the uptake or secretion of solutes. Driving force for this transport results from concentration, hydrostatic and potential gradients, and is mediated by ion channels or carrier molecules in the apical and basolateral cell membranes (transcellular pathway) and by pore-forming proteins within the tight junction between two adjacent cells (paracellular pathway). Tight junctions can block as well as selectively admit transport of ions, macromolecules and water. This selectivity varies between different tissues and can be altered under physiological or pathophysiological conditions.

Electrical properties of epithelia can be depicted as an equivalent circuit (Fig. 1a). The present work is based on a two-membrane model for ion and water transport, which implies an apical capacitance C^{ap} and resistance R^{ap} as well as a basolateral capacitance C^{bl} and resistance R^{bl} and further a conductive pathway between epithelial cells (R^{para}).

While the overall transepithelial resistance ($R_T = R^{sub} + R^{epi}$) can easily be measured, and a method to discriminate between transcellular ($R^{trans} = R^{ap}R^{bl}/(R^{ap} + R^{bl})$) and paracellular resistance has recently been published [1],

K. Diamantaras, W. Duch, L.S. Iliadis (Eds.): ICANN 2010, Part I, LNCS 6352, pp. 211–216, 2010.

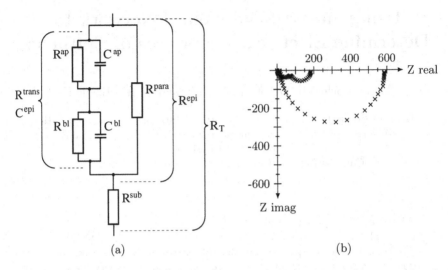

(a)   (b)

Fig. 1. (a) Equivalent electrical circuit for a model discriminating between the apical (index ap) and the basolateral (index bl) side of an epithelium. In this model, C^{epi} is composed of C^{ap} and C^{bl} ($C^{epi} = \frac{C^{ap}C^{bl}}{C^{ap}+C^{bl}}$). (b) Overlap of two Nyquist diagrams obtained from colonic carcinoma HT-29/B6 cells at 42 different AC frequencies between 1.3 and 16,000 Hz. At high AC frequencies Z_{re} approaches R^{sub}, at low frequencies $R_T = R^{sub} + R^{epi}$. C^{epi} can be calculated from the frequency ω at which Z_{im} reaches a minimum ($C^{epi} = \frac{1}{\omega Z_{im\,min} R^{epi}}$). In untreated cells the Nyquist diagram yields a semicircle, as $\tau^{ap} \approx \tau^{bl}$. Apical application of the ionophor nystatin causes a decrease in R^{ap} and τ^{ap} and a deviation of the curve from its original semicircular form.

existing techniques fail to provide a fast and reliable way of determining all parameters for the model given in Fig. 1a.

A technique suggested in 1998 allowed computer-aided dynamic modeling for intact epithelia [2]. By using conventional transepithelial voltage clamp and a least squares algorithm, the total membrane capacitance C^{epi} could be estimated with a confidence of 99 per cent. For single model parameters like C^{ap} or C^{bl}, however, only a precision of $\pm20\%$ was possible.

Here, we introduce an ANN based approach for estimating C^{ap}, C^{bl}, R^{ap} and R^{bl} with less than 20 per cent error rate from epithelial measurements.

2   Principles of Data Processing

Network training and testing is based on impedance spectra obtained from experiments on epithelial cell layers. Whereas the testing data are actually measured impedance spectra, the training data are calculated according to the electrical model (Fig. 1a) and by deriving information from the actual measurement.

It is an essential prerequisite that the testing impedance spectra are obtained from a cell layer in the presence of a substance altering either R^{ap} or R^{bl}. Such alteration affects the relation $\tau^{ap} \sim \tau^{bl}$. Fig. 1b shows data from an experiment where R^{ap} has been decreased by apical drug application, leading to $\tau^{ap} \ll \tau^{bl}$. A second prerequisite is that the values for C^{epi} and R^{para} have to be determined, e.g. by two-path impedance spectroscopy as described by Krug et al. [1].

Impedance spectroscopy is a well-established method for analysis of electrical properties of solid state bodies, but also common in electrophysiological analysis of tissues and cells (see e.g. [1,3,4]). During an impedance measurement an alternating current (AC) of known frequency ω and amplitude I_0 is applied to a system, while amplitude V_0 and phase difference ϕ of the concomitant electrical potential are measured. Z can be expressed as a complex number $Z = R + iX$. Real part Z_{re} and imaginary part Z_{im} describe the resistance R and the reactance X, respectively.

It has been demonstrated that the subepithelial resistance R^{sub} and the epithelial resistance R^{epi} (Fig. 1a) can be determined by impedance measurements [3]. In a plot of Z_{re} versus Z_{im} (Nyquist diagram, Fig. 1b) the lower root indicates the value for R^{sub}, and the upper root for $R_T = R^{sub} + R^{epi}$.

Considering all components in Fig. 1a, the equation for an impedance Z_T at a specific frequency ω can be derived. As the ohmic resistances R^{sub}, R^{para}, R^{ap}, R^{bl}, and the reactances $(= \frac{1}{i\omega C})$ of the capacitors C^{ap} and C^{bl} are used, an epithelial impedance Z^{epi} can be derived as:

$$Z^{epi}(\omega) = Z_T - R_{sub} \tag{1}$$

$$= \frac{R^{para}(R^{ap} + R^{bl}) + i\omega[R^{para}(R^{ap}\tau^{bl} + R^{bl}\tau^{ap})]}{R^{ap} + R^{bl} + R^{para}(1 - \omega^2\tau^{bl}\tau^{ap}) + i\omega[R^{para}(\tau^{ap} + \tau^{bl}) + R^{ap}\tau^{bl} + R^{bl}\tau^{ap}]}$$

3   Creating Appropriate Training Data

As an impedance can be deduced from the electrical model (Eq. (1)), the following relation between a Nyquist diagram consisting of n impedance data points (with frequencies $\omega_0, \omega_1, \ldots, \omega_{n-1}$) and the electrical model ensues:

$$(Z_{\omega_0}, Z_{\omega_1}, \ldots, Z_{\omega_{n-1}}) \sim (R^{ap}, C^{ap}, R^{bl}, C^{bl}, R^{para}, R^{sub}) \tag{2}$$

While R^{para} and C^{epi} are given as prerequisite, R^{sub} and R^{epi} have to be determined or extrapolated from the Nyquist diagram of the sample. If R^{epi} and R^{para} are known, R^{trans} can easily be deduced from the electrical model.

Varying R^{ap}, R^{bl}, C^{ap} and C^{bl} allows to simulate Nyquist diagrams for different hypothetical experiment settings for the test measurement:

$$(R^{ap}, C^{ap}, R^{bl}, C^{bl}) \in (\mathbb{R}_+ \times \mathbb{R}_+ \times \mathbb{R}_+ \times \mathbb{R}_+) \tag{3}$$

However, there are implicit constraints. Values for R^{ap} are limited by $R^{ap} \leq R^{trans}$, values for C^{ap} are limited by $C^{ap} \geq C^{epi}$. Unfortunately, no feasible upper limit C_{max} can be calculated; this value has to be specified manually. Values for R^{bl} depend on R^{trans} and R^{ap}, as $R^{bl} = R^{trans} - R^{ap}$. Values for C^{bl}

depend on C^{epi} and C^{ap}, as $\frac{1}{C^{bl}} = \frac{1}{C^{epi}} - \frac{1}{C^{ap}}$. To ensure efficient ANN training, equally distributed subsets of possible values have to be used.

It is extremely important to note that the model of the electrical properties of epithelia used here can lead to identical impedance data (or Nyquist diagrams respectively) for different parameter tuples $(R^{ap}, R^{bl}, C^{ap}, C^{bl})$. This is due to the symmetry of the RC components of the transcellular pathway (Fig. 1a). Training an ANN more than once with the same input data will decrease training efficiency and estimation quality if the correlated output is not identical.

There are two scenarios, in which such harmful redundancy can appear:

- Interchanging $R^{ap} \leftrightarrow R^{bl}$, $C^{ap} \leftrightarrow C^{bl}$: Assuming two pseudo measurements with corresponding tuples $(R^{ap}_1, R^{bl}_1, C^{ap}_1, C^{bl}_1)$ and $(R^{ap}_2, R^{bl}_2, C^{ap}_2, C^{bl}_2)$, calculations will result in the same impedances if:

$$R^{ap}_1 = R^{bl}_2, \quad R^{bl}_1 = R^{ap}_2, \quad C^{ap}_1 = C^{bl}_2, \quad C^{bl}_1 = C^{ap}_2 \quad (4)$$

- $\tau^{ap} = \tau^{bl}$: If the apical and basolateral time constants $\tau = RC$ are of same value, it is not possible to distinguish apical or basolateral properties from a Nyquist diagram. But moreover, distinct tuples $(R^{ap}_1, C^{ap}_1, R^{bl}_1, C^{bl}_1)$ and $(R^{ap}_2, C^{ap}_2, R^{bl}_2, C^{bl}_2)$ - that do not appear in the first scenario - can lead to identical values for τ^{ap} and τ^{bl} and therefore cause redundancy.

The easiest way to ensure that the first scenario is not produced, is to add less-than relation constraints $(R^{ap} < R^{bl}, C^{ap} < C^{bl})$. The second scenario can be avoided by simply excluding tuples where $\tau^{ap} = \tau^{bl}$. Note that this exclusion of tuples does not prevent feasible approximation of parmeter values. Only apical/ basolateral assignment for resistances and capacitances is lost; actual values will be correct. The assignment can be deduced from experiment settings, i.e. if two-path impedance spectroscopy has been used to determine R^{para}.

4   ANN Architecture and Test Settings

The present approach was examplarily tested with two different ANN approaches using the ANN simulation tool FAST [5]. Both architectures are based on a fixed equally distributed subset of eight data points of the Nyquist diagrams. In both approaches, standard backpropagation was used as learning rule.

The first approach used the network construction algorithm FlexNet [6] to determine an appropriate architecture. FlexNet allows network construction for given data with a basically unlimited number of hidden layers and units. Special features of this algorithm, such as cross-cut connections, were not exploited.

As a second approach, a bottle neck architecture with 20 hidden units in three layers was used (layer structure: 16-8-4-8-4). Each unit in the first hidden layer represents an impedance Z, or data point of a Nyquist diagram respectively, where Z_{re} and Z_{im} are represented each by an input unit. The parameters of interest $(R^{ap}, R^{bl}, C^{ap}, C^{bl})$ are represented by four output units.

Prerequisitory parameters. Values for C^{epi} and R^{para} were derived from a physiological experiment: $C^{epi} = 3.5\ \mu F/cm^2$, $R^{para} = 4069\ \Omega cm^2$. For determination of R^{sub} and R^{epi} an ideal estimation has been assumed: $R^{sub} = 9.8\ \Omega cm^2$, $R^{epi} = 772\ \Omega cm^2$. R^{trans} was deduced to amount to $952\ \Omega cm^2$.

Training data. Each vector starts with 16 inputs values representing Z_{re} and Z_{im} each. The four following values are the values of the corresponding parameters of interest. R^{ap} and R^{bl} have been chosen with value distances of $10\ \Omega cm^2$ and C^{ap} and C^{bl} with value distances of $0.1\ \mu F/cm^2$; C_{max} was chosen as 15 $\mu F/cm^2$. This resulted in a total of 61,664 training vectors.

Test data. The τ quotient was assumed to be ≥ 5.0, and parameter tuples chosen appropriately. Values for R^{ap} and R^{bl} ranged between $111.111\ \Omega cm^2$ and $841.639\ \Omega cm^2$, values for C^{ap} and C^{bl} ranged between $4.111\ \mu F/cm^2$ and $14.444\ \mu F/cm^2$. A total of five impedance measurements matching the prerequisitory constraints were calculated according to section 2 and used as test data.

5 Results

Without avoiding harmful redundancy error rates cannot be notably reduced for FlexNet or for the standard backpropagation during the training progress; instead, oscillation is observed. Therefore, these redundancies in the training data were eliminated as described in section 3. Notable reduction of error rate for both ANN approaches, however, was only observed with very small learning rates. With a learning rate ≤ 0.0001, FlexNet could achieve error rates $\leq 5\%$ for known and $\leq 20\%$ for unknown Nyquist diagrams (Fig. 2a). Same holds true for the standard backpropagation architecture (Fig. 2b).

A learning rate of 0.00001 showed only minimal distortions (like oscillation) while steadily reducing the error rate. By this, the above mentioned error rates

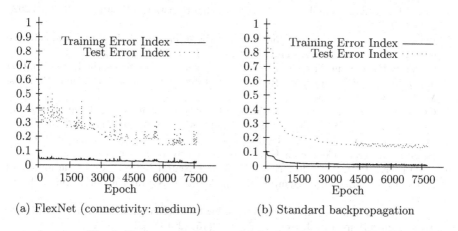

(a) FlexNet (connectivity: medium)   (b) Standard backpropagation

Fig. 2. Progress of training with learning rate 0.00001

were achieved within less than 7,500 epochs for both approaches. Estimations were, however, considerably more unprecise, if test data were used where the apical and basolateral time constant did not differ at least by a factor of five.

The network architecture built by FlexNet consisted of 20 units in two hidden layers. Although the same number of units is used as for the standard backpropagation, the structure is different here (16-10-10-4).

6 Discussion and Conclusions

Pattern recognition based on the electrical model for epithelia showed good learning progress and small error rates. The foreseen problems in creating appropriate training data could be solved. No notable oscillation was observed. For a learning rate of 0.00001 the slope of the error rate graph was <0.

A crucial point is that typical impedance measurements consist of 40-50 data points. Using all data points as input is not efficient. However, focussing on an equally distributed subset of impedance data points is only acceptable if there is evidence that this is the optimal subset. This is not the case here. Therefore, appropriate feature selection algorithms [7] have to be investigated in the future.

Nevertheless, with the present work a new computational approach for determining electrical properties of epithelia has been successfully introduced. Our tests showed that theoretical considerations on calculating training data were correct. Thus, the present work represents a proof of concept.

Moreover, the precision of the estimations even with the present unsophisticated ANN approaches were already better than the error rates reported by Bertrand et al. [2]. Further optimization of our approach appears therefore to be promising and will be the subject of further investigations.

References

1. Krug, S.M., Fromm, M., Günzel, D.: Two-path Impedance Spectroscopy for Measuring Paracellular and Transcellular Epithelial Resistance. Biophys. J. 97(8), 2202–2211 (2009)
2. Bertrand, C.A., et al.: System for Dynamic Measurements of Membrane Capacitance in Intact Epithelial Monolayers. Biophys. J. 75(6), 2743–2756 (1998)
3. Gitter, A.H., Fromm, M., Schulzke, J.D.: Impedance Analysis for the Determination of Epithelial and Subepithelial Resistance in Intestinal Tissues. J. Biochem. Biophys. Methods 37(1-2), 35–46 (1998)
4. Clausen, C., Lewis, S.A., Diamond, J.M.: Impedance Analysis of a Tight Epithelium Using a Distributed Resistance Model. Biophys. J. 26(2), 291–317 (1979)
5. Mohraz, K., Arras, M.K.: FORWISS Artificial Neural Network Simulation Toolbox. Bavarian Reserach Center for Knowledge-Based Systems (1996)
6. Mohraz, K., Protzel, P.: FlexNet - A Flexible Neural Network Construction Algorithm. In: 4th European Symposium on Artificial Neural Networks, pp. 111–116 (1996)
7. Kavzoglu, T., Mather, P.M.: The Role of Feature Selection in Artificial Neural Network Applications. Int. J. Remote Sens. 23(15), 2919–2937 (2001)

Machine Learning and Personalized Modeling Based Gene Selection for Acute GvHD Gene Expression Data Analysis

Maurizio Fiasché[1,2], Maria Cuzzola[2], Roberta Fedele[2],
Pasquale Iacopino[2], and Francesco C. Morabito[1]

[1] DIMET, University "Mediterranea" of Reggio Calabria, Italy
[2] Transplant Regional Center of Stem Cells and Cellular Therapy,
"A. Neri", Reggio Calabria, Italy
maurizio.fiasche@unirc.it

Abstract. In this paper a novel gene selection method based on personalized modeling is proposed and is compared with classical machine learning techniques to identify diagnostic gene targets and to use them for a successful diagnosis of a medical problem - acute graft-versus-host disease (aGvHD). An analysis using the integrated approach of new data with the existing models is evaluated. Identifying a compact set of genes from gene expression data is a critical step in bioinformatics research. Personalized modeling is a recently introduced technique for constructing clinical decision support systems. This is a novel study which utilises both computational and biological evidence and the use of a personalized modeling for the analysis of this disease. Directions for further studies are also outlined.

Keywords: Gene selection, GvHD, machine learning, personalized modeling, wrapper.

1 Introduction

Identifying a compact set of informative genes from microarray data (gene expression data) is critical in the construction of an efficient clinical decision support system. Microarray analysis might help to identify unique markers (e.g. a set of gene) of clinical importance. Diagnosis and prediction of a biological state/disease is likely to be more accurate by identifying clusters of gene expression profiles (GEPs) performed by macroarray analysis. Based on a genetic profile, it is possible to set a diagnostic test, so a sample can be taken from a patient, the data related to the sample processed, and a profile related to the sample obtained [1]. We apply this approach here to detect acute graft-versus-host disease (aGvHD) in allogeneic hematopoietic stem cell transplantation (HSCT), a curative therapy for several malignant and non malignant disorders. Acute GvHD remains the major complication and the principal cause of mortality and morbidity following HSCT [2], and its diagnosis is merely based on clinical criteria and may be confirmed by biopsy of one of the 3 target organs (skin, gastrointestinal tract, or liver) [2]. There is no definitive diagnostic blood test for aGvHD. In the current project, our primary objective was to validate a novel and not

K. Diamantaras, W. Duch, L.S. Iliadis (Eds.): ICANN 2010, Part I, LNCS 6352, pp. 217–223, 2010.

invasive method to confirm the diagnosis of aGvHD in HSCT patients at onset of clinical symptoms. In medical area, personalized modeling has significant potential to benefit the patients who need tailored treatment, such as cancer diagnosis and drug response. The main idea of personalized modeling is to create a model for each objective sample, which is able to discover the most important information specifically for this sample. Since personalized modeling focuses on the individual sample rather than simply on the global problem space, it can be more appropriate to build clinical decision support systems for new patients. Previous work has reported that using personalized modeling can achieve better classification results than the results from global modeling [1][4]. This study used a *Personalized Modeling based Gene Selection method* (PMGS) proposed in [3] for macroarray data analysis integrating new data with the existing models [1]. The organization of the rest of this paper is as follows: section 2 gives an overview about gene selection methods describing the PMGS algorithm and personalized modelling; section 3 describes results about the experiments conducted with the integrated approach for new data samples; section 4 gives conclusions inferred with some possible future applications.

2   Gene Selection Methods and Personalized Modeling

Many attempts have been made to identify which genes are most important for diagnosing different diseases (e.g. cancer diagnosis) and prognosis task using microarray and macroarray technology. Generally, most developed gene selection methods can be categorized into two groups, filter and wrapper methods. The performance from wrapper methods is usually superior to that from filter methods, because the result comes from the optimized classification model. A standard wrapper gene selection method can be found in [5]. Wrapper gene selection methods can generally yield high classification accuracy using a particular classifier with an expensive computational cost. In wrapper method, the gene selection process is heavily dependent on a search engine, a search area (data), and an evaluation criterion for optimizing the learning model [3]. We have seen in [4] the critical state of the global modelling. More importantly, it is difficult to incorporate previous developed models or existed knowledge into global modeling. Personalized modeling is a relative new method in bioinformatics research, which is less found in literature. A representative work is published in [4]. One main difficulty in gene selection is how to optimize the learning function to evaluate the candidate genes during the training process. Genetic algorithm(GA) is a powerful method that is capable of exploring the combination of features and principally able to converge to the best solution. However, classical GA is often criticized for its huge computational cost and the difficulty of parameter setting. Compact genetic algorithm(cGA) [6] is a GA based algorithm that drives the evolution towards a better probability distribution. Compared to classical GA, compact GA is able to discover and maintain the relationships between the features through the entire optimization, which creates a much faster discovery of the global optimum.

2.1   Algorithm of PMGS Method

In this study, we propose and want to compare with classical wrapper (global model), a new gene selection method based on personalized modeling for GEP based on macroarray method data analysis, especially for aGvHD diagnosis and prognosis. In the proposed PMGS method, we employ wrappers to search candidate gene sets and then use the selected most important genes to profile individual data sample. This gene selection method can incorporate any classifier models for optimizing the learning function during the training process. In this study, we have investigated two classification algorithms, including Weighted distance K-nearest neighbor (WKNN) [4] and NaiveBayes to make a comparison. The algorithm and the block diagram of the PMGS method has been described in [3], and is not explained here for brevity.

3 Experiment

The goal of this study is to design a model to select a compact set of genes that can profile the pattern of objective microarray data.

3.1 Data

Fifty-nine HSCT patients were enrolled in our study between March 2006 and July 2008 in Transplants Regional Center of Stem Cells and Cellular Therapy "A. Neri" Reggio Calabria, Italy, during a Governative Research Program of minister of the Health with the title: *"Project of Integrated Program: Allogeneic Hemopoietic Stem Cells Transplantation in Malignant Hemopathy and Solid Neoplasia Therapy - Predictive and prognostic value for graft vs. host disease of chimerism and gene expression"*. Because experimental design plays a crucial role in a successful biomarker search, the first step in our design was to choose the most informative specimens and achieve adequate matching between positive cases aGvHD (YES) and negative controls aGvHD (NO) to avoid bias. This goal is best achieved through a database containing high-quality samples linked to quality controlled clinical information. Patients with clinical signs of aGvHD (YES) were selected, and in more than 95% of them aGvHD was confirmed by biopsy including those with grade I. We used 26 samples from aGvHD (YES) patients that were taken at the time of diagnosis and we selected 33 samples from patients that didn't experienced aGvHD (NO). All together YES/NO patient groups comprised a validation set. Total RNA was extracted from whole peripheral blood samples using a RNA easy Mini Kit (Qiagen) according to the manufacturer's instructions. Reverse transcription of the purified RNA was performed using Superscript III Reverse Transcriptase (Invitrogen). A multigene expression assay to test occurrence of aGvHD were carried out with TaqMan® Low Density Array Fluidic (LDA-macroarray card) based on Applied Biosystems 7900HT comparative dd CT method, according to manufacturer's instructions. Expression of each gene was measured in triplicate and then normalized to the reference gene 18S mRNA, who was included in macroarray card. About the project of macroarray card, we selected 47 candidate genes from the published literature, genomic databases, pathway analysis. The 47 candidate genes were involved in immune network and inflammation pathogenesis. Finally a group of new patients is enrolled for testing the new approach explained in this paper.

Table 1. The 13 genes selected from CFS, the 7 genes selected through the wrapper- naïve Bayes method [5] are marked with °, the 5 genes selected with SVM are marked with *. Names and meaning of genes are shown in [5].

Gene Name		
BCL2A1	EGR2°	SELP
CASP1°*	FAS	SLPI°
CCL7	ICOS°*	STAT6
CD83	IL4	Foxp-3 *
CXCL10°	IL10°*	CD52 °*

3.2 Experimental Setup – Wrapper Approach

In table 1 is shown some results published in previous [5], with the addition of a new wrapper analysis with SVM as Classifier. The global dataset has been divided in training data set with 29 patient samples (13 aGvHD(Yes) and 16 aGvHD(No)) and in testing   data set consisted of 30 patient samples (13 aGvHD(Yes) and 17 aGvHD(No)). Here as classifier we have used a SVM. SVMs use a kernel function to implicitly map data to a high dimensional space. Then, they construct the maximum margin hyperplane by solving an optimization problem on the training data. Sequential minimal optimization (SMO) [7] has been used in this paper to train a SVM. However, due to the high computational cost it is not very practical to use the wrapper method to select genes for SVMs. Also here, consistently with the analysis in [5] the search algorithm was the best-first with forward selection, starting with the empty set of genes. The search for the best subset is based on the training data only. Once the best subset has been determined, and a classifier has been built from the training data (reduced to the best features found), the performance of that classifier is evaluated on the test data. The 5 Genes selected using the wrapper method are shown in table 1 in comparison with gene selected from the previous analysis [5]. A leave-one-out cross validation (LOOCV) procedure was performed to investigate the robustness of the method over the training set: in 29 runs, the subset of 5 genes was selected 29 times (100%) by the SMO. Section 3.5 has shown the performance of this technique estimated on the testing data.

3.3 Experimental Setup – Personalized Modeling Based Gene Selection Method

Here we want to employ the PMGS approach described in the 2, to compare it with the techniques used in 3.2 and to integrate these models with new data. For each data sample, the final selected most important genes may be different. The selected frequency of some genes is significantly high, which means they can be recognized highly representative of the data pattern. For example *CASP1, FOXP3, ICOS, CD52* are the most important genes for sample 20 and CASP1 is often present in the best subgroups. As previous shown the main goal of developing PMGS method is to discover the personalized information for each sample (can be a patient clinical evidence sample), rather than simply to compare the classification accuracy with published results in literature. For this purpose, PMGS is designed to be able to give a detailed profile for the new testing data sample(a new patient sample), which can contribute to clinical decision support system. However, LOOCV was performed to investigate the robustness of the method over the training set: in 29 runs, the personalized best subset was selected 29 times (100%). Section 3.5 has shown the performance of this technique estimated on the testing data.

3.4 Experimental Setup – Integrated Approach for New Data and Existing Models

Here we want to employ the PMGS approach described in section 2, to compare it with the techniques used in 3.2 and to integrate these models with new data. For this aim, we have used a group of 7 new patients as new dataset D [1], [5],with 3 case of aGvHD, in a different subspace of the problem space and we have obtained a very good modeling of the pathology. We have used like the other models training and testing dataset. Section 3.6 has shown the performance of this technique estimated on the testing data.

3.5 Experimental Results

In this study SVM classifier and classifiers previously used [5] obtain similar results with the PMGS method. The results confirm that it is possible to diagnose the aGvHD using a selected number of variables. Only one case escaped all our classification models, which achieved 97% accuracy in a LOOCV on the testing data set. Experimental results are shown in Table 2.

3.6 Experimental Results of the Integrated Approach

For the 7 patients of the new dataset D we have a new situation for the clinical symptoms and for the general clinical situation, furthermore a different modality of infusion of the cell is occurred, so, in particular in these situations the integration of the existing models is a good method. The Model M seen above, does not perform very well on the new data D. The model is used to train on a dataset $D0$ in a subspace of the problem space where it performs well. The new dataset D is in another subspace of the problem space. Data $D0tr$ extracted from $D0$ is first used to evolve one of the models seen above $M0$, and with the rule extracted the model M is transformed into equivalent local models. The model $M0$ is further evolved on Dtr into a new model $Mnew$, the first representing data $D0tr$ and the last two, data Dtr. Although on the test data $D0tst$ both models performed equally well, $Mnew$ generalizes better on $Dtst$. Building alternative models of the same problem could help to understand the problem better and to choose the most appropriate model for the task. The new model created for each step is trained ($D0tr$) with the personalized model for 50 runs (9 cases has been removed because not clinically good for the training) and a LOOCV (92% for the integrated method) is calculated in comparison with single standard methods on the new dataset D of 7 patients (table 2).

Table 2. Experimental results of a CFS with ANN classifier and a wrapper method combined with SVM and of the PMGS with naïve bayes and with WKNN. The starting set has been divided in training set and test set, a LOOCV has been calculated for the two subsets. Experimental results of a CFS with ANN classifier and a wrapper method combined with SVM with PMGS. In the last two rows the Integrated approach marked with (i).

Method	Test set (Dtst)	Training set	Test set
CFS-ANN	3(7)	28(29)	29(30)
Wrapper-SVM	4(7)	29(29)	29(30)
PMGS-naïve Bayes	3(7)	27(29)	29(30)
PMGS-WKNN	4(7)	29(29)	29(30)
(i)PMGS- naïve Bayes	6(7)	-	-
(i)PMGS- WKNN	6(7)	-	-

4 Biomedical Conclusions and Future Work

We examined the immune transcripts to study the applicability of gene expression profiling (macroarray) as a single assay in early diagnosis of aGVHD. From a biological point of view, the results are reliable, as reported in [5]. Others have reasoned that Th2 cell therapy could rapidly ameliorate severe aGVHD via IL-4 and IL-10 mediated mechanisms [8]. It is noteworthy that in our study a set of genes, indicated by computational analysis, included same mediators of Th2 response such as IL10, and signal transducer and activator of transcription 6, interleukin-4 induced (STAT6). In our study increased expression levels of CXCL10 and CCL7 were identify as informative biomarker of alloreactive disease. Altogether our results strongly outlined the importance and utility of non-invasive tool for aGVHD diagnosis based on GEP. As a clinical trial, tissue biopsies were performed to confirm the above diagnostic results. In conclusion, our models may prevent the need for an invasive procedure. This study demonstrated, for the first time, that the proposed integrated methodology for the personalized selection of gene diagnostic targets and their use for diagnosis of aGVHD results in a satisfactory 92% accuracy over independent test data set of HSCT population. We plan to extend the system including all clinical and genetic variables [9], testing with new data samples this method and for a larger group of patients to capture their peculiarity. The authors are engaged in this direction.

References

1. Kasabov, N.: Evolving Connectionist Systems: The Knowledge Engineering Approach, 2nd edn. Springer, London (2007)
2. Weisdorf, D.: Graft vs. Host disease: pathology, prophylaxis and therapy: GVHD overview. Best Pr. & Res. Cl. Haematology 21(2), 99–100 (2008)
3. Hu, Y., Song, Q., Kasabov, N.: Personalized modeling based gene selection for microarray data analysis. In: Koeppen, M., Kasabov, N., Coghill, G. (eds.) ICONIP 2008. LNCS, vol. 5506, pp. 1221–1228. Springer, Heidelberg (2009)
4. Kasabov, N.: Global, local and personalised modelling and profile discovery in Bioinformatics: An integrated approach. Pattern Recognition Letters 28(6), 673–685 (2007)

5. Harik, G.R., Lobo, F.G., Goldberg, D.E.: The compact genetic algorithm. IEEE Trans. Evolutionary Computation 3(4), 287–297 (1999)
6. Fiasché, M., Verma, A., Cuzzola, M., Iacopino, P., Kasabov, N., Morabito, F.C.: Discovering Diagnostic Gene Targets and Early Diagnosis of Acute GVHD Using Methods of Computational Intelligence over Gene Expression Data. In: Alippi, C., Polycarpou, M., Panayiotou, C., Ellinas, G. (eds.) ICANN 2009. LNCS, vol. 5769, pp. 10–19. Springer, Heidelberg (2009)
7. Platt, J.: Fast training of support vector machines using sequential minimal optimization. In: Advances in Kernel Methods–Support Vector Learning. MIT Press, Cambridge (1998)
8. Foley Jason, J.E., Mariotti, J., Ryan, K., Eckhaus, M., Fowler, D.H.: The cell therapy of established acute graft-versus-host disease requires IL-4 and IL-10 and is abrogated by IL-2 or host-type antigen-presenting cells. Biology of Blood and Marrow Transplantation 14, 959–972 (2008)
9. Fiasché, M.: Implementations of Evolving Integrated Multimodel Systems, Algorithms and Applications in Biomedical Field. PhD Thesis. DIMET, University "Mediterranea" of Reggio Calabria (2010)

Supervised Associative Learning in Spiking Neural Network

Nooraini Yusoff and André Grüning

Department of Computing, Faculty of Engineering and Physical Sciences,
University of Surrey, Guildford, GU2 7XH Surrey, UK
{n.yusoff,a.gruning}@surrey.ac.uk

Abstract. In this paper, we propose a simple supervised associative learning approach for spiking neural networks. In an excitatory-inhibitory network paradigm with Izhikevich spiking neurons, synaptic plasticity is implemented on excitatory to excitatory synapses dependent on both spike emission rates and spike timings. As results of learning, the network is able to associate not just familiar stimuli but also novel stimuli observed through synchronised activity within the same subpopulation and between two associated subpopulations.

Keywords: Spiking neural network, Associative learning, Supervised learning, Excitatory-Inhibitory network, Izhikevich spiking neurons.

1 Introduction

There is evidence in neurophysiology that long-term association between stimuli, which involves synaptic plasticity, is triggered by overlapping short-term activity, which only involves activity dynamics (e.g. [1], [7] and [8]), linking neuronal activity and long-term memory.

Associative-based learning can be implemented using unsupervised or supervised approaches [6]. For unsupervised learning, perhaps the temporal variant of Hebbian learning known as spike-timing dependent plasticity (STDP) is the most biologically plausible approach. However, the purely unsupervised approach is often not suitable for goal-oriented applications, so it is used in this paper with prescribed target stimuli as a form of supervision. Such supervisory signal could be assumed to come from another part of the brain [2].

In this study, we explore a supervised associative learning algorithm as a combination of spike emission rate dependent and STDP approaches from [9] on a learning task similar to [8]. Supervision in learning is only through intensified currents into paired target neuron subpopulations. Learning is performed by associating two different stimuli with synchronisation of network activity within and between subpopulations of neurons as the key measure of stimulus association.

2 Simulation Model

For our simulation, the network structure is an adaptation of excitatory-inhibitory neural network model similar to [7]-[8]. The neuron model used with simple computational

K. Diamantaras, W. Duch, L.S. Iliadis (Eds.): ICANN 2010, Part I, LNCS 6352, pp. 224–229, 2010.

properties is based on the Izhikevich spiking neuron (IM) with standard parameters governing the dynamics of membrane potential (further details of the IM can be found in [3] and [4]).

The network is composed of 1000 neurons ($N=1000$) with 800 excitatory neurons ($N_E=800$) and 200 inhibitory neurons ($N_I=200$). Each neuron receives synaptic contacts from 20% of excitatory neurons ($C_E=0.2N_E$) and 20% of inhibitory neurons ($C_I=0.2N_I$), randomly. The excitatory neurons population is divided into subpopulations that each represents an object for the memory under study, meanwhile the inhibitory subpopulation acts as the global network inhibition. In our simulations, there are four ($p=4$, P1-P4) subpopulations of excitatory neurons with 160 (selectivity, $f=0.2 \rightarrow fN_E=160$) units each with the following allocation: P1: neurons 1-160, P2: neurons 161-320, P3: neurons 321-480 and P4: neurons 481-640, while neurons from 801-1000 are inhibitory and the remaining excitatory neurons 641-800 are the nonselective pool of neurons. The connection strengths of excitatory synapses on excitatory neurons are denoted $W_{1/0/a}$, excitatory on inhibitory neurons W_{EI}, inhibitory on excitatory neurons W_{IE}, and inhibitory on inhibitory W_{II}. Within $W_{1/0/a}$, W_1 are the synaptic connections within the same subpopulation, W_a is the synaptic connection between two associated subpopulations and W_0 labels the non-associated subpopulation.

3   Learning Implementation

For our simulation experiments, learning is performed through implementation of synaptic plasticity on excitatory to excitatory synapses ($W_{1/0/a}$). Other synapses (W_{EI}, W_{IE}, and W_{II}) are set to random values with moduli drawn uniformly the range from between 0 and 1 and with signs of connections depending on the type of the neuron (excitatory or inhibitory).

Learning is implemented in a Hebbian paradigm, considering both spike rate and timings of both pre-synaptic and post-synaptic neurons in a learning window [9]. In a learning trial with 500 milliseconds (ms) simulated time, the time window is divided into 100 ms ($T=100$) wide overlapping bins at 50 ms intervals (Fig. 1). For each learning time bin, the average spike rate of every excitatory neuron (S_{pre} and S_{post}) is estimated as the ratio of the number of spikes emitted in the bin divided by T [8]. The weight adjustments, ΔW are calculated as a function of time difference, $\Delta t = t_j^{(f)} - t_i^{(f)}$, where $t_j^{(f)}$ and $t_i^{(f)}$ are the last firing times of post-synaptic neuron j and pre-synaptic neuron i, respectively, within the learning time bin (Fig. 2) [9]. To avoid saturation of synaptic strength values infinitely, we keep the values within the range 0 to 3.

A synapse W is highly potentiated (if $W(t)) = 0$) to the maximal synaptic strength ($w_{max} = 3$) if both pre- and postsynaptic neurons emit spikes above the high rate threshold T_+ and only if the time difference of the last firing between the pre- and postsynaptic neurons is above 0 ($\Delta t > 0$). W is weakly potentiated with an amount of ΔW (derived from Fig. 2), if the pre synaptic (postsynaptic) neuron emits spikes with rate above T_+ whilst the postsynaptic (pre synaptic) neuron spike emission rate is below T_+ but above the low threshold, T_a. For depression of W, where $\Delta t < 0$ from Fig. 2, it is applied if the pre synaptic (postsynaptic) neuron emits spikes above T_+ and the

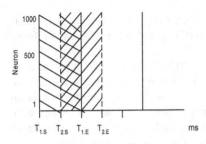

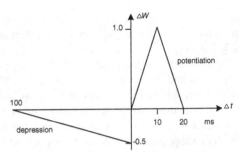

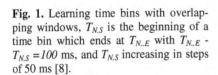

Fig. 1. Learning time bins with overlapping windows, $T_{N.S}$ is the beginning of a time bin which ends at $T_{N..E}$ with $T_{N..E} - T_{N.S} = 100$ ms, and $T_{N.S}$ increasing in steps of 50 ms [8].

Fig. 2. A function of time difference between last firing of pre-, $t_i^{(f)}$, and post synaptic neuron, $t_j^{(f)}$, $\Delta t = t_{post} - t_{pre} = t_j^{(f)} - t_i^{(f)}$, on excitatory neurons [9], Fig. 2.

post-synaptic (pre synaptic) neuron emits spikes below T_a. The synaptic plasticity rules are summarised in 1-3.

$$W_{ij}(t+1) = \begin{cases} w_{max}, & W_{ij}(t) = 0, \; (S_{pre} \geq T_+ , \; S_{post} \geq T_+) , \; \Delta t > 0 \quad (1) \\ max(w_{min}, min(w_{max}, W_{ij}(t)+\Delta W), & \begin{aligned}[& (S_{pre} \geq T_+, T_a < S_{post} < T_+) ; \\ & (T_a < S_{pre} < T_+ , \; S_{post} \geq T_+)], \; \Delta t > 0 \end{aligned} \quad (2) \\ max(w_{min}, min(w_{max}, W_{ij}(t) - |\Delta W|), & \begin{aligned}[& (S_{pre} \geq T_+ , \; S_{post} \leq T_a) ; \\ & (S_{post} \geq T_+ , \; S_{pre} \leq T_a)], \; \Delta t < 0 \end{aligned} \quad (3) \end{cases}$$

4   Simulation Results

In our simulation, for every ms in each trial, each neuron receives background noisy external currents $\xi_i(t)$, where $\xi_i(t)$ is Gaussian noise with mean μ and stdev σ. Excitatory and inhibitory neurons receive external currents with standard deviations $\sigma_{Ne}=3$ and $\sigma_{Ni}=1$, respectively. During a learning trial, for $t>150$ to $t \leq 350$ ms, the external current distribution to target stimulus subpopulation 1 is changed to a uniform one from range 0 to γ with $\gamma=30$. Then, for $t>250$ to $t \leq 450$ ms, the target stimulus subpopulation 2 is stimulated with the same range of currents as its subpopulation to be associated. We ran two batches of simulations: 1) learning with familiar stimuli and 2) learning with novel stimuli. For (1), a stimulus is assumed to have been learned prior to establishing relationship between two different stimuli, while for (2) only a small subset of synapses are initialised with some strength values.

4.1   Learning with Familiar Stimuli

For implementing associative learning with familiar stimulus, neurons in the same subpopulation are connected with a set of random W_1 values in the range of 0 and 3. With such pre-initialised synaptic connections, neurons in the same subpopulation always fire synchronously. An example of associative learning results between two stimuli, P1 and P3 is depicted in Fig. 3.

A. Trial 1

B. Trial 2

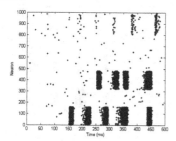
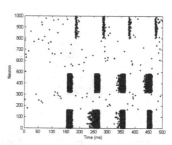

Fig. 3. Synchronisation of neuronal network activity after two learning trials for a pair of familiar stimuli P1 ↔ P3. Currents to excitatory subpopulation neurons of P1 (neurons: 1-160) are intensified for 200 ms ($t>150$ to $t<=350$ ms), then P3 (neurons: 321-480) is stimulated for the same duration ($t>250$ to $t<=450$ ms). Association of patterns is measured based on synchronous activity in each member of a stimuli learning pair subpopulation. A) Learning trial 1: activation of P1 is observed in between *350 to 450 ms*, B) Learning trial 2: activation of P3 (in between $t>150$ to $t<=250$ ms) and activation of P1 (in between $t>350$ to $t<=450$ ms) as the results of pattern association.

After two trials, association of P1 ↔ P3 could be established. Initially, intensified currents to subpopulations P1 and P3 activate their respective subpopulation only. Then, at times $350 < t \leq 450$ ms, there exists prolonged activity of P1 by activation through P3. In trial 2, prospective activity can be observed with activation of P3 within stimulation period of P1 (in $150 < t \leq 250$ ms) and activation of P1 within stimulation period of P3 (in $350 < t \leq 450$ ms).

4.2 Learning with Novel Stimuli

For learning with novel stimuli, only 20% of neurons within the same subpopulation are initialised with W_I values in the range of 0 and 1. The initial values of W_I represent some random connectivity assumed to result from any previous learning. Initially, in our simulation, the so intialised synaptic connections are not enough to have synchronous activity within a subpopulation compared to when learning with familiar stimuli. Results of association learning with novel stimuli P1 and P3 are depicted in Fig. 4.

From Fig. 4, during the early phase of learning, after stimulations to P1 and P3, the neurons in both subpopulations only fire asynchronously caused by the injected current within $t>150$ to $t\leq350$ ms and $t>250$ to $t\leq450$ ms for P1 and P3, respectively. A spill-over of activity from P1 to P3 and vise-versa can only be observed after ten trials.

A. Trial 1

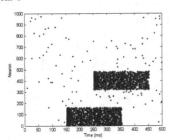

B. Trial 10

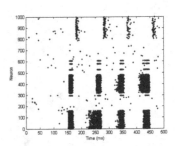

Fig. 4. Neuronal network activity after one and ten learning trials for stimuli pair P1 ↔ P3. Currents to excitatory subpopulation neurons of P1 is intensified for 200 ms ($t>150$ to $t<= 350$ ms), then P3 is stimulated for the same duration ($t>250$ to $t<= 450$ ms). A) In the early phase of learning, after one trial, neurons in subpopulations P1 and P3 fire asynchronously as both stimuli are novel and activity are only dependent on the external currents. B) After ten trials, neuronal activity within each subpopulation is more synchronised as the result of learning. Activation of P3 (within $t>150$ to $t<= 250$ ms) and activation of P1 (within $t>400$ to $t<= 500$ ms) indicate association of P1 ↔ P3.

5 Conclusion

We have explored a simple associative learning scheme utilising Hebbian learning both for spike rates and timings (STDP) for synaptic plasticity, similar to [9]. Unlike other supervised approaches [5] where neuronal activity is forced to have relatively precise spike timing to match the desired target spike train, this scheme uses supervisory currents to establish an association between two stimuli. And unlike previous approaches [8], that only rely on sliding average spike rates, our approach has a plausibility advantage by incorporating spike timings, too [9]. However, it remains to examine whether a single branch (1), (2) or (3) of the weight update rule has a dominating affect on learning. The associations show in spill-over of activity between the two stimuli involved. This demonstrates once more that long-term associations between stimuli involving synaptic plasticity are triggered by overlapping short-term activity involving only short-term activity dynamics. We have run a series of simulation experiments for learning associations of familiar stimuli and novel stimuli. For learning with familiar stimuli, associations between pair patterns are learned faster compared to novel stimuli.

Acknowledgments. This research has been funded by a PhD grant from the Ministry of Higher Education (Malaysia).

References

1. Bloom, F., Nelson, C.A., Lazerson, A.: Brain, Mind, and Behaviour, 3rd ed. Educational Broadcasting Corporation, US (2001)
2. Crick, F.: The recent excitement about neural networks. Nature 337(1989), 129–132 (1989)

3. Izhikevich, E.M.: Simple Model of Spiking Neurons. IEEE Trans. Neural Networks 14(6), 1569–1572 (2003)
4. Izhikevich, E.M.: Which model to use for cortical spiking neurons. IEEE Trans. Neural Networks 15(5), 1063–1070 (2004)
5. Kasinski, A., Ponulak, F.: Comparison of Supervised Learning Methods for Spike Time Coding in Spiking Neural Networks. Int. J. Appl. Math. Comput. Sci. 16(1), 101–113 (2006)
6. Dayan, P., Abbot, L.F.: Theoretical Neuroscience: Computational and Mathematical Modeling of Neural Systems. MIT, Cambridge (2005)
7. Brunel, N., Lavigne, F.: Semantic Priming in a Cortical Network Model. Journal of Cognitive Neuroscience 21(12), 2300–2319 (2009)
8. Mongillo, G., Amit, D.J., Brunel, N.: Retrospective and prospective persistent activity induced by Hebbian learning in a recurrent cortical network, vol. 18, pp. 2011–2024 (2003)
9. Paugam-Moisy, H., Martinez, R., Bengio, S.: Delay learning and polychnization for reservoir computing. Neurocomputing 71(7-9), 1143–1158 (2008)

Dynamics and Function of a CA1 Model of the Hippocampus during Theta and Ripples

Vassilis Cutsuridis* and Michael Hasselmo

Center for Memory and Brain, Boston University, Boston, MA, USA
vcut@bu.edu

Abstract. The hippocampus is known to be involved in spatial learning in rats. Spatial learning involves the encoding and replay of temporally sequenced spatial information. Temporally sequenced spatial memories are encoded and replayed by the firing rate and phase of pyramidal cells and inhibitory interneurons with respect to ongoing network oscillations (theta and ripples). Understanding how the different hippocampal neuronal classes interact during these encoding and replay processes is of great importance. A computational model of the CA1 microcircuit [3], [4], [5] that uses biophysical representations of the major cell types, including pyramidal cells and four types of inhibitory interneurons is extended to address: (1) How are the encoding and replay (forward and reverse) of behavioural place sequences controlled in the CA1 microcircuit during theta and ripples? and (2) What roles do the various types of inhibitory interneurons play in these processes?

Keywords: Computational model, microcircuit, inhibitory interneurons, STDP, calcium, theta, ripples, medial septum, CA1.

1 Introduction

Spatial memories in the hippocampus are encoded (stored) and replayed by the firing frequency and spike timing of pyramidal cells and inhibitory interneurons during network oscillations. Theta oscillations (4-10 Hz) are observed in rats during exploration and rapid eye movement (REM) sleep, whereas sharp wave-associated ripples (100-200 Hz) are observed during immobility, slow-wave sleep (SWS) and consummatory behaviours. During exploration hippocampal place cells have been shown to systematically shift their firing phase with respect to theta as the animal transverses the place field (a phenomenon known as phase precession) [19].

Many theories have been proposed over the years trying to understand how memories in the hippocampus are encoded and replayed during network oscillations [7],[15]. Buzsaki's two-stage memory model [15] hypothesized that both theta and sharp-wave (ripple) states of the hippocampus are essential to memory trace encoding and replay. During theta (exploratory behavior) neocortical

---

* Corresponding author.

K. Diamantaras, W. Duch, L.S. Iliadis (Eds.): ICANN 2010, Part I, LNCS 6352, pp. 230–240, 2010.
© Springer-Verlag Berlin Heidelberg 2010

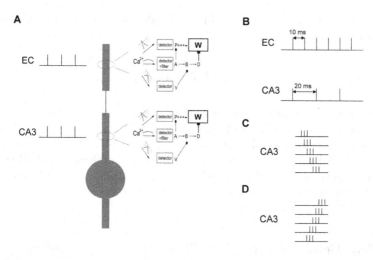

Fig. 1. (A) Pyramidal cell model with calcium detectors in distal and proximal dendrites. (B) Entorhinal cortical (EC) and Schaffer collateral (CA3) inputs during theta rhythm. (C) Forward replay of CA3 spatial memories used as inputs to CA1 during ripple activity (location A in figure 2). (D) Reverse replay of CA3 spatial memories used as inputs to CA1 during ripple activity (location B in figure 2).

information is transmitted to the hippocampus via the dentate gyrus, where it is encoded by pyramidal cells via synaptic plasticity mechanisms. During the sharp-wave associated ripple state the pyramidal cells initiate population bursts, which then cause the already stored memories in the hippocampus to reach the neocortex and hence to be replayed. Hasselmo's and colleagues' oscillatory model [7] hypothesized that hippocampal theta rhythm (4-7 Hz) can contribute to memory formation by separating encoding (storage) and retrieval of memories into independent functional sub-cycles. Recent experimental evidence has shown that in the CA1 area of the hippocampus the same set of excitatory and inhibitory cells, which fire at specific phases during theta, are active at completely different phases during ripples [10], [11], [12]. Similarly, medial septal GABAergic neurons differentially phase their activities with respect to theta and ripple [14], [17].

Here we investigate, via computer simulations, the biophysical mechanisms by which encoding and replay of behaviourally relevant spatial memory sequences are achieved by the CA1 microcircuitry. A model of the CA1 microcircuit [3], [4], [5], [6] is extended that uses simplified biophysical representations of the major cell types, including pyramidal cells (PCs) and four types of inhibitory interneurons: basket cells (BCs), axo-axonic cells (AACs), bistratified cells (BSCs) and oriens lacunosum-moleculare (OLM) cells. Inputs to the network come from the entorhinal cortex (EC), the CA3 Schaffer collaterals and medial septum (MS). Our model addresses three important issues: (1) How is the mechanism of phase precession of place cells in the CA1 microcircuit achieved in presence of various types of inhibitory interneurons? (2) How are the encoding and replay (forward and reverse) of behavioural place sequences controlled in the CA1 microcircuit during theta and ripples? and (3) What roles do the various types of inhibitory interneurons play in these processes?

2 Model Architecture and Properties

The CA1 network model consisted of 4 pyramidal cells and four types of inhibitory interneurons: two basket cells, an axoaxonic cell, a bistratified cell and an oriens lacunosum-moleculare (OLM) cell. Hodgkin-Huxley mathematical formalism was used to describe the ionic and synaptic mechanisms of all cells. All simulations were performed using XPPAUT [20] running on a PC under windows XP. The biophysical properties of each cell were adapted from cell types reported in the literature [5], [9].

Pyramidal Cells. Each pyramidal cell consisted of 4 compartments: an axon, a soma, a proximal dendrite and a distal dendrite. Active properties included a fast Na^+ current, a delayed rectifier K^+ current, an LVA L-type Ca^{2+} current, an A-type K^+ current, and a calcium activated mAHP K^+ current. No recurrent connections between pyramidal cells in the network were assumed.

Each pyramidal cell received proximal and distal excitation (AMPA and NMDA) from the CA3 Schaffer collaterals and entorhinal cortex (EC), respectively, and synaptic inhibition ($GABA_A$) from the BC, AAC, BSC, and OLM cells in the soma, axon, proximal dendrite and distal dendrite, respectively.

A mechanism for spike timing dependent plasticity (STDP) in each dendrite was used to measure plasticity effects. The mechanism had a modular structure consisting of three biochemical detectors, which responded to the instantaneous calcium level and its time course in the dendrite [1]. The detection system consisted of: (1) a potentiation (P) detector which detected calcium levels above a high-threshold (e.g. $4\mu M$) and triggered LTP, (2) a depression (D) detector which detected calcium levels exceeding a low threshold level (e.g. $0.6\mu M$), remained above it for a minimum time period and triggered LTD, and (3) a veto (V) detector which detected levels exceeding a mid-level threshold (e.g. $2\mu M$) and triggered a veto to the D response. Calcium entered the neuron through: (1) voltage-gated calcium channels (VGCCs), and (2) NMDA channels located at each dendrite. Calcium influx from neither channels alone elicited plasticity. Plasticity resulted only from the synergistic action of the two calcium sources (NMDA and VGCC). A graphical schematic of the model pyramidal cell and its calcium detectors for STDP is shown in Figure 1A.

Inhibitory Interneurons. All inhibitory interneurons consisted of a single compartment (soma). Active properties of BC, AAC and BSC included a fast Na^+, a delayed rectifier K^+ and a type-A K^+ currents [5]. Active properties of the OLM cell included a fast Na^+ current, a delayed rectifier K^+ current, a persistent Na^+ current and an h-current [9]. During theta, axoaxonic and basket cells received excitatory inputs from the EC perforant path and the CA3 Schaffer

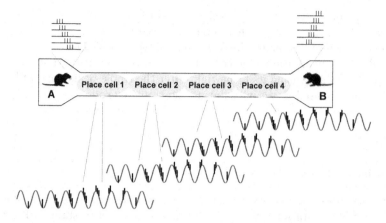

Fig. 2. Virtual linear track paradigm used. The rat must transverse the track starting from location A and stopping at location B. Gray filled ellipses represent the place fields (PF) of three pyramidal cells (PCs) in the network. Note their fields are non-overlapping. As the rat transverses the PF, each PC shifts its firing to earlier phases of the theta rhythm. At locations A and B the rats retrieve either the track locations to be transversed or the track locations already transversed, respectively.

collateral, inhibition from the medial septum, and recurrent excitation from the pyramidal cells. Basket cells recurrently inhibited each other and received additional inhibition from the bistratified cells. Bistratified cells were excited by the CA3 Schaffer collateral input only, inhibited by the medial septum, synaptically excited by PC recurrent excitation and synaptically inhibited by the basket cell. OLM cells received recurrent excitation from the PCs and forward inhibition from the medial septum. During ripples, the AAC, BC and BSC were excited only by the CA3 Schaffer collaterals and inhibited by the MS cells (see MODEL INPUTS subsection for details). The OLM cell was excited by the PCs and inhibited by the MS cells (see MODEL INPUTS subsection for details).

Model Inputs. Excitatory inputs (spikes) to network cells originated from the entorhinal cortex (EC) and CA3 Schaffer collaterals, whereas external inhibitory one from the medial septum (MS). During theta, the EC and CA3 inputs were continuously present, but at different frequencies (see Figure 1B). The interspike interval of the EC input was set to 10ms (100Hz), whereas the ISI of the CA3 input was set to 20ms (50Hz) [22]. Both EC and CA3 inputs arrived at the same time in the CA1-PC dendrites. The MS inputs were modelled as burst cells, which fired at specific phases of the theta rhythm. One MS burst cell fired at the peak of the extracellular theta (*type 1*) [14], whereas the other one at its trough (*type 2*) [17]. MS cells inhibited only the network inhibitory interneurons.

During ripples, the CA1 PCs received forward or reversed excitatory rippled input only from the CA3 Schaffer collaterals (see Figure 1C and 1D) [15], [21]. The inhibitory inputs from the MS cells were of two types: (1) a cell with a theta-like oscillation during the ripple-centered epoch, pausing its activity before the ripple peak and increasing its firing right after the ripple peak (*type 1*) [17], and (2) a cell that paused its activity during the ripple episode (*type 2*) [17].

3   Results

3.1   Virtual Linear Track

Our virtual linear track consisted of a rat running from station A to station B (see Figure 2). In stations A and B the rat was allowed to stand still awaiting for the GO signal to transverse the linear track. The linear track consisted of four non-overlapping place field representations of equal dimensions ($\approx 25cm$). The virtual rat took 2.25 sec (9 theta cycles) to tranverse through one place field. Figure 4 shows the firing activities of two place cells (PC 1 and PC4) and all inhibitory interneurons in two place fields (PF1 and PF4 in Figure 2). Each place field was encoded by the firing of a single pyramidal cell, whose phase of firing shifted with respect to the external theta rhythm [19]. As the rat entered a place field (first theta cycle) of a given pyramidal cell, the first spikes occured close to the trough of the theta cycle. As the rat was approaching the end of the field (last theta cycle), they occured near the peak of the cycle, having precessed almost 180 degrees over the course of 9 theta cycles (see figure 4) [23]. This was accomplished by the constantly increasing strength of the proximal synapses due to the STDP learning rule, which increased the tendency of PCs to fire at earlier theta phases in the presence of a constant level inhibitory threshold (BSC inhibition) (simulation result not shown). Once the rat reached station B, it was rewarded and allowed to be engaged into consummatory behaviours. At the stations A and B, our hippocampal simulation entered a different state of waking without theta rhythmic oscillations, where sharp wave associated ripple activity dominated the input and output of CA1 [16], [18]. As experimental studies have shown at station A the rat experienced forward replay of neural activity coding the track locations to be transversed [16], whereas at station B the rat experienced reverse replay of neural activity coding the track locations it has just tranversed [18].

3.2   Encoding of Spatiotemporal Memories during Theta

Figure 3 depicts the encoding process of spatiotemporal memories during theta. During theta, input from EC enters the distal dendrite of the CA1 PC cells, whereas input from CA3 Schaffer collaterals enters the proximal dendrite of the PC cells. On their own, the EC inputs generate dendritic spikes in the distal dendrites, which get attenuated on their way to the soma (see figure 3A) [2]. The CA3 inputs generate excitatory postsynaptic potentials (EPSPs), which fail to

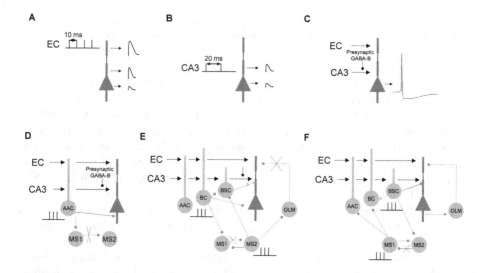

Fig. 3. Schematic of encoding of spatiotemporal memories during the theta rhythm (see text for details)

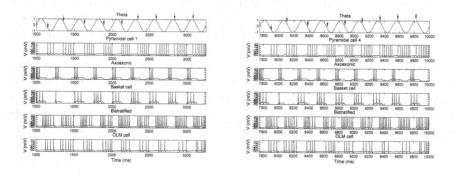

Fig. 4. (Left) Firing activities of pyramidal cell 1 and all inhibitory interneurons with respect to theta rhythm. (Right) Firing activities of pyramidal cell 4 and all inhibitory interneurons with respect to theta rhythm. Vertical arrows indicate phase precession of pyramidal cell firings in every theta cycle. Nine theta cycles comprise a pyramidal cell's (place cell's) place field.

generate somatic action potentials, because they are presynaptically inhibited by $GABA_B$ (see figure 3B) [8]. The presynaptic $GABA_B$ inhibition in CA1 cyclically changed its strength with respect to theta (active during the first half of theta, inactive during the second half) [8]. During the first half of theta, the strength of CA3 input to PC proximal dendrites was reduced by 50%. When the EC and CA3 inputs were concident in the proximal dendrites of the PCs, then action potentials are generated in the PC somas (figure 3C).

Figure 3D-F depicts which cells are active during theta. Figure 4 depicts the firing activities of all network cells during theta. During the first half-cycle of theta (0-180 degrees), we propose the following: the coincident EC and CA3 inputs cause first the AAC to fire action potentials with interspike interval (ISI) equal to 20ms, which inhibit the PCs at their axons and prevent them from firing APs (Figure 3D) [11]. Once the AAC stops firing, BCs, which are modeled as slow integrators [11], start to fire due to the coincident EC and CA3 inputs to their somas. Because of their mutual recurrent inhibition, each BC fires every 40ms as in [11]. The role of BCs is to inhibit the PCs and prevent them from firing, pace subthreshold theta oscillations in PCs [13] and prevent the BSC from ruining learning in the PC proximal dendrite by inhibiting it (Figure 3E). BSC, along with the OLM cell, is also inhibited by the type 2 MS cell (Figure 3E). The type 2 MS cell also inhibits the type 1 MS cell, which in turn disinhibits the AAC and BCs and allows them to fire and carry-on with their inhibitory duties (Figure 3E).

Figure 3F depicts the second sub-cycle of theta, which begins as the presynaptic $GABA_B$ inhibition to CA3 Schaffer collateral input to PC synapses declines and type 1 MS cell approach maximum activity. Because of this septal input, the basket and axoaxonic cells are now inhibited, releasing pyramidal cells, bistratified cells and OLM cells from inhibition. Pyramidal cells may now fire more easily, thus, allowing previously learned memories to be recalled. Type 1 MS cell also inhibits the type 2 MS cell, which in turn disinhibits the BSC and OLM cell. To ensure the correct place memory of the sequence is recalled, the disinhibited BSC broadcasts to all PCs a non-specific inhibitory signal, which allows the PCs that learned the place memory to recall it, while quenching all other spurious places memories (e.g. subsequent memories in the sequence). The OLM cell, which gets activated by the PCs, in turn send an inhibitory signal to the distal PC dendrite, which prevents the EC input from interfering with the recall of the pattern.

3.3 Forward and Backward Replay of Memories during Ripple Activity

Figure 5 depicts the replay processes during a ripple episode. In contrast to theta (figure 4), during the ripple episode (forward or reverse) the firing patterns of inhibitory interneurons in the network change (figure 6) [11], [12]. During ripple activity what was *locally* learned during theta oscillations, it is now retrieved by the subiculum, entorhinal cortex and the neocortex, where it reached consciousness [15]. The synaptic weights of the proximal dendrite are now fixed (no changing). Forward and reverse replay activity arise from the highly synchronous activity of the CA3 PCs [15], [21]. This highly synchronous activity excites first the AAC, which is disinhibited by the type 1 MS cell (as we mentioned before the type 1 MS cell pauses its activity for about 25ms before the peak of the ripple episode and increases it right after it), and in turn inhibit the axons of all CA1 PCs in the network. The duration of this axonal inhibition is short (less than

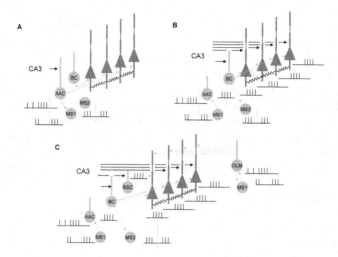

Fig. 5. Schematic of the forward and backward replay processes of spatiotemporal memories during ripple activity (see text for details). Vertical dashed gray line indicates the peak of the ripple episode.

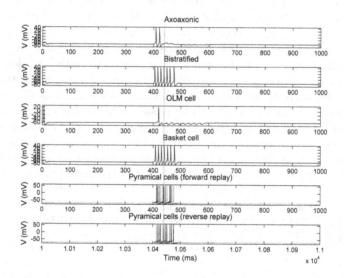

Fig. 6. Firing activities of all network cells with respect to ripples during both forward and reverse replay of spatiotemporal memories. Dashed yellow line indicates peak amplitude of ripple episode. Axoaxonic, basket, bistratified and OLM cells fire the same way during both forward and reverse replay of memories [11], [12]. During forward replay, pyramidal cells fire in a specific order: black, blue, red, and green. During reverse replay the order is reversed: green, red, blue, and black.

25 ms), since the AAC pauses its firing right after the peak of ripple episode due to increased activity of the type 1 MS cell. The role of the AAC is to silence the CA1 network and prepare it for the appropriate retrieval of information based on the current context. Similar firing activity has the OLM cell in the network, because it is also (dis)inhibited by a type 1 MS cell. The role of the OLM cell is to prevent the EC input from interfering with the recall of the memory.

Next, BCs and BSC, which were inhibited by the type 2 MS cells during the start of the ripple episode are now disinhibited by them and become active from the highly synchronous CA3 input. The role of the BSC is to provide a non-specific inhibition to all PCs, allowing this way only the "appropriate" PCs that learned the pattern(s) to recall it(them). The role of the BCs is to maintain the highly syncronous ripple activity of the PCs. A similar role is played by the gap channels in the PC axons [24].

4   Conclusion

A reduced version of a previously published CA1 microcircuit model [3], [4], [5], [6] is extended to simulate how spatiotemporal patterns are encoded and retrieved in the CA1 area of the hippocampus during theta and ripples. Our model demonstrates: (1) How is phase precession of place cells in CA1 achieved in the presence of various types of inhibitory interneurons? and (2) How are encoding and replay (forward and reverse) of behavioural sequences of spatial memories controlled in CA1 during theta and ripples in the presence of various types of inhibitory interneurons. Much more work is needed to further explore why the model place cells don't precess beyond 180 degrees with respect to theta. Does a full 360 degrees phase precession result from the interactions of a larger and noiser network of cells or is it driven by phase precessed CA3 inputs? How does a larger number of simulated theta cycles contribute to phase precession? Also, what happens to network dynamics and its ability to learn when the presentation frequencies of inputs change? Finally, what role does dopamine in CA1 play in binding together temporally sequenced spatial memories?

Acknowledgement. This work was funded by NSF Science of Learning Center CELEST grant SMA 0835976, NIMH R01 MH61492, NIMH R01 MH60013 and NIMH Silvio Conte Center grant P50 MH71702.

References

[1] Rubin, J.E., Gerkin, R.C., Bi, G.Q., Chow, C.C.: Calcium time course as signal for spike-timing-dependent plasticity. J. Neurophysiol. 93, 2600–2613 (2005)
[2] Jarsky, T., Roxin, A., Kath, W.L., Spruston, N.: Conditional dendritic spike propagation following distal synaptic activation of hippocampal CA1 pyramidal neurons. Nat. Neurosci. 8(12), 1667–1676 (2005)

[3] Cutsuridis, V., Cobb, S., Graham, B.P.: Encoding and Retrieval in a CA1 Micro-circuit Model of the Hippocampus. In: Kurkova, V., et al. (eds.) ICANN 2008,, Part II. LNCS, vol. 5164, pp. 238–247. Springer, Heidelberg (2008)

[4] Cutsuridis, V., Cobb, S., Graham, B.P.: Hippocampus, microcircuits and associative memory. Neural Networks 22(8), 1120–1128 (2009)

[5] Cutsuridis, V., Cobb, S., Graham, B.P.: Encoding and retrieval in the hippocampal CA1 microcircuit model. Hippocampus 20(3), 423–446 (2010)

[6] Graham, B.P., Cutsuridis, V., Hunter, R.: Associative Memory Models of Hippocampal Areas CA1 and CA3. In: Cutsuridis, V., et al. (eds.) Hippocampal Microcircuits: A Computational Modeller's Resource Book, pp. 461–494. Springer, Heidelberg (2010)

[7] Hasselmo, M., Bodelon, C., Wyble, B.: A proposed function of the hippocampal theta rhythm: separate phases of encoding and retrieval enhance reversal of prior learning. Neural Comput. 14, 793–817 (2002)

[8] Molyneaux, B.J., Hasselmo, M.: GABA$_B$ presynaptic inhibition has an in vivo time constant sufficiently rapid to allow modulation at theta frequency. J. Neurophys. 87(3), 1196–1205 (2002)

[9] Kunec, S., Hasselmo, M.E., Kopell, N.: Encoding and retrieval in the CA3 region of the hippocampus: a model of theta-phase separation. J. Neurophysiol. 94(1), 70–82 (2005)

[10] Klausberger, T., Somogyi, P.: Neuronal diversity and temporal dynamics: the unity of hippocampal circuit operations. Science 321, 53–57 (2008)

[11] Klausberger, T., Magill, P.J., Marton, L.F., David, J., Roberts, B., Cobden, P.M., Buzsaki, G., Somogyi, P.: Brain-state- and cell-type-specific firing of hippocampal interneurons in vivo. Nature 421, 844–848 (2003)

[12] Klausberger, T., Marton, L.F., Baude, A., Roberts, J.D., Magill, P.J., Somogyi, P.: Spike timing of dendrite-targeting bistratified cells during hippocampal network oscillations in vivo. Nat. Neurosci. 7(1), 41–47 (2004)

[13] Cobb, S.R., Buhl, E.H., Halasy, K., Paulsen, O., Somogyi, P.: Synchronization of neuronal activity in hippocampus by individual GABAergic interneurons. Nature 378(6552), 75–78 (1995)

[14] Borhegyi, Z., Varga, V., Szilagyi, N., Fabo, D., Freund, T.F.: Phase segregation of medial septal GABAergic neurons during hippocampal theta activity. J. Neurosci. 24(39), 8470–8479 (2004)

[15] Buzsaki, G.: Two stage model of memory trace formation: a role for "noisy" brain states. Neurosci. 31(3), 551–570 (1989)

[16] Diba, K., Buzsaki, G.: Forward and reverse hippocampal place-cell sequences during ripples. Nat. Neurosci. 10(10), 1241–1242 (2007)

[17] Dragoi, G., Carpi, D., Recce, M., Csicsvari, J., Buzsaki, G.: Interactions between hippocampus and medial septum during sharp waves and theta oscillation in the behaving rat. J. Neurosci. 19(14), 6191–6199 (1999)

[18] Foster, D.J., Wilson, M.A.: Reverse replay of behavioural sequences in hippocampal place cells during the awake state. Nature 440, 680–683 (2006)

[19] O'Keefe, J., Recce, M.L.: Phase relationship between hippocampal place units and the EEG theta rythm. Hippocampus 3(3), 317–330 (1993)

[20] Ermentrout, B.: Simulating, analyzing, and animating dynamical systems: A guide to XPPAUT for researchers and students. SIAM, Philadelphia (2002)

[21] Koene, R.A., Hasselmo, M.E.: Reversed and forward buffering of behavioral spike sequences enables retrospective and prospective retrieval in hippocampal regions CA3 and CA1. Neural Networks 21, 276–288 (2008)

[22] Colgin, L.L., Denninger, T., Fyhn, M., Hafting, T., Bonnevie, T., Jensen, O., Moser, M.B., Moser, E.I.: Frequency of gamma oscillations routes flow of information in the hippocampus. Nature 462(19), 353–358 (2009)

[23] Schmidt, R., Diba, K., Leibold, C., Schmitz, D., Buzsaki, G., Kempter, R.: Single-trial phase precession in the hippocampus. J. Neurosci. 29(42), 13232–13241 (2009)

[24] Traub, R.D., Draguhn, A., Whittington, M.A., Baldeweg, T., Bibbig, A., Buhl, E.H., Schmitz, D.: Axonal gap junctions between principal neurons: a novel source of network oscillations, and perhaps epileptogenesis. Rev. Neurosci. 13, 1–30 (2002)

A Probabilistic Neural Network for Assessment of the Vesicoureteral Reflux's Diagnostic Factors Validity

Dimitrios Mantzaris[1], George Anastassopoulos[1], Lazaros Iliadis[2],
Aggelos Tsalkidis[3], and Adam Adamopoulos[4]

[1] Medical Informatics Laboratory, Democritus University of Thrace, GR-68100,
Alexandroupolis, Greece
anasta@med.duth.gr
[2] Department of Forestry & Management of the Environment and Natural Resources,
Democritus University of Thrace, GR-68200, Orestiada, Hellas
liliadis@fmenr.duth.gr
[3] Pediatric Clinics, Democritus University of Thrace, GR-68100, Alexandroupolis, Greece
atsalkid@med.duth.gr
[4] Medical Physics Laboratory, Democritus University of Thrace, GR-68100,
Alexandroupolis, Greece
adam@med.duth.gr

Abstract. This study examines Probabilistic Neural Network (PNNs) models in terms of their classification efficiency in the Vesicoureteral Reflux (VUR) disease. PNNs were developed for the estimation of VUR risk factor. The obtained results lead to the conclusion that in this case the PNNs can be potentially used towards VUR risk prediction. There is a redundancy in the diagnostic factors, so pruned PNN was used in order to evaluate the contribution of each one. Moreover, the Receiver Operating Characteristic (ROC) analysis was used in order to select the most significant factors for the estimation of VUR risk. The results of the pruned PNN model were found in accordance with the ROC analysis. The obtained results may support that a number of the diagnostic factors that are recorded in patient's history may be omitted with no compromise to the fidelity of clinical evaluation.

Keywords: Artificial Neural Networks, Probabilistic Neural Networks, ROC analysis, Vesicoureteral Reflux.

1 Introduction

Medical prognosis is the attempt of a physician to reach a valid decision upon the nature of a patient's disease, to predict its likely expected course and to foresee the chances of recovery based on an objective set of criteria that are applicable to the particular case. Clinician's decision is based on accurately classifying the findings of an examination into groups of high and low risk factors. The problem of generating prognosis for medical diseases is complex due to the non linear interaction between different diagnostic factors [1].

K. Diamantaras, W. Duch, L.S. Iliadis (Eds.): ICANN 2010, Part I, LNCS 6352, pp. 241–250, 2010.
© Springer-Verlag Berlin Heidelberg 2010

Effective simulating methods based on computer usage for assessing of medical diseases diagnostic factors were searched. Computer simulations became more effective and they started to assist in experiments or clinical and laboratorial examinations. The prognosis possibility of a disease is valuable for physicians as well as for patients, bringing also measurable advantages, because time-consuming and expensive examinations are reduced to the indispensable minimum [2].

Artificial Neural Networks (ANNs) are suitable for disease prognosis since there is no need to posses the function of input and output parameter in evident form. If the function exists, it will be established through the network during the training process and it will be written down as weighted individual neurons. Nowadays, ANNs have been widely used in medicine [3], successfully, such as oncology [4], urology [4], [5], [6], [7], surgery [8], [9], orthopaedics [10], cardiology [11], pediatrics [5], pediatric surgery [12] etc.

This study implements Probabilistic Neural Networks (PNN) which have not been used in similar research efforts in the past [5], [6], [7]. The main purpose of this paper is the estimation of the significant Vesicoureteral Reflux (VUR) risk factors in neonates, infants and children, as reliable and on-time detection of VUR is crucial in the effective treatment of the disease and the avoidance of relapses.

Moreover, the available data underwent to statistical processing using the Receiver Operating Characteristic (ROC) analysis [13] in order to select the most significant factors for the estimation of VUR risk.

2 Vesicoureteral Reflux and Factors Related to the Prognosis

Urinary Tract Infections (UTIs) are diagnosed by the identification of bacteria in urine culture (in concentration greater than 10^5/ml), irrespectively of the microorganism the route and the level of infection. The frequency of UTI in neonates is about 1-2% and 2-4% in infants and children [14], [15].

The type and the frequency that bacteria cause urinary tract infection depend on the age, sex, and the presence or not of renal tract anatomical abnormalities. The most common bacteria are: E.Coli, Proteus, Klembsiella, Pseudomonas, Streptococcus and others.

The clinical presentation (Systsymp) is usually whit non specific symptoms like: fever, vomiting, diarrhea, feeding problems. Patients have failure to thrive or even lose weight. Older children may present dysuria, enuresis, frequency or loin pain [16].

Today's clinical routine for diagnosis is based on positive urine cultures. An antibiogramme is very important in order to find out the sensitivity of the causative organism and to provide the most appropriate antibiotic treatment. Urine collection is obtained, always under aseptic conditions, by urine bag, suprapubic aspiration or catheterization, depending on the age of the patient and the severity of the clinical presentation. It is also necessary a blood laboratory testing that includes FBC (Full Blood Count), (where WBC: number of white blood cells, WBC type, Ht: haematocrite, Hb: haemoglobine, PLT: platelets). Erythrocyte Sedimentation Rate (ESR) and C-Reactive Protein (CRP) (positive or negative) are also tested [15].

A young child with documented UTI should be further evaluated with renal / bladder ultrasound and Cysteourethrogram (CUG) in order to detect VUR, obstruction or other congenital abnormality.

The normal flow of urine begins in the collecting system of each kidney. Urine then flows out of each kidney and into a tube called ureter. Each ureter leads into the bladder, where the urine collects until it is passed out of the body. Normally, urine should flow only in this direction. In VUR, however, urine that has already been collected in the bladder is able to flow backwards from the bladder, along the ureter, and back into the collecting system of the kidney. VUR may be present in either one or both ureters [16].

The VUR is an anatomical and functional disorder with potentially serious consequences because the bacteria have direct access to the kidneys and cause a kidney infection (pyelonephritis) [14]. In particular, when the ureter inserts into the trigone, the distal end of the ureter courses through the intramural portion of the bladder wall at an oblique angle. The intramural tunnel length–to–ureteral diameter ratio is 5:1 for a healthy non-refluxing ureter. As the bladder fills with urine and the bladder wall distends and thins, the intramural portion of the ureter also stretches, thins out, and becomes compressed against the detrusor backing. This process allows a continual antegrade flow of urine from the ureter into the bladder but prevents retrograde transmission of urine from the bladder back up to the kidney; thus, a healthy intramural tunnel, within the bladder wall, functions as a flap-valve mechanism for the intramural ureter and prevents urinary reflux.

An abnormal intramural tunnel (i.e. short tunnel) results in a malfunctioning flap-valve mechanism and VUR. When the intramural tunnel length is short, urine tends to reflux up the ureter and into the collecting system. Pacquin reports that refluxing ureters have an intramural tunnel length–to–ureteral diameter ratio of 1.4:1. To prevent reflux during ureteral reimplantation, the physician must obtain a minimum tunnel length–to–ureteral diameter ratio of 3:1.

The human kidney contains two types of renal papillae: simple (convex) papilla and compound (concave) papilla. Compound papillae predominate at the polar regions of the kidney, whereas simple papillae are located at nonpolar regions. Approximately 66% of human papillae are convex and 33% are concave.

Intrarenal reflux or retrograde movement of urine from the renal pelvis into the renal parenchyma is a function of intrarenal papillary anatomy. Simple papillae possess oblique, slitlike, ductal orifices that close upon increased intrarenal pressure. Thus, simple papillae do not allow intrarenal reflux. However, compound papillae possess gaping orifices that are perpendicular to the papillary surface that remain open upon increased intrarenal pressure. These gaping orifices allow free intrarenal reflux.

In children, particularly those in the first 6 years of life, urinary infection can cause kidney damage [15]. The VUR is recognized in 25-40% of causes of UTIs in children [16].

CUG is obtained by catheterization of the bladder, infusion of a special dye-contrast material. Then a series of images with x-ray radiation are taken. This is a painful procedure and demands the exposure of the patient in radiation and also maltreats the patient's genitals. Despite the negative side-effects, the use of CUG is essential, in today's clinical routine, in order to identify anatomical abnormalities and to provide information for the appropriate therapy and prophylaxis avoiding the creation of renal scarring and subsequenty renal dysfunction.

Time interval between the appearance of the symptoms and UTI diagnosis (DUR-SYMPT) and time interval between the appearance of the symptoms and the initiation of treatment (STARTTRE) are very crucial for the best possible management in the acute phase and the prevention of long term consequences in the renal function of the subjects.

The VUR data, which are used at the design of proposed ANN structure, are obtained from the Pediatric Clinical Information System (CIS) of Alexandroupolis' University Hospital, Greece.

The clinical and laboratorial parameters that were considered for VUR diagnosis were 21, namely, sex, age, siblings, utsymp, systsymp, WBC, WBC type, hematocrit, hemoglobin, platelets, ESR, CRP, bacteria, sensitivity, ultrasound, Dimercaptosuccinic Acid (DMSA) scintigraphy, symptoms duration, start treatment, risk factor, collect and resistance. These parameters have been explained previously. Both of utsymp and DMSA scintigraphy were not known for all cases, so they were dropped from the data set, thus reducing the number of parameters to 19. It is emphasized that some of the parameters may take more than one values simultaneously. For example, the parameter age can have a value between 1 and 3, depending on the child's age, less than 1 year old, or between 1 and 5 years old, or greater than 5 years old. In the other hand, the parameter sensitivity has 6 available values, *penic, cephal2, chephal3, aminogl, sulfonamides* and *other*, and it is possible the patient's clinical results of this parameter to be simultaneouly *cephal3* and *aminogl*. The insertion of sensitivity's values to ANN demands the division of this parameter to 6 independent subparameters instead of a universal parameter. Similar process is applied at systsymp and risk factor. As a result, the number of parameters for ANN was extended to 34.

The VUR clinical and laboratorial parameters and their values are depicted in Table 1. The 1st column of Table 1 is corresponded the ANN inputs with VUR parameters, which are represented in 2nd column of the table. The existence of a range of NN inputs means that the corresponding VUR parameter can have, simultaneously, more than one value.

Table 1. Vesicoureteral reflux clinical and laboratorial factors and their values

NN inputs	Factors	Factors' Values					
1	**Sex**	Boy	Girl				
2	**Age**	< 1 year	1 – 5 years	> 5 years			
3	**Siblings**	1	2	3			
4–8	**Systsymp**	Fever	Vomiting / diarrhea	Anorexia	Loss of weight	Others	
9	**WBC**	< 4500	4500–10500	> 10500			
10	**WBCtype**	n	L	m	E	b	
11	**HT**	< 37	37 – 42	> 42			
12	**HB**	< 11.5	11.5 – 13.5	> 13.5			
13	**PLT**	< 170	170 – 450	> 450			
14	**ESR**	< 20	20 – 40	> 40			
15	**CRP**	+	-				
16	**Bacteria**	e.coli	proteus	kiebsielas	strep	stapf	psedom	others
17–22	**Sensitiv**	penic	cephal2	cephal3	aminogl	sulfonamides	other
23	**Ultrasoun**	rsize nrm	rsize abn	rstract nrm	rstract abn	Normal	other
24	**Dursymp**	2 days	3 days	4 days	5 days	> 5 days	
25	**Starttre**	2 days	3 days	4 days	5 days		
26–27	**Riskfact**	Age <	Ttreat				
28	**Collect**	u-bag	catheter	Suprapubi			
29–34	**Resistan**	Penicillin	Kefalosp2	Kefalosp3	Aminoglyc	Sulfonam	Others
	Utsymp	Dysouria	Frequency	Burning	Enuresis	Abdominal pain	
	DMSA	+	-				

As mentioned above, CUG is the principal medical examination for VUR diagnosis. At the same time, this imaging technique is dangerous for children patients' health and there is no alternative method for diagnosis of VUR. This paper proposes a computational method, which is based on ANNs, predicting VUR existence, without the exposure of children in radiation.

The VUR data used at the design of PNN model, were obtained from the Pediatric Clinical Information System of Alexandroupolis' University Hospital in Greece.

The present study is based on a dataset consisting of 160 cases (children patients with UTI). Some of these patients presented VUR. This data set was divided into a set of 120 records for the training of PNNs and another set of 40 records for the evaluation and testing of their classification efficiency.

3 PNNs for VUR Prediction

The proposed pattern recognition models for VUR factor classification are based on a non-symbolic computational intelligence method implemented by ANN [5]. The development of such an ANN demands the determination of a number of parameters, such as the type of ANN, the number of neurons in each layer and the applied learning algorithm.

PNNs are a variant of Radial Basis Function Networks and approximate Bayesian statistical techniques, combining new input vectors with existed storage data in order to classify correctly the input data; a process familiar to human behavior [17].

PNNs are based on Parzen's Probabilistic Density Function (PDF) estimator [18] and their aim is the correct classification of input vectors to one of the available target classes of the problem. A PNN is a three-layer feed-forward network, consisting of an input layer, a radial basis and a competitive layer [19]. The first layer transfers the input data to a hidden layer. The radial basis function layer computes distances from the input vector to the training input vectors and produces a vector whose elements indicate how close the input is to a training input. The third layer sums these contributions for each class of inputs to produce as its net output a vector of probabilities. Finally, a competitive transfer function on the output of the third layer classifies the input vector into a specific class because this one has the maximum probability of being correct.

The PNNs do not require iterative learning process, so that may managed magnitude of data faster that other ANN architectures. This PNNs' feature results by the Bayesian technique's behavior.

The number of input nodes of PNN equals to the number of variables of the problem and the number of nodes for output layer equals to the number of classes, as they are defined by the problem. It was clarified in section 2 that input parameters are thirty four and output classes are two; consequently, in this study, the input layer consists of thirty four neurons and the output layer has two neurons that determines the patients' VUR risk factor. The number of nodes for hidden layer is the number of patterns during the PNN's construction. Consequently, the proposed PNN had 120 neurons for hidden layer, as the available data set for PNN implementation, consisted of 120 cases. PNNs' design is straightforward and does not depend on training, thus no learning algorithm was selected during PNN's implementation [20].

The PNNs architecture is constrained by the available features of specific problem, however, the width of the calculated Gaussian curve for each probability density function have to be defined. In the present study, this spread factor varied from 0.1 to 100.

4 PNNs' and ROC Analysis Results

The construction and the classification efficiency of the developed PNNs were based on MATLAB Neural Network Toolbox, due to its effectiveness and user-friendly interface [20].

The three level architecture of the PNNs is 34-120-2. The spread of the radial basis function, representing the width of the Gaussian curve, varied during the experimental design phase of the PNNs. The spread's value ranged from 0.1 to 5.0.

The evaluation criterions for PNNs' performance are the percentages of successful prognosis over pathological and overall cases. The obtained results of PNNs with satisfactory performance are summarized in Table 2. The second column of the Table presents the spread's value of the RBF. The performance of the proposed PNNs is depicted in columns third through eighth. The classification efficiency of PNNs was based on the percentages of correct classified cases over testing (40 cases), training (120 cases) and overall data set (160 cases) they are presented in columns third to fifth. The proper classification of pathological cases is a critical feature for the evaluation of the PNNs' generalization ability. The implemented PNNs have to recognize patients with increased VUR risk factor, so the fields 6th to 8th store the percentage of pathological cases that have been categorized correctly, for testing, training and overall data, respectively.

Table 2. The PNNs for the VUR risk factor prediction

ANN model	Spread	Percentage of Successful Prognosis			Percentage of Successful Prognosis Over Pathological Situations		
		Testing Set	Training Set	Overall Set	Testing Set	Training Set	Overall Set
PNN₁	0.4	87.50	100.00	96.88	100.00	100.00	100.00
PNN₂	1.5	85.00	99.12	95.63	61.12	90.91	85.57

The results of PNN_1 and PNN_2 simulations, as they are presented in Table 2, conclude that their classification efficiency is similar. However, the proposed PNN_2 misclassified VUR cases as normal cases, as obtained by results of Table 2. On the other hand, PNN_1 did not misclassify VUR cases as normal, as obtained by the results of Table 2. It is an important feature of the PNN_1's behavior, as it has the ability to distinguish the VUR patients by diagnostic factors. It is clear the satisfactory performance of PNN_1 in terms of VUR estimation. Therefore, the PNN can be potentially used towards VUR risk prediction.

The PNN_1 was used for the significance estimation of the diagnostic risk factors and it was trained with 34 pruned data sets. Each of these sets used values related to 33 diagnostic factors instead of the total 34 ones. In other words, one different diagnostic factor was omitted in each data set. The PNN_1 was constructed and tested with the pruned data sets.

As it was shown in Table 1, the number of diagnostic factors is N = 34, so the possible combinations of input data subsets are given by N!/k!(N-k)! , for k = 1 ... 34. The total number of combinations is 17.179.869.183, so exhaustive search is time-consuming.

Table 3. Experimental results using Pruned PNN

Omitted Factors	Percentage of Successful Prognosis			Percentage of Successful Prognosis over Pathological Situations			AUC	AUC
	Testing Set	Training Set	Overall Set	Testing Set	Training Set	Overall Set		
Sex	80.00	100.00	95.00	78.13	100.00	94.21	0.549	0.549
Age	81.98	100.00	97.32	92.50	100.00	94.00	0.523	0.523
Siblings	97.62	100.00	98.12	100.00	100.00	100.00	0.468	0.532
Systsymp1 (Fever)	98.23	100.00	98.78	100.00	100.00	100.00	0.445	0.555
Systsymp2 (Vomitting/ diarrhea)	97.62	100.00	98.12	100.00	100.00	100.00	0.460	0.540
Systsymp3 (anorexia	98.23	100.00	98.78	100.00	100.00	100.00	0.445	0.555
Systsymp4 (Loss of weight)	87.50	100.00	96.85	100.00	100.00	100.00	0.503	0.503
Systsymp5 (Others)	82.89	100.00	97.82	100.00	100.00	100.00	0.515	0.515
WBC	97.11	100.00	97.86	100.00	100.00	100.00	0.477	0.523
WBCtype	97.11	100.00	97.86	100.00	100.00	100.00	0.475	0.525
HT	87.50	100.00	96.85	100.00	100.00	100.00	0.504	0.504
HB	98.53	100.00	99.11	100.00	100.00	100.00	0.428	0.572
PLT	98.53	100.00	99.11	100.00	100.00	100.00	0.420	0.580
ESR	62.50	100.00	90.63	50.00	100.00	89.71	0.603	0.603
CRP	97.11	100.00	97.86	100.00	100.00	100.00	0.473	0.527
Bacteria	70.00	100.00	92.25	72.13	100.00	93.86	0.576	0.576
Sensitiv1 (penic)	99.32	100.00	99.68	100.00	100.00	100.00	0.380	0.620
Sensitiv2 (cephal2)	98.53	100.00	99.11	100.00	100.00	100.00	0.430	0.570
Sensitiv3 (cephal3)	81.18	100.00	96.12	100.00	100.00	100.00	0.535	0.535
Sensitiv4 (aminogl)	98.23	100.00	98.78	100.00	100.00	100.00	0.443	0.557
Sensitiv5 (Sulfonamides)	99.67	100.00	99.80	100.00	100.00	100.00	0.339	0.661
Sensitiv6 (others)	82.89	100.00	97.82	100.00	100.00	100.00s	0.518	0.518
Ultrasound	80.00	100.00	95.00	72.18	100.00	93.71	0.569	0.569
Dursympt	97.62	100.00	98.12	100.00	100.00	100.00	0.468	0.532
Starttre	98.92	100.00	99.28	100.00	100.00	100.00	0.404	0.596
Riskfact1 (Age < 1 year)	98.92	100.00	99.28	100.00	100.00	100.00	0.411	0.589
Riskfact2 (Ttreat)	98.40	100.00	99.02	100.00	100.00	100.00	0.437	0.563
Collect	82.89	100.00	97.82	100.00	100.00	100.00	0.518	0.518
Resistan1 (Penicillin)	81.18	100.00	96.12	100.00	100.00	100.00	0.537	0.537
Resistan2 (Kefalosp2)	80.00	100.00	95.00	78.13	100.00	94.21	0.548	0.548
Resistan3 (Kefalosp3)	87.50	100.00	96.85	100.00	100.00	100.00	0.503	0.503
Resistan4 (Aminoglyc)	97.62	100.00	98.12	100.00	100.00	92.86	0.452	0.548
Resistan5 (Sulfonal)	80.00	100.00	95.00	78.13	100.00	94.21	0.544	0.544
Resistan6 (Others)	87.50	100.00	96.85	100.00	100.00	100.00	0.504	0.504

The available data set of VUR's records was processed by ROC analysis. The aim of this data processing was the evaluation of importance role of each diagnostic factor for VUR estimation. The Area Under Curve (AUC) is an important statistic of ROC analysis. The mathematical expressions for AUC, sensitivity and specificity are explained in [13]. A value of area larger than 0.5, indicates the importance contribution of a specific diagnostic factor.

The obtained results for pruned PNN and ROC analysis are summarized in Table 3. The diagnostic factor which was not considered during the PNN₁'s development is presented in the first column of the Table 3. The 2nd to 7th columns depict the performance of PNN₁ for each of pruned data sets. The results of the 2nd to 4th columns are the percentages of successful prognosis over testing (40 cases), training (120 cases) and overall pruned data sets (160 cases). The 5th to 7th columns records the percentage of successful prognosis of pathological cases for testing, training and overall pruned data sets. The eighth column presents the AUC of ROC for the diagnostic factor in the first column.

The obtained results of PNN's simulation with pruned data sets as well as the ROC analysis exhibit that some diagnostic factors reinforce the VUR estimation, while other diagnostic factors reduce the classification efficiency of PNN1. As it is shown in Table 3, the percentages of successful prognosis for pathological and normal cases are unchangeable and equal to 100%. This behavior of pruned PNN1 declares that the proposed neural network has adaptation ability, so that the training patterns can be classified correctly during the simulation process.

There is not improvement of pruned PNN1 in terms of the percentages of successful prognosis over pathological situations; due to the PNN1 with full-sized data set achieved the optimal classification for pathological cases. However, the percentages of successful prognosis for testing, training and overall pruned data sets are significantly increased due to PNN1's implementations omitted some diagnostic factors.

The results of the pruned PNN₁ were compared to the ones related to the full-sized PNN₁. The performance of PNN₁ is significantly decreased in the case of the omission of the sex, age, ESR, bacteria, ultrasound, resistan2 (Kefalosp2) and resistan5 (Sulfonal) diagnostic factors.

The omission of the resistan1 (Penicillin), sensitiv3 (Cephal3), sensitiv6 (others), collect and systsymp5 (others) diagnostic factors improves the pruned PNN₁'s classification efficiency of normal cases according to experimental values as presented in Table 3. Both the simulation results of pruned PNN₁ and ROC analysis' values show that performance of pruned ANN is unchanged in case of the systsym4 (loss of weight), HT, resistan3 (Kefalosp3) and resitstan6 (others) were not considered during the PNN₁'s development. The PNN₁'s implementation, without the sensitiv5 (Sulfonamides), yields satisfactory results in terms of the discrimination of pathological and normal cases.

5 Conclusions

Urinary tract infections (UTIs) are one of the most frequent diseases in infants and children. The VUR has serious consequences as the bacteria have direct access to the kidneys and cause a kidney infection (pyelonephritis). Despite the serious complications of VUR, no investigation has been done on the effectiveness and weightiness of the various diagnostic factors in the clinical evaluation of the patients with UTIs. A method for the evaluation of the most significant diagnostic factor towards VUR risk is proposed in the present work. The method presented here utilized an optimal PNN. The PNN was designed, implemented and tested with data sets of 33 parameters instead of full-sized data set.

The obtained results of pruned PNN_1 were in accordance with ones of the ROC analysis. The most significant diagnostic factors for VUR risk estimation, as proposed by PNN_1 with pruned data sets, are sex, age, ESR, bacteria, ultrasound, resistan2 (Kefalosp2) and resistan5 (Sulfonal). Consequently, a number of diagnostic factors may be omitted without any loss in the clinical assessment validity. From this point of view, the obtained results may support that a number of recorded diagnostic factors that are recorded in patient's history may be omitted with no compromise to the fidelity of clinical evaluation.

In future work, it would be used advanced optimization searching techniques, such as Genetic Algorithms search, in order to be defined a complete set of diagnostic factors for VUR estimation.

References

1. McGuire, W., Tandom, A., Allred, D., Chamnes, G., Clark, G.: How to Use Orognostic Factors in Axillary Node-negative Breast Cancer Patients. J. Natl. Cancer Inst. 82, 1006–1015 (1990)
2. Papik, K., Molnar, B., Schaefer, R., Dombovari, Z., Tulassay, Z., Feher, J.: Application of Neural Networks in Medicine - A Review. Med. Sci. Monit., 538–546 (1998)
3. Jigneshkumar, P., Ramesh, G.: Applications of Artificial Neural Networks in Medical Science. Current Clinical Pharmacology 2, 217–226 (2007)
4. Anagnostou, T., Remzi, M., Djavan, B.: Artificial Neural Networks for Decision-Making in Urologic Oncology. Reviews in Urology 5, 15–21 (2003)
5. Mantzaris, D., Anastassopoulos, G., Tsalkidis, A., Adamopoulos, A.: Intelligent Prediction of Vesicoureteral Reflux Disease. WSEAS Trans. Systems 9, 1440–1449 (2005)
6. Knudsona, M., Austina, C., Walda, M., Makhloufb, A., Niederb, C.: Computational Model for Predicting the Chance of Early Resolution in Children with Vesicoureteral Reflux. The Journal of Urology 178, 1824–1827 (2007)
7. Shiraishia, K., Matsuyamaa, H., Neppleb, K., Waldb, M., Niederbergerc, C.: Validation of a Prognostic Calculator for Prediction of Early Vesicoureteral Reflux Resolution in Children. The Journal of Urology 182, 687–691 (2009)
8. Papadopoulos, H., Gammerman, A., Vovk, V.: Confidence Predictions for the Diagnosis of Acute Abdominal Pain. In: AIAI 2009, pp. 175–184 (2009)
9. Mantzaris, D., Anastassopoulos, G., Iliadis, L., Adamopoulos, A.: An Evolutionary Technique for Medical Diagnosis Risk Factor Selection. IFIP International Federation for Information Processing 296, 195–203 (2009)
10. Mantzaris, D., Anastassopoulos, G., Lymperopoulos, K.: Medical Disease Prediction Using Artificial Neural Networks. In: 8th IEEE International Conference on BioInformatics and Bio.Engineering (2008)
11. Tjoa, M., Dutt, D., Lim, Y., Yau, B., Kugean, R., Krishnan, S., Chan, K.: Artificial Neural Networks for the Classification of Cardiac Patient States Using ECG and Blood Pressure Data. In: Proceedings of the Seventh Australian and New Zealand Intelligent Systems Conference, pp. 323–327 (2001)

12. Mantzaris, D., Anastassopoulos, G., Adamopoulos, A., Stephanakis, I., Kambouri, K., Gardikis, S.: Selective Clinical Estimation of Childhood Abdominal Pain Based on Pruned Artificial Neural Networks. In: Proceedings of the 3rd WSEAS International Conference on Cellular and Molecular Biology, Biophysics and Bioengineering, pp. 50–55 (2007)
13. Streiner, D., Cairney, J.: What's Under the ROC? An Introduction to Receiver Operating Characteristics Curves. The Canadian Journal of Psychiatry 52, 121–128 (2007)
14. Nelson, C., Koo, H.: Vesicoureteral Reflux (2005),
    http://www.emedicine.com/ped/topic2750.htm
15. Youngerman-Cole, S.: Vesicoureteral Reflux (2004),
    http://www.uhseast.com/147424.cfm
16. Thompson, M., Simon, S., Sharma, V., Alon, U.S.: Timing of Follow-Up Voiding Cystourethrogram in Children with Primary Vesicoureteral Reflux: Development and Application of a Clinical Algorithm. Pediatrics 115, 426–434 (2005)
17. Orr, R.: Use of a Probabilistic Neural Network to Estimate the Risk of Mortality after Cardiac Surgery. J. Medical Decision Making 17, 178–185 (1997)
18. Parzen, E.: On Estimation of a Probability Density Function and Mode. Annals of Mathematical Statistics 33, 1065–1076 (1962)
19. Iliadis, L.: Intelligent Information Systems and Applications in Risk Estimation. Stamoulis Publishing, Thessaloniki (2007)
20. Howard, D., Mark, B.: Neural Network Toolbox User's Guide, The Math Works, Inc. (2008),
    http://www.mathworks.com/access/helpdesk/help/
    pdf_doc/nnet/nnet.pdf

Shape-Based Tumor Retrieval in Mammograms Using Relevance-Feedback Techniques

Stylianos D. Tzikopoulos[1], Harris V. Georgiou[1],
Michael E. Mavroforakis[2], and Sergios Theodoridis[1]

[1] National and Kapodistrian University of Athens, Dept. of Informatics
and Telecommunications, Panepistimiopolis, Ilissia, Athens 15784, Greece
[2] University of Houston, Department of Computer Science, PGH 219, 4800 Calhoun
Rd., Houston, TX 77204-3010, USA

Abstract. This paper presents an experimental "morphological analysis" retrieval system for mammograms, using Relevance-Feedback techniques. The features adopted are first-order statistics of the Normalized Radial Distance, extracted from the annotated mass boundary. The system is evaluated on an extensive dataset of 2274 masses of the DDSM database, which involves 7 distinct classes. The experiments verify that the involvement of the radiologist as part of the retrieval process improves the results, even for such a hard classification task, reaching the precision rate of almost 90%. Therefore, Relevance-Feedback can be employed as a very useful complementary tool to a Computer Aided Diagnosis system.

1 Introduction

Over the recent years, content-based image retrieval (CBIR) systems are gaining in importance [1,2,3]. Such systems extract visual features from the "query" image, e.g. color, texture or shape and perform a comparison of it with the available images in a database, using specific *similarity measures*. The most *similar* images are returned to the user.

The scenario described above uses low-level features, which are not capable of capturing the image semantics, e.g. the high-level semantic concept that is meaningful for a user. This is known as the *semantic gap*. In order to address this gap, Relevance Feedback techniques have been developed since the early and mid-1990's [4,5]. In such a system, the user interacts with the search engine and marks the images that he perceives as relevant or non-relevant. Taking into account this feedback information, the engine "learns" and improved results are returned to the user during the next iteration.

The search engine is usually a classifier, trained by the relevant and non-relevant samples, labelled by the user [6]. Support Vector Machines (SVMs) [7] are often chosen for this classification scheme. They allow fast learning and evaluation, they do not need restrictive assumptions regarding the data, they are flexible and they turn out to be less sensitive, compared to density-based learners with respect to the problem of class imbalance. Therefore, many Relevance Feedback schemes use the 2-class SVMs for the classification step [8,9,10,11].

K. Diamantaras, W. Duch, L.S. Iliadis (Eds.): ICANN 2010, Part I, LNCS 6352, pp. 251–260, 2010.
© Springer-Verlag Berlin Heidelberg 2010

The type of the patterns that the search engine returns to the user for labelling is of high importance. For example in [11], the user labels patterns that have been classified as relevant with high confidence, e.g., the furthest patterns to the positive (relevant) side of the classifier. This can be easier for the user, but gives no useful information to the system, leading to slow convergence. More popular approaches adopt the active technique [9]. This approach provides the user with the most informative patterns, e.g. the patterns closest to the decision boundary, in order to improve the speed of the convergence.

Besides image retrieval, Relevance Feedback can also be employed to other systems. In fact, Relevance Feedback was first introduced for the retrieval of text documents [12], music [13], 3D objects [14] and more recently it was used for medical image retrieval [15,16,17,18]. In such a context, the aim of a retrieval system is to function in conjunction with a Computer Aided Diagnosis (CAD) system. The radiologists can be provided with relevant past cases -according to the query-, along with proven pathology and other information, making the diagnosis more reliable. Relevance Feedback seems an ideal scheme for the improvement of the performance of medical image retrieval systems, as it incorporates the radiologist's judgement, in order to capture the some higher-level semantic concepts of the medical images. The judgement of such an expert is the result of a very complex and vague procedure, combining a multitude of quantitative and qualitative facts, as well as the radiologist's experience, and therefore should be taken into consideration.

From these works, only the one in [18] is referred to mammograms. However, it restricts to a small number of images and focuses on micro-calcification clusters, in contrast to our work, which is based on a larger database and focuses on masses. Furthermore, the whole approach is different, as it will become clear in the following sections.

In this work, a Relevance Feedback scheme for the retrieval of mammograms is presented. The system retrieves mammograms containing masses of the same morphology as the query image. The system is tested on a dataset of 2274 masses of the DDSM database [19], that originate from 7 distinct classes. The adopted features for the shape description are first-order statistics of the mass boundary. The latter is given as part of the annotation of the database. The obtained results are promising, according to specific statistical measures and they show a convergence of the relevant retrieved images, reaching the success rate of almost 90%.

The rest of the paper is organized as follows: In section 2, the mammographic image database used is presented. The shape features extracted and the classifier used are described in detail in section 3. Section 4 presents the results obtained, while discussion and conclusion are summarized in section 5.

2   Dataset

The methodology presented in this work was applied to images of the Digital Database of Screening Mammography (DDSM), that are provided and described in [19], available online freely for scientific purposes. This database consists of 2589 cases and each case corresponds to four mammograms, representing the two breasts at craniocaudal (CC) and mediolateral (MLO) oblique views. The images of the database are the result of a digitization procedure, using three different scanners. All the images are analysed by expert radiologists and the corresponding abnormalities (4775) are annotated as calcifications (2201), masses (2556) or other abnormalities (18). Each abnormality has been associated by pixel-level ground truth information, provided by a radiologist, and a complete description of the abnormality is given, including diagnostic assessment, subtlety and proven pathology, as described in [19]. In addition, in case of calcifications, information about the type and the distribution are available and in case of masses, the description includes the mass shape and the mass margin.

The spatial resolution of the images is 50 μm/pixel or 43.5 μm/pixel and the bit depth is 12 or 16 bits, according to the scanner used. A typical image of the database is shown at figure 1.

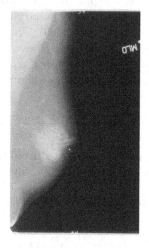

Fig. 1. Left MLO image of the case 3088 of the database

3   Methods

3.1   Feature Extraction

For the case of a mass abnormality of a mammogram, a detailed pixel-based ground-truth description is available, as figure 2(a) shows. In addition, characterization of the mass shape is given, including the following classes: Architectural Distortion, Irregular, Lobulated, Lymph Node, Oval, Round, Tubular or Other. Our goal is to predict the class of the shape, using the morphological characteristics of the boundary. The features adopted for this purpose are first-order statistics of the Normalized Radial Distance, as presented in [20,21]. Obviously, other features may also be used. Our choice is justified, by the simplicity of these two features and by the high accuracy that is finally obtained.

First, the centroid of the mass is calculated, using cumulative distributions of the projections in both x and y axes. Then, the radial distance sequence of the centroid and the border pixels are extracted, using equation (1).

$$d\left(i\right) = \sqrt{\left(\left(x\left(i\right) - X_0\right)^2 + \left(y\left(i\right) - Y_0\right)^2\right)}, \ i = 1, 2, ..., N \tag{1}$$

where the point (X_0, Y_0) is the centroid and $x\left(i\right), y\left(i\right)$ are the parametric data series of length N, corresponding to the border pixels.

In order to overcome problems associated with the non-convex shape of the boundary, in relation to the mass centroid, the Radial Distance Function samples are calculated from the mass perimeter towards the centroid (and not vice versa, as commonly used), as it has been pointed out in [22]. In addition, a pre-processing stage of image dilation [23], using a 3×3 mask, is applied before acquiring the borderline curve, so that to avoid problems with edge-following techniques in cases of sharp corners. The boundary is traced at pixel level, starting from the pixel that corresponds to angle 0. The sequence of the pixels continues to follow the mass boundary counter-clockwise as figure 2(a) illustrates. Finally, a normalization step is adopted using equation (2). The Normalized Radial Distance extracted from the mass boundary of figure 2(a) is shown at figure 2(b).

$$d_n\left(i\right) = \frac{d\left(i\right) - d_{min}}{d_{max} - d_{min}} \tag{2}$$

Seven simple curve features are now extracted from the Normalized Radial Distance, meaning the d_n sequence, using the following equations (3)–(9).

1. The mean value is estimated using equation (3)

$$m = \frac{1}{N} \sum_{i=1}^{N} d_n\left(i\right) \tag{3}$$

2. The standard deviation is calculated using equation (4)

$$s = \sqrt{\frac{1}{N} \sum_{i=1}^{N} \left(d_n\left(i\right) - m\right)^2} \tag{4}$$

3. The mass circularity is extracted according to equation (5)

$$C = \frac{P^2}{A} \tag{5}$$

where A is the area and P the perimeter of the mass.

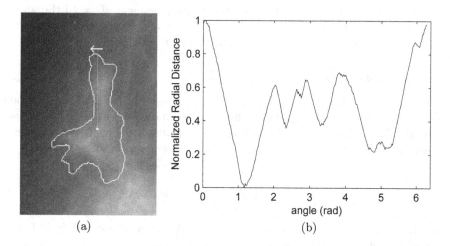

(a)   (b)

Fig. 2. a) The segmented mass of the right MLO mammogram of case 3129, annotated as Irregular, the mass centroid and the starting pixel on the boundary, and b) the corresponding normalized radial distance signal.

4. The entropy is calculated using equation (6)

$$E = \sum_{i=1}^{B} P_k \log (P_k)$$ (6)

where P_k are the probability values estimated using a $B = 100$ bins histogram.

5. The area ratio parameter is estimated by equation (7)

$$A_R = \frac{1}{m \cdot N} \sum_{i=1}^{N} (d_n (i) - m)$$ (7)

where $A_R = 0$, $\forall d (i) \le m$.

6. The zero-crossing count Z_c is computed as a count of the number of times the d_n signal crossed the average d_n value.

7. The roughness index R is calculated by dividing the d_n signal into small segments of equal length and then estimating a roughness index for each one of them according to equations (8) and (9)

$$R(j) = \sum_{i=j}^{L+j} |d(i) - d(i+1)|, \ j = 1, \ldots, \lceil \frac{N}{L} \rceil$$ (8)

$$R = \frac{\sum_{j=1}^{k} \left(R(j) + \frac{L_{k+1}}{L} \cdot R(k+1) \right)}{k + \frac{L_{k+1}}{L}}, \ k = \lceil \frac{N}{L} \rceil - 1$$ (9)

where $R(j)$ is the roughness index for the j segment, $L = 16$ the number of boundary points in each segment, k denotes the last segment of length L and N is the total number of boundary points available.

3.2   Classification

For the classification of the masses of the database at step 0 of the Relevance Feedback procedure, a simple Euclidean minimum distance classifier [24] is used. The Euclidean distance E_i of query pattern q from all the available patterns p_i, where $i = 1, 2, \ldots, N_t$, is estimated according to equation (10).

$$E_i = \sqrt{\sum_{j=1}^{S} (q(j) - p_i(j))^2} \qquad (10)$$

where N_t is the number of all the patterns of the database and $S = 7$ is the dimension of the feature space.

On the next steps of the process, an SVM classifier [25,26] is trained according to the feedback of the user. In the simple SVM case, the system returns the most "confident" relevant patterns for labelling, while in the active SVM case, the system returns the most "ambiguous" patterns for labelling, as described in section 1.

4   Experiments and Results

For the evaluation of the Relevance Feedback scheme, the 2556 masses, included in the database, are used. Note that apart from the detailed boundary of each mass, a classification of the shape of the masses in the following classes is also available: Architectural Distortion, Irregular, Lobulated, Lymph Node, Oval, Round, Tubular or Other. The masses corresponding to the Architectural Distortion class are excluded from the experiments, as this characterization can be extracted mainly by a comparison between the pair of breasts and not from a mass boundary itself. We further exclude 27 masses that have been annotated to belong to more than one classes. Thus the resulting size of the database is 2274 masses with 7 distinct classes. In order to evaluate the performance of the retrieval results at each round of the RF, the *precision curve* [27] is used. The precision at each round is defined as $pr = \frac{R}{N}$, where $N = 10$ is the total number of returned images to the user and R are the relevant images among them.

The experiments were carried out according to the following scenario:

- The user chooses a mass from the database as query image
- Repeat for steps 0 (no feedback yet) to 10 (user gave feedback 10 times)
    • The system returns to the user 10 images for evaluation and the precision is estimated
    • The system returns to the user 10 images to label
    • The user labels a subset of the images, as "relevant" or "non-relevant"
    • The system is re-trained, using the feedback of the user as new information

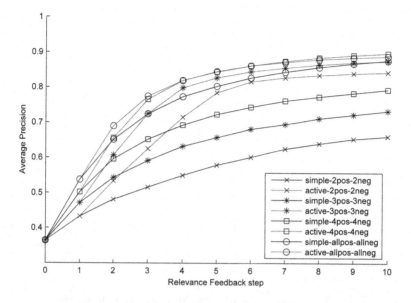

Fig. 3. Average precision at different steps of the RF procedure

The above scenario is repeated for all the images of the database, in order to achieve more focused results. The system uses the simple SVM scheme [11], according to which the user labels the most confident relevant patterns, or the active SVM scheme [9], where the user labels the most uncertain patterns that lie closest to the classifier's decision boundary. In addition, the user is modeled as follows:

- The 'patient' user, that marks all the patterns returned by the system at each step as relevant or non-relevant, that can lead to imbalanced training sets.
- The less 'patient' user, that marks up to four relevant and four non-relevant patterns, among the patterns that the system returns at each step.
- The 'impatient' user, that marks up to three relevant and three non-relevant patterns, among the patterns that the system returns at each step.
- The 'lazy' user, that marks up to two relevant and two non-relevant patterns, among the patterns that the system returns at each step.

The average precision achieved at each iteration step for all the above configurations is shown in figure 3. Note that all the curves start from the same point at step 0, as no information is given from the user. At step 1, the simple and active techniques of the same type of user achieve equal precision rate, as the available images at step 0 for each user type are the same for these two scenarios. However, at step 1 the user of the active scenario provides more informative feedback than the one of the simple scenario, leading to a quicker convergence of the classifier. This is the reason for the fact that active SVM outperforms the simple SVM at steps greater than or equal to 2, always for the same type of user.

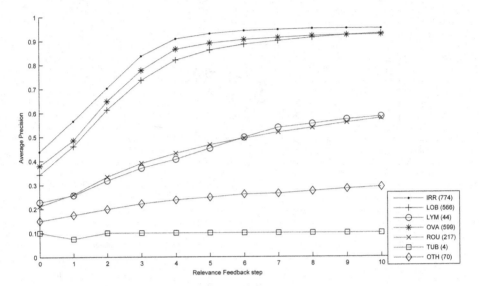

Fig. 4. Average precision per class for active-3pos-3neg scenario

The maximum precision rate of 89.7% is observed for the case of active scenario that the user marks up to 4 relevant and 4 non-relevant patterns and not for the 'patient' user, because probably the latter one creates sometimes imbalanced training sets.

Figure 4 shows the average precision for each one of the 7 classes for the scenario of active SVM and a usual user -not 'patient', nor 'lazy'- labeling at most 3 relevant and 3 non-relevant images at each step. The size of each class is given in parenthesis, indicating the number of the masses in the database that belong to each class. It is obvious that all the precision curves, except for the one of the Tubular class (only 4 samples), are increasing monotonically. Therefore, the retrieval process gives better results, on average, for all the classes as the Relevance Feedback proceeds.

5   Discussion and Conclusion

In this work, Relevance Feedback has been employed as a complementary tool to a Computer Aided Diagnosis system, that retrieves masses with similar shape as the query one. The judgement of the radiologist is considered to be of high importance to such a sensitive system as a medical application, where the errors should be eliminated and therefore it is suggested to be taken into consideration. The results, which almost reach 90% precision rate, show that the retrieval process can be improved significantly, when the radiologist is incorporated in the retrieval process, even for a hard classification task of 7 classes, using features of first-order statistics.

The system converges much faster when the user is more actively involved in the process, by labeling more samples as "relevant" or "non-relevant". In addition, the active technique converges faster to better results than the simple one, while the average precision for each class (figure 4) follows the rules of the Relevance Feedback scheme. The mammographic dataset used for the evaluation is rather extensive, consisting of the large number of 2274 masses, categorized in 7 distinct classes; these facts ensure that the results presented are very useful, reliable and consistent.

The system is also available online for any user at [28].

References

1. Smeulders, A., Worring, M., Santini, S., Gupta, A., Jain, R.: Content-based image retrieval at the end of the early years. IEEE Transactions on pattern analysis and machine intelligence 22(12), 1349–1380 (2000)
2. Gevers, T., Smeulders, A.: Content-based image retrieval: An overview. Prentice-Hall, Englewood Cliffs (2004)
3. Datta, R., Li, J., Wang, J.: Content-based image retrieval: approaches and trends of the new age. In: Proceedings of the 7th ACM SIGMM International Workshop on Multimedia Information Retrieval, Citeseer, pp. 10–11 (November 2005)
4. Zhou, X., Huang, T.: Relevance feedback in image retrieval: A comprehensive review. Multimedia Systems 8(6), 536–544 (2003)
5. Rui, Y., Huang, T., Ortega, M., Mehrotra, S.: Relevance feedback: A power tool for interactive content-based image retrieval. IEEE Transactions on circuits and systems for video technology 8(5), 644–655 (1998)
6. Crucianu, M., Ferecatu, M., Boujemaa, N.: Relevance feedback for image retrieval: a short survey. State of the Art in Audiovisual Content-Based Retrieval, Information Universal Access and Interaction, Including Datamodels and Languages
7. Vapnik, V.: Estimation of dependencies based on empirical data. Series in Statistics. Springer, Heidelberg (1982)
8. Hong, P., Tian, Q., Huang, T.: Incorporate support vector machines to content-based image retrieval with relevant feedback. In: Proceedings of the 7th IEEE International Conference on Image Processing, Citeseer, pp. 750–753 (2000)
9. Tong, S., Chang, E.: Support vector machine active learning for image retrieval. In: Proceedings of the Ninth ACM International Conference on Multimedia, pp. 107–118. ACM, New York (2001)
10. Liu, R., Wang, Y., Baba, T., Uehara, Y., Masumoto, D., Nagata, S.: SVM-based active feedback in image retrieval using clustering and unlabeled data, pp. 954–961 (2008)
11. Drucker, H., Shahrary, B., Gibbon, D.: Relevance feedback using support vector machines, pp. 122–129 (2001)
12. Salton, G.: Automatic information organization and retrieval. McGraw Hill Text, New York (1968)
13. Chen, G., Wang, T., Herrera, P.: Relevance Feedback in an Adaptive Space with One-Class SVM for Content-Based Music Retrieval. In: Proceedings of the International Conference on Audio, Language and Image Processing, ICALIP 2008 (2008)
14. Papadakis, P., Pratikakis, I., Trafalis, T., Theoharis, T., Perantonis, S.: Relevance Feedback in Content-based 3D Object Retrieval: A Comparative Study, vol. 5 (2008)

15. Rahman, M., Bhattacharya, P., Desai, B.: A framework for medical image retrieval using machine learning and statistical similarity matching techniques with relevance feedback. IEEE transactions on Information Technology in Biomedicine 11(1), 58–69 (2007)

16. Zhang, Q., Tai, X.: A Relevance Feedback Method in Medical Image Retrieval Based on Bayesian Theory. In: International Conference on BioMedical Engineering and Informatics, BMEI 2008, vol. 1 (2008)

17. Song, W., Huangshan, C., Hua, T.: Analytic Implementation for Medical Image Retrieval Based On FCM Using Feature Fusion With Relevance Feedback. In: Proceedings of the 2nd International Conference on Bioinformatics and Biomedical Engineering, ICBBE 2008, pp. 2590–2595 (2008)

18. El-Naqa, I., Yang, Y., Galatsanos, N., Nishikawa, R., Wernick, M.: A similarity learning approach to content-based image retrieval: application to digital mammography. IEEE Transactions on Medical Imaging 23(10), 1233–1244 (2004)

19. Heath, M., Bowyer, K., Kopans, D., Moore, R., Kegelmeyer, P.: The digital database for screening mammography, pp. 212–218 (2000)

20. Kilday, J., Palmieri, F., Fox, M.: Classifying mammographic lesions using computerized image analysis. IEEE Transactions on Medical Imaging 12(4), 664–669 (1993)

21. Bruce, L., Adhami, R.: Classifying mammographic mass shapes using the wavelet transform modulus-maxima method. IEEE Transactions on Medical Imaging 18(12), 1170–1177 (1999)

22. Georgiou, H., Mavroforakis, M., Dimitropoulos, N., Cavouras, D., Theodoridis, S.: Multi-scaled morphological features for the characterization of mammographic masses using statistical classification schemes. Artificial Intelligence in Medicine 41(1), 39–55 (2007)

23. Gonzalez, R., Woods, R.: Digital Image Processing. Prentice-Hall, Englewood Cliffs (2007)

24. Theodoridis, S., Koutroumbas, K.: Pattern Recognition, 4th edn. Academic Press, London (2009)

25. Mavroforakis, M.E., Theodoridis, S.: A geometric approach to support vector machine (svm) classification. IEEE Trans. Neural Netw. 17(3), 671–682 (2006)

26. Mavroforakis, M.E., Sdralis, M., Theodoridis, S.: A geometric nearest point algorithm for the efficient solution of the SVM classification task. IEEE Transactions on Neural Networks 18(5), 1545–1549 (2007)

27. Luo, J., Nascimento, M.: Content-based sub-image retrieval using relevance feedback, 9 (2004)

28. Image Processing Techniques for Mammographic Images, http://mammo.di.uoa.gr

Efficient Domain Decomposition for a Neural Network Learning Algorithm, Used for the Dose Evaluation in External Radiotherapy

Marc Sauget[1], Rémy Laurent[1], Julien Henriet[1], Michel Salomon[2],
Régine Gschwind[1], Sylvain Contassot-Vivier[3], Libor Makovicka[1],
and Charles Soussen[4]

[1] Femto-ST, ENISYS/IRMA,
F-25210 Montbéliard, France
marc.sauget@univ-fcomte.fr
[2] University of Franche-Comté, LIFC/AND,
F-90000 Belfort, France
[3] University of Nancy, LORIA, Campus Scientifique,
BP 239 F-54506 Vandoeuvre-lès-Nancy Cedex France
[4] Faculté des sciences et techniques, CRAN,
F-54506 Vandoeuvre-lès-Nancy Cedex France

Abstract. The purpose of this work is to further study the relevance of accelerating the Monte Carlo calculations for the gamma rays external radiotherapy through feed-forward neural networks. We have previously presented a parallel incremental algorithm that builds neural networks of reduced size, while providing high quality approximations of the dose deposit. Our parallel algorithm consists in a regular decomposition of the initial learning dataset (also called learning domain) in as much subsets as available processors. However, the initial learning set presents heterogeneous signal complexities and consequently, the learning times of regular subsets are very different. This paper presents an efficient learning domain decomposition which balances the signal complexities across the processors. As will be shown, the resulting irregular decomposition allows for important gains in learning time of the global network.

Keywords: Pre-clinical studies, Doses Distributions, Neural Networks, Learning algorithms, External radiotherapy.

1   Introduction

The work presented in this paper takes place in a multi-disciplinary project called *Neurad* [2], involving medical physicists and computer scientists whose goal is to enhance the treatment planning of cancerous tumors by external radiotherapy. In our previous works [4,9], we have proposed an original approach to solve scientific problems whose accurate modeling and/or analytical description are difficult. That method is based on the collaboration of computational codes and neural networks used as universal interpolator. Thanks to that method, the

K. Diamantaras, W. Duch, L.S. Iliadis (Eds.): ICANN 2010, Part I, LNCS 6352, pp. 261–266, 2010.

Neurad software provides a fast and accurate evaluation of radiation doses in any given environment (possibly inhomogeneous) for given irradiation parameters.

More precisely, the *Neurad* project proposes a new mechanism to simulate the dose deposit during a clinical irradiation.The neural network is used to obtain the deposit in a homogeneous environment whereas the specific algorithm expresses the rules to manage any inhomogeneous environment. The feasibility of this original project has been clearly established in [3]. It was found that our approach results in an accuracy similar to the Monte Carlo one and suppresses the time constraints for the external radiotherapy evaluation. The accuracy of the neural network is a crucial issue; therefore it is the subject of many research works on neural network learning algorithms. To optimize the learning step, we have proposed to learn regular subdomains of the global learning dataset. Although satisfactory results were obtained, we could observe different level of accuracy among the subdomains. Thus, in this paper we describe a new decomposition strategy of the global learning set to solve this problem.

2   Quantification of the Complexity of the Learning Domain

The goal of this work is to propose a solution allowing a decomposition of a data set in subdomains taking into account the complexity of the data to learn. Complexity influences the time and the accuracy of the learning step for a neural network. Therefore a work about the complexity management is necessary to ensure a homogeneous learning in both time and accuracy for all subdomains composing the global data set.

To identify the complexity of our learning domain, we have chosen to study the variance between the data. The interest of this technique, used in many contexts, is to establish precisely the local and the global complexities of a domain. In our case, we have evaluated the learning domain complexity using the following variation function for the following function:

$$lC_{i,j} = \sum_{x=i-r,x\neq i}^{i+r} \sum_{y=j-r,y\neq j}^{j+r} \frac{|f(x,y) - f(i,j)|}{||\overrightarrow{(x,y)} - \overrightarrow{(i,j)}||} \tag{1}$$

So, in order to evaluate the local complexity $lC_{i,j}$ at spatial point (i,j), we use the variations between that point and a given set of its neighbors (x,y), each of them being distance weighted. The interest of this function is to take into account all informations of complexities composing the dataset after a sampling of the dose values. The global complexity of a global learning domain is described by the sum of all the local complexities (in absolute value). The r parameter allows to determine the size of the neighborhood taken into account to evaluate the local complexity of a point. We do not use the average of local complexities, because the number of values in a subdomain has a direct impact on the final accuracy of the learning, and even more on the learning time.

3   Decomposition Strategy

In our previous works [1] we have used a classical dimensional strategy to subdivide the learning domain. This first choice was only motivated by its simplicity of use and the regularity of the resulting subdomains: as it can be seen in our previous results, a regular decomposition only based on the dimension characteristic does not provide a set of subdomains with a constant degree of complexity. In spite of that, we propose to use another decomposition strategy based on a tree structure. This strategy of decomposition, denoted URB (Unbalanced Recursive Bisection) in the literature, was proposed by Jones and Plassman [7,8].

The URB strategy divides each dimension alternatively in two parts to obtain two subdomains having approximately the same complexity estimation. The two parts are then further divided by applying the same process recursively. Finally, this algorithm provides a simple geometric decomposition for a given number of processors. One of its advantages is to provide rectangular sub-parts which do not imply any sensible management overhead. In our case, dividing the dimension alternatively gives quickly subdomains which are spatially unbalanced. To further highlight this difference, we facilitate the comparison between the complexities of the subdomains by rescaling them between 0 and 100, so that 100 corresponds to the highest complexity. And again, we can see a very important difference between the two strategies. On the one hand the regular strategy exhibits a wide range of complexities: from 4.9 to 100; on the other hand the URB strategy presents a limited range: from 30.9 to 35.4. Consequently, the proposed local correlation based on irregular domain decomposition allows us to build subdomains with homogeneous complexities. The remainder of this article shows why this characteristic is important in the context of neural network learning.

4   Experimental Results

In this section, both quality and performance of our algorithm are experimentally evaluated. Our algorithm has been implemented in standard C++ with Open-MPI for the parallel part, and all computations were performed at Mesocentre de calcul de Franche-Comte machine.

4.1   Data Description

In the context of external radiotherapy, an essential parameter is the width of the beam. The radiation result is directly dependant on this parameter. Indeed, if the beam has a small width, it cannot reach the electronic balance and does not present a tray as large as could be seen in Figure 1. The main constraint in the scope of our work is the limited tolerance about the final learning error. Indeed, the neural network described here represents one tool in a very complex chain of treatments for the global evaluation of the dose deposit in complex environments. The use of the neural network is central in our overall project and

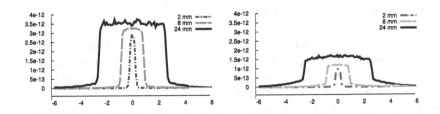

Fig. 1. Dose deposits at the depth of 60 mm in water and in TA6V4

a too large error at this stage could imply that our final solution may be out of the medical error tolerance.

For these experiments, we have trained our network using a set of data provided by Monte Carlo simulations [5]. These data represent the doses deposit for different beams. We have chosen to work specifically on small width beams to study the different behaviors of the learning process for data with and without electronic stability. The dataset is built from the result of irradiation in water and TA6V4 for three widths (2, 15 and 30 mm). The water is the principal element composing the human body (similar to the human tissue composition and used for medicinal accelerator calibrations) and the TA6V4 is a common compound used in prosthesis [6].

Since the dataset is generated using a grid of 120x100 points and considering two materials with three beam widths for each one, it is composed of 120x100x3x2 elements. Each element has seven input components: the position in the three spatial dimensions; the beam width (min and max information); the environment density and the distance between it and the irradiation source. We propose to test different decomposition configurations to quantify the accuracy of the learning and to determine the limits of our solution.

4.2   Decomposition Results

First, we will study how the complexities are balanced by comparing decompositions induced by our URB based algorithm to regular ones. Therefore Table 1 describes the minimum, maximum and means complexity value obtained for the different subdomains with increasing levels of partitioning. As explained previously, the global data set is composed of irradiation results corresponding to different configurations (two materials, three beam widths). To evaluate the complexity value of a subdomain, we have chosen to use only the sum of its local complexities. The objective is to get a finer partitioning in the areas of larger complexities. The values in Table 1 show clearly the good behavior of our approach: the complexities are better balanced with our algorithm than with the regular partitioning.

4.3   Learning Results

As shown in the previous subsection, our approach is able to produce dataset partitions with less heterogeneity across the complexity values. Similar complexity values should mean similar learning tasks and thus similar learning times. From Table 1, which presents also the training times , we can observe that these times are still not very homogeneous. This can be explained by the complexity of the learning domain which is evaluated for each curve of dose deposit independently. Indeed, it is not realistic to find any correlation parameter between the different simulation results. The choice to use the sum of the local complexities to evaluate the global complexity does take into account all situations. This explains why all the learning times gained for URB based decomposition are not equal. Fortunately, in all cases the mean learning times resulting from our decomposition clearly outperform the ones obtained with the regular decomposition.

Table 1. Global evaluation of our solution with a selection and the full dataset

subdomaine	Initial test						Full dataset	
	Decomposition		learning times				Qualitative evaluation	
	URB	REG	URB		REG		URB	REG
	SD^1	SD	SD	$Means^2$	SD	Means	Means	Means
4	1.0	87.9	270	424	1122	739	*	*
8	3.5	73.3	291	348	2399	880	1604	11498
16	3.1	60.7	72	26	1225	273	1098	8632
24	8.7	47.6	125	23	355	100	113	5259

4.4   Qualitative Evaluation

With this test, we want to control the quality of the learning and the accuracy of interpolation induced by of our neural networks. For this, we have enlarge the training set by adding two more beam widths (9 and 23 mm) for both water and TA6V4. The learning dataset is thus composed of 120x100x5x2 points. Globally, we can say that our optimized URB based decomposition approach gives more precise results. Furthermore, and more important, we can note very shorter computing times (Table 1) with our approach. Those overall good performances (accuracy and learning times) show the relevance of our work, and are crucial for the ongoing of the whole medical project.

5   Conclusion and Future Work

A strategy for the domain decomposition has been presented. Its principle is based on a domain decomposition on the input parameters of the learning data set taking into account the complexity of the dose deposit signal in order to

---

[1] Standard Deviation (in %).
[2] Means of the learning time (in seconds).

266   M. Sauget et al.

balance the learning times and to improve the global accuracy. Qualitative and quantitative evaluations of the algorithm have been performed experimentally on real data sets. They confirm the good behavior of our algorithm in terms of performance and quality. The small differences between the subdomain learning times show the improvement of our solution in a realistic context of use. In the following of the Neurad project, it should be interesting to add another important feature to our learning process which is a dynamic load balancing who could have some interests in the context of very large learning. And with this efficient parallel learning algorithm we have the capabilities to learn all the data necessary to the medicinal context.

Acknowledgments. The authors thanks the LCC (Ligue Contre le Cancer) for the financial support, the Franche-Comté region and the CAPM (Communauté d'Agglomération du Pays de Montbéliard).

References

1. Bahi, J., Contassot-Vivier, S., Sauget, M., Vasseur, A.: A parallel incremental learning algorithm for neural networks with fault tolerance. In: Palma, J.M.L.M., Amestoy, P.R., Daydé, M., Mattoso, M., Lopes, J.C. (eds.) VECPAR 2008. LNCS, vol. 5336, pp. 502–515. Springer, Heidelberg (2008)
2. Bahi, J.M., Contassot-Vivier, S., Makovicka, L., Martin, E., Sauget, M.: Neurad. Agence pour la Protection des Programmes.
No: IDDN.FR.001.130035.000.S.P.2006.000.10000 (2006)
3. Bahi, J.M., Contassot-Vivier, S., Makovicka, L., Martin, E., Sauget, M.: Neural network based algorithm for radiation dose evaluation in heterogeneous environments. In: Kollias, S.D., Stafylopatis, A., Duch, W., Oja, E. (eds.) ICANN 2006. LNCS, vol. 4132, pp. 777–787. Springer, Heidelberg (2006)
4. Bahi, J.M., Contassot-Vivier, S., Sauget, M.: An incremental learning algorithm for functional approximation. Advances in Engineering Software 40(8), 725–730 (2009) doi:10.1016/j.advengsoft.2008.12.018
5. BEAM-nrc. NRC of Canada, http://www.irs.inms.nrc.ca/BEAM/beamhome.html
6. Buffard, E., Gschwind, R., Makovicka, L., David, C.: Monte Carlo calculations of the impact of a hip prosthesis on the dose distribution. Nuclear Instruments and Methods in Physics Research Section B: Beam Interactions with Materials and Atoms 251(1), 9–18 (2006)
7. Jones, M.T., Plassmann, P.E.: Computational results for parallel unstructured mesh computations (1994)
8. Jones, M.T., Plassmann, P.E.: Parallel algorithms for the adaptive refinement and partitioning of unstructured meshes. In: Proceedings of the Scalable High-Performance Computing Conference, pp. 478–485. IEEE, Los Alamitos (1997)
9. Makovicka, L., Vasseur, A., Sauget, M., Martin, E., Gschwind, R., Henriet, J., Salomon, M.: Avenir des nouveaux concepts des calculs dosimétriques basés sur les méthodes de Monte Carlo. Radioprotection 44(1), 77–88 (2009)

Towards Better Receptor-Ligand Prioritization: How Machine Learning on Protein-Protein Interaction Data Can Provide Insight Into Receptor-Ligand Pairs

Ernesto Iacucci and Yves Moreau

KULeuven, ESAT/SISTA, Kasteelpark Arenberg 10,
3001 Leuven-Heverlee, Belgium
{Ernesto.Iacucci,Yves.Moreau}@esat.kuleuven.be

Abstract. The prediction of receptor-ligand pairs is an active area of biomedical and computational research. Oddly, the application of machine learning techniques to this problem is a relatively under-exploited approach. Here we seek to understand how the application of least squares support vector machines (LS-SVM) to this problem can improve receptor-ligand predictions. Over the past decade, the amount of protein-protein interaction (PPI) data available has exploded into a plethora of various databases derived from various wet-lab techniques. Here we use PPI data to predict receptor ligand pairings using LS-SVM. Our results suggest that this approach provides a meaningful prioritization of the receptor-ligand pairs.

Keywords: Bioinformatics, Machine Learning, Kernels, Protein-Protein Interaction, Receptor, Ligand, LS-SVM.

1 Introduction

The prediction of receptor-ligand pairs is an active area of biomedical and computational research. Oddly, the application of machine learning techniques to this problem is a relatively under-exploited approach. Here we seek to understand how the application of least squares support vector machines (LS-SVM) to this problem can improve receptor-ligand predictions. Over the past decade, the amount of protein-protein interaction (PPI) data available has exploded into a plethora of various databases derived from various wet-lab techniques [1]. Here we use PPI data to predict receptor ligand pairings using LS-SVM.

As the task of pairing receptors and ligands is essentially the elucidation of a subgraph of a much larger PPI network, much can be learned from use of the rest of the graph. Given a well defined PPI network, we consider the first neighbors of the receptors and ligands to be informative; as different ligands and receptors can regulate the same processes, the neighbors will likely be involved in the same processes as those regulated by the putative receptor-ligand pairing. In order to integrate PPI information without any bias from know receptor ligand pairs we consider the first neighbors excluding any receptor-ligand edges.

K. Diamantaras, W. Duch, L.S. Iliadis (Eds.): ICANN 2010, Part I, LNCS 6352, pp. 267–271, 2010.

We look into the use of creating a kernel classifier to carry out the receptor-ligand learning task. While many kernel-based machine learning techniques have been applied to the PPI task [2,3], it has hitherto never, to our understanding, been used on the receptor-ligand problem. Kernel learning provides the means to utilize related data and perform classification in higher dimensional space via methods. In our work, we use a least-squared support vector machine (LS-SVM) method based on the work presented by Suykens *et al.* (2002)[4].

We organize the work presented here by first describing our data sources. Following this we describe the building and tuning of the the kernel classifer. We then follow with a presentation of results. We conclude with a discussion of the results and future directions for this work.

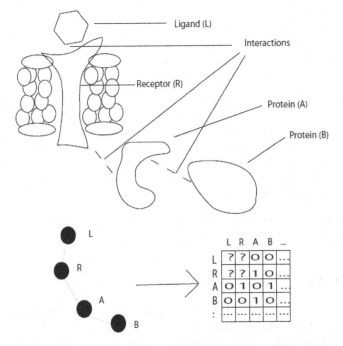

Fig. 1. Schematic of receptor-ligand and protein-protein intereaction model. The top image is a representation of in-vivo interact of proteins and receptors and ligands while the bottom image is the graph representation from which the adjacency matrix is derived.

2 Methods

Our objective is to prioritize receptor-ligand candidates using a LS-SVM classifier based on PPI data.

2.1 Data Sources

The PPI profile of each candidate protein was created by taking PPI sub-graph defined by the candidates and their first neighbors, a PPI vector for each candidate protein was then created by indicating the presence of a PPI with each member of the subgraph with a '1' and absence of by '0'(or rather, an adjacency matrix was created). The PPI kernel was generated from this data.

We take as our "Golden Standard" the receptor-ligand dataset from the The Database of Ligand-Receptor Partners (DLRP) [5]. This is an experimentally derived dataset of known receptors and their corresponding ligands. These interactions are an recorded in an adjacency matrix where known interaction is represented as a '1' and lack of interaction is represented as a '0'. These are the values which are used to train the classifier and are the values which the classifer is trying to predict.

2.2 Kernels and LS-SVM Classifier

The PPI vectors (described above) were used to create the PPI kernel. A LS-SVM [4] was trained using this kernel to predict outcomes for the receptor-ligand pairs known from our "Golden Standard".

Creating the kernel involved trials with several different kernel functions, linear functions being found to give the best performance in all cases. The regularization parameters for the LS-SVMs was tuned using a two tier grid search which first uniformly ranged from 10^{-6} to 10^{+6}. in $10^{1.0}$ steps followed by a second finer search with $10^{0.1}$ steps. Data was partitioned into training, testing, and validation (10% of data). The model was checked for over-fitting by observation of lack of decrease in performance in the test data.

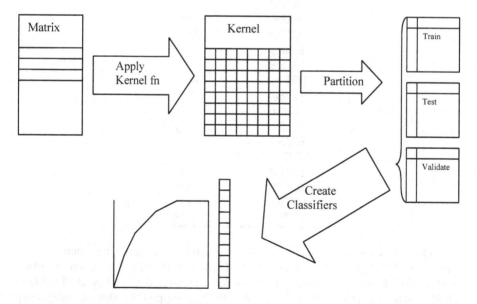

Fig. 2. Workflow of the kernel classifier creation and use. The PPI vectors are organized into a PPI matrix. A PPI kernel is derived from this matrix. The data is then partitioned into training, testing, and validation segments. The LS-SVM is used to create a classifier and then applied to the data. The method is then evaluated using receiver operating characteristic curves.

3 Results and Discussion

The known tgfβ receptor-ligand set used here consisted of 80 known receptor-ligand pairs. We assessed the performance of our kernel classifier with the ligands of this family. The results are summarized in table 1. We examined the area under the curve (AUC) of the receiver operating characteristic curves for each. We find that the average AUC was 0.71.

When we do not consider the family members which have the fewest number of known partners (AMH, TGFB1, TGFB2, and TGFB3) the results increase dramatically, with a range of AUC values from 0.7 to 1.0 with an average AUC of 0.89. This observation suggests that an increase in training examples is important for better classification.

Evaluation of the receptor-ligand predictions via AUC value reflects a real-word practicality as we expect that wet-lab investigation of the predictions would have to be prioritized as candidates are numerous and the ability to investigate putative pairs scarce due to the expense and time involved in in-vivo investigation.

Table 1. AUC values for the ligands which are members of the tgfβ family as predicted by the kernel classifier method

Ligand	AUC
TGFB2	0
BMP7	1.0
AMH	0
TGFB1	0.25
BMP5	1.0
BMP8	0.7
TGFB3	0.78
INHBA	0.75
INHA	0.7
BMP4	1.0
BMP2	1.0
BMP15	1.0
BMP3	1.0
BMP6	0.89
INHBB	1.0
BMP10	0.78

Looking forward, we expect to exend our method to include other sources of information. This has certainly worked in the broader field of PPI prediction. Bhrdwaj et al. (2005) [6] used this strategy to introduce expression data to predict PPI data in addition to the use phylogenetic data. Their findings support the idea that integrating these two types of data (gene expression profile and phylogenetic) increases the accuracy of predictions rather than phylogenetic analysis alone. Co-expression data can be seen as as an indicator of protein-protein interaction as proteins which interact for the purpose of performing a similar function are likely to be co-expressed to carry-out their biological activity [7,8].

Certainly, the ever-expanding amount of high-throughput data which continues to become available to the bioinformatics community represents an excellent opportunity to enhance the kernel classifier prioritization method presented here.

Acknowledgments. The authors would like to thank Dr. Shi Yu and Dr. Anneleen Daemen and Mr. Fabian Ojeda for their thoughtful suggestions.

References

[1] Keshava Prasad, T.S., Goel, R., Kandasamy, K., et al.: Human Protein Reference Database–2009 update. Nucleic Acids Res. 37, D767–D772 (2009)

[2] Kim, S., Yoon, J., Yang, J., et al.: Walk-weighted subsequence kernels for protein-protein interaction extraction. BMC Bioinformatics 11, 107 (2010)

[3] Miwa, M., Saetre, R., Miyao, Y., et al.: Protein-protein interaction extraction by leveraging multiple kernels and parsers. Int. J. Med. Inform. 78, e39–e46 (2009)

[4] Suykens, J.A., De Vandewalle Jr., M.B.: Optimal control by least squares support vector machines. Neural Netw. 14, 23–35 (2001)

[5] Graeber, T.G., Eisenberg, D.: Bioinformatic identification of potential autocrine signaling loops in cancers from gene expression profiles. Nat. Genet. 29, 295–300 (2001)

[6] Bhardwaj, N., Lu, H.: Correlation between gene expression profiles and protein-protein interactions within and across genomes. Bioinformatics 21, 2730–2738 (2005)

[7] Grigoriev, A.: A relationship between gene expression and protein interactions on the proteome scale: analysis of the bacteriophage T7 and the yeast Saccharomyces cerevisiae. Nucleic Acids Res. 29, 3513–3519 (2001)

[8] Ge, H., Liu, Z., Church, G.M., et al.: Correlation between transcriptome and interactome mapping data from Saccharomyces cerevisiae. Nat. Genet. 29, 482–486 (2001)

The DAMNED Simulator for Implementing a Dynamic Model of the Network Controlling Saccadic Eye Movements

Anthony Mouraud[1,3], Alain Guillaume[2,3], and Hélène Paugam-Moisy[1,4]

[1] LIRIS, UMR CNRS 5205, Université de Lyon, F-69676 Bron, France
[2] LNC, UMR CNRS 6155, Université de Provence, F-13331 Marseille, France
[3] Fac. Sc. Sport, Université de la Méditerranée, F-13288 Marseille, France
[4] INRIA-Saclay, LRI, Université Paris Sud 11, F-91405 Orsay, France
anthony.mouraud@gmail.com, alain.guillaume@univmed.fr,
helene.paugam-moisy@univ-lyon2.fr

Abstract. The DAMNED simulator is a Distributed And Multithreaded Neural Event-Driven framework designed for implementing Spiking Neuron Networks (SNNs). This paper shows the power of DAMNED for simulating the temporal dynamics of a biologically inspired model of the system controlling saccadic eye movements. A fundamental neural structure for the saccade generation is the Superior Colliculus (SC). The proposed model relies on two pathways leaving this structure: A first one supervises the motor error and the movement initiation and a second one provides a direct drive to premotor centers. This simple model, its SNN implementation and its dynamic behaviour reproduce the evolution of movement amplitude as a function of activity location in the SC. It also accounts for classical results obtained when the SC is subjected to electrical stimulations.

Keywords: Spiking neuron network, event-driven simulation, distributed simulation, saccadic eye movement control.

1 Introduction

Many models are proposed by neuroscientists for explaining how the neural activity could be the basis of behavioural control or cognitive mechanisms. The models are mostly defined by a scheme on a paper, and they are very useful for designing experiments on human or animals, but they are seldom implemented in a way that may show how they work and behave through time. A gap is thus induced between models and experiments, the latter accounting more and more for temporal recordings. However, Spiking Neuron Networks (SNNs) are excellent candidates for simulating the dynamics of interactions between several neural substrates in a biologically plausible way.

The DAMNED simulator has been designed for realizing simulations of biologically plausible large scale SNNs in a distributed and event-driven way [1]. The present paper proposes to take advantage of the DAMNED simulator to implement and analyze the dynamic behaviour of a theoretical model of the brainstem neural network involved in the saccadic eye movements generation. Saccades are the high velocity displacements of the eye produced to align the greatest accuracy zone of the retina, the fovea, with

K. Diamantaras, W. Duch, L.S. Iliadis (Eds.): ICANN 2010, Part I, LNCS 6352, pp. 272–281, 2010.

targets of interest. The saccadic part of the oculomotor system has been studied since decades through animal and human experiments [2,3,4]. A fundamental characteristic of this system is its organization in a feedback loop that would control the amplitude of the saccade [2]. The precise description of the neural circuit that produces saccades has been attractive for modelling. Many models of the saccadic system have already been proposed [5] but none of them has been implemented with spiking neuron networks. All these computational models have brought both informations and hypotheses about the interactions of the underlying neural networks. In the present paper we propose a slightly different model that tests a new hypothesis for the organization of the feedback loop in the brainstem. For validation, the model has been implemented in the form of a modular SNN and its dynamics has been simulated with DAMNED.

Section 2 briefly outlines the simulator characteristics. Section 3 presents the model proposed for the sub-collicular saccade generation system. Section 4 details the experimental protocols applied to the SNN simulating the model and the functionalities of the saccadic system studied in simulation. Section 5 comments the behaviour observed through time in the eye movement control system and discusses the model validation.

2   Simulation Framework

DAMNED is not the only spiking neuron networks simulator but to our best knowledge DAMNED is the only one that gathers event-driven, distributed and multithreaded characteristics as the basis of its design [6]. The computational performance of the simulator has been tested on a common hardware architecture and analyzed for large scale SNNs [7]. The principles of the DAMNED simulation framework previously defined in [1] are summarized in the following subsections.

2.1   The DAMNED Simulator

The simulator takes advantage of both distributed hardware and concurrent threads. Communications via message passing between CPUs (multi-core, computer network, cluster or parallel machine), and also local concurrency between calculation and communication (threads), speed up the computation and enlarge the available memory, compared to sequential SNN simulation. Figure 1 proposes a layered view of the DAMNED global architecture. The first layer is the distributed hardware (processor/memory couples). DAMNED achieves communications between hardware resources via the Message Passing Interface (MPI) with ssh (secured shell) for the message delivery (second and third layers). In case of a multiprocessor hardware, messages are passed through the local bus. For each MPI node the DAMNED simulator creates two threads (fourth layer): A CoMmunication Controller (CMC) sends and receives spike event messages and a ComPutation Controller (CPC) allocates each time-stamped spike event to an Event-driven Cell (EC), aka the target spiking neuron that computes the event and eventually creates a new spike event in response. The last layer is the SNN to be simulated.

2.2   Mapping an SNN on DAMNED

Through a user interface, the simulator allows the definition of network structures based on specification of populations and projections between them. User defined models of

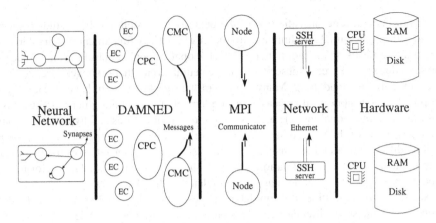

Fig. 1. Layered view for the global architecture of the DAMNED simulator

neuron, synapse and projection can be registered in the simulator through the interface. An environment process gives input stimulations to the simulated network and gets back output activities. This behaviour lets the environment free to use neural activities during the simulation, for instance to drive motor commands of robotic devices. At the end of the simulation the user may also access spikes, membrane potentials or synaptic weights and display their evolution during the simulation. DAMNED simulates the network activity in discrete time with an event-driven strategy [8]. The time scale used for simulation is up to the user. In present experiments the time scale is 0.1 ms. Mapping the SNN onto the hardware is also user defined through the simulator interface. Each neuron is identified by an index and ranges of neuron indexes are associated with each simulation node.

3   Model of Saccade Generation

3.1   Physiological Background

In the brain, the neural network that generates motor commands for orienting the line of sight (i.e. to displace the eye to orient the fovea) toward stimulus of interest is among the best understood sensorimotor system, notably in its output part. The superior colliculus (SC), a paired and layered structure located at the roof of the brainstem (Fig. 2), plays a pivotal role to control saccadic eye displacement. Each SC controls saccades toward targets in the contralateral visual hemifield. The intermediate and deep layers of this structure are organized in a motor map with the amplitude and the direction of the movement respectively represented on its rostro-caudal and medio-lateral axes. Activities of several cortical areas involved in gaze orientation (Lateral Intra-Parietal area, Frontal Eye Field, Supplementary Eye Field) converge on this motor map. Collicular neurons send their axons toward premotor centers housing neurons called "Excitatory Burst Neurons" (EBNs). These neurons in turn directly control motoneurons of extraocular muscles.

Importantly, EBNs form an homogeneous pool without topography: The amplitude of the saccade is coded through the frequency and duration of the discharge. Hence, a spatial to temporal transformation has to be performed between the SC and the premotor centers. This spatio-temporal transformation is performed through a synaptic density gradient as anatomically observed between SC and EBNs [9,10] : neurons located in the SC rostral pole make less synaptic boutons than those in the caudal pole (graded strength). In addition, the amplitude of the movement is controlled by a feedback loop [2] driving EBNs to discharge until a desired displacement signal is nullified.

The central mesencephalic reticular formation (cMRF) is another structure involved in gaze control. It is reciprocally connected with the SC [11] and projects notably toward a particular pool of neurons called omnipause neurons (OPNs) [4]. These OPNs are neurons that strongly inhibit EBNs. They are tonically active during fixation and silent during saccades. The shut off of their discharge is required for the initiation of the saccade. Given cMRF afferences from the SC and projections toward the OPNs, some neurons in this structure could be inhibitory interneurons that inhibit OPNs to trigger the saccade initiation.

To sum up, activity at the level of the SC is transmitted to at least two downstream structures: cMRF and EBNs. Finally, it is also known that the cMRF receives feedback from the EBNs.

3.2 Theoretical Model

Several papers proposed schemes including the cMRF but to our best knowledge no model including the cMRF has been yet implemented and tested. In previous schemes, roles assigned to the cMRF mostly concern the regulation and the update of SC activity. Indeed connections between SC and cMRF are reciprocal [11]. We propose that the cMRF could in addition be the point of comparison of the feedback loop.

In the present paper, for the sake of simplification, only the ouput part of the network is modelled. This simplification corresponds in fact to an experimental situation of electrical stimulation of the SC that evokes saccadic eye movements similar to natural ones [12,13]. We based our model on the following characteristics of the saccadic system. First, the feedback loop closes downstream of the SC [14]. Second, rather than organizing the feedback loop around a single output pathway from the SC, like for already proposed models [5], we suggest that one output pathway of the SC (the cMRF) could contain the desired displacement signal and that another one would be the forward branch of the organization through EBNs toward motoneurons. In addition, the EBNs activity would also be fed back to cMRF through an inhibitory interneuron. When the activity in cMRF neurons (the desired displacement) is reduced to zero through the feedback coming from EBNs, the inhibition of OPNs is removed and the saccade stops.

3.3 Modular Spiking Neuron Network

A modular spiking neuron network is proposed for implementing the theoretical model of saccade generation (Figure 2). The sub-collicular feedback loop relies on the interaction between three neuron populations. First, a population made of 100 EBNs which show a burst activity during saccade. Second a population of 100 OPNs which are tonically active before and after a saccade. Third, a population of 100 cMRF neurons. OPNs

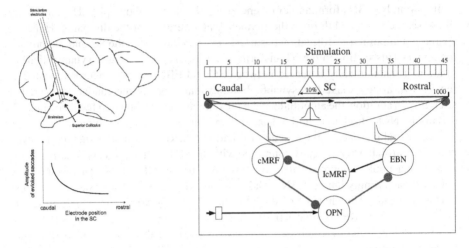

Fig. 2. Left : Anatomical locating of the Superior Colliculus at the top of the brainstem (top) and relationship between the amplitude of evoked saccades and the position of an electrical stimulation (bottom). Right : Topology of the modular spiking neural network. Black arrows show excitatory influence and red round ended arrows show inhibitory influence.

and cMRF populations are inhibitory and EBNs population is excitatory. An inhibitory intermediate 100 neurons population (IcMRF) between EBNs and cMRF is introduced to implement the inhibitory influence of EBNs upon cMRF. OPNs inhibit EBNs and receive a constant external input activity in order to maintain a tonic activity before and after a saccade. cMRF in turn inhibits OPNs to trigger saccade initiation and ending.

As OPNs shut off under cMRF influence, the hyperpolarisation of EBN neurons is released. EBNs emit a burst of action potential indicating the saccade velocity (frequency of the burst). The discharge ends when the EBNs inhibition on cMRF, mediated by IcMRF, becomes stronger than the SC influence on cMRF. The saccade amplitude is determined by the frequency and duration of the EBNs burst.

As shown in Figure 2, a unidimensionnal 1000 neurons population of the Superior Colliculus (SC) is implemented and projects on both EBNs and cMRF populations. This SC population represents a rostro-caudal line in the right colliculus. The projection weights from SC to EBNs and cMRF are exponentially decreasing from the caudal to the rostral pole of the SC map. Consequently a range of horizontal saccade amplitudes to the left can be generated by such a saccade generation model. Excitatory gaussian shaped lateral excitation and long range inhibition are implemented in the collicular map to generate activation in a subpart of the SC map depending on the position of the stimulation.

Stimulations of the SC map at predefined positions are achieved by a 45 electrodes array. In the model each electrode is implemented as a cell connected to a subpart of the SC map. Stimulations are applied by making these cells fire spikes like impulsions to the connected neurons. The neuron model implemented in this network is a conductance based leaky integrate and fire neuron (LIF) [15].

4   Experiments and Results

4.1   Experimental Protocols

The electrical microstimulation of SC evokes saccadic gaze shifts similar to natural ones [12,13]. This artificial situation implies that the feedbacks to SC, for example from the cMRF, are neglected.

Each of the 45 electrodes generates an excitatory potential on the targeted neurons on the SC map. The impact range of the electrodes reaches 10% of the map around the electrode (Fig. 2). A competition between lateral excitations and long range inhibitions in the SC recruits about 20% of the map when the stimulation occurs. A supplementary electrode stimulates the OPNs during the whole experiment.

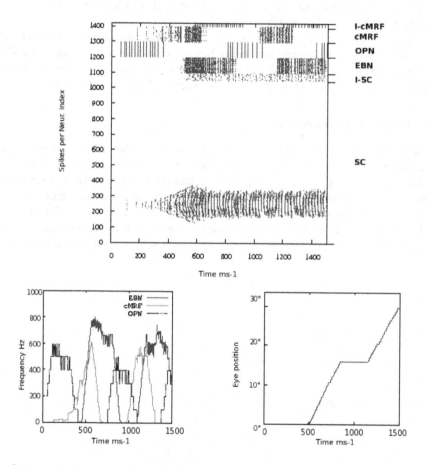

Fig. 3. Example of a generated saccade. Top : spike raster plot for each neuron function of time. Bottom left : instantaneous discharge frequencies of OPNs, EBNs and cMRF populations (averaged for all neurons in the populations). Bottom right : horizontal eye displacement in terms of number of EBNs spikes through time.

Stimulations on the SC are applied during 150 ms with a frequency set to 300 Hz and generates an activity in the map of 500 to 600 Hz on average. The OPNs population receives a constant external input at 400 Hz during the same period. An example of the network model response to stimulation is shown on Figure 3. Time is in ms^{-1}.

4.2   Stimulation Position

The network model have been stimulated at seven different sites on the SC map to evaluate its ability to reproduce saccade amplitudes observed in biological microstimulation experiments. Saccade amplitude is computed from the number of fired EBNs spikes. The EBNs discharge frequency represents the eye velocity (Fig. 3). Despite the sustained stimulation on the SC map, saccades terminate with an amplitude that depends on the stimulation site. A caudal stimulation leads to a larger saccade amplitude than more rostral stimulations (Fig. 4).

The non-linearity of the relationship between stimulation site position and saccade amplitude that is found in experimental studies is also present in our model. The SNN dynamic simulation confirms that the phenomenon is a logical consequence of the exponential weight gradient of the projection between the SC map and EBNs.

4.3   Stimulation Parameters

Both current intensity and pulse frequency variations have been observed in the model. The influence of these variations has been tested on two stimulation sites on the electrodes array : position 10 and position 30. Current intensity in the model is given by the weight (w) and radius (r in % of the SC map) of the electrodes impact on the SC map. In standard conditions, the values of these parameters are set to $w = 3.7$ and $r = 5$ and allow to elicit a range of saccade amplitudes comparable to those obtained in biological studies (Figure 4). For the sake of comparison with experimental studies, let us

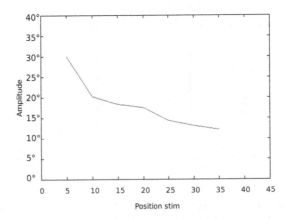

Fig. 4. Saccade amplitude function of the position on the SC map. Position is given in terms of the electrodes indexes.

label this condition as the $2 \times T$ condition, where T is the threshold value of the couple (w,r) necessary to elicit a saccade in response to electrical input. In order to study the behaviour of the model when varying current intensity, the model has been stimulated with three distinct intensities : $1, 3 \times T$ ($w = 2.8, r = 3.25$), $2 \times T$ ($w = 3.7, r = 5$) and $6 \times T$ ($w = 11, r = 15$). The saccade amplitudes obtained are shown on Figure 5 (left).

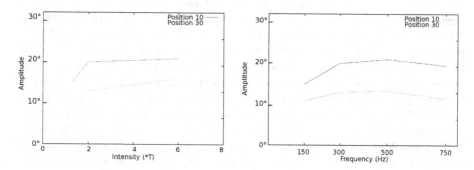

Fig. 5. Left : Saccade amplitude function of the stimulus intensity. Right : Saccade amplitude function of the stimulation frequency. Stimulations are applied at sites 10 and 30 on the electrode array.

Decreasing the current intensity ($1, 3 \times T$) leads to a decrease in saccade amplitude. Conversely, increasing the intensity ($6 \times T$) does not result in a clear substantial increase in saccade amplitude. This pattern is in accordance with biological observations.

Tested stimulation pulse frequencies range from 150 Hz to 750 Hz. The stimulation frequency in control condition was set to 300 Hz. Results show that from 300 Hz to 500 Hz, the amplitude of evoked saccades remains constant (Fig. 5, right). If the frequency is lowered (below 300 Hz) or increased (beyond 500 Hz), the saccade amplitude decreases.

5   Discussion

A new organization of the neural network controlling saccadic eye movements has been proposed. The behaviour of the theoretical model has been simulated through time by implementing several neural populations in a modular spiking neuron network. The dynamics of the SNN has been observed and analyzed in event-driven simulations computed with the DAMNED simulator.

The control of saccadic eye movements is supposed to rely on a mechanism of feedback loop. Initially the required movement is coded on a motor map that is present in the SC. This collicular activity is transmitted to two downstream structures, the cMRF and the EBNs. The cMRF would control the movement initiation and contain a signal of desired displacement. The activity of the EBNs would produce the eye displacement and would be fed back to decrease the cMRF activity. When the activity in the cMRF is

280 A. Mouraud, A. Guillaume, and H. Paugam-Moisy

terminated, the eye movement stops. We show that our proposition based on two output pathways from the SC - one handling the desired displacement and one corresponding to a direct drive toward pre-motor neurons - is defensible when implemented with a modular SNN. Indeed, experimental results in simulation account for the classical results observed for electrical stimulations in the SC.

Despite its simplicity, the present scheme integrates the two major known projections from the SC to cMRF and to EBNs [11]. Given the implementation of projection gradients, moving the stimulation site toward the caudal pole of the SC leads to an increase in the amplitude of evoked saccades. The well-established organization in motor map is respected. Regarding the influence of the current intensity used for electrical stimulations, it is classically observed that increasing this parameter leads to a first phase of saccade amplitude increase, followed by a saturation when the site specific amplitude is reached (the amplitude for which cells under the electrode discharge for natural saccades) [12]. This pattern of amplitude evolution as a function of current intensity is obtained in the present work. The amplitude saturation is due to a saturation in the development of the activity at the level of the SC, itself due to intrinsic connectivity in the map (short range excitation and long range inhibition). Concerning frequency variation, results are also qualitatively similar to biological ones: A first phase of amplitude increase is followed by a saturation and later by an amplitude decrease [13]. This observation could result from local interactions in the SC, delays and/or refractory period of the LIF neuron model implemented. Interestingly, in the saturation range, the increase in stimulation frequency results in an increase of the displacement velocity. This is also an observation made in biological experiments.

The scheme proposed in the present paper remains very simple and several improvements could be considered. For example, the well described projection from the cMRF to the SC have been neglected since simulations have been limited to the condition of electrical stimulations. In future work, these projections would be added to capture the dynamics of the network in the situation of natural saccades toward visual target.

In conclusion, the DAMNED simulator has proved to be an excellent tool for testing by SNN implementation the dynamic behaviour of a new scheme for the organization of the neural network controlling saccade generation. Simulations have shown that our theoretical model accurately accounts for the dynamics of neural activities involved in the control of saccadic eye movements.

Acknowledgments

This work has been partially supported by the ANR "MAPS", grant BLAN07-1_185594.

References

1. Mouraud, A., Paugam-Moisy, H., Puzenat, D.: A distributed and multithreaded neural event driven simulation framework. In: PDCN, pp. 212–217 (2006)
2. Robinson, D.A.: Oculomotor control signals. In: G., L., y Rita P., B. (eds.) Basic Mechanisms of Ocular Motility and their Clinical Implications, pp. 337–374. Pergamon, Oxford (1975)
3. Büttner, U., Büttner-Ennever, J.A.: Present concepts of oculomotor organization. In: B&, J. (ed.) Neuroanatomy of the Oculomotor System. Prog. Brain Res. Elsevier, vol. 151, pp. 1–42 (2006)

4. Horn, A.K.: The reticular formation. Prog. Brain Res. 151, 127–155 (2006)
5. Girard, B., Berthoz, A.: From brainstem to cortex: Computational models of saccade generation circuitry. Prog. Neurobiol. 77(4), 215–251 (2005)
6. Brette, R., Rudolph, M., Carnevale, N.T., Hines, M.L., Beeman, D., Bower, J.M., Diesmann, M., Morrison, A., Goodman, P., Friederick, H.J., Zirpe, M., Natschläger, T., Pecevski, D., Ermentrout, G.B., Djurfeldt, M., Lansner, A., Rochel, O., Vieville, T., Muller, E., Davidson, A., El Boustani, S., Destexhe, A.: Simulation of networks of spiking neurons: A review of tools and strategies. J. Comp. Neur. 23(3), 349–398 (2007)
7. Mouraud, A., Puzenat, D.: Simulation of large spiking neural networks on distributed architectures, the ¨damned ¨ simulator. In: Palmer-Brown, D., Draganova, C., Pimenidis, E., Mouratidis, H. (eds.) EANN. Communications in Computer and Information Science, vol. 43, pp. 359–370. Springer, Heidelberg (2009)
8. Watts, L.: Event-driven simulation of networks of spiking neurons. In: Cowan, J.D., Tesauro, G., Alspector, J. (eds.) Advances in Neural Information Processing System, vol. 6, pp. 927–934. MIT Press, Cambridge (1994)
9. Ottes, F., Van Gisbergen, J.A., Eggermont, J.: Visuomotor fields of the superior colliculus: a quantitative model. Vis. Res. 26(6), 857–873 (1986)
10. Moschovakis, A.K., Kitama, T., Dalezios, Y., Petit, J., Brandi, A.M., Grantyn, A.A.: An anatomical substrate for the spatiotemporal transformation. J. Neurosci. 18(23), 10219–10229 (1998)
11. Chen, B., May, P.J.: The feedback circuit connecting the superior colliculus and central mesencephalic reticular formation: a direct morphological demonstration. Exp. Brain Res. 131, 10–21 (2000)
12. Robinson, D.A.: Eye movements evoked by collicular stimulation in the alert monkey. Vis. Res. 12, 1795–1808 (1972)
13. Guillaume, A., Pélisson, D.: Gaze shifts evoked by electrical stimulation of the superior colliculus in the head-unrestrained cat. i. effect of the locus and of the parameters of stimulation. Eur. J. Neur. 14, 1331–1344 (2001)
14. Kato, R., Grantyn, A., Dalezios, Y., Moschovakis, A.K.: The local loop of the saccadic system closes downstream of the superior colliculus. Neuroscience 143(1), 319–337 (2006)
15. Brette, R.: Exact simulation of integrate-and-fire models with synaptic conductances. Neur. Comp. 18(8), 2004–2027 (2006)

A Model of Basal Ganglia in Saccade Generation

Ravi Krishnan[1], Shivakesavan Ratnadurai[2],
Deepak Subramanian[3], and Srinivasa Chakravarthy[4]

[1] Indian Institute of Management, Ahmedabad, India
[2] University of Florida, Gainsville, USA
[3] Dept. of Neurological Sciences,Christian Medical College, Vellore
[4] Department of Biotechnology, Indian Institute of Technology Madras,
Chennai 600036, India

Abstract. We model the role played by the Basal Ganglia (BG) in generation of voluntary saccadic eye movements. Performance of the model is evaluated on a set of tasks such as feature and conjunction searches, directional selectivity and a successive saccade task. Behavioral phenomena such as independence of search time on number of distracters in feature search and linear increase in search time with number of distracters in conjunction search are observed. It is also seen that saccadic reaction times are longer and search efficiency is impaired on diminished BG contribution, which corroborates with reported data obtained from Parkinson's Disease (PD) patients.

Keywords: Saccades, basal ganglia, reinforcement learning, Parkinson's disease.

1 Introduction

Saccades are rapid, frequent eye movements that shift the fovea onto objects of interest. Several areas of the brain, including the frontal cortical areas, Lateral Intraparietal (LIP) cortex, Basal Ganglia (BG), Superior Colliculus (SC) and the brainstem reticular formation are believed to be involved in saccade generation. Models of saccade generation, however, tend to focus heavily on the determination of saccadic saliency in the Superior Colliculus and eye movement dynamics thereafter. The aim of this paper is to emphasize the role played by the BG in modulating SC activity during voluntary saccades.

1.1 Basal Ganglia

The Basal Ganglia (BG) [1] are a set of seven deep brain nuclei believed to be involved in several forms of motor learning and function, including generation of voluntary saccades. They receive projections from the cortex through the Striatum, and send projections back to the cortex via the Thalamus.

A prominent school of thought on BG function regards this circuit as a Reinforcement Learning (RL) [2] engine that uses reward information from the environment to inform and modulate sensory-motor cortex engaged in motor function. Particularly, the neurotransmitter dopamine released by mesencephalic nuclei like the Ventral

K. Diamantaras, W. Duch, L.S. Iliadis (Eds.): ICANN 2010, Part I, LNCS 6352, pp. 282–290, 2010.

Tegmental Area (VTA) and Substantia Nigra pars compacta (SNc) is thought to represent Temporal Difference (TD) error signal. The proposed BG model has explicit representations of the 5 key BG nuclei: Striatum, Globus Pallidus externa (GPe), Subthalamic Nucleus (STN), Substantia Nigra pars reticulata (SNr) and Substantia Nigra pars compacta (SNc). Reward information conveyed by dopamine release to BG nuclei switches striato-pallidal transmission between the direct pathway and indirect pathways of the BG.

1.2 Saccades

Robinson [3] proposed one of the earliest models of saccade generation in which the desired eye position is compared with an internally generated estimate; the resulting error signal is used to correct eye position. Since SC receives convergent afferents from several cortical visual and cognitive centers, it is believed to be the location for the integration of signals from various information pathways in the brain for saccadic control. Hence, models typically focused on the role played by the SC in controlling saccades and in determining the firing pattern observed in brainstem motor and premotor neurons (e.g. [4], [5], [6]). Most of these models attempted to explain observed effects of various well-studied paradigms such as the removal of fixation, presence of distracters, the gap effect and the anti-saccade task on Saccade Reaction Times (SRT). Arbib and Dominey [7] model the role of BG in controlling sequential eye movements. Their model includes a large number of structures subserving saccade control like SC, Thalamus, Caudate, Frontal Eye Fields and SNr but does not include the indirect pathway of BG. In the proposed model, the IP plays an important complementary role to DP, as will be described in Section 2.

2 Model Implementation

Figure 1 shows the architecture of the BG involved in saccade generation. The circuitry of the BG is often divided into two major pathways, the *Direct Pathway* (DP) and the *Indirect Pathway* (IP). The DP is formed by inhibitory GABA-ergic projections from the striatum (input layer of BG) to neurons in the SNr (output layer of BG). Striatal activation inhibits neurons in SNr, which in turn disinhibits the SC. The IP consists of projections from striatum to SNr via the STN-GPe loop. Various well-studied paradigms such as conjunction search and feature search are simulated. Effect of diminished BG output on saccade reaction time and search efficiency is studied to understand PD saccade behavior.

2.1 Visual Stimuli and Feature Maps

The visual stimuli used in the present simulation study consist of oriented (vertical/horizontal), colored (red/green) bars. Therefore, in the model, the cortical inputs to the BG comprises of maps of various features (red and green colors, and horizontal and vertical orientations), which are assumed to be generated in the relevant visual cortical areas. Orientation information is extracted using Gabor filters. Sections of the maps representing the foveated portion of the scene are given higher resolution. We assume that color is a basic feature and color information is available at all points of the visible scene, while orientation is a higher level feature and the strength of orientation information diminishes with increasing distance from the point of fixation.

2.2 Striatum and Value Function

The striatum (Caudate) is modeled as two 2D Continuous Attractor Neural Networks (CANNs) [8]. One of these, comprising of neurons of the D1 receptor type, sends projections along the Direct Pathway to SNr; the other, comprising of neurons of the D2 receptor type, sends projects along the Indirect Pathway to the GPe. Cortical afferents to the striatum are passed through a weight stage, before it is input to each striatum as follows:

$$I_{ij}^{StrD1} = \sum_{k=1}^{M} W_k^{Ctx\_StrD1} I_{ijk}^{Ctx} \qquad (1)$$

This is presented as input to each of the CANNs that comprise the striatum. The state of a node with index (i,j) is given by:

$$\tau_u \frac{du_{ij}^{StrD1}}{dt} = -u_{ij}^{StrD1} + \sum_{p,q} w_{ij,pq}^{StrD1} s_{pq}^{StrD1} \kappa_x + I_{ij}^{StrD1} \qquad (2)$$

where τ is the time constant, κ_x is a scaling factor, s_{ij}^{StrD1} is the normalized square of u_{ij}^{StrD1} given by:

$$s_{ij}^{StrD1} = \frac{(u_{ij}^{StrD1})^2}{1 + \frac{1}{2}\sum_{pq}(u_{pq}^{StrD1})^2 \kappa_x} \qquad (3)$$

The lateral connections consist of short-range excitation and long-range inhibition given as:

$$w_{ij,pq}^{StrD1} = Ae^{-\frac{d^2}{2\sigma_w^2}} - C; \quad d = \sqrt{(i-p)^2 + (j-q)^2} \qquad (4)$$

The output, U_{ij}^{StrD1}, of the neuron at (i,j) in STRIATUM_D1 is given as:

$$U_{ij}^{StrD1} = \tanh(\lambda^{StrD1} s_{ij}^{StrD1}) \qquad (5)$$

where λ^{StrD1} is the slope of activation function of neurons in STRIATUM_D1.

Note that though eqns. (2-5) commonly describe dynamics of the two CANNs (consisting of D1 and D2 neurons respectively) only one set of equations is shown for the sake of brevity of presentation. Both the CANNs receive the same cortical afferents I_{str} (of eqn. (1)). Activity of striosomes in the dorsal striatum is believed to correspond to net expected future reward [9], which is nothing but the value function associated with the current state. We compute value function from the net input coming into D1-receptive striatal neurons:

$$V(t) = \sum_i \sum_j I_{ij}^{StrD1}(t) \tag{6}$$

2.3 STN-GPe Loop

The STN-GPe modules are connected in feedforward-feedback fashion in such a way that their joint activity produces oscillations. We had earlier shown that if inhibitory interactions dominate lateral interactions in GPe, the STN-GPe system produce complex activity; when excitatory interactions dominate, STN-GPe neurons exhibit regular forms of activity like traveling waves and synchronized bursts [10]. Electrophysiological data from STN-GPe reveal that these structures exhibit complex spiking activity in an intact brain; under dopamine-deficient conditions, as in Parkinson's disease, the activity here degrades to synchronized bursting patterns. In light of the above considerations, we had earlier hypothesized that if the BG is a reinforcement learning machine, STN-GPe is the Explorer [11]. The STN-GPe model of (Gangadhar et al,[10]) is used in the present model.

2.4 Dopamine Signal and Direct/Indirect Pathways

The Temporal Difference (TD) error is interpreted as dopamine signal and calculated as:

$$\delta(t) = r(t) + \gamma V(t+1) - V(t) \tag{7}$$

where r(t) represents the reward delivered at time t. The $\delta(t)$ signal is broadcast to striatum where it switches transmission of corticostriatal signals between DP and IP. The switching is done by differentially controlling the steepness of activation functions of the D1 and D2 sublayers of the striatum as follows:

$$\lambda^{StrD1} = A_1 \left(\frac{1}{1+e^{-\alpha(\delta-\beta_2)}} + \frac{1}{1+e^{-\alpha(\beta_3-\delta)}} - 1 \right) \tag{8}$$

$$\lambda^{StrD2} = A_2 \left(\frac{1}{1+e^{-\alpha(\beta_1-\delta)}} \right) \tag{9}$$

where α denotes the slope of the activation function, β_1, β_2 and β_3 denotes the thresholds for dopamine regimes 1, 2 and 3 respectively. In the simulation we have used values of $\alpha = 30$, $\beta_1 = -0.3$, $\beta_2 = 0.3$, and $\beta_3 = 3$.

2.5 Substantia Nigra Pars Reticulata

The SNr is simply a summing unit, which adds the contributions along the DP coming from the striatum and those along IP coming from the STN.

2.6 Training

Training takes place at three levels, Cortico-striatal DP & IP and from STN → SNr. A set of weights is used for each of the levels. The DP Cortico-striatal weights are trained such that the striatum learns the most rewarding feature(s). The training rule used is:

$$\Delta W_k^{Ctx\_StrD1} = \eta_1 \delta \sum_i \sum_j U_{ij}^{StrD1} I_{ijk}^{Ctx} \tag{10}$$

where η_1 is the learning rate, δ is the dopamine signal (TD error), U_{ij}^{StrD1} is the current output of the D1 CANN and I_{ijk}^{Ctx} is the cortical input to striatum as defined before (see eqn (1)).

The IP cortico-striatal weights are trained to activate non-rewarding features(s) so that the D2 CANN activates and suppresses inputs at the corresponding points. The training rule used here is:

$$\Delta W_k^{Ctx\_StrD2} = -\eta_1 \delta \sum_i \sum_j U_{ij}^{StrD2} I_{ijk}^{Ctx} \tag{11}$$

where η_3 is the learning rate and U_{ij}^{StrD2} is the current output of the D2 CANN. This ensures that when δ is highly negative, the weights are trained in the direction of enhancing the activity of the D2 CANN.

These weights are trained with the objective of enhancing the negative connections from the STN to SNr so that the output at the SNr is negative for regime 1 operation. They are initialized to take a value of -1 initially and subsequently trained according to the rule:

$$\Delta W_{ij}^{IP\_SNr} = \eta_4 \delta U_{ij}^{STN} U_{ij}^{SNr} \tag{12}$$

where η_4 is the learning rate, U_{ij}^{STN} and U_{ij}^{SNr} are the current outputs of the STN and SNr grids respectively.

2.7 Superior Colliculus

The activity of SNr is given as input to the SC along with the direct input from the Feature Maps, which represent the cortical input. Note that BG output (from SNr) modulates the direct cortical inputs to SC as follows:

$$I_{ij}^{SC} = (A_1 + A_2 U_{ij}^{SNr}) \sum_{k=1}^{M} I_{ijk}^{Ctx} \tag{13}$$

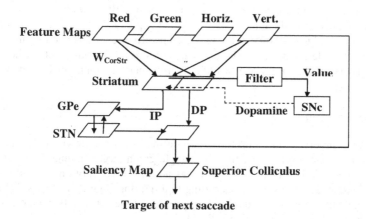

Fig. 1. Model Architecture

3 Results

We applied the model to learn a series of voluntary saccade paradigms, as discussed below. In all the cases the input scene is a 240x240 grid, the central 80x80 window of which contains the targets involved in the task.

3.1 Saccading to a Single Target

Figure 2 shows the contribution of the BG and the corresponding dopamine levels in a single target saccade task where a reward is administered on saccading to it. Before training, the value of a scene containing the target is low so that δ on target appearance is low (=0.02). However, positive reward is administered on saccading to the target, and therefore δ increases (=0.998) (figure 2a). After training, the Value of the

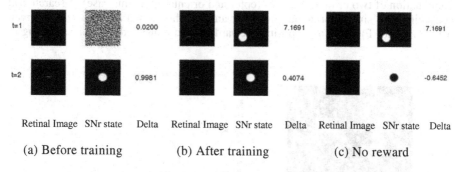

(a) Before training   (b) After training   (c) No reward

Fig. 2. BG Contribution for a Single Target Task. Three cases (a,b & c) are shown. Each case is depicted by a 2 X 2 array of images: the rows (t=1 & 2) represent the instants when the target is presented (t=1) and when the saccade is made to the target (t=2), and the columns represent the retinal image (left) and the state of the SNr (right). The number on the right of each case denote instantaneous values of δ at t=1 & 2.

scene containing the target becomes high, and a positive fluctuation in δ (=7.17) ("do-pamine burst") occurs right at the instant of target appearance (figure 2b). Moreover, δ takes a negative value (=-0.645) if the expected positive reward is not administered on making the saccade (figure 2c). These results are strongly reminiscent of the experimentally observed response properties of dopamine neurons found in a monkey reaching for food [9].

3.2 Feature Search

Feature search involves searching for targets defined by a unique visual feature (color in this case). A search grid consisting of a single green target amongst red distractors was used (Figure 3a). A positive reward was administered only on saccading to the green dot and negative reward on saccading to a red dot. Figure 3b shows that search time does not show significant dependence on the number of targets, which conforms to human behavioral data on similar tasks [12].

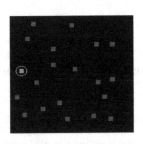
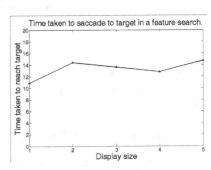

Fig. 3. (a) Feature Search grid. (b) Effect of Display Grid Size on Search time.

3.2 Conjunction Search

The target in a conjunction search is not defined by any single visual feature, but by a combination of two or more features (color and orientation in this case). A search grid consisting of a single horizontal green bar amongst horizontal red and vertical green bars was used (Figure 4 a). A positive reward was administered only on saccading to

Fig. 4. (a) Conjunction Search grid. (b) Effect of Display Grid Size on Feature search time.

the horizontal green bar and negative reward on saccading to any other bar. Figure 4b shows that search time increases almost linearly with the number of distracters, which conforms to human behavioral data on such tasks [12].

3.3 Effect of Lowered BG Output

BG contribution to saccade generation comes in three forms: 1) representation of error in dopamine signal (δ), 2) use of δ for learning the saccade task, 3) the exploratory influence of the Indirect Pathway than enables moving away of the eye from the current point of fixation. It was observed that the model failed to perform even simple feature search when the BG output was scaled down by a factor < 0.5. Figure 5a compares the number of saccades needed to reach the target in case of normal and lowered (by a factor of 0.6) BG output in a feature search. Search time increases very sharply for display size > 3.

As shown by figure 5b, it was also observed that average reaction times were longer in case of weakened BG output (We measured reaction times in terms of the time taken by the saliency map to reach a peak of height > 95% of the maximum value it can reach). This is consistent with the increase in saccade reaction times observed in MPTP-infused monkeys (MPTP infusion results in degeneration of dopaminergic fibers to the striatum and results in a net lower BG output) by Kato et al [14].

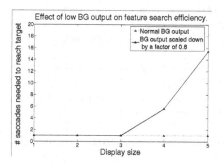 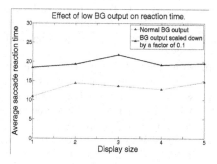

Fig. 5. Effect of lower BG output on (a) Feature search Efficiency, and (b) Saccade reaction time

4   Discussion

We propose here that the role of the BG in voluntary saccades is to either reinforce the parts of the saliency map that correspond to rewarding positions and suppress those corresponding to unrewarding ones. The BG circuit is modeled as a comprehensive reinforcement learning machinery in which the DP subserves exploitation while the IP is engaged in exploration. Dopamine signal to the striatum, which is interpreted as the TD error, switches the onward transmission of corticostriatal signals between DP and IP. A key feature incorporated is the calculation of the value of a scene in the striatum based on corticostriatal input. Dopaminergic cell activity strongly resembles experimental data [9]. The proposed model describes the role the BG plays in both learning and performance of voluntary saccade tasks. In feature and conjunction searches, the pattern of dependence of search time on display size is shown to conform to behavioral data. Increased saccade reaction time with scaled-down BG output agrees with data obtained from monkeys in dopamine-depleted condition [14].

References

1. Gerfen, C.R., Wilson, C.J.: The basal ganglia. In: Swanson, L.W., Bjorklund, A., Hokfelt, T. (eds.) Handbook of Chemical Neuroanatomy, pp. 371–468. Elsevier, Amsterdam (1996)
2. Sutton, R.S., Barto, A.G.: Reinforcement Learning: An Introduction. MIT Press, Cambridge (1998)
3. Robinson, D.: Oculomotor Control Signals. In: Lennerstrands, G., Bach-y-Rita, P. (eds.) Basic Mechanisms of Ocular Motility and their Clinical Implications. Pergammon Press, Inc., New York (1975)
4. Lefevre, P., Galiana, H.L.: Dynamic feedback to the superior colliculus in a neural network model of the gaze control system. Neural Networks 5, 871–890 (1992)
5. Arai, K., Keller, E.L., Edelman: Two-dimensional neural network model of the primate saccadic system. Neural Networks 7, 1115–1135 (1994)
6. Optican, L.: Control of saccade trajectory by the superior colliculus. In: Contemporary Oculo-Motor and Vestibular Research: A Tribute to DA Robinson, pp. 98–105 (1994)
7. Dominey, P.F., Arbib, M.A.: A Cortico-Subcortical Model for Generation of Spatially Accurate Sequential Saccades. Cerebral Cortex 2, 153–175 (1992)
8. Standage, D.I., Trappenberg, T.: Modelling divided visual attention with a winner-take-all network. Neural Networks 18(5-6), 620–627 (2005)
9. Schultz: Predictive Reward Signal of Dopamine Neurons. J. Neurophysiol. 80, 1–27 (1998)
10. Gangadhar, G., Joseph, D., Chakravarthy, V.S.: Understanding Parkinsonian Handwriting using a computational model of basal ganglia. Neural Computation 20, 1–35 (2008)
11. Sridharan, D., Prashanth, P.S., Chakravarthy, V.S.: The role of the basal ganglia in exploration in a neural model based on reinforcement learning. International Journal of Neural Systems 16, 111–124 (2006)
12. Wolfe, J.M.: Guided search 2.0: A revised model of visual search. Psychonomic Bulletin and Review 1, 202–238 (1994)
13. Montague, P.R., Dayan, P., Person, C., Sejnowski, T.J.: A framework for mesencephalic dopamine systems based on predictive Hebbian learning. J. Neurosc. 16, 1936–1947 (1996)
14. Kato, M., Miyashita, N., Hikosaka, O., Matsumura, M., Usui, S., Kori, A.: Eye movements in monkeys with local dopamine depletion in caudate nucleus. J. Neuroscience 15(1), 912–927 (1995)

Computational Inferences on Alteration of Neurotransmission in Chemotaxis Learning in *Caenorhabditis elegans*

Michiyo Suzuki[1], Tetsuya Sakashita[1], Toshio Tsuji[2], and Yasuhiko Kobayashi[1]

[1] Microbeam Radiation Biology Group, Japan Atomic Energy Agency,
1233 Watanuki, Takasaki, Gunma 370-1292, Japan
{suzuki.michiyo,sakashita.tetsuya,kobayashi.yasuhiko}@jaea.go.jp
[2] Graduate School of Engineering, Hiroshima University,
1-4-1 Kagamiyama, Higashi-Hiroshima, Hiroshima, 739-8527, Japan
tsuji@bsys.hiroshima-u.ac.jp

Abstract. *Caenorhabditis elegans* changes its NaCl-associated behavior from attraction to avoidance following exposure to NaCl in the absence of food (salt chemotaxis learning). To understand the changes induced by chemotaxis learning at the neuronal network level, we modeled a neuronal network of chemotaxis and estimated the changes that occurred in the nervous system by comparing the neuronal connection weights prior to and after chemotaxis learning. Our results revealed that neurotransmission involving ASE and AIA neurons differed prior to and after chemotaxis learning. This partially corresponded to the experimental findings of previous studies. In addition, our computational inference results suggest the involvement of novel synapse connections in chemotaxis learning. Our approach to estimate changes of neurotransmission corresponding to learning may help in planning experiments in order of importance.

Keywords: Computational neuroscience, neuronal network model, salt chemotaxis learning, neurotransmission, *C. elegans*.

1 Introduction

The nematode *C. elegans* is one of the major model organisms for the nervous system. Its neuronal networks consisting of 302 neurons [1] enable it to respond adequately to various stimuli such as attractant/repellent chemicals, variations in temperature, and mechanical stimulation [2]. *C. elegans* typically approaches NaCl, as a soluble chemoattractant. Behavioral plasticity is observed in this organism after it experiences a particular combination of multiple stimuli [3]; for example, *C. elegans* modifies its movement response to NaCl from attraction to avoidance following exposure to NaCl in the absence of food for several hours (see Fig. 1). Since the anatomical structure of the nervous system in *C. elegans* is well-characterized [1] and does not change at the adult stage, by using this organism it may be possible to understand the specific changes in neuronal states (the

K. Diamantaras, W. Duch, L.S. Iliadis (Eds.): ICANN 2010, Part I, LNCS 6352, pp. 291–300, 2010.
© Springer-Verlag Berlin Heidelberg 2010

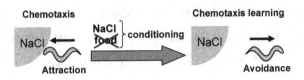

Fig. 1. Salt chemotaxis learning in *C. elegans*

response-characteristic of a neuron and the synaptic transmission efficiency at a certain time) corresponding to behavioral changes. Because of this advantage, in recent years many studies on the mechanisms of learning and memory have been carried out using *C. elegans* [3]–[6].

The behavioral plasticity in response to NaCl, termed 'salt chemotaxis learning', can be explained, at the neuronal network level, as the changes over time of both the response-characteristics of each neuron and the degree of synapse transmission (neurotransmission). In the previous studies, the involvement of some neurons in learning was determined from molecular experiments. However, even using physiologic and/or advanced imaging techniques [7]–[8], it is not possible to measure signal transduction in whole synapse connections and gap junctions in *C. elegans* at the same time. For this reason, whether the change of neuronal states corresponding to the behavioral changes extends to the whole nervous system or only to a limited part of the nervous system is not known.

Therefore, to understand the behavioral changes induced by learning at the neuronal network level, we here propose a novel approach in which the neuronal network is modeled based on the actual neuronal connections, and the neuronal changes corresponding to learning are estimated. The purpose of our computational inference study is to provide novel information that cannot be obtained using conventional experimental techniques. These results will help us to plan experiments in order of importance. This paper covers estimation of the neuronal changes relating particularly to salt chemotaxis learning.

2   Computational Inference of Neuronal States Using a Neuronal Network Model

2.1   Stimulation Response in *C. elegans* and Its Neuronal Structure

C. elegans has a simple cylindrical body approximately 1 mm in length and the body is composed of 959 cells. Neuronal networks consisting of 302 neurons include approximately 5000 chemical synapse connections, approximately 600 gap junctions and approximately 2000 connections between neurons and muscles [1]. The neuronal network processes information from various kinds of stimuli inside and outside the body, and produces differing types of movement appropriate for each stimulus; for example, avoiding obstacles or repellent chemicals. As mentioned previously, in addition to transient responses, *C. elegans* has the capacity to learn some amount of environmental information [3]. Although *C. elegans* usually prefers NaCl and approaches the high-concentration area of a NaCl gradient,

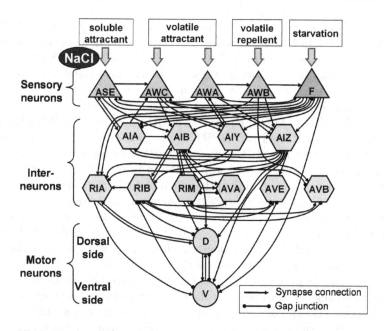

Fig. 2. A model of the chemotactic neuronal network in *C. elegans*

after having experienced starvation and NaCl at the same time, the response changes to avoidance of NaCl. Neurons of *C. elegans* are classified into three main groups by function: sensory neurons, interneurons and motor neurons. The sensory neurons detect external stimuli first, and then the interneurons process information from the stimuli. Finally, the motor neurons control the muscles on the basis of signals from the interneurons. These neuronal networks enable *C. elegans* to respond adequately to various stimuli.

2.2   A Model of the Chemotactic Neuronal Network in *C. elegans*

Estimation of the neurotransmission prior to and after chemotaxis learning is meaningful towards an understanding of the changes in the nervous system induced by learning. Therefore, we here propose a neuronal network model of *C. elegans*, and use this model to estimate the changes in neurotransmission relating particularly to salt chemotaxis learning. Figure 2 shows a model of the neuronal network in relation to chemotaxis, in which the neuronal connections were connected based on the anatomical structure [1] of *C. elegans*. There are 66 connections in this model.

'ASE' represents a pair of sensory neurons as one neuron, in which the sensory neurons ASEL and ASER, which sense soluble chemicals such as NaCl, were simplified. We expressed the other sensory neurons relating to chemotaxis in our model, in which AWA(L/R) and AWC(L/R) sense volatile chemoattractants and AWB(L/R) senses volatile repellents. Neurons that have the same function were presented as one neuron in the same way as ASE neuron. On the other hand, the details of the neurons that sense starvation are not known. We here focused on sensory neurons, ADF(L/R), ASG(L/R) and ASI(L/R), which relate to the formation of dauer larvae under conditions without food at the larval stage [9] and/or sense stress at the adult stage [10]. We represented these as a sensory neuron 'F' that sense starvation. Subsequently, 10 types of interneurons, AIA(L/R), AIB(L/R), AIY(L/R), AIZ(L/R), RIA(L/R), RIB(L/R), RIM(L/R), AVA(L/R), AVE(L/R) and AVB(L/R), connecting with the 5 sensory neurons were included in this model. Finally, we modeled motor neurons. For various types of movement such as turn and locomotion in *C. elegans*, muscles are controlled by motor neurons existing in the whole body. In fact, turns in response to stimuli are considered to be dependent on neuromuscular controls in the head. Therefore, we considered only the outputs of 14 motor neurons for head control, and these neurons were simplified as only 2 neurons, i.e., a dorsal (D) motor neuron and a ventral (V) motor neuron, where the former controls the dorsal side of the head and the latter controls the ventral side.

In this model, multiple connections existing between a pair of neurons were simplified as a single connection and the efficiency (information content) of neurotransmission of each connection was expressed by the connection weight, w_i ($i = 1, 2, \cdots, 66$). Signal transductions on chemical synapse connections are one way transductions, while gap junctions are interactive. A positive value of w_i indicates an excitatory signal and a negative value signifies an inhibitory signal.

2.3   Description of the Characteristics of Neurons

Output of the sensory neurons O_j ($j \in$ {ASE, AWC, AWA, AWB, F} was expressed by the following nonlinear equation based on the general neuronal characteristics:

$$O_j = c_j/[1 + \exp\{-a_j(I_j - b_j)\}] \tag{1}$$

where a_j is an inclination with output function, b_j is the value of the stimulation input at which the output of the neuron takes a central value, and c_j is a gain ($0 < c_j \leq 1$) to the output and is equivalent to the stimulation reception sensitivity. The input I_j to each neuron is the sum of a value that multiplies the connection weight w_i by the stimulation input S_j and/or the output of the connected neuron. Stimulation inputs S_j to sensory neurons are the step-less inputs of the range of [0, 1], which quantifies the strength of the stimulation. Therefore, O_j outputs the continuation value of [0, 1] which is normalized by the maximum output from the actual neuron. The output characteristics O_k ($k \in$ {AIA, AIB, AIY, AIZ, RIA, RIB, RIM, AVA, AVE, AVB, D, V}) of interneurons and motor neurons were also represented by Eq. (1).

2.4   Settings for Output of Motor Neurons Based on Behavior

In the proposed model of the neuronal network, if the output of motor neurons D and V corresponding to stimulation input sensed by sensory neurons is known,

Table 1. Settings for output of motor neurons based on behavior

Stimulation	Behavior	Motor neuron	State	Output
Non-stimuli	Forward	D	Inhibition	$T_{\mathrm{D}} = 0$
	(Nomal)	V	Inhibition	$T_{\mathrm{V}} = 0$
Attractants	Forward	D	Excitation	$T_{\mathrm{D}} = 1$
	(Attraction)	V	Excitation	$T_{\mathrm{V}} = 1$
Repellents	Dorsal-side turn	D	Excitation	$T_{\mathrm{D}} = 1$
(Case 1)	(Avoidance)	V	Inhibition	$T_{\mathrm{V}} = 0$
Repellents	Ventral-side turn	D	Inhibition	$T_{\mathrm{D}} = 0$
(Case 2)	(Avoidance)	V	Excitation	$T_{\mathrm{V}} = 1$

we can estimate the neurotransmission for each synapse connection and each gap junction on the basis of the input-output relationship. However, it is impossible to measure the output of each motor neuron even using advanced techniques.

Therefore, we provided the output of the motor neurons from the corresponding behavioral responses, such as forward movement or turn. Here we assumed that *C. elegans* moves forward when the internal states of 2 motor neurons balance, and it turns when the states do not balance. Turns are classified into 2 cases, i.e., the dorsal-side turn (Case 1) and ventral-side turn (Case 2). Motor neuron D is in an excited state when the dorsal-side muscles contract and *C. elegans* turns to its dorsal side, and motor neuron V is in an excited state when the ventral-side muscles contract and the worm turns to its ventral side. Based on this, the settings for outputs of the motor neurons corresponding to each stimulation input were provided as shown in Table 1. Outputs for forward movement (attraction) were given as $T_{\mathrm{D}} = T_{\mathrm{V}} = 1$. In the same way, for turn (avoidance), the desired outputs were given as $T_{\mathrm{D}} = 1$ and $T_{\mathrm{V}} = 0$ or $T_{\mathrm{D}} = 0$ and $T_{\mathrm{V}} = 1$. Therefore, in the case of normal chemotaxis (prior to learning), response to stimulation sensed by the ASE, AWC or AWA neurons is forward movement, and the desired outputs of the motor neurons were $T_{\mathrm{D}} = T_{\mathrm{V}} = 1$. Also, the response to stimulation sensed by the AWB neuron is turn, and the desired outputs of the motor neurons were $T_{\mathrm{D}} = 1$ and $T_{\mathrm{V}} = 0$ or $T_{\mathrm{D}} = 0$ and $T_{\mathrm{V}} = 1$.

2.5   Optimization of the Neuronal Network Model by a Real-Coded Genetic Algorithm (GA)

In this study, the desired outputs of the motor neurons, T_{D} and T_{V}, were provided so as to correspond to each of u $(u = 1, 2, \cdots, U = 10)$ patterns of stimulation inputs to sensory neurons. Note that T_{D} and T_{V} for responses after learning were set to different values from those for prior to learning only in the response to NaCl which was sensed by the ASE neuron. To search for an adequate set of neuronal connection weights that fulfills the input-output relationship provided in Table 2, we employed a real-coded genetic algorithm (GA) that we previously used for parameter tuning of some neuronal network models of *C. elegans* and confirmed its effectiveness [11]. All the connection weights, w_i $(i = 1, 2, \cdots, 66)$, included

Table 2. Desired outputs of motor neurons corresponding to stimulation inputs (Case 1)

u	Input					Output prior to learn.			Output after learn.		
	S_{ASE}	S_{AWC}	S_{AWA}	S_{AWA}	S_F	T_D	T_V	Behav.	T_D	T_V	Behav.
1	1	0	0	0	0	1	1	FW	1	0	DT
2	0	1	0	0	0	1	1	FW	1	1	FW
3	0	0	1	0	0	1	1	FW	1	1	FW
4	0	0	0	1	0	1	0	DT	1	0	DT
5	0	0	0	0	1	0	0	FW	0	0	FW
6	1	0	0	0	1	1	1	FW	1	0	DT
7	0	1	0	0	1	1	1	FW	1	1	FW
8	0	0	1	0	1	1	1	FW	1	1	FW
9	0	0	0	1	1	1	0	DT	1	0	DT
10	0	0	0	0	0	0	0	FW	0	0	FW

FW denotes forward movements and DT denotes dorsal-side turns.

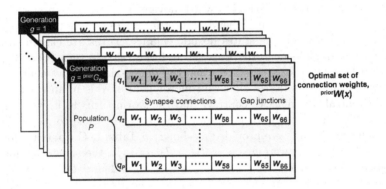

Fig. 3. The outline of the GA method for searching for an adequate set of connection weights prior to chemotaxis learning. The method for connection weights after learning is similar to this.

in the model shown in Fig. 2 were represented as individual genes (see Fig. 3). A string including all the connection weights (genes) of the model was treated as an individual in the GA, and the procedures, (1) selection, (2) crossover, and (3) mutation, were repeated at each generation g ($g = 1, 2, \cdots, G_{fin}$). An individual of a GA consisted of a string arraying a set of connection weights included in the neuronal network model.

For each GA generation, the adequacy of each individual was evaluated to determine which individuals will be included in the next generation. The function for evaluating error values during GA-searching was defined by the following equation.

$$F(p) = \sum_{u=1}^{U} (|T_D(u) - O_D(p, u)| + |T_V(u) - O_V(p, u)|) \tag{2}$$

where p $(p = 1, 2, \cdots, P)$ is the serial number of the GA individual. Searching for an adequate set of connection weights for prior to and after learning was conducted using a GA in each case, and a set of connection weights that provides a minimal value of $F(p)$ in the final generation, G_{fin} ($\in \{^{\text{prior}}G_{\text{fin}}$ (for weights prior to learning), $^{\text{after}}G_{\text{fin}}$ (for weights after learning)$\}$) was employed in the model.

3   Estimated Changes in Neurotransmission After Chemotaxis Learning

In searching for an adequate set of connection weights by a GA, we set the desired outputs of motor neurons corresponding to sensory inputs prior to and after chemotaxis learning as shown in Table 2. We repeated the search $^{\text{prior}}N = 50$ times under the same calculation conditions to ensure statistical power, and 50 distinct sets of neuronal connection weights were thus obtained. On the other hand, searching for connection weights for after learning was conducted where each of the previous 50 sets of connection weights were used as initial values, and the calculations were repeated $^{\text{after}}N = 50$ times for each set of initial values. Finally, the average variation in the sets of connection weights after learning was derived from the results of 2500 (50 50) sets of connection weights. Because turns to another direction occurred, we partially changed the desired outputs (Case 2), in which the outputs of motor neurons for turn were inverted from those of Case 1 shown in Table 2. Under these settings, we conducted the same searching as described above.

We evaluated quantitatively the change in neurotransmission on each neuronal connection after salt chemotaxis learning, based on a variation, $v_i(x, y)$. The variation of neurotransmission of each neuronal connection, prior to and after learning, was calculated by the following equation:

$$v_i(x, y) = |^{\text{prior}}w_i(x) - ^{\text{after}}w_i(x, y)| \tag{3}$$

where $^{\text{prior}}w_i(x)$ is the i $(i = 1, 2, \cdots, 66)$-th connection weight prior to learning that is included in the x $(x = 1, 2, \cdots, ^{\text{prior}}N)$-th adequate set of weights, and $^{\text{after}}w_i(x, y)$ is the i-th connection weight after learning that was obtained from an initial value of $^{\text{prior}}w_i(x)$ and is included in the y $(y = 1, 2, \cdots, ^{\text{after}}N)$-th adequate set of weights. Subsequently, the mean variation of $\bar{v}_i(x)$ was calculated by:

$$\bar{v}_i(x) = \frac{1}{^{\text{after}}N} \sum_{y=1}^{^{\text{after}}N} v_i(x, y) \tag{4}$$

For each of the 50 sets of initial connection weights prior to learning, this calculation was performed and the integrated value of mean variation V_i of each neuronal connection was calculated by:

$$V_i = \sum_{x=1}^{^{\text{prior}}N} \bar{v}_i(x) \tag{5}$$

Note that V_i in Case 1 and Case 2 were individually calculated.

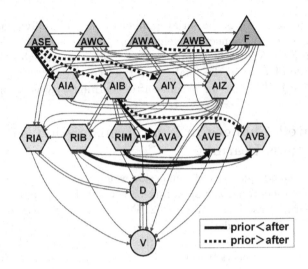

Fig. 4. Estimated changes in neuronal networks induced by salt chemotaxis learning

We focused on the neural connections whose connection weight changed in the same way in the 2 types of input-output settings (Case 1 and Case 2). Ten connections where substantial changes ($V_i > 20$) occurred are shown as heavy lines in Fig. 4. The solid lines denote connections that resulted in excitatory neurotransmission, and the dotted lines denote those that resulted in inhibitory neurotransmission. Among the 10 connections, 4 connections connected with ASE neuron. It is known that ASE sensory neuron and AIY interneuron play a significant role in chemotaxis learning [4]. In addition, the activity of ASE neuron is inhibited by the function of AIA neuron, which results in the inhibition of neurotransmission to AIB or AIY neuron from an ASE neuron [5]. Our results partially corresponded to this experimental finding.

Furthermore, the connections at which neurotransmission was barely altered ($V_i < 10$) were concentrated in those connections from the F sensory neuron (Figure not shown). This indicates that neurotransmission relating to starvation maintains a constant level regardless of learning. The weights of neuronal connections from the F neuron were values in the range of -0.3 to 0.3 on average, which were lower than that of other connections. These results suggest the possibility that salt chemotaxis learning can be realized by inhibiting the activity of neurotransmission involving ASE neuron. Nevertheless, the substantial changes corresponding to chemotaxis learning were newly estimated in this study on synapse connections to AVA and AVB interneurons. Although biological experiments using advanced imaging techniques could measure the changes of neurotransmission at a few neuronal-levels, our method could estimate the changes in neurotransmission concerned with learning at a neuronal network level.

4   Discussion and Conclusions

The purpose of our study was to establish a novel computational approach, which provides information that cannot be obtained using well-known physiological and/or advanced imaging techniques, and that provides information for selecting experiments in order of importance. To understand the changes induced by chemotaxis learning in *C. elegans* at the neuronal network level, we modeled the chemotactic neuronal network based on the actual neuronal connections. In this model, we simplified the neuronal connections and properties of neurons on the basis of their function and estimated the changes that occurred in the nervous system by comparing the neuronal connection weights prior to and after salt chemotaxis learning.

The results revealed that signal transduction in several connections, such as that from AIA interneuron to ASE sensory neuron, differed prior to and after salt chemotaxis learning. This corresponded partially to the experimental findings of previous studies which suggested the involvement of some synapse connections in salt chemotaxis learning. The significant point is that we used the simplified model and obtained results similar to the actual experimental results. These results are meaningful with respect to discussions concerning the adequacy of simplification and assumptions on modeling of living organisms. Another important point is that we could estimate involvement of some novel neuronal connections in chemotaxis learning by computational approach. The involvement in chemotaxis learning will need to be examined in greater detail through biological experiments at the neuronal-level.

On the other hand, comparative studies on learning dynamics between the neuronal network model and the actual *C. elegans* are also important, particularly focusing on the effects of external noisy input and the time needed for learning. These results will provide suggestive knowledge on learning. We will investigate these relationships through more-detailed analyses of the data presented in this paper. Furthermore, updating the model to correspond to the novel knowledge is important to obtain more accurate results. Since it is much important to establish a framework for estimation of neurotransmission that does not change even if the targeted model is changed, we developed such the method for computational inferences in this study. The method we proposed is not dependent on a model and can also be applied to the distinct neuronal-network model for estimating changes in neurotransmission prior to and after learning. We will use the proposed method to estimate the neurotransmission underlying various types of phenomena.

Acknowledgments

The authors thank Dr Hisao Ohtake for his helpful suggestions on the modeling and simulations. This study was partially supported by a Grant-in-Aid for JSPS Fellows (00186258) to M.S. and a Grant-in-Aid for Scientific Research on Innovative Areas from MEXT (20115010) to M.S. and T.T.

300   M. Suzuki et al.

References

1. White, J.G., Southgate, E., Thomson, J.N., Brenner, S.: The Structure of the Nervous System of the Nematode *Caenorhabditis elegans*. Philos. Trans. R. Soc. Lond. B. Biol. Sci. 314, 1–340 (1986)
2. Hobert, O.: Behavioral Plasticity in *C. elegans* Paradigms, Circuits, Genes. J. Neurobiol. 54, 203–223 (2003)
3. Saeki, S., Yamamoto, M., Iino, Y.: Plasticity of Chemotaxis Revealed by Paired Presentation of a Chemoattractant and Starvation in the Nematode *Caenorhabditis elegans*. J. Exp. Biol. 204, 1757–1764 (2001)
4. Ishihara, T., Iino, Y., Mohri, A., Mori, I., Gengyo-Ando, K., Mitani, S., Katsura, I.: HEN-1, a Secretory Protein with an LDL Receptor Motif, Regulates Sensory Integration and Learning in *Caenorhabditis elegans*. Cell 109, 639–649 (2002)
5. Tomioka, M., Adachi, T., Suzuki, H., Kunitomo, H., Schafer, W.R., Iino, Y.: The Insulin/PI 3-kinase Pathway Regulates Salt Chemotaxis Learning in *Caenorhabditis elegans*. Neuron 51, 613–625 (2006)
6. Kuhara, A., Mori, I.: Molecular Physiology of the Neural Circuit for Cal-cineurin-dependent Associative Learning in *Caenorhabditis elegans*. J. Neurosci. 13-26, 9355–9364 (2006)
7. Lockery, S.R., Goodmann, M.B.: Tight-seal Whole-cell Patch Clamping of *Caenorhabditis elegans* Neurons. In: Conn, P.M. (ed.) Methods in Enzymology 293, pp. 201–217. Academic Press, San Diego (1998)
8. Feinberg, E.H., VanHoven, M.K., Bendesky, A., Wang, G., Fetter, R.D., Shen, K., Bargmann, C.I.: GFP Reconstitution Across Synaptic Partners (GRASP) Defines Cell Contacts and Synapses in Living Nervous Systems. Neuron 57, 353–363 (2008)
9. Bargmann, C.I., Horvitz, H.R.: Control of Larval Development by Chemosensory Neurons in *Caenorhabditis elegans*. Science 251, 1243–1246 (1991)
10. Chang, A.J., Chronis, N., Karow, D.S., Marletta, M.A., Bargmann, C.I.: A Distributed Chemosensory Circuit for Oxygen Preference in *C. elegans*. PLoS Biology 4, 1588–1602 (2006)
11. Suzuki, M., Tsuji, T., Ohtake, H.: A Model of Motor Control of the Nematode *C. elegans* with Neuronal Circuits. Artif. Intell. Med. 35, 75–86 (2005)

Neuro-symbolic Representation of Logic Programs Defining Infinite Sets

Ekaterina Komendantskaya[1], Krysia Broda[2], and Artur d'Avila Garcez[3]

[1] School of Computing, University of Dundee, UK[*]
[2] Department of Computing, Imperial College, London, UK
[3] Department of Computing, City University London, UK

Abstract. It has been one of the great challenges of neuro-symbolic integration to represent recursive logic programs using neural networks of finite size. In this paper, we propose to implement neural networks that can process recursive programs viewed as inductive definitions.

Keywords: Neurosymbolic integration, Structured learning, Mathematical theory of neurocomputing, Logic programming.

1 Introduction

Neuro-symbolic integration is the area of research that endeavours to synthesize the best of two worlds: neurocomputing and symbolic logic. The area was given a start in 1943 by the pioneering paper of McCulloch and Pitts that showed how Boolean logic can be represented in neural networks; we will call these *Boolean networks*. Neuro-symbolism has since developed different approaches to inductive, probabilistic and fuzzy logic programming [2,3,11].

Various neuro-symbolic approaches that use logic programs run over finite domains have been shown effective as a hybrid machine learning system [3]. However, when it comes to recursive logic programs that describe infinite sets, Boolean networks become problematic, for they may require networks of infinite size. Some approaches to solve this problem use finite approximations of such networks, [1,5], but the approximations may be difficult to obtain automatically.

In this paper, we propose to take a new look at recursive logic programs, that is, to approach them not from the point of view of *first-order logic*, but from the point of view of functional programming [9]. As an example, consider how a formal grammar generates the strings of a language. Grammars are inductive definitions, i.e. rules that generate a set. In [7], we have introduced neuro-symbolic networks that can process inductive definitions given in a functional language, and applied these networks to data type recognition. In this paper, we show how this neuro-symbolic construction can be applied to processing recursive logic programs. The idea is that inductive definitions can be used as set *generators* or term *recognisers*. The former can generate elements of a set from the inductive definition, the latter can recognise whether an element satisfies the inductive definition, and hence belongs to the defined set.

---

[*] The work was supported by EPSRC, UK; PDRF grant EP/F044046/2.

K. Diamantaras, W. Duch, L.S. Iliadis (Eds.): ICANN 2010, Part I, LNCS 6352, pp. 301–304, 2010.
© Springer-Verlag Berlin Heidelberg 2010

2   Neural Networks as Inductive Generators

In the standard formulations of logic programming [8], a logic program consists of a finite set of clauses (or rules) of the form $A \leftarrow A_1, \ldots, A_n$ where A and the A_i's are atomic formulae, typically containing free variables; and $A_1, \ldots, A_n$ denotes the conjunction of the A_i's. Note that n may be 0, such clauses are called *facts*. We assume that the logical syntax has a numerical encoding suitable for neural networks, cf. [6]. Let us start with an example.

Example 1. The program below corresponds to the inductive definition of the set of natural numbers in functional languages, where S(n)=n+1. Using the syntax below, number 3 will be given by a term S(S(S(0))).
```
nat(0) <- // zero is a natural number
nat(S(n)) <- nat(n) // if n is a natural number, so is S(n)
```

Recursive clauses require the predicate (e.g. nat) appearing on the left-hand side (called the head) of a clause to appear also on the right-hand side (called the body) of the clause, and variables (e.g. n) appearing in the head to appear in the body within the same predicate. The head must contain a function symbol (e.g. 0 or S); such functions play the role of constructors in the inductive definitions of functional languages. Certain inductive definitions do not contain recursion of any kind. Such programs inductively define finite sets.

Example 2. Logic program defining the set of boolean values:
```
bool(t) <-//true is a boolean    bool(f) <-//false is a boolean
```

The last distinction we need to make is between *simple* and *dependent* definitions. All the inductive definitions we have considered so far were simple, in that they did not depend on other inductive definitions. Consider the example of the dependent inductive definition of lists of elements of a certain type, e.g. nat. The definition of this type not only involves recursion, but it is also dependent on another inductive definition: nat. See [7]. Inductive definitions have two common uses: read from right to left they can be used to *generate* the elements of a set, and read from left to right they can be used for type-checking expressions. Both implementations require finite and terminating computations. Figure 1 shows some network architectures for generating and recognising expressions.

3   Neural Networks as Recursive Recognisers

We now turn to networks that can process recursive logic programs viewed as inductive definitions, see [7] for the full formal analysis of these networks. It has been shown in [7] that there exists a general method that allows to construct the networks from the specification of an inductive definition. Given a recursive clause $X(C(y)) \leftarrow X(y)$, the *recursive recogniser* for C is a one layer network, consisting of $n > 1$ neurons with the following properties. The length n of the single layer is the length of the input vector that the network will process. Each neuron has one input connection, with weight 1. The biases of all but the first neuron are set to 0; the bias of the first neuron is set to $-n_C$, where n_C is a numerical representation of C. The first neuron has an *output connection* that can be received externally. The outputs of the 2nd to nth neurons, called *recursive outputs*, are connected to the same layer, as follows: the output connection of the kth neuron ($k \in 2, \ldots, n$) is sent as an input to the $k - 1$ neuron. Note

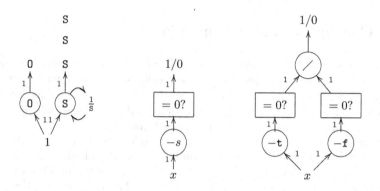

Fig. 1. Left: Generating elements of set **nat**. The input 1 is sent to the two neurons with zero biases and activation functions $f(x) = x * O$ and $f(x) = x * S$, where $O(S)$ are the numerical encodings of $O(S)$. The recursive weight is set to $\frac{1}{S}$. At time 1, the network outputs O and S standing for natural numbers 0 and 1, at time 2, it will generate another S, standing for $S(S(0))$ - or natural number 2. In the diagram - it is time 3, and the term $S(S(S(O)))$ is formed. **Centre:** Recognising symbol s. The input is sent to the neuron with bias $-s$; it outputs 0 if the input matches s and some non-zero value otherwise. This neuron may be connected to a zero-recogniser (in the square box) that outputs 1 whenever the signal 0 is computed. **Right:** Recognising expressions satisfying inductive definition **bool** from Example 2.

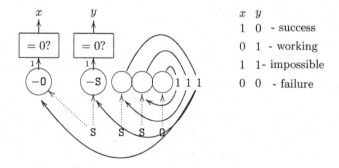

x	y	
1	0	- success
0	1	- working
1	1	- impossible
0	0	- failure

Fig. 2. This network decides whether $S(S(S(0)))$ satisfies the inductive definition of **nat**. Such network receives an input vector i, given by numerical encoding of the term - $S(S(S(0)))$. Dotted arrows show the initial input to the network; solid arrows show the connections with weight 1. The network has an 0-recogniser, and recursive S-recogniser: the recursive outputs from neurons in the S-recogniser layer are sent to the same layer.

that the first neuron of such network is the symbol recogniser for the function
C. The other $n-1$ neurons in the layer are designed to recursively process the
remaining $n-1$ elements of the input vector, see Figure 2.

It is possible to connect vectors of neurons in a cascade to recognise dependent
types. For example, to recognise a symbolic term of type list(nat), composed of
nested cons in the standard way, we can use two layers of neurons: a lower layer
to recognise the list structure, and an upper layer to recognise nat structure, [7].

4   Conclusions and Future Work

In this paper, we have applied the general method [7] to recursive logic programs.
We have explained two neuro-symbolic methods that work with inductive definitions: *inductive generators* and *recursive recognisers*. The methods can be
applied to logic programs with infinite Herbrand bases for which the traditional
model-theoretic methods cannot be applied directly.

Taking on board the "logic programs as inductive definitions" idea, we wish
to revise the traditional methods of building neuro-symbolic networks. The goal
is to compare results with the traditional implementations of semantic operators
and proof systems, resolution and unification. The hope is that the functional
approach would be more natural to integrate with neural networks [4,10].

References

1. Bader, S., Hitzler, P., Hölldobler, S.: Connectionist model generation: A first-order
   approach. Neurocomputing 71, 2420–2432 (2008)
2. d'Avila Garcez, A., Broda, K.B., Gabbay, D.M.: Neural-Symbolic Learning Systems: Foundations and Applications. Springer, Heidelberg (2002)
3. d'Avila Garcez, A., Lamb, L.C., Gabbay, D.M.: Neural-Symbolic Cognitive Reasoning. In: Cognitive Technologies, Springer, Heidelberg (2008)
4. Gartner, T., Lloyd, J., Flach, P.: Kernels and distances for structured data. Machine Learning 3(57), 205–232 (2004)
5. Gust, H., Kühnberger, K.-U., Geibel, P.: Learning models of predicate logical
   theories with neural networks based on topos theory. In: Perspectives of Neural-
   Symbolic Integration, pp. 233–264. Springer, Heidelberg (2007)
6. Komendantskaya, E.: Unification neural networks: Unification by error-correction
   learning. J. of Algorithms in Cognition, Informatics, and Logic (2009) (in print)
7. Komendantskaya, E., Broda, K., d'Avila Garcez, A.: Using inductive types for
   ensuring correctness of neuro-symbolic computations. In: CIE 2010 booklet (2010)
8. Lloyd, J.: Foundations of Logic Programming, 2nd edn. Springer, Heidelberg (1987)
9. Paulson, L.C., Smith, A.W.: Logic programming, functional programming, and
   inductive definitions. In: ELP, pp. 283–309 (1989)
10. Smolensky, P., Legendre, G.: The Harmonic Mind. MIT Press, Cambridge (2006)
11. Wang, J., Domingos, P.: Hybrid markov logic networks. In: Proc. AAAI 2008, pp.
    1106–1111 (2008)

A Model for Center-Surround Stimulus-Dependent Receptive Fields

José R.A. Torreão and Silvia M.C. Victer

Instituto de Computação, Universidade Federal Fluminense
24210-240 Niterói RJ, Brazil

Abstract. A model for image coding based on Gabor-like stimulus-dependent receptive fields has been recently introduced, where the parameters of the coding functions are obtained from the Fourier transform of the input. Here we extend such model, by showing that it can also be based on center-surround structures, such as found in the retina and the lateral geniculate nucleus. Consistent with the interpretation of these early visual stages as providing a decorrelated signal to the cortex, we propose center-surround stimulus-dependent receptive fields which yield whitened representations of natural inputs. Our model receptive fields are found to replicate properties of the mammalian center-surround structures.

1 Introduction

The classical description of the receptive field assumes a fixed spatial organization, but this has been challenged by neurophysiological findings which indicate that the receptive-field structure changes with neuronal input [1,2,3]. Motivated by these, we have recently proposed a model for image coding by the mammalian visual cortex [4], in terms of Gabor-like, signal-dependent receptive field functions of the form

$$\psi_c(x, y; \omega_x, \omega_y) = e^{i[\omega_x x + \omega_y y + \varphi_{\tilde{I}}]} e^{-\left(\frac{x^2 + y^2}{2\sigma_c^2}\right)} \qquad (1)$$

where $\varphi_{\tilde{I}}$ is the phase of the signal's Fourier transform, and σ_c is related to its magnitude as

$$\sigma_c(\omega_x, \omega_y) = \frac{1}{(2\pi)^{3/2}} \sqrt{|\tilde{I}(\omega_x, \omega_y)|} \qquad (2)$$

A representation of the signal $I(x, y)$, assumed square-integrable, has been obtained, in terms of the ψ_c functions, as

$$I(x, y) = \int_{-\infty}^{\infty} \int_{-\infty}^{\infty} d\omega_x d\omega_y e^{i(\omega_x x + \omega_y y)} * \psi_c(x, y; \omega_x, \omega_y) \qquad (3)$$

where the asterisk denotes spatial convolution. Although Eq. (3) holds exactly only over an infinite domain, it has been shown to remain approximately valid over finite windows, with different σ_c values computed at each window. For a

K. Diamantaras, W. Duch, L.S. Iliadis (Eds.): ICANN 2010, Part I, LNCS 6352, pp. 305–310, 2010.

typical image, the coding functions ψ_c show properties which are consistent with those of the receptive fields of the cortical simple cells, what lends neurophysiological plausibility to the model (see [4] for details).

Here we show how the above approach can be extended to receptive fields with a center-surround organization, such as found in the retina and in the lateral geniculate nucleus (LGN). The center-surround organization has been explained, based on information theoretic principles, by assuming that the early visual system produces a decorrelated version of the input signal, which is then relayed, for further processing, to the cerebral cortex [5,6]. Neural cells in the retina and the LGN would thus have developed receptive field structures which are best suited to whiten natural images, whose Fourier spectra are known to decay, approximately, as the inverse magnitude of the frequency − i.e., $\sim (\omega_x^2 + \omega_y^2)^{-1/2}$ [7]. Consistent with such interpretation, we introduce circularly symmetrical, stimulus-dependent coding functions in terms of which a similar representation as Eq. (3) is defined for the whitened input. The resulting coding functions are found to replicate properties of the neurophysiological receptive field structures.

2   Center-Surround Signal-Dependent Representation

We propose to represent the output of the center-surround cells as

$$I_{white}(x, y) = \int_{-\infty}^{\infty} \int_{-\infty}^{\infty} d\omega_x d\omega_y e^{i(\omega_x x + \omega_y y)} * \psi(r; \omega_x, \omega_y) \tag{4}$$

where $I_{white}(x, y)$ is a whitened image, modeled as the convolution of the input image and a suitable zero-phase whitening filter, $W(x, y)$:

$$I_{white}(x, y) = W(x, y) * I(x, y) \tag{5}$$

The receptive field is here modeled by $\psi(r; \omega_x, \omega_y)$ − for $r = \sqrt{x^2 + y^2}$ −, which is a circularly symmetrical coding function, chosen under the form

$$\psi(r; \omega_x, \omega_y) = -\frac{e^{i\varphi_{\tilde{I}}(\omega_x, \omega_y)}}{\pi r} \{1 - \cos[\sigma(\omega_x, \omega_y)\pi r] - \sin[\sigma(\omega_x, \omega_y)\pi r]\} \tag{6}$$

where $\varphi_{\tilde{I}}$ is the phase of the Fourier transform of the input signal, as already defined, and $\sigma(\omega_x, \omega_y)$ is related to the magnitude of the transform, as shown in the Appendix, as

$$\sigma(\omega_x, \omega_y) = \frac{\rho}{\pi} \sqrt{1 - \left[1 + \frac{\rho \tilde{W}(\omega_x, \omega_y)|\tilde{I}(\omega_x, \omega_y)|}{4\pi}\right]^{-2}} \tag{7}$$

In the above, $\tilde{W}(\omega_x, \omega_y)$ is the Fourier transform of the whitening filter, and we have defined ρ as the frequency magnitude: $\rho = \sqrt{\omega_x^2 + \omega_y^2}$.

The absolute value of the function $\psi(r; \omega_x, \omega_y)$ reaches a maximum of σ, at $r = 0$, its first zero appears at $r = r_0 = 1/2\sigma$, and the second one at $r = r_1 = 2/\sigma$, the range between them, of length $3/2\sigma$, defining the surround of the model receptive field. There are additional zeros for $r > r_1$, and thus additional side lobes, but the depth of those is less than one third of that of the first lobe. The coding function therefore displays a single dominant surround whose size will depend on the spectral content of the input image, and on the choice of whitening filter (see Eq. 7). Following the interpretation proposed in [5,6], we assume that the center-surround receptive field structures are such as to equalize the spectrum of natural images — which decays as $1/\rho$, as already noted —, at the same time suppressing high-frequency noise. We therefore chose the whitening filter spectrum as

$$\tilde{W}(\omega_x, \omega_y) = \frac{\rho}{1 + \kappa\rho^2} \tag{8}$$

where κ is a free parameter. Other filters with the same general spectral properties could have been chosen, without substantially altering our model.

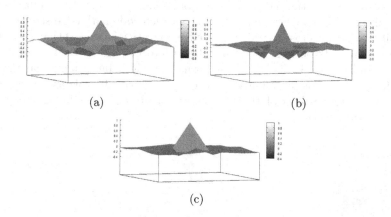

(a)   (b)

(c)

Fig. 1. Plots of the magnitude of the coding functions of Eq. (6), obtained from a 3×3 fragment of the original image in Fig. 2a. The represented frequencies, (ω_x, ω_y), in (a), (b) and (c), are (0,1), (2,0), and (3,1), respectively.

Fig. 1 shows examples of the coding functions resulting from the above approach. These have been obtained from a 3×3 patch of the natural image shown in Fig. 2a, and serve to illustrate the general behavior of our signal-dependent receptive fields. The figure displays the magnitude of $\psi(r; \omega_x, \omega_y)$ divided by σ, such that all functions reach the same maximum value of 1 (when the phase factor $e^{i\varphi_I(\omega_x,\omega_y)}$, in Eq. (6), is considered, we obtain both center-on and center-off structures). It is easy to see that our model does not respond to uniform inputs, since, when $\rho = 0$, σ is also zero, and the coding function vanishes. On the other hand, at low frequencies, as illustrated by Fig. 1a, the receptive fields show a marked center-surround organization. As ρ increases, the surround tends to become less important (Fig. 1b), all but disappearing at the higher frequencies (Fig. 1c). Such behavior has been found to hold irrespectively of the κ value chosen (we considered $0.05 < \kappa \leq 1$), and is in keeping with our whitening model: the relative weight of the low frequencies − which tend to be dominant in the natural images − should be attenuated; that of the middle-range ones should be enhanced, and the high-frequency noise should be suppressed. Therefore, the low-frequency receptive fields would tend to be of bandpass character, while the high-frequency ones would tend to be low-pass, what is consistent with the profiles in Fig. 1 (a similar change in receptive field structure, associated with the change in mean luminance level, has been reported for retinal ganglion cells [8]).

Fig. 2 shows examples of natural images (from the van Hateren database [9]) coded by the signal-dependent receptive fields. We present the input image − from which $\sigma(\omega_x, \omega_y)$ and the coding function (receptive field) $\psi(r; \omega_x, \omega_y)$ are obtained − and the resulting whitened representation, obtained by computing Eq. (4) over finite windows. For comparison, the log-log spectra of the input and whitened signals are also presented (in the plots, the vertical axis is the rotational average of the log magnitude of the Fourier transforms, and the horizontal axis is $\log \rho$). It is apparent that the representation tends to equalize the input spectra, the resulting images looking like edge maps which code both edge strength (the intensity variation across the edge) and edge polarity (the sign of that variation). We present results obtained with 3×3 and 5×5 windows, for $\kappa = 0.05$. The smaller window gives better definition for narrow edges, but can miss larger ones. The effect of κ is not pronounced, but, consistent with its role as a measure of noise level, larger values of the parameter usually enhance the low-frequency portion of the spectra.

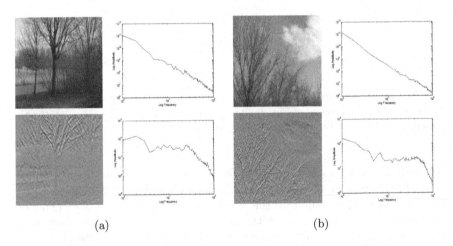

(a)   (b)

Fig. 2. a) Top: input image and its log-log spectrum (see text). Bottom: whitened image and its log-log spectrum. Similarly for b). We have used 5×5 (a) and 3×3 (b) windows, with $\kappa = 0.05$. The images are 192×192.

3   Concluding Remarks

We have introduced a model for stimulus-dependent center-surround receptive fields, extending an earlier approach used for modeling Gabor-like neurons [4].

As we have shown, besides performing whitening, our model receptive fields present the following neurophysiologically plausible properties: they appear both with center-on and with center-off organization; they do not respond to uniform inputs; they are frequency-dependent; their surrounds tend to be better defined for lower frequencies, and less so for higher frequencies — what lends them the character of a bandpass filter in the first case, and of a low-pass filter, in the latter. All such properties have been experimentally verified either for retinal ganglion cells or for cells of the lateral geniculate nucleus.

The center-surround receptive fields presented here can be associated with the Gabor-like ones introduced in [4], to configure a general model of signal-dependent representation and processing in the visual pathway, between the retina and V1: the output of the center-surround cells would define the Gabor-like receptive fields (see Eq. (1)), and these would then act as projection filters, to generate a sparse signal representation, as advocated, for instance, in [10].

Acknowledgment. This work has been partially supported by CNPq-Brasil.

References

1. Allman, J., Miezin, F., McGuinness, E.: Stimulus specific responses from beyond the classical receptive field: Neurophysiological mechanisms for local-global comparison in visual neurons. Annu. Rev. Neuroscience 8, 407–430 (1985)
2. David, S.V., Vinje, W.E., Gallant, J.L.: Natural stimulus statistics alter the receptive field structure of V1 neurons. The Journal of Neuroscience 24(31), 6991–7006 (2004)
3. Bair, W.: Visual receptive field organization. Current Opinion in Neurobiology 15(4), 459–464 (2005)
4. Torreão, J.R.A., Fernandes, J.L., Victer, S.M.C.: A model for neuronal signal representation by stimulus-dependent receptive fields. In: Alippi, C., Polycarpou, M., Panayiotou, C., Ellinas, G. (eds.) ICANN 2009. LNCS, vol. 5768, pp. 356–362. Springer, Heidelberg (2009)
5. Atick, J.J., Redlich, A.N.: What does the retina know about natural scenes. Neural Comp. 4, 196–210 (1992)
6. Dan, Y., Atick, J.J., Reid, R.C.: Efficient coding of natural scenes in the lateral geniculate nucleus: experimental test of a computational theory. J. Neurosci. 16(10), 3351–3362 (1996)
7. Ruderman, D.L., Bialek, W.: Statistics of natural images: Scaling in the woods. Phys. Rev. Lett. 73(6), 814–817 (1994)
8. Derrington, A.M., Lennie, P.: The influence of temporal frequency and adaptation level on receptive field organization of retinal ganglion cells in cat. J. Physiol (London) 333, 343–366 (1982)
9. van Hateren, J.H., van der Schaaf, A.: Independent component filters of natural images compared with simple cells in primary visual cortex. Proc. R. Soc. Lond. B 265, 359–366 (1998)

10. Olshausen, B.A., Field, D.J.: Emergence of simple-cell receptive field properties by learning a sparse code for natural images. Nature 381, 607–609 (1996)
11. Enroth-Cugell, C., Robson, J.G., Schweitzer-Tong, D.E., Watson, A.B.: Spatiotemporal interactions in cat retinal ganglion cells showing linear spatial summation. J. Physiol. 341, 279–301 (1983)

Appendix

Here we obtain the parameter $\sigma(\omega_x, \omega_y)$ of the coding function $\psi(r; \omega_x, \omega_y)$, given in Eq. (7).

Taking the Fourier transform of both sides of Eq. (4) (with the integration variables changed to ω'_x and ω'_y), using Eq. (5) and the sifting property of the delta, we find

$$\tilde{W}(\omega_x, \omega_y)\tilde{I}(\omega_x, \omega_y) = 2\pi \int \int d\omega'_x d\omega'_y \delta(\omega'_x - \omega_x, \omega'_y - \omega_y)\tilde{\psi}(\rho; \omega'_x, \omega'_y) =$$

$$= 2\pi\tilde{\psi}(\rho; \omega_x, \omega_y) \tag{9}$$

for $\rho = \sqrt{\omega_x^2 + \omega_y^2}$, and with $\tilde{W}$ and $\tilde{\psi}$ denoting, respectively, the Fourier transforms of the filter and of the coding function. The latter can be found, from Eq. (6), as

$$\tilde{\psi}(\rho; \omega_x, \omega_y) = -2e^{i\varphi_{\tilde{I}}(\omega_x, \omega_y)} \left\{ \frac{1}{\rho} - \frac{1 - \text{cyl}(\rho/2\pi\sigma)}{\sqrt{\rho^2 - \pi^2\sigma^2}} - \frac{\text{cyl}(\rho/2\pi\sigma)}{\sqrt{\pi^2\sigma^2 - \rho^2}} \right\} \tag{10}$$

where $\text{cyl}(\rho/2\pi\sigma) = 1$, if $0 \leq \rho \leq \pi\sigma$, and zero, otherwise.

Using the above in Eq. (9), this can be solved for $\sigma(\omega_x, \omega_y)$, and we will get two different solutions, depending on wheter we assume $\sigma < \rho/\pi$ or $\sigma \geq \rho/\pi$. As already noted, the length of the surround region of the model receptive field defined by $\psi(r; \omega_x, \omega_y)$ is $3/2\sigma$. Since the retinal and LGN cells are experimentally found to have large surround areas, we chose to work here with the solution for $\sigma < \rho/\pi$ (we noticed very little change in our results, when the alternative solution was used). In this case, Eqs. (9) and (10) yield

$$\tilde{W}(\omega_x, \omega_y)|\tilde{I}(\omega_x, \omega_y)| = -4\pi \left[\frac{1}{\rho} - \frac{1}{\sqrt{\rho^2 - \pi^2\sigma^2}} \right] \tag{11}$$

where we have identified $\tilde{I}(\omega_x, \omega_y) = |\tilde{I}(\omega_x, \omega_y)|e^{i\varphi_{\tilde{I}}(\omega_x, \omega_y)}$. Through a straightforward manipulation, the above can be solved for σ, yielding the result in Eq. (7), and thus proving the validity of the representation in Eq. (4).

We conclude by remarking that the most commonly used model for center-surround receptive fields, the difference of Gaussians [11], has not been used here, because it would have required two parameters (the width of the two Gaussians) for the definition of the coding functions, while the above approach provides a single equation for this purpose.

Simple Constraints for Zero-Lag Synchronous Oscillations under STDP

Florian Hauser*, David Bouchain, and Günther Palm

Institute of Neural Information Processing, Ulm University, Germany
{florian.hauser,david.bouchain,guenther.palm}@uni-ulm.de

Abstract. Zero-lag synchronous oscillations have been confirmed several times in biological experiments as well as successfully reproduced and simulated by theoreticians. But it has not been analyzed yet how synaptic changes develop through STDP (spike timing-dependent plasticity) in a neural network of this type, and which physiological parameters have a qualitative influence on the synaptic strengths in long-term behavior. We analytically calculate these synaptic changes based on a simplified scheme which enables us to make conclusions about local and global connectivity patterns with the ability to produce zero-lag synchronous oscillations.

1 Introduction

Zero-lag synchronous oscillations between different cortical areas over large distances have been observed many times in different studies ([1], [2], [3], [4]). Moreover, it is commonly believed that oscillations observed in LFP (local field potential) measurements correspond to zero-lag synchronisation as well. Oscillation frequencies, especially those in the gamma band ($40 - 80$ Hz), are considered correlates of higher cognitive functions in the mammalian brain ([5]) and are exemplarily used in our investigation. Experimentalists and theoreticians agree on the importance of this phenomenon. Several EEG (electroencephalography) and MEG (magnetoencephalography) studies recorded such oscillations and theoreticians tried to model these in artificial neural networks ([6], [7]). Two popular connectivity principles originated from this idea: Local, mutually exciting neural groups (*local assemblies*) and more global bidirectionally coupled populations, distributed across two or more cortical areas (*global assemblies*).

Although we already know that artificial neural networks of this kind can be built, the precise synaptic changes which co-occur with their activity are often neglected. STDP is the most recently found category of local synaptic learning ([8], [9]). Today people tend to use STDP models instead of symmetric Hebbian rules, but usually in their pair-based and additive framework. There is much debate which STDP model accounts for the biologically most plausible learning rule. But we show what kind of problems arise if we confine ourselves to the simplest STDP framework.

---

* Corresponding author.

K. Diamantaras, W. Duch, L.S. Iliadis (Eds.): ICANN 2010, Part I, LNCS 6352, pp. 311–316, 2010.

By considering just the pre- and post-synaptic spike patterns as in experimental methods without extensive modeling of neural activity we can simplify our analytical calculations. Although measured oscillations give us the amount of neural activity in a certain time window of a few milliseconds, we can assume that at every peak of an oscillation period the majority of neurons are zero-lag synchronized. This allows us to look at a two-neuron scheme and investigate their synaptic changes over time. Although zero-lag synchronization is an idealized concept rarely found in experimental data, jittering applied to the STDP function does not result in a qualitative change in the synaptic modification. Fig. 1 (left) visualizes this by convolving the STDP function with a Gaussian distribution of temporal jittering.

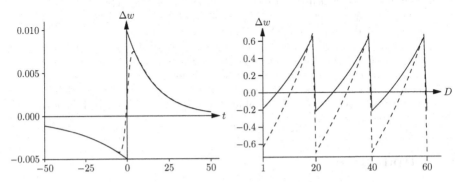

Fig. 1. *Left*: STDP window with parameters $A_+ = 0.01, A_- = -0.005, \tau_+ = 16$ ms and $\tau_- = 33$ ms (solid). Same STDP window convolved with $\mathcal{N}(0, \sigma)$, the Gaussian with $\sigma = 2$ ms (dashed). Difference of post- and pre-synaptic spike times in milliseconds on the t axis and amounts of weight change on the Δw axis. *Right*: Plot of synaptic change Δw with axonal delays D in realistic ranges ([10]) after an experiment duration of 2 seconds, i.e. $D \in [1, 60]$ ms, $N = 100$ and pairing frequency $\rho = 50$ Hz. STDP parameters are the same as in left plot. The solid line corresponds to $\Delta w^{\text{NN}}(D, N)$ and the dashed one to $\Delta w^{\text{U}}(D, N)$.

2   Simplified Scheme

To keep the analytical investigation simple, we abstract from any neural or synaptical dynamics and its consequent neural network towards an experimental setup akin to the work of physiologists which already studied several kinds of long-term potentiation and depression mechanisms ([11]). The so called pairing of pre- and post-synaptic events given a certain repetition frequency ρ is the standard procedure used by experimentalists. STDP results in the evolution of weight changes depending on the order of the pre-synaptic EPSP onset (excitatory post-synaptic potential) and post-synaptic AP (action potential). If the pre-synaptic event precedes the post-synaptic, the weight of the synapse is increased by a certain amount (and decreased when the order is reversed). We use a scheme for our investigation with only two neurons which are connected through one synapse. If we take into account another recurrent synapse with equal axonal delay, no qualitative change occurs because both synapses undergo the same changes over time. Therefore we can approximate synchronized feedforward as well as recurrent structures. If pre- and post-synaptic neurons fire synchronously, the pre-synaptic AP always arrives later at the synapse due to the axonal delay. Varying the axonal delays enables modeling of local and global structures as well as different post-pre-pairing times in experimental setups and gives an insight into qualitative changes of weight evolution. Given a certain oscillation period T which corresponds with the experimentalist's pairing frequency ρ and an axonal delay D, our artificial experimental setup is fully described.

3   Synaptic Changes

We use the standard additive STDP function $W(\Delta t)$ from the review [12] on phenomenological models of STDP. Using a pre-synaptic event as reference, we can distinguish between a Nearest-Neighbor and an Unrestricted (also called All-to-All, [13]) interaction. Whereas in the first case a pre-synaptic event is paired with the both nearest post-synaptic ones in time, the Unrestricted interaction considers all possible pairing combinations. For every interaction scheme we look for a function $\Delta w(D, N)$ which gives us the amount of changes at a synapse with axonal delay D after N pairings. These explicit pairings always belong to the post-pre case due to the positive axonal delay. With an previously given initial synaptic strength w_0, $w(D, N) = w_0 + \Delta w(D, N)$ gives us the final synaptic strength. So we are able to get explicit equations for the single synapse, mentioned in Section 2. For better readability we set $k = \lfloor \frac{D}{T} \rfloor$. The resulting equation for the Nearest-Neighbor interaction is given by

$$\Delta w^{\mathrm{NN}}(D, N) = (N - k)A_- e^{-\frac{D - kT}{\tau_-}} + (N - k - 1)A_+ e^{-\frac{(k+1)T - D}{\tau_+}}$$
$$+ \sum_{i=1}^{k} A_- e^{-\frac{D - (k-i)T}{\tau_-}} . \tag{1}$$

The Unrestricted interaction leads to equation

$$\Delta w^{\mathrm{U}}(D, N) = \sum_{i=1}^{N-1-k} \sum_{j=k+1}^{N-i} A_+ e^{-\frac{jT - D}{\tau_+}}$$
$$+ \sum_{i=1}^{N-k} \sum_{j=-k}^{i-1} A_- e^{-\frac{D + jT}{\tau_-}}$$
$$+ \sum_{i=N-k+1}^{N} \sum_{j=-N+i}^{i-1} A_- e^{-\frac{D + jT}{\tau_-}} . \tag{2}$$

Fig. 1 (right) shows plots of Eq. 1 and Eq. 2 with STDP parameters which satisfy Eq. 3, i.e. $A_+ = 0.01, A_- = -0.005, \tau_+ = 16$ ms, $\tau_- = 33$ ms and $T = 20$ ms. The number of pairings is fixed to $N = 100$, matching an overall time of 2 seconds.

4 Results

The STDP function $W(\Delta t)$ depends on the amplitude parameters A_+, A_- and time constants τ_+, τ_-. All together this gives us a certain time window in which both, potentiation and depression, are able to interact. Roughly speaking, if we take into account a repetition frequency $\rho = \frac{1}{T}$ such that T is smaller than the STDP time window, post-pre pairings coincide with previous ones and vice versa, which is indeed the case for the gamma band considering physiological measured values for the STDP parameters. To determine how the STDP parameters influence the long-term behavior of synaptic changes we can use standard analysis. If we want to draw conclusions about the existence of several types of neural networks under the additive STDP regime, the moment of change to exclusively potentiation for all axonal delays has to be the point of interest. Our first definition is a stability criterion ([14]) which is often considered when choosing the STDP parameters. This means if we think of independent pre- and post-synaptic firing rates which are chosen from stationary Poisson statistics, depression has to outweigh potentiation which can be assured by requiring $\int_{-\infty}^{\infty} W(\Delta t) d\Delta t < 0$ leading to the inequality

$$A_+ \tau_+ + A_- \tau_- < 0 \qquad (3)$$

for Unrestricted interaction under the assumptions $A_+, \tau_+, \tau_- > 0$ and $A_- < 0$. This constraint will also be used for the Nearest-Neighbor interaction as a consequence of the satisfiability of Eq. 4.

On the other hand we want to find an interval in the STDP parameter space which leads to potentiation in our experiments, i.e. lower and upper bounds for some parameters which then can be tested within experimental ranges. In the Nearest-Neighbor case the desired result can be achieved by taking $\frac{\partial \Delta w^{\mathrm{NN}}(D,N)}{\partial N} > 0$ which is N-independent and looking at the limit value for $D \to 0$. So potentiation occurs if $W(T) > -A_-$ holds which also implies $A_+ > -A_-$. Inserted into the stability inequality we further constrain $\tau_- > \tau_+$. It should be noted that the potentiation criterion additionally depends on the pairing frequency $\rho = \frac{1}{T}$ as desired. To test our derived inequalities in combination, we deduce the potentiation constraint[1]

$$\frac{\tau_-}{\tau_+} > \frac{A_+}{-A_-} > e^{\frac{T}{\tau_+}}. \qquad (4)$$

The same procedure can be used for Unrestricted interaction except that the left-hand side of $\frac{\partial \Delta w^{\mathrm{U}}(D,N)}{\partial N} > 0$ is still a function in N so we have to look at $N \to \infty$ as well. As a result of combining the inequality again with the STDP stability criterion we obtain

$$\frac{\tau_-}{\tau_+} > \frac{A_+}{-A_-} > e^{\frac{T}{\tau_+}} \left(\frac{1 - e^{\frac{-T}{\tau_+}}}{1 - e^{\frac{-T}{\tau_-}}} \right). \qquad (5)$$

---

[1] E.g. for $T = 20$ ms we need $\tau_+ > 30$ ms such that $A_+ \leq -2A_-$. It follows that $\tau_- > 2\tau_+ \geq 60$ ms.

The difference between both interaction schemes results in a scaling factor > 1 on the right-hand side of Eq. 5 if the constraint $\tau_- > \tau_+$ holds which is usually the case in physiological measurements. As a consequence the Unrestricted interaction causes a different interval of synaptic strenghts dependent on both time constants.

5   Discussion and Conclusions

We notice for our example plot in Fig. 1 (right) that a reset of potentiation strength occurs at every multiple of the oscillation frequency. So a consequent sharp transition constraint of the delay-specific strengthening arises together with the oscillation frequency. To overcome this problem with regard to local assemblies, i.e. small delays, we derived upper and lower bounds for STDP parameter relationships. We tested these inequalities with several STDP parameter settings from experimental measurements ([9],[15], [16]) with a 50 Hz pairing frequency and didn't find a single satisfying setting. As a consequence it appears that pair-based additive STDP as defined by e.g. [12] does not permit the persistence of local assemblies and strongly controls delay-specific strengthing of synapses of global assemblies. Similar results were produced by [17] and [18] through simulations which can now be explained in terms of physiological parameters and their exact dependencies among each other.

On the other hand, recent studies indicate that pair-based models are not sufficient, especially in high frequency pairing experiments ([19], [20]). So one should specify STDP models more carefully in future simulations. There are already a few recent models which take into account triplet or even quadrupel settings which are able to reproduce experimental findings to a much more satisfying degree ([21], [22], [20]). We will investigate those rules in the near future.

Acknowledgements. This research has been supported by a scholarship from the Graduate School of *Mathematical Analysis of Evolution, Information and Complexity* at Ulm University. Special thanks to Andreas Knoblauch who read early drafts of the manuscript and made a number of valueable suggestions and corrections.

References

1. Castelo-Branco, M., Neuenschwander, S., Singer, W.: Synchronization of visual responses between the cortex, lateral geniculate nucleus, and retina in the anesthetized cat. The Journal of Neuroscience 18 (1998)
2. Engel, A.K., König, P., Kreiter, A., Singer, W.: Interhemispheric synchronization of oscillatory neuronal responses in cat visual cortex. Science 252 (1991)
3. Roelfsema, P.R., Engel, A., Knig, P., Singer, W.: Visuomotor integration is associated with zero time-lag synchronization among cortical areas. Nature 385 (1997)
4. Schneider, G., Nikolic, D.: Detection and assessment of near-zero delays in neuronal spiking activity. Journal of Neuroscience Methods 152 (2006)

5. Buzsaki, G., Draguhn, A.: Neuronal oscillations in cortical networks. Science 304 (2004)
6. Sommer, F., Wennekers, T.: Associative memory in networks of spiking neurons. Neural Networks Special Issue 14 (2001)
7. Vicente, R., Golo, L., Mirasso, C., Fischer, I., Pipa, G.: Dynamical relaying can yield zero time lag neuronal synchrony despite long conduction delays. PNAS 105 (2008)
8. Markram, H., Luebke, J., Frotscher, M., Sakmann, B.: Regulation of synaptic efficacy by coincidence of postsynaptic aps and epsps. Science 275 (1997)
9. Bi, Q.Q., Poo, M.M.: Synaptic modification in cultured hippocampal neurons: Dependence on spike timing, synaptic strength, and postsynaptic cell type. J. Neurosc. 18, 10464–10474 (1998)
10. Swadlow, H.: Information flow along neocortical axons. Time and the Brain, Conceptual Advances in Brain Research (2000)
11. Malenka, R.C., Bear, M.F.: LTP and LTD: An embarrassment of riches. Neuron 44 (2004)
12. Morrison, A., Diesmann, M., Gerstner, W.: Phenomenological models of synaptic plasticity based on spike timing. Biol. Cyb. 98, 459–478 (2008)
13. Sjoestroem, J., Gerstner, W.: Spike-timing dependent plasticity. Scholarpedia 5 (2010)
14. Kempter, R., Gerstner, W., van Hemmen, J.L.: Hebbian learning and spiking neurons. Physical Review E 59, 4498–4514 (1999)
15. Froemke, R., Dan, Y.: Spike-timing-dependent synaptic modification induced by natural spike trains. Nature 416 (2002)
16. Froemke, R., Poo, M.M., Dan, Y.: Spike-timing-dependent synaptic plasticity depends on dendritic location. Nature 434 (2005)
17. Knoblauch, A., Sommer, F.T.: Synaptic plasticity, conduction delays, and inter-areal phase relations of spike activity in a model of reciprocally connected areas. Neurocomputing, 52–54 (2003)
18. Knoblauch, A., Sommer, F.T.: Spike-timing-dependent synaptic plasticity can form zero lag links for cortical oscillations. Neurocomputing 58-60 (2004)
19. Sjoestroem, P., Turrigiano, G., Nelson, S.: Rate, timing, and cooperativity jointly determine cortical synaptic plasticity. Neuron 32 (2001)
20. Wang, H.X., Gerkin, R.C., Nauen, D.W., Bi, G.Q.: Coactivation and timing-dependent integration of synaptic potentiation and depression. Nature Neuroscience 8 (2005)
21. Pfister, J.P., Gerstner, W.: Triplets of spikes in a model of spike timing-dependent plasticity. The Journal of Neuroscience 26 (2006)
22. Froemke, R., Tsay, I., Raa, M., Long, J., Dan, Y.: Contribution of individual spikes in burst-induced long-term synaptic modification. Journal of Neurophysiology 95 (2006)

Multilinear Decomposition and Topographic Mapping of Binary Tensors

Jakub Mažgut[1], Peter Tiňo[2], Mikael Bodén[3], and Hong Yan[4]

[1] Faculty of Informatics and Information Technologies,
Slovak University of Technology, 81219 Bratislava, Slovakia
mazgut@fiit.stuba.sk
[2] School of Computer Science, The University of Birmingham,
Birmingham B15 2TT, UK
P.Tino@cs.bham.ac.uk
[3] Institute of Molecular Bioscience and School of Information Technology
and Electrical Engineering,
The University of Queensland, QLD 4072, Australia
m.boden@uq.edu.au
[4] Dept. Electronic Engineering, City University of Hong Kong, Kowloon, Hong Kong
h.yan@cityu.edu.hk

Abstract. Current methods capable of processing tensor objects in their natural higher-order structure have been introduced for real-valued tensors. Such techniques, however, are not suitable for processing binary tensors which arise in many real world problems, such as gait recognition, document analysis, or graph mining. To account for binary nature of the data, we propose a novel generalized multi-linear model for principal component analysis of binary tensors (GML-PCA). We compare the performance of GML-PCA with an existing model for real-valued tensor decomposition (TensorLSI) in two experiments. In the first experiment, synthetic binary tensors were compressed and consequently reconstructed, yielding the reconstruction error in terms of AUC. In the second experiment, we compare the ability to reveal biologically meaningful dominant trends in a real world large-scale dataset of DNA sequences represented through binary tensors. Both experiments show that our GML-PCA model is better suited for modeling binary tensors than the TensorLSI.

Keywords: Generalized multilinear principal component analysis, binary data, tensor objects, dimensionality reduction.

1 Introduction

Traditional methods for data dimensionality reduction, such as principal component analysis (PCA), have been designed to process data objects in the form of vectors. To use these methods for tensorial data decomposition, one needs to break the natural higher order tensor structure and reshape the tensors into vectors. However, higher order dependencies presented in the data structure of tensors can

K. Diamantaras, W. Duch, L.S. Iliadis (Eds.): ICANN 2010, Part I, LNCS 6352, pp. 317–326, 2010.
© Springer-Verlag Berlin Heidelberg 2010

potentially lead to more compact and useful representations [1]. Moreover, vectorization of tensors often results in high-dimensional vectors. Since PCA involves eigendecomposition of the covariance matrix, processing of such vectors could be computationally infeasible.

An increasing number of practical applications involves manipulation of multidimensional tensors, stimulating development of new methods for processing tensorial data in their natural higher-order structure, without the need for data vectorization (e.g. [1,2]). Many real world problems involve data in the form of binary tensors, for example gait recognition [1], document analysis [2], or graph mining (with graphs represented by adjacency tensors). However, to the best of our knowledge, at present, there is no systematic framework capable of processing tensors with binary values. In this contribution we propose a principled framework for decomposing binary tensors – a generalized multi-linear model for principal component analysis of binary tensors (GML-PCA).

2   Overview of Basic Multilinear Algebra

We denote vectors by lowercase boldface letters (e.g. $\mathbf{u}$), matrices by italic uppercase (e.g. U), and tensors by calligraphic letters, (e.g. $\mathcal{A}$). Elements of an N-th order tensor $\mathcal{A} \in \mathbb{R}^{I_1 \times I_2 \times ... \times I_N}$ are addressed by N indices i_n ranging from 1 to I_n, $n = 1, 2, ..., N$. For convenience, we will often write a particular index setting $(i_1, i_2, ..., i_N) \in \Upsilon = \{1, 2, ..., I_1\} \times \{1, 2, ..., I_2\} \times ... \times \{1, 2, ..., I_N\}$ for a tensor element using vector notation $\mathbf{i} = (i_1, i_2, ..., i_N)$, so that instead of writing $\mathcal{A}_{i_1,i_2,...,i_N}$ we write $\mathcal{A}_{\mathbf{i}}$.

A rank-1 tensor $\mathcal{A} \in \mathbb{R}^{I_1 \times I_2 \times ... \times I_N}$ can be obtained as an outer product of N vectors $\mathbf{u}^{(n)} \in \mathbb{R}^{I_n}$, $n = 1, 2, ..., N$: $\mathcal{A} = \mathbf{u}^{(1)} \circ \mathbf{u}^{(2)} \circ ... \circ \mathbf{u}^{(N)}$. If we consider an orthonormal basis $\{\mathbf{u}_1^{(n)}, \mathbf{u}_2^{(n)}, ..., \mathbf{u}_{I_n}^{(n)}\}$ for the n-mode space $\mathbb{R}^{I_n}$, any tensor $\mathcal{A}$ can be expressed as a linear combination of $\prod_{n=1}^{N} I_n$ rank-1 basis tensors $(\mathbf{u}_{i_1}^{(1)} \circ \mathbf{u}_{i_2}^{(2)} \circ ... \circ \mathbf{u}_{I_n}^{(N)})$:

$$\mathcal{A} = \sum_{\mathbf{i} \in \Upsilon} \mathcal{Q}_{\mathbf{i}} \cdot (\mathbf{u}_{i_1}^{(1)} \circ \mathbf{u}_{i_2}^{(2)} \circ ... \circ \mathbf{u}_{i_N}^{(N)}) \tag{1}$$

with expansion coefficients stored in the Nth order tensor $\mathcal{Q} \in \mathbb{R}^{I_1 \times I_2 \times ... \times I_N}$, so that each tensor element $\mathcal{A}_{\mathbf{j}}$, $\mathbf{j} \in \Upsilon$ is equal to

$$\mathcal{A}_{\mathbf{j}} = \sum_{\mathbf{i} \in \Upsilon} \mathcal{Q}_{\mathbf{i}} \cdot \prod_{n=1}^{N} u_{i_n, j_n}^{(n)}. \tag{2}$$

Several methods have been proposed for reduced rank representations of real-valued tensors [3,4]. For example, one can assume that a reduced set of basis tensors in the expansion (2) is sufficient to approximate all tensors in a given dataset:

$$\mathcal{A} \approx \sum_{\mathbf{i} \in K} \mathcal{Q}_{\mathbf{i}} \cdot (\mathbf{u}_{i_1}^{(1)} \circ \mathbf{u}_{i_2}^{(2)} \circ ... \circ \mathbf{u}_{i_N}^{(N)}), \tag{3}$$

where $K \subset \Upsilon$. In other words, tensors in a given dataset can be found 'close' to the $|K|$-dimensional hyperplane in the tensor space spanned by the rank-1 basis tensors $(\mathbf{u}_{i_1}^{(1)} \circ \mathbf{u}_{i_2}^{(2)} \circ ... \circ \mathbf{u}_{i_N}^{(N)})$, $\mathbf{i} \in K$.

Note that orthonormality of the basis vectors $\{\mathbf{u}_1^{(n)}, \mathbf{u}_2^{(n)}, ..., \mathbf{u}_{I_n}^{(n)}\}$ for the n-mode space $\mathbb{R}^{I_n}$ can be relaxed. It can be easily shown that as long as for each mode $n = 1, 2, ..., N$, the vectors $\mathbf{u}_1^{(n)}, \mathbf{u}_2^{(n)}, ..., \mathbf{u}_{I_n}^{(n)}$ are linearly independent, their outer products $(\mathbf{u}_{i_1}^{(1)} \circ \mathbf{u}_{i_2}^{(2)} \circ ... \circ \mathbf{u}_{i_N}^{(N)})$, $\mathbf{i} \in \Upsilon$, will be linearly independent as well. If all the n-mode space basis are orthonormal, the tensor decomposition is known as the Higher-Order Singular Value Decomposition (HOSVD) [3]. Extending matrix (2nd-order tensor) decompositions (such as SVD) to higher-order tensors is not straightforward. Familiar concepts such as rank become ambiguous and more complex. However, the main purpose of the decomposition remains unchanged: represent a tensor as a sum of rank-1 tensors.

3 The Model

Consider a set of Nth-order binary tensors $\mathcal{D} = \{\mathcal{A}_1, \mathcal{A}_2, ..., \mathcal{A}_m, ..., \mathcal{A}_M\}$, where $\mathcal{A}_m \in \{0, 1\}^{I_1 \times I_2 \times ... \times I_N}$ and each tensor element $\mathcal{A}_{m,\mathbf{i}}$ is independently generated from a Bernoulli distribution with mean $\mathcal{P}_{m,\mathbf{i}}$ (all mean parameters for the data are collected in the tensor $\mathcal{P} \in [0, 1]^{M \times I_1 \times I_2 \times ... \times I_N}$ of order $N + 1$). Assuming independence among the data tensors, the model likelihood reads

$$L(\mathcal{P}) = \prod_{m=1}^{M} \prod_{\mathbf{i} \in \Upsilon} P(\mathcal{A}_{m,\mathbf{i}}|\mathcal{P}_{m,\mathbf{i}}) = \prod_{m=1}^{M} \prod_{\mathbf{i} \in \Upsilon} \mathcal{P}_{m,\mathbf{i}}^{\mathcal{A}_{m,\mathbf{i}}} \cdot (1 - \mathcal{P}_{m,\mathbf{i}})^{1 - \mathcal{A}_{m,\mathbf{i}}}. \quad (4)$$

A more detailed model description can be found in [5].

Our goal is to find a lower dimensional representation of the binary tensors in $\mathcal{D}$ while still capturing the data distribution well. The mean Bernoulli parameters are confined to the interval $[0, 1]$. To solve our problem in an unbounded domain, we rewrite the Bernoulli distribution using the log-odds parameters $\theta_{m,\mathbf{i}} = \log [\mathcal{P}_{m,\mathbf{i}}/(1 - \mathcal{P}_{m,\mathbf{i}})]$ and the logistic link function $\sigma(\theta_{m,\mathbf{i}}) = (1 + e^{-\theta_{m,\mathbf{i}}})^{-1} = \mathcal{P}_{m,\mathbf{i}}$. We thus obtain the log-likelihood

$$\mathcal{L}(\Theta) = \sum_{m=1}^{M} \sum_{\mathbf{i} \in \Upsilon} \mathcal{A}_{m,\mathbf{i}} \log \sigma(\theta_{m,\mathbf{i}}) + (1 - \mathcal{A}_{m,\mathbf{i}}) \log \sigma(-\theta_{m,\mathbf{i}}), \quad (5)$$

where we collect all the natural parameters $\theta_{m,\mathbf{i}}$ in a tensor $\Theta \in \mathbb{R}^{M \times I_1 \times I_2 \times ... \times I_N}$. Now, $\theta_{m,\mathbf{i}} \in \mathbb{R}$, which allows us to easily constrain all the Nth-order parameter tensors θ_m to lie in a subspace spanned by a reduced set of rank-1 basis tensors $(\mathbf{u}_{r_1}^{(1)} \circ \mathbf{u}_{r_2}^{(2)} \circ ... \circ \mathbf{u}_{r_N}^{(N)})$, where $r_n \in \{1, 2, ..., R_n\}$, and $R_n \leq I_n$, $i = 1, 2..., N$. The indices $\mathbf{r} = (r_1, r_2, ..., r_N)$ take values from the set $\rho = \{1, 2, ..., R_1\} \times \{1, 2, ..., R_2\} \times ... \times \{1, 2, ..., R_N\}$.

We further allow for an Nth-order bias tensor $\Delta \in \mathbb{R}^{I_1 \times I_2 \times \cdots \times I_N}$, so that the parameter tensors θ_m are constrained onto an affine space. Using (2) we get

$$\theta_{m,\mathbf{i}} = \sum_{\mathbf{r} \in \rho} \mathcal{Q}_{m,\mathbf{r}} \cdot \prod_{n=1}^{N} u_{r_n,i_n}^{(n)} + \Delta_{\mathbf{i}}. \tag{6}$$

To get analytical parameter updates in the maximum likelihood framework, we use the the trick of [6] and take advantage of the fact that while the log-likelihood of the constrained model is not convex in the parameters, it is convex in any of these parameters, if the others are fixed. Derivation of the parameter updates is rather involved and (due to space limitations) we refer the interested reader to [5], where details of the derivations, as well as the update formulas can be found.

3.1 Decomposing Unseen Binary Tensors

Note that our model (5-6) is not fully generative (the expansion coefficients are not explicitly governed by a distribution). To decompose an N-th order tensor $\mathcal{A}' \in \{0,1\}^{I_1 \times I_2 \times \cdots \times I_N}$ not included in the training dataset $\mathcal{D}$ we maximize the model log-likelihood with respect to the expansion coefficients $\mathcal{Q}_{\mathbf{r}}$, while keeping the basis vectors and the bias tensor fixed. When using gradient ascent, the updates take the form [5]

$$\mathcal{Q}_{\mathbf{r}} \leftarrow \mathcal{Q}_{\mathbf{r}} + \eta \sum_{\mathbf{i} \in \Upsilon} C_{\mathbf{r},\mathbf{i}} \left[\mathcal{A}'_{\mathbf{i}} - \sigma \left(\sum_{\mathbf{v} \in \rho} \mathcal{Q}_{\mathbf{v}} \, C_{\mathbf{v},\mathbf{i}} + \Delta_{\mathbf{i}} \right) \right], \tag{7}$$

where $C_{\mathbf{r},\mathbf{i}} = \prod_{n=1}^{N} u_{r_n,i_n}^{(n)}$.

4 Experiments

In this section we present two types of experiments designed to evaluate:

(1) the amount of preserved information in compressed tensor representations by decomposing and consequently reconstructing synthetic binary tensors and **(2)** the ability to topographically organize binary tensors representing a real word large-scale dataset of DNA subsequences originating from different functional regions of genomic sequences.

In the experiments we compare our GML-PCA model with an existing real-valued tensor decomposition method (TensorLSI) [2].

4.1 Synthetic Data

We first generated 10 synthetic data sets, each containing 10,000 2nd-order binary tensor of size (250,30). Each data set was sampled from a different Bernoulli natural parameter (linear) subspace determined by 10 randomly generated linearly independent basis tensors. The order and size of the synthetic tensors were selected to match the sizes of tensors representing DNA sub-sequences in the second experiment.

On each synthetic data set, both models (GML-PCA and TensorLSI) were used to find latent subspaces spanned by different number of basis tensors ($L = 1, 2, 4, 6, 8, 10, 15, 20, 30$) using 80% (8,000) of the tensors (training sets). To evaluate the amount of preserved information in the low dimensional representations, tensors in each hold out set (2,000 tensors) were projected onto the reduced-dimensionality latent space (see section 3.1) and then reconstructed back into the original binary tensor space.

Both models yield a real-valued "prediction" for every binary value in tensors to be reconstructed. To evaluate the match between the real-valued "predictions" and the target binary values we employ the area under the ROC curve (AUC). Let $\{x_1, x_2 \ldots x_J\}$ and $\{y_1, y_2 \ldots y_K\}$ represent the model outputs for all nonzero and zero elements of tensors from the test set (targets). The AUC value for that particular prediction (reconstruction) of the test set of tensors can be calculated as a normalized Wilcoxon-Mann-Whitney statistic [7],

$$\text{AUC} = \frac{\sum_{j=1}^{J} \sum_{k=1}^{K} C(x_j, y_k)}{J \cdot K}, \quad C(x_j, y_k) = \begin{cases} 1 & \text{if } x_j > y_k, \\ 0 & \text{otherwise,} \end{cases}$$

where J and K are the total number of nonzero and zero tensor elements in the test set, respectively, and C is a scoring function. Reconstruction results in terms of AUC for different dimensionality of the latent space are shown in figure 1. Higher AUC values imply more accurate reconstructions. Our GML-PCA clearly outperforms TensorLSI in a statistically significant manner.

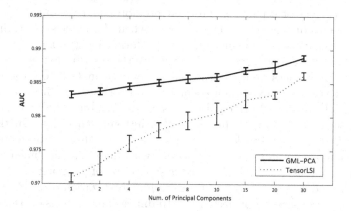

Fig. 1. AUC analysis of hold-out binary tensor reconstructions obtained by GML-PCA and TensorLSI using different tensor subspace dimensionalities. Shown are the means and standard deviations across 10 synthetic data sets.

4.2 Topographic Mapping of DNA Sequences

Current systems for analyzing and predicting promoter regions in DNA sequences are based on the underlying principle that sub-sequences from different
functional regions differ in local term[1] composition [8]. To capture both the term
composition and position, we represent the DNA sequences as binary second-
order tensors $\mathcal{A}$ where rows i_1 represent terms, columns i_2 positions within the
sequence, and the binary tensor element $\mathcal{A}_{i_1,i_2}$ is an indicator whether the sequence represented by $\mathcal{A}$ has a term i_1 at position i_2.

To reveal natural groupings of sub-sequences from different functional regions,
we employ GML-PCA and TensorLSI models to compress their representations
into a principal subspace and visualize their distributions. As a dataset we use
30,964 human promoter sequences of length 250 nucleotides and the same number of intronic sequences (of length 250) employed in [8]. Promoters and introns
represent two different functional regions of DNA. Promoters are special regions
upstream of a gene that contain regulatory binding sites controlling the process
of gene expression. Introns, on the other hand, may contain important control
signals for splicing a gene product.

Terms used in the binary tensor representation of DNA sequences were found
using a suffix tree construction that identified terms that were statistically significant longest words preserving the within-class frequencies [5]. Having identified
31 such terms, each DNA subsequence was represented by a binary 2nd-order
tensor with 31 rows (terms) and 250 columns (positions).

The binary sequence representations were decomposed via TensorLSI using
10 principal tensors and via GML-PCA model using 5 column and 2 row basis
vectors[2]. Such decompositions assign to each sequence a 10-dimensional vector of expansion coefficients. Based on the assumption of different local term
composition of sequences from different functional regions of DNA, one would
expect some level of separation between promoter and intronic sequences in
the principal 10-dimensional subspace, even when the models are trained in a
completely unsupervised manner (no class information (promoter vs. intron)
supplied during the model fitting). To visualize the distribution of sequences in
the principal subspaces we used principal component analysis to project the 10-
dimensional vectors of expansion coefficients onto the three-dimensional space
spanned by the leading 3 principal vectors (figure 2). TensorLSI decomposition
fails to discriminate between promoter and intronic sequences. On the other
hand, GML-PCA analysis clearly separates a large subset of promoters from
intronic sequences. Analyzing the sequences with higher latent dimensionalities
of GML-PCA/TensorLSI did not improve separation of promoters from introns.

For a more detailed analysis of topographic organization of DNA sequences
in the latent subspace we projected the 10-dimensional expansion vectors onto
the two-dimensional principal subspace (see figure 3) and analyzed how the

---

[1] As a term, we denote a short and widespread sequence of nucleotides that has or
may have a biological significance.

[2] For GML-PCA model, outer products of 5 column and 2 row basis vectors give 10
principal tensors, which is equivalent with TensorLSI settings of 10 basis tensors.

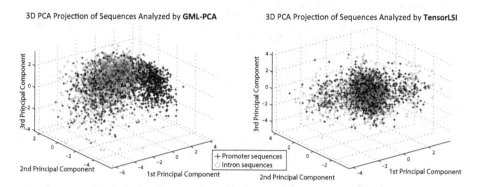

Fig. 2. Three-dimensional PCA projections of 10% randomly sampled promoter and intronic sequences from the tensor space spanned by 10 basis tensors obtained by the GML-PCA (left) and TensorLSI (right)

sequence composition depends on the positions in the two-dimensional plot. The study (not reported here) reveals that well separated promoter sequences from introns have frequent occurrences of CG di-nucleotides around the transcription start sites (TSS). These so-called CpG islands are known to be associated with functional promoter regions-approximately 60% of mammalian genes [9]. On the other hand, intronic sequences from intron-rich regions have a higher concentration of terms GT and AT which are known signals for splicing and are thus expected to occur in introns. We manually selected one intron and two promoter sequences, and in figure 3 visualized their binary tensor representations. In the binary matrices we highlighted important terms (marked with black dots) that have a strong influence on the sequence position. Well separated and "close" promoters (P-1,P-2) have similar term composition structure and higher occurrences of terms (GGCG and GCG) that contain di-nucleotids CG. On the other hand, the intron (I-1) is characterized by high occurrences of terms GT and AT.

To further investigate the relevance of topographic mapping of DNA sequences by GML-PCA, we searched the compressed feature space for biologically relevant structure. Genes that are transcribed by the same factors are often functionally similar [10]. Carrying specific biologically relevant features, suitable representations of promoters should correlate with the roles assigned to their genes. If the topographic mapping highlights such features, it is an indication that our method can be valuable for screening of biological sequences in terms of their biological function. To assign biologically meaningful labels to promoters, all sequences were mapped to gene identifiers using the Gene Ontology (GO; [11]). We could assign zero or more GO terms (labels) to each promoter sequence. In total there are 8051 unique GO terms annotating 14619 promoters.

To evaluate whether promoters deemed similar by GML-PCA are also functionally similar, we need a methodology for calculating a "distance" between each pair of promoters. Euclidean distance between the 10-dimensional expansion vectors is not appropriate as a distance measure for two reasons: first, the basis

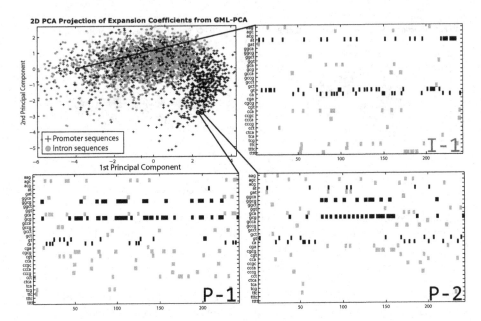

Fig. 3. Detailed visualization of second-order binary tensors for manually selected promoter and intron sequences. Important terms that have a strong influence on the sequence coordinates in the top left 2D plot are marked with black dots.

tensors are not orthogonal; second, they span a subspace of Bernoulli natural parameters that have a nonlinear relationship with the data values. To determinate the model-based 'distance' between two promoter sequences m and l in a principled manner, we calculated the sum of average symmetrized Kullback-Leibler divergences between noise distributions for all corresponding tensor elements $\mathbf{i} \in \Upsilon$:

$$\mathrm{D}(m,l) = \sum_{\mathbf{i} \in \Upsilon} \left(\frac{\mathrm{KL}[p_{m,\mathbf{i}} \| p_{l,\mathbf{i}}] + \mathrm{KL}[p_{l,\mathbf{i}} \| p_{m,\mathbf{i}}]}{2} \right),$$

where KL represents the KL divergence between two Bernoulli distributions defined by their means $p_{m,\mathbf{i}}$ and $p_{l,\mathbf{i}}$.

The following test aims to analyze if the compressed tensorial promoter representations are biologically meaningful. For each labeled promoter m in the dataset, we label the group of all promoters l within a pre-specified distance $\mathrm{D}(m,l) < \mathrm{D}_0$ as "positives" and all others as "negatives".

In the tests we consistently use a distance of $\mathrm{D}_0 = 25$, usually rendering over one hundred "positives". For each GO term that was assigned at least to one promoter, Fisher's exact test resolves if it occurs more often amongst "positives" than would be expected by chance. The null hypothesis is that the GO term is not attributed more often than by chance to the topological neighborhood "positives". A small p-value indicates that the term is "enriched" at the position of the reference promoter m. We adjust for multiple hypothesis testing and set the threshold at which to report a term as significant accordingly ($p < 5 \cdot 10^{-7}$). To understand the tendency of false discovery, we also repeated the tests (with the same significance threshold) after shuffling the points assigned to promoters. Re-assuringly, in no case did this permutation test identify a single GO term as significant.

In total, at the given level of significance, we found 75 GO terms that were locally enriched around one or more reference promoters in the two-dimensional plot of promoters shown in figure 3. The observation that a subset of promoter sequences are functionally organized after decomposition into 10 basis tensors adds support to the methods' ability to detect variation at an information-rich level. More specifically, we find a number of terms that are specifically concerned with chromatin structure (that packages the DNA), e.g. GO:000786 "Nucleosome", GO:0006333 "Chromatin assembly or disassembly" and GO:0065004 "Protein-DNA complex assembly". Interestingly, we found several enriched terms related to development, e.g. GO:0022414 "Reproductive process" and GO:0007565 "Female pregnancy". Anecdotally, we note that CpG islands (that are clearly distinct in the promoter sequence data) are associated with open DNA, leading to constitutive gene expression.

5 Conclusion

Traditionally, dimensionality reduction is formulated on vectorial data. However, an increasing number of practical applications involves manipulation of tensors. In order to apply methods developed for vectorial data to tensors, one is forced to break the natural higher order tensor structure and reshape the tensors into vectors. Moreover, many real world problems involve data in the form of binary tensors. At present, there is no systematic framework for processing tensors with binary values.

We have introduced a novel generalized multilinear model for principal component analysis of binary tensors (GML-PCA). The model is designed to account for binary nature of the data by modeling the tensor elements with Bernoulli noise distribution and constraining their natural parameters to lie in a subspace spanned by a reduced set of principal tensors.

In two experiments we have shown that our GML-PCA model is better suited for modeling binary tensors than the existing real-valued tensor decomposition method (TensorLSI). In the first experiment, synthetic binary tensors were compressed and consequently reconstructed, yielding the reconstruction error in terms of AUC. In the second second experiment, we compare the ability to reveal biologically meaningful dominant trends in a real world large-scale dataset of DNA sequences represented through binary second-order tensors. Experimentation with higher-order binary tensors is a matter for future work and the results will be published elsewhere.

Acknowledgments. J. Mažgut was supported by the Scientific Grant Agency of Republic of Slovakia, grant No. VEGA 1/0508/09. P. Tiňo was supported by the DfES UK/Hong Kong Fellowship for Excellence. M. Bodén was supported by the ARC Centre of Excellence in Bioinformatics and the 2009 University of Birmingham Ramsay Research Scholarship Award. H. Yan was supported by a grant from the Hong Kong Research Grant Council (Project CITYU123809).

References

1. Lu, H., Plataniotis, K.N., Venetsanopoulos, A.N.: MPCA: Multilinear Principal Component Analysis of Tensor Objects. IEEE Trans. on Neural Networks 19, 18–39 (2008)
2. Cai, D., He, X., Han, J.: Tensor Space Model for Document Analysis. In: Proc. 29th Annu. ACM SIGIR Int. Conf. Research and Development in Information Retrieval, Seatlle, WA, pp. 625–626 (August 2006)
3. De Lathauwer, L., De Moor, B., Vandewalle, J.: A Multilinear Singular Value Decomposition. SIAM Journal on Matrix Analysis and Applications 21(4), 1253–1278 (2000)
4. Wang, H., Ahuja, N.: Compact Representation of Multidimensional Data Using Tensor Rank-One Decomposition. In: Proc. 17th Int. Conf. Pattern Recognition, Cambridge, UK, pp. 44–47 (August 2004)
5. Mažgut, J., Tiňo, P., Bodén, M., Yan, H.: Generalized Multi-Linear Principal Component Analysis of Binary Tensors. Technical Report CSRP-07-10, University of Birmingham, School of Computer Science, UK (2010), http://www.cs.bham.ac.uk/~pxt/PAPERS/bin_tensor_tr.pdf
6. Schein, A., Saul, L., Ungar, L.: A Generalized Linear Model for Principal Component Analysis of Binary Data. In: 9th Int. Workshop Artificial Intelligence and Statistics, Key West, FL (January 2003)
7. Cortes, C., Mohri, M.: AUC Optimization vs. Error Rate Minimization. In: Advances in Neural Information Processing Systems, Banff, AL, Canada, vol. 16, pp. 313–320 (July 2003)
8. Li, X., Zeng, J., Yan, H.: PCA-HPR: A Principle Component Analysis Model for Human Promoter Recognition. Bioinformation 2(9), 373–378 (2008)
9. Cross, S., Clark, V., Bird, A.: Isolation of CpG islands from large genomic clones. Nucleic Acids Res. 27(10), 2099–2107 (1999)
10. Bodén, M., Bailey, T.L.: Associating transcription factor-binding site motifs with target GO terms and target genes. Nucleic Acids Res. 36(12), 4108–4117 (2008)
11. Ashburner, M., Ball, C.A., Blake, J.A., Botstein, D., Butler, H., Cherry, J.M., Davis, A.P., Dolinski, K., Dwight, S.S., Eppig, J.T., Harris, M.A., Hill, D.P., Issel-Tarver, L., Kasarskis, A., Lewis, S., Matese, J.C., Richardson, J.E., Ringwald, M., Rubin, G.M., Sherlock, G.: Gene Ontology: tool for the unification of biology. The Gene Ontology Consortium. Nature Genetics 25(1), 25–29 (2000)

Evolutionary q-Gaussian Radial Basis Functions for Improving Prediction Accuracy of Gene Classification Using Feature Selection

Francisco Fernández-Navarro[1], César Hervás-Martínez[1], Pedro A. Gutiérrez[1], Roberto Ruiz[2], and José C. Riquelme[3]

[1] Department of Computer Science and Numerical Analysis, University of Cordoba, Rabanales Campus, Albert Einstein building 3 floor, 14071, Córdoba, Spain
[2] Area of Computer Science, Pablo de Olavide University, School of Engineering, Spain
[3] Department of Computer Science, University of Seville, Avda. Reina Mercedes s/n. 41012 Seville, Spain

Abstract. This paper proposes a Radial Basis Function Neural Network (RBFNN) which reproduces different Radial Basis Functions (RBFs) by means of a real parameter q, named q-Gaussian RBFNN. The architecture, weights and node topology are learnt through a Hybrid Algorithm (HA) with the $iRprop+$ algorithm as the local improvement procedure. In order to test its overall performance, an experimental study with four gene microarray datasets with two classes taken from bioinformatic and biomedical domains is presented. The Fast Correlation–Based Filter (FCBF) was applied in order to identify salient expression genes from thousands of genes in microarray data that can directly contribute to determining the class membership of each pattern. After different gene subsets were obtained, the proposed methodology was performed using the selected gene subsets as the new input variables. The results confirm that the q-Gaussian RBFNN classifier leads to promising improvement on accuracy.

1 Introduction

The importance of the use of Artificial Neural Networks (ANNs) in the classification of microarray gene expression as an alternative to other techniques was stated in serveral research works [1,2] due to their flexibility and high degree of accuracy to fit to experimental data. In this work, we focus on Radial Basis Function Neural Networks (RBFNNs) which have been succesfully employed in different pattern recognition problems including the classification of microarray gene [2].

In high-dimensional space, the distances to the nearest and furthest neighbours look nearly identical. Therefore, in this kind of problem, the distances are concentrated and the Gaussian kernel looses its interpretation in terms of locality around its centre [3]. For that reason, we propose a novelty RBF based on

K. Diamantaras, W. Duch, L.S. Iliadis (Eds.): ICANN 2010, Part I, LNCS 6352, pp. 327–336, 2010.

the q-Gaussian Distribution which parametrize the standard Normal distribution by replacing the exponential expressions for q-exponential expressions, and maximizing Tsallis entropy [4] under certain constraints [5]. This novelty basis function incorporates a real parameter q (besides the centers and width of the RBF) which can relax or contract the shape of the kernel. This basis function matches better the shape of the kernel and the distribution of the distances, since the modification of the q parameter allows representing different basis functions (Cauchy RBF, Gaussian RBF, etc). Due to severe ill-conditioning of the coefficient matrix of the q-Gaussian RBF, a Hybrid Evolutionary Algorithm (HEA) based on heuristics is employed to select the parameters of the model.

The motivation for applying feature selection (FS) techniques has shifted from being an optional subject to becoming a real prerequisite for model building. The main reason is the high–dimensional nature of many modelling task in this field. A typical microarray dataset may contain thousands of genes but only a small number of samples (often less than two hundred).

Based on the generation procedure, FS can be divided into individual feature ranking (FR) and feature subset selection (FSS). FR measures the feature-class relevance, then rank features by their scores and select the top–ranked ones. In contrast, FSS attempts to find a set of features with good performance. Hybrid models were proposed to handle large datasets to take advantage of the above two approaches (FR, FSS). In this work, the relevant features were obtained by the Fast Correlation–Based Filter (FCBF), a hybrid approach proposed in [6].

One of the major advantages of the proposed method is the reduced number of features and q-Gaussian RBFs included in the final expression, since the HEA reduces its complexity by pruning connections and removing hidden nodes. Therefore, using the proposed approach, the feature selection is performed in two stages: Firstly, in the preprocessing by means of the features selector and secondly, in the HEA by pruning connections.

This paper is organized as follows: Section 2 formally presents the q-Gaussian RBF model considered in this work and the main characteristics of the algorithm used for training the model. Section 3 introduces the feature selection algorithm used in this paper. Section 4 describes the experiments carried out and discusses the results obtained. Finally, Section 5 completes the paper with the main conclusions and future directions suggested by this study.

2   Classification Method

2.1   Related Works

A RBFNN is a three-layer feed-forward neural network. Let the number of nodes of the input layer, of the hidden layer and of the output layer be p, m and 1 respectively. For any sample $\mathbf{x} = [x_1, x_2, \ldots, x_p]$, the output of the RBFNN is $f(\mathbf{x})$. The model of a RBFNN can be described with the following equation:

$$f(\mathbf{x}) = \beta_0 + \sum_{i=1}^{m} \beta_i \cdot \phi_i(d_i(\mathbf{x})) \tag{1}$$

where $\phi_i(d_i(\mathbf{x}))$ is a non-linear mapping from the input layer to the hidden layer, $\boldsymbol{\beta} = (\beta_1, \beta_2, \ldots, \beta_m)$ is the connection weight between the hidden layer and the output layer, and β_0 is the bias. The function $d_i(\mathbf{x})$ can be defined as:

$$d_i(\mathbf{x}) = \frac{\|\mathbf{x} - \mathbf{c}_i\|^2}{\theta_i^2} \tag{2}$$

where θ_i is the scalar parameter that defines the width for the i-th radial unit, $\|.\|$ represents the Euclidean norm and $\mathbf{c_i} = [c_1, c_2, \ldots, c_p]$ the center of the RBFs. The standard RBF (SRBF) is the Gaussian function, which is given by:

$$\phi_i(d_i(\mathbf{x})) = e^{-d_i(\mathbf{x})}, \tag{3}$$

The radial basis function $\phi_i(d_i(\mathbf{x}))$ can take different forms, including the Cauchy RBF (CRBF) or the Inverse Multiquadratic RBF (IMRBF). Fig. 1a ilustrates the influence of the choice of the RBF in the hidden unit activation. One can observe that the Gaussian function presents a higher activation close to the radial unit center than the other two RBFs. In this paper, we propose the use of the q-Gaussian function as RBF. This basis function is obtained by replacing the exponential expression of the SRBF for a q-exponential expression [5]. The q-Gaussian can be defined as:

$$\phi_i(d_i(\mathbf{x})) = \begin{cases} (1 - (1-q)d_i(\mathbf{x}))^{\frac{1}{1-q}} & \text{if } (1 - (1-q)d_i(\mathbf{x})) \geq 0 \\ 0 & \text{Otherwise.} \end{cases} \tag{4}$$

The q-Gaussian can reproduce different RBFs for different values of the real parameter q. As an example, when the q parameter is close to 2, the q-Gaussian is the CRBF, for $q = 3$, the activation of a radial unit with an IMRBF for $d_i(\mathbf{x})$ turns out to be equal to the activation of a radial unit with a q-Gaussian RBF for $d_i(\mathbf{x})/2$ and, finally, when the value of q converges to 1, the q-Gaussian converges to the Gaussian function (SRBF). Fig. 1b presents the radial unit activation for the q-Gaussian RBF for different values of q.

2.2 q-Gaussian RBF for Classification

To construct a probabilistic classification model, we consider a RBFNNs with softmax outputs and the standard structure: an input layer with a node for every input variable; a hidden layer with several RBFs; and an output layer with 1 node. There are no connections between the nodes of a layer and none between the input and output layers either. The activation function of the i-th node in the hidden layer $(\phi_i(d_i(\mathbf{x})))$ is given by Eq. 4 and the activation function of the output node $(f(\mathbf{x}))$ is defined in Eq 1. The transfer function of all output nodes is the identity function.

In this work, the outputs of the neurons are interpreted from the point of view of probability through the use of the softmax activation function.

$$g(\mathbf{x}) = \frac{\exp f(\mathbf{x})}{1 + \exp f(\mathbf{x})} \tag{5}$$

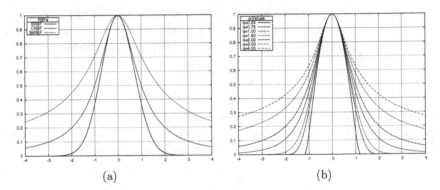

Fig. 1. Radial unit activation in one-dimensional space with $c = 0$ and $\theta = 1$ for different RBFs: (a) SBRF, CRBF and IMRBF and (b) q-Gaussian with different values of q

where $g(\mathbf{x})$ is the probability that a pattern $\mathbf{x}$ belongs to class 1. The probability a pattern $\mathbf{x}$ has of belonging to class 2 is $1 - g(\mathbf{x})$.

The error surface associated with the model is very convoluted. Thus, the parameters of the RBFNNs are estimated by means of a HEA (detailed in Section 2.3). The HEA was developed to optimize the error function given by the negative log-likelihood for N observations, which is defined for a classifier g:

$$l(g) = \frac{1}{N} \sum_{n=1}^{N} [-y_n f(\mathbf{x}_n) + \log \exp f(\mathbf{x}_n)] \tag{6}$$

where y_n is the class that the pattern n belongs to.

2.3   Hybrid Evolutionary Algorithm

The basic framework of the HEA is the following: the search begins with an initial population of RBFNNs and, in each iteration, the population is updated using a population-update algorithm which evolves both its structure and weights. The population is subject to operations of replication and mutation. We consider $l(g)$ as the error function of an individual of the population. The fitness measure needed for evaluating the individuals is a strictly decreasing transformation of the error function $l(g)$ given by $A(g) = \frac{1}{1+l(g)}$, where $0 < A(g) \leq 1$. Figure 2 describes the procedure to select the parameters of the radial units. The main characteristics of the algorithm are the following:

1. *Initialization of the Population.* First, $5,000$ random RBFNNs are generated. The centers of the radial units are firstly defined by the k-means algorithm for different values of k, where $k \in [M_{min}, M_{max}]$, being M_{min} and M_{max} the minimum and maximum number of hidden nodes allowed for any RBFNN model. The widths of the RBFNNs are initialized to the geometric mean of

1: **Hybrid Algorithm**:
2: Generate a random population of size N
3: **repeat**
4:    Calculate the fitness of every individual in the population
5:    Rank the individuals with respect to their fitness
6:    The best individual is copied into the new population
7:    The best 10% of population individuals are replicated and they substitute the worst 10% of individuals
8:    Apply parametric mutation to the best (p_m)% of individuals
9:    Apply structural mutation to the remaining $(100 - p_m)$% of individuals
10: **until** the stopping criterion is fulfilled
11: Apply *iRprop+* to the best solution obtained by the EA in the last generation.

Fig. 2. Hybrid Algorithm (HA) framework

the distance to the two nearest neighbours and the q parameter to values near to 1, since when $q \to 1$ the q-Gaussian reduces to the standard Gaussian RBFNN. A random value in the $[-I, I]$ interval is assigned for the weights between the hidden layer and the output layer. Finally, the initial population is obtained by selecting the best 500 RBFNNs.

2. *Parametric and Structural Mutations.* Parametric mutation consists of a simulated annealing algorithm. Structural mutation implies a modification in the structure of the RBFNNs. There are four different structural mutations: hidden node addition, hidden node deletion, connection addition and connection deletion. More information about genetic operators proposed can be seen in [7,8]. It is important to describe the structural and parametric mutations of the q parameter:

   - Structural Mutation: If the structural mutator adds a new node in the RBFNN, the q parameter is assigned to 1, since when $q = 1$ the q-Gaussian RBF reproduce to the Gaussian RBF.
   - Parametric Mutation: The q parameter is updated by adding a ε value, where $\varepsilon \in [-0.25, 0.25]$, since the modification of the q-Gaussian is very sensible to q variation.

3. *iRprop+ Local Optimizer.* The local optimization algorithm used in our paper is the *iRprop+* [9] optimization method. In the proposed methodology, we run the EA and then apply the local optimization algorithm to the best solution obtained by the EA in the last generation.

3   Feature Selection: Fast Correlation–Based Filter (FCBF)

The limitations of FR and FSS approaches in high-dimensional spaces, clearly suggest the need for a hybrid model. The FCBF method can be labelled as this kind of framework, Hybrid–Generation Feature Selection.

In feature subset selection, it is a fact that two types of features are generally perceived as being unnecessary: features that are irrelevant to the target concept, and features that are redundant given other features.

Notions of feature redundancy are normally in terms of feature correlation. It is widely accepted that two features are redundant to each other if their values are completely correlated. There are two widely used types of measures for the correlation between two variables: linear and non–linear. In the linear case, the Pearson correlation coefficient is used, and in the non–linear case, many measures are based on the concept of entropy, or measure of the uncertainty of a random variable. Symmetrical uncertainty (SU) is frequently used, defined as

$$SU(\mathbf{x}, \mathbf{y}) = 2 \left[\frac{IG(\mathbf{x}|\mathbf{y})}{H(\mathbf{x}) + H(\mathbf{y})} \right]$$

where $H(\mathbf{x}) = -\sum_i^p p(x_i) \log_2(p(x_i))$ is the entropy of a variable $\mathbf{x}$ and $IG(\mathbf{x}|\mathbf{y}) = H(\mathbf{x}) - H(\mathbf{x}|\mathbf{y})$ is the information gain from $\mathbf{x}$ provided by $\mathbf{y}$. Both of them are between pairs of variables. However, it may not be as straightforward in determining feature redundancy when one is correlated with a set of features. [10] apply a technique based on cross–entropy, named Markov blanket filtering, to eliminate redundant features.

FCBF calculates SU–correlation between any feature F_i and the class C generating a list in descending order, and heuristically decides a feature F_i to be relevant if it is highly correlated with the class C, i.e., if $SU_{i,c} > \delta$, where δ is a relevance threshold which can be determined by users. The selected relevant features are then subject to redundancy analysis. Similarly, FCBF evaluates the SU–correlation between individual features for redundancy analysis based on an approximate Markov blanket concept. For two relevant features F_i and F_j ($i \neq j$), F_j can be eliminated if $SU_{i,c} \geq SU_{j,c}$ and $SU_{i,j} \geq SU_{j,c}$. The iteration starts from the first element in the ranking and continues as follows. For all the remaining features, if F_i happens to form an approximate Markov blanket for F_j, F_j will be removed from list. After one round of filtering features based on F_i, the algorithm will take the remaining feature right next to F_i as the new reference to repeat the filtering process. The algorithm stops until no more features can be eliminated.

4 Experiments

This section presents the experimental results and analysis of q-Gaussian RBF models on 4 public microarray datasets with high dimensionality/small sample size and two classes (Table 1). At the beginning, the datasets and several machine learning algorithms used in this analysis are briefly described. Subsequently, experimental results are given and discussed from different aspects.

4.1 Microarray Data

These datasets were taken from bioinformatic and biomedical domains. They are often used to validate the performance of classifiers and gene selectors. Due

Table 1. Characteristics of the four datasets used for the experiments: number of instances (Size), number of Real (R), Binary (B) and Nominal (N) input variables, total number of inputs (#In.), number of classes (#Out.), per-class distribution of the instances (Distribution) and the number of generations (#Gen.)

Dataset	Source	Size	R	B	N	In	Out	Distribution	*Gen*
Breast	Van't Veer et al [11]	97	493	-	-	493	2	(46,51)	100
CNS	Pomeroy et al [12]	60	170	-	-	170	2	(21,39)	10
Colon	Alon et al [13]	62	59	-	-	59	2	(40,22)	10
Leukemia	Golub et al [14]	72	203	-	-	203	2	(42,25)	50

Table 2. Comparison of the proposed method to other probabilistic methods: Results of accuracy ($C_G(\%)$), Root Mean Square Error ($RMSE_G$) and Area Under Curve (AUC_G) on the generalization set

Dataset	Metric	RBFN Result	MLogistic Result	SLogistic Result	C4.5 Result	LMT Result	SVM Result	QRBF *Mean ± std*
Breast	C	80.00	*84.00*	*84.00*	64.00	*84.00*	76.00	**85.00 ± 3.05**
CNS	C	86.66	**100.00**	80.00	60.00	80.00	66.67	*97.38 ± 1.02*
Colon	C	**87.50**	75.00	81.25	75.00	75.00	62.50	*85.35 ± 2.06*
Leukemia	C	*94.44*	*94.44*	83.33	83.33	83.33	66.67	**100.00 ± 0.00**
Breast	AUC	0.85	*0.91*	**0.96**	0.71	**0.96**	0.81	0.88 ± 0.08
CNS	AUC	0.78	**1.00**	0.78	0.58	0.78	0.50	*0.93 ± 0.03*
Colon	AUC	*0.86*	0.75	**0.90**	0.70	**0.90**	0.50	0.83 ± 0.12
Leukemia	AUC	*0.95*	*0.95*	0.80	0.83	0.80	0.50	**1.00 ± 0.00**
Breast	RMSE	0.41	0.37	*0.34*	0.57	*0.34*	0.42	**0.32 ± 0.02**
CNS	RMSE	0.37	**0.00**	0.46	0.61	0.46	0.47	*0.23 ± 0.05*
Colon	RMSE	*0.33*	0.50	0.36	0.48	0.39	0.49	**0.29 ± 0.08**
Leukemia	RMSE	*0.23*	*0.23*	0.40	0.39	0.40	0.47	**0.00 ± 0.00**

The best result is in bold face and the second best result in italics.

to high dimensionality and small sample size, gene selection is an essential prerequisite for further data analysis. The selected datasets were: Breast [11], CNS [12], Colon [13] and Leukemia [14]. In these 4 microarray datasets, all expression values of genes are reals. For convenience, they were standarized before our experiments, that is, for each represented gene, its mean and standard deviation were zero and one, respectively, after the standarized operation had been performed. Finally, in the preprocessing stage, the number of features was reduced by means of the FCBF feature selector.

4.2 Alternative Statistical and Artificial Intelligence Methods Used for Comparison Purposes

Different state-of-the-art Statistical and Artificial Intelligence algorithms have been implemented for comparison purposes. Specifically, the results of the following algorithms have been compared with the q-Gaussian RBF (QRBF) model presented in this paper:

1. A Gaussian Radial Basis Function Network (RBFN), deriving the centres and width of hidden units using k-means, and combining the outputs obtained from the hidden layer using logistic regression.
2. The MultiLogistic (MLogistic) algorithm. It is a method for building a multinomial logistic regression model with a ridge estimator to guard against overfitting by penalizing large coefficients.
3. The SimpleLogistic (SLogistic) algorithm. It is based on applying LogitBoost algorithm with simple regression functions and determining the optimum number of iterations by a five fold cross-validation.
4. The C4.5 classification tree inducer.
5. The Logistic Model Tree (LMT) classifier.
6. The Support Vector Machine (SVM) classifier with RBF kernels.

These algorithms have been selected because many of these approaches have also been tested before in the classification problem of microarray gene expression. The detailed description and some previous results of these methods can be found in [15].

4.3 Experimental Design

The evaluation of the different models has been performed using three different measures: Correctly Classified Rate (C) or accuracy, Root Mean Square Error ($RMSE$) and Area Under the ROC Curve (AUC) because they have been identified as three of the most commonly used metric to determine the performance of a classifier [16]. C represents threshold metrics, AUC is a probability metric, and $RMSE$ is a rank metric.

All the parameters used in the HA (Section 2.3) except the number of generations ($\#Gen$) have the same values in all problems analyzed below (Table 1). The maximun and minimun number of RBFs in the hidden layer ($[M_{\min}, M_{\max}]$) is $[1,3]$. The connections between hidden and output layer are initialized in the $[-5,5]$ interval (i.e. $[-I, I] = [-5, 5]$). The size of the population is $N = 500$.

For the selection of the SVM hyperparameters (regularization parameter, C, and width of the Gaussian functions, γ), a grid search algorithm has been applied with a ten-fold cross-validation, using the following ranges: $C \in \{2^{-5}, 2^{-3}, \dots, 2^{15}\}$ and $\gamma \in \{2^{-15}, 2^{-13}, \dots, 2^{3}\}$.

The experimental design was conducted using a holdout cross validation procedure with $3n/4$ instances for the training dataset and $n/4$ instances for the generalization dataset. In order to evaluate the stability of the methods, the evolutionary algorithm is run 30 times.

The HA and the model proposed was implemented in JAVA. We also used "libsvm" [17] to obtain the results of the SVM method, and WEKA to obtain the results of the remaining methods.

4.4   Results

Table 2 shows the results of the correct classification rate (C_G), Root Mean Square Error ($RMSE_G$) and Area Under the ROC Curve (AUC_G) in the generalization set for each dataset and the RBFN, MLogistic, SLogistic, C4.5, LMT, SVM and QRBF methods.

From the analysis of the results, it can be concluded, from a purely descriptive point of view, that the QRBF model obtained the best results for two datasets in C_G, for one datasets in AUC_G and for three datasets in $RMSE_G$. Importantly, the perfect classification is obtained with the best QRBF model for leukemia dataset. The results confirm that the QRBF classifier leads to promising improvement on accuracy.

Finally, since the proposed model (QRBF) is stochastic and the remaining classifiers are deterministic, the use of statistical tests for comparison of means or ranking would not make much sense.

5   Conclusions

In this paper, we propose a methodology (composed by two stages) for microarray gene classification that allows reducing the number of features of thousands to tens. This reduction of features is obtained by applying the FCBF feature selector algorithm, in the preprocessing stage and by means of performing the operations of remove connections and hidden nodes that incorporates the Hybrid Evolutionary Algorithm (HEA) which evolves the proposed base classifier, namely q-Gaussian Radial Basis Function Neural Networks. The proposed methodology achieved for the best models, the best results in C_G over all datasets, which justifies the proposal.

Finally, because of the reduced number of features that included the best models, it is possible to interpret them and then analyze the causal relationship between gene characteristics and the probability of belonging to each class.

Acknowledgement

This work has been partially subsidized by the TIN 2008-06681-C06-03 project of the Spanish Inter-Ministerial Commission of Science and Technology (MICYT), FEDER funds and the P08-TIC-3745 project of the "Junta de Andalucía" (Spain). The research of Francisco Fernández-Navarro has been funded by the "Junta de Andalucia" Predoctoral Program, grant reference P08-TIC-3745.

References

1. Lancashire, L.J., Powe, D.G., Reis-Filho, J.S., Rakha, E., Lemetre, C., Weigelt, B., Abdel-Fatah, T.M., Green, A.R., Mukta, R., Blamey, R., Paish, E.C., Rees, R.C., Ellis, I.O., Ball, G.R.: A validated gene expression profile for detecting clinical outcome in breast cancer using artificial neural networks. Breast cancer research and treatment 120(1), 83–93 (2010)

2. Chu, F., Wang, L.: Applying rbf neural networks to cancer classification based on gene expressions. In: IEEE International Conference on Neural Networks - Conference Proceedings, pp. 1930–1934 (2006)

3. Verleysen, M., François, D., Simon, G., Wertz, V.: On the effects of dimensionality on data analysis with neural networks. In: Mira, J., Álvarez, J.R. (eds.) IWANN 2003. LNCS, vol. 2687, II105–II112. Springer, Heidelberg (2003)

4. Tsallis, C.: Possible generalization of boltzmann-gibbs statistics. Journal of Statistical Physics 52(1-2), 479–487 (1988)

5. Tsallis, C., Mendes, R.S., Plastino, A.R.: The role of constraints within generalized nonextensive statistics. Physica A: Statistical Mechanics and its Applications 261(3-4), 534–554 (1998)

6. Yu, L., Liu, H.: Efficient feature selection via analysis of relevance and redundancy. Journal of machine learning research 5, 1205–1224 (2004)

7. Martínez-Estudillo, A.C., Martínez-Estudilo, F.J., Hervás-Martínez, C., Garcá, N.: Evolutionary product unit based neural networks for regression. Neural Networks 19(4), 477–486 (2006)

8. Hervás-Martínez, C., Martínez-Estudillo, F.J., Carbonero-Ruz, M.: Multilogistic regression by means of evolutionary product-unit neural networks. Neural Networks 21(7), 951–961 (2008)

9. Igel, C., Hüsken, M.: Empirical evaluation of the improved rprop learning algorithms. Neurocomputing 50(6), 105–123 (2003)

10. Koller, D., Sahami, M.: Toward optimal feature selection. In: 13th Int. Conf. on Machine Learning, pp. 284–292 (1996)

11. Van't Veer, L.J., Dai, H., Van de Vijver, M.J., He, Y.D., Hart, A.A.M., Mao, M., Peterse, H.L., Van Der Kooy, K., Marton, M.J., Witteveen, A.T., Schreiber, G.J., Kerkhoven, R.M., Roberts, C., Linsley, P.S., Bernards, R., Friend, S.H.: Gene expression profiling predicts clinical outcome of breast cancer. Nature 415(6871), 530–536 (2002)

12. Pomeroy, S.L., Tamayo, P., Gaasenbeek, M., Sturla, L.M., Angelo, M., McLaughlin, M.E., Kim, J.Y.H., Goumnerova, L.C., Black, P.M., Lau, C., Allen, J.C., Zagzag, D., Olson, J.M., Curran, T., Wetmore, C., Biegel, J.A., Poggio, T., Mukherjee, S., Rifkin, R., Califano, A., Stolovitzky, G., Louis, D.N., Mesirov, J.P., Lander, E.S., Golub, T.R.: Prediction of central nervous system embryonal tumour outcome based on gene expression. Nature 415(6870), 436–442 (2002)

13. Alon, U., Barka, N., Notterman, D.A., Gish, K., Ybarra, S., Mack, D., Levine, A.J.: Broad patterns of gene expression revealed by clustering analysis of tumor and normal colon tissues probed by oligonucleotide arrays. Proceedings of the National Academy of Sciences of the United States of America 96(12), 6745–6750 (1999)

14. Golub, T.R., Slonim, D.K., Tamayo, P., Huard, C., Gaasenbeek, M., Mesirov, J.P., Coller, H., Loh, M.L., Downing, J.R., Caligiuri, M.A., Bloomfield, C.D., Lander, E.S.: Molecular classification of cancer: Class discovery and class prediction by gene expression monitoring. Science 286(5439), 527–531 (1999)

15. Witten, I.H., Frank, E.: Data Mining: Practical Machine Learning Tools and Techniques, Data Management Systems, 2nd edn. Morgan Kaufmann, Elsevier (2005)

16. Sokolova, M., Lapalme, G.: A systematic analysis of performance measures for classification tasks. Information Processing and Management 45, 427–437 (2009)

17. Chang, C., Lin, C.: Libsvm: a library for support vector machines (2001)

Sparse Coding for Feature Selection on Genome-Wide Association Data

Ingrid Brænne[1,2,3,*], Kai Labusch[1], and Amir Madany Mamlouk[1,3]

[1] Institute for Neuro- and Bioinformatics
[2] Medizinische Klinik II
[3] Graduate School for Computing in Medicine and Life Sciences
University of Lübeck,
Ratzeburger Allee 160, 23563 Lübeck, Germany
{labusch,braenne,madany}@inb.uni-luebeck.de
http://www.inb.uni-luebeck.de

Abstract. Genome-wide association (GWA) studies provide large amounts of high-dimensional data. GWA studies aim to identify variables that increase the risk for a given phenotype. Univariate examinations have provided some insights, but it appears that most diseases are affected by interactions of multiple factors, which can only be identified through a multivariate analysis. However, multivariate analysis on the discrete, high-dimensional and low-sample-size GWA data is made more difficult by the presence of random effects and nonspecific coupling. In this work, we investigate the suitability of three standard techniques (p-values, SVM, PCA) for analyzing GWA data on several simulated datasets. We compare these standard techniques against a sparse coding approach; we demonstrate that sparse coding clearly outperforms the other approaches and can identify interacting factors in far higher-dimensional datasets than the other three approaches.

Keywords: Sparse Coding, GWA, SNP, Feature Selection, Machine Learning.

1 Introduction

Genome-wide association (GWA) studies provide large amounts of high-dimensional genotype data. The aim of these studies is to reveal the genetic factors that explain an increase in risk e.g. for myocardial infarction. Modern GWA techniques can simultaneously genotype over one million single nucleotide polymorphisms (SNPs) for a human genome and thus enable extensive comparisons between groups with and without a specific phenotype. There is a growing body of studies – mainly focusing on single-SNP statistics (p-values) – that have identified genetic loci influencing the risk of complex diseases such as diabetes [1], myocardial infarction [2,3], and Crohn's disease [4].

---

* Corresponding author.

K. Diamantaras, W. Duch, L.S. Iliadis (Eds.): ICANN 2010, Part I, LNCS 6352, pp. 337–346, 2010.
© Springer-Verlag Berlin Heidelberg 2010

To date, however, these findings have had only limited impact on risk assessment and clinical treatments [5]. This is probably due to the fact that a disease effect may come about only through the interaction of multiple loci. A search for single-locus effects alone is not likely to reveal the more complex genetic mechanisms underlying multifactorial traits [1,6,7]. Analyzing the enormous GWA datasets for more than just single effects is however not straightforward: Not only are we dealing with extremely high-dimensional data (typically hundreds of thousands of genetic loci), we also face the additional challenge of having a relatively small sample size, as even large GWA datasets typically consist of only several thousands of individuals (see e.g. [8]). A further challenge is that, most likely, not all of the affected individuals (cases) consistently express the same characteristic disease pattern, making the search for these patterns even more difficult.

A standard approach for classification and multivariate feature selection is the support vector machine (SVM)[9,10]. SVMs have successfully been applied in several GWA studies [1,11,12]. However, because we are searching for small subgroups of individuals with similar genetic patterns rather than looking for a perfect two-class classification, the SVM might not be the most appropriate method.

Principal component analysis (PCA), one of the most commonly used feature selection methods, has also been used in a number of GWA studies. In these studies, however, PCA was primarily used not for feature selection but to correct for population stratification [13,14,15]. In datasets with a large number of SNPs, PCA may not be able to identify the disease-specific patterns due to the presence of a large number of randomly formed patterns. It would therefore be desirable to use a feature selection method that is more robust against noise.

In this work, we propose Sparse Coding (SC) as such a feature selection method. We will compare SC against the standard techniques described above (single-SNP statistics, SVM, PCA) on simulated GWA datasets containing multifactorial patterns. As we will show, only PCA and SC are able to identify the multifactorial patterns at all, and SC can detect patterns in datasets with large numbers of SNPs where PCA no longer works well. A fundamental advantage of SC in this respect is that, whereas the principal components of the PCA are constrained to be orthogonal, the codebook vectors of SC are not subject to this constraint [16]. SC will thus not miss the disease-specific patterns due to non-orthogonal alignment to random structures.

2   Data and Methods

2.1   Simulated GWA Data

Up to now, most GWA studies have mainly identified single SNPs that influence the risk of a given phenotype. Some studies have combined these SNPs to develop risk scores [17]. Single SNPs that do not show any effect on the phenotype might increase the risk of a disease in combination with other SNPs. However, we do not expect all cases to have the same SNP-pattern; otherwise it could be easily identified.

Furthermore, there are diseases where the phenotype label might be rather fuzzy, i.e., we have a large group of individuals that are labeled as cases but the labeling might not be due to genetic patterns but rather due to other factors. In other words, we seek to find disease-specific genetic patterns for subgroups of the data. Furthermore, we also expect structures in the data that are present across the population without any disease-specific effect.

To obtain synthetic datasets with these properties, we proceeded as follows: First we simulated datasets by random sampling with the constraint of genotype distributions according to the Hardy Weinberg Equilibrium (HWE) [18] with a minor allele frequency of 0.4–0.5. This was done twice, once for the cases and once for the controls.

The next step was to integrate SNP patterns for a subset of the cases. In order to obtain a dataset as described above, we cannot change the distribution of the SNPs since this would result in a significant difference between cases and controls (small p-values) as well as a deviation from the HWE. The pattern was thus introduced by resorting the genotypes. The resorting was realized by swapping the genotypes for a number of SNPs, one at a time, so that the predefined subgroup featured the same genotypes. In this way, we retain the original non-significant distribution of the SNPs as well as a disease-specific pattern.

To account for unspecific patterns in the data, we additionally introduced patterns covering subsets of cases as well as controls. This was done in the same way as for the disease-associated pattern, but this time for both the cases as well as the controls with equal pattern sizes. For evaluation purpose we simulated several datasets of varying dimensions and pattern sizes as shown in Table (1).

In the following, we will introduce a set of points $X = (\mathbf{x}_1, \ldots, \mathbf{x}_N)$, $x_i \in \mathbb{R}^D$, consisting of the simulated individuals $\mathbf{x}_i$, described by D features (here SNPs), which are the dimensions that actually span our feature space. Further we introduce the corresponding class information $Y = (y_1, \ldots, y_N)$, $y_i \in \{1, -1\}$ that denotes whether a individual $\mathbf{x}_i$ belongs to the cases ($y_i = 1$) or to the controls ($y_i = -1$).

2.2   Single SNP Statistics

The significant differences of the distribution of the SNP alleles for each SNP respectively were calculated with the Chi-square statistic. The SNPs were subsequently ranked according to their p-values. The 100 best ranked SNPs were selected and the number of the known relevant SNPs among them counted.

2.3   SVM

We consider given data samples X and corresponding class information Y. In the SVM approach one looks for a hyperplane that separates the two classes of data samples with maximum margin. The SVM can be used for feature selection by considering the influence of each data dimension on the margin.

Table 1. For each kind of dataset we varied the total amount of SNPs as well as the patternsizes. The first datatype consist of 1 disease specific pattern and 1 unspecific pattern. The second datatype hold 1 disease specific pattern as well as 5 unspecific patterns. All the patterns for each dataset respectively are of the same size.

	pattern size/ 15000 SNPs	pattern size/ 20000 SNPs	pattern size/ 25000 SNPs	pattern size/ 30000 SNPs
1 disease specific pattern 1 unspecific pattern	10 20 30 40 50	10 20 30 40 50	10 20 30 40 50	10 20 30 40 50
1 disease specific pattern 5 unspecific pattern	10 20 30	10 20 30	10 20 30	10 20 30

In order to find the maximum margin solution one considers a constant margin of 1 and minimizes the norm of the normal vector of the separation hyperplane which is an equivalent problem, i.e., one solves the following optimization problem

$$\hat{\mathbf{w}} = \arg\min_{\mathbf{w}} \mathbf{w}^T\mathbf{w} \text{ subject to } y_i\left(\mathbf{w}^T\mathbf{x}_i - b\right) \geq 1 \tag{1}$$

where $\hat{\mathbf{w}}$ is the normal vector of the maximum margin separation hyperplane.

In the linear case the influence of a data dimension on the margin can be measured by considering the absolute value of the entries of $\hat{\mathbf{w}}$. In the experiments, we trained a linear hard-margin SVM on the simulated data and sorted the data dimensions according to the absolute values of the corresponding entries of $\hat{\mathbf{w}}$ in descending order. We took the first 100 data dimensions and counted how many of the relevant data dimensions were found among them.

2.4 PCA

Again, we consider given data samples X and corresponding class information Y. For each of the two classes we separately compute the principal components that correspond to the M largest eigenvalues, i.e., M largest directions of variance. Let $V^1 = (\mathbf{v}_1^1, \ldots, \mathbf{v}_M^1)$ contain the principal components of class 1 and $V^{-1} = (\mathbf{v}_1^{-1}, \ldots, \mathbf{v}_M^{-1})$ contain the principal components of class -1.

The larger the absolute value of an entry of a principal component is, the larger the contribution of the corresponding primal data dimension to this direction of variance is. In order to find data dimensions that contribute differently to the variance of both classes, i.e., in order to measure how different the primal data dimension j contributes to the directions of maximum variance in class 1 and -1, we consider

$$r_j = |\max_i |(\mathbf{v}_i^1)_j| - \max_i |(\mathbf{v}_i^{-1})_j|| \tag{2}$$

We sort the data dimensions according to the rank r_j in descending order. Again, we consider the first 100 data dimensions and check how many of the relevant dimensions can be found among them. We tested a number of choices for M, the number of principal components. Finally, we used $M = 5$ which provided the best results.

2.5 Sparse Coding

Sparse coding employs low-dimensional subspaces in order to encode high-dimensional signals, i.e., it looks for a dictionary $C \in \mathbb{R}^{D \times M}$ that minimizes the representation error

$$\frac{1}{L} \sum_{i=1}^{L} \|\mathbf{x}_i - C\mathbf{a}_i\|_2^2 \tag{3}$$

where $\mathbf{x}_i^{\text{opt}} = C\mathbf{a}_i$ with $\mathbf{a}_i = \arg\min_{\mathbf{a}} \|\mathbf{x}_i - C\mathbf{a}\|$,$\|\mathbf{a}\|_0 \leq k^1$ denotes the best k-term representation of $\mathbf{x}_i$ in terms of C. There is a similarity between Sparse Coding and PCA, i.e., the columns of the dictionary matrix C also correspond to directions of large variance, however in contrast to PCA there isn't any orthogonality constraint imposed on the directions of large variance. Furthermore due to the constraint on the maximum number of non-zero entries of the coefficient vectors $\mathbf{a}_i$, it is possible to control the dimensionality of the subspaces that are used to cover the data, independently from the number of directions that are used. In order to evaluate if the additional control capabilities can be used to improve feature selection performance, we separately learned a dictionary for class 1, i.e., $C^1 = (\mathbf{c}_1^1, \ldots, \mathbf{c}_M^1)$ and class -1, i.e., $C^{-1} = (\mathbf{c}_1^{-1}, \ldots, \mathbf{c}_M^{-1})$. We used a combination of neural gas and the bag of pursuits method, which was proposed in [16].

As for PCA, the larger the absolute value of an entry of a direction $\mathbf{c}$ is, the larger the contribution of the corresponding primal data dimension to this direction of variance is. Hence, we obtain a feature ranking of the data dimensions in the same way. In order to obtain the rank of primal data dimension j, we consider

$$r_j = |\max_i |(\mathbf{c}_i^1)_j| - \max_i |(\mathbf{c}_i^{-1})_j|| \tag{4}$$

In contrast to PCA, SC has two parameters that have to be chosen by the user, M, the number of non-orthogonal directions to consider and k, the number of non-zero entries in the coefficient vectors $\mathbf{a}$. Again, we experimented with different choices for these parameters and took those values that provided the best results, i.e., $M = 5$ and $k = 4$.

As for PCA, we sort the data dimensions according to the rank r_j in descending order. Then again, we consider the first 100 data dimensions and check how many of the relevant dimensions can be found among them.

---

[1] $\|\mathbf{a}\|_0$ is equal to the number of non-zero entries of $\mathbf{a}$.

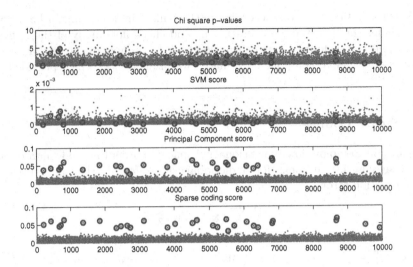

Fig. 1. Selection by p-values, SVM, PCA and SC score on a 10000 dimensional dataset with one disease specific pattern and 5 random patterns. The pattern specific SNPs are marked with red circles. In contrast to the first two algorithms, the pattern specific SNPs stand out through scoring with PCA and SC. For the scoring with PCA we used the first 5 principal components (M=5). The number of columns of the dictionary C is the same as the number of principal components (M=5), and the number of non zero entries k in the coefficient vector a_i is 4.

3   Results and Discussion

In order to measure the performance of the algorithm on GWA datasets, we simulated datasets with a minor allele frequency of 0.4-0.5 and genotypes according to Hardy Weinberg equilibrium.

3.1   Comparing Feature Selection Methods

In the first experiment, we compared the performance of different feature selection approaches, i.e., feature selection by p-values, SVM, PCA and SC, by simulating a 10000 dimensional dataset containing a pattern that was specific for a subgroup of 100 cases as well as a 5 noise pattern of 100 cases and 100 controls. All patterns consisted of 30 pairwise disjunct SNPs (see the Section 2.1 for further details).

We applied a Chi-square test and ranked the SNPs according to their significance values (p-values) as described in section 2.2. We trained a SVM on the data and ranked the SNPs by their influence on the classification hyperplane as described in section 2.3. For the feature selection by PCA, we calculated a score based on the contribution of the SNPs to the directions of maximum variances as described in section 2.4. For the SC approach we calculated the score in the same way but the directions of large variance were obtained from a sparse coding algorithm (see the Section (2.5) for further details).

As shown in Figure (1) selecting SNPs on the basis of their p-values will not lead to the identification of the SNP pattern that is specific for a subgroup of the cases. The weakness of this approach is obvious; SNPs that are part of a multi-dimensional pattern might only have a combined effect and not an effect for each SNP respectively. Hence, the pattern will not become visible when only one SNP at a time is considered.

The feature selection by SVM also fails to identify the SNPs. In contrast to the selection by the p-values, the SVM allows for a classification of the classes by implementing a multi-dimensional decision boundary. However, its weakness lies in the attempt of solving a two-class problem. Due to the nature of the data, i.e. only a rather small group of the cases contains the pattern of interest, we do not deal with a pure two class problem, but aim to identify subgroups that can be identified by sets of SNPs that have the same value for a large number of persons.

In contrast to the previously discussed approaches, feature selection by PCA and SC successfully identifies the targeted SNPs. Randomly distributed genotypes will have similar variances. However, if there is a pattern present in the data, due to the non-random distribution of the SNPs that belong to this pattern, directions of large variance will point in the direction of the pattern. The principal components cover as much of the variability of the data as possible, thus the class-specific SNPs will have a high influence on the class-specific principal components and thus be identified by PCA. Like PCA, SC also looks for directions of large variance but does this in low dimensional subspaces.

3.2 PCA and SC on High Dimensional Data

Next, we evaluated the performance of SC and PCA by varying the number of dimensions as well as the pattern size. To compensate for the random variations in the experiments, a total of 10 random datasets were generated for each dimensionality and pattern size. We assessed the quality of the results by counting how many of the targeted SNPs were found among the first 100 ranked SNPs.

First, we measured the performance on datasets where 1 pattern specific for a subgroup of the cases, and 1 noise pattern (pattern is present in both cases and controls) was present. The results are shown in Figure (2).

The power to detect the SNPs decreases with increasing dimensionality of data and with decreasing fraction of case-specific SNPs. This can be explained by the increasing probability of having random patterns in the data that have properties similar to the targeted SNPs. However, SC seems to be more robust against this effect than PCA.

Both PCA and SC provide a poor performance when applied to datasets where the size of case specific patterns is small. However, since the performance does not change substantially with an increasing number of dimensions, we assume that there exists a minimal pattern size that is required in order to be able to identify case specific patterns.The performance of both algorithms in the case of large patterns is close to 100%, thus implying that these settings do not challenge the algorithms to their limit.

In order to study the effect of a greater number of random structures in the data in the second round we repeated the experiments but this time with 5 noise patterns that were present in cases and controls. Since we want to compare the algorithms at their limits, we only run the algorithms on pattern sizes up to 30 SNPs. The results are shown in Figure (3).

The mean performance of PCA tends to decrease compared to the performance on the datasets where only one noise pattern is present whereas the performance of SC remains more stable. Due to the weaker performance of the PCA, SC significantly outperforms PCA for these more complex datasets.

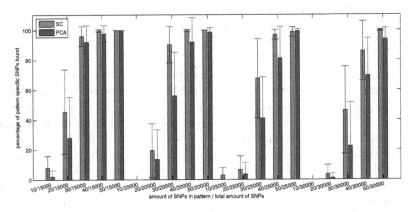

Fig. 2. The plot shows the mean percentage of identified pattern specific SNPs with the corresponding standard deviations for the varying amount of dimensions and pattern size for datasets with 1 noise patterns. The parameters are the same as described in figure 1. SC works more robustly than PCA for critical scenarios.

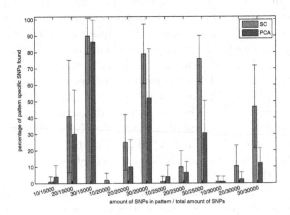

Fig. 3. This plot corresponds to Figure 2, except this time 5 noise patterns are used, and the pattern size is only varying from 10 to 30, since bigger patterns do not challenge whether PCA nor SC.

The improved performance of SC compared to PCA might be due to the orthogonality constraint that holds for PCA. Due to this constraint it might not be possible to learn certain directions if there are other stronger (random) structures in the data that allow only learning of structures that are orthogonal to these random structures. These restrictions are not present in the sparse coding approach.

4 Conclusion

The demand for identifying SNP interaction becomes more and more present for GWA studies. However because of the complexity and computational burden the number of studies reporting interacting loci remain small relative to the amount of GWA studies. In this work, we have shown that extracting SNPs by their p-values will not lead to the identification of multivariate gene patterns. The prominent multivariate SVM approach also fails to identify the disease specific patterns. A pattern that is present in only a small subset of the cases will not be detected due to the fact that the SVM seeks a good classification of all the cases and controls and hence for a random dataset the SNPs with the largest differences in the distribution of the genotypes (low p-values) be a good choice for the classifier.

PCA as a feature extraction shows good results for large pattern sizes with only a low number of noise patterns. However by introducing greater numbers of patterns to simulate disease unspecific coupling between SNPs, as it is likely to appear in real data, the performance of PCA is weakened.

The proposed sparse coding (SC) approach clearly outperforms SNP selection by p-values and SVM scores. In addition it demonstrated a significant higher stability on high-dimensional datasets with multiple noise patterns.

SC can thus be used as a preprossessing tool to select a subset of relevant SNPs. The relatively small amount of identifyed SNPs can subsequently be further analyzed in order to establish a risk prediction or for classification purpose.

Acknowledgments. The authors thank Martin Böhme for fruitful discussions on the manuscript. This work was supported by the Graduate School for Computing in Medicine and Life Sciences funded by Germany's Excellence Initiative [DFG GSC 235/1].

References

1. Wei, Z., Wang, K., Qu, H.Q.Q., Zhang, H., Bradfield, J., Kim, C., Frackleton, E., et al.: From disease association to risk assessment: an optimistic view from genome-wide association studies on type 1 diabetes. PLoS genetics 5(10), e1000678+ (2009)
2. Samani, N.J., Erdmann, J., Hall, A.S., Hengstenberg, C., Mangino, M., Mayer, B., Dixon, R.J., et al.: Genomewide Association Analysis of Coronary Artery Disease. N. Engl. J. Med. 357(5), 443–453 (2007)

3. Erdmann, J., Groszhennig, A., Braund, P.S., Konig, I.R., Hengstenberg, C., Hall, A.S., Linsel-Nitschke, P., et al.: New susceptibility locus for coronary artery disease on chromosome 3q22. 3. Nat. Genet. 41(3), 280–282 (2009)
4. Raelson, J.V., Little, R.D., Ruether, A., Fournier, H., Paquin, B., Van Eerdewegh, P., Bradley, W.E., et al.: Genome-wide association study for crohn's disease in the quebec founder population identifies multiple validated disease loci. Proc. Natl. Acad. Sci. U. S. A. 104(37), 14747–14752 (2007)
5. Ioannidis, J.P.: Prediction of cardiovascular disease outcomes and established cardiovascular risk factors by genome-wide association markers. Circ. Cardiovasc. Genet. 2(1), 7–15 (2009)
6. Wray, N.R., Goddard, M.E., Visscher, P.M.: Prediction of individual genetic risk of complex disease. Current Opinion in Genetics and Development 18(73), 257–263 (2008)
7. Moore, J.H.: The ubiquitous nature of epistasis in determining susceptibility to common human diseases. Human heredity 56(1-3), 73–82 (2003)
8. Consortium, T.W.T.C.C.: Genome-wide association study of 14,000 cases of seven common diseases and 3,000 shared controls. Nature 447(7145), 661–678 (2007)
9. Guyon, I., Elisseeff, A.: An introduction to variable and feature selection. J. Mach. Learn. Res. 3, 1157–1182 (2003)
10. Guyon, I., Weston, J., Barnhill, S., Vapnik, V.: Gene selection for cancer classification using support vector machines. Machine Learning 46, 389–422 (2002)
11. Yoon, Y., Song, J., Hong, S.H., Kim, J.Q.: Analysis of multiple single nucleotide polymorphisms of candidate genes related to coronary heart disease susceptibility by using support vector machines. Clin. Chem. Lab. Med. 41(4), 529–534 (2003)
12. Ban, H.J., Heo, J.Y., Oh, K.S., Park, K.: Identification of type 2 diabetes-associated combination of snps using support vector machine. BMC Genet. 11(1), 26 (2010)
13. Paschou, P., Ziv, E., Burchard, E.G., Choudhry, S., Rodriguez-Cintron, W., Mahoney, M.W., Drineas, P.: Pca-correlated snps for structure identification in worldwide human populations. PLoS Genet. 3(9), 1672–1686 (2007)
14. Black, M., Watanabe, R.: A principal-components-based clustering method to identify multiple variants associated with rheumatoid arthritis and arthritis-related autoantibodies. BMC Proceedings 3(suppl. 7), S129 (2009)
15. Price, A.L., Patterson, N.J., Plenge, R.M., Weinblatt, M.E., Shadick, N.A., Reich, D.: Principal components analysis corrects for stratification in genome-wide association studies. Nature Genetics 38(8), 904–909 (2006)
16. Labusch, K., Martinetz, T.: Learning Sparse Codes for Image Reconstruction. In: Verleysen, M. (ed.) Proceedings of the 18th European Symposium on Artificial Neural Networks, d-side, pp. 241–246 (2010)
17. Kathiresan, S., Melander, O., Anevski, D., Guiducci, C., et al.: Polymorphisms Associated with Cholesterol and Risk of Cardiovascular Events. N. Engl. J. Med. 358(12), 1240–1249 (2008)
18. Crow, J.F.: Hardy, Weinberg and Language Impediments. Genetics 152(3), 821–825 (1999)

Self-adaptive Artificial Neural Network in Numerical Models Calibration

Anna Kučerová and Tomáš Mareš

Czech Technical University in Prague, Faculty of Civil Engineering,
Department of Mechanics, Thákurova 7,
16629 Prague, Czech Republic
{anicka,marestom}@cml.fsv.cvut.cz

Abstract. The layered neural networks are considered as very general tools for approximation. In the presented contribution, a neural network with a very simple rule for the choice of an appropriate number of hidden neurons is applied to a material parameters' identification problem. Two identification strategies are compared. In the first one, the neural network is used to approximate the numerical model predicting the response for a given set of material parameters and loading. The second mode employs the neural network for constructing an inverse model, where material parameters are directly predicted for a given response.

Keywords: Artificial neural network, multi-layer perceptron, approximation, nonlinear relations, back-propagation, parameter identification.

1 Introduction

A variety of engineering tasks nowadays leads to an inverse analysis problem, where the goal is to identify parameters of a numerical model describing properly the experiment. In overall, there are two main philosophies to solution of identification problems [4]. A forward (classical) mode is based on the definition of an error function of the difference between outputs of the model and experimental measurements. A solution comes with the minimum of this function. This mode of identification could be considered as more general and robust, but repeated application is relatively computationally expensive. The second philosophy, an inverse mode, assumes the existence of an inverse relationship between outputs and inputs. If such relationship is established, then the retrieval of desired inputs is a matter of seconds and could be easily executed repeatedly.

Artificial neural networks (ANNs) [2] are powerful computational systems consisting of many simple processing elements – so-called neurons – connected together to perform tasks analogously to biological brains. Their main feature is ability to change their structure based on external information that flows through the ANN during the learning (training) phase. A particular type of ANN is so-called feedforward neural network, which consists of neurons organized into layers where outputs from one layer are used as inputs into the following layer.

K. Diamantaras, W. Duch, L.S. Iliadis (Eds.): ICANN 2010, Part I, LNCS 6352, pp. 347–350, 2010.
© Springer-Verlag Berlin Heidelberg 2010

In this contribution, two different applications of ANN to parameter identification are presented. In the forward mode of identification, ANN is used to approximate the computationally expensive numerical model. ANN can be then efficiently used in the phase of parameter optimization where the huge number of numerical model evaluations is replaced by very fast evaluations of ANN. In the inverse mode, the ANN is applied to approximate the inverse relation between inputs and outputs. This problem is often ill-posed, but once such relation is established, it can be very quickly and repeatedly used for estimation of parameters from any new experiment.

When dealing with ANNs, the key point is the choice of its architecture. The number of units in an input and output layer is usually given, but it remains to decide the number of units in hidden layer. In this contribution, a very simple self-adaptive ANN is applied to parameters identification of the microplane model M4 [1]. The forward and inverse strategy is compared.

2 Architecture of Artificial Neural Network

Despite of ANN's popularity there are only few recommendations for the choice of ANN's architecture. The authors, e.g. in [3], show that ANN with any of a wide variety of continuous nonlinear hidden-layer activation functions, one hidden layer with an arbitrarily large number of units suffices for the "universal approximation" property. Therefore, we limit our numerical experiments to such a case. But there is no theory yet to decide how many hidden units are needed to approximate any given function.

In general the choice of the number of hidden units (*NH*) depends on many factors such as the number of input and output units, the number of training samples, the complexity of the function to be approximated etc. The choice of *NH* can be driven by following principles: (i) if ANN produces a high error on both the training and testing data due to so-called *underfitting*, ANN's architecture is probably too simple and more hidden units should be added; (ii) if ANN produces relatively small error on training data, but in orders of magnitude higher error on testing due to *overfitting*, there are probably too many hidden units and some of them should be eliminated. Regarding these principles, we employ a simple ANN with the ability to adapt the number of hidden neurons. The ANN starts with one hidden neuron and the process of ANN's training is executed. We compute the average absolute error on training data *ETR* and testing data *ETE*. When the ETE/ETR ratio is smaller than a chosen value of testing to training error ratio TTER, new hidden neuron is added into the ANN and the training process and testing of ETE/ETR is repeated till it is smaller than TTER. The value of TTER is fixed to 3.2 with respect to the study presented in [5].

3 Application of ANN in Parameters Identification of Microplane Model M4

Concrete is a heterogeneous material and therefore the simulation of its behaviour encounters serious difficulties, both theoretical and numerical. The microplane model M4 [1] is a fully three-dimensional material law, which includes different types of material loading. The major disadvantage of this model, however, is an enormous computational cost associated with structural analysis and phenomenological material parameters without clear physical interpretation. Here, we would like to present two possible applications of the ANN in parameters identification of the microplane model.

Because of the limited space for this contribution, we focus on identification of three parameters – Young's modulus E, k_1 and c_{20} – which should be identified from the uniaxial compression test. When simulating uniaxial compression, the model output is a stress-strain diagram. We discretize the stress-strain diagram into 18 discrete points corresponding to fixed values of strain. Because of high computational demands of each compression test simulation, only 60 and 10 samples were generated for a training and a testing set, respectively.

We start by the inverse mode of identification where ANN is supposed to approximate the inverse relation between model outputs and model parameters (here, considered as inputs). Only several values of stresses are chosen with respect to their correlation with parameters. The computed values of correlation are presented e.g. in [4]. To simplify the training process, one ANN is trained with adaptivity for each model parameter. The set of inputs and resulting architecture together with resulting relative errors of ANN's predictions are described in Table 1.

Table 1. Inverse mode of identification

Parameter	Inputs	Architecture	Av. ETR [%]	Av. ETE [%]
E	σ_1, σ_2, σ_3	$3 - 5 - 1$	0.18	0.34
k_1	σ_5, σ_{18}, σ_{peak}, σ_{peak}, $E_{prediction}$	$5 - 4 - 1$	0.46	0.86
c_{20}	σ_6, σ_8, σ_{12}, σ_{16}, $E_{predict.}$, $k_{1,predict.}$	$6 - 3 - 1$	10.44	22.43

One can see that ANN can very precisely find the inverse relation for prediction Young's modulus and parameter k_1, but it is unable to approximate the inverse relation for parameter c_{20} with satisfactory precision. So the application of ANN in the inverse mode is not always trivial.

In the case of the forward mode, the ANN can be used for the approximation of the numerical model itself. In that case, however, there is a relatively small number of ANN's inputs – only four model parameters (Poison's ratio, which cannot be identified only from axial deformation, but has still an indispensable influence on its shape, is added). But there is a larger number of outputs corresponding to discrete points of stress-strain diagram. In order to predict stress values in these points, there are two possibilities of ANN implementation.

In the first scenario, one independent ANN can be trained to predict the stress in one chosen point. Such ANN can be very simple, the training process can be also fast and easy, but we must train 18 different ANNs. Fig. 1(a) shows the prediction error for each ANN predicting the stress value in one of 18 points. One can see that an average error on both the training and testing data of all ANNs is smaller than 4% and worst cases have not exceeded the error of 8%. The only disadvantage of this approach remains the necessity of training a number of independent ANNs.

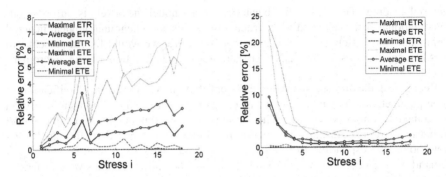

Fig. 1. Forward mode of identification: (a) Relative errors in predictions of 18 simple ANNs; (b) Relative errors in prediction of one complex ANN

In the second scenario, only one ANN can be trained, if we add the value of strain as the fifth input. 60 training and 10 testing diagrams consisting of 18 points change to 1080 training and 10 testing samples. The relation to be approximated becomes of course more complicated. Prediction errors computed relatively to bounds of stresses corresponding to particular diagram points are depicted in Fig. 1(b). When comparing to the first scenario of the forward mode, the errors are in general higher, but the usage of one ANN is of course simpler.

4   Conclusions

In the presented contribution, we focus on an application of artificial neural networks in parameters identification. A very simple adaptive ANN is applied to parameters identification of the microplane model. Three different scenarios are demonstrated and their particular advantages and drawbacks are discussed.

Acknowledgement. The financial support of this work by research project MSM 6840770003 is gratefully acknowledged.

References

1. Bažant, Z.P., Caner, F.C., Carol, I., Adley, M.D., Akers, S.A.: Microplane model M4 for concrete. Journal of Engineering Mechanics 126(9), 944–961 (2000)
2. Gurney, K.N.: An introduction to neural networks. UCL Press, London (2002)
3. Hornik, K.: Some new results on neural network approximation. Neural Networks 6, 1069–1072 (1993)
4. Kučerová, A.: Identification of nonlinear mechanical model parameters based on softcomputing methods, Ph.D. thesis, Ecole Normale Supérieure de Cachan, Laboratoire de Mécanique et Technologie (2007)
5. Kučerová, A., Mareš, T.: Artificial Neural Network as Universal Approximation of Nonlinear Relations. In: Proceedings of International Conference on Modelling and Simulation 2010 in Prague (2001)

Measuring Adjective Spaces*

Timo Honkela, Tiina Lindh-Knuutila, and Krista Lagus

Adaptive Informatics Research Centre
Aalto University of Science and Technology
P.O. Box 15400, FI-00076 Aalto

Abstract. In this article, we use the model adjectives using a vector space model. We further employ three different dimension reduction methods, the Principal Component Analysis (PCA), the Self-Organizing Map (SOM), and the Neighbor Retrieval Visualizer (NeRV) in the projection and visualization task, using antonym test for evaluation. The results show that while the results between the three methods are comparable, the NeRV performs best of the three, and all of them are able to preserve meaningful information for further analysis.

1 Introduction

Large number of studies indicate that methods using co-occurrence data provide useful information on the relationships between the words, as words with similar or related meaning will tend to occur in similar contexts [1]. This intuition has been carefully assessed, in particular, for nouns and verbs. In this article, we study whether co-occurrence statistics provide a basis for automatically creating a representation for a group of adjectives as well. Further, we compare dimension reduction methods, in particular, the Principal Component Analysis [2], the Self-Organizing Map [3] and Neighbor Retrieval Visualizer (NeRV) [4] affect the quality of the final representation. We study the neighborhoods of the adjectives in the created vector space, and use antonyms pairs to evaluate the result.

Nouns and verbs have received much more attention than adjectives in language technology, knowledge engineering and related research fields. For instance, the nodes of ontologies are mainly entities labeled with nouns. In linguistics, verbs have been the subject of very active study as verbs usually serve as the ordering elements of a sentence. Adjectives are not very well described in ontologies, but Wordnet and EuroWordnet have considered including a small set of lexical conceptual relations that allow to encode adjectives.

The Self-Organizing Map has been earlier used in several studies to create word clusters automatically from statistical features obtained from corpora. In [5], analysis of 150 English word types was carried out using the self-organzing map. The resulting map divided into separate areas of verbs and nouns, with nouns further dividing into areas of animate and inanimate nouns. The verbs were studied in [6], where a verb map was created using features, such as case marking and adverbs. The resulting verb

---

* This work has been supported by the Academy of Finland and the Finnish Funding Agency for Technology and Innovation.

K. Diamantaras, W. Duch, L.S. Iliadis (Eds.): ICANN 2010, Part I, LNCS 6352, pp. 351–355, 2010.

clusters depicted organization related to emotional content. In addition, [7], an adjective map based on emotive aspects of words was created with manually provided features.

2 Methods

The word vector space model is a standard method for representing text data in numerical form. In the model, words are represented as feature vectors. Features of a word are often words that co-occur with it in a certain context or window [8]. We obtain feature vectors statistically from a corpus, using a window of a small size, and counting the co-occurrences of the feature words that appear with the target word in this window. The similarity of the words can be then measured as the Euclidean distance between them in the vector space.

The original dimensionality of the vector space is usually high and dimesion reduction methods are needed. This can be done by either feature selection, i.e. selecting a subset of the original features that give most information of the object in question, or by feature extraction, using features that are combinations of original dimensions. Both are frequently applied to word vector spaces.

Generally, a dimension reduction method is good, if the neighbors of the data points in the original space can be retrieved well based on the projected points in the visualization. We use three feature extraction methods that project the data to two dimensions for visualization purposes, the Principal Component Analysis [2] the Self-Organizing Map (SOM) [3] and the Neighbor Retrieval Visualizer (NeRV) [4]. In the following, we give the basic details of each method.

The PCA is an orthogonal linear transformation which transforms the possibly correlated data into new variables, in such a way that the greatest variance lies on the first principal component and most of the variance is contained in a few first principal components. This makes it a practical tool for dimension reduction, as the remaining components can be dropped with minimal loss of information.

The SOM is a classical unsupervised learning method which typically produces a two-dimensional discretized representation of the input space. It preserves the topological properties of the input space, which makes it an useful tool for visualizing high-dimensional data.

The novel NeRV method for nonlinear dimensionality reduction and data visualization [4] conceptualises the dimensionality reduction as an information retrieval problem and rigorously quantifies the goodness of the dimension reduction method in terms of precision and recall. The NeRV algorithm [9] is able to optimise the cost function (1) that allows an optimal balance between these two. The cost function is given as

$$E_{NeRV} = \lambda[E_i[D(p_i,q_i)]] + (1-\lambda)E_i[D(q_i,p_i)] \ , \tag{1}$$

where $E_i[D(p_i,q_i)]$ is the number of misses and $E_i[D(q_i,p_i)]$ the number of false positives. Minimising $E_i[D(p_i,q_i)]$ maximizes the recall, and minimizing $E_i[D(q_i,p_i)]$ maximizes the precision. The relative cost parameter λ can be used to focus to either of them.

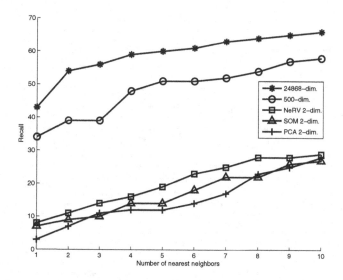

Fig. 1. Comparison of different methods used to create an adjective space based on word co-occurrence statistics. The y-axis shows the percentage of antonyms successfully found for the 72 test adjectives among the n nearest neighbors and the x-axis provides different values of n, from 1 to 10. The high-dimensional spaces are marked with an asterisk (24868 dimensions) and a circle (500 dimensions). The methods for creating the 2-dimensional projection from the 500-dimensional data are the NeRV (marked with a square), the SOM (marked with a triangle), and the PCA (marked with a plus sign).

3   Experiments

The objective of the experiments was to study the effect of the dimension reduction on the data and see whether there are differences in the dimension reduction methods. The text collection used in the experiments was extracted from English Wikipedia articles. The statistics of the two closest context words were collected for each of the 72 adjectives included in the analysis. For each adjective, a 24868-dimensional feature vector was created. The original feature dimensionality contains all the words that occur in the collection over 100 times. We then reduced the dimensionality of matrix by feature selection: Only the 500 words that occur most frequently with the 72 adjectives are included. Further, we use the matrix with 500-dimensional feature vectors to project the data into two dimensions using the PCA, the SOM and the NeRV. The PCA was implemented using standard Matlab functionalities, the SOM with its common functionalities using the SOM Toolbox. The NeRV is implemented in the dredviz software package developed for information visualization.[1]

---

[1] The software package, developed in the Adaptive Informatics Research Centre, Aalto University School of Science and Technology, is available at
http://www.cis.hut.fi/projects/mi/software/dredviz/

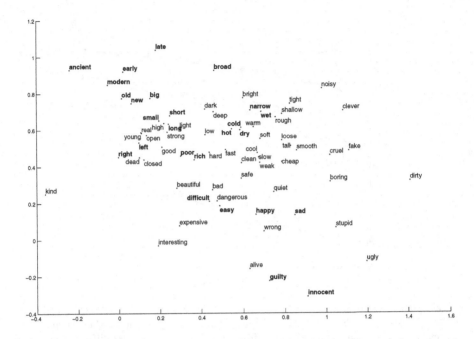

Fig. 2. The set of adjectives used in the study projected into a 2-dimensional space using the Neighbor Retrieval Visualizer (NeRV) method. The words in bold have the antonym in their local neighborhood.

There does not seem to exist a consensus among linguists on how adjectives should be divided into categories in general. We then considered two alternatives, i.e., synonyms and antonyms. Antonyms are words that have an opposite meaning, and synonymous words have a same or almost the same meaning. They both offer a means for evaluating the ordering of the obtained vector space. As synonymity is not clearly defined, we used the antonyms for which the definitions are clearer. Each adjective had an antonym in the set: long–short, good–bad, etc. We then calculated the recall, that is checked whether the antonym could be found within the $[1, 2, \ldots 10]$ nearest neighbors. The result of this experiment is presented in Fig. 1.

The fact that the high-dimensional spaces provide higher percentages than the 2-dimensional spaces is understandable. Lower-dimensional spaces are often used to reach lower computational complexity. Moreover, a 2-dimensional space is particularly useful in visualization. Thus, it is to be noted that the nearest neighbors in the case of SOM, NeRV and PCA were calculated in the 2-dimensional space. The NeRV method seems to reach better performance than the SOM which again exceeds the performance of the PCA method. Figure 2 shows the results for the NeRV. We can see that many antonym pairs are located close to each other in the visualization. The pairs ancient-modern, old-new and early-late form their own cluster in the top-left corner of the figure. Another group is formed by the pairs hot-cold, dry-wet in close vicinity with cool and warm. Other pairs close to each other include poor-rich, innocent-guilty, happy-sad and difficult-easy.

4   Conclusions and Discussion

In this article, we studied the representation of the adjectives based on the short context they appear in. The results, based on an antonym test, show that the context provides a reasonably good means for automatically extracting meaningful relationship between adjectives. While the NeRV performs best in this setting, based on this evaluation, all methods tested preserve meaningful information for further analysis.

The antonym test is a very simple evaluation method which only measures one side of the problem: whether the words with opposite meaning can be found close to each other in the word vector space. A closer look at Fig. 2 reveals that there are several other words for which the meaning is close or which seem to belong to a same category as well. To obtain concrete results, though, we would need linguistically or semantically defined groupings of adjectives and lists of adjectives in each group - which we could then use as a basis of more thorough evaluation.

Acknowledgements

We wish to thank Jaakko J. Väyrynen and Sami Virpioja who have helped us by gathering the basic data used in the experiments and by providing assistance in the data analysis.

References

1. Firth, J.R.: Papers in linguistics 1934-1951. Oxford University Press, Oxford (1957)
2. Jolliffe, I.T.: Principal Component Analysis. Springer, Heidelberg (2002)
3. Kohonen, T.: Self-Organizing Maps. Springer, Heidelberg (2001)
4. Venna, J., Peltonen, J., Nybo, K., Aidos, H., Kaski, S.: Information retrieval perspective to nonlinear dimensionality reduction for data visualization
5. Honkela, T., Pulkki, V., Kohonen, T.: Contextual relations of words in Grimm tales, analyzed by self-organizing map. In: Proceedings of ICANN 1995, Nanterre, France, vol. II, pp. 3–7. EC2 (1995)
6. Lagus, K., Airola, A.: Semantic clustering of verbs – analysis of morphosyntactic contexts using the SOM algorithm. In: Acquisition and Representation of Word Meaning: Theoretical and computational perspectives, Pisa, Roma. Linguistica Computazionale. Instituti Editoriali E Poligrafici Internazionali, vol. XXII-XXIII, pp. 263–287 (2005)
7. Honkela, T.: Adaptive and holistic knowledge representations using self-organizing maps. In: Proceedings of Int. Conference on Intelligent Information Processing, IIP 2000, pp. 81–86. IFIP (2000)
8. Schütze, H.: Word Space. In: Advances in Neural Information Processing Systems, NIPS Conference, vol. 5, pp. 895–902. Morgan Kaufmann Publishers Inc., San Francisco (1993); Journal of Machine Learning Research 11, 451–490 (2010)
9. Venna, J., Kaski, S.: Nonlinear dimensionality reduction as information retrieval. In: Proceedings of the 11th International Conference on Artificial Intelligence and Statistics, AISTATS 2007 (2007)

Echo State Networks with Sparse Output Connections

Hans-Ulrich Kobialka and Umer Kayani

Fraunhofer Institut Intelligente Analyse- und Informationssysteme IAIS
Schloss Birlinghoven, 53754 Sankt Augustin, Germany
Hans-Ulrich.Kobialka@iais.fraunhofer.de

Abstract. An Echo State Network transforms an incoming time series signal into a high-dimensional state space, and, of course, not every dimension may contribute to the solution. We argue that giving low weights via linear regression is not sufficient. Instead irrelevant features should be entirely excluded from directly contributing to the output nodes. We conducted several experiments using two state-of-the-art feature selection algorithms. Results show significant reduction of the generalization error.

Keywords: Echo State network, feature selection.

1 Introduction

Machine learning methods minimize the training error, i.e. they approximate a model which might have produced the training data. In case of high-dimensionality data, machine learning algorithms exploit also redundant and irrelevant features if these (by chance) minimize the training error. A model trained like this may not perform well later on previously unseen data. This problem is known as 'overfitting'.

Echo State Networks (ESNs) are a recent approach of training recurrent neural networks which showed excellent performance on learning temporal tasks [1] [2]. In the very end, training boils down to determining the weights of the connections to the output nodes using a single large linear regression. The connection weights inside the net are sparse, generated randomly, and not changed during training.

Regression computes weights for every output connection. Many of these weights may be small, but this possibly leads to the effect described above, i.e. redundant or irrelevant nodes are considered if they minimize the training error.

Sparse connectivity has been observed in biological brains and there are many scientists which advocate that sparsity is also beneficial in artificial neural networks [3]. The internal layer of ESNs is sparsely connected, and so it seems to be a contradiction that each output node is connected to all internal nodes.

The hypothesis we investigate in this paper is: The reduction of output connections reduces the generalization error, i.e. the error when trained ESNs are applied on previously unseen data.

2 Echo State Networks

An Echo State Network is an artificial recurrent neural network (RNN) which at each time step t computes its output $y(t)$ based on its internal state $x(t)$.

K. Diamantaras, W. Duch, L.S. Iliadis (Eds.): ICANN 2010, Part I, LNCS 6352, pp. 356–361, 2010.

$$y(t) = f_{out} \left(x(t)^T W_{out} \right) . \tag{1}$$

where W_{out} is the output weight matrix, and ^{T} denotes the transpose of a matrix. $f_{out}(.)$ is the output activation function. We use identity $(f_{out}(.) = x)$ in this paper. State $x(t)$ of internal nodes is computed based on the input $u(t)$, and the previous state $x(t\text{-}1)$. Optionally the previous net output $y(t\text{-}1)$ can be fed back to the net.

$$x(t) = f \left(W_{in} u(t) + W x(t\text{-}1) + W_{fb} y(t\text{-}1) \right) . \tag{2}$$

where W, W_{in}, and W_{fb} are weight matrices of the connections between the internal nodes, (W) between the input nodes and the net (W_{in}) and between the output nodes and the net (W_{fb}).

An ESN is constructed in the following way. First, the number of input nodes, output nodes, and internal nodes are chosen. The weight matrices W, W_{in} and, optionally, W_{fb} are chosen randomly. The weight matrix W connecting the internal nodes has to be sparse, i.e. only a few connection weights (e.g. 10%) are non-zero. Furthermore, matrix W has to ensure the echo state property [4] [5].

After the ESN is constructed, the training data (the input u_{train} and the given train outputs y_{train}) is fed into the net thereby computing states $x_{train}(t)$ according to (2).

$$x_{train}(t) = f \left(W_{in} u_{train}(t) + W x_{train}(t\text{-}1) + W_{fb} y_{train}(t\text{-}1) \right) . \tag{3}$$

All collected training states $x_{train}(t)$ are collected in a state matrix X_{train} and all given train outputs in matrix Y_{train}. In case of a single output node, Y_{train} is a vector.

$$X_{train} = \begin{bmatrix} x_{train}^T(1) \\ x_{train}^T(2) \\ \vdots \\ x_{train}^T(N_{train}) \end{bmatrix} , \quad Y_{train} = \begin{bmatrix} y_{train}(1) \\ y_{train}(2) \\ \vdots \\ y_{train}(N_{train}) \end{bmatrix} \tag{4}$$

were N_{train} is the number of training samples. Then according to equation (1), and with $f_{out}(.) = x$, the following should hold.

$$Y_{train} = X_{train} W_{out}. \tag{5}$$

As X_{train} and Y_{train} are given, the output weight matrix W_{out} can be computed via regression. Regression can be computed in several ways, e.g. SVM regression [6]. One simple but effective way is Ridge Regression which introduces a penalty term λ for preventing high weights thereby reducing the sensitivity to noise and overfitting.

$$W_{out} = (X_{train}^T X_{train} + \lambda^2 I)^{-1} X_{train}^T Y_{train} . \tag{6}$$

with I being the identity matrix and $^{-1}$ the inverse of a matrix.

3 ESN Training as a Feature Selection Problem

The idea is to exclude irrelevant (or superfluous) states in X_{train} from W_{out} (i.e. setting connection weights in W_{out} to zero). The remaining connection weights are then computed via regression.

The states of an internal node can be regarded as values of a stochastic variable. Therefore we treat the selection of non-zero output connection weights as a variable selection problem, in the literature more often known as 'feature selection' [7].

Feature selection is an iterative process where different subsets of features are evaluated. The number of all possible feature subsets is 2^N, with N being the number of features. For large numbers of features, feature selection algorithms are needed to search the solution space within a reasonable time. In this paper, we use a greedy algorithm, 'Backward Elimination' (also known as 'Backward Deletion' or 'Backward Selection') [8], and a genetic one, 'Markov blanket-embedded genetic algorithm' (MBEGA) [9].

3.1 Fitness Function

For both algorithms, the performance of a particular feature set has to be assessed by computing the training error. In case of ESNs, this can be divided into two steps.

1. Computation of W_{out}. First the columns corresponding to the features to be excluded are deleted from matrix X_{train}. Then W_{out} is computed using Ridge regression, using equation (6).
2. Using W_{out} to compute the error. Applying the ESN on possibly another training data set creates another X'_{train}. Again, the columns of deleted features have to be reduced, and Y is computed: $Y = X'_{reduced_{train}} W_{out}$. Finally from the difference between Y and Y_{train} the RMSE is computed.

This scheme allows doing different things in these steps, in particular using different data sets, and we benefited from this during our experiments.

4 Experiments

4.1 ARTINOS Data

The data sets we used for the experiments were coming from a, so called, 'electronic nose' sensor, named ARTINOS [11]. Each measurement consists of a time series coming from a sensor array of 16 elements over 142 time steps. The ESN has to detect the concentration of dangerous gases. The problem is that the sensors operate in freight containers containing all possible kinds of goods and smells. The sensor signal also contains the influence of these atmospheres present in a container, thus the signal-to-noise-ratio could be bad and the gas isn't detectable. But when target gases are detectable, the background noise in the signal can't be predicted, i.e. we are unable to construct a training data set which represents the noise of the learning task properly.

Therefore in our experiments, we divided the training and test data sets such that they contain data from different measurements (having different background noise) in order to be realistic.

4.2 ARTINOS Data Used in the Experiments

The ARTINOS data consists of 1365 measurements taken at different days over a period of 3 weeks. We divided the data into 7 sets, each measured at different days, and therefore taken from different freight containers each having its own kind of background noise in the measurement data. Five of these sets were chosen to be used for training, while the remaining two were left for testing.

Using Backward Elimination, the feature set is reduced during each round based on the training data until only one feature is left. All the feature sets found during this procedure are evaluated on one test set and the best one is selected to be the final feature set. This feature set is finally assessed using the other test set.

4.3 Backward Elimination with Variations in Computing Error Estimations

In experiment A, the 5 training data sets are separated for weight computation (3 data sets) and error estimation (2 data sets), as explained in 3.1. In experiment B, we joined all 5 training data sets into one matrix X_{train} and use it for both weight computation and error estimation. In experiment C, weight computation was done as in experiment B (using one big state matrix X_{train}) but error was computed by cross validation, i.e. computing X^i_{train} and the error for each of the 5 training data sets, and then used the mean error.

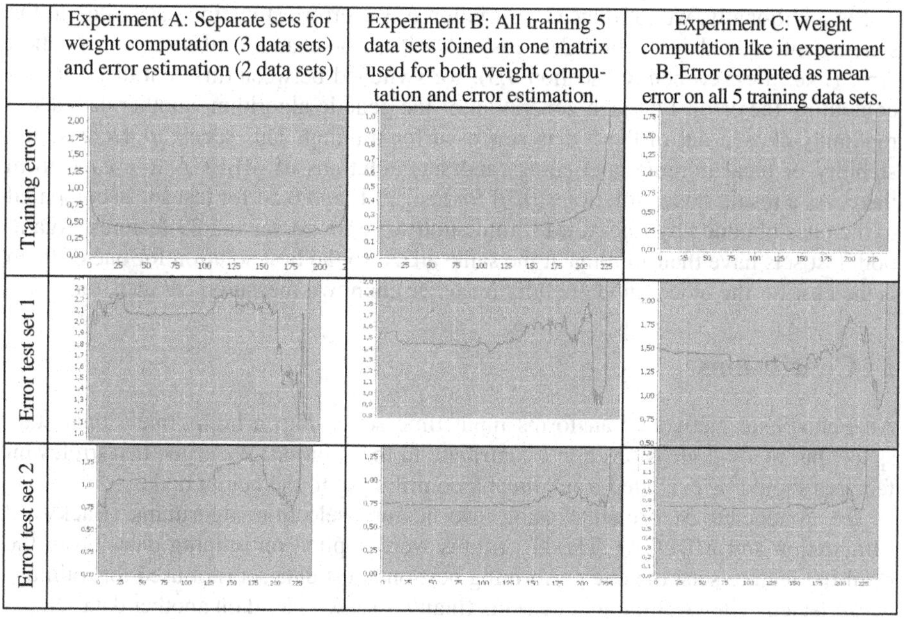

	Experiment A: Separate sets for weight computation (3 data sets) and error estimation (2 data sets)	Experiment B: All training 5 data sets joined in one matrix used for both weight computation and error estimation.	Experiment C: Weight computation like in experiment B. Error computed as mean error on all 5 training data sets.
Training error			
Error test set 1			
Error test set 2			

Fig. 3. Error on training data and two test sets when applying Backward Elimination

Experiment A performed worse and experiment C performed slightly better than B. Obviously it is advantageous to exploit the whole training set for both weight computation and error estimation. Instead of computing the error on all training data (experiment B), it seems to be better to compute the error in a cross validation manner (experiment C).

More interesting than the differences between the experiments are their similarities. The test error can be improved in all cases. The improvements for test set 1 and test set 2 both have their minimum error in the same region (7 to 15 features). The error on test set 1 can be reduced from 1.49 down to 0.87 (with 10 features) and the error of test set 2 goes down from 0.74 to 0.69 (with the same 10 features). It is astonishing that a feature set of 230 features can be pruned down to less than 5%.

4.4 Experiments Using MBEGA

Greedy algorithms, like Backward Elimination, are computationally expensive. Genetic algorithms usually reach acceptable solutions rather quick. But during experiments, MBEGA searched in rather irrelevant areas of the solution space. The reason for this was the fitness function used. It looks for minimizing the error and thus search gets stuck in some local minima..

Then we used MBEGA to optimize the result of Backward Elimination. After finding promising feature set sizes using Backward Elimination (section 4.3), we used MBEGA with a cost function which raises a penalty for feature set sizes above 30. But even with this modified cost function, MBEGA did not yield better solutions.

So, additionally, we introduced a variation of the error estimation, according to the scheme introduced in section 3.1. Instead using, for example, the cross validation error (like in experiment C, section 4.3), we switched between different data sets for computing the error. For each generation of the genetic algorithm, another data set is randomly chosen out of the 5 data sets used for training. This seems to decrease the stability of local minima, and eases candidate solutions of MBEGA to escape from there. As a result, better solutions (0.78 for test set 1, and 0.54 for test set 2) compared to the ones obtained by Backward Elimination were found, having 29 features. Again, both test sets have their minima at the same areas, so the best solution for one of them is the best for the other, and hopefully for other unknown measurement data, too.

5   Conclusions

An Echo State Network transforms input time series into a high-dimensional state space, but many dimensions don't contribute to the solution. We argue that irrelevant features should be excluded from directly contributing to the output nodes.

We conducted experiments using two feature selection algorithms (Backward Elimination and MBEGA). The algorithms were applied on training data. From the resulting feature sets, the one performing best on a test data set (not used for training) was selected. The resulting feature set is finally assessed based on another data set.

In the fitness function (of both Backward Elimination and MBEGA), we separated error estimation from the computation of connection weights (see section 3.1). During experiments, we investigated several ways of doing error estimation, and improved the results of the two feature selection algorithms.

The results of the experiments (including experiments on other ARTINOS data and the Japanese Vowels data set [12]. These experiments are not described here due to space restrictions) were quite surprising. Improvements were achieved in each case, even they vary depending on the dataset between twenty and several hundred percent of the test error. The best feature set is always only a small fraction of the total feature set.

The initial hypothesis, that the reduction of output connections reduces the generalization error of ESNs, holds for the experiments performed so far. This work is in line with the results of Dutoit et. al. [10] who also showed excellent results (i.e. error reduction by a factor of 5) by applying pruning and regularization techniques on ESN output connections. We expect that feature selection on output connection will become a commonly used technique for improving ESN performance.

Acknowledgment. This work is part of the project DEGENA funded by the German Federal Ministry of Education and Research (BMBF).

References

1. Jaeger, H., Maass, W., Principe, J. (eds.): Special Issue Echo State Networks and Liquid State Machines. Neural Networks 20(3), 287–432 (2007)
2. Lukosevicius, M., Jaeger, H.: Reservoir computing approaches to recurrent neural network training. Computer Science Review 3(3), 127–149 (2009)
3. Labusch, K., Barth, E., Martinetz, T.: Sparse Coding Neural Gas: Learning of Overcomplete Data Representations. Neurocomputing 72(7-9), 1547–1555 (2009)
4. Jaeger, H.: The "echo state" approach to analysing and training recurrent neural networks. GMD Report 148, German National Research Center for Information Technology (2001)
5. Jaeger, H.: Erratum note,
   http://www.faculty.jacobs-university.de/hjaeger/pubs/
   EchoStatesTechRepErratum.pdf
6. Shi, Z., Han, M.: Support vector echo-state machine for chaotic time-series prediction. IEEE Transactions on Neural Networks 18(2), 359–372 (2007)
7. Guyon, I., Elissee, A.: An introduction to variable and feature selection. Journal of Machine Learning Research 3, 1157–1182 (2003)
8. Kohavi, R., John, G.: Wrappers for feature subset selection. Artificial Intelligence 97(1-2), 273–324 (1996)
9. Zhu, Z., Ong, Y.S., Dash, M.: Markov blanket-embedded genetic algorithm for gene selection. Pattern Recognition 40(11), 3236–3248 (2007)
10. Dutoit, X., Schrauwen, B., Van Campenhout, J., Stroobandt, D., Van Brussel, H., Nuttin, M.: Pruning and regularisation in reservoir computing. Neurocomputing 72, 1534–1546 (2009)
11. DEGENA project, http://www.sysca-ag.de/degena/index.htm
12. Kudo, M., Toyama, J., Shimbo, M.: Data, http://kdd.ics.uci.edu

On Estimating Mutual Information for Feature Selection

Erik Schaffernicht[1], Robert Kaltenhaeuser[1],
Saurabh Shekhar Verma[2], and Horst-Michael Gross[1]

[1] Neuroinformatics and Cognitive Robotics Lab,
Ilmenau University of Technology, Germany
Erik.Schaffernicht@tu-ilmenau.de
[2] College of Technology, GBPUAT, Pantnagar, India

Abstract. Mutual Information (MI) is a powerful concept from information theory used in many application fields. For practical tasks it is often necessary to estimate the Mutual Information from available data. We compare state of the art methods for estimating MI from continuous data, focusing on the usefulness for the feature selection task. Our results suggest that many methods are practically relevant for feature selection tasks regardless of their theoretic limitations or benefits.

Keywords: Mutual Information, Probabilitty Density Estimation, Feature Selection.

1 Introduction

Mutual Information (MI) is a well known concept from information theory and has been utilized to capture the dependence structure between pairs of random variables X and Y. In contrast to approaches like correlation coefficients MI is not limited to the linear dependencies but includes any nonlinear ones. In an information theoretic sense, MI quantifies the information variable X contains about Y and vice versa.

Identifying relevant features for a given learning problem in order to eliminate irrelevant and redundant inputs that complicate the learning process is defined as the feature selection task. Applying Mutual Information to calculate the relevance of a given input channel is a very intuitive and common approach. In its most simple form it allows a feature ranking, but there are more sophisticated filter approaches based on MI.

The practical challenge of using Mutual Information for feature selection is the estimation of this measure from the available data. Similar to [1], we compare different approaches of estimating MI, but in contrast we include new approaches for estimation and focus on the feature selection task.

A brief recap of all the considered methods will be given in the next section. The results of our tests will be shown in section 3, where we draw conclusion about the usefulness of different methods for feature selection.

K. Diamantaras, W. Duch, L.S. Iliadis (Eds.): ICANN 2010, Part I, LNCS 6352, pp. 362–367, 2010.

2   Methods for Estimating Mutual Information

The goal is to estimate the mutual information, which is given by

$$I(X;Y) = \int \int p(x,y) log_2 \frac{p(x,y)}{p(x)p(y)} dx dy \qquad (1)$$

In this paper, we consider the histogram estimation with Scott's rule [2], Cellucci's adaptive partitioning of the XY plane [3], an approach using an ensemble of histograms, kernel density estimation (KDE) [4], least-squares mutual information (LSMI) [5] and k-nearest neighbor estimation (K-NN) [6].

This selection is far from complete, literature thrives with other methods, but it captures the intuitive methods (Histogram and KDE) as well as the current standard method (K-NN) and a very recent method that claims superiority to this (LSMI).

2.1   Histogram Approach

The standard histogram partitions the axes into distinct bins of width w_i and then counts the number n_i of observation falling into the bin i. In order to turn this count into a normalized probability density, we simply divide by the total number N of observations and by the width w of the bins to obtain probability values

$$p_i = \frac{n_i}{N w_i} \qquad (2)$$

for which $\int p(x)dx = 1$. This gives a model for the density $p(x)$ that is constant over the width of each bin.

The mutual information between X and Y given by eqn.1 changes to eqn.3

$$I(X;Y) = \sum_i \sum_j P_{ij} log_2 \left(\frac{P_{ij}}{P_i P_j} \right) \qquad (3)$$

where $P_i = p_i \cdot w$ is the probability of bin i in the marginal space and $P_{ij} = p_{ij} \cdot w^2$ is the probability of bin ij in the joint space. We use Scott's rule [2] to approximate the value of the bin width.

2.2   Ensemble of Histograms

Histograms, especially histograms with a constant bin width, are highly dependent on the choice of the width of the bins. Histograms with different bin widths applied to the same dataset can provide very different results of Mutual Information due to estimation errors.

One possibility to handle this problem is using an ensemble of many histograms, all using different bin widths. We use Scott's rule and the parameter λ to determine the size of the ensemble n and the width of the bins or the number of bins, respectively. Let k_{Scott} be the number of bins calculated by Scott's rule. All integer values in the interval $[\lceil k_{Scott}/\lambda \rceil, \lfloor k_{Scott} \cdot \lambda \rfloor]$ provide the number of bins for one instance.

After creating the histograms and estimating the values for the mutual information for each different bin width $I_i(X;Y)$ as shown in the previous section (Eqn. 3), the final Mutual Information can be calculated by using the arithmetic average over the estimated mutual information values.

2.3   Adaptive Partitioning of the XY Plane

Instead of using a constant bin width, it is possible to define variable sized bins based on the data. One of these methods is Cellucci's adaptive partitioning of the XY plane [3]. The plane is partitioned by dividing each axis into multiple equiprobable segments. Additionally it should satisfy the Cochran criterion on the expectancies $E(n_{ij})$ of the bins, which requires $E(n_{ij}) \geq 1$ for all elements of the partition and $E(n_{ij}) \geq 5$ for at least 80% of the bins.

To obtain this, each axis is partitioned that $P_x(i) = 1/k$ and $P_y(j) = 1/k$, where $P_x(i)$ is the probability of segment i of the x-axis and k denotes the number of bins in the marginal space and should be equal for each axis.

The bins in the marginal space are chosen such that each one has an occupancy of N/k points. Eqn. 3 is used to compute the values.

2.4   Kernel Density Estimation (KDE)

With kernel density estimation, the probability density function of X can be estimated by the superposition of a set of kernel functions $k(u)$, centered on the data points:

$$p(x) = \frac{1}{Nh^d} \sum k\left(\frac{x - x_n}{h}\right) \tag{4}$$

In general, the kernel function satisfies $k(u) \geq 0$ and $\int k(u)du = 1$. Using Gaussian kernel funtions, the probability density functions are given as

$$p(x,y) = \frac{1}{N} \sum \frac{1}{2\pi h^2} exp\left(-\frac{(x - x_n)^2 + (y - y_n)^2}{2h^2}\right). \tag{5}$$

2.5   Least-Squares Mutual Information (LSMI)

The least-squares Mutual Information [5] uses a concept named density ratio estimation. Instead of approximating the probability density functions $p(x)$, $p(y)$ and $p(x,y)$ separately, the density ratio function

$$\omega(x,y) = \frac{p(x,y)}{p(x)\,p(y)} \tag{6}$$

is estimated here in a single shot. The advantage of doing this is to avoid the division by estimated densities, which tend to magnify the estimation error.

Therefore, the approximated density ratio function $\hat{\omega}_\alpha(x, y)$ is modeled by a linear model $\hat{\omega}_\alpha(x, y) := \alpha^T \varphi(x, y)$ where $\alpha = (\alpha_1, ..., \alpha_b)^T$ is a vector of parameters to be learned from samples, $\varphi(x, y) = (\varphi_1(x, y), ..., \varphi_b(x, y))^T$ denotes a vector of basis functions, such that $\varphi(x, y) \geq 0$ for all $(x, y) \in D_x \times D_y$. To determine α the squared error J_0 is minimized

$$J_0(\alpha) = \frac{1}{2} \int_x \int_y (\hat{\omega}_\alpha(x, y) - \omega(x, y))^2 p(x)\, p(y)\, dx\, dy. \qquad (7)$$

2.6   K-Nearest Neighbor Approach(K-NN)

The K-NN approach uses a fixed number k of nearest neighbors to estimate the MI. For each point in the dataset, the minimum volume V that encompasses K points is determined. By counting the number of points inside this volume in the marginal spaces the Mutual Information can be estimated.

The Mutual Information is estimated as

$$I(X; Y) = \psi(k) - \frac{1}{k} - \frac{1}{N} \sum_{i=1}^{N} [\psi(n_x(i)) + \psi(n_y(i))] + \psi(N) \qquad (8)$$

where $\psi(x)$ is the digamma function and n_x denotes the neighbours in one dimension.

It can be expanded easily to m variables approximating the Joint Mutual Information (JMI):

$$I(X_1; ...; X_m) = \psi(k) - \frac{m-1}{k} - \frac{1}{N} \sum_{i=1}^{N} [\psi(n_{x_1}(i)) + ... + \psi(n_{x_m}(i))] + (m-1)\,\psi(N)$$

$$(9)$$

3   Experiments

Our first batch of experiments resembles those presented in [1]. All approaches had to approximate the MI between two variables where the real Mutual Information was known due to the design of experiments. This includes linear, quadratic and trigonometric dependencies with different levels of noise and a changing number of available samples. For details, refer to [1]. The results are in line with those presented by Khan. The most precise and most consistent results were achieved by the K-NN, which proved to be the standard everyone has to compare to, and the KDE approach. The adaptive histogram approach turned out to be very inconsistent in case of sparse data, while LMSI showed a tendency for strong deviations of the MI for different data sets. The ensemble of histograms evinced small benefits compared to the basic histogram in high noise scenarios.

For the second batch of experiments, we focused on the feature selection tasks. For feature extraction the exact value of the Mutual Information is secondary,

Table 1. Results on the UCI data sets. Given is the balanced error rate, bold entries mark the best results.

Method	Ionosphere	German Credit	Breast Cancer	Parkinsons	Hearts
Histogram	0.0994	0.3791	**0.0463**	0.1601	0.3679
Ensemble	0.1193	0.3791	**0.0463**	0.1601	0.3752
Adapt. Hist	0.1009	**0.3596**	0.0639	0.0921	0.4554
KDE	0.1193	0.3693	**0.0463**	0.1576	0.3752
LSMI	**0.0817**	0.3693	0.0548	0.1356	0.3621
KNN	0.1126	0.3956	0.0632	**0.0647**	0.4068
KNN JMI	0.1432	0.3866	0.0775	0.1632	**0.3512**

more important is the correct ranking of the features, where systematic estimation errors will cancel out each other.

For the actual feature selection two different algorithms were used. The first is MIFS - Mutual Information for Feature Selection [7], which is a simple approximation of the JMI. At each step of the algorithm, the feature is selected, which possesses the highest MIFS value:

$$MIFS = I(X_i; Y) - \beta \sum_{s \in S} I(X_i; s) \tag{10}$$

where S denotes the set of already selected features, X_i is the feature for which the MIFS value is calculated and Y are the labels. Furthermore, β is a free parameter stating the influence of the already selected features on the remaining candidate features. β was heuristically determined to keep the MIFS value positive for the first eight features. This method was combined with all approaches to consider multi-dimensional influences presented in Sec. 2.

The second algorithm uses a forward selection strategy based on the Joint Mutual Information (JMI) [8]. In each step the feature that possesses the maximum JMI between the candidate feature, the already selected features and the labels is chosen. The computation of the JMI was done using the K-NN approach.

The feature selection test were performed on five different datasets from the UCI Machine Learning repository [9]. We used the algorithms to extract the eight best features from the data sets and tested them by using a nearest neighbor classifier and the leave one out strategy to compute the balanced error rate. The resulting error rates are shown in Tab. 1. Equal error rates for different methods are the result of selecting the same features (not necessarily in the same order).

On one hand, the table shows that each method achieves for one data set the best results. On the other hand, every method is inferior to others for some data sets. The most consistent results based on the ranking were achieved by LMSI, the KDE and the histogram approach, while the worst outputs are resulting from the K-NN approach directly estimating the JMI. This particular way of handling the JMI is outperformed by the MIFS approximation on a regular basis. In terms of computational costs, the histogram and KDE are cheapest, while the LSMI is the most expensive method due to the inherent cross validation.

4   Conclusions

In this paper, we investigated methods for estimating Mutual Information from data. For application scenarios, in which the exact value is required, our results are very similar to those published in [1]. The conclusion is to use either the Kernel Density Estimation or the Kraskov's Nearest Neighbor method.

Concerning the feature selection task only a correct ranking of the input variables is required. Most consistent performers are the Least Squares Mutual Information, the Kernel Density Estimation and simple Histogram estimation. The most problematic approach is the direct estimation of the Joint Mutual Information using the Kraskov Nearest Neighbor Method, in almost every case it was outperformed by the MIFS approximation.

The basic conclusion to be drawn from these investigations is that there is no best method to estimate Mutual Information in the feature selection context, but all considered method are more or less useful depending on the data. Nevertheless, we suggest using the KDE method, because of its good results in both types of experiments.

References

1. Khan, S., Bandyopadhyay, S., Ganguly, A.R., Saigal, S., Erickson, D.J., Protopopescu, V., Ostrouchov, G.: Relative performance of mutual information estimation methods for quantifying the dependence among short and noisy data. Physical Review E 76, 026209 (2007)
2. Scott, D.W.: Multivariate density estimation: theory, practice and visualization. John Wiley & Sons, New York (1992)
3. Cellucci, C.J., Albano, A.M., Rapp, P.E.: Statistical validation of mutual information calculations: Comparison of alternative numerical algorithms. Physical Review E 71(6), 066208 (2005)
4. Silverman, B.W.: Density Estimation for Statistics and Data Analysis. Chapman and Hall, London (1986)
5. Suzuki, T., Sugiyama, M., Sese, J., Kanamori, T.: A least-squares approach to mutual information estimation with application in variable selection. In: Proceedings of the 3rd Workshop on New Challenges for Feature Selection in Data mining and Knowledge Discovery (FSDM 2008), Antwerp, Belgium (2008)
6. Kraskov, A., Stögbauer, H., Grassberger, P.: Estimating mutual information. Physical Review E 69, 066138 (2004)
7. Battiti, R.: Using mutual information for selecting features in supervised neural net learning. IEEE Transactions on Neural Networks 5(4), 537–550 (1994)
8. Kwak, N., Choi, C.H.: Input feature selection by mutual information based on parzen window. IEEE Transactions on Pattern Analysis and Machine Intelligence 24(12), 1667–1671 (2002)
9. Asuncion, A., Newman, D.: UCI machine learning repository (2007), http://archive.ics.uci.edu/ml/

Using Correlation Dimension for Analysing Text Data*

Ilkka Kivimäki, Krista Lagus, Ilari T. Nieminen,
Jaakko J. Väyrynen, and Timo Honkela

Adaptive Informatics Research Centre,
Aalto University School of Science and Technology
firstname.lastname@tkk.fi
http://www.cis.hut.fi/research/

Abstract. In this article, we study the scale-dependent dimensionality
properties and overall structure of text data with a method that measures correlation dimension in different scales. As experimental results,
we present the analysis of text data sets with the Reuters and Europarl
corpora, which are also compared to artificially generated point sets. A
comparison is also made with speech data. The results reflect some of the
typical properties of the data and the use of our method in improving
various data analysis applications is discussed.

Keywords: Correlation dimension, dimensionality calculation, dimensionality reduction, statistical natural language processing.

1 Introduction

Knowing the *intrinsic dimensionality* of a data set can be a benefit, for instance,
when deciding the parameters of a dimension reduction method. One popular
technique for determining the intrinsic dimensionality of a finite data set is
calculating its correlation dimension, which is a fractal dimension. This is usually
done according to the method introduced by Grassberger and Procaccia in [1].
Usually the goal in these dimensionality calculations is to characterise a data
set by a single statistic. Not much emphasis is always put to the notion of the
dependence of correlation dimension on the scale of observation. However, as
we will show, the scale-dependent dimensionality properties can vary between
different data sets according to the nature of the data. Most neural network and
statistical methods such as singular value decomposition or the self-organising
map are usually applied without considering this fact. Even in papers studying
dimensionality calculation methods (e.g. [2] and [3]) the scale-dependence of
dimensionality is noted, but usually left without further discussion.

We focus on natural language data. It has been observed that the intrinsic
dimensionality of text data, such as term-document matrices, is often much

---

* This work has been supported by the Academy of Finland and a grant from the
Department of Mathematics and Statistics at the University of Helsinki (IK).

K. Diamantaras, W. Duch, L.S. Iliadis (Eds.): ICANN 2010, Part I, LNCS 6352, pp. 368–373, 2010.
© Springer-Verlag Berlin Heidelberg 2010

lower than the dimensionality of the original data space due to its sparseness and correlation in the data. In addition to term-document matrices, we also consider speech data and data about co-occurences of words inside the same sentence, which is another approach of encoding semantic information in text.

In a research closely related to ours, [4] studies the local dimensionality of a word space concluding that the small-scale dimensionality is very low compared to the dimensionality of the data space. In that paper, the word space was built with the random indexing method, whereas we use a more standard setting. In [5] a method for calculating dimensionality is presented and the effect of different term-weighting methods on the dimensionality estimates is studied. Also in [6] dimensionality calculations were made for natural language data, in this case partly with the same data sets that we use. For the calculations, they used a modified version of a method originally proposed by [7] based on eigenvalue information of the autocorrelation matrix of the data.

2   The Scale-Dependent Correlation Dimension

Correlation dimension can be measured for a finite data set $\{x_1, \ldots x_N\} \subset \mathbb{R}^n$ by the Grassberger-Procaccia (GP) algorithm [1]. First we define the *correlation sum* $C(r)$ as the probability of a randomly chosen pair of data points being within distance r from each other:

$$C(r) = \frac{2}{N(N-1)} \sum_{i=1}^{N} \sum_{j=i}^{N} I(\rho(x_i, x_j) < r),$$

where $I(x)$ is the indicator function (i.e. 1, if the argument condition holds and 0 otherwise) and ρ is the metric. We will use the Euclidean distance as the metric. In the usual implementation of the GP-algorithm the correlation dimension is then defined as the slope of the linear segment in the plot of the correlation sum $C(r)$ against r in double logarithmic coordinates.

In other words, one first finds a *scale* $[r_i, r_j]$, where the loglog-plot of the correlation sum appears linear and then computes the correlation dimension $\hat{\nu}$ as the logarithmic derivative on this interval:

$$\hat{\nu} = \hat{\nu}(r_i, r_j) = \frac{\log(C(r_j)/C(r_i))}{\log(r_j/r_i)}.$$

However, instead of defining only one segment or *scale* $[r_i, r_j]$, the dimensionality of a data set can actually be measured scale-dependently by studying the local derivatives with different r. For estimating these dimensionality curves, we decided throughout the paper (after experimenting with different values) to use 100 measuring points $r_1, \ldots, r_{100}$, distributed logarithmically on the interval $[r_1 = \min \rho(x_i, x_j), r_{100} = \max \rho(x_i, x_j)]$. For illustration purposes, we use an additional smoothing method by a simple triangular kernel of window length w.

The window length then defines the width of the scale of observation. Thus we can finally define the scale-dependent dimensionality of the data set as

$$\nu(r) = \frac{1}{2w} \sum_{\substack{j=i-w, \\ j\neq i}}^{i+w} \hat{\nu}(r_i, r_j), \text{ when } r \in [r_i, r_{i+1}]. \tag{1}$$

Again, after experimenting with different window lengths, we fixed the value at $w = 6$ throughout the paper.

3   Experiments

3.1   Reuters

The first data set for experiments with the method presented above is a document collection gathered from the Reuters corpus of news articles [8]. We took a subset of the corpus consisting of 10 000 articles. The documents have been preprocessed by removing stop words and reducing all words into their stems. The frequencies of the subset's 300 most frequent terms were counted for each article resulting in a matrix of 10 000 vectors with dimensionality 300. As a common preprocessing method, a term frequency–inverse document frequency or *tf/idf*–weighting [9] was performed for the raw frequencies.

The dimensionality curve for the Reuters data set is shown in Figure 1(a). The curve indicates some essential properties of a term-document matrix. Starting from the large scale on the right end of the curve, the dimensionality starts increasing from zero as the scale narrows down from the diameter of the data set. It soon reaches a maximum value which would traditionally be interpreted as the dimensionality of the set. For our 10 000 article subset of the Reuters collection the dimensionality would thus be approximately $\nu(r) = 7.5$. Continuing on to smaller scales on the left of the maximum value, the dimensionality decreases significantly.

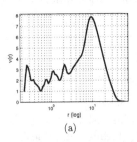
(a)

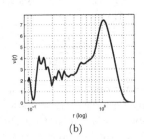
(b)

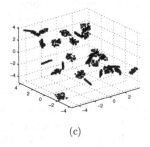
(c)

Fig. 1. The dimensionality curve of $\nu(r)$ for the Reuters data set (a), the data set consisting of 200 3-D clusters with 40 points scattered in 20-D space (b) and the illustration of 2-D clusters scattered in 3-D space

The low values of $\nu(r)$ with small r mean that the data shows high auto-correlation locally. We will simulate this kind of behaviour with an artificially generated set of points that consists of low-dimensional clusters scattered in a high-dimensional embedding space. This idea is illustrated in Figure 1(c), which shows 2-dimensional clusters scattered in 3-dimensional space. Our example data set contains 200 subsets of 40 points from uniform distribution in a 3-dimensional unit cube. These 200 clusters are each rotated by a random rotating matrix and then shifted by a randomly generated vector in a 20-dimensional embedding space. The dimensionality curve for this data set is shown in Figure 1(b).

The high autocorrelation at small distances suggests that the documents differ only in the frequencies of a few different key terms from each other. This phenomenon can cause problems with large document collections because there is not enough information for making a detailed analysis of the collection. Thus the dimensionality curve could possibly be used to evaluate the differentia-bility of a word-document data set and to develop a better feature selection method through a hierarchical clustering. For instance, expanding the feature space within proper clusters with terms that are significant to the documents in that cluster making the differentiation of the document vectors easier. Related work has already been done in [10] and also in [11].

3.2 ISOLET

To contrast the shape of the dimensionality curve for text data we will use the ISOLET speech data set [12]. It consists of 7797 samples of spoken English letters of which 617 acoustic features were measured resulting in 7797 vectors in 617-dimensional space. The dimensionality curve is shown in Figure 2(a)[1]. One can interpret a part with linear behaviour in the correlation integral in the scale between $r = 4.7$ and $r = 6.8$, where we get a rough estimate of $\nu(r) = 13.3$.

An interesting feature of the ISOLET data set dimensionality curve is in the small scale where the dimensionality value seems to explode. This explosion is caused by the noise in the acoustic speech data which produces variance in small scale in all the noisy feature components of the embedding space. Again we use an artificially generated data set to support this observation. Figure 2(b) shows the dimensionality curve of a data set consisting of 8000 random points from the 3-dimensional unit hypercube to which 20-dimensional Gaussian white noise with a variance of 10^{-3} has been added.

Figures 1(b) and 2(b) can now be compared to each other. The sets represented by the curves differ quite a lot in their scale-dependent dimensionalities, but show also similarity in dimensionalities in certain scales. In the extreme case, a bad method or a careless examination could lead to an interpretation of the sets having the same dimensionality. This again supports the significance of investigating dimensionality properties of data sets in several scales.

---

[1] Here we omitted the smallest point-pair distance from further analysis as it was several magnitudes smaller than the rest of the distances forcing the curve to drop to zero at the left end.

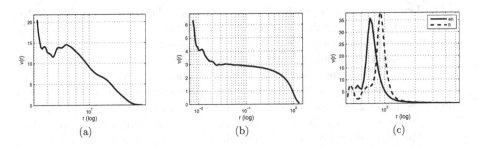

Fig. 2. $\nu(r)$ for the ISOLET data set (a), the 3-D data set with 20-D Gaussian white noise (b) and for the English (solid line) and Finnish (dashed line) Europarl data sets (c)

3.3   Europarl

The Europarl corpus version 3 contains the minutes from the sessions of the EU parliament from the years 1997-2006 in 11 languages [13]. We used it to study dimensionality properties of word co-occurence data. Only the results of experiments conducted with the English and Finnish parts of the corpus are presented here. We used a subset of the corpus containing the sessions of 591 days that were recorded for both languages. Both of the subsets were preprocessed by first removing the XML-tagging used in the files, then applying sentence boundary detection, tokenization and removal of punctuation and special characters.

The data matrix had the 1 000 most frequent words as the term vectors and the 20 000 most frequent words as the context features. For the elements of the matrix, we counted the frequencies of each term and feature word occuring in the same sentence. Finally, we took the logarithm of the frequencies increased by one as is done in the *tf/idf*-method, however preserving the frequency rank information in this case.

The dimensionality curves for the English and Finnish Europarl data sets are shown in Figure 2(c). The overall shape of both curves looks the same. The long and thin right tails imply that some of the 1 000 data points in both sets are spread very far from the others and also that there are large scale correlations in the data. However, the sharp peak in both curves shows that the interpoint distances are concentrated on a narrow scale causing rather high dimensionality estimates in both cases. The peak dimensionality values are 35.9 for English and 38.1 for Finnish. On the left of the peak value, the dimensionality curves both descend showing low-dimensionality in small scales for both data sets. However, this effect is not as pronounced as with the Reuters data set because of the shortness of the left tail in both curves. One more thing worth noting is the different positioning of the curves on the horizontal axis. Further experiments, not reported here, suggest that the location of the peak value on the horizontal axis correlates highly with the average sentence length in words of the language, but also the word type/token ratio may have an impact on this phenomenon.

4   Conclusions and Discussion

We have presented a method for observing the scale-dependent dimensionality of a finite data set based on the Grassberger-Procaccia algorithm. The dimensionality curves obtained with our method give interesting information about the structure of the data set and show some typical characteristics of the phenomenon causing the data. We illustrated the method with natural language data and artificially generated data discussing its indications and benefits.

The relevance of scale-dependent dimensionality for dimensionality reduction, clustering and other data analysis methods seems to be an interesting topic for future research, which, according to our knowledge, has not received much attention before. Also the reliability of the GP-algorithm, as used in our study, needs to be studied more. An additional interesting question is how different data analysis methods respond to scale invariance or self-similarity (or the lack of them) in a data set. These ideas and questions will get the authors' attention in future investigations and also serve as the motivation to the whole content of this article.

References

1. Grassberger, P., Procaccia, I.: Characterization of strange attractors. Phys. Rev. Lett. 50(5), 346–349 (1983)
2. Camastra, F.: Data dimensionality estimation methods: a survey. Pattern Recognition 36(12), 2945–2954 (2003)
3. Theiler, J.: Estimating fractal dimension. Journal of the Optical Society of America A 7, 1055–1073 (1990)
4. Karlgren, J., Holst, A., Sahlgren, M.: Filaments of meaning in word space. Advances in Information Retrieval, pp. 531–538 (2008)
5. Kumar, C.A., Srinivas, S.: A note on effect of term weighting on selecting intrinsic dimensionality of data. Journal of Cybernetics and Information Technologies 9(1), 5–12 (2009)
6. Kohonen, T., Nieminen, I.T., Honkela, T.: On the quantization error in SOM vs. VQ: A critical and systematic study. In: Proceedings of WSOM 2009, pp. 133–144 (2009)
7. Fukunaga, K., Olsen, D.R.: An algorithm for finding intrinsic dimensionality of data. IEEE Trans. Comput. 20, 176–183 (1971)
8. Lewis, D.D., Yang, Y., Rose, T.G., Li, F.: Rcv1: A new benchmark collection for text categorization research. J. Mach. Learn. Res. 5, 361–397 (2004)
9. Manning, C.D., Schütze, H.: Foundations of statistical natural language processing. MIT Press, Cambridge (1999)
10. Vinay, V., Cox, I.J., Milic-Frayling, N., Wood, K.R.: Measuring the complexity of a collection of documents. In: Lalmas, M., MacFarlane, A., Rüger, S.M., Tombros, A., Tsikrika, T., Yavlinsky, A. (eds.) ECIR 2006. LNCS, vol. 3936, pp. 107–118. Springer, Heidelberg (2006)
11. Cai, D., He, X., Han, J.: Document clustering using locality preserving indexing. IEEE Transactions on Knowledge and Data Engineering 17(12), 1624–1637 (2005)
12. Cole, R., Fanty, M.: Spoken letter recognition. In: HLT 1990: Proceedings of the Workshop on Speech and Natural Language, pp. 385–390 (1990)
13. Koehn, P.: Europarl: A parallel corpus for statistical machine translation. In: Machine Translation Summit X, pp. 79–86 (2005)

Designing Simple Nonlinear Filters Using Hysteresis of Single Recurrent Neurons for Acoustic Signal Recognition in Robots

Poramate Manoonpong[1], Frank Pasemann[2],
Christoph Kolodziejski[1], and Florentin Wörgötter[1]

[1] Bernstein Center for Computational Neuroscience (BCCN)
University of Göttingen, D-37077 Göttingen, Germany
{poramate,kolo,worgott}@bccn-goettingen.de
[2] Institute of Cognitive Science
University of Osnabrück, D-49069 Osnabrück, Germany
frank.pasemann@uni-osnabrueck.de

Abstract. In this article we exploit the discrete-time dynamics of a single neuron with self-connection to systematically design simple signal filters. Due to hysteresis effects and transient dynamics, this single neuron behaves as an adjustable low-pass filter for specific parameter configurations. Extending this neuro-module by two more recurrent neurons leads to versatile high- and band-pass filters. The approach presented here helps to understand how the dynamical properties of recurrent neural networks can be used for filter design. Furthermore, it gives guidance to a new way of implementing sensory preprocessing for acoustic signal recognition in autonomous robots.

Keywords: Neural networks, Digital signal processing, Non-speech recognition, Autonomous robots, Walking robots.

1 Introduction

To date, recurrent neural networks (RNNs) have been employed to a wide field of applications due to their excellent properties, like robustness, adaptivity, and dynamics. Examples include the use of RNNs in chaotic systems [1], [2], robot control and learning [3], trajectory generation [4], and others. Many applications require effective learning methods [5], [6] to train the networks. As a consequence, the networks, in particular for signal processing [7], [8], [9], end up with a massive connectivity or cascaded recurrent structures. The complexity of such networks requires a large memory during learning. In addition, their high dimensionality makes it difficult to analyze them and even to understand the neural dynamics in detail. However, a thorough understanding of the network dynamics is one important part to further develop and apply these networks to other applications, like robot control. This is also a basic step towards the development of complex systems [10]. As a small step forward in this direction, we want to show here how neural dynamics, e.g., hysteresis effects, can be applied to systematically

K. Diamantaras, W. Duch, L.S. Iliadis (Eds.): ICANN 2010, Part I, LNCS 6352, pp. 374–383, 2010.

design simple nonlinear low-pass, high-pass, and even band-pass filters. With one or only a few neurons such filters can be used for sensory signal processing in autonomous robots, where preprocessed signals will drive (complex) robot behavior, e.g., for (non-speech) sound recognition.

The following section shortly describes the discrete-time dynamics of a single recurrent neuron. Section 3 explains how we develop low-pass filters by utilizing hysteresis effects of the single recurrent neuron. Sections 4 and 5 show the extension of the low-pass filters to high- and band-pass ones. Section 6 presents an application of using the proposed neural filers for acoustic signal recognition in a walking robot. The last section provides summary and discussion.

2   Discrete Dynamics of a Single Recurrent Neuron

A single neuron with self-connection (see Fig. 1(a)) has several interesting (discrete) dynamical features[11]. For example, an excitatory self-connection leads to a hysteresis effect, while stable oscillation with period-2 orbit can be observed for an inhibitory self-connection. Both phenomena occur for specific parameter domains, where the input and the strength of the self-connection are considered as parameters. In this article, hysteresis effects are utilized for designing simple filters. The corresponding discrete-time dynamics is parameterized by the input I and the self-connection w_s (see Fig. 1(a)), and for a recurrent neuro-module is given by $a(t+1) = w_s f(a(t)) + \theta$ with the sigmoidal transfer function $f(a) = \tanh(a)$. The parameter θ stands for the sum of the fixed bias term b and the variable input I to the neuron. $O(t) = f(a(t))$ is the output signal. We refer the reader to [12] for the presentation of the dynamics of a neuron with excitatory self-connection in the (θ, w_s)-parameter space.

3   Low-Pass Filters

In this section we describe how simple low pass filters can be designed based on the hysteresis effect of the single recurrent neuron mentioned above. We simulate a sine wave input signal varying from 100 Hz to 1000 Hz (compare Fig. 1(b)). It is used as an input signal for the recurrent neuro-module configured as a hysteresis element L (see Fig. 1(a)). The network is constructed and analyzed using the Integrated Structure Evolution Environment (ISEE) [5] which is a software platform for developing and evolving recurrent neural networks. To observe the low-pass filter characteristics of the network, we fixed the presynaptic weight ($w_{i1} = 1.0$) from the input to the neuron and the bias term ($b_1 = -0.1$) while the self-connection w_{s1} of the output unit is varied (see Fig. 1(c)). Using this setup, the network performs as a low-pass filter at different cutoff frequencies according to the strength of w_{s1}. Figure 1(c) presents the correlation between w_{s1} and the cutoff frequency. For example, selecting $w_{s1} = 2.42$ the network suppresses signals with frequencies higher than 500 Hz. This effect together with the characteristic curve of this network is shown in Fig. 2.

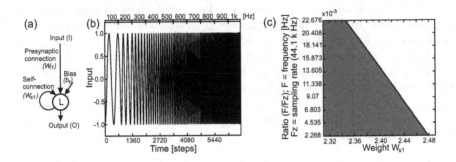

Fig. 1. Low-pass filter setup. (a) Recurrent neuro-module realizing a simple low-pass filter. Its input weight w_{i1} and bias term b_1 are fixed to 1.0 and -0.1, respectively, while the weight w_{s1} is changeable in order to obtain certain cutoff frequencies. (b) Example of the input signal at increasing frequencies (from 100 Hz to 1 kHz, 44.1 kHz sampling rate). (c) Cutoff frequency of a low-pass filter module depending on the self-connection w_{s1}. The x -axis represents the self-connection w_{s1} and the y-axis represents the ratio between frequency [Hz] and sampling rate (44.1 kHz). Note that this diagram will be used later for defining lower cutoff frequencies f_L of the band-pass filters described below.

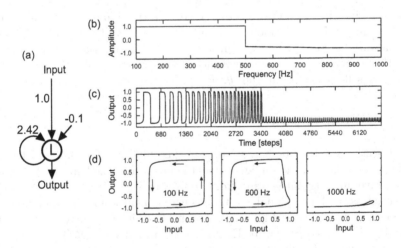

Fig. 2. Example of a low-pass filter. (a) A 500 Hz low-pass filter neuro-module. (b) Characteristic curve of the network with its cutoff frequency at 500 Hz. (c) Output signal of the network according to the given input shown in Fig. 1(b). (d) The hysteresis effect between input and output signals at certain frequencies. Due to the hysteresis effect, the shape of the output signal is distorted, e.g., 100 Hz and 500 Hz. Arrows show how the output develops according to the change of the input.

To visualize the hysteresis effect of the 500 Hz low-pass filter, output versus input signals are plotted in Fig. 2(d). This shows that the hysteresis effect disappears for the high-frequency signals (e.g., 1000 Hz), whereas for low-frequency signals (e.g., 100 Hz and 500 Hz) the hysteresis switches the amplitude between (almost) saturation values (approximately -1 and $+1$). As the bias term defines the base activity of the neuron, the amplitude of the high-frequency output oscillates with a small magnitude between around -0.6 and -0.998. Eventually it will never rise above 0.0 again. Due to the slowness of the transient dynamics and the bias term the upper saturation domain (high stable fixed points ($\approx +1$)) is never reached if high frequency signals are applied. Furthermore, because of the hysteresis effects, the low-pass filter output is slightly shifted and its shape is distorted. Therefore, the system acts as a nonlinear low-pass filter.

4   High-Pass Filters

Having established a single neuron low-pass filter, the following step is to derive networks, which behave like high-pass filters based on the presented low-pass. The simplest way to do this would be to subtract the low-pass filter output (see, e.g., Fig. 2(c)) from the input (see Fig. 1(b)). In other words, the low-pass filter neuron L (see Figs. 1(a) and 3(a)) would here act as an inhibiting neuron which inhibits transmission of all low-frequency signals of the input. However, due to the hysteresis effect, the low-pass filter output is shifted and its shape is distorted compared to the input (see Fig. 2(d)). Thus the input cannot be directly subtracted. To overcome this problem, we again utilize the hysteresis effect to shape the input to match it to the low-pass filter output. For doing this, we simply add one more hysteresis unit H (see Fig. 3(a)) receiving its input via a fixed presynaptic weight ($w_{i2} = 1.0$). Its neural parameters (self-connection w_{s2} and bias term b_2, see Fig. 3(a)) are experimentally adjusted and we set them to $w_{s2} = 2.34$ and $b_2 = -0.1$ for which a suitable hysteresis loop is achieved (see Fig. 3(b)). According to this specific weight and bias term, this hidden neuron H actually performs as a low-pass filter with a cutoff frequency of around 1000 Hz. Thus it shapes the input and allows all signals having frequencies up to around 1000 Hz to pass through. After preprocessing at H, the shaped input signal is transmitted to the output neuron O through a positive connection weight ($w_{c2} = 1.0$, see Fig. 3(a)). It is then subtracted by the low-pass filter output due to a negative connection weight ($w_{c1} = -1.0$, see Fig. 3(a)). Still the resulting signal consists of a few spikes in the low frequency components. Therefore, we add a self-connection w_{s3} together with a bias term b_3 at O to obtain an appropriate third hysteresis loop (see Fig. 3(c)) that eliminates these spikes. The neural parameters of this output unit are experimentally tuned and they are set to $w_{s3} = 2.45$ and $b_3 = -1.0$. The resulting network structure is show in Fig. 3. Using this network, we then obtain high-pass filters at certain cutoff frequencies by tuning only the weight w_{s1} shown in Fig. 1(c). For example, choosing $w_{s1} = 2.39$ the network functions as a 700 Hz high-pass filter. This high-pass effect and the characteristic curve of the network are shown in Fig. 4.

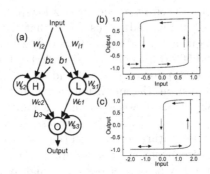

Fig. 3. High-pass filter setup. (a) Recurrent neural network realizing a simple high-pass filter. All weights and bias terms are fixed ($w_{i1,2} = 1.0$, $w_{s2} = 2.34$, $w_{s3} = 2.45$, $w_{c1} = -1.0$, $w_{c2} = 1.0$, $b_{1,2} = -0.1$, and $b_3 = -1.0$), while the weight w_{s1} is changeable according to Fig. 1(c) in order to obtain certain cutoff frequencies. (b), (c) Hysteresis effect between the input and output of the hidden neuron H and the output neuron O, respectively. The input of H varies between -1.0 and $+1.0$ while the sum of the inputs of O varies between -2.0 and $+2.0$. Due to the hysteresis effect the output of H and O has its low (≈ -1.0) and high ($\approx +1.0$) activations at different points. The output of H will show high activation when the input increases to values above 0.88. On the other hand, it will show low activation when the input decreases below -0.68. For the output of O, it will show high activation when the input increases to values above 1.86 while it will show low activation when the input decreases below 0.135. Arrows show how the output develops according to the change of the input.

5   Band-Pass Filters

In this section, we describe how band-pass filters can be achieved by simply changing the self-connections of the high-pass filter network (see Fig. 3(a)) while its structure remains unchanged. Interestingly, due to the fact that the output neuron of the network (see Fig. 3(a)) behaves as a hysteresis element, we only need to increase its self-connection w_{s3} (i.e., increasing its hysteresis size [12]) up to a certain point. As a consequence of the transient dynamics [12], the high frequency signals will then be suppressed.

To observe this phenomenon, we first let the network behave as a 100 Hz high-pass filter; i.e., it passes only signals with frequencies above 100 Hz. The neural parameters are given as follows: $w_{i1,2} = 1.0$, $w_{s1} = 2.479$, $w_{s2} = 2.34$, $w_{s3} = 2.45$, $w_{c1} = -1.0$, $w_{c2} = 1.0$, $b_{1,2} = -0.1$, and $b_3 = -1.0$. Now gradually increasing w_{s3} from approximately 2.47 to 2.57 the high frequency boundary of the network decreases. Thus, in order to design our band-pass filters, this weight will be used to set the upper cutoff frequency f_U. It defines the upper limit at which the frequencies pass through. Beyond this limit, signals will be cancelled out. The correlation between weight w_{s3} and the upper cutoff frequency f_U is shown in Fig. 5(a). As shown in the previous sections, the self-connection

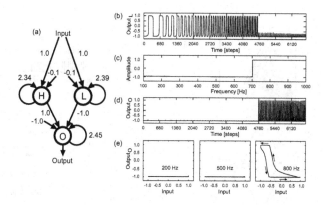

Fig. 4. Example of a high-pass filter. (a) The 700 Hz high-pass filter network. (b) Output of the low-pass filter neuron L according to the given input shown in Fig. 1(b). It suppresses the signal at frequencies above $\approx$ 700 Hz. (c) Characteristic curve of the network with its cutoff frequency at approximately 700 Hz. (d) Output signal of the network according to the given input shown in Fig. 1(b). Only the high frequency signals remain at high amplitude while the amplitude of the lower ones is reduced. (e) Relation between input and output signals at certain frequencies. Due to the hysteresis effect and the subtraction process, the shape of the output signal is distorted, e.g., 800 Hz. Arrows show how the output develops according to the change of the input.

w_{s1} is generally applied to set the frequency at which the signal will be passed (for high-pass filters) or filtered (for low-pass filters). Here we make use of this weight (w_{s1}, see Fig. 1(c)) to set the lower cutoff frequency f_L which allows only signals having frequencies *above* this point to pass. For example, selecting $w_{s1} = f_L = 2.47$ and $w_{s3} = f_U = 2.51$ from the ($w_{s1,3}$, cutoff frequencies)-spaces shown in Figs. 1(c) and 5(a), the network (see Fig. 5(b)) lets signals pass which have frequencies between 200 Hz and 850 Hz (see Fig. 5(c)). Decreasing w_{s1} to 2.455 but increasing w_{s3} to 2.532 the signal bandwidth is reduced to the range from around 300 Hz to around 600 Hz (see Fig. 5(d)). Furthermore, it is even possible set the weights to narrow the frequency range to around 500 Hz by choosing, e.g., $w_{s1} = 2.43$ and $w_{s3} = 2.542$ (see Fig. 5(e)). Thus, the network behaves as a versatile band pass filter.

6   Robot Behavior Control

To show the capability of the neural filters presented here for real world applications, we have applied, e.g., a 400 Hz low-pass filter network (see Fig. 1(a)), to generate acoustic-driven walking behavior (see Fig. 6) of our hexapod robot [2], [12]. The network receives the input–a multi frequency signal mixing between a target low frequency signal (e.g., 300 Hz) and unwanted noise from

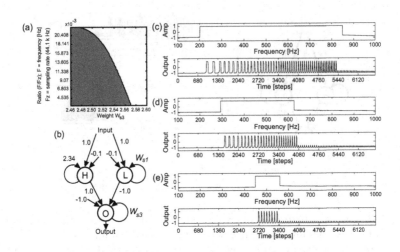

Fig. 5. Example of a band-pass filter. (a) Upper cutoff frequency f_U of a band-pass filter network depending on the weight w_{s3}. (b) The band-pass filter network. The self-connection w_{s1} of neuron L defines the lower cutoff frequencies (cf. Fig. 1(c)) while w_{s3} of the output neuron O is for controlling the upper cutoff frequencies (a). (c) Response of the network for $w_{s1} = 2.47$, $w_{s3} = 2.51$. Upper panel: Characteristic curve of the network with bandwidth from 200 Hz to 850 Hz. Lower panel: Output signal of the network according to the input given in Fig. 1(b). (d) Response of the network for $w_{s1} = 2.455$, $w_{s3} = 2.532$. Upper panel: Characteristic curve of the network with bandwidth from around 300 Hz to around 600 Hz. Lower panel: Output signal of the network using the same input as above. (e) Response of the network for $w_{s1} = 2.43$, $w_{s3} = 2.542$. Upper panel: Characteristic curve of the network with its bandpass of around 500 Hz. Lower panel: Output signal of the network. Note that Amp means the amplitude of neuron activation.

motors as well as locomotion (see Figs. 6(a)–(c))–from an acoustic sensor system of the robot. It suppresses the unwanted noise including acoustic signals having frequencies above 400 Hz (see Figs. 6(d) and (e)) while the low frequency signals pass through (see Fig. 6(f)). As a consequence, it enables the robot to autonomously react on a specific acoustic signal in a real environment; i.e., the robot changes its gait from a slow wave gait (default gait, see Figs 6(g) and (h)) to a fast one (acoustic-driven gait, see Fig. 6(i)) as soon as it detects the signal at the carrier frequency of 300 Hz. The video clip of the experiments can be seen at http://www.manoonpong.com/ICANN2010/AcousticDrivenBehavior.mpg.

These acoustic-driven walking behavioral experiments show that the simple recurrent neural filters are appropriate for robot applications like background noise elimination, and/or non-speech sound recognition.

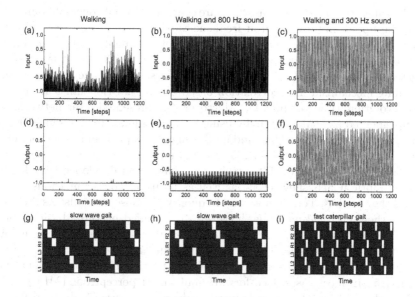

Fig. 6. Input and output signals of the 400 Hz low-pass filter network and corresponding walking patterns in three example situations (only walking (left), walking and receiving 800 Hz sound (middle), and walking and receiving 300 Hz sound (right)). (a)–(c) The input signal to the network for the different conditions. (d)–(f) The output of the network according to the given input for the different conditions. (g)–(i) Examples of the corresponding walking patterns in a certain period for the different conditions. The x-axis represents time and the y-axis represents the legs. During the swing phase (white blocks) the feet have no ground contact. During the stance phase (black blocks) the feet touch the ground. R1: Right front leg, R2: Right middle leg, R3: Right hind leg, L1: Left front leg, L2: Left middle leg, L3: Left hind leg. Note that we use an additional low-pass filter neuron to eliminate the remaining noise ((d), (e)) and smooth the desired acoustic signal (f) before activating the desired walking pattern (here, caterpillar-like gait (i) through modular neural locomotion control [2].

7 Discussion and Conclusions

In this study, we have addressed the exploitation of hysteresis effects and transient dynamics of a single neuron with an excitatory self-connection to design different filters. Starting from one single recurrent neuron, we have observed that this simple network with its specific parameters has the property of a low-pass filter. As such it has comparable properties of an infinite impulse response filter in digital filter theory (IIR filter) because its recurrent connection provides feedback to the system as the output of the IIR filter does. Based on this simple low-pass filter network, by adding two recurrent neurons we obtained high- and band-pass filters, where these neurons also act as hysteresis elements. The cutoff frequencies of the high-pass filter are controlled by only one self-connection; while the upper and lower cutoff frequencies of the band-pass filter are determined by two self-connections. An advantage of the small number and limited range of all relevant parameters ($w_{s1,3}$, see Figs. 1(c) and 5(a)) is that these parameters could be self-adjusted for obtaining a desired frequency range through a learning mechanism, like correlation based differential Hebbian learning [13], or by evolutionary algorithms [5]. Moreover, the presented filter networks can be implemented as analog filters by using Schmitt trigger circuits which also exhibit the hysteresis effect. This kind of filtering technique is different from many others [14], [15], [16], [17], [8], [7], [9] which are in use.

Several successful digital filter techniques have been developed, like Butterworth, Elliptic, Chebyshev filters, as well as by using Fourier methods [14]. In general they are based on impulse and frequency response methods. As described by [15], these classical methods, however, are founded on three basic assumptions: linearity, stationary, and second-order statistics with particular emphasis on Gaussian characteristic. Thus advanced techniques like artificial neural networks have become an alternative way for in particular nonlinear signal processing [15]. In most cases, feed-forward multi layer perceptrons (MLP) with a gradient descend based learning algorithm have been extensively used for this [16], [17]. On the other hand, the use of recurrent neural networks for digital signal processing applications is now increasing, too. For example, Hagen et al. [8] presented a multi-loop recurrent network with a cascaded structure to predict an acoustic signal. Becerikli [7] used dynamic neural networks with Levenberg-Marquardt based fast training for nonlinear filtering design. Squartini et al. [9] employed echo state networks for identification of nonlinear dynamical systems for digital audio processing. Compared to many of these approaches, we present here a minimal and analyzable filter set based on simple neural dynamics. Due to the neural dynamics, these filters provide a sharp cut-off but the shape of the output signal is distorted; i.e., the filter networks act as nonlinear filters. Thus, these networks are appropriate for applications like background noise elimination, or non-speech sound recognition as shown here. One can also combine different filter modules or modify the neural structure to achieve more complex signal preprocessing [12]. To this end, we believe that here the described technique for filter design may lead to another way of modelling sensory preprocessing for robotic systems. More demanding tasks will be a deeper investigation of the mathematical properties of these filter networks and their dynamical behavior (e.g., spectral characteristics) using the framework of a nonlinear autoregressive moving average (NARMA) model [18]. We will also intensively evaluate the capability of our networks by comparing them to conventional liner filters (i.e. IIR filters).

Acknowledgments. We thank Tomas Kulvicius for technique advises. This research was supported by the PACO-PLUS project (IST-FP6-IP-027657) as well as by BMBF (Federal Ministry of Education and Research), BCCN (Bernstein Center for Computational Neuroscience)–Göttingen W3.

References

1. Dayhoff, J.E., Palmadesso, P.J., Richards, F.: Oscillation Responses in a Chaotic Recurrent Network. In: Recurrent Neural Networks: Design and Applications, pp. 153–177. CRC Press, Boca Raton (1999)
2. Steingrube, S., Timme, M., Wörgötter, F., Manoonpong, P.: Self-Organized Adaptation of a Simple Neural Circuit Enables Complex Robot Behaviour. Nature Physics 6, 224–230 (2010)
3. Ziemke, T.: On Parts and Wholes of Adaptive Behavior: Functional Modularity and Dichronic Structure in Recurrent Neural Robot Controllers. In: 6th International Conference on Simulation of Adaptive Behavior, pp. 115–124 (2000)
4. Zegers, P., Sundareshan, M.K.: Trajectory Generation and Modulation using Dynamic Neural Networks. IEEE T. Neural Networ. 14(3), 520–533 (2003)
5. Hülse, M., Wischmann, S., Pasemann, F.: Structure and Function of Evolved Neuro-Controllers for Autonomous Robots. Connect. Sci. 16(4), 249–266 (2004)
6. Williams, R.J., Peng, J.: An Efficient Gradient–Based Algorithm for On–Line Training of Recurrent Network Trajectories. Neural Comput. 2(4), 490–501 (1990)
7. Becerikli, Y.: Nonlinear Filtering Design using Dynamic Neural Networks with Fast Training. In: Yazıcı, A., Şener, C. (eds.) ISCIS 2003. LNCS, vol. 2869, pp. 601–610. Springer, Heidelberg (2003)
8. Hagen, M.T., De Jesus, O., Schultz, R.: Training Recurrent Networks for Filtering and Control. In: Recurrent Neural Networks: Design and Applications, pp. 325–354. CRC Press, Boca Raton (1999)
9. Squartini, S., Cecchi, S., Rossini, M., Piazza, F.: Echo State Networks for Real-Time Audio Applications. In: Liu, D., Fei, S., Hou, Z., Zhang, H., Sun, C. (eds.) ISNN 2007. LNCS, vol. 4493, pp. 731–740. Springer, Heidelberg (2007)
10. Beer, R.D.: The Dynamics of Active Categorical Perception in an Evolved Model Agent. Adapt. Behav. 11(4), 209–243 (2003)
11. Pasemann, F.: Dynamics of a Single Model Neuron. Int. J. Bifurcat. Chaos 3(2), 271–278 (1993)
12. Manoonpong, P.: Neural Preprocessing and Control of Reactive Walking Machines: Towards Versatile Artificial Perception-Action Systems. In: Cognitive Technologies, Springer, Heidelberg (2007)
13. Kolodziejski, C., Porr, B., Wörgötter, F.: Mathematical Properties of Neuronal TD-Rules and Differential Hebbian Learning: A Comparison. Biol. Cybern. 98(3), 259–272 (2008)
14. Oppenheim, A.V., Schafer, R.W., Buck, J.R.: Discrete-time Signal Processing. Prentice-Hall, Englewood Cliffs (1999)
15. Haykin, S.: Neural Networks Expand SP's Horizons. IEEE Signal Processing Magazine, 24–49 (1996)
16. Hanna, A.I., Mandic, D.P., Razaz, M.: A Normalised Backpropagation Learning Algorithm for Multilayer Feed-Forward Neural Adaptive Filters. In: The 2001 IEEE Workshop on Neural Networks for Signal Processing, pp. 63–72 (2001)
17. Uncini, A.: Audio Signal Processing by Neural Networks. Neurocomputing 55(3-4), 593–625 (2003)
18. Mandic, D., Chambers, J.: Recurrent Neural Networks for Prediction: Learning Algorithms, Architectures and Stability. Wiley, Chichester (2001)

Automatic Segmentation of Color Lip Images Based on Morphological Filter

Meng Li and Yiu-ming Cheung

Department of Computer Science, Hong Kong Baptist University
mli@comp.hkbu.edu.hk, ymc@comp.hkbu.edu.hk

Abstract. This paper addresses the problem of lip segmentation in color space, which is a crucial issue to the success of a lip-reading system. We present a new segmentation approach to lip contour extraction by taking account of the color difference between lip and skin in color space. Firstly, we obtain a lip segment sample via a color transformation sequence in 1976 CIELAB and LUX color spaces. Secondly, we establish a Gaussian model and make use of the hue and saturation value of each pixel within the lip segment to estimate the model parameters. Subsequently, the memberships of lip and non-lip regions are calculated, respectively. Thirdly, we employ morphological filters to obtain the desirable lip region approximately based on the memberships. Finally, we extract the lip contour via convex hull algorithm with the prior knowledge of the human mouth shape. Experiments show the efficacy of the proposed approach in comparison with the existing lip segmentation methods.

1   Introduction

In the past decade, lip segmentation has received considerable attention from the community because of its widespread applications[1], [2]. In general, lip segmentation is a non-trivial task because the color difference between the lip and the skin regions is not so noticeable sometimes. In the literature, a few image segmentation techniques have been proposed. One class of methods is based on the clustering with color features [3] provided that the number of clusters is known in advance. However, from the practical viewpoint, the number of clusters should be selected adaptively. Consequently, such a method is unable to operate fully automatically. Another class of widely-used methods is model-based ones [1]. Empirical studies have shown its success, but manually work on landmarks is needed for training.

In this paper, we will present a new method for automatic segmentation of lip images provided that the lower part of a face (i.e. the part between nostril and chin) has been available. A color transformation sequence is proposed to enlarge the distinction between the lips and the skin. Different from the existing methods, the proposed one only extracts a segment of lip rather than the whole lip region. Then, based on the lip segment sample, we establish a Gaussian model in a modified HSV color space so that the memberships of lip and non-lip region are calculated, respectively. We further utilize morphological filters to obtain the lip region candidate based on the two memberships. Finally, convex hull algorithm is employed to extract lip contour. Experiments have shown the efficacy of the proposed approach in comparison with the existing methods.

K. Diamantaras, W. Duch, L.S. Iliadis (Eds.): ICANN 2010, Part I, LNCS 6352, pp. 384–387, 2010.

2   Lip Membership Based on Color Space Transformation

We transform the source image into 1976 CIELAB color space and employ the histogram equalization to cover the a^* component to the range of $[0, 255]$, denoted as I_{a^*}. Furthermore, we get the U component via the method proposed in [4] with histogram equalization, denoted as I_U.

Let $I_{sub} = I_{a^*} - I_U$.[1] We establish a Gaussian model for I_{sub} based on the gray-level value for each non-zero pixel with the mean $\hat{\mu}_{sub}$ and the standard deviation $\hat{\sigma}_{sub}$. The candidate lip segment can be obtained by

$$I_{candidate} = \begin{cases} 0 \ if \quad I_{sub} \leq \hat{\mu}_{sub} - 2\hat{\sigma}_{sub}, \\ 1 \ otherwise. \end{cases} \tag{1}$$

The morphological reconstruction based method proposed in [5] is performed to suppress border connected noisy structures. The output image is denoted as $I^*_{candidate}$. In $I^*_{candidate}$, the nearest connected foreground block to gravity center, as the extracted segment, makes a segment sample that corresponds to the lip segment. Note that it is enough to extract a part of lip rather than the whole region because the extracted segment is used for sample data so as to establish a probability model.

For each pixel in HSV image, we perform the following transformation to get a vector: $C = (H \cdot cos(2\pi \cdot S), H \cdot sin(2\pi \cdot S))^T$. Then, we establish a probability model as follows:

$$P = \frac{1}{2\pi\sqrt{\hat{\Sigma}}} \cdot exp(-\frac{(X - \hat{\mu})\hat{\Sigma}^{-1}(X - \hat{\mu})^T}{2}) \tag{2}$$

where the mean $\hat{\mu}$ and the covariance matrix $\hat{\Sigma}$ can be evaluated by C vectors of the pixels in source image restricted by the lip segment region in the previous steps. As the input of the model of Eq.(2), the C vector for each pixel in the whole source image is obtained. Thus, we can calculate the lip membership denoted as M_{lip}.

Similarly, we can also establish a probability model to calculate the non-lip membership as $M_{non-lip}$. Moreover, considering the convenience of visibility, we project the memberships from $[0, 1]$ to $[0, 255]$.

3   Lip Contour Extraction

We obtain a mask image by letting

$$Mask = 255 - M_{non-lip} - I_U. \tag{3}$$

While the lip membership is labeled as marker, morphological reconstruction operation can be employed.

We further utilize a gray-level threshold selection method proposed in [6] to transform the reconstruction result into a binary image denoted as B_{RT} with boundary

---

[1] In this paper, all equations are employed in positive area. That is, as long as a result is negative, it will be set at 0 automatically.

connected structures suppressed, and mark the biggest continued foreground block by B_{lip_1}.

According to the following equation

$$I_{TTM} = I_U - I_{a^*}, \tag{4}$$

the region we have obtained covers the teeth, tongue and some parts of oral cavity approximately.

We further transform I_{TTM} into a binary image as B_{TTM} by the threshold selection method. Then, morphological closing is employed to $B_{RT} \cup B_{TTM}$ by performing a 5×5 structuring element operation. We select the biggest foreground block denoted as B_{lip_2} in the closing operation result. Hence, the binary image $B_{lip_1} \cup B_{lip_2}$ can represent the whole lip region. Furthermore, we utilize morphological opening with 3×3 structuring element to smooth the edge, resulting as B_{lip}. Finally, the quickhull algorithm proposed in [7] is employed to draw the contour of lip.

4   Experimental Results

Comparison is made to demonstrate the performance of the proposed approach with Liew03 proposed in [3], and Guan08 in [8]. Four databases: (1) AR face database [9], (2) CVL face database [10], (3) GTAV face database, and (4) a database established by ourselves, are used to test the accuracy and robustness in different capture environments. We randomly selected 800 images in total and manually segmented the lip to serve as the ground truth. Some segmentation results can be found in Figure 1.

Two measures (OL and SE) defined in [3] are used to evaluate the performance of the algorithms. Table 1 shows the segmentation results on the four different databases.

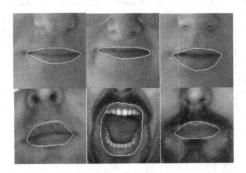

Fig. 1. Some samples of lip contour extraction in different databases

Table 1. The segmentation results across the four databases

Algorithm	Liew03	Guan08	Proposed Approach
average OL, %	80.73	45.10	**90.12**
average SE, %	20.15	55.21	**9.33**

5   Conclusion

In this paper, we have proposed a new approach to automatic lip segmentation via the probability model in color space and morphological filter. This approach features the high stability of lip segmentation and robust performance against the disparate capture environment and different skin color. Experiments have shown the promising result of the proposed approach in comparison with the existing methods.

Acknowledgment

The work described in this paper was supported by the Faculty Research Grant of Hong Kong Baptist University with the project code: FRG2/08-09/122 and FRG2/09-10/098, and by the Research Grant Council of Hong Kong SAR under Project HKBU 210309.

References

1. Matthews, I., Cootes, T., Bangham, J.: Extraction of visual features for lipreading. IEEE Transactions on Pattern Analysis and Machine Intelligence 24, 198–213 (2002)
2. Cetingul, H., Yemez, Y., Erzin, E., Tekalp, A.: Discriminative analysis of lip motion features for speaker identification and speech-reading. IEEE Transaction on Image Processing 15(10), 2879–2891 (2006)
3. Liew, A.W., Leung, S., Lau, W.: Segmentation of color lip images by spatial fuzzy clustering. IEEE Transactions on Fuzzy Systems 11(4), 542–549 (2003)
4. Lievin, M., Luthon, F.: Nonlinear color space and spatiotemporal mrf for hierarchical segmentation of face features in video. IEEE Transactions on Image Processing 13(1), 63–71 (2004)
5. Soille, P.: Morphological Image Analysis: Principles and Applications. Springer, Heidelberg (1999)
6. Otsu, N.: A threshold selection method from gray-level histograms. IEEE Transactions on Systems, Man, and Cybernetics 9(1), 62–66 (1979)
7. Barber, C., Dobkin, D., Huhdanpaa, H.: The quickhull algorithm for convex hulls. ACM Transactions on Mathematical Software 22(4), 469–483 (1996)
8. Guan, Y.: Automatic extraction of lips based on multi-scale wavelet edge detection. Computer Vision, IET 2(1), 23–33 (2008)
9. Martinez, A., Benavente, R.: The ar face database. CVC Technical Report No.24 (June 1998)
10. Solina, F., Peer, P., Batagelj, B., Juvan, S., Kovac, J.: Color-based face detection in the '15 seconds of fame' art installation. In: Proceedings of Conference on Computer Vision / Computer Graphics Collaboration for Model-based Imaging, Rendering, Image Analysis and Graphical Special Effects, Versailles, France, pp. 38–47 (2003)

Learning in a Unitary Coherent Hippocampus

Charles Fox and Tony Prescott

Adaptive Behaviour Research Group, University of Sheffield S10 2TN, UK

Abstract. A previous paper [2] presented a model (*UCPF-HC*) of the hippocampus as a unitary coherent particle filter, which combines the classical hippocampal roles of associative memory and spatial navigation, using a Bayesian filter framework. The present paper extends this model to include online learning of connections to and from the CA3 region. Learning in the extended neural network is equivalent to learning in a temporal restricted Boltzmann machine under certain assumptions about neuromodulatory effects on connectivity and learning during theta cycles, which suggest detailed neural mappings for Bayesian inference and learning within sub-stages of a theta cycle. After-depolarisations (ADP) are hypothesised to play a novel role to enable reuse of recurrent prior information across sub-stages of theta.

1 Introduction

Anatomy. The principal input structures of the hippocampus are the superficial layers of Entorhinal Cortex (ECs). ECs projects to Dentate Gyrus (DG) which is believed to sparsify the encoding of ECs. Both ECs and DG project to CA3, which also receives strong recurrent connections that are disabled [3] by septal ACh. CA3 and ECs project to CA1, which in turn projects to the deep layers of Entorhinal cortex (ECd), closing a loop if ECd sends information back to ECs. ECs, CA1 and ECd outputs appear to share a coding scheme, as evidenced by one-to-one topographic projections. In contrast, DG and CA3 outputs are thought to work in a second basis or latent space. In a second loop, ECs and CA1 both project to Subiculum (Sub), which projects to the midbrain Septum (Sep) via fornix. Septal ACh and GABA fibres project back to all parts of hippocampus.

  UCPF-HC model. A previous paper [2], mapped this hippocampal circuit onto a modified Temporal Restricted Boltzmann machine (TRBM, [8]). The TRBM assumes Boolean observation vectors (including a bias node), z'; Boolean hidden state vectors (including a bias node), x'; weight matrices $W_{x'z'}$ and $W_{x'x'}$, and specifies joints,

$$P(x_t, x_{t-1}, z_t) = \frac{1}{Z} \exp \sum_t (-x_t' W_{x'x'} x_{t-1}' - x_t' W_{x'z'} z_t'). \qquad (1)$$

Unlike the standard TRBM, UCPF-HC uses the following deterministic update to obtain maximum *a posteriori* estimates:

$$\hat{x}_t \leftarrow \arg\max P(x_t|\hat{x}_{t-1}, z_t) = \{\hat{x}_t(i) = (P(x_t(i)|\hat{x}_{t-1}, z_t) > \tfrac{1}{2})\}_i \qquad (2)$$

which is the zero-temperature limit of an annealed sequential Gibbs sampler.

K. Diamantaras, W. Duch, L.S. Iliadis (Eds.): ICANN 2010, Part I, LNCS 6352, pp. 388–394, 2010.

The noisy inputs $z_t = y_t + \epsilon_t$ are mapped to the combined ECs and DG, where the DG activations are functions of the ECs activations, $z_t = (ECs_t, DG_t(ECs_t))$. CA3 is mapped to the hidden state, x_t. CA1 performs a partial decoding into the DG basis. Finally the estimated de-noised output is mapped to ECd, $\hat{y}_t = ECd_t$. Each neural population is a Boolean vector at each discrete time step t.

A major problem with UCPF-HC tracking is tracking loss, as it approximates the whole posterior with a single sample. To deal with this, performance of the filter is monitored to heuristically detect when tracking is lost – by thresholding a moving average of discrepancy between observed and denoised sensors – then the priors are disabled when lostness is detected. In UCPF-HC, the Subiculum-Septum circuit performs this monitoring. Sub then compares the partially decoded CA1 information against the original ECs input, receiving one-to-one connections from both regions. If they differ for an extended period of time, this indicates loss of tracking. *Tonic* cholinergic projections from Sep, activated via Sub, are well-placed to disable the CA3 priors when lostness occurs, as they are known [3] to disable the recurrent connections in CA3.

The present study presents a new version of UCPF-HC, using the plus maze environment detailed in [2], and extendend with ADP to perform learning in CA3. The plus-maze consists of 13 discrete locations as shown in fig. 4(a). The agent sees unique visual markers if facing two of the arms; it also has touch sensors to report walls to its immediate left, right and front. The original UCPF-HC model included mechanisms to perform path integration in the grid and heading cells using odometry and denoised ECd states – to simplify the present study we assume that grid and heading cells give uncorrelated noisy (Global Positioning System style) estimates of location and orientation, as would be obtained if the UCPF-HC's outputs were always perfect or known to be lost but the odometry was noisy.

ADP Physiology. CA3 pyramidal cells [1] exhibit a single cell short-term memory effect called after-depolarisation (ADP), illustrated in fig. 4(b). A spike (1) in membrane potential, V, is followed by a fast after-hyper-polarisation (AHP, 2), then an after-depolarisation (ADP, 3) and a second, slower AHP (4), before returning to its resting potential (5). (See [7] sections 5.2.5 and 5.3.5 for a detailed review.) ADP has previously been suggested [5] as a basis for multiplexed short-term memories in hippocampus, enabling around seven patterns to be stored simultaneously by re-activating themselves after other patterns, using the ADP gain plus an external excitatory oscillator. We will suggest a related but novel role for ADPs, allowing priors to be restored during separate wake and sleep cycles [4] in a temporal network. ADP is dependent on the presence of ACh or 5HT [6], and septal *phasic* ACh has been suggested to play a role in the hippocampal theta rhythm [3].

2 On-Line Learning for the UCPF-HC Model

The previous version [2] of UCPF-HC did not perform any realistic learning. CA3 cell semantics were specified by hand – for example cells were specified to respond to conjunctions of places, headings and light states. Ideal CA3 responses were computed

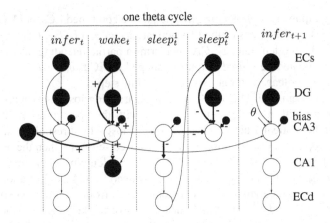

Fig. 1. The four substeps, $infer, wake, sleep^1, sleep^2$ within one theta cycle in the learning neural network model. Circles denote populations of neurons. Arrows indicate fully connected neural network projections (this is *not* a Bayesian network diagram). Thick arrows indicate connections whose weights are updated with Hebbian (+) and anti-Hebbian (-) rules. Dotted arrows indicate where learning occurs but no information is projected (i.e. when the child population is clamped from elsewhere). Filled-in nodes are fixed values at each substep, unfilled nodes are to be computed. The bias population contains a single neuron which is always on, and abstracts the threshold values in CA3. In the first substep of the next cycle, $infer_{t+1}$, CA3 receives a θ signal which disconnects the recurrent connections and switches to ADP recurrent activation.

offline, from these hand-set specifications and ground truth data sets, then weights for each input population to CA3, *pop*, were set using independent wake-sleep [4] updates,

$$\Delta w_{ij} = \alpha(\langle CA3_i pop_j \rangle_{\hat{P}(pop,CA3|b)} - \langle CA3_i pop_j \rangle_{P(pop,CA3|b)}) \qquad (3)$$

where $\hat{P}$ is the empirical data distribution including the hand-set ideal hidden values; P is the model's generative distribution; and b is the set of hidden nodes biases, preset empirically to model priors on the handset semantics. This was not indented as a realistic learning model, rather just a computational method to set the weights. In particular the computation was greatly simplified by having access to ground-truth hidden states, which made the weights mutually independent given the bias. In reality the agent does not have access to ground truth hidden states – only to sensors.

We do not give the new model access to ideal CA3 states or hand-set their semantics – this time the semantics must be learned. The semantics of DG and CA1, and hence the weights $W_{EC \to DG}$ and $W_{CA1 \to EC}$ remain set by hand – we focus only on extending the model to learn all connections to and from CA3: namely $W_{ECs \to CA3}$, $W_{DG \to CA3}$, $W_{CA3 \to CA3}$ and $W_{CA3 \to CA1}$.

To simplify both the presentation and implementation of the learning model, we will first present the hippocampal learning algorithm for the UCPF-HC neural network as a *fait accompli*, then describe a graphical model simplification used in the implementation. The graphical model formulation also provides insight into the purposes of the neural network processes, which were in fact derived from the graphical model during

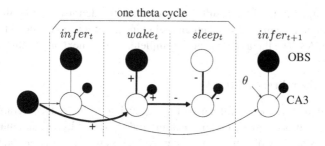

Fig. 2. The reduced TRBM model. This network is equivalent to the neural network, but includes undirected connections, and groups the information from EC,DG and CA1 into a single observable population, OBS.

development. The algorithm is based on the wake-sleep process but is now intended as a biological model.

2.1   Neural Network Model

The neural learning algorithm is based on the wake-sleep algorithm [4] and is illustrated in fig. 1. It assumes that for every discrete time step t there are four substeps, $infer_t, wake_t, sleep_t^1, sleep_t^2$ corresponding to different phases of one hippocampal theta cycle. These substeps have differing connectivity and learning dynamics, which might be controlled by neuromodulators during the theta cycle. The substeps occur sequentially. But importantly, CA3 activation during the $infer_t$ substep is required to directly influence CA3 at $wake_t$; and CA3 activation at $infer_t$ is required to directly influence CA3 at $infer_{t+1}$; as shown by the arrows in the figure. We tentatively suggest that ADP, discussed in section 1, might play a role in such temporally incontiguous transmission of information.

The $infer_t$ substep is identical to inference in the UCPF-HC model. ECs sensor data is observed; deterministic DG activations (via handset $W_{EC \to DG}$) are computed, and thus act as observations too. We assume that the state of CA3 at $infer_{t-1}$ was inferred exactly and correctly by the UCPF, and is available as an input via recurrent transmission weights $W_{CA3 \to CA3}$. Using these inputs, CA3 is updated with a Gibbs sampling step at temperature $T = 0$. CA1 and ECd decode it to retrieve denoised sensor estimates.

In the $wake_t$ substep, the same input vector is maintained in EC and DG; and CA1 activation becomes clamped by a training signal from the ECs input. We assume that conjunctions of facts from ECs are represented perfectly in CA1 by this process, as in DG. We require a delayed copy of the recurrent CA3 input from $infer_{t-1}$ as was received in the $infer_t$ step – *not* a recurrent CA3 input from $infer_t$ – as the recurrent input to CA3 in $wake_t$. CA3 is resampled at $T = 1$ and Hebbian learning is performed at all synapses to and from CA3. In the $sleep_t^1$ substep, the recurrent CA3 connections are used directly so that CA3's state now is influenced by its previous state, $wake_t$. Its connections from ECs and DG are made ineffectual. CA3 is sampled again at temperature $T = 1$, then CA1 and ECd is decoded from it. In $sleep_t^2$ we assume that ECs becomes clamped to the ECd result – feeding back the denoised output into the input. CA3 is resampled again at $T = 1$ and antihebbian learning is performed in all synapses to and from CA3. The theta cycle is now complete, and the next one begins at $infer_{t+1}$.

2.2 Reduced Undirected Model

We next explain why the neural network is equivalent to the reduced graphical model shown in fig. 2. It is a new variant of the temporal restricted Boltzmann machine [8].

DG consists entirely of cells whose receptive fields are copies or conjunctions of ECs fields. In the reduced model, we form a single population, OBS, which contains both DG and ECs cells. CA1 in the neural model consists of cells with identical fields to DG cells, which are thus also implicitly contained in OBS. The weights $W_{OBS-CA3}$ are undirected as in the TRBM, though the steps of learning them correspond to the steps learning the weights in the neural model.

In phase $infer_t$, CA3 is driven by inputs from EC and DG in the directed neural model, which is equivalent to the undirected link to the observed OBS population in the reduced model. (The bias link is also changed from directed to undirected in the reduced model – again this is an equivalence as the bias is always observed.) In this phase, the temperature is zero so the inferences are always the MAPs. This gives the best denosied estimate of the state of the world.

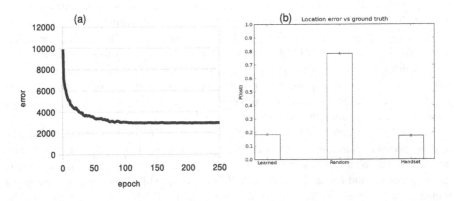

Fig. 3. (a) Training errors. Error is the sum of ECs-ECd discrepancies over all training data in each epoch. (b) Lostness probabilities in learned, random and handset-semantics weights. Error bars show one standard deviation of uncertainty about the population mean.

In phase $wake_t$, the drivers of CA3 are the same, but the temperature is $T = 1$. In the neural model, CA1 is clamped to EC, and Hebbian learning occurs in $W_{EC \rightarrow CA3}$, $W_{DG \rightarrow CA3}$ and $W_{CA3 \rightarrow CA1}$. This is equivalent to clamping OBS again in the reduced model, and Hebbian learning on $W_{CA3-CA1}$. As in the neural model there is also Hebbian learning on the recurrent CA3 connections.

In phase $sleep_t$ of the undirected model, a CA3 sample is drawn conditioned on its recurrent state only. Then an OBS sample is drawn conditioned on CA3, and finally a new CA3 sample is drawn conditioned on its recurrents and on the OBS sample. Antihebbian learning is performed on all connections to CA3. This is equivalent to the process in the neural model's $sleep_t^1$ and $sleep_t^2$, and is a standard TRBM sleep step.

Phase $infer_{t+1}$ is the start of the next cycle, and like the neural model, requires historical CA3 input from $infer_t$, as might be obtained using ADP.

3   Results

We tested the learning algorithm in the plus-maze world (see [2]), using a path of 30,000 random walk steps. The path was replayed for several epochs until the weights converged. For computational simplicity, learning was performed used the equivalent reduced model, though inference was performed with the full neural model, sharing the learned weights. Python code for the simulation is available from the authors. There is some subtlety in handling learning for cases where the Sub-Sep lostness circuit is activated, which is detailed in the appendix. Fig. 5(a) shows the training errors during learning – using a learning rate of $\alpha = 0.001$ – most of the learning takes place in the first 10 epochs. As in the original [2] UCPF-HC model, the neural network is used to infer denoised ECd estimates of position and sensors. Fig. 5(b) shows the average rate of location errors using the learned weights, compared against the handset semantic of the original UCPF-HC model. A run with randomised, untrained weights is shown for comparison. Inspecting the receptive fields of CA3 cells learned by the training, we find cells in fig. 4(a) responding to individual places (3 and 4); regions around a place (2); the ends of the arms (5); and less well defined fields (1 and 6).

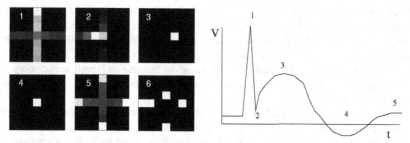

(a) Examples of learned CA3 receptive fields, over the plus maze.

(b) Typical membrane time course following a spike under ADP dynamics.

Fig. 4.

4   Discussion

We have presented a top-down mapping of a wake-sleep learning algorithm onto the biological hippocampal circuit and existing UCPF-HC model. The UCPF-HC model was extended by adding detailed substeps within theta cycles, which specify the connectivity and learning operations required by the algorithm, as biological hypotheses. Our revised model demonstrates a biological plausible online learning mechanism for CA3 pyramidal cells, and thus lends support to our general hypothesis that the hippocampal system may operate as a unitary coherent particle filter. This type of mapping necessarily makes strong predictions about what neurons would be required to do to implement the algorithm. In particular we have relied on specific timing features of ADP and on ACh to switch between recurrent CA3 activation and ADP-based CA3 memories. It remains to be seen whether biological ADP and ACh are able to provide these functions.

The inference step was performed at zero temperature, separately from higher temperature wake and sleep steps. There are several possible variations on this theme. First, both wake and sleep could be performed at zero temperature, removing the need for a separate inference step, and resulting in a different type of optimisation during learning (minimising $KL[Q^T||P^T]$ rather than $KL[Q||P]$. In the limit $Q = P$ they would give the same result). Second, wake and sleep steps could be extended to run for several steps. This would result in longer sequences of uninterrupted tracking of observations, alternating with longer 'hallucinated' sequences of generated samples. The latter would resemble sequence replay and preplay known to take place in CA3.

Future work could implement the neural learning model directly, in place of the reduced simplification. It could also consider memories of the agent's own actions as way to increase the predictability of plus maze sequences. Finally the agent should iteratively estimate the amount of error in its own location estimates rather than rely on the artificial noisy GPS assumption used in this proof-of-concept implementation.

References

1. Ceaser, M., Brown, D.A., Gahwiler, B.H., Knopfel, T.: Characterization of a calcium-dependent current generating a slow afterdepolarization of CA3 pyramidal cells in rat hippocampal cultures. Eur. J. Neuroscience 5, 560–569 (1993)
2. Fox, C., Prescott, T.: Hippocampus as unitary coherent particle filter. In: Proceedings of the International Joint Conference on Neural Networks, IJCNN (2010)
3. Hasselmo, M.E., Schnell, E., Barkai, E.: Dynamics of learning and recall at excitatory recurrent synapses and cholinergic modulation in rat hippocampal region CA3. Journal of Neuroscience 15, 5249–5262 (1995)
4. Hinton, G.E., Dayan, P., Frey, B.J., Neal, R.M.: The wake-sleep algorithm for unsupervised neural networks. Science 268, 1158–1161 (1995)
5. Jensen, O., Idiart, M.A.P., Lisman, J.E.: Physiologically realistic formation of autoassociative memory in networks with theta/gamma oscillations: role of fast NMDA channels. Learning and Memory 3, 243–256 (1996)
6. Lisman, J., Idiart, M.A.P.: Storage of 7+/-2 short-term memories in oscillatory subcycles. Science 267, 1512–1515 (1995)
7. Spruston, N., McBain, C.: Structure and functional properties of hippocampal neurons. In: Andersen, P., Morris, R., Amaral, D., Bliss, T., O'Keefe, J. (eds.) The Hippocampus Book. Oxford University Press, Oxford (2007)
8. Taylor, G.W., Hinton, G.E., Roweis, S.T.: Modeling human motion using binary latent variables. In: Schölkopf, B., Platt, J., Hoffman, T. (eds.) NIPS 19 (2007)

Collaborative Filtering through SVD-Based and Hierarchical Nonlinear PCA

Manolis G. Vozalis, Angelos Markos, and Konstantinos G. Margaritis

Department of Applied Informatics, University of Macedonia,
156 Egnatia Street, P.O. Box 1591, 54006, Thessaloniki, Greece
{mans,amarkos,kmarg}@uom.gr

Abstract. In this paper, we describe and compare two distinct algorithms aiming at the low-rank approximation of a user-item ratings matrix in the context of Collaborative Filtering (CF). The first one implements standard Principal Component Analysis (PCA) of an association matrix formed from the original data. The second algorithm is based on h-NLPCA, a nonlinear generalization of standard PCA, which utilizes an autoassociative network, and constrains the nonlinear components to have the same hierarchical order as the linear components in standard PCA. We examine the impact of the aforementioned approaches on the quality of the generated predictions through a series of experiments. Experimental results show that the latter approach outperforms the standard PCA approach for most values of the retained dimensions.

Keywords: Collaborative Filtering,Low-rank Approximation, Artificial Neural Networks, Principal Component Analysis.

1 Introduction

With the term Collaborative Filtering (CF) we refer to intelligent techniques which are employed by Recommender Systems (RSs) and are used to generate personalized recommendations. The basic idea of CF is that users who have agreed in the past tend to agree in the future. A common and successful approach to collaborative prediction is to fit a factor model to the original rating data, and use it in order to make further predictions. A factor model approximates the observed user preferences in a low dimensionality space in order to uncover latent features that explain user preferences. In this paper, we will focus on two PCA implementations, aiming at the low-rank approximation of the corresponding user-item ratings matrix.

PCA is a well-established data analysis technique that relies on a simple transformation of recorded observations, to produce statistically independent score variables. It has been extensively used for lossy data compression, feature extraction, data visualization, and most recently in the field of Collaborative Filtering [1,2,3]. The linear assumption underlying PCA makes it insufficient for capturing nonlinear patterns among variables. Artificial Neural Network (ANN) models, a class of nonlinear empirical modeling methods, allow for nonlinear

K. Diamantaras, W. Duch, L.S. Iliadis (Eds.): ICANN 2010, Part I, LNCS 6352, pp. 395–400, 2010.
© Springer-Verlag Berlin Heidelberg 2010

mappings between the original and the reduced dimensional spaces. Various ANN methods have been described in a PCA framewok [4,5,6,7]. ANNs have been utilized for the generation of CF predictions: Billsus and Pazzani [8] formulate CF as a classification problem by feeding their data matrix of reduced dimensions to an ANN. Lee et al. [9] put users into clusters by using a Self-Organizing Map neural network, and then apply CF on those clusters in order to extract recommendations. Gong and Ye [10] utilize a backpropagation neural network to fill the missing values of the original data matrix, and then apply item-based CF to form the item neighborhood.

The aim of this paper is to examine two implementations of PCA in the context of CF. The first implementation utilizes PCA through the Singular Value Decomposition (SVD) of the covariance matrix. For our second implementation we apply a hierarchical nonlinear PCA algorithm, denoted as h-NLPCA [11]. The primary contribution of this work lies in the application of h-NLPCA, which is based on a multi-layer perceptron with an auto-associative topology, for the generation of personalized recommendations. The main advantage of h-NLPCA is that it enforces a hierarchical order of principal components which always yields the same solution of uncorrelated features.

The remainder of this paper is organized as follows: Section 2 is devoted to a general presentation of the two PCA approaches, through SVD and ANNs, respectively. Section 3 discusses the proposed algorithms in the context of CF, outlining the distinct implementation steps. The efficiency of each approach is demonstrated in Section 4 through a set of experiments on a publicly available data set. The paper concludes in Section 5.

2   Two PCA Implementations

2.1   SVD-Based PCA

PCA summarizes the variation in correlated multivariate attributes to a set of non-correlated components, called principal components, each of which is a particular linear combination of the original variables [1]. PCA can be performed by applying the SVD to either a covariance or a correlation matrix of the original data set, in order to extract the smallest number of components while retaining as much of the original variance as possible. The eigenvalues of the covariance (correlation) matrix indicate the amount of variance along the direction given by the corresponding eigenvector. That is, when a covariance matrix $\mathbf{A}$ is decomposed by SVD, i.e., $\mathbf{A} = \mathbf{USV}^T$, the matrix $\mathbf{U}$ contains the variables' loadings for the principal components, and the matrix $\mathbf{S}$ has the corresponding variances along the diagonal [1]. A reduction to k dimensions is obtained by projecting the original data matrix on the subspace consisting of eigenvectors corresponding to the largest k eigenvalues of the covariance matrix.

2.2   h-NLPCA

Nonlinear PCA is based on a multi-layer perceptron (MLP) with an autoassociative topology, also known as an *autoencoder*. The network consists of two parts:

the first part represents the extraction function, $\Phi_{extr} : X \rightarrow Z$. The second part represents the inverse, reconstruction function, $\Phi_{gen} : Z \rightarrow \hat{X}$. A hidden layer in each part enables the network to perform nonlinear mapping functions [11]. The autoassociative network performs an identity mapping, which means that the input is approximated at the output layer with the highest possible accuracy. This property of the network is achieved by minimizing the squared reconstruction error $E = \frac{1}{2}||\hat{x} - x||^2$. This task, which is nontrivial, is accomplished by a 'bottleneck' layer in the middle, of smaller dimension than either the input or output layers. Thus, the data have to be projected or compressed into a lower dimensional representation Z, for the subsequent layers to reconstruct the input. If network training succeeds in finding an acceptable solution, we may assume that data compression achieved at the 'bottleneck' layer may force hidden units to represent significant features in data.

Hierarchical nonlinear PCA (h-NLPCA), as proposed by Scholz et al. [11], provides the optimal nonlinear subspace spanned by components, but also constrains the nonlinear components to have the same hierarchical order as the linear components in standard PCA. This means that the first n components explain the maximal variance that can be covered by an n-dimensional subspace and that the i-th component of an n component solution is identical to the i-th component of an m component solution.

E_1 and $E_{1,2}$ are the squared reconstruction errors when using one or two components in the 'bottleneck' layer, respectively. In order to perform the h-NLPCA, we have to minimize both $E_{1,2}$ (as in plain NLPCA, or s-NLPCA), and E_1. In practice, this is equal to minimizing the hierarchical error, E_H:$E_H = E_1 + E_{1,2}$. The optimal network weights for a minimal error in h-NLPCA can be found by using the conjugate gradient descent algorithm [31]. At each algorithm's iteration, the single error terms E_1 and $E_{1,2}$ have to be calculated separately. In standard s-NLPCA, this is performed by a network with either one or two units in the 'bottleneck' layer. In the case of h-NLPCA, one network is the subnetwork of the other. The hierarchical error function can be easily extended to k components ($k \leq d$): $E_H = E_1 + E_{1,2} + E_{1,2,3} + \cdots + E_{1,2,3,\ldots,k}$.

In other words, for the minimization of E_H, we search for a k-dimensional subspace of minimal mean square error (MSE) under the constraint that the $(k-1)$-dimensional subspace is also of minimal MSE. This requirement is extended so that all $1, \ldots, k$ dimensional subspaces are of minimal MSE. Hence, each subspace represents the data with regard to its dimensionalities best. Hierarchical nonlinear PCA can therefore be seen as a true and natural nonlinear extension of standard linear PCA [11].

3   The Proposed Algorithms

In this section we will describe how the aforementioned PCA implementations can be combined with CF in order to make prediction generation both scalable and effective. In both cases, once PCA is applied for the low rank approximation of the original user-item ratings matrix, we compute a neighborhood for each user. Finally, user similarity is utilized for the generation of the requested prediction.

3.1 CF through h-NLPCA

We start with the following basic definitions. For $i = 1, \ldots, n$ users, ratings on $j = 1, \ldots, m$ items are collected in the $n \times m$ data matrix $\mathbf{R}$. Each of the corresponding items takes on k different rating values (levels or categories) from a given range, i.e. $(1, 2, 3, 4, 5)$.

Step 1. Data representation. Impute the missing values in the original user-item matrix, $\mathbf{R}$, with the corresponding *column* average, $\bar{r}_j$, which leads to a new filled-in matrix, $\mathbf{A}$.

Step 2. Low rank approximation. The conjugate gradient descent algorithm [11] is used to train the h-NLPCA network as described in Section 2. The hierarchical error E_h is minimized at each training iteration. The reduced or reconstructed matrix is denoted as $\mathbf{A}_k$, where k is the number of retained components.

Step 3. Neighborhood Formation. Calculate the similarity measure between each user and his closest neighbors in order to form the user neighborhood. To find the proximity between two users, u_a and u_i, we utilize the Pearson correlation coefficient, which is computed as follows:

$$cor_{ai} = \frac{\sum_{j=1}^{l} r_{aj} r_{ij}}{\sqrt{\sum_{j=1}^{l} r_{aj} \sum_{j=1}^{h} r_{ij}}}$$

where r_{ij} denotes the rating of user u_i on item i_j. Note that the summations over j are calculated over the l items for which both users u_a and u_i have expressed their opinions.

Step 4. Prediction Generation. Prediction generation requires that a user neighborhood of size h is already formed for the active user, u_a. Then, we compute the prediction rating p_{aj} for user u_a on item i_j, using the following equation:

$$p_{aj} = \bar{r}_j + \frac{\sum_{i=1}^{h} rr_{ij} * cor_{ai}}{\sum_{i=1}^{h} |cor_{ai}|}$$

It is important to note that the user ratings, rr_{ij}, are taken from the reduced matrix $\mathbf{A}_k$. Also, we have to add the original item average back, $\bar{r}_j$, since it was subtracted during the normalization step of the preprocessing.

3.2 CF through SVD-Based PCA

Step 1. Data representation and normalization. Impute the missing values in the original user-item matrix, $\mathbf{R}$, with the corresponding *column* average, $\bar{r}_j$. Then obtain the column centered matrix $\mathbf{A}$.

Step 2. Low rank approximation. Compute the SVD of $\mathbf{A}$ and keep only the first k eigenvalues. This is equivalent to the factorization of the covariance matrix

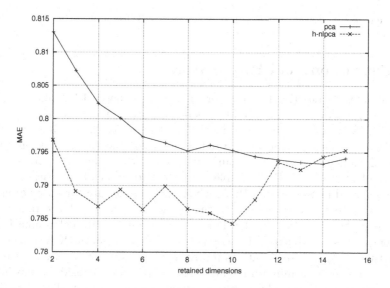

Fig. 1. Comparison of PCA and h-NLPCA for different values of retained dimensions

$\frac{1}{m-1}\mathbf{A}^{\mathbf{T}}\mathbf{A}$ [1]. The reduced or reconstructed matrix is denoted as $\mathbf{A}_k$, where k is the number of retained components.

Neighborhood formation and prediction generation (steps 3 and 4) are executed as described in the h-NLPCA implementation.

4 Experiments

In this section the efficiency of each approach is demonstrated through a series of experiments. We utilized MovieLens, a dataset publicly available from the GroupLens research group, which consists of 100,000 ratings, assigned by 943 users on 1682 movies. The sparsity of the data set is high, at a value of 93.7%. Starting from the initial data set, a distinct split of training (80%) and test (20%) data was utilized. Mean Absolute Error (MAE) was the metric we employed to evaluate the accuracy of the methods. MAE measures the deviation of predictions generated by the RSs from the true rating values, as they were specified by the user.

For our experiments, we kept a fixed user neighborhood size and evaluated the effect of a varying number of retained dimensions, k, on prediction accuracy. Figure 1 depicts the MAE for values of k ranging between 2 and 15. Based on that figure, it is clear that h-NLPCA outperformed SVD-based PCA for almost all the values of retained dimensions. In particular, h-NLPCA generated the overall most accurate prediction, MAE=0.7843, for k=10, meaning that only 10 *pseudo*-items, out of the 1682 original ones, were able to capture the latent relations existing in the initial user-item ratings matrix. In contrast, SVD-based

PCA reached its lowest error value, MAE=0.7933, for a slightly larger value of k, $k=14$.

5   Conclusions and Future Work

In this paper we described two factor models, SVD-based PCA and h-NLPCA for the low-rank approximation of a user-item ratings matrix in the context of CF. h-NLPCA, which can be considered as a neural based non-linear extension of PCA, gave the most accurate predictions according to MAE when applied to the MovieLens dataset. The main advantage of the proposed approach stems from the fact that h-NLPCA is able to account for more of the variance in the data compared to SVD-based PCA, when the variables are (or may be) nonlinearly related to each other. However, the prediction accuracy of a certain method depends on the structure of the data it is used on. A detailed comparison on different data sets is beyond the scope of this article. In both PCA implementations, the sparse user-item ratings matrix is filled using the average ratings for users to capture a meaningful latent relationship. Future considerations include PCA methods that are robust against missing data and that allow for missing value estimation. For example, non linear PCA approaches, such as Kernel PCA and Regularized PCA [1], may provide a valuable insight into the CF framework.

References

1. Jolliffe, I.T.: Principal Component Analysis, 2nd edn. Springer, Heidelberg (2002)
2. Goldberg, K., Roeder, T., Gupta, D., Perkins, C.: Eigentaste: A constant time collaborative filtering algorithm. Information Retrieval Journal 4, 133–151 (2001)
3. Kim, D., Yum, B.J.: Collaborative filtering based on iterative principal component analysis. Expert Systems with Applications 28, 823–830 (2005)
4. Oja, E.: A simplified neuron model as a principal component analyzer. Journal of Mathematical Biology 15(3), 267–273 (1982)
5. Diamantaras, K.I., Kung, S.Y.: Principal Component Neural Networks: Theory and Applications. John Wiley & Sons, New York (1996)
6. Kramer, M.A.: Nonlinear principal component analysis using autoassociative neural networks. AIChE Journal 37(2), 233–243 (1991)
7. Tan, S., Mayrovouniotis, M.L.: Reducing data dimensionality through optimizing neural network inputs. AIChE Journal 41(6), 1471–1480 (1995)
8. Billsus, D., Pazzani, M.J.: Learning collaborative information filters. In: 15th International Conference on Machine Learning, Madison, WI, pp. 46–53 (1998)
9. Lee, M., Choi, P., Woo, Y.: A hybrid recommender system combining collaborative filtering with neural network. In: Bra, P.D., Brusilovsky, P., Conejo, R. (eds.) Adaptive Hypermedia and Adaptive Web-Based Systems, pp. 531–534. Springer, Heidelberg (2002)
10. Gong, S., Ye, H.: An item based collaborative filtering using bp neural networks prediction. In: 2009 International Conference on Industrial and Information Systems, Haikou, China, pp. 146–148 (2009)
11. Scholz, M., Fraunholz, M., Selbig, J.: Nonlinear principal component analysis: Neural network models and applications. In: Principal Manifolds for Data Visualization and Dimension Reduction, pp. 44–67. Springer, Heidelberg (2007)

A Novel Tuning Method for Neural Oscillators with a Ladder-Like Structure Based on Oscillation Analysis

Yuya Hattori[1,2], Michiyo Suzuki[2], Zu Soh[1],
Yasuhiko Kobayashi[2], and Toshio Tsuji[1]

[1] Graduate School of Engineering, Hiroshima University,
1-4-1 Kagamiyama, Higashi-Hiroshima, Hiroshima 739-8527, Japan
{hattori,sozu,tsuji}@bsys.hiroshima-u.ac.jp
[2] Microbeam Radiation Biology Goup, Japan Atomic Energy Agency,
1233 Watanuki, Takasaki, Gunma 370-1292, Japan
{suzuki.michiyo,kobayashi.yasuhiko}@jaea.go.jp

Abstract. Neural oscillators with a ladder-like structure is one of the central pattern generator (CPG) model that is used to simulate rhythmic movements in living organisms. However, it is not easy to realize rhythmical cycles by tuning many parameters of neural oscillators. In this study, we propose an automatic tuning method. We derive the tuning rules for both the time constants and the coefficients of amplitude by linearizing the nonlinear equations of the neural oscillators. Other parameters such as neural connection weights are tuned using a genetic algorithm (GA). Through numerical experiments, we confirmed that the proposed tuning method can successfully tune all parameters.

Keywords: Central pattern generator (CPG), neural oscillators, parameter tuning, genetic algorithm, *C. elegans*.

1 Introduction

The central pattern generator (CPG) is a network of neuronal cells that control rhythmic reciprocating movements such as walking (humans), meandering (snakes), and swimming (fish) [1]. The CPG generates rhythmic electric signals via signal transduction between neurons. These internally-generated signals are then modified on the basis of sensory information about the external environment, received via sensory neurons. A number of mathematical models, termed 'neural oscillators', have been developed to describe how CPG's function [2], [3].

Recently, several research groups have simulated rhythmic movements in animals using neural oscillators [3], [4]. For example, Ekeberg developed a neural oscillator for the lamprey CPG which was then used to conduct swimming simulations [3]. Suzuki et al. constructed a neural network model of the nematode *C. elegans* [4], [5] using Matsuoka's neural oscillators and then used this model to simulate rhythmic movements such as sinusoidal locomotion [4], [6].

K. Diamantaras, W. Duch, L.S. Iliadis (Eds.): ICANN 2010, Part I, LNCS 6352, pp. 401–410, 2010.

In all of these simulations, the neural oscillators had a ladder-like structure. This structure incorporates a large number of parameters which makes tuning difficult when attempting to reproduce rhythmic reciprocating movements on a computer. Parameter-tuning rules and the methods for tuning for these parameters to generate the desired output have only been evaluated for neural oscillators that are composed of a small number of oscillators [7], [8]. There is currently no effective tuning method for setting the parameters of a neural oscillator that is composed of a large number of oscillators. Thus, the parameters included in neural oscillators that have a ladder-like structure are currently tuned by trial-and-error.

In this dissertation, we propose an automatic tuning method for all parameters included in neural oscillators with a ladder-like structure. In this method, the tuning rules for both the time constants and the coefficient of amplitude are derived by linearizing the nonlinear equations of neural oscillators. Other parameters, such as the neural connection weights, are tuned using a genetic algorithm (GA) [9]. To avoid stagnation in GA-based tuning ('tuning' denotes 'learning' in a GA) for a large number of parameters, we propose a two-step GA. This consists of a GA for the early stages of tuning and a GA for the mid-late stage of tuning. The former GA reduces large scale learning errors and the latter reduces errors for each oscillator individually. We evaluate the effectiveness of the proposed method through numerical experiments of rhythmic-signal generation in *C. elegans*.

2   Characteristic Analysis of Neural Oscillators with a Ladder-Like Structure

2.1   Neural Oscillators with a Ladder-Like Structure [2]

Matsuoka's model is representative of neural oscillators that have a ladder-like structure. This model is composed of excitatory oscillators (white circle in Fig. 1) and inhibitory oscillators (gray circle in Fig. 1). An excitatory oscillator connects with adjacent excitatory oscillators that are located in the Nth column of the 2nd row. An inhibitory oscillator connects with the corresponding excitatory oscillator. The strength of signal transduction of the neural connection between

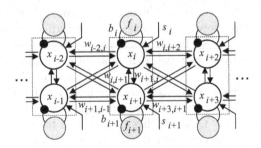

Fig. 1. Schematic of the neural oscillator with a ladder-like structure

two excitatory oscillators is represented by the connection weight $w_{i,j}$ ($i \neq j \in \{1, 2, \ldots, 2N\}$). Three types of signals are input to each excitatory oscillator from adjacent oscillators. These include signals from excitatory oscillators, $w_{i,j}x_j$, signals coding for an adaptation effect from an inhibitory oscillator, $b_i f_i$, and a sensory feedback signal, s_i. b_i is a fatigue coefficient and f_i is an output of the inhibitory oscillator. The output x_i of the excitatory oscillator and the output f_i of the inhibitory oscillator are represented by the following equations [2]:

$$T_{\mathrm{r}i}\frac{dx_i}{dt} + x_i = \sum_{j=1,\; j\neq i}^{2N} w_{i,j}h(x_j) - b_i f_i + s_i \tag{1}$$

$$T_{\mathrm{a}i}\frac{df_i}{dt} + f_i = h(x_i) \tag{2}$$

$$h(\epsilon) = \max(\epsilon, 0) \tag{3}$$

$$y_n = \alpha_n\left(h(x_{2n}) - h(x_{2n-1})\right) \tag{4}$$

where, $T_{\mathrm{r}i}$ and $T_{\mathrm{a}i}$ are the time constants and $h(\epsilon)$ is a threshold function of x_j. y_n is the total output of a pair of oscillators in the n ($n \in \{1, 2, \ldots, N\}$)th column. α_n is a coefficient of the output amplitude. To generate a desired output for each pair of oscillators, $w_{i,j}$, b_i, $T_{\mathrm{r}i}$, $T_{\mathrm{a}i}$, and α_n must be properly tuned.

2.2   Derivation of the Tuning Parameters Based on Oscillation Analysis of the Neural Oscillators

Although proper tuning of the parameters included in a neural oscillator is important to generate the desired output, a detailed analysis of a neural oscillator is difficult because of its nonlinear characteristics. Therefore, we evaluated the relationship between the neural oscillator output and the input parameters. The nonlinear equations that describe the neural oscillator are linearized at the equilibrium position as follows:

First, equation (3) is approximated by the differentiable function $\tilde{h}(\epsilon) = \epsilon/(1 + e^{-T\epsilon})$, where, T is a constant with a large value. Under this condition, equations (1) and (2) are linearized with an equilibrium position $\bar{x}_i$ of $dx_i/dt = 0$ and $\bar{f}_i$ of $df_i/dt = 0$, respectively. Thus, equations (1) and (2) are represented by the following:

$$T_\beta r_i\frac{dx_i}{dt} + x_i = \sum_{j=1,\; j\neq i}^{2N} w_{i,j}\tilde{h}'(\bar{x}_j)x_j - b_i f_i \tag{5}$$

$$T_\beta a_i\frac{df_i}{dt} + f_i = \tilde{h}'(\bar{x}_i)x_i \tag{6}$$

where, $\tilde{h}' = d\tilde{h}/d\epsilon$. The time constants $T_{\mathrm{r}i}$ and $T_{\mathrm{a}i}$ are represented by $T_{\mathrm{r}i} = T_\beta r_i$ and $T_{\mathrm{a}i} = T_\beta a_i$. T_β is a time constant that is common in all oscillators, and r_i and a_i are coefficients of the time constant. In equation (5), s_i is deleted because of the time-invariant input. To solve the simultaneous linear differential equations (5) and (6), these equations are expressed using the following matrices:

$$\left.\begin{array}{c} \begin{bmatrix} \dot{\mathbf{X}} \\ \dot{\mathbf{F}} \end{bmatrix} = \frac{1}{T_\beta} \mathbf{A} \begin{bmatrix} \mathbf{X} \\ \mathbf{F} \end{bmatrix} \\[2em] \mathbf{A} = \begin{bmatrix} \mathbf{W'} & \mathbf{B'} \\ \mathbf{H'} & \mathbf{T'} \end{bmatrix} \end{array}\right\} \tag{7}$$

where, $\mathbf{X}$, $\mathbf{F}$, $\dot{\mathbf{X}}$, and $\dot{\mathbf{F}}$ are matrices relating to the output of the excitatory oscillator x_i and the inhibitory oscillator f_i. These matrices are represented by:

$$\dot{\mathbf{X}} = \begin{bmatrix} \frac{dx_1}{dt} \\ \frac{dx_2}{dt} \\ \vdots \\ \frac{dx_{2N}}{dt} \end{bmatrix}, \dot{\mathbf{F}} = \begin{bmatrix} \frac{df_1}{dt} \\ \frac{df_2}{dt} \\ \vdots \\ \frac{df_{2N}}{dt} \end{bmatrix}, \mathbf{X} = \begin{bmatrix} x_1 \\ x_2 \\ \vdots \\ x_{2N} \end{bmatrix}, \mathbf{F} = \begin{bmatrix} f_1 \\ f_2 \\ \vdots \\ f_{2N} \end{bmatrix}$$

$\mathbf{W'}$, $\mathbf{B'}$, $\mathbf{H'}$, and $\mathbf{T'}$ are matrices describing the neural connection weight $w_{i,j}$, the fatigue coefficient b_i, and the coefficients of the time constants r_i and a_i. These matrices are represented by:

$$\mathbf{W'} = \begin{bmatrix} -\frac{1}{r_1} & \frac{w_{1,2}\tilde{h}'(\bar{x}_2)}{r_1} & \cdots & \frac{w_{1,2N}\tilde{h}'(\bar{x}_{2N})}{r_1} \\ \frac{w_{2,1}\tilde{h}'(\bar{x}_1)}{r_2} & -\frac{1}{r_2} & \cdots & \frac{w_{2,2N}\tilde{h}'(\bar{x}_{2N})}{r_2} \\ \vdots & \vdots & \ddots & \vdots \\ \frac{w_{2N,1}\tilde{h}'(\bar{x}_1)}{r_{2N}} & \frac{w_{2N,2}\tilde{h}'(\bar{x}_2)}{r_{2N}} & \cdots & -\frac{1}{r_{2N}} \end{bmatrix}, \mathbf{B'} = \begin{bmatrix} -\frac{b_1}{r_1} & 0 & \cdots & 0 \\ 0 & -\frac{b_2}{r_2} & \cdots & 0 \\ \vdots & \vdots & \ddots & \vdots \\ 0 & 0 & \cdots & -\frac{b_{2N}}{r_{2N}} \end{bmatrix},$$

$$\mathbf{H'} = \begin{bmatrix} \frac{\tilde{h}'(\bar{x}_1)}{a_1} & 0 & \cdots & 0 \\ 0 & \frac{\tilde{h}'(\bar{x}_2)}{a_2} & \cdots & 0 \\ \vdots & \vdots & \ddots & \vdots \\ 0 & 0 & \cdots & \frac{\tilde{h}'(\bar{x}_{2N})}{a_{2N}} \end{bmatrix}, \mathbf{T'} = \begin{bmatrix} -\frac{1}{a_1} & 0 & \cdots & 0 \\ 0 & -\frac{1}{a_2} & \cdots & 0 \\ \vdots & \vdots & \ddots & \vdots \\ 0 & 0 & \cdots & -\frac{1}{a_{2N}} \end{bmatrix}$$

Therefore, solving for the output x_i of the excitatory oscillator in equations (1) and (2) is represented by:

$$x_i = \sum_{k=1}^{4N} C_{qk} Q_{i,k} e^{\frac{\gamma_k}{T_\beta}t} \left[\cos(\frac{\lambda_k}{T_\beta}t) + i\sin(\frac{\lambda_k}{T_\beta}t) \right] \tag{8}$$

where, $Q_{k,k}$ is an eigenvector of $\mathbf{A}$, and γ_k ($k \in \{1, 2, \ldots, 4N\}$) and λ_k are the real and imaginary numbers of $Q_{k,k}$, respectively. C_{qk} is calculated using the initial values of x_i and f_i. A solution for x_i can be expressed by an oscillation equation that is a compound trigonometric function. The equation indicates that the angular frequency of x_i is decided by λ_k/T_β. Thus, the relationship between the input parameters and the output of the neural oscillator is partially explained. In the next section, the tuning rules for the time constants and the amplitude of the oscillatory output are derived based on equation (8).

3 Parameter-Tuning Method of Neural Oscillators with a Ladder-Like Structure

The parameters included in the neural oscillators are divided into the following three groups: (1) time constants, T_{ri} and T_{ai}, (2) the amplitude coefficient, α_n, and (3) the connection weight, $w_{i,j}$, and fatigue coefficient, b_i. The parameters in groups (1) and (2), but not (3), were derived using tuning rules that were based on the oscillation analysis in **2.2**. The parameters in group (3) were tuned using a genetic algorithm (GA) [9].

In the proposed tuning algorithm, the tuning methods for (1) and (2) are combined with a GA for (3). The parameters are tuned by both a local GA and a global GA. The former is used for all parameters during the early stages of tuning whereas the latter is used for a limited pair of oscillators at the mid-late stage of tuning. This two-step tuning method is designed to avoid learning stagnation during GA-based tuning. A procedure of the proposed parameter-tuning algorithm is outlined below.

Step 0: Initialization
The parameters for each pair of oscillators are arranged in order (shown in Fig. 2). All the parameters included in the neural oscillators are represented as individual genes. A string including all the parameters (genes) of the neural oscillator is treated as an individual in the GA. During the initialization step, P individuals are produced and the initial value for each gene is given as a uniform random number.

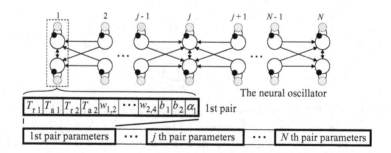

Fig. 2. A string of a GA

Step 1: Global Parameter-Tuning Using a GA (GA1)

(1) The tuning rule of the time constants
Based on the oscillation analysis in **2.2**, the output-cycle length for neural oscillators with a ladder-like structure is proportional to the time constants. Thus, when a desired output-cycle length C_s^D is given, the time constants after tuning, T_{ri}^{new} and T_{ai}^{new}, are represented by:

$$T_{ri}^{new} = \frac{C_s^D}{C_s} T_{ri}^{old} \tag{9}$$

$$T_{ai}^{new} = \frac{C_s^D}{C_s} T_{ai}^{old} \tag{10}$$

where C_s is the output-cycle length of the neural oscillators and T_{ri}^{old} and T_{ai}^{old} are time constants prior to tuning. Thus, the time constants T_{ri} and T_{ai} at the g ($g \in \{1, 2, \ldots, G_1\}$) th generation may be set to a unique value as T_{ri}^{new} and T_{ai}^{new} that are calculated from equations (9) and (10) using T_{ri}^{old}, T_{ai}^{old} and C_s at the $g - 1$th generation.

(2) **The tuning rule of the amplitude coefficient**

In equation (4), the output, y_n, of the neural oscillator in the n ($n \in \{1, 2, \ldots, N\}$)th column is calculated by multiplying the difference in output between a pair of excitatory oscillators by α_n. Thus, the error between the total output y_n of a pair of oscillators and its desired output y_n^D is decreased by tuning α_n. An amplitude error, $e^{\alpha_n}(l)$ ($l \in \{1, 2, \ldots, L\}$) denotes an output error between $y_n(l)$ and its desired output $y_n^D(l)$, where y_n is discretized with L and the output from the lth sampling is $y_n(l)$. A square summation of $e^{\alpha_n}(l)$ is expressed by:

$$E^{\alpha_n} = \sum_{l=1}^{L} \left(y_n(l) - y_n^D(l) \right)^2 \tag{11}$$

The amplitude coefficient α_n that minimizes E^{α_n} is given by the following equation:

$$\alpha_n^{new} = \frac{\sum_{l=1}^{L} \left(y_n(l) y_n^D(l) \right)}{\sum_{l=1}^{L} \left(y_n(l) \right)^2} \alpha_n^{old} \tag{12}$$

where, α_n^{new} is the amplitude coefficient after tuning and α_n^{old} is the coefficient before tuning. y_n is expressed by $y_n = \alpha_n^{old} \left(h(x_{2n}) - h(x_{2n-1}) \right)$. Thus, the amplitude coefficient α_n at the gth generation is set to a unique value of α_n^{new} that is calculated from equation (12) using α_n^{old} at the $(g - 1)$th generation.

(3) **Genetic evolution-inspired operation for parameter optimization**

An individual of a GA consists of a string arraying a set of parameters included in the neural oscillators. For each GA generation, the adequacy of each individual is evaluated to determine which individuals will be included in the next generation. The function for evaluating error values during tuning is defined by the following equation.

$$J = \frac{1}{N} \frac{1}{L} \sum_{n=1}^{N} \sum_{l=1}^{L} \left| y_n(l) - y_n^D(l) \right| \tag{13}$$

where the desired output y_n^D is given by an arbitrary function. The value of J decreases accordingly with a decrease in the error between the total output $y_n(l)$ of the nth pair of neural oscillators and its desired output $y_n^D(l)$. At each generation, individuals are sorted into ascending order based on J. J_{elite} denotes the smallest value of J that is obtained by an elite individual. Based on this evaluation, individuals with greater diversity are produced by a series of GA-operation with (a) selection, (b) crossover, and (c) mutation.

The above procedures from (1) to (3) are repeated until g_1 reaches G_1.

Step 2: Local Parameter-Tuning with a GA (GA2)

During local parameter-tuning using a GA (GA2), the parameters (T_{ri}, T_{ai}, b_i, α_n, and $w_{i,j}$) that are arranged for each pair of oscillators from the first column to the Nth column are tuned individually. All parameters are tuned simultaneously using GA1, whereas the tuning is limited to the parameters in one column of the neural oscillator using GA2. During this process, the following procedures: (1) tuning of the time constants, (2) tuning of the amplitude coefficient, and (3) genetic evolution-inspired operation for parameter optimization, are conducted for each column of the neural oscillator until g_2 reaches G_2. The parameters of the first column are tuned first. The process is then repeated up to the Nth column. Once the parameter tuning of Nth column is completed, the tuning is repeated for individual columns using a GA2, beginning with first column. During this phase of individual tuning, the parameters, except those of the column targeted for tuning, are set to their previously tuned values. The tuning process is then repeated until the total generation, g_{total}, for GA1 and GA2 reaches G_{total}.

4   Numerical Experiments

We evaluated the effectiveness of the proposed tuning method of the ladder-like neural oscillators. As an example to reproduce the complex rhythmic signals like living animals, we applied the proposed tuning method to a rigid link model of *C. elegans*, which includes 12 pairs of neural oscillators [4]. We conducted the parameter tuning by using the conventional method (the 'simple tuning method') as well as the proposed method, and compared these results.

4.1   Acquisition of *C. elegans* Rhythmic Signal

The rigid link model for *C. elegans* [4] used in this experiment represents the body of *C. elegans* and is based on the actual neuromuscular structure, innervated by 12 pairs of motor neurons (see Fig. 3). The angle q_n of the nth link is controlled by the output y_n of the nth pair of ladder-like neural oscillators. To acquire observations of rhythmic signals in *C. elegans*, five or more animals were placed on a plate containing nematode growth medium [5]. Their sinusoidal locomotion was recorded using a video camera mounted on a stereomicroscope for approximately 1 min at 24 frames per second. Each frame of the video was

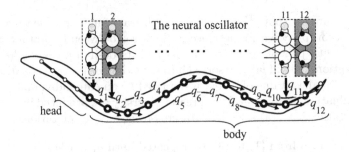

Fig. 3. A rigid link model of *C. elegans*

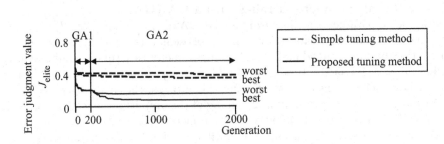

Fig. 4. Evolution of the error judgment value, J_{elite}

processed using the following procedures: (a) binarization, (b) denoising, (c) skeletonizing, and (d) division of body line into the 16 parts, using image processing software. Because the rhythmic signals acquired from *C. elegans* had high levels of background noise, the signal was approximated using the following equation:

$$q_n^{\mathrm{D}} = A_{0\,n}^{\mathrm{D}} + \sum_{k=1}^{K} A_{n,k}^{\mathrm{D}} \sin \left(\frac{2k\pi}{C_{\mathrm{s}}^{\mathrm{D}}} t - d_{n,k}^{\mathrm{D}} \right) \tag{14}$$

$A_{0\,n}^{\mathrm{D}}$ is a bias, $A_{n,k}^{\mathrm{D}}$ is the amplitude of oscillatory output, $C_{\mathrm{s}}^{\mathrm{D}}$ is the output-cycle length, and $d_{n,k}^{\mathrm{D}}$ is the phase. The link angle was approximated by $K = 2$. The data were discretized by sampling L, and were set to the desired link angle $q_n^{\mathrm{D}}(l)$. In addition, $q_n^{\mathrm{D}}(l)$ was normalized to the maximum value of the desired link angle and denoted as the desired output $y_n^{\mathrm{D}}(l)$ of the corresponding pair of oscillators.

4.2   *C. elegans* 's Rhythmic Signal Generation

To generate the desired outputs from the 12 columns of ladder-like neural oscillators, the parameters were tuned using the proposed tuning method. The number of neural oscillator columns was set to $N = 12$, and the desired output of the nth pair of oscillators was calculated using data acquired from *C. elegans*. The range of parameters used in this study were $T_{\mathrm{r}\,i} = [0, \infty)$ [sec], $T_{\mathrm{a}\,i} = [0, \infty)$ [sec], $w_{i,j} = (-\infty, \infty)$, $b_i = [0, \infty)$, $s_i = 1.0$. The generation number of tuning method

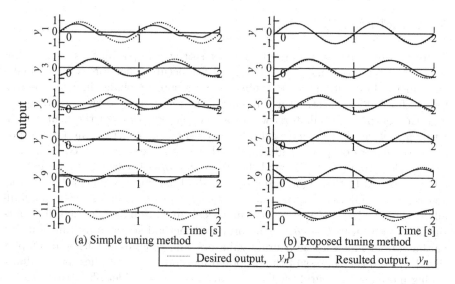

(a) Simple tuning method   (b) Proposed tuning method

⋯⋯⋯ Desired output, y_n^D —— Resulted output, y_n

Fig. 5. Results of reproduction of the rhythmic signals in *C. elegans*)

were $G_1 = 200$, $G_2 = 20$, and $G_{\text{total}} = 2,000$. To reduce the computational load, the time constants T_r, T_a and the fatigue coefficient b_i were represented by equivalence at all oscillators.

We conducted five trials using different initial values for both tuning methods, the proposed tuning method and simple tuning method. The best trial T^{best} was the one that yielded the lowest error judgment value, J, at $G_{\text{total}} = 2,000$th generation of a GA among five trials. The worst trial T^{worst} yielded the highest value of J. The values for J in the elite individual at each GA generation in the two trials, T^{best} and T^{worst}, are shown in Fig. 4. The solid line represents J_{elite} the proposed tuning method and the dotted line represents the simple tuning method. The evolution curves, J_{elite} produced by the proposed tuning method decreased smoothly prior to the 200th generation in comparison with J_{elite} of the simple tuning method. In addition, J_{elite} was lower for the proposed tuning method than for the simple tuning method at the 2,000th generation. The total output, y_n, of the nth pair of oscillators which used the parameters tuned by T^{best} in Fig. 4 is shown in each panel of Fig. 5 (solid line; data not shown for $n = 2, 4, 6, 8, 10, 12$). Panels (a) and (b) illustrate the results of the proposed and simple tuning methods, respectively. The dotted line represents the desired outputs, y_n^D, of the nth pair of the oscillator. From the results, we confirmed that the outputs of all pairs of oscillators correlate with the desired output for the parameters tuned using the proposed method. In contrast, the output of a few pairs of oscillators did not reproduce the desired output using the simple tuning method. Although, it has been difficult to tune the parameters for 12 pairs of neural oscillators to generate complex signals of animals [4], the proposed tuning method appears to generate the desired oscillatory outputs (shown in Fig. 5).

5 Conclusions

There was no effective tuning method for setting the parameters of a nonlinear neural oscillators that have a ladder-like structure. Therefore, we proposed a novel method for automatically tuning the parameters included in neural oscillators with a ladder-like structure. To clarify the relationship between parameters and each output of oscillators, we linearized the equations of the neural oscillators and derived the tuning rules for both the time constants and amplitude of the oscillatory outputs. Underivable other parameters were tuned by using a genetic algorithm (GA). To avoid the stagnation of GA-learning, we formulated a two-step GA. In this algorithm after tuned all parameters of neural oscillators generally by a Global GA, parameters of each pair of oscillators were individually tuned by a Local GA. Based on numerical simulation of mimicked rhythmic-signal generation in *C. elegans*, the proposed method successfully tuned all the parameters included in the neural oscillators, and generated sinusoidal complex signals. Given the success of the proposed method, future studies may evaluate tuning methods for neural oscillators that have a non-ladder-like structure.

References

1. Fred, D.: Foundation of Neurobiology. W. H. Feeman and Company, New York (1999)
2. Matsuoka, M.: Sustained oscillations generated by mutually inhibiting neurons with adaptation. Bio. Cybern. 52, 367–376 (1985)
3. Ekeberg, Ö.: A combined neuronal and mechanical model of fish swimming. Bio. Cybern. 69, 363–374 (1993)
4. Suzuki, M., Tsuji, T., Ohtake, H.: A model of motor control of the nematode *C.elegans* with neuronal circuits. Artif. Intell. Med. 35, 75–86 (2005)
5. Brenner, S.: The genetics of *Caenorhabditis elegans*. Genetics 77, 71–94 (1974)
6. Suzuki, M., Goto, T., Tsuji, T., Ohtake, H.: A dynamic body model of the nematode C. elegans with neuronal oscillators. J. Robotics Mechatronics 17(3), 318–326 (2005)
7. Artur, M.A.: On stability and tuning of neural oscillators: Application to rhythmic control of a humanoid robot. Neural Networks 1, 99–104 (2004)
8. Dinggou, Z., Kuanyi, Z.: Computer simulation study on central pattern generator: From biology to engineering. Int. J. of Neural Sys. 16(6), 6–16 (2006)
9. Goldberg, D.E.: Genetic Algorithms in Search, Optimization and Machine Learning. Addison-Wesley Publishing, Reading (1989)

Ensemble-Based Methods for Cancellable Biometrics

Anne Canuto[1,2,*], Michael Fairhurst[2], Laura E. A. Santana[1],
Fernando Pintro[1], and Antonino Feitosa Neto[1]

[1] Dep of Informatics and Applied Mathematics Federal University of RN, Natal Brazil
[2] School of Engineering and Digital Arts University of Kent, Canterbury, UK
anne@dimap.ufrn.br

Abstract. In this paper, we investigate the use of genetic algorithms and ensemble systems in cancellable biometrics, using fingerprint-based identification to illustrate the possible benefits accruing. The main aim is to analyze the performance of these well-established structures on transformed biometric data to determine whether they have a positive effect on the performance of this complex and difficult task.

1 Introduction

Cancellable biometrics use intentionally-distorted data instead of original sample data for template protection in biometric identification [2,5]. Proposed methods are divided into two broad classes [2]: biometric cryptosystems and feature transform approaches. In the latter, a transformation function (*f*) is applied to the biometric template and only the transformed template is stored. These schemes can be further categorized as *salting* (*f* is invertible) and noninvertible transforms. Here, we focus on the use of noninvertible transformation functions. Various functions are proposed for different biometrics, but the fingerprint modality has offered the most template protection methods [4, 6, 7]. Although the use of cancellable biometrics balances the convenience of biometric authentication with security, there is a risk that using such transformed data will decrease performance, since the complexity of the transformed biometric is much higher than that of the original. Hence a good tradeoff between discriminability and noninvertibility is essential when using feature transformations. We present a way to achieve this by using established classification structures (single classifiers and ensemble systems [1,3]) in both original and transformed fingerprint images. In order to increase effectiveness, we use a genetic algorithm to distribute the attributes among the ensemble elements. A modified version of a non-invertible transformation [4] is presented. The aim is to analyze performance on transformed biometric data and investigate the benefits available in the transformed domain.

2 The Transformation Function

The transformation method we use is a modified version of [4], as follows:

---

* Corresponding author.

K. Diamantaras, W. Duch, L.S. Iliadis (Eds.): ICANN 2010, Part I, LNCS 6352, pp. 411–414, 2010.
© Springer-Verlag Berlin Heidelberg 2010

1. Choose a minutia to be the reference minutia;
2. Define a 3D dimensional array in which the width (W_X) and height (W_Y) of the array are twice the size of an input fingerprint image and the depth (W_Z) is 2π.
3. Map the reference minutia into the 3D array with the reference minutia in the centre of the array. The other minutiae are rotated and translated to align the orientation of the reference minutia into the x-axis of the array.
4. Define the values of the cells of the 3D array such that the cell is set to 1 if it contains more than one minutia, and otherwise, the cell is set to 0;
5. A 1D bit-string is generated and the order of the array is permuted. This permutation is based on the type of reference minutiae and the user's PIN.
6. If the number of reference minutiae has reached its maximum, stop. Otherwise, go to step 1.

According to step 5 of the algorithm, a 1D string is defined for each reference minutia. This action brings two problems: the first concerns the definition of the exact number of minutiae to be used. The definition of a small number means that some useful minutiae information might be lost. In contrast, the use of a large number means that the fingerprint samples with few minutiae should be either disregarded or looped. The second problem is related to the large dimension of the input pattern.

To address these problems, we use a simpler version of the original transformation where, instead of creating one 3D array for each minutia, a 3D array is created for all reference minutiae and the values of all corresponding 3D array cells are summed. Thus, the resulting array is not binary, but represents the frequency of minutia present in that particular 3D cell. However, it can be easily transformed into binary form by means of simple thresholding. In using this modified algorithm, all minutiae are used as reference and the complexity of the problem is low. In addition, we still use a 1D binary string, as was proposed in the original version.

3 Methods and Materials

For our investigation, the original and transformed fingerprint data will be processed by individual classifiers and also by both homogeneous and heterogeneous ensemble structures. Initial experiments have shown that the simpler transformation function has a similar performance to the original, and thus we have used only the modified function presented above in analysing classification performance. The main components of our experimental work [2] are as follows: Individual classifiers: k-NN (nearest neighbour), C4.5 (decision tree) and MLP neural network; Combination Methods: Sum, weighted sum, majority voting, support vector machine (SVM) and k-NN; Ensemble size: 3, 6 and 12 individual classifiers; Dataset division: 10-fold cross validation; Statistical test: T-test with $\alpha = 0.05$.

It is important to emphasize that the heterogeneous structures include ensembles with 2 and 3 different types of classifiers taken into consideration. As there are several possibilities for each structure, the average accuracy delivered by all possibilities within the corresponding structure is determined. Our individual classifiers and combination methods were exported from the WEKA machine learning visual package (http:www.cs.waikato.ac.nz/~ml/weka). Some of the combination methods are trainable. In this sense, a validation set is used. For the weighted sum, the simple recognition rate over a validation set was used as weights.

Genetic algorithms are used for finding the optimal subset of attributes. A binary chromosome (size L (number of classifiers) x N (number of attributes)) is used to represent a possible solution for the problem, and a population of 30 chromosomes is used. Termination occurs after a maximum number of iterations (500 for transformed and 2500 for original data). The fitness of the possible solutions is analyzed in terms of a intra-classifier correlation, a criterion that defines the correlation within one classifier. The correlation of each classifier is calculated and then averaged to provide the intra-class correlation. Finally, as the genetic algorithm is a non-deterministic technique, 10 runs were performed.

We use the FVC2001 database [8], which consists of 800 fingerprint images (8 samples of 100 users). Minutiae are extracted, each generating 7 features: (x-y coordinates), direction, reliability measure, minutia type, feature type and feature identifier. To choose the target minutiae, a standard core detection procedure was applied and the N (N=10 here) closest minutiae to the core selected. In the transformation procedure, only x and y coordinates and direction information are used. The cell sizes used were as in [3], Cx=Cy=30 and Cz = $\pi/3$.

4   Results and Discussion

Table 1 illustrates the accuracy and standard deviation of the classification structures. The best results achieved by the classification methods in each row are in bold. The statistical test compared the best results with the other results, on a two-by-two basis. Statistically significant results are underlined. It is seen that classification accuracy increases for the transformed fingerprint data, showing that adopting the transformation functions was positive for all configurations. This is because the transformation function utilizes all the extracted fingerprint minutiae. However, the improvement can also be analyzed from a statistical viewpoint. Classification accuracy with the transformed data was compared to that using the original data, statistically significant improvements being observed in all cases.

Table 1. The accuracy level of the classification systems using three ensemble sizes (3,6 and 12), with ensembles homogeneous (HOM) and heterogeneous (HET)

	Ind	k-NN	SVM	Sum	Voting	WS
Original Dataset						
3-HOM	19.08±7.41	59.13±13.42	65.29±12.19	**66.29±10.32**	52.63±11.1	59.54±10.95
3-HET	49.84±5.16	60.73±7.23	**67.68±5.56**	65.55±3.81	52.89±8.26	62.59±6.73
6-HOM	63.11±6.7	77.63±7.52	**79.38±6.63**	78.79±7.11	76.29±9.05	77.08±8.55
6-HET	63.24±3.06	81.55±2.49	**83.21±1.5**	82.3±1.55	79.54±2.69	81.36±1.75
12-HOM	62.86±5.61	81.38±3.91	**82.79±2.37**	80.03±4.18	78.58±5.55	77.96±6.97
12-HET	63.09±2.41	84.09±1.83	**84.98±1.12**	83.39±2.04	81.71±2.93	82.57±2.81
Transformed dataset						
3-HOM	71.29±7.02	79.38±8.84	**81.46±8.25**	80.08±11.19	75.54±7.65	80.88±8.2
3-HET	71.37±2.74	78.2±4.19	**82.77±1.7**	81.63±3.38	77.5±1.72	82.59±1.62
6-HOM	70.9±6.84	84.79±4.56	87.42±2.59	**89.0±2.47**	87.42±1.55	89.0±3.0
6-HET	71.02±2.66	87.34±1.48	89.27±1.13	90.73±0.89	89.91±0.79	**90.91±1.37**
12-HOM	75.22±9.41	87.67±5.6	90.71±1.8	**93.13±1.94**	92.58±1.85	92.96±1.87
12-HET	75.24±6.64	90.15±1.65	92.04±0.65	94.13±0.85	93.54±1.04	**94.69±0.82**

Classification accuracy increases considerably with the number of component classifiers. Hence, the improvement achieved by the ensemble systems is higher for systems with 12 classifiers than for 3. As expected, ensembles with fewer classifiers were more unstable, with a high standard deviation. This means that both combination method and individual classifier choice is more critical. From a statistical viewpoint, there were 14 statistically significant improvements for ensembles with size 3 and 6, while there were 16 for ensembles with size 12.

When comparing the accuracy of the different ensemble structures, it is seen that the accuracy of heterogeneous structures was higher than homogeneous structures in all cases. In addition, the improvement in the accuracy comparing original and transformed data was higher for heterogeneous structures than homogeneous case.

Of the combination methods, SVM generated the best results in 7 cases (out of 12), while weighted sum provided the best results in 3 cases, sum in 4 cases and weighted sum in 2 cases. It is important to note that SVM provided the highest accuracy for the most difficult situations (original dataset and small number of individual classifiers).

5 Final Remarks

This paper has presented an analysis of ensemble systems as a tool to enhance the performance of cancellable fingerprint recognition processing. This has demonstrated that the use of our modified version of a non-invertible transformation function produces an increase in classification accuracy of. This gain was more marked for the ensemble systems than for individual classifiers. The results obtained are very promising since the performance of the ensemble structure improved in the transformed space, using a simpler transformation procedure than the original version proposed in [4]. The use of other transformation functions as well as the use of other modalities is the subject of on-going research.

References

1. Canuto, A., Abreu, M., Oliveira, L.M., Xavier Junior, J.C., Santos, A.: Investigating the influence of the choice of the ensemble members in accuracy and diversity of selection-based and fusion-based methods for ensembles. Patt. Recog. Letters 28, 472–486 (2007)
2. Jain, A.K., Nandakumar, K., Nagar, A.: Biometric Template Security. EURASIP Journal on Advances in Signal Processing, Special Issue on Biometrics (January 2008)
3. Kuncheva, L.I.: Combing Pattern Classifiers. Wiley, New Jersey (2004)
4. Lee, C., Kim, J.: Cancelable fingerprint templates using minutiae-based bit-strings. J Network Comput Appl. (2010) doi:10.1016/j.jnca,12.011
5. Maltoni, D.M., Jain, A.K., Prabhakar, S.: Handbook of Fingerprint Recognition. Springer, Berlin (2003)
6. Nagar, A., Jain, A.K.: On the Security of Non-invertible Fingerprint Template Transformed. In: IEEE Workshop on Information Forensics and Security, WIFS (2009)
7. Ratha, N.K., Chikkerur, S., Connell, J.H., Bolle, R.M.: Generating cancelable fingerprint templates. IEEE Trans. on Pattern Analysis and Machine Intelligence 29(4), 561–572 (2007)
8. FVC (2004), http://bias.csr.unibo.it/fvc2004/

A Privacy-Preserving Distributed and Incremental Learning Method for Intrusion Detection

Bertha Guijarro-Berdiñas, Santiago Fernandez-Lorenzo,
Noelia Sánchez-Maroño, and Óscar Fontenla-Romero

Faculty of Informatics, University of A Coruña, Spain
{cibertha,sfernandezl,noelia,ofontenla}@udc.es
http://www.dc.fi.udc.es/lidia/

Abstract. Computer systems are facing an increased number of security threats, specially regarding Intrusion detection (ID). From the point of view of Machine learning, ID presents many of the new cutting-edge challenges: tackle with massive databases, distributed learning and privacy-preserving classification. In this work, a new approach for ID capable of dealing with these problems is presented using the KDDCup99 dataset as a benchmark, where data have to be classified to detect an attack. The method uses Artificial Neural Networks with incremental learning capability, Genetic Algorithms and a feature selection method to determine relevant inputs. As supported by the experimental results, this method is able to rapidly obtain an accurate model based on the information of distributed databases without exchanging any compromised data, obtaining similar results compared with other authors but offering features that make the proposed approach more suitable for an ID application.

Keywords: Intrusion detection, distributed machine learning, large scale learning, artificial neural networks, genetic algorithms.

1 Introduction

With the rapid expansion of Internet in recent years, computer systems are facing an increased number of security threats. One aspect receiving a great deal of attention is the detection of intruders. The earliest reference in the field of intrusion detection (ID) can be credited to J.P.Anderson [6] who discussed the need for adapting system auditing mechanisms for investigating possible attacks. Later on, the IDES (Intrusion Detection Expert System) [7] appeared that employed statistical techniques and heuristic rules to detect security breaches. After that, several ID systems began to figure in the literature. All of them have used different techniques for ID, being the most successful and popular that based on signatures rules. This technique, however, has a major drawback in that it is only capable of detecting known attacks and requires an expert to create the rules for detecting each attack. Other approaches based on the use of artificial

K. Diamantaras, W. Duch, L.S. Iliadis (Eds.): ICANN 2010, Part I, LNCS 6352, pp. 415–421, 2010.

neural networks [9], genetic algorithms [8], or simulations of the human immuno-
logical system have also been attempted. However, the question of security in
the computerized world is a highly complex and active one, and we are still a
long way from obtaining systems that are highly reliable and secure.

In order to be able to detect any suspicious activities in the system, an Intrusion Detection System (IDS) must analyze network traffic data. It is, therefore,
interesting to develop systems able to learn from data how to identify an attack.
Moreover, new kinds of attacks are constantly appearing and an IDS must be
able to easily incorporate this new knowledge. For these reasons, ID is an adequate problem to be treated with machine learning (ML) techniques. However,
from the point of view of ML, intrusion detection presents many of the new
cutting-edge ML challenges: 1) tackle with massive and complex databases, 2)
learning in a distributed environment, and 3) preserving the privacy of data used
for classification. As it is not an easy ML problem, in 1999 the KDD (Knowledge
Discovery and Data Mining Tools Conference) Cup competition [3] proposed an
ID challenge in which, using data derived from the DARPA[1], the problem was
to distinguish among four types of attacks or a non-attack by using as inputs
several variables extracted from traffic data. It is a hard dataset for the sake of
classification because of its large size (it contains an enormous number of connection records) and the complexity of the input features, some of them with
unbalanced values. This set has become a valuable benchmark to test IDS and,
broadly, to test pattern recognition and machine learning algorithms.

Nowadays, this challenge remains opened and new works have been appearing
to overcome the competition winner. However, all are focused only on improving
the classification accuracy and they do not tackle other aspects of the environment of an ID system to be truly applicable. In this paper, a new approach
for ID in computer networks capable of dealing with the aforementioned problems is presented. This method is based on a combination of feature selection,
a novel classification method using Artificial Neural Networks with incremental
learning capability and Genetic Algorithms. Using the KDDCup99 dataset as a
benchmark its results are compared with that obtained by other authors.

2   The KDD Cup 99 Dataset and Data Preprocessing

The KDDCup99 dataset [3] was constructed in 1998 from a simulation performed
by DARPA to deal with the ID problem [1]. It contains about 5 million connection records that are sequences of TCP packets represented by 41 continuous
and discrete attributes. Each connection is labeled as either normal, or as an
attack. There exists 38 training attack types grouped into four main categories.
As in general, the interest is distinguishing between attack and no-attack, the
KDDCup99 problem can be treated as a binary classification problem.

As established in [13] the KDDCup99 training dataset is a good candidate to
feature selection. Feature Selection techniques try to eliminate irrelevant and/or
redundant attributes. Classification algorithms benefit from the decrease in the

---

[1] Defense Advanced Research Project Agency.

number of features, improving their predictive accuracy and shortening their learning period. In fact, one of the main problems when facing the KDDCup99 dataset is the computational efficiency due to its enormous size. In this paper we employed a method [13] combining discretization algorithms and filters to achieve an important reduction in the number of input features. Specifically, the Consistency-Based filter [10] and the Entropy Minimization Discretization (EMD) [11] were used. The consistency-based filter evaluates the worth of a subset of features by the level of consistency in the class values when the training instances are projected onto the subset of attributes. However, this filter cannot deal directly with numerical attributes and, in addition, some features of the KDDCup99 dataset present high imbalance and variability. These problems, that may cause a malfunction in most classifiers, are softened up by using discretization methods and, therefore, the EMD was employed in this work.

3   The Proposed Method for Intrusion Detection

The KDDCup99 on ID represents several important challenges to current ML methods. Among them, it is the necessity of moving towards the construction of scalable learning methods able to deal with massive databases, as many sophisticated ML methods found problems due to their memory or processing-time requirements. The scalability problem can be tackled by horizontally partitioning the training data and building a global model with the models derived from all the data splits, that is, by distributing learning. This is the approach taken in this paper. However, new problems arise. On one hand, it has to be determined how to combine the knowledge locally acquired to obtain a unique classifier. The second problem is related with privacy-preserving when the local models are distributed over a network, as no party wants to disclose its private data set to each other or any third party. The aim of this research area is therefore to develop efficient methods that enable this type of computation while minimizing the amount of the private information each party has to disclose to the other.

On the other hand, from the ID point of view similar and parallel characteristics arise: a machine can receive thousands of new connections records to be analyzed every day; the ID system must be able to rapidly learn from these new data in order to detect new types of attacks; and, in a real network training data is originally geographically distributed, i.e., every computer in the network suffers its own attacks. Therefore, a distributed machine learning approach is very suitable also to tackle with the described ID scenario.

In order to obtain a global classifier able to learn from several distributed local classifiers, each one obtained from different data partitions, we have developed a model based on genetic algorithms and artificial neural networks [5]. In our approach, first, several local classifiers, as many as data partitions, are built. These local classifiers are single layer neural networks using a fast linear learning method [4]. The advantages of this method for our purposes are:

- it obtains the optimal weights of the network by solving a system of linear equations with a matrix of coefficients C by applying classical methods of linear algebra with a complexity of $O(J(I+1)^2)$ (I number of network's inputs and J number of outputs), thus requiring much less computational resources than classical iterative methods.

- It presents incremental and distributed learning capacity. This can be achieved by summing the corresponding matrices of coefficients C of the systems of linear equations of the M trained networks and then obtaining the new weights by solving the system of equations for this new matrix of coefficients.

Although the chosen local model present several advantages it is very sensitive to skewness. For this reason, instead of constructing the global model by simply summing all local models, we have developed a merging method based on genetic algorithms. Each individual of the population is a local model represented by the coefficients C from which networks' weights are obtained. Once each local network is trained, they are sent to the genetic algorithm. Taking advantage of the incremental learning capability of the local classifiers, the genetic algorithm is used to combine these local models. New generation of networks are obtained by crossing individuals (summing their coefficients matrices C) and mutation (changing any number in C). At the end, the best individual will be selected as the final global classifier. In addition to improve the scalability, our proposed scheme of distributed learning is specially suited for the ID domain. Thus, on a real ID system, when the system starts there is only one node alive, called the *central node*, whose objective is to combine the local neural networks along the time. The first time a new *client node* is deployed, it asks the central node if there is any available neural network to be used as its local classifier and, if it is the case, the coefficients C are sent to the client node. From this point, every local classifier is autonomous, i.e. they can work and protect its client node without communicating with other classifiers. Moreover, they can improve over time by incrementally learning from new connections to the client node they are protecting. In order to combine the existing knowledge along a network of local classifiers, the central node periodically requests all the local neural networks and combine them by employing the genetic algorithm approach. Once the new classifier has been obtained, it will be sent again to all client nodes. As evolution always improves, or at least equals, the existing classifier success rate, it is expectable that the system will gradually tend towards a better approach.

It is important to remark that, thanks to the incremental learning capacity of the local models, distributed learning is done without exchanging connection records between the different entities involved, as only the coefficients C of the system of linear equations are sent, thus preserving privacy and very much reducing the amount of data that needs to be transmitted.

4   Experimental Results over the KDD Cup 99 Dataset

In this work, the experimental study performed involves applying the proposed method to the binary version of the KDDCup99 dataset.

4.1 Experimental Conditions

Although our proposed system is able to deal with larger datasets, in this study we employed a subset of 10% of the original DARPA training set to get results comparable with other authors as this was the dataset used in the original competition. This subset of 494.021 instances was further partitioned into 3 new sets: 45% of instances were used to train the local neural networks, 45% were used by the genetic algorithm to obtain new generations, and 10% were used by the genetic algorithm to select the best individual. For the test set, we used the original KDDCup99 dataset containing 331.029 patterns. In every case, 20% of the datasets are normal patterns (no attacks).

Regarding the genetic algorithm, we tested different number of individuals and generations (25, 50, 75 and 100 in both cases), allowing 1% of mutation rate. As fitness function the Error rate $E = (FP + FN)/(TP + FP + TN + FN)$ was employed where FP, FN, TP and TN are, respectively, the number of false positives, false negatives, true positives and true negatives, taking the attack class as the positive one. For each experiment, a 7-trial, 10-fold cross validation was used to train and test the classifier. Three performance measures –standard for previous authors– were calculated in terms of average error in the testing data across trials: Error(E), already defined, indicates the overall error rate for both classes –Normal and Attack–; True Positive Rate (TPR), or Attack Detection Rate, shows the overall rate of detected attacks; and False Positive Rate (FPR), indicates the proportion of normal patterns erroneously classified as attacks.

4.2 Results

Table 1 presents the Error, the TPR and the FPR obtained over the test set employing different number of generations and individuals.

Table 1. Error(%), TPR(%) and FPR(%) obtained over the Test Set. Font in boldface indicates the best results. Mean training simulations time (in seconds) for the proposed method is also included.

	Generations															
	Error(%)				TPR(%)				FPR(%)				Time (s)			
ind	25	50	75	100	25	50	75	100	25	50	75	100	25	50	75	100
25	8.89	8.88	8.86	8.85	89.56	89.58	89.63	89.66	**2.47**	2.51	2.61	2.65	59	116	172	230
50	8.87	8.84	8.83	8.82	89.60	89.66	89.68	**89.72**	2.53	2.62	2.68	2.79	116	225	340	459
75	8.87	8.82	8.83	8.83	89.60	89.68	89.67	89.70	2.52	2.65	2.65	2.74	176	346	521	681
100	8.85	8.82	**8.81**	**8.81**	89.64	89.70	**89.72**	**89.72**	2.58	2.70	2.75	2.77	235	458	674	894

Being the *training time* a critical aspect when dealing with massive databases, we have also measured the mean training time as shown in column 4 of Table 1.

Finally, we have selected as the best results those obtained using a population of 75 individuals and 50 generations, as it presents Error, TPR and FPR near to the minimum but requiring less computational time to learn. Hereafter, the results of the proposed method for the best individual are compared with those obtained by other authors [12,14,13,15,16], as can be seen in Table 2.

Table 2. Comparison with the results obtained by other authors over the test set

Method	Error	TPR	FPR	Method	Error	TPR	FPR
Proposed method	8.82	89.68	2.65	5FNs exp	6.70	92.75	0.75
KDD Winner	6.70	91.80	0.55	SVM Linear	6.89	91.83	1.62
PKID+Cons+C4.5	**5.14**	**94.08**	1.92	SVM RBF	6.86	91.83	1.43
EMD+INT+C4.5	6.69	91.81	0.49	ANOVA ens.	6.88	91.67	0.90
5FNspoly	6.48	92.45	0.86	Pocket 2cl.	6.90	91.80	1.52
5FNs fourier	6.69	92.72	0.75	PKID+Cons+FVQIT	5.95	92.73	**0.48**

5 Conclusions

We have described an algorithm that hybridizes the classification power of ANN algorithms with the search and optimization power of the genetic algorithm. The result is an algorithm that requires computational capabilities above that of the ANN algorithm alone, but handles correctly the problems of scalability, privacy and data distribution. Although the results over the KDDCup obtained by previous authors are from a 2% upto a 5% better, the proposed algorithm provides some other remarkable advantages for ID like:

- The system is able to handle massive datasets. Even if the dataset is distributed geographically (as it could occur in a real ID system) or if it is a one-file massive dataset (like the KDDCup file) the proposed model is suitable, as a file can be partitioned and distributed along local nodes in a unique or several machines. In fact, our method achieves good results using the complete KDDCup99 in just 59 seconds while most of the previous works have to use a subset of the training set containing less than 50.000 instances.
- A normal approach to exchange classifiers between different nodes is by sending training patterns through the network. In this case two problems arise: firstly, as the dimensions of the dataset are high it would be a very time-consuming task and, secondly, exchanging patterns would be against preserving data privacy. In this paper, we propose another way of exchanging knowledge. The unique data which is really necessary to exchange among learning nodes are the neural networks coefficients C, which were obtained with each partition of the dataset. The transmitting cost of C is depreciable if we compare it with the cost of sending patterns.
- Finally, the developed IDS using the proposed scheme will be able to learn through time as new data is acquired without the need to gather old training samples as no retrain is needed due to its incremental learning properties.

Currently, we are working on introducing this learning scheme into a multiagent system whose aim will be intrusion detection in computer networks.

Acknowledgments. The authors acknowledge financial support from the Xunta de Galicia and the Ministerio de Ciencia e Innovacion (projects TIN2009-10748 and PGIDIT06PXIB105205PR partially supported by the EU ERDF).

References

1. Lippmann, R.P., Fried, D.J., Graf, I., et al.: Evaluating Intrusion Detection Systems: the 1998 DARPA Off-Line Intrusion Detection Evaluation. In: 2000 DARPA Information Survivability Conference and Exposition, pp. 12–26 (2000)
2. Saad, Y.: Practical use of polynomial preconditionings for the conjugate gradient method. SIAM Journal of Scientific and Statistical Computing 6, 865–881 (1985)
3. KDDCup (1999), http://kdd.ics.uci.edu/databases/kddcup99/kddcup99.html
4. Castillo, E., Fontenla-Romero, O., Guijarro-Berdiñas, B., Alonso-Betanzos, A.: A global optimum approach for one-layer neural networks. Neural Comput. 14(6), 1429–1449 (2002)
5. Guijarro-Berdiñas, B., Martinez-Rego, D., Fernandez-Lorenzo, S.: Privacy-Preserving Distributed Learning based on Genetic Algorithms and Artificial Neural Networks. In: 2nd Int. Symp. on DCAI, pp. 195–202 (2009)
6. Anderson, J.P.: Computer Security Threat Monitoring and Surveillance. Technical Report, James P. Anderson Co. (1980)
7. Lunt, T.F., et al.: IDES: The Enhanced Prototype. A Real-Time Intrusion-Detection Expert System. Tech. Rep. SRI Project 4185-010, CSL SRI International (1988)
8. Crosbie, M., Spafford, G.: Active Defense of a Computer System Using Autonomous Agents. Tech. Rep., Purdue University (1995)
9. Lippmann, R.P., Cunningham, R.K.: Improving Intrusion Detection Using Keyword Selection and Neural Networks. Computer Networks 34, 597–603 (2000)
10. Dash, M., Liu, H.: Consistency-based Search in Feature Selection. Artificial Intelligence Journal 151, 155–176 (2003)
11. Fayyad, U.M., Irani, K.B.: Multi-Interval Discretization of Continuous-Valued Attributes for Classification Learning. In: Proc. 13th IJCNN, pp. 1022–1029 (1993)
12. Elkan, C.: Results of the KDD 1999 Classifier Learning. ACM SIGKDD Explorations Newsletter 1(2), 63–64 (2000)
13. Bolon-Canedo, V., Sanchez-Marono, N., Alonso-Betanzos, A.: A Combination of Discretization and Filter Methods for Improving Classification Performance in KDD Cup 1999 Dataset. In: Proc. IJCNN, pp. 305–312. IEEE Press, Los Alamitos (2009)
14. Fugate, M., Gattiker, J.R.: Computer Intrusion Detection with Classification and Anomaly Detection, using SVMs. Int. J. Pattern Recognition and Artif. Intell. 17(3), 441–458 (2003)
15. Alonso-Betanzos, A., Sanchez-Marono, N., Carballal-Fortes, F.M., Suarez-Romero, J., Perez-Sanchez, B.: Classification of Computer Intrusions Using Fuctional Networks. A Comparative Study. In: Proc ESANN 2007, pp. 25–27 (2007)
16. Porto-Diaz, I., Martinez-Rego, D., Alonso-Betanzos, A., Fontenla-Romero, O.: Combining Feature Selection and Local Modelling in the KDD Cup 1999 Dataset. In: Alippi, C., Polycarpou, M., Panayiotou, C., Ellinas, G. (eds.) ICANN 2009. LNCS, vol. 5768, pp. 824–833. Springer, Heidelberg (2009)

Using Evolutionary Multiobjective Techniques for Imbalanced Classification Data

Sandra García, Ricardo Aler, and Inés María Galván

Computer Science Departament, Carlos III University of Madrid
Avda. Universidad 30, 28911 Leganes, Spain
http://www.evannai.inf.uc3m.es

Abstract. The aim of this paper is to study the use of Evolutionary Multiobjective Techniques to improve the performance of Neural Networks (NN). In particular, we will focus on classification problems where classes are imbalanced. We propose an evolutionary multiobjective approach where the accuracy rate of all the classes is optimized at the same time. Thus, all classes will be treated equally independently of their presence in the training data set. The chromosome of the evolutionary algorithm encodes only the weights of the training patterns missclassified by the NN. Results show that the multiobjective approach is able to consider all classes at the same time, disregarding to some extent their abundance in the training set or other biases that restrain some of the classes of being learned properly.

1 Introduction

Classification is one of the main areas within Machine Learning. Typically, classification is formulated as an optimization problem: given a family of parameterized functions, the goal is to find the optimal that minimizes some error or loss function on the training set. For instance, the function might be the family of Feed-Forward Neural Networks (NN) with a given architecture and a set of connection weights [9].

Different optimization algorithms can be used, however, most of the optimization approaches are single-objective. Yet, classification problems lead very easily to considering several objectives, for instance, in order to avoid overfitting [4].

So, it is possible to consider classification as a Multiobjective Optimization problem. Several works on Evolutionary Multiobjective Machine Learning (EMOML) have shown that generalization can be improved [5,7].

The aim of this paper is to improve the generalization in classification problems for NN where classes are imbalanced. This means that there is much more data for some of the classes than for the rest (see for instance [6,13]). Usually, learning algorithms that minimize the training error, tend to focus in majority classes at the expense of the rest. In this paper we have found that it is not always the case that it is the minority classes that obtain low accuracies, but it is common that there is some bias against some of the classes. In order to avoid this problem, we propose an EMOML approach where the accuracy rates of all

K. Diamantaras, W. Duch, L.S. Iliadis (Eds.): ICANN 2010, Part I, LNCS 6352, pp. 422–427, 2010.

the classes are optimized at the same time. Thus, during learning all classes will be treated equally, independently of their abundance in the training set or other biases. At the end of the learning process, the evolutionary algorithm will produce a Pareto front that represents the tradeoff between the learning rates of the different classes. There remains the issue of selecting this point from the front that will be discussed in next section.

Our approach is closely related to the optimization of ROC curves. They have been used in Machine Learning as an alternate way of comparing different algorithms, specially if classes are imbalanced or not all classes have the same cost[1,3]. The goal of our study is not finding the optimal ROC curve, but to use the accuracy rates as secondary objectives with the aim of indirectly optimize the total accuracy.

In the present work the chromosome encodes the weights for some of the training data. The learning algorithm will use the weighted sample instead of the original dataset. The rationale behind this decision is that it gives to the evolutionary algorithm the possibility of focusing in some of the classes by increasing the weights of some of its instances. The idea of adaptive weights for training data has been successfully used in several areas of Machine Learning [12]. In this paper we follow a similar approach of Boosting: the chromosomes will be defined as an ordered list of weights. Each weight is a real number that tells how many times the correspondient pattern from the missclassified sample must be replicated. Each chromosome will have an associated NN, constructed by means of backpropagation on a training sample made of the correctly classified patterns and the set of missclassified samples, replicated according to chromosome.

The NN have been chosen because it is known that they are sensitive to reweighting of the training sample. Training will be carried out with Standard Backpropagation [9] which is an algorithm for training multilayer NN. NSGA-II [11] has been the evolutionary multiobjective optimization algorithm.

2 Multiobjective Approach for Imbalanced Classification Data

As NSGA-II must optimize all class accuracies at the same time, our encoding allows NSGA-II to improve some of the classes by replicating some of its patterns. However, this might worsen some of the other classes. Thus, the evolutionary algorithm is in charge of finding the best weighting for all the classes involved. Its output is the best non-dominated set (the front) available at the end of the search. However, we want to produce a single classifier, and not a whole set so we will choose the classifier that minimizes the total error on the same training set. In case that more than one individual have the same total error, we will choose the one which has the smaller sum of weights. After that, the generalization of the NN selected will be evaluated on a separate test set.

As mentioned before, chromosomes only contain the weights of the missclassified samples. Chromosomes will be defined as an ordered list of real numbers (the weights [1]): $z = z_i, i = 1 : |M|$. Each weight z_i tells how many times pattern i from the missclassified sample M must be replicated.

But before calling to the NSGA-II, several steps have to be carried out:

- A NN is trained with the original training set T.
- The set of missclassified patterns M is computed. The set of correctly classified patterns is $T - M$.
- The lenght of the chromosomes is set to $|M|$.
- The performance of a NN trained by backpropagation depends on the training data but also on the initial connections weights w_0, which are typically a set of small values generated randomly. This means that during the search process, a chromosome might outperform another, not because it is intrinsically better, but because of the initial weights. This adds some noise to the fitness function. In order to remove the noise, a set of random initial weigths w_0 is fixed. Therefore, the backpropagation algorithm will always start from the same fixed set of initial weights w_0 for all neural networks created during the search process, instead of generating new random weights everytime backpropagation is run.

Now, the NSGA-II algorithm can start. Initially, all the chromosomes will be generated randomly by NSGA-II, the weights will be random numbers, uniformly generated in the range $[0, K]$, where K is a parameter. Every generation, the chromosomes are evaluated by the fitness function, which is computed as follows:

- The replicated sample M_z is computed, according to weights in z.
- A neural network is trained with the correctly classi ed sample $T - M$ and the replicated one M_z. Backpropagation is used for training, it starts from the set of weights w_0 generated before running NSGA-II.
- Those values are returned to NSGA-II.

We can define the NSGA-II objectives as: let C the number of classes in the problem and $|T_c|$ the number of patterns belonging to class c. $T_c = \{(x_i, c), i = 1 : |T_c|\}$ is the set of patterns belonging to class c. As NSGA-II is a minimization algorithm, the class errors will be used instead of class accuracies. The error for class c is the 0-1 loss for neural network NN_z associated to chromosome z, is defined in Eq.1. E_c is computed on the original training sample (not the replicated one). Therefore, the set of goals to be minimized by NSGA-II is $E_c, c = 1 : C$.

$$E_c(z) = \frac{1}{|T_c|} * \sum_{i=1}^{i=|T_c|} \delta(y_i, NN_z(x_i)) \tag{1}$$

3   Experimental Validation

3.1   Experimental Setup

Table 1 shows a summary of the characteristics of the data sets used in this work. The data sets have been selected from the UCI Machine Learning Repository [2]

---

[1] Not to be confused with the NN weights w0.

and the Proben Repository [8]. Balance-scale, Car,and Thyroid have the largest differences between the majority and the minority classes, whereas Card displays almost no imbalance. Breast-cancer and Ionosphere show some imbalance.

Table 1. Classification Domains

Dataset	N. of Attributes	N. of Classes	N. of Patterns	N. Class Patterns	Source
Thyroid	21	3	7200 (3428 Test)	166/368/6666	Proben
Car	6	4	1728	1210/384/69/65	UCI
Balance Scale	4	3	645	288/49/288	UCI
Breast Cancer - W	9	2	699	241/458	Proben
Ionosphere	34	2	351	225/126	UCI
Card	51	2	690	307/383	Proben

First of all, different architectures of NN have been trained for each domain, in order to select an appropriate number of hidden neurons. In this work, the number of hidden neurons of the NN must be fixed from the start, under the hypothesis that a wide range of architectures will provide similar performance. The objective of this study is to show the advantage of using a multiobjective approach, not to find the optimal architecture for the NN.

All NN are trained with the backpropagation algorithm during 500 iterations and a learning rate of 0.1. They are composed by 3 hidden layers each of them with 15 neurons. The FANN software library has been used [10].

The genes in the NSGA-II chromosome are randomly initialized with real numbers in the interval [0,5]. The population size was set to 30 and NSGA-II was run for 50 generations with a crossover and mutation probabilities of 0.5 and 0.01, respectively.

3.2   Experimental Results

In this paper we will use "total classification rate" to refer to the percentage accuracy classification rate of the dataset. "Class classification rate" will be employed to refer to classification rates broken down for each one of the different classes in the problem. Table 2 shows both the total and the class rates obtained by the initial NN for test. 5-fold cross validation has been used for all domains except "Thyroid", because the latter is provided with a test set. Majority and minority classes have been marked with + and −, respectively. It can be observed that, in some of the imbalanced domains (Thyroid, Balance-Scale, and Ionosphere), the NN obtains much lower classification rates for the minority classes than for the rest. However, this is not true for Car and Breast Cancer.

The multiobjective algorithm provides a Pareto front with non-dominated individuals. Using the criteria selection described in section 2 we choose one individual and check its classification success rate (studying the total one and the rate per each class). These rates are also shown in Table 2.

The largest increment in total classification rate (+5.22%) occurs in the Balance Scale data set. This improvement is due to a +57.35% increase in the

Table 2. Classification Rate

Dataset	Test Initial NN	Test MO Aproach
	Total — Class Classification Rate (%)	Total — Class Classification Rate (%)
Thyroid	$97.81 - 71.23^-/94.31/98.61^+$	$98.24 - 72.60^-/95.45/98.99^+$
Car	$94.21 - 93.55^+/80.41/88.75^-/96.46^-$	$95.25 - 97.43^+/86.46/93.57^-/98.46^-$
Balance Scale	$89.14 - 90.74^+/26.98^-/99.29^+$	$94.36 - 92.85^+/84.33^-/98.13^+$
Breast Cancer	$96.42 - 96.72^-/96.96^+$	$96.70 - 97.38^-/95.42^+$
Ionosphere	$88.59 - 97.34^+/73.74^-$	$89.15 - 97.73^+/74.8^-$
Card	$82.75 - 79.70^-/85.33^+$	$82.46 - 82.23^-/82.65^+$

minority class, without decreasing significantly the rest of the classes. The Car domain also shows a total rate improvement (+1%). In this case, all classes are improved with no particular focus on the minority classes. The accuracy increases range from +2.0% to +6.05%. Let us remember that in Car, the NN obtained higher accuracies for the minority classes, therefore it makes sense that the multiobjective approach will focus on the majority classes. In the Thyroid, and Ionosphere domains, there is some total rate improvement over the initial NN (less than 1%). It does so by focusing mainly on the minority classes. In the Breast Cancer and Card domains there is no significant change over the initial NN results. For the Breast Cancer this is reasonable because it is hard to improve the classification rate for the classes already provided by the NN (96.72% and 96.96% respectively). With regard to Card, the classes were not imbalanced, so the multiobjective approach could not take advantage of focusing in some of the classes in order to improve results.

4   Conclusions

In this paper we have explored a multiobjective evolutionary technique to deal with imbalanced classification problems with Neural Networks (NN). The NN Backpropagation algorithm tends to learn better some of the classes (typically the majority ones) at the expense of the rest of the classes. In order to remove this tendency, we have proposed an evolutionary multiobjective approach that uses NSGA-II, where the accuracy rates of all the classes is optimized at the same time. At the end of the evolutionary process, a Pareto front of NN is obtained. The aim is to improve the accuracies of all the classes but at the same time, increase the total classification rate. The latter is achieved by selecting the NN with maximum total classification rate among the NN in the Pareto front. If there are more than one point with the same total rate, the one with minimum sum of weights was chosen.

In order to generate a diverse front of NN, NSGA-II explored the space of training instance weighs: each input-output pair was associated to a weight. Thus, NN were trained not on the original sample, but on a weighted sample. The NSGA-II chromosomes contain different weighting sets that give rise to different NN after being trained by Backpropagation on the weighted sample. In order to work with shorter chromosomes, only weights for the training instances missclassified by an initial NN were considered.

The experiments show that in some of the cases, the total classification rate is improved by focusing on the classes that were not learned well by the initial NN. In other cases the total rate was not significantly improved but in general, the accuracy rates of some of the classes improved without decreasing the total classification rate. In summary, the algorithm gives equal opportunity to all classes, independently of their abundance in the training set or independently of other biases, because they are all optimized at the same time.

Acknowledgments. This work is funded by the Spanish Ministry of Science under contract TIN2008-06491-C04-03 (MSTAR) and TSI-020110-2009-137.

References

1. Bradley, A.P.: The use of the area under the roc curve in the evaluation of machine learning algorithms. Pattern Recognition 30, 1145–1159 (1997)
2. Merz, C.J., Blake, C.L.: UCI repository of machine learning databases. Technical report, University of California, Irvine, Dept. of Information and Computer Sciences (1998), http://www.ics.uci.edu/mlearn/MLRepository.htm
3. Fieldsend, J.E., Everson, R.M.: Multi-class roc analysis from a multi-objective optimisation perspective. Pattern Recognition Letters. Special Issue: ROC Analysis in Pattern Recognition 27, 918–927 (2006)
4. Senhoff, B., Graning, L., Yaochu, J.: Generalization improvement in multi-objective learning. In: International Joint Conference on Neural Networks (2006)
5. Yaochu, J.: Multi-Objective Machine Learning, pp. 151–172. Springer, Heidelberg (2006)
6. Stephen, S., Japkowicz, N.: The class imbalance problem: A systematic study. Intelligent Data Analysis Journal 6(5), 429–449 (2002)
7. Deb, K., Knowles, J., Corne, D.: Multiobjective Problem Solving from Nature. From Concepts to Applications, pp. 155–176. Springer, Heidelberg (2008)
8. Prechelt, L.: Proben1. a set of neural network benchmarking problems and benchmarking rules. Technical report, Dept. of Computer Science, University of Karlsruhe, Germany (1994),
http://www.ubka.uni-karlsruhe.de/cgi-bin/psview?document=/ira/1994/21&search=/ira/1994/21
9. Rojas, R.: Neural Networks: A Systematic Introduction, pp. 55–180. Springer, Heidelberg (1996)
10. Nissen, S.: Implementation of a fast artificial neural network library (fann). Technical report, Dep. of Computer Science. University of Copenhagen (2003),
http://leenissen.dk/fann/
11. Deb, K., Pratap, A., Agarwal, S., Meyarivan, T.: A fast and elitist multiobjective genetic algorithm: Nsga-ii. IEEE Transactions on Evolutionary Computation 6, 182–197 (2002)
12. Wang, H., Wang, X.: Classification by evolutionary ensembles. Pattern Recognition 39, 595–607 (2006)
13. Feldkamp, L.A., Murphey, Y.L., Guo, H.: Neural learning from unbalanced data. Applied Intelligence, 117–128 (2004)

Modeling the Ase 20 Greek Index Using Artificial Neural Nerworks Combined with Genetic Algorithms

Andreas S. Karathanasopoulos[1], Konstantinos A. Theofilatos[2],
Panagiotis M. Leloudas[2], and Spiridon D. Likothanassis[2]

[1] Liverpool Business School, CIBEF John Moores University, Liverpool, England
[2] Pattern Recognition Laboratory, Dept. of Computer Engineering & Informatics,
University of Patras, 26500, Patras, Greece
theofilk@ceid.upatras.gr, andreas.kara@hotmail.com,
leloudas@ceid.upatras.gr, likothan@cti.gr

Abstract. The motivation for this paper is to investigate the use of alternative novel neural network architectures when applied to the task of forecasting and trading the ASE 20 Greek Index using only autoregressive terms as inputs. This is done by benchmarking the forecasting performance of 4 different neural network training algorithms with some traditional techniques, either statistical such as an autoregressive moving average model (ARMA), or technical such as a moving average convergence/divergence model (MACD), plus a naïve strategy. For the best training algorithm found, we used a genetic algorithm to find the best feature set, in order to enhance the performance of our models. More specifically, the trading performance of all models is investigated in a forecast and trading simulation on ASE 20 fixing time series over the period 2001-2009 using the last one and half year for out-of-sample testing. As it turns out, the combination of the neural network with genetic algorithm, does remarkably well and outperforms all other models in a simple trading simulation exercise and when more sophisticated trading strategies as transaction costs were applied.

Keywords: Quantitative Trading Strategies, transaction costs, genetic algorithms, feedforward neural networks, momentum and backpropagation.

1 Introduction

The use of intelligent systems for market predictions has been widely established. This paper deals with the application of combined computing techniques for forecasting the Greek stock market. The development of accurate techniques is critical to economists, investors and analysts. The traditional statistical methods, on which the forecasters were reliant in recent years, seem to fail to capture the interrelationship among market variables. This paper encourages search of methods capable of identifying and capturing all the discontinuities, the nonlinearities and the high frequency multipolynomial components characterizing the financial series today. The category that promises such effective results is the combination of Genetic algorithms with Neural Networks named Genetic-trainlm model. Many researchers have argued that

K. Diamantaras, W. Duch, L.S. Iliadis (Eds.): ICANN 2010, Part I, LNCS 6352, pp. 428–435, 2010.
© Springer-Verlag Berlin Heidelberg 2010

combining many models for forecasting gives better estimates by taking advantage of each model's capabilities and comparing them with single time series models.

The literature review using that index in academic research is quite enough, with first Dunis et al. (2010a) proved that combined models can have better forecasting accuracy. Dunis et al (2010b) continues to show better results in terms of annualized return, using another mixed neural network model. Moreover the ASE-20 has been used in a BA dissertation (2009) and lastly when Dunis et al. (2010c) tried to compare the genetic programming algorithms with neural networks using as forecasting index the ASE-20, they came up with the interesting result, that GP algorithm can give us better forecasting performance.

2 The ASE 20 Greek Index and Related Financial Data

For Futures on the FTSE/ASE-20 that are traded in derivatives markets the underlying asset is the blue chip index FTSE/ASE-20. The FTSE/ASE-20 index is based on the 20 largest ASE stocks. It was developed in 1997 by the partnership of ASE with FTSE International and is already established benchmark. It represents over 50% of ASE's total capitalization and currently has a heavier weight on banking, telecommunication and energy stocks.

Table 1. Explanatory variables for Neural Networks

Number	Variable	Lag
1	Athens Composite all share return	1
2	Athens Composite all share return	2
3	Athens Composite all share return	3
4	Athens Composite all share return	4
5	Athens Composite all share return	5
6	Athens Composite all share return	6
7	Athens Composite all share return	7
8	Athens Composite all share return	8
9	Moving Average of the Athens Composite all share return	10
10	Athens Composite all share return	11
11	Athens Composite all share return	12
12	Athens Composite all share return	14
13	Moving Average of the Athens Composite all share return	15
14	Athens Composite all share return	16

The FTSE/ASE 20 index is traded as a futures contract that is cash settle upon maturity of the contract with the value of the index fluctuating on a daily basis. The cash settlement of this index is simply determined by calculating the difference between the traded price and the closing price of the index on the expiration day of the contract. Furthermore, settlement is reached between each of the participating counterparties. Whilst the futures contract is traded in index points the monetary value of the contract is calculated by multiplying the futures price by the multiple of 5 euro per point. For example, a contract trading at 1,400 points is valued at 7,000 EUR.

The ASE 20 Futures is therefore adapted to a level in which to suit institutional trading. As a result, our application is deemed more realistic and specific to the series that we investigate in this paper.

The observed ASE 20 time series is non-normal (Jarque-Bera statistics confirms this at the 99% confidence interval) containing slight skewness and high kurtosis. It is also non-stationary and we decided to transform the ASE 20 series into stationary series of rates of return.

As inputs to our neural networks, based on the autocorrelation function and some ARMA experiments we selected 1 set of autoregressive and moving average terms of the ASE 20 returns.

In order to train the neural networks we divided our dataset as follows:

- The Total Dataset with 2283 days from 1/1/2001 to 30/9/2009
- The Training Dataset with 1874 days from 24/1/2001 to 31/3/2008
- The Test Dataset with 350 days from 28/11/2006 to 31/3/2008
- The out-of-sample Dataset with 392 days from 1/4/2008 to 30/9/2009.

3   Forecasting Models

3.1   Benchmark Models

In this paper, we benchmark our neural network models with 3 traditional strategies, namely an autoregressive moving average model (ARMA), a moving average convergence/divergence technical model (MACD) and a naïve strategy [5, 6].

The naïve strategy takes the most recent period change as the best prediction of the future change.

The MACD strategy used is quite simple. Two moving average series are created with different moving average lengths. The decision rule for taking positions in the market is straightforward. Positions are taken if the moving averages intersect. If the short-term moving average intersects the long-term moving average from below a 'long' position is taken. Conversely, if the long-term moving average is intersected from above a 'short' position is taken.

Autoregressive moving average models (ARMA) assume that the value of a time series depends on its previous values (the autoregressive component) and on previous residual values (the moving average component). Using as a guide the correlogram in the training and the test sub periods we have chosen a restricted ARMA (12,12) model. All of its coefficients are significant at the 99% confidence interval. The null hypothesis that all coefficients (except the constant) are not significantly different from zero is rejected at the 99% confidence interval.

3.2   Combining Genetic Algorithms with Neural Networks

Genetic Algorithms are general search algorithms, based on evolutions principles of nature, able to solve tough problems. Holland (1975) was the first to implement those using chromosomes of bit-strings. Genetic Algorithms are useful and efficient if the search space is big and complicated or there is not any available math analysis of the problem. They have been used in many problems in the past including timetabling problems[1], neural networks[2], health and medical problems[3], scheduling problems[4] etc.

Genetic Algorithms have their root in biology where every living organism has cells and every cell has the same number of chromosomes. Chromosomes are DNA strings, used as a model of the organism.

In Genetic Algorithms, chromosome is the solution of a problem, consisted of genes, which are the optimizing parameters. A Genetic Algorithm creates an initial population of chromosomes, evaluates this population and evolves it through several generations searching the best solution for the problem. The chromosomes that achieved the biggest evaluation score are more likely to be selected for the evolution of the population.

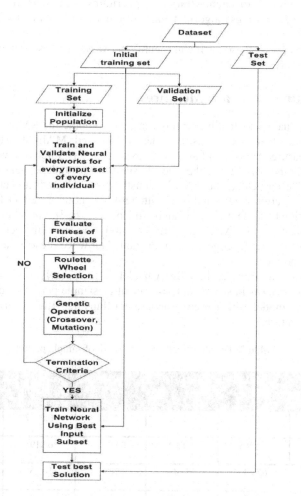

Fig. 1. Architecture of the proposed method

In this specific application, we used genetic algorithms in order to extract the best feature set which we must use for modeling the ASE index Greek index. The structure of the proposed method is shown in figure 1. In this method, genetic algorithms with artificial neural networks were used for determining the best set of inputs and then artificial neural networks were used for building the finale forecasting model.

In this paper, we used feed forward neural networks. A feed-forward neural network is an artificial neural network where connections between the units do not form a directed cycle. This is different from recurrent neural networks.

The feed-forward neural network was the first and arguably simplest type of artificial neural network devised. In this network, the information moves in only one direction, forward, from the input nodes, through the hidden nodes (if any) and to the output nodes. There are no cycles or loops in the network.

In order to use the best training algorithm for the artificial neural networks, we experimented with 3 different training algorithms (TRAINLM, TRAINGDM, TRAINGDA) [9]. All these algorithms are different variations of the back propagation algorithm.

For implementing these artificial neural networks we used the Matlab 7.9.0 (R2009b) Toolbox.

4 Forecasting Accuracy Measures

In order to evaluate statistically our forecasts, we compute the RMSE, the MAE, the MAPE and the THEIL-U statistics. The RMSE and MAE statistics are scale-dependent measures but give a basis to compare volatility forecasts with the realized volatility while the MAPE and the Theil-U statistics are independent of the scale of the variables. In particular, the Theil-U statistic is constructed in such a way that it necessarily lies between zero and one, with zero indicating a perfect fit. A more detailed description of these measures can be found on [5, 6, 7]. For all three of the error statistics retained (RMSE, MAE, MAPE) the lower the output, the better the forecasting accuracy of the model concerned. In the table below we present our results for the out of sample period.

As we can see in Table 2, the ARMA model do remarkably well and presents the most accurate forecasts in statistical terms in out-of-sample period. Second comes the neural network model which used genetic algorithms and RNN comes third in our statistical evaluation.

Table 2. The statistically results in out of sample period

	NAIVE	MACD	ARMA	Genetic Algorithm with trainlm	traingdm
RMSE	0.0349	0.0272	0.0261	0.0267	0.0278
MAE	0.0265	0.0201	0.0192	0.0195	0.0199
MAPE	635.9%	352.4%	151.5%	172.5%	287.1%
THEIL-U	0.6786	0.7497	0.8848	0.7684	0.7559

	traingda	trainlm
RMSE	0.0548	0.0287
MAE	0.0285	0.0200
MAPE	372.46%	168.51%
THEIL-U	0.7283	0.07736

4.1 Empirical Trading Simulation Results

The trading performance of all the models considered in the out of sample subset is presented in table 3. We choose the network with the higher profit in the test sub-period. Our trading strategy applied is simple and identical for all the models: go or stay long when the forecast return is above zero and go or stay short when the forecast return is below zero. As shown in table 3 below the Genetic Algorithm with trainlm perform significantly better than the other neural networks.

Table 3. Out-of-sample results

	NAIVE	MACD	ARMA	Genetic Algorithm with trainlm	traingdm
Information Ratio (excluding costs)	0.65	0.38	0.28	0.78	0.66
Annualized Volatility (excluding costs)	39.26%	40.86%	40.87%	40.83%	40.84%
Annualized Return (excluding costs)	25.49%	15.72%	11.56%	31.76%	26.85%
Maximum Drawdown (excluding costs)	-46.10%	-50.63%	-30.295%	-45.29%	-63.82%
Positions Taken (annualized)	117	38	198	118	117
Transaction costs	16.38%	5.32%	27.72%	16.52%	16.38%
Annualized Return (including costs)	9.11%	10.4%	-16.15%	15.24%	10.47%

	traingda	trainlm
Information Ratio (excluding costs)	0.69	0.71
Annualized Volatility (excluding costs)	40.84%	40.83%
Annualized Return (excluding costs)	28.18%	28.98%
Maximum Drawdown (excluding costs)	-31.01%	-69.17%
Positions Taken (annualized)	103	120
Transaction costs	14.42%	16.08%
Annualized Return (including costs)	13.76%	12.8

Following [6], we check for potential improvements to our models through the application of transaction costs. A transaction cost is trading strategy devised to filter out those trades with expected returns below a threshold d around zero. They suggest to go long when the forecast is above d and to go short when the forecast is below d. According to the Athens Stock Exchange, transaction costs for financial institutions and fund managers dealing a minimum of 143 contracts or 1 million Euros is 10 Euros per contract (round trip). Dividing this transaction cost of the 143 contracts by average size deal (1 million Euros) gives us an average transaction cost for large players of 14 basis points (1 base point=1/100 of 1%) or 0.14% per position.

Putting the models in order and despite larger drawdowns it is easy to understand that the best model is Genetic Algorithm with trainlm and second comes the trainlm. With small differences traingda model comes third and lastly is the traingdm.

5   Concluding Remarks

In this paper, we apply a combination of genetic algorithm with neural networks, a traingdm neural network, a traingda neural network and a trainlm neural network to a one-day-ahead forecasting and trading task of the ASE 20 fixing series with only autoregressive terms as inputs. We use a naïve strategy, a MACD and an ARMA model as benchmarks. We develop these different prediction models over the period 2001 - 2008 and validate their out-of-sample trading efficiency over the following period from September 2008 through 2009.

The Genetic Algorithm-Neural Network demonstrates the highest trading performance in terms of annualized return and information ratio before transaction costs and when more elaborate trading strategies are applied. When refined trading strategies are applied and transaction costs are considered the Genetic Algorithm-neural network again continues to outperform all other models achieving the highest annualized return. The traingdm, the traingda and the trainlm neural network models perform remarkably well and seem to have great ability in providing good forecasts when autoregressive series are only used as inputs.

Finally, the application of genetic algorithms reduced the inputs which should be used by the artificial neural networks while improving the models' performance.

References

[1] Beligiannis, G., Moschopoulos, C., Kaperonis, G., Likothanassis, S.: Applying evolutionary computation to the school timetabling problem: The Greek case. Computers & Operations Research 35, 1265–1280 (2008)
[2] Georgopoulos, E.F., Adamopoulos, A.V., Likothanassis, S.D.: A Tool for Evolving Artificial Neural Networks. In: 1st International Workshop on Combinations of Intelligent Methods and Applications, CIMA 2008 (2008)
[3] Theofilatos, K., Georgopoulos, E., Likothanassis, S.: Modeling the Magnetoencephalo-Gram (MEG) Of Epileptic Patients Using Genetic Programming and Minimizing the Derived Models Using Genetic Algorithms. In: Numerical Analysis AND Applied Mathematics: International Conference on Numerical Analysis and Applied Mathematics 2009, Vol. 1, Vol. 2 (2009)

[4] Pezzellaa, F., Morgantia, G., Ciaschetti, G.: A genetic algorithm for the Flexible Job-shop Scheduling Problem. Computers & Operations Research 35(10), 3202–3212 (2008)

[5] Dunis, C., Laws, J., Karathanasopoulos, A.: Modelling and Trading the Greek Stock Market with Hybrid ARMA-Neural Network Models, CIBEF Working Papers (2010a), http://www.cibef.com

[6] Dunis, C., Laws, J., Karathanasopoulos, A.: Modelling and Trading the Greek Stock Market with mixed-Neural Network Models, CIBEF Working Papers (2010a), http://www.cibef.com

[7] Dunis, C., Laws, J., Karathanasopoulos, A.: GP Algorithm versus Hybrid and Mixed neural networks, CIBEF Working Papers (2010a), http://www.cibef.com

[8] Michos, T.: BA dissertation, Modelling and Trading the ASE 20 Greek Index with Neural Network Models (2009)

[9] Matlab 7.9.0 (R2009b) Toolbox

A Hybrid Approach for Artifact Detection in EEG Data

Jacqueline Fairley[1], George Georgoulas[2], Chrysostomos Stylios[2], and David Rye[1]

[1] Emory University, School of Medicine
Dept. of Neurology, Atlanta, Georgia, USA
{jafairl,drye}@emory.edu
[2] Laboratory of Knowledge and Intelligent Computing, Dept. of Informatics
and Communications Technology, TEI of Epirus, Kostakioi, 47100, Artas
Greece georgoul@gmail.com, stylios@teiep.gr

Abstract. This paper presents a hybrid approach for extreme artifact detection in electroencephalogram (EEG) data, recorded as part of the polysomnogram (psg). The approach is based on the selection of an "optimal" set of features guided by an evolutionary algorithm and a novelty detector based on Parzen window estimation, whose kernel parameter h is also selected by the evolutionary algorithm. The results here suggest that this approach could be very helpful in cases of absence of artifacts during the training process.

Keywords: Genetic Algorithms, Feature Selection, Parzen Novelty Detection, Artifact Detection.

1 Introduction

Valid automated computer-based sleep analysis system development relies upon the creation of efficient automated computer-based artifact processing methodologies [1]. This paper introduces a hybrid computational based method for the automated detection of a commonly observed electroencelphalogram (EEG) artifact within human psg data [2]. The artifact of interest is usually created by excessive patient movement (EPM), which is visually characterized by increased signal amplitude and variance values within the EEG. However, the characteristics of EPM make the underlying physiological EEG signal attributes visually unrecognizable and interfere with sleep technician and physician psg analysis [3]. During automated/computerized psg analysis these body movements may also be misinterpreted [4].

Due to the common occurrence of EPM artifacts within human psg recordings the signal analysis approaches obtained within this study are vital to the establishment of an efficient automated computer-based artifact processing methodology. Implementation of the latter will advance the development of a valid automated computer-based sleep analysis system, which will directly impact the diagnosis and treatment of people affected by sleep related illnesses. Further emphasis on the importance of this work is provided by the National Institutes of Health which states, "At least 40 million

K. Diamantaras, W. Duch, L.S. Iliadis (Eds.): ICANN 2010, Part I, LNCS 6352, pp. 436–441, 2010.

Americans each year suffer from chronic, long-term sleep disorders each year. These disorders account for an estimated $16 billion in medical costs each year" [5].

Presently, no standardized approaches for psg computer-based automated artifact removal and/or compensation are widely accepted within clinical practice of human sleep analysis. However, two main research approaches are used to address artifacts within human psg data and have been cited in the literature, which include psg artifact prevention and treatment [1], [2]. The second approach, artifact treatment focuses, on artifact removal by utilizing computational artifact data elimination and compensation techniques. The primary focus of this work is computational artifact data elimination.

The artifact problem can be formulated as a two class classification problem. However when one class is either under-sampled or not present at all, then the problem becomes more difficult and a different approach is needed. In the latter case a novelty detector can be used [6], which attempts to model, only, the known class.

2 Materials and Methods

As mentioned in the introductory section, the main idea behind this research work is to treat the artifact detection as a novelty (anomaly) detection or as a one class classification problem [6]. By this approach, we treat artifacts as anomalous situations and we focus on modeling the normal EEG behavior. Deviations from the "Standard EEG Model" are considered artifact.

As in the general two-class (or multi-class) classification problems, we usually have to move from the original space (the "raw data" space) to a feature space of a (much) smaller dimension through a feature extraction process. By doing so, we hope to condense the relevant information and get rid of potential "noise" and also alleviate the problem of the curse of dimensionality. Therefore we often tend to extract more features than are necessary based upon expert knowledge and intuition and then employ a feature selection stage to come up with a near optimum set of variables [7].

2.1 Data Description

The proposed work was tested using a psg record sampled at 200 Hz for a total duration of 7.25 hours provided in compliance with Emory University Institutional Review Board protocol by the Emory Clinic Sleep Disorders Center (ECSDC) located in Atlanta, Georgia, USA.

In order to extract the psg recording, surface electrodes from calibrated sleep monitoring equipment were attached to subjects by sleep technicians at the ECSDC. The electroencephalogram (EEG) data channel C3-A2 was extracted from the central electrode (C3) and referenced to anterior electrodes (A2), according to the international 10-20 electrode placement system [8].

A visual example of a 30 second epoch/segment of EPM artifact contamination in the EEG is displayed in the top panel of Figure 1. Increased EEG signal amplitude (C3-A2) is shown in the vertical axis displaying an amplitude value exceeding 700μV indicated by the arrow.

Twenty features (Table 1) were extracted from 1 sec time windows, EEG (C3-A2), after consultations with sleep physicians at ECSDC, an exhaustive review of prior bio-signal/psg data artifact detection methods, and a detailed visual analysis of the signal characteristics of EPM artifact and Non-artifact corrupted psg data sets [9].

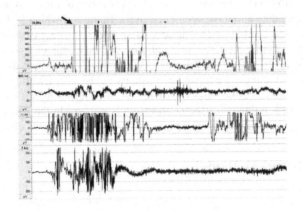

Fig. 1. Example of EPM artifact displayed in the top panel EEG channel

2.2 Genetic Algorithm Feature Selection Stage

Feature selection can be performed in more than one way utilizing different criteria [13]. In this work, a wrapper [10] approach was adopted to assist in selecting a set of features that maximizes a portion of the area under the ROC curve (AUC) [11].

More specifically a GA is utilized to select the features that are used by the novelty detector (which at the same time tries to optimize a design parameter of the detector). The GA population consists of binary chromosomes divided into five competing subpopulations [12]. Each of the subpopulations (containing different mutation rate ranges that provide varying degrees of search space exploration) competes for resources with the subpopulation having the best performance given a greater number of chromosomes/individuals [12].

The GA was implemented using the GEATBx toolbox [12] and it run for 500 "generations". Apart from twenty bits reserved to encode the selected set, we also genetically encoded the kernel parameter h of the Parzen detector using ten more bits.

Fitness Function. Due to the imbalanced nature of the data set, the selection of accuracy (overall classification rate) as a metric is not the best choice for this case. Thus, the classifiers are compared by using their corresponding receiver operating characteristic (ROC) curves. The ROC curve plots the True Positive (TP) rate (such that positive are the artifact free segments and negative are artifact segments) against the False Positive (FP) rate as an acceptance threshold is varied (Figure 2). AUC is a single scalar value that can be used for classifier comparison [11].

For this work because we were also looking for a high True Negative (TN) rate we substituted the AUC for a portion of the area that was between specific (small) values (0.005-0.05) of the FP rate which corresponded to high TN rates (Figure 2).

Table 1. Extracted Features

Feature Number	Feature Name	Symbol
1	Mean Absolute Amplitude	MAA
2	Curve Length	L
3	Mean Energy	MnE
4	Power Spectrum Sub-band, Delta Power	{Delta}
5	Power Spectrum Sub-band, Theta Power	{Theta}
6	Power Spectrum Sub-band, Alpha Power	{Alpha}
7	Power Spectrum Sub-band, Spindle Power	{Spindle
8	Power Spectrum Sub-band, Beta Power	{Beta}
9	Mean/Expected Value	E
10	Variance	Var
11	Standard Deviation	Std
12	Spectral Edge Frequency	SEF
13	Kurtosis	Kurt
14	Skewness	Skew
15	Mobility	Mobi
16	Complexity	CmP
17	Zero Crossing	C
18	Entropy	EnT
19	75th Amplitude Percentile	75 Amp
20	Non-Linear Energy	NE

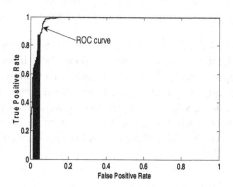

Fig. 2. Typical ROC curve for an imbalanced data set ("negative" class under-sampled)

2.3 Parzen Novelty Detector

In this work the Parzen window method is used to estimate the probability density function of the training data (the underlying stochastic model). It is a non-parametric kernel based method and the most widely used kernel is the Gaussian kernel which is controlled by a single parameter h. The latter is employed with h being automatically selected by the GA (10 bit encoding –(0.005-2.0 phenotype)).

The Parzen detector was implemented using the Data Description Toolbox [13]. The threshold to decide whether a sample comes from the underlying statistical model is put such that a fraction (a user defined parameter) of the training objects is rejected (0.01 in our case).

2.4 Experimental Procedure

In order to test the proposed approach we used manually labeled EPM artifacts within the EEG data sets. Manual/expert EPM artifact labeling was based upon instruction from ECSDC physicians and technicians in visual artifact identification. A total of 26098 epochs (25882 not artifact and 216 artifact epochs) were involved in this work.

We employed the k-fold cross validation with k set equal to five. Due to the abundant number of non-artifact samples we used only part of the available non-artifact data in order to reduce processing time. After that, we divided the non-artifact training data into two sets and we used 70% of them to train the novelty detector (to build the statistical model and select the corresponding threshold) and the remaining 30% along with the corresponding artifact data to calculate the performance measure (the portion of the AUC as described above).

3 Results

The procedure described in section 2.4 was repeated 5 times and the results were averaged. The overall achieved performance was 98.44%±0.41 (mean±standard deviation) for the non artifact segments and 80.93%±11.33 for the artifacts. The TP rate is close to the expected value since a 0.01 rejection error was selected during the training process. The TN rate is worse but it can be improved on the expense however of the TP rate.

The GA always selected the curve length and the standard deviation in all but one repetition. Surprisingly it did not select the, variance which might be considered a viable feature based upon Figure1. It also frequently selected the mean energy and the nonlinear energy. The highest number of features selected were 8 with the most occurrences at 5 features being selected 7 times and the lease occurrences with 1 feature being selected zero times. Therefore, the GA was "biased" toward parsimonious solutions, selecting on average five (out of the original twenty) features.

4 Conclusions

In this paper, we proposed a novel hybrid approach to artifact detection based on a combination of a GA algorithm for feature selection and a novelty detector. The results indicate that this approach can be used as an alternative to the standard two class classification approach especially when the information about the artifact class is missing.

Even though the feature selection module was not directly dictated to favor solutions with a lower number of features it frequently used only ¼ of the original variables resulting in a more compact representation of the problem. It is important to mention that most of the features were selected in a concise manner revealing a certain inherent pattern of the problem.

On the other hand the results are not as good as in the case of a two class formulation [14]. Nevertheless they are promising and the proposed approach can be applied toward cases where minimal to zero information about the artifacts exist.

Acknowledgments. The authors would like to thank the National Institute of Neurological Disorders and Stroke along with the National Science Foundation sponsored program Facilitating Academic Careers in Engineering and Science (FACES) at the Georgia Institute of Technology and Emory University for providing research funding for this project. Authors would also like to thank the Operational Programme Education and Lifelong Learning of the Greek Ministry of Education, Lifelong Learning and Religious Affairs co-financed by the Greece and the European Union for its sponsoring. Gratitude is also extended to the technicians at ECSDC for data collection and technical assistance in psg interpretation.

References

1. Anderer, P., Roberts, S., Schlogl, A., Gruber, G., Klosch, G., Herrmann, W., Rappelsberger, P., Filz, O., Barbanoj, M.J., Dorffner, G., Saletu, B.: Artifact processing in computerized analysis of sleep EEG – a review. Neuropsychobiology 40, 150–157 (1999)
2. Klass, D.W.: The continuing challenge of artifacts in the EEG. American Journal of Eeg Technology 35(4), 239–269 (1995)
3. Butkov, N.: Atlas of Clinical Polysomnography, vol. I. Ashland, Synapse Media Inc. (1996)
4. Foundation, N.S.: Sleep in America Poll (2005),
   http://www.sleepfoundation.org
5. NINDS, N.: Brain Basics: Understanding Sleep in Brain Resources and Information Network (BRAIN) NINDS, Editor. National Institutes of Health, Bethesda (2007)
6. Tax, D.M.J.: One-class classification; concept-learning in the absence of counterexamples. Ph.D. thesis, Delft University of Technology (2001)
7. Sa, M.J.P.: Pattern recognition. Concepts, methods, and applications. Springer, Heidelberg (2001)
8. Bloch, K.E.: Polysomnography: a systematic review. Technol. Health Care 5(4), 285–305 (1997)
9. Fairley, J.: Statistical Modeling of the Human Sleep Process via Physiological Recordings, Ph.D. thesis, Electrical and Computer Engineering, p.167, Georgia Institute of Technology: Atlanta. (2008)
10. Guyon, I., Elisseeff, A.: An introduction to variable and feature selection. J. Machine Learning Research 3, 1157–1182 (2003)
11. Bradley, A.P.: The use of the area under the ROC curve in the evaluation of machine learning algorithms. Pattern Recognition 30(7), 1145–1159 (1997)
12. GEATbx The Genetic and Evolutionary Algorithm Toolbox for Matlab,
    http://www.geatbx.com/
13. The Data Description Toolbox,
    http://homepage.tudelft.nl/n9d04/dd_tools.html
14. Fairley, J., Johnson, A., Georgoulas, G., Vachtsevanos, G., Rye, D.: Multiple Intelligent Feature Selection vs. Single Feature Thresholding for Extreme Artifact Detection in EEG Data (2010) (in preparation)

Improving the Scalability of Recommender Systems by Clustering Using Genetic Algorithms

Olga Georgiou and Nicolas Tsapatsoulis

Cyprus University of Technology,
P.O. Box 50329, 3036, Lemesos, Cyprus
{olga.georgiou,nicolas.tsapatsoulis}@cut.ac.cy
http://www.cut.ac.cy

Abstract. It is on human nature to seek for recommendation before any purchase or service request. This trend increases along with the enormous information, products and services evolution, and becomes more and more challenging to create robust, and scalable recommender systems that are able to perform in real time. A popular approach for increasing the scalability and decreasing the time complexity of recommender systems, involves user clustering, based on their profiles and similarities. Cluster representatives make successful recommendations for the other cluster members; this way the complexity of recommendation depends only on cluster size. Although classic clustering methods have been often used, the requirements of user clustering in recommender systems, are quite different from the typical ones. In particular, there is no reason to create disjoint clusters or to enforce the partitioning of all the data. In order to eliminate these issues we propose a data clustering method that is based on genetic algorithms. We show, based on findings, that this method is faster and more accurate than classic clustering schemes. The use of clusters created, based on the proposed method, leads to significantly better recommendation quality.

Keywords: Recommender systems, collaborative filtering, user clustering, genetic algorithms.

1 Introduction

Recommender systems have been proved to be an important response to the information overload problem; they provide users with more proactive and personalized information. One of the most successful variations of recommender systems, called collaborative filtering, has been developed and improved over the past decade to the point where a wide variety of algorithms exist for generating recommendations [7], [6]. Contemporary recommendation systems in order to tackle the scalability problem, caused by the increasing number of users, group users into clusters based on their preferences (ratings) toward similar data objects (like movies, jokes, etc) [1], [10]. From each cluster a user, or a group of users, are identified, are used as reference for recommendations to the other cluster members [2]. Traditional clustering algorithms create disjoint clusters and

K. Diamantaras, W. Duch, L.S. Iliadis (Eds.): ICANN 2010, Part I, LNCS 6352, pp. 442–449, 2010.

attempt to assign every data point to exactly one cluster [8]. However, in recommender systems it is desirable to allow users to belong to several clusters based on different properties of their profile or based on there on line choices [11]. On the other hand, cluster-based recommendation must be based on clearly defined clusters; sparse clusters are of limited importance [3] and may lead to wrong predictions and unsuccessful recommendations. Furthermore, the time complexity of clustering algorithms [9] is a very important issue since typical recommender systems include hundreds of thousands users per cluster [6],[4].

In this paper we propose a data clustering method which is based exclusively on genetic algorithms [5]. It creates dense clusters sharing common elements and converges rapidly even in very high dimensional spaces like the ones encountered in recommender systems. Challenging cases, like the existence of users, with extremely high total ratings difference, in the same cluster, were impossible using the traditional clustering methods. Additionally for maximizing the reduction of time complexity, we introduce the identification of representative users, from each cluster using an appropriate similarity metric. The efficiency of the proposed method is tested along two axes: The sparsity of each cluster is measured using the *Minkowski* distance while the efficiency of prediction is used to prove the appropriateness of this method for recommender systems.

2   User Clustering and Recommender Systems

The recommendation problem can be formulated as follows: Let C be the set of users (customers) and let I be the set of all possible items that the users can recommended, such as books, movies, or restaurants. Let also u be a utility function that measures the usefulness (as may expressed by user ratings) of item i to user c_j, i.e., $u : C \times I \rightarrow \Re$. The usefulness of all items to all users can be expressed as a matrix U with rows corresponding to users and columns corresponding to items. An entry $u(c_j, i)$ of this matrix may have either positive value indicating the usefulness (rating) of item i to user c_j or a zero value indicating that the usefulness $u(c_j, i)$ has not been evaluated. The recommendation problem can be seen as the estimation of zero values of matrix U from the non-zero ones.

Recommendation in the collaborative filtering approach requires some similarity $r(c_a, c_b)$ between users c_a and c_b to be computed based on the items that both of them evaluated with respect to their usefulness. The most popular approaches for user similarity computation are Pearson correlation and Cosine-based metrics. Both of these methods produce values $r(c_a, c_b) \in [-1 \; 1]$. In this paper we use the Pearson correlation to calculate the similarity of users:

$$r(a, b) = \frac{\sum_{i \in I_{c_a, c_b}} (u(c_a, i) - \bar{u}_{c_a})(u(c_b, i) - \bar{u}_{c_b})}{\sqrt{\sum_{i \in I_{c_a, c_b}} (u(c_a, i) - \bar{u}_{c_a})^2} \sqrt{\sum_{i \in I_{c_a, c_b}} (u(c_b, i) - \bar{u}_{c_b})^2}} \quad (1)$$

where $u(c_a, i)$ and $u(c_b, i)$ are the ratings of users c_a and c_b on item i, $\bar{u}_{c_a}$ and $\bar{u}_{c_b}$ are the average ratings over all rated items for c_a and c_b, and the set I_{c_a, c_b} stands for the items co-rated by user c_a and c_b. It is important to note that Pearson coefficient can be computed only if $I_{c_a, c_b} \neq \emptyset$.

Collaborative filtering based recommender systems build a neighborhood of users having similar preferences. The neighborhood formation process is actually the model-building or learning process for a recommender system algorithm. The aim of neighborhood formation, is to find for an active user c_a, an ordered list of k users $N^a = \{N_1, N_2, ..., N_k\}$ such that $c^a \notin N^a$ and $r(c_a, N_1) \geq r(c_a, N_2)... \geq r(c_a, N_k)$. Recommendations for user c_a are obtained either as predicted usefulness values $\hat{u}(c_a, i)$ for a particular item i, or as a recommendation list of N items, $I^a = \{I_1, I_1, ..., I_N\}$ that the active user will like the most. The recommended list consists of items not already rated by the active user. The latter form of recommendation is known as *Top-N recommendation* while the former is usually referred to as *prediction*.

Nearest neighbor based recommender systems suffer from the *scalability* problem: the computation grows with both the number users and items making it difficult to provide successful recommendations in reasonable time. Furthermore, the estimation of an appropriate value for k is very difficult since it depends on the active user as well as on the form of the user similarity matrix R (defined as a 2D matrix with entries $r(c_a, c_b) \in \Re$, and $c_a, c_b \in N$). In most of these approaches, the similarity between two users is based on the ratings of common items, therefore many pairs of users have no correlation at all, facing the known *sparsity* problem. In an attempt to moderate the scalability and sparsity problems clustering methods were employed. A cluster is a collection of data objects that are similar to one another within the same cluster and are dissimilar to the objects in other clusters. A cluster's sparsity can be defined with the aid of *Minkowski* distance. Let $\mathbf{X} = \{\underline{x}_1, \underline{x}_2, ..., \underline{x}_n\}$ be a set of vectors. A measure of sparsity for set $\mathbf{X}$ is defined as:

$$d(\mathbf{X}) = \sqrt{\sum_{\underline{x}_i, \underline{x}_j \in \mathbf{X}, i \neq j} \|\underline{x}_i - \underline{x}_j\|} \tag{2}$$

where $\|\underline{x}\|$ denotes the magnitude of vector $\underline{x}$. Obviously, the lowest the sparsity of set, the highest its compactness.

In order for clustering methods to be efficient, in the context of a recommender system, the clusters that are created must be dense and the data points should not necessarily classified into exactly one cluster. Clusters should be allowed to overlap while some data points might not be assigned to any cluster. In this way it is secured that the cluster members that will be used for recommendations do share common properties. Finally, a representative data object of a cluster is usually used for the recommendation to address time complexity.

3   Clustering Using Genetic Algorithms

Let us consider again the usefulness matrix U, introduced in the beginning of Section 2, whose rows correspond to users and columns correspond to items. By applying a threshold T to all matrix entries we get a binary matrix $\mathbf{B}$ whose entries $b(c_j, i)$ indicate that the user c_j either liked item i ($b(c_j, i) = 1$) or disliked / not rated it $(b(c_j, i) = 0)$. Assuming that the usefulness ratings $u(c_j, i)$ take values in the interval $[0 \; r_{max}]$ a reasonable choice for threshold T is $0.6 r_{max}$. The rows of matrix $\mathbf{B}$ express a simplified form of user preferences by encoding the items they liked.

In order to apply a genetic algorithm optimization for cluster creation we consider a set binary vectors $\mathbf{G} = \{g_i | i = 1, \ldots, P_N\}$, with $g_i \in \mathcal{R}^L$. Each vector g_i corresponds to an initial cluster formation. Thus, the length L, of vector g_i is equal to the total number of users of the recommender system while the positions of the ones in vector g_i indicate that the corresponding users belong to the cluster. According to this formulation P_N is the number of initial solutions (clusters). Once the initial population has been created the process of creating new generations starts and consists, typically, of three stages:

1. A fitness value (measure of "optimality") of each string in the random population is calculated.
2. Genetic operators, corresponding to mathematical models of simple laws of nature, like reproduction, crossover and mutation are applied to the population and result in the creation of a new population.
3. The new population replaces the old one.

In our case optimization aims to increase both the number of users included in a cluster as well as the number of items these users co-rated high. Let us consider a set of indexes $J^{\mathbf{g}_i} = \{j | g_{ij} = 1\}$, where g_{ij} is the j-th element of vector $\mathbf{g}_i$. Let also $I^{\mathbf{g}_i} = \bigcap_{j \in J^{\mathbf{g}_i}} \mathbf{b}_j$ be the intersection of the rows $\mathbf{b}_j, \; j \in J^{\mathbf{g}_i}$ corresponding to the preferences of users belonging to cluster $\mathbf{g}_i$. The non-zero elements of vector $I^{\mathbf{g}_i}$ correspond to the highly co-rated items by these users. Thus, the fitness value of cluster $\mathbf{g}_i$ is given by:

$$F(\mathbf{g}_i) = N^{I^{\mathbf{g}_i}} + N^{J^{\mathbf{g}_i}} \qquad (3)$$

where $N^{I^{\mathbf{g}_i}}$ is the number of non-zero elements of vector $\mathbf{g}_i$ and $N^{J^{\mathbf{g}_i}}$ is the cardinality of set $J^{\mathbf{g}_i}$. The objective is to find binary strings $\mathbf{g}_i$ that maximize the fitness function $F(\mathbf{g}_i)$. The realization of the genetic operators reproduction, mutation and crossover is as follows:

Reproduction. The fitness function $F(\mathbf{g}_i)$ is used in the classical "roulette" wheel reproduction operator that gives higher probability of reproduction to the strings with better fitness according to the following procedure:

1. An order number, q, is assigned to the population strings. That is q ranges from 1 to P_N, where P_N is the size of population.
2. The sum of fitness values (F_{sum}) of all strings in the population is calculated.
3. The interval $[0 \; F_{sum}]$ is divided into P_N sub-intervals each of one being $[SF_{q-1} \; SF_q]$
   where $SF_{q-1} = \sum_{j=1}^{q-1} F(\mathbf{g}_i)$ for $q > 1$ and $SF_{q-1} = 0$ for $q = 0$ or $q = 1$, and $SF_q = \sum_{j=1}^{q} F(\mathbf{g}_i)$ for every q.
4. A random real number R_0 lying in the interval $[0, F_{sum}]$ is selected.

5. The string having the same order number as the subinterval of R_0 is selected
6. Steps (4) and (5) are repeated P_N times in order to produce the intermediate population to which the other genetic operators will be applied.

Crossover. Given two strings of length k (parents) an integer number is randomly selected. The two strings retain their gene values up to gene r and interchange the values of the remaining genes creating two new strings (offspring).

Mutation. This operator is applied to each gene of a string and it alters its content, with a small probability. The mutation operator is actually a random number that is selected and depending on whether it exceeds a predefined limit it changes the value of a gene.

4   Experimental Evaluation

The aim of experimental evaluation is to prove the efficiency of the proposed clustering based recommendation method with the aid of real data. The averaged density of the created clusters is measured for various number of clusters and comparisons are made against, the widely used in recommender systems, K-means clustering algorithm. The quality of recommendation is also measured and compared against the traditional collaborative filtering method, and the K-means clustering method.

4.1   Evaluation Framework

Experimental evaluation of the proposed method was done with the aid of Dataset 1 of the Joke Recommender System [4]. This datasets contains over than 4.1 million continuous ratings [−10.00   10.00] of 100 jokes from 73421 users. It is one of the most widely used dataset for evaluating algorithms for recommender systems. We divided the dataset ratings into 60% for training and 40% for test set producing two matrics $T_r \in \Re^{U \times J_1}$ and $T_s \in \Re^{U \times J_2}$ respectively, where $U = 73421$, $J_1 = 60$ and $J_2 = 40$.

Our experiments where conducted on a typical PC, running Windows XP, and with the aid of Matlab platform (http://www.mathworks.com/). First, the proposed GA-based clustering algorithm was applied to the training set to create 100 user clusters. This resulted in clusters of an average cardinality of 35 users, while the average jokes commonly rated by cluster members was 25. Due to cluster overlapping the total number of users selected by GA-clustering was 1603. In order to have a fair comparison with the K-means algorithm as well as to the other recommendation methods we have used the training and test data for these users only. The K-means algorithm was used to partition the 1603 users into a varying number of clusters. Then we identify the representative user (user with highest similarity score), from each cluster, with the aid of Pearson coefficient (see eq.1).

Recommendations were considered to be the jokes rated by representative users, higher than a threshold T (set a $T = 2$ but threshold value does not actually affects the experiment). Let C_i^j be the i-th member of the j-th cluster and C_r^j be the representative of that cluster. Let us, also, denote the set of items rated by C_i^j as $\mathbf{I}_i^j$ and the set of high rated items of the same user as $\mathbf{H}_i^j$ (obviously $\mathbf{H}_i^j \subseteq \mathbf{I}_i^j$). For each cluster member two values are computed: the satisfaction without recommendation s_i^j and the satisfaction after receiving recommendation by the cluster representative $\widetilde{s}_i^j$. The last value was computed using three different methods: the representatives of clusters created using GA, the representatives of clusters created using K-means and the nearest neighbor (across all users) recommendation (1-NN). The s_i^j and $\widetilde{s}_i^j$ values are computed as follows:

$$s_i^j = \frac{Car(\mathbf{H}_i^j)}{Car(\mathbf{I}_i^j)} \qquad \widetilde{s}_i^j = \frac{Car(\mathbf{H}_i^j \cap \mathbf{H}_r^j)}{Car(\mathbf{I}_i^j) \cap \mathbf{H}_r^j)} \tag{4}$$

where $Car(\mathbf{X})$ denotes the cardinality of set $\mathbf{X}$.

4.2   Results and Discussion

Figure 1 presents the average cluster sparsity for a varying number clusters created using genetic algorithms and K-means. The average sparsity value is computed with the aid of eq.2 across all the clusters of a given partitioning of user space. The genetic algorithm clustering creates far more dense clusters (lower sparsity value). GA based clustering allows cluster overlapping; as a result the average sparsity remains constant and independent of the number of created clusters. This is a very important result because as the number of users is increased the number of clusters is also increased, therefore, keeping the size of clusters almost constant guarantees scalability both in time complexity as well as in recommendation quality. The average sparsity of K-means clusters reduces as the number of partitions increases; this is due to the fact that the more the cluster the less the cluster members. The latter, however, leads to deterioration of recommendation quality (see also Figure 2).

Figure 2 shows recommendation quality as a function of the number of clusters for three methods: 1-NN, GA based clustering and K-means clustering. For comparison we plot also the user satisfaction without receiving any recommendation. The latter, as well as the nearest neighbor method, are independent of the cluster number since they are computed across all user population. The GA-based clustering method presents almost constant performance. The recommendation quality is always higher than that of K-means and 1-NN. We should note here that the time complexity for nearest neighbor estimation is prohibitive for real time performance. The K-means clustering algorithm presents pour performance as the number of clusters increases. in some cases also, the quality was worsed when recommendations was used, as opposed, when it was not used. Results were expected, since the fixed number of users, lead to an increase of clusters number and decrease of clusters size. Cluster overlapping preserves cluster cardinality and causing high quality.

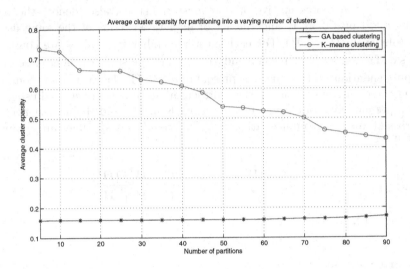

Fig. 1. Average cluster sparsity for partitioning into a varying number of clusters using (a) Genetic Algorithms (b) K-means

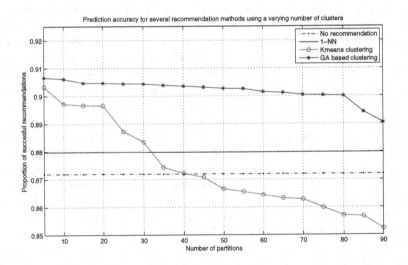

Fig. 2. Recommendation quality using one representative per cluster (methods GA based clustering and K-means) and the 1-NN method. Benchmarking against no recommendation is also shown.

5   Conclusion and Further Work

In order to keep up with this information explosion the scalability of recommender systems must be improved while the time complexity of recommendation algorithms must be kept low. These are the main reasons the clustering based recommendation systems gain attention. In this paper, we have proposed a genetic algorithm based clustering method which creates dense clusters appropriate for recommendation systems. The clusters are allowed to overlap; thus both density of clusters and recommendation efficiency are kept almost constant and independent of the number of clusters. Given that the number of clusters increase proportionally with the number of data objects the proposed method ensures scalability. In addition, recommendations are made by cluster representatives minimizing the time complexity.

Future work includes testing the proposed method in sparse datasets. The creation of dense clusters in such datasets is challenging. In addition Top-N recommendation methods will be investigated using all cluster members recommendations instead of the ones of clusters' representatives. Finally, methods for choosing the best cluster representatives will be also explored.

References

1. Braak, P.t., Abdullah, N., Xu, Y.: Improving the Performance of Collaborative Filtering Recommender Systems through User Profile Clustering. In: The 2009 IEEE/ACM Int'l Joint Conference on Web Intelligence and Intelligent Agent Technology, vol. 03, pp. 147–150. IEEE Computer Society, Washington (2009)
2. O'Donovan, J., Smyth, B.: Trust in recommender systems. In: 10th Int'l Conference on Intelligent User Interfaces (IUI 2005), pp. 167–174. ACM, New York (2005)
3. Ester, M., Kriegel, H.-P., Sander, J., Xu, X.: A density-based algorithm for discovering clusters in large spatial databases with noise. In: 2nd International Conference on Knowledge Discovery and Data Mining, Portland, OR, pp. 226–231 (1996)
4. Goldberg, K., Roeder, T., Gupta, D., Perkins, C.: Eigentaste: A Constant Time Collaborative Filtering Algorithm. Information Retrieval 4(2), 133–151 (2001)
5. Goldberg, D.: Genetic Algorithms. Addison-Wesley, Reading (1989)
6. The GroupLens Research Project, http://www.grouplens.org/
7. Herlocker, J.L., Konstan, J.A., Terveen, L.G., Riedl, J.T.: Evaluating collaborative filtering recommender systems. ACM Transactions on Information Systems 22(1), 5–53 (2004)
8. Jain, A.K., Dubes, R.C.: Algorithms for Clustering Data. Prentice Hall Publishers, Englewood Cliffs (1988)
9. Kim, K., Ahn, H.: A recommender system using GA K-means clustering in an online shopping market. Expert Systems with Applications: An International Journal 34(2), 1200–1209 (2008)
10. Min, S.-H., Han, I.: Dynamic Fuzzy Clustering for Recommender Systems. In: Ho, T.-B., Cheung, D., Liu, H. (eds.) PAKDD 2005. LNCS (LNAI), vol. 3518, pp. 480–485. Springer, Heidelberg (2005)
11. Truong, K., Ishikawa, F., Honiden, S.: Improving Accuracy of Recommender System by Item Clustering. IEICE - Transactions on Information and Systems E90-D(9), 1363–1373 (2007)

A Directional Laplacian Density for Underdetermined Audio Source Separation

Nikolaos Mitianoudis

School of Science and Technology, International Hellenic University,
14th km Thessaloniki-Moudania, 57001 Thessaloniki, Greece
n.mitianoudis@ihu.edu.gr
http://www.tech.ihu.edu.gr/

Abstract. In this work, a novel probability distribution is proposed to model sparse directional data. The Directional Laplacian Distribution (DLD) is a hybrid between the linear Laplacian distribution and the von Mises distribution, proposed to model sparse directional data. The distribution's parameters are estimated using Maximum-Likelihood Estimation over a set of training data points. Mixtures of Directional Laplacian Distributions (MDLD) are also introduced in order to model multiple concentrations of sparse directional data. The author explores the application of the derived DLD mixtures to cluster sound sources that exist in an underdetermined two-sensor mixture.

Keywords: Audio Source Separation, Mixture Models, Directional Data, Sparse Data Modelling.

1   Introduction

Circular Statistics is the branch of statistics that addresses the modeling and inference from *circular* or *directional* data, i.e. data with rotating values. Many interesting circular models can be generated from known probability distributions by either wrapping a linear distribution around the unit circle or transforming a bivariate linear r.v. to its directional component [1]. There also exist several distributions that are periodic by definition and can therefore be employed to model directional data. The *von Mises distribution* (also known as the circular normal distribution) is a continuous probability distribution on the unit circle [1]. It may be considered the circular equivalent of the normal distribution and is defined by:

$$p(\theta) = \frac{e^{k\cos(\theta - m)}}{2\pi I_0(k)} \quad , \forall \ \theta \in [0, 2\pi) \tag{1}$$

where $I_0(k)$ is the modified Bessel function of order 0, m is the mean and $k > 0$ describes the "width" of the distribution. The von Mises distribution has been extensively studied and many methods that fit the distribution or its mixtures to normally distributed circular data have been proposed [2,1,3,4].

This study proposes a novel distribution to model directional sparse data. *Sparsity* is mainly used to describe data that are mostly close to their mean

K. Diamantaras, W. Duch, L.S. Iliadis (Eds.): ICANN 2010, Part I, LNCS 6352, pp. 450–459, 2010.

value with the exception of several large values. There are several sparse models that have been proposed for linear sparse data [5] and several attempts to model circular sparse signals by wrapping a Laplace distribution [6,7]. This paper proposes a Directional Laplacian Distribution (DLD) as a direct modelling solution for circular sparse data. The Maximum Likelihood estimates (MLE) of the model's parameters are derived, along with an Expectation-Maximisation (EM) algorithm that estimates the parameters of a Mixture of Directional Laplacian Distributions (MDLD).

One application where directional statistical modelling is essential is *Under-determined Audio Blind Source Separation* (BSS) [5,7,8]. Assume that a set of K sensors $x(n) = [x_1(n), \ldots, x_K(n)]^T$ observes a set of L $(K < L)$ sound sources $s(n) = [s_1(n), \ldots, s_L(n)]^T$. The instantaneous mixing model can be expressed in mathematical terms, by $x(n) = As(n)$, where A represents the *mixing matrix* and n the sample index. The blind source separation problem provides an estimate of the source signals s, based on the observed microphone signals and some general source statistical profile. The two-channel $(K = 2)$ BSS scenario is often reduced to an angular clustering problem of sparse data, which has been addressed using Wrapped Laplacian Mixtures [7]. The proposed DLD model is tested with several synthetic modelling experiments and in real audio BSS examples.

2   A Directional Laplacian Density

2.1   Definition

Assume a r.v. θ modelling directional data with π-periodicity.

Definition 1. *The following probability density function models directional Laplacian data over $[0, \pi)$ and is termed* Directional Laplacian Density *(DLD):*

$$p(\theta, m, k) = c(k)e^{-k|\sin(\theta - m)|} \quad, \forall \; \theta \in [0, \pi) \qquad (2)$$

where $m \in [0, \pi)$ defines the mean, $k > 0$ defines the "width" (approximate variance) of the distribution, $c(k) = \frac{1}{\pi \hat{I}_0(k)}$ and $\hat{I}_0(k) = \frac{1}{\pi} \int_0^\pi e^{-k \sin \theta} d\theta$.

The normalisation coefficient $c(k) = 1/\pi \hat{I}_0(k)$ can be easily derived from the fundamental property of density functions. In Figure 1, the DLD is depicted for $m = 0.1$ and various values of k. The DLD is a heavy-tailed density that exhibits a π periodicity. The above definition can be amended to reflect a "fully circular" phenomenon (2π), however, we will continue with the π periodicity since it is required by our source separation application.

2.2   Maximum Likelihood Estimation Using Directional Laplacian Priors

Assume a population of angular data $\Theta = \{\theta_1, \ldots, \theta_n, \ldots, \theta_N\}$ that follow a Directional Laplacian Distribution. Maximum Likelihood Estimation (MLE) can

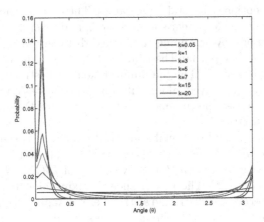

Fig. 1. The proposed Directional Laplacian Density (DLD) for $m = 0.1$ and various values of k

be used to fit the proposed Directional Laplacian Distribution to a set of angular data Θ. Assuming statistical independence between the observed data points, the MLE problem [9] can solve by maximising the log-likelihood function $J(\Theta, m, k)$ in terms of m, k. Assuming a DLD prior, the log-likelihood function $J(\Theta, m, k)$ can be expressed, as follows:

$$J(\Theta, m, k) = -N \log \pi - N \log \hat{I}_0(k) - k \sum_{n=1}^{N} |\sin(\theta_n - m)| \qquad (3)$$

To estimate the parameters that maximise the log-likelihood, alternating updates for m and k iteratively yields an optimum of the log-likelihood. It is not straighforward to obtain a closed-form solution by solving the equations $\partial J(\Theta, m, k)/\partial m = 0$ and $\partial J(\Theta, m, k)/\partial k = 0$ for m and k respectively. Thus, one has to resort to alternative solutions to estimate m and k.

Estimation of m. Iterative optimisation is employed to estimate m. To achieve faster convergence, a Newton-step optimisation will be pursued. The Newton-step updates for m can be given by the following update equation [9]:

$$m^+ \leftarrow m + \left[\frac{\partial^2 J(\Theta, m, k)}{\partial m^2} \right]^{-1} \frac{\partial J(\Theta, m, k)}{\partial m} \qquad (4)$$

where m^+ denotes the new update of the estimated parameter and

$$\frac{\partial J(\Theta, m, k)}{\partial m} = \sum_{n=1}^{N} k \operatorname{sgn}(\theta_n - m) \cos(\theta_n - m) \qquad (5)$$

$$\frac{\partial^2 J(\Theta, m, k)}{\partial m^2} = \sum_{n=1}^{N} k(\delta(\theta_n - m) + |\sin(\theta_n - m)|) \qquad (6)$$

The Newton-step for m is independent from k and can be estimated, as follows:

$$m^+ \leftarrow m + \frac{\sum_{n=1}^{N} \operatorname{sgn}(\theta_n - m) \cos(\theta_n - m)}{\sum_{n=1}^{N} \delta(\theta_n - m) + |\sin(\theta_n - m)|} \qquad (7)$$

Estimation of k. In order to avoid the iterative update of k via gradient ascent on the log-likelihood [9], an alternative solution is to solve $\partial J(\Theta, m, k)/\partial k = 0$ numerically. From the first derivative of $J(\cdot)$ along k, and

$$\frac{\partial^p}{\partial k^p} \hat{I}_0(k) = (-1)^p \frac{1}{\pi} \int_0^\pi \sin^p \theta e^{-k \sin \theta} d\theta = (-1)^p \hat{I}_p(k) \qquad (8)$$

it is straightforward to derive the following:

$$\frac{\hat{I}_1(k)}{\hat{I}_0(k)} = \frac{1}{N} \sum_{n=1}^{N} |\sin(\theta_n - m)| \qquad (9)$$

Calculating k from the ratio $\hat{I}_1(k)/\hat{I}_0(k)$ analytically is not very straightforward. However, through numerical evaluation, it can be shown that the ratio $\hat{I}_1(k)/\hat{I}_0(k)$ is a monotonic $1-1$ function of k. In Figure 2, the ratio $\hat{I}_1(k)/\hat{I}_0(k)$ is estimated for uniformly sampled values of $k \in [0.01, 30]$. Since this ratio is not dependent on data, one can create a look-up table for a variety of k values and use interpolation to estimate k from an arbitrary value of $\hat{I}_1(k)/\hat{I}_0(k)$. This look-up table solution is more efficient compared to iterative optimisation approaches and generally accelerates the model's training.

Initialisation of the ML Approach. In [2], there exists a methodology to estimate closed-form solutions for m, k in the case of the Von-Mises distribution. The methodology can not yield direct solutions of m, k for the DLD prior, however, one can employ the strategy in [2] to derive an upper bound of the log-likelihood in (3). The derived upper bound can be used to extract closed-form estimates of m_{init} that can be used as initialisations of the iterative solutions proposed in the previous section. Let $C = \sum_n |\cos \theta_n|$, $S = \sum_n |\sin \theta_n|$, $R = \sqrt{C^2 + S^2}$, $\bar{\theta} = \operatorname{atan}(S/C)$, $|\cos \bar{\theta}| = C/R$, $|\sin \bar{\theta}| = S/R$. Using the triangular inequality $|x| - |y| \le |x \pm y| \le |x| + |y|$, we manipulate the last term of the log-likelihood in (3).

$$\sum_n |\sin(\theta_n - \bar{\theta} + \bar{\theta} - m)| \ge \sum_n |\sin(\theta_n - \bar{\theta})||\cos(\bar{\theta} - m)| - \sum_n |\cos(\theta_n - \bar{\theta})||\sin(\bar{\theta} - m)|$$

$$= \sum_n |\sin \theta_n \cos \bar{\theta} - \cos \theta_n \sin \bar{\theta}||\cos(\bar{\theta} - m)| - \sum_n |\cos \theta_n \cos \bar{\theta} + \sin \theta_n \sin \bar{\theta}||\sin(\bar{\theta} - m)|$$

$$\ge (S|\cos \bar{\theta}| - C|\sin \bar{\theta}|)|\cos(\bar{\theta} - m)| - \sum_n (|\cos \theta_n||\cos \bar{\theta}| + |\sin \theta_n||\sin \bar{\theta}|)|\sin(\bar{\theta} - m)|$$

$$\ge (S\frac{C}{R} - C\frac{S}{R}) - \frac{C^2 + S^2}{R}|\sin(\bar{\theta} - m)| = -R|\sin(\bar{\theta} - m)|$$

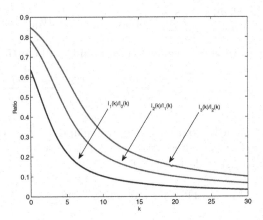

Fig. 2. The ratio $\hat{I}_p(k)/\hat{I}_{p-1}(k)$ is a monotonic $1-1$ function of k

Thus, the log-likelihood appears to have the following upper bound:

$$J(m,k) \leq kR|\sin(\bar{\theta}-m)| - N\log\pi - N\log\hat{I}_0(k) = J_u(m,k) \qquad (10)$$

To find the maximum of the bound, we set

$$\frac{\partial J_u}{\partial m} = -\text{sgn}(\sin(\bar{\theta}-m))\cos(\bar{\theta}-m) = 0 \qquad (11)$$

The above equation yields the solutions $m = \bar{\theta}$ or $m = \bar{\theta} \pm \pi/2$. For the second solution set, only the $m = \bar{\theta} + \pi/2$ solution can be valid, since $m \in [0,\pi)$ and $\bar{\theta} \in [0,\pi/2)$. The two solutions arose to account for the use of absolute values in the estimation of $\bar{\theta}$ and thus $\bar{\theta}$ is restricted to $\bar{\theta} \in [0,\pi/2)$. A simple method to define the correct solution is to evaluate the expression $\text{sgn}(\sum_{n=1}^{N} \text{atan}\tan\theta_n)$. If the expression is positive, the correct solution is $m_{init} = \bar{\theta}$. In the opposite case, the correct solution is $m_{init} = \bar{\theta} + \pi/2$. In Figure 3, a comparison between the estimated optimum m_{init} and the actual m for all values of $m \in [0,\pi)$ is performed for two values of k. The accuracy of the bound seems to depend on the value of m. In addition, the tightness of the bound depends clearly on the value of k. For great values of k, the estimated bound approximates the actual cost function accurately, thus the estimated m_{init} is very close to the actual m. For low values of k, the accuracy of the estimated m_{init} depends on the actual m. In general, the optimal value m_{init} that was estimated in this section can only serve as a valid initialisation of the ML approach.

2.3   Mixtures of Directional Laplacian Distributions

In a similar fashion to Gaussian Mixture Models (GMM), one can employ *Mixtures of Directional Laplacian Distributions* (MDLD) in order to model a mixture of directional "heavy-tailed signals".

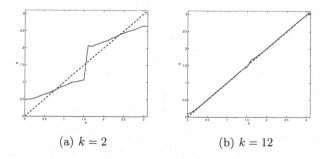

(a) $k = 2$ (b) $k = 12$

Fig. 3. The estimated optimum m_{init} (red line) compared to the actual m (blue dotted line) for all values of $m \in [0, \pi)$ for $k = 2$ (left) and $k = 12$ (right). The tightness of the bound depends on the value of k.

Definition 2. Mixtures of Directional Laplacian Distributions *are defined by the following pdf:*

$$p(\theta, m_i, k_i) = \sum_{i=1}^{M} a_i c(k_i) e^{-k_i |\sin(\theta - m_i)|} \quad , \forall \, \theta \in [0, \pi) \tag{12}$$

where a_i denotes the weight of each distribution in the mixture, m_i, k_i denote the mean and the approximate variance of each distribution and M the number of DLDs used in the mixture.

Training via Expectation-Maximisation (EM). A common method that can be employed to train a mixture model is the *Expectation-Maximization* (EM) algorithm. Bilmes estimates Maximum Likelihood mixture density parameters using the EM [10]. Assuming N training samples for θ_n and Directional Laplacian mixtures (12), the log-likelihood of these training samples takes the following form:

$$J(a_i, m_i, k_i) = \sum_{n=1}^{N} \log \sum_{i=1}^{M} \frac{a_i}{\pi \hat{I}_0(k_i)} e^{-k_i |\sin(\theta_n - m_i)|} \tag{13}$$

Introducing unobserved data items that can identify the components that "generated" each data item, we can simplify the log-likelihood of (13) for MDLD, as follows:

$$I(a_i, m_i, k_i) = \sum_{n=1}^{N} \sum_{i=1}^{M} (\log \frac{a_i}{\pi} - \log \hat{I}_0(k_i) - k_i |\sin(\theta_n - m_i)|) p(i|\theta_n) \tag{14}$$

where $p(i|\theta_n)$ represents the probability of sample θ_n belonging to the ith Directional Laplacian of the MDLD. In a similar fashion to Gaussian Mixture Models, the updates for $p(i|\theta_n)$ and α_i can be given by the following equations:

$$p(i|\theta_n) \leftarrow \frac{a_i c(k_i) e^{-k_i|\sin(\theta_n - m_i)|}}{\sum_{i=1}^{M} a_i c(k_i) e^{-k_i|\sin(\theta_n - m_i)|}} \tag{15}$$

$$a_i \leftarrow \frac{1}{N} \sum_{n=1}^{N} p(i|\theta_n) \tag{16}$$

Based on the derivation of the MLE estimates for DLD prior, it is straightforward to derive the following updates for the MDLD parameters m_i and k_i, by optimising $I(a_i, m_i, k_i)$. The means m_i are estimated using a Newton-step on $I(a_i, m_i, k_i)$, as follows:

$$m_i^+ \leftarrow m_i + \frac{\sum_{n=1}^{N} \mathrm{sgn}(\theta_n - m_i) \cos(\theta_n - m_i) p(i|\theta_n)}{\sum_{n=1}^{N} (\delta(\theta_n - m_i) + |\sin(\theta_n - m_i)|) p(i|\theta_n)} \tag{17}$$

To estimate k_i, we will resort to the numerical estimation of k_i. The first derivative is given by:

$$\frac{\partial I(a_i, m_i, k_i)}{\partial k_i} = \sum_{n=1}^{N} (\frac{\hat{I}_1(k_i)}{\hat{I}_0(k_i)} - |\sin(\theta_n - m_i)|) p(i|\theta_n) \tag{18}$$

Equating (18) to zero yields:

$$\frac{\hat{I}_1(k_i)}{\hat{I}_0(k_i)} = \frac{\sum_{n=1}^{N} |\sin(\theta_n - m_i)| p(i|\theta_n)}{\sum_{n=1}^{N} p(i|\theta_n)} \tag{19}$$

Using the lookup table solution that was discussed in the previous section, one can estimate k_i directly from (19).

Training Initialisation. The training of a mixture model is dependent on the initialisation of its parameters, especially the means m_i. Depending on different initialisations, in general, the EM algorithm may yield different mixture models that approximate the observed pdf, implying that the EM algorithm may get trapped in several local maxima. In a similar fashion to Gaussian Mixture Model initialisation, a *Directional K-Means* [11] is used to initialise the means m_i of the DLDs in the MDLD EM training, described in the previous section.

3   Experiments

In this section, we evaluate the efficiency of the derived EM algorithms for the estimation of the Directional Laplacian Density Mixtures. To generate 1D Directional Laplacian data, we employed the Inverse Transform Sampling technique [12]. We created a mixture of 5 concentrations of DLD samples centred at $0.3, 0.9, 1.5, 2.5, 3$ respectively. The values of k_i for each DLD were $12, 10, 12, 14, 14$. Each of the 5

Table 1. Parameter Estimation for a Mixture of Directional Laplacian ($M = 5$) using the proposed EM algorithm. Average parameter results for 50 independent runs.

	m_i	k_i	a_i	$\hat{m}_i$	$|\hat{k}_i - k_i|/k_i$	$\hat{a}_i$
DLD$_1$	0.3	12	0.1071	0.4743	0.0616	0.0906
DLD$_2$	0.9	10	0.2143	0.9001	0.1735	0.2377
DLD$_3$	1.5	12	0.3571	1.5068	0.0403	0.3576
DLD$_4$	2.5	14	0.1429	2.4262	0.1946	0.1307
DLD$_5$	3	14	0.1786	2.9650	0.0281	0.1834

Table 2. The proposed MDLD approach is compared in terms of SDR (dB) with MoL-EM_hard, MoWL-EM_hard and Hyvärinen's approach and the average SDR of the mixtures

	Groove Dataset				Latino Dataset			
	s_1	s_2	s_3	s_4	s_1	s_2	s_3	s_4
Mixed Signals	-30.02	-10.25	-6.14	-21.24	-2.47	-11.8	-2.04	-9.14
MDLD-EM	4.20	-4.32	-0.75	2.07	9.31	-0.04	8.17	3.53
MoWL-EM_hard	4.32	-4.35	-1.16	3.27	8.72	-0.04	8.13	3.03
MoL-EM_hard	2.85	-4.47	-0.86	3.28	8.65	-0.075	8.15	3.51
Hyvärinen	3.79	-3.72	-1.13	1.49	10.03	-1.74	8.16	3.42

concentrations contained different number of samples in order to create different contributions to the overall density. The total number of samples was set to 3000. We ran 50 independent runs of the EM-algorithm as described in Section 2.3. An average of the estimated $\hat{m}_i$, $\hat{k}_i$ and $\hat{a}_i$ is shown in Table 1. In most of the 50 cases, we witnessed accurate estimation of the underlying concentrations. However, there were several cases (5-6 out of 50), where the initialisation offered by the Directional K-Means was not accurate for some of the clusters. Since most mixture estimation algorithms are sensible to initialisation, this resulted into a drop of the average accuracy in mixture training. Nonetheless, most of the clusters were correctly identified and the overall results are promising. Also it is important to mention that two of the cluster centres were chosen to be at 0.3 and 3 which are very close to the borders π and 0 that would be causing problems in the linear case. The MDLD is not affected at all, since it it is circular by definition.

The next step is to evaluate the proposed algorithm for audio source separation. Moving the sensor signals to a sparser domain (MDCT domain), the sources become sparser and thus smaller coefficients are more probable and most of the signal's energy is concentrated in few large values. Therefore, the density of the data in the mixture space shows a tendency to cluster along the directions of the mixing matrix columns and the two-sensor multiple-source separation problem is reduced to an angular clustering problem of $\theta_n = \text{atan}(x_2(n)/x_1(n))$ [7,8]. In these experiment, we will use Hyvärinen's clustering approach [13], the MoL-EM [7] and the WMoL-EM [8] for comparison. After Mixture fitting with the EM algorithm, separation will be performed using hard thresholding, as described in our previous work [7,8]. In order to quantify the performance of the algorithms, we are estimating the *Signal-to-Distortion Ratio* (SDR) from the BSS_EVAL Toolbox [14]. The frame length for the MDCT analysis is set to 64 msec for the test signals sampled at 16 KHz and to 46.4 msec for those at 44.1 KHz. We initialise the parameters of the MoL, MoWL and MDLD as follows: $\alpha_i = 1/N$ and $c_i = 0.001$, $T = [-1, 0, 1]$ (for MoWL only) and $k_i = 15$ (for Circular Laplacian only). The centres m_i were initialised in either case using the Directional *K-means* step.

We tested the algorithms with the *Groove* and the *Latino* dataset, available by (BASS-dB) [15], sampled at 44.1 KHz. The "Groove" dataset features four widely spaced sources: bass (far left), distorted guitar (center left), clean guitar (center right) and drums (far right). The "Latino" dataset features four widely spaced sources: bass (far left), drums (center left), keyboards (center right) and distorted guitar (far right). In Table 2, we can see the results for the four methods in terms of SDR. The average SDR of the two input signals, treating them as estimates of each input signal, is also provided for comparison (Mixed Signals row). The proposed MDLD approach seems to provide the best performance for most of the audio sources with small difference though. The important advantage of the proposed MDLD approach is that it is not susceptible to bordering effects. It is slightly slower compared to the original MoL approach and also faster compared to the previous MoWL, since the proposed EM is more efficient compared to the one for MoWL.

4 Conclusions

In this paper, the author addresses the problem of modelling Directional Sparse data. Sparsity is often modelled using the Laplacian density for data with infinite linear support, which is not directly applicable in the case of directional or circular data. This work is building on previous work on directional Gaussian models (i.e. the von-Mises densities) to propose a novel Directional Laplacian model for modelling directional sparse data. ML estimates and an EM-algorithm were introduced to handle sparse circular data modelling problems. The proposed circular density was applied to the underdetermined source separation problem. The proposed solution featured a complete solution to the problem, compared to previous efforts. For future work, the author is planning to expand the model to handle multi-dimensional circular data.

References

1. Jammalamadaka, S., Sengupta, A.: Topics in Circular Statistics. World Scientific, Singapore (2001)
2. Bentley, J.: Modelling circular data using a mixture of von Mises and uniform distributions. Simon Fraser University, MSc thesis (2006)
3. Mardia, K., Kanti, V., Jupp, P.: Directional Statistics. Wiley, Chichester (1999)
4. Dhillon, I., Sra, S.: Modeling Data using Directional Distributions. Technical report, Technical Report TR-03-06, University of Texas at Austin, Austin, TX (2003)

5. Lewicki, M., Sejnowski, T.: Learning Overcomplete Representations. Neural Computation 12, 337–365 (2000)
6. Jammalamadaka, S., Kozubowski, T.: A new family of Circular Models: The Wrapped Laplace distributions. Technical report, Technical Report No. 61, Department of Mathematics, University of Nevada, Reno, NV (2002)
7. Mitianoudis, N., Stathaki, T.: Underdetermined Source Separation using Mixtures of Warped Laplacians. In: International Conference on Independent Component Analysis and Source Separation (ICA), London, UK (2007)
8. Mitianoudis, N., Stathaki, T.: Batch and Online Underdetermined Source Separation using Laplacian Mixture Models. IEEE Transactions on Audio, Speech and Language Processing 15(6), 1818–1832 (2007)
9. Moon, T., Stirling, W.: Mathematical Methods and Algorithms for Signal Processing. Prentice-Hall, Upper Saddle River (2000)
10. Bilmes, J.: A gentle tutorial of the EM algorithm and its application to parameter estimation for Gaussian Mixture and Hidden Mixture Models. Technical report, Department of Electrical Engineering and Computer Science, U.C. Berkeley, California (1998)
11. Banerjee, A., Dhillon, I.S., Ghosh, J., Sra, S.: Clustering on the Unit Hypersphere using von Mises-Fisher Distributions. Journal of Machine Learning Research 6, 1345–1382 (2005)
12. Devroye, L.: Non-Uniform Random Variate Generation. Springer, New York (1986)
13. Hyvärinen, A.: Independent Component Analysis in the presence of Gaussian Noise by Maximizing Joint Likelihood. Neurocomputing 22, 49–67 (1998)
14. Févotte, C., Gribonval, R., Vincent, E.: BSS EVAL Toolbox User Guide. Technical report, IRISA Technical Report 1706, Rennes, France (April 2005), http://www.irisa.fr/metiss/bsseval/
15. Vincent, E., Gribonval, R., Fevotte, C., Nesbit, A., Plumbley, M., Davies, M., Daudet, L.: BASS-dB: the blind audio source separation evaluation database, http://bass-db.gforge.inria.fr/BASS-dB/

Frontal View Recognition Using Spectral Clustering and Subspace Learning Methods[*]

Anastasios Maronidis, Anastasios Tefas and Ioannis Pitas

Aristotle University of Thessaloniki, Department of Informatics
Box 451, 54124 Thessaloniki, Greece
{amaronidis,tefas,pitas}@aiia.csd.auth.gr

Abstract. In this paper, the problem of frontal view recognition on still images is confronted, using subspace learning methods. The aim is to acquire the frontal images of a person in order to achieve better results in later face or facial expression recognition. For this purpose, we utilize a relatively new subspace learning technique, Clustering based Discriminant Analysis (CDA) against two well-known in the literature subspace learning techniques for dimensionality reduction, Principal Component Analysis (PCA) and Linear Discriminant Analysis (LDA). We also concisely describe spectral clustering which is proposed in this work as a preprocessing step to the CDA algorithm. As classifiers, we use the K-Nearest Neighbor the Nearest Centroid and the novel Nearest Cluster Centroid classifiers. Experiments conducted on the XM2VTS database, demonstrate that PCA+CDA outperforms PCA, LDA and PCA+LDA in Cross Validation inside the database. Finally the behavior of these algorithms, when the size of training set decreases, is explored to demonstrate their robustness.

Keywords: Dimensionality Reduction, Subspace Learning, Spectral Clustering.

1 Introduction

Frontal view recognition is a binary approach to the more general head pose estimation problem. Pose estimation means to infer the orientation of a person's head relative to the view of the camera. Given an image that depicts a person's head, actually frontal view recognition aims at classifying it to frontal or non-frontal.

Frontal view recognition is very important to bridge the gap in communication between humans and computers and could be integrated to many available technologies. For instance, it should be used as a preprocessing task in order to achieve better results in later face or facial expression recognition. The point is that face and facial expression recognition techniques require frontal view images

---

[*] This work has been funded by the Collaborative European Project MOBISERV FP7-248434 (http://www.mobiserv.eu), An Integrated Intelligent Home Environment for the Provision of Health, Nutrition and Mobility Services to the Elderly.

K. Diamantaras, W. Duch, L.S. Iliadis (Eds.): ICANN 2010, Part I, LNCS 6352, pp. 460–469, 2010.
© Springer-Verlag Berlin Heidelberg 2010

because they convey more information about the face and its expressions than non-frontal images.

The ability to gain efficient results with a little computational effort is an issue that arises at this point. There is a variety of methods that have been proposed for head pose estimation and specifically for frontal view recognition. In [1] the authors organize all of these methods into categories, according to the fundamental approach that underlies the implementation of them. The categories that they present are: Appearance Template methods, Detector Array methods, Nonlinear Regression, Manifold Embedding, Flexible Models, Geometric Methods, Tracking Methods and Hybrid Methods which combine the above.

In this paper we have focused on the Manifold Embedding Methods. The problem that becomes apparent is that usually initial images lie on a high dimensional space, which is, of course, intractable. To resolve this issue, these methods seek for low-dimensional manifolds which lie on the initial high-dimensional space and model the continuous variation of the head pose. In this category, several methods have been proposed. Some of them are: Principal Component Analysis (PCA), Linear Discriminant Analysis (LDA) and their kernelized versions, Isomap, Locally Linear Embedding (LLE), Laplacian Eigenmaps (LE) and the linear approximations of the latter two, Locally Embedded Analysis (LEA) and Locality Preserving Projections (LPP), respectively.

Here, we have utilized three linear subspace learning methods, PCA, LDA and CDA. This approach simplifies the problem of dimensionality reduction to a simple multiplication between a matrix (transformation matrix) and a vector (initial image). While PCA is an unsupervised method, (in that it does not need any prior information about the labeling of the data points into classes), the other two are supervised. Specifically CDA introduces a different kind of labeling which relies on the clustering of the data points.

Clustering techniques are unsupervised methods to extract groups of "similar" data points in a data set. Formally speaking, given a set $\mathcal{X} = \{x_1, x_2, \cdots, x_N\}$ of N data points and the desired number K of groups, clustering means to find a partition $(\mathcal{X}_k)_{k=1}^{K}$ of the set $\mathcal{X}$ such that $\cup_{k=1}^{K} (\mathcal{X}_k) = \mathcal{X}$ and $\mathcal{X}_k \cap \mathcal{X}_l = \emptyset$ if $k \neq l$. There are many approaches to cluster the points of a given data set. Here we have employed a category of clustering algorithms, called Spectral Clustering. The great advantage of the Spectral Clustering algorithms is that they are simple to implement by using basic knowledge of Linear Algebra.

From the above discussion, someone may ask how should the number K of groups be extracted, and additionally if is there any method to automatically learn this number using the data set. In [2] the authors propose an automatic multiscale data clustering to extract different plausible data partitionings by using the eigenvalues of an affinity matrix. In parallel, the proposed method associates each partition to a numerical measure that indicates its plausibility.

Obviously, after the clustering step, every data point gets a new label that denotes the group in which it belongs to. CDA makes use of this supervised information to project the data from their initial dimensionality to a lower dimensionality in a manner that the classes in which they belong to, become more discriminant. The difference between LDA and CDA is that LDA may not be able to separate samples from different classes if multiple clusters per class exist in input feature space. Conversely, CDA tries to benefit from this additional information and it is expected to work well in problems characterized by the existence of clusters inside the classes. As we will see in Section 5, the frontal view recognition problem is indeed one such. In the following analysis, every 2D image has been decomposed to a 1D vector by row-wise scanning. From now on, these vectors are denoted as data-points.

2   Spectral Clustering

As it became apparent in the previous section, clustering of the data-points is an important and imperative step of the CDA algorithm. Thus, we need an algorithm to cluster our data in a meaningful way. In our study, we have utilized the Spectral Clustering technique which has become one of the most popular clustering algorithms and it often outperforms traditional clustering algorithms such as K-means algorithm.

Two important mathematical tools for the development of spectral clustering are the similarity graph and the affinity matrix. Consider a set of data-points $\mathcal{X} = \{x_1, x_2, \cdots, x_N\}$ lying on the data space $\mathbb{R}^m$, a metric $d(x_m, x_n)$ and some parametric monotonically decreasing function $f_{mn}(\sigma) = f(d(x_m, x_n), \sigma)$ which measures the similarity between every pair of such data points. We define the similarity graph as the graph $(\mathcal{X}, \mathcal{E})$, where $\mathcal{X}$ is the set of the data points and $\mathcal{E}$ is the set of the edges between the data-points. The weights of the edges calculated with the similarity function f constitute a matrix W which has at position (m, n) the weight $f_{mn}(\sigma)$ between the m, n edges. Of course, W has to be a symmetric matrix. Relying on this new concept, we may interpret the problem of clustering in a nice new way: Find a partition of the graph such that the edges between different groups have very low weights (which means that points in different clusters are dissimilar from each other) and the edges within a group have high weights (which means that points within the same cluster are similar to each other) [3].

The affinity matrix P is an $N \times N$ matrix, where N is the number of data points and contains the whole information about the neighboring of the data. There are several ways to define the affinity matrix. Here we have used the random walk approach:

$$P = D^{-1}W. \tag{1}$$

D is called the degree matrix. It is diagonal with $D_{nn} = \sum_{i=1}^{N} f_{ni}$. W is the weight matrix defined above. P can be interpreted as the transition table of a random walk among the set of vertices $\mathcal{X}$. Each row of P sums to 1.

Given the number K of clusters, Spectral Clustering algorithm firstly computes the K largest eigenvalues of P. Then constructs an $N \times K$ matrix who has as columns the K corresponding eigenvectors. It has been shown in [3] that the rows of this matrix could be used as a new representation of the initial data, which is more useful from a clustering perspective. Thus on this new data representation any common clustering algorithm should be employed in a more efficient way. Here, for our needs, we have employed the K-means algorithm.

An issue that arises from the above discussion is how to estimate the "correct" number of clusters. There is a variety of methods in the literature (e.g. isodata), but the purpose here is to stay in the framework that has been presented. A tool that has been widely used in this framework is the eigengap heuristic:

- Perform eigenanalysis on the affinity matrix $\boldsymbol{P}$
- Rank the eigenvalues in descending order: $(\lambda_1, \lambda_2, \cdots, \lambda_N)$
- Find the maximum gap δ between consecutive eigenvalues $(\lambda_i, \lambda_{i+1})$
- Use the index i as an estimation of the total number of clusters
- Use this eigengap δ as a plausibility measure, where δ takes values between 0 and 1.

A. Azran and Z. Ghahramani in [2] extended this heuristic. They showed that by letting the random walk take multiple steps, different scales of partitioning are explored. In the case where the number of steps is M, the transition matrix is given by multiplying $\boldsymbol{P}$ with itself M times and is then called the Mth order transition matrix. This matrix contains the probabilities of the random walk to transit from one state to another in M steps. The idea behind this approach is to use the eigengap heuristic to these Mth order transition matrices for several values of M. It can be easily shown that the set of the eigenvalues of $\boldsymbol{P}^M$ is $\left(\lambda_1^M, \lambda_2^M, \cdots, \lambda_N^M\right)$. Using the eigengap heuristic on these sets for diverse values of M $(1 \leq M \leq M_{max})$, results in a set of eigengaps $\{\delta(M)\}_M$. The local maxima of this set are estimations of different scales of partitioning with plausibility measured by the corresponding δ.

3   Subspace Learning Methods

Subspace learning methods aim at finding a projection subspace, of the initial data, in which a specific criterion is optimized in order to achieve better representation or better discrimination. Usually, the subspace is of lower dimensionality in order to overcome the curse of dimensionality of initial high dimensional datapoints. Discriminant subspace methods aim at reducing the dimensionality of a data set in a way that increases the discriminative power of the data. This is done by the optimization of an objective function, which usually leads to the eigenvalue decomposition of a matrix or the generalized eigenvalue decomposition of two matrices. Here we have utilized three such methods, PCA, LDA and CDA. In our analysis we have firstly used PCA as a preprocessing step retaining a cumulative percentage of the total variation of the data [4]. This percentage essentially indicates the proportion of information been retained. When PCA is not referred, it is implicitly considered that a 100% percentage of the total variance has been retained. Thus, in this case we have rejected the zero eigenvalues of the covariance matrix of the data. This is done in order to keep as many dimensions as the number of non-zero eigenvalues of the covariance matrix of the data.

Linear Discriminant Analysis (LDA) [5] as mentioned is a supervised method for dimensionality reduction. Let x be an m dimensional random vector. LDA tries to find a transform to a low-dimensional space such that when x is projected, classes are well separated. Let us denote by c the total number of classes, by μ_i the mean vector of class i, by μ the mean vector of the whole data set and by n_i the number of samples belonging to class i. The objective of LDA is to find W that maximizes

$$J(W) = \frac{tr\{W^T S_B W\}}{tr\{W^T S_W W\}}. \tag{2}$$

where $tr\{\cdot\}$ denotes the trace of a matrix,

$$S_B = \sum_{i=1}^{c} (\mu_i - \mu)(\mu_i - \mu)^T. \tag{3}$$

is the between-class scatter and

$$S_W = \sum_{i=1}^{c} \sum_{k=1}^{N_i} (x_k^i - \mu_i)(x_k^i - \mu_i)^T. \tag{4}$$

is the within-class scatter matrix. In a few words LDA tries to separate the means of classes while gathering the points inside every class. The solution of this problem is given by the generalized eigenvalue decomposition of $S_W^{-1} S_B$. The transformation matrix W consists of the eigenvectors which correspond to the largest eigenvalues. LDA in contrast to PCA, takes into consideration both the within-class scatter and the between-class scatter carrying more discriminant information of the data. In LDA, the maximum number of retained dimensions is confined to $c - 1$, where c is the total number of classes.

Clustering Based Discriminant Analysis (CDA) [6], like LDA, looks for a transform W, such that the projections $z = W^T x$ for each class are well separated. The difference with LDA is that the classes might contain many clusters (subclasses). Let us denote the total number of classes by c, the total number of clusters inside the i-th class by d_i and the mean vector for the j-th cluster of the i-th class by μ_j^i. CDA tries to maximize

$$J(W) = \frac{tr\{W^T R W\}}{tr\{W^T C W\}}. \tag{5}$$

where

$$R = \sum_{i=1}^{c-1} \sum_{l=i+1}^{c} \sum_{j=1}^{d_i} \sum_{h=1}^{d_l} (\mu_j^i - \mu_h^l)(\mu_j^i - \mu_h^l)^T. \tag{6}$$

is the between-cluster scatter and

$$C = \sum_{i=1}^{c} \sum_{j=1}^{d_i} \sum_{s} (x_s - \mu_j^i)(x_s - \mu_j^i)^T. \tag{7}$$

is the within-cluster scatter matrix [6]. In a few words, CDA tries to separate clusters belonging to different classes while minimizing the within scatter in every cluster. Also it puts no constraints on clusters of the same class. The solution is given by the generalized eigenvalue decomposition of $C^{-1}R$, keeping again the largest eigenvalues. As already mentioned, the main advantage of CDA against LDA is that CDA exploits clustering information to separate the classes. One more advantage is that CDA is capable of retaining $d - 1$ dimensions, where d is the total number of clusters of the data. Of course $d - 1$ is greater than or at least equal to $c - 1$, which is the maximum retained dimensionality by LDA. It is worth stressing that if no clusters are found on data classes, then CDA is identical to LDA. We propose the use of spectral clustering as described in the previous Section in order to automatically extract both the number of clusters in each class and the samples that belong to each cluster.

4   Classifiers

The next task after the dimensionality reduction of initial data points is the classification of the data into classes. Since the number of retained dimensions is small, due to the use of subspace learning methods, it is able to avoid the use of complex classifiers, like SVMs. Here we have employed the K-Nearest Neighbor (KNN), the Nearest Centroid (NC) and the Nearest Cluster Centroid (NCC) classifiers. The K-Nearest Neighbor is a non-linear voting classifier. A datapoint is assigned to the most common class among its K nearest neighbors. In Nearest Centroid the centroids of the several classes are calculated and the data-point is assigned to the class with the nearest centroid to it. Finally, the Nearest Cluster Centroid is a modified version of NC. The difference is that NCC takes into consideration the clusters of the classes. In NCC the centroids of the several clusters are calculated and the data-point is assigned to the class in which the nearest cluster centroid belongs to. In our experiments, for the PCA and LDA algorithms we have used the Nearest Centroid while for the CDA algorithm we have used the Nearest Cluster Centroid.

5   Experimental Results

Experiments were performed on XM2VTS database. The XM2VTS database has been acquired at the University of Surrey. It contains four recordings of 295 subjects from the university. The volunteers visited the recording studio of the university four times at approximately one month intervals. On each visit (session) two recordings (shots) were made. The first shot consisted of speech whilst the second consisted of rotating head movements. Digital video equipment was used to capture the entire database [7]. Face tracking was applied on the head rotation shot videos that depict people that start from a frontal pose, turn their heads to their right profile, back to frontal pose then to the left profile. The images were then resized to 40 × 30. There are 1000 facial images captured this way. 500 of them are frontal and 500 non-frontal. Fig. 1 depicts some image examples from the database. The first row contains frontal examples and the second row contains non-frontal examples.

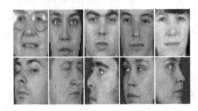

Fig. 1. Image examples from database (*1st row: Frontal, 2nd row: Non-frontal*)

Due to the lack of another testing database we confined our analysis inside this database. Firstly, we conducted a 10-fold cross validation to compare PCA, LDA, CDA, PCA+LDA and PCA+CDA one against each other. Secondly, we conducted a series of reverse cross validation experiments, (by reducing the number of the training data samples), to assess the robustness of the algorithms and to find out whether they collapse. We actually reversed the training set with the test set, so that increasing the number of cross validation steps, the size of the training set decreased.

5.1   10-Fold Cross Validation

On clustering step, we have used the Euclidean metric

$$d\left(\boldsymbol{x_m}, \boldsymbol{x_n}\right) = \sqrt{\sum_{i=1}^{i=M} \left(x_m^i - x_n^i\right)^2}. \tag{8}$$

and as similarity function the Gaussian similarity function which is defined as:

$$f_{mn}\left(\sigma\right) = \exp\left(-\frac{d\left(\boldsymbol{x_m}, \boldsymbol{x_n}\right)}{\sigma^2}\right). \tag{9}$$

The parameter σ plays the role of the variance and determines the scale of the neighborhood of every data point. Our empirical study, has shown that $\sigma = 0.25 \cdot E\left(d\left(\boldsymbol{x_m}, \mathbf{x}_n\right)\right)$ is a value which offers intuitively satisfactory results. Using this value as σ, Spectral clustering systematically returned 2 clusters on non-frontal class and 3 clusters on frontal class at every step of cross validation procedure. In PCA+CDA, Spectral Clustering was performed after the PCA step, as proposed in [6]. The centroid image of every cluster is depicted on Fig. 2 (a). It is interesting to observe that the first cluster of non-frontal class consists of those faces that are turned to their left profiles and the second cluster consists of those turned to their right. Also, careful inspection shows that the 3 clusters of the frontal class consist of a group of dark faces, a group of medium brightness faces and a group of brighter faces respectively.

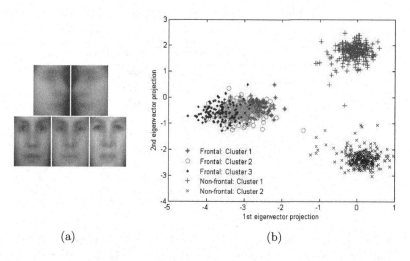

Fig. 2. (a) Centroid images of clusters. (*First row: Non-frontal, Second row: Frontal*), (b) 2D projection of the data

Using these 5 clusters extracted by the spectral clustering algorithm, CDA was capable of retaining up to 4 dimensions by keeping the four eigenvectors which correspond to the greatest four eigenvalues of $C^{-1}R$. Fig. 2 (b) depicts the projections of initial data points to the first two eigenvectors. The several clusters of the data are clearly shown on this figure.

On table 1 we present the accuracy values that the several algorithms achieved at the 10-fold cross validation procedure. The approach that has been used is given on the 1st column. The proportion of the energy retained by PCA is given on the 2nd column. The accuracy value achieved by the specific method utilizing the NC and the NCC classifiers for PCA/LDA and CDA respectively, are given on the 3rd column. The accuracy values utilizing KNN classifier with $K = 1$ and $K = 3$, are given on the 4th and 5th column respectively. The bold value indicates the best performance. Its value is 98.9% and it has been reached by the PCA(95%)+CDA approach combined with the Nearest Cluster Centroid classifier. It is interesting to observe that PCA+KNN has similar performance to PCA+CDA approach and outperforms PCA+LDA approach.

5.2   Reducing the Size of the Training Set

In the next experiment we compared the robustness of PCA(95%)+CDA+NC, PCA(95%)+LDA+NC and PCA+NC to the size of the training set. For the Spectral Clustering preprocessing we fixed the value of σ to $0.25 \cdot E\left(d\left(\boldsymbol{x}_m, \boldsymbol{x}_n\right)\right)$ as before. Fig. 3 demonstrates how does the size of the training set affect the accuracy value of the several algorithms. On the horizontal axis the size of the training set is given and on the vertical axis the accuracy value is depicted. There are three curves corresponding to the three aforementioned methods. Of

Table 1. 10-fold cross validation rates

Dim. Reduction		Classification		
approach	$PCA(\%)$	NC/NCC	1-NN	3-NN
PCA	-	91.9	98.3	98.2
	100	97.8	97.8	97.7
LDA	95	98.1	97.7	97.9
	90	98.1	97.7	98.1
	80	97.1	97	97.7
	100	98	98.3	98
CDA	95	**98.9**	98.6	98.7
	90	98.3	98.7	98.8
	80	97.9	98.8	98.8

course, as can be seen, as the size of the training set decreases, the performance of all three methods also decreases. However, it is clear that the PCA and LDA algorithms are more robust than CDA. The numbers on the edges of the PCA(95%)+CDA curve indicate the mean number of the clusters returned for the specific size of the training set. An explanation about the instability of the CDA algorithm can be given with the help of these numbers. We can see that while the size of the training set decreases, the number of clusters returned increases in a way that it no more represents the actual clustering structure of the data. For instance, there might arise a situation where a data point (e.g. outlier) constitutes a whole cluster on its own. In this case the CDA algorithm achieves the opposite results.

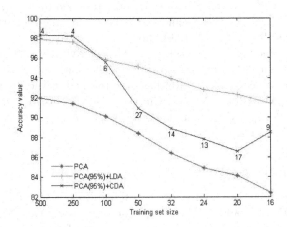

Fig. 3. Consecutive cross validation experiments

One reason for this unsuccessful clustering of the data is the fact that the Spectral Clustering algorithm is very sensitive to the choice of parameter σ. So, by fixing it to a standard value across the experiments makes the algorithm inflexible.

6   Conclusions

Frontal view recognition on still images has been explored in this paper. Subspace learning techniques (PCA, LDA and CDA) have been used for this purpose to achieve computationally easy and efficient results. Due to the low dimensionality of the reduced feature vectors, the use of complex classifiers like SVMs has been avoided and instead the K-Nearest Neighbor, Nearest Centroid and Nearest Cluster Centroid classifiers have been employed. Spectral Clustering performed on the XM2VTS database yielded interesting results which indicate that the problem of frontal view recognition is characterized by the existence of clusters inside the classes. 10-fold cross validation on the same database yielded an accuracy value equal to 98.9%, which was reached by the PCA(95%)+CDA approach. A set of eight consecutive experiments indicated that even though PCA+CDA beats PCA and PCA+LDA in 10-fold cross validation, however the latter two are more robust than CDA when the size of the training set decreases. Actually, what has been shown is the strong dependance of the CDA on the clustering of the data and the sensitivity of the clustering to the σ parameter.

References

1. Murphy-Chutorian, E., Trivedi, M.M.: Head pose estimation in computer vision: A survey. IEEE Transactions on Pattern Analysis and Machine Intelligence 31, 607–626 (2009)
2. Azran, A., Ghahramani, Z.: Spectral methods for automatic multiscale data clustering. IEEE Conference on Computer Vision and Pattern Recognition (CVPR) 1(1), 190–197 (2006)
3. von Luxburg, U.: A tutorial on spectral clustering 17(4), 395–416 (2007)
4. Jolliffe, I.: Principal Component Analysis. Springer, Heidelberg (1986)
5. Belhumeur, P.N., Kriegman, J.P.H., Kriegman, D.J.: Eigenfaces vs fisherfaces: Recognition using class specific linear projection. IEEE Transactions on Pattern Analysis and Machine Intelligence 19(7), 711–720 (1997)
6. wen Chen, X., Huang, T.: Facial expression recognition: a clustering-based approach. Pattern Recognition Letters 24, 1295–1302 (2003)
7. Messer, K., Matas, J., Kittler, J., Luttin, J., Maitre, G.: XM2VTSDB: The extended M2VTS database. In: Second International Conference on Audio and Video-based Biometric Person Authentication (AVBPA), pp. 72–77 (1999)

Improving the Robustness of Subspace Learning Techniques for Facial Expression Recognition*

Dimitris Bolis, Anastasios Maronidis, Anastasios Tefas, and Ioannis Pitas

Aristotle University of Thessaloniki, Department of Informatics
Box 451, 54124 Thessaloniki, Greece
{mpolis,amaronidis,tefas,pitas}@aiia.csd.auth.gr

Abstract. In this paper, the robustness of appearance-based, subspace learning techniques for facial expression recognition in geometrical transformations is explored. A plethora of facial expression recognition algorithms is presented and tested using three well-known facial expression databases. Although, it is common-knowledge that appearance based methods are sensitive to image registration errors, there is no systematic experiment reported in the literature and the problem is considered, a priori, solved. However, when it comes to automatic real-world applications, inaccuracies are expected, and a systematic preprocessing is needed. After a series of experiments we observed a strong correlation between the performance and the bounding box position. The mere investigation of the bounding box's optimal characteristics is insufficient, due to the inherent constraints a real-world application imposes, and an alternative approach is demanded. Based on systematic experiments, the database enrichment with translated, scaled and rotated images is proposed for confronting the low robustness of subspace techniques for facial expression recognition.

Keywords: Facial Expression Recognition, Appearance Based Techniques, Subspace Learning Methods.

1 Introduction

Visual communication plays a central role in human communication and interaction. Verbal information does not consist the total information used in human communication. Facial expressions and gestures are also of great importance in everyday life, conveying information about emotion, mood and ideas. Consequently, the successful recognition of facial expressions will significantly facilitate the human-computer interaction.

Research in psychology [1] has indicated that at least six emotions (anger, disgust, fear, happiness, sadness and surprise) are universally associated with

---

* This work has been funded by the Collaborative European Project MOBISERV FP7-248434 (http://www.mobiserv.eu), An Integrated Intelligent Home Environment for the Provision of Health, Nutrition and Mobility Services to the Elderly.

K. Diamantaras, W. Duch, L.S. Iliadis (Eds.): ICANN 2010, Part I, LNCS 6352, pp. 470–479, 2010.

distinct facial expressions. According to this approach these are the basic emotional states which are inherently registered in our brain and recognized globally. Several other facial expressions corresponding to certain emotions have been proposed but remain unconfirmed as universally discernible. In this paper we focus on the facial expressions deriving from these particular emotions and the neutral emotional state.

A transparent way of monitoring emotional state is by using a video camera, which automatically detects human face and captures the facial expressions. Following this approach the data used for input to the expression analyst tool would be a video stream, namely successive luminance images. Many techniques have been proposed in the literature for facial expression recognition [2]. Among them, appearance based methods followed by subspace learning methods are the most popular approach. In subspace techniques the initial image is decomposed in a 1-D vector by row-wise scanning and bases that optimize a given criterion are calculated. Then, the high dimensionality of the initial image space is reduced into a lower one. A simple distance measure is usually applied at the new space in order to perform classification. Various criteria have been employed in order to find the bases of the low dimensional spaces. Some of them have been defined in order to find projections that express the population in an optimal way without using the information about the way the data are separated to different classes, (e.g., Principal Component Analysis (PCA) [3], Non-Negative Matrix Factorization (NMF) [4]). While, other criteria deal directly with the discrimination between classes, e.g. Discriminant NMF (DNMF) [5], Linear Discriminant Analysis (LDA) [6].

The appearance based methods disadvantage is their sensitivity to image registration errors. However, for all the cases, the problem of image registration prior to recognition is considered solved and isn't discussed. As a result, the preprocessing steps are not clearly described, implying that only small displacements of the bounding box may occur, which cannot result in considerable lower performance. This is not the case in automatic real-world applications, which, often, significantly fail to calculate the optimal geometrical characteristics of the bounding box, when even slight distortions could lead in great differences regarding the performance.

The aim of this paper is two fold. Firstly, to illustrate the sensitivity of appearance based subspace learning methods when the registration of the face prior to recognition fails, even for one pixel. Secondly, to propose a training set enrichment approach and the corresponding subspace learning methods for improving significantly the performance of these techniques in the facial expression recognition problem.

In the analysis done in this paper, the 2-D images have been decomposed into 1-D vectors in order to be used as inputs in the subspace techniques. The remainder of the paper is organized as follows: Section 2 is devoted to Subspace Learning Techniques. It is divided into three subsections. PCA, LDA and DNMF are presented in each of them respectively. In Section 3 K-Nearest Neighbor (KNN), Nearest Centroid (NC) and Support Vector Machines (SVM) classifiers are concisely described while in Section 4 a number of experimental results on BU, JAFFE and KOHN-KANADE databases are presented. Finally, in Section 5 the conclusion is drawn.

2 Subspace Techniques

2.1 Principal Component Analysis

Principal Component Analysis (PCA) is an unsupervised subspace learning technique. Let $\mathbf{x} \in \mathbb{R}^M$ be a random vector. The objective in PCA is to find projection vectors $\mathbf{w}_i$ that maximize the variance of the projected samples $\mathbf{z}_i = \mathbf{w}^T\mathbf{x}$. Assuming that the expected value of $\mathbf{x}$ is zero, the problem of finding the projections $\mathbf{w}_i$ is an eigenanalysis problem of the covariance matrix $\mathbf{C} = E[\mathbf{x}\mathbf{x}^T]$. The transformation matrix $\mathbf{W} = [\mathbf{w}_1\mathbf{w}_2\cdots\mathbf{w}_N]$ comprises by the eigenvectors of $\mathbf{C}$ that correspond to the M' maximum eigenvalues of $\mathbf{C}$. Any data point (vector) $\mathbf{x}$ from the initial space can now be approximated by a linear combination of the M' first eigenvectors to produce a new M'-dimensional vector. This approach achieves projection of the data from the initial space to a new feature space with a predefined dimensionality. In PCA someone has to decide beforehand on the new dimensionality M' or alternatively the new dimensionality may be defined by the percentage of the total sum of the eigenvalues that should be retained after the projection. This percentage essentially indicates the proportion of the information to be retained. The main property of PCA is that it generates uncorrelated variables from initial possibly correlated ones. The disadvantage of PCA is that it might lose much discriminative information of the data, since it does take into account the class labels of the data.

2.2 Linear Discriminant Analysis

Linear Discriminant Analysis (LDA) in contrast to PCA is a supervised method for dimensionality reduction. It tries to find a transform to a low-dimensional space such that when $\mathbf{x}$ is projected, classes are well separated. Let us denote by C the total number of classes, by $\boldsymbol{\mu}_i$ the mean vector of class i, by $\boldsymbol{\mu}$ the mean vector of the whole data set and by N_i the number of samples belonging to class i. The objective of LDA is to find $\mathbf{w}$ that maximizes

$$J(\mathbf{W}) = \frac{tr[\mathbf{W}^T\mathbf{S}_B\mathbf{W}]}{tr[\mathbf{W}^T\mathbf{S}_W\mathbf{W}]},$$

where $tr[\cdot]$ denotes the trace of a matrix and

$$\mathbf{S}_B = \sum_{i=1}^{C}(\boldsymbol{\mu}_i - \boldsymbol{\mu})(\boldsymbol{\mu}_i - \boldsymbol{\mu})^T$$

is the between-class scatter and

$$\mathbf{S}_W = \sum_{i=1}^{C}\sum_{k=1}^{N_i}(\mathbf{x}_k^i - \boldsymbol{\mu}_i)(\mathbf{x}_k^i - \boldsymbol{\mu}_i)^T$$

is the within-class scatter. That is, LDA tries to maximize the distance between the mean vectors of the classes, while minimizing the variance inside each class. The solution of this problem is given by the generalized eigenvalue decomposition of $\mathbf{S}_W^{-1}\mathbf{S}_B$ keeping again the largest eigenvalues. LDA in contrast to PCA, takes into consideration both the within-class scatter and the between-class scatter carrying more discriminant information of the data. LDA is capable of retaining up to $C-1$ dimensions, where C is the total number of classes.

2.3   Discriminant Non-negative Matrix Factorization

The DNMF is a supervised NMF based method that decomposes the feature vectors into parts enhancing the class separability at the same time. The 2-D image of F pixels is row-wise scanned resulting in the vector $\mathbf{x} = [x_1, x_2, \cdots, x_F]^T$. The NMF then tries to approximate the vector $\mathbf{x}$ with a linear combination of the columns of the vector $\mathbf{h}$ such that $\mathbf{x} \simeq \mathbf{Zh}$, where $\mathbf{h} \in \mathbb{R}_+^M$. In general, $M < F$, namely the NMF produce a vector of a lower dimension, compared to the initial vector $\mathbf{x}$. The matrix $\mathbf{Z} \in \mathbb{R}_+^{F \times M}$ is a non negative matrix, whose columns sum to one. The approximation $\mathbf{x} \simeq \mathbf{Zh}$ imposes a certain error, whose value is calculated using the Kullback- Leibler divergence $KL(\mathbf{x}\|\mathbf{Zh})$ [7]. The decomposition cost is the sum of the KL divergences for the total number of the feature vectors. This way the following metric can be calculated:

$$D(\mathbf{X}\|\mathbf{ZH}) = \sum_j KL(\mathbf{x}_j\|\mathbf{Zh}_j) =$$

$$= \sum_{i,j} \left(x_{i,j} \ln \left(\frac{x_{i,j}}{\sum_k z_{i,k} h_{k,j}} \right) + \sum_k z_{i,k} h_{k,j} - x_{i,j} \right)$$

as the measure of the cost for approximating $\mathbf{X}$ with $\mathbf{ZH}$ [7]. The NMF is the outcome of the following optimization problem:

$$\min_{\mathbf{Z},\mathbf{H}} D(\mathbf{X}\|\mathbf{ZH}) \quad \text{subject to}$$

$$z_{i,k} \geq 0, h_{k,j} \geq 0, \sum_i z_{i,j} = 1, \forall j.$$

All the elements of $\mathbf{Z}$ and $\mathbf{H}$ should be non negative real numbers. This way, the vector $\mathbf{h}_j$ represents the weight vector and the $\mathbf{Z}$ matrices the M basis images, whose linear combination result in the initial image, permitting only additions between the different basis images.

The DNMF algorithm can be considered as an alternative to NMF plus LDA method [5]. In the case of DNMF, discriminant constraints are incorporated inside the cost of NMF. This form of decomposition leads to the creation of basis images that correspond to discreet parts of the face (e.g., mouth, eyes).

The modified divergence is constructed deriving from the minimization of the Fisher criterion using the new cost function given by:

$$D_d\left(\mathbf{X}\|\mathbf{ZH}\right) = D\left(\mathbf{X}\|\mathbf{ZH}\right) + \gamma tr[\mathbf{S}_w] - \delta tr[\mathbf{S}_b],$$

where γ and δ are constants and $tr[\cdot]$ is the trace of its argument. The minimization of this function is done by finding the minimum for the $tr[\mathbf{S}_w]$ term, and the maximum for the $tr[\mathbf{S}_b]$ one.

The vector $\mathbf{h}_j$ that corresponds to the j-th column of the matrix $\mathbf{H}$, is the coefficient vector for the ρ-th facial image of the r-th class and will be denoted as $\mathbf{h}_\rho^{(r)} = [h_{\rho,1}^{(r)}, h_{\rho,2}^{(r)}, \cdots, h_{\rho,M}^{(r)}]^T$. The mean vector of the vectors $\mathbf{h}_\rho^{(r)}$ for the rth class is denoted as $\boldsymbol{\mu}_\rho^{(r)} = [\mu_1^{(r)}, \mu_2^{(r)}, \cdots, \mu_M^{(r)}]^T$ and the mean of all the classes as $\boldsymbol{\mu} = [\mu_1, \mu_2, \cdots, \mu_M]^T$. Then, the within scatter for the coefficient vectors $\mathbf{h}_j$ is defined as:

$$\mathbf{S}_w = \sum_{r=1}^{K} \sum_{\rho=1}^{N_r} \left(\mathbf{h}_\rho^{(r)} - \boldsymbol{\mu}^{(r)}\right) \left(\mathbf{h}_\rho^{(r)} - \boldsymbol{\mu}^{(r)}\right)^T,$$

whereas the between scatter matrix is defined as:

$$\mathbf{S}_b = \sum_{r=1}^{K} N_r \left(\boldsymbol{\mu}^{(r)} - \boldsymbol{\mu}\right) \left(\boldsymbol{\mu}^{(r)} - \boldsymbol{\mu}\right)^T.$$

The matrix $\mathbf{S}_w$ defines the scatter of the sample vector coefficients around their class mean and a convenient measure for the dispersion of the samples is the trace of $\mathbf{S}_w$. While, the matrix $\mathbf{S}_b$ denotes the between-class scatter matrix and defines the scatter of the mean vectors of all classes around the global mean $\boldsymbol{\mu}$. At this point become obvious why by minimizing and maximizing the traces of $\mathbf{S}_w$ and $\mathbf{S}_b$ respectively, we shrink the classes and increase the separability among them.

This class-specific decomposition is intuitively motivated by the theory that humans use specific discriminant features of the human face for memorizing and recognizing them [8].

All the above methods, aim at projecting the initial high-dimensional datapoints to a feature space with low dimensionality. In that new space, the datapoints are likely to be classified in a more efficient way. In our study, we use three well-known in the literature classifiers, the K-Nearest Neighbor (KNN), the Nearest Centroid (NC) and the Support Vector Machines (SVMs). They are all concisely described in the following paragraph.

3   Classifiers

The K-Nearest Neighbour is a non-linear voting classifier. A datapoint is assigned to the most common class among its K nearest neighbours. In NC the centroids of the several classes are calculated and the datapoint is assigned to the class with the nearest centroid to it.

A support vector machine tries to calculate the optimal hyperplane or set of hyperplanes in a high dimensional space. Intuitively, a good separation is achieved by the hyperplane that maximizes the functional margin, since, in general, the larger the margin the lower the generalization error of the classifier. The SVMs used for our experiments were proposed in [9], and use a modified method to calculate the maximum functional margin, inspired by the Fisher's discriminant ratio. The SVMs are successively applied for a 2-class problem each time. The winning class is then compared with one of the remaining classes following the same method and the procedure is repeated until the prevailing class for each test sample is found.

4   Experimental Results

For our experiments we used the BU [10], JAFFE [11] and COHN- KANADE [12] databases for facial expression recognition. BU contains images from 100 subjects, captured in four facial expressions intensities for each of the six, universally recognized, emotions (anger, disgust, happiness, fear, sadness, surprise) and one neutral pose for each person, namely a total of 2500 images. It contains subjects (56% female, 44% male), ranging from 18 years to 70 years old, with a variety of ethnic/racial ancestries, including White, Black, East-Asian, Middle-east Asian, Indian and Hispanic Latino. We used the most expressive of each facial expression. Thus, the final database we utilized consisted of 700 images.

The JAFFE database contains 213 images of the 7 aforementioned facial expressions, posed by 10 Japanese female models. Each image has been rated on these emotion adjectives by 60 Japanese subjects. Finally, from the COHN-KANADE we used 407 images from 100 subjects. Subjects, in this case, range in age from 18 to 30 years. Sixty-five percent were female; 15 percent were African-American and three percent Asian or Latino. In Figures 1 and 2 typical examples of the six expressions and the neutral case for the JAFFE and COHN-KANADE database are illustrated, respectively.

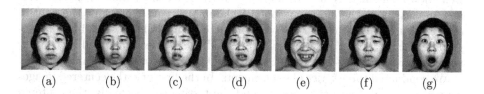

(a)   (b)   (c)   (d)   (e)   (f)   (g)

Fig. 1. The JAFFE Facial Expression Database (a) neutral, (b) angry, (c) disgusted, (d) feared, (e) happy, (f) sad, (g) surprised

We preprocessed the images manually in order to have the eyes in fixed predefined positions in the frame. Firstly, we gathered the coordinates of the eyes in the initial images. The initial distance between the eyes was calculated and the image was down-scaled in an isotropic way, in order to succeed a 16-pixel eyes

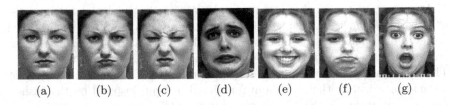

(a)   (b)   (c)   (d)   (e)   (f)   (g)

Fig. 2. The Cohn-Kanade Facial Expression Database (a) neutral, (b) angry, (c) disgusted, (d) feared, (e) happy, (f) sad, (g) surprised

distance. In the final step we cropped the image to the size of 40×30 producing a bounding box centered to the subject's face. The image cropping was based on the eyes due to their inherent attribute of maintaining fixed position, independently to the various facial expressions. Other features of the face (e.g., mouth, eye-brows) have the tendency to be shifted in other positions, regarding certain expressions. For example, in the case of surprise the eye-brows appear in higher position in comparison with the neutral expression. Thus, manual cropping based on other features, apart from the eyes, could produce discriminant information on itself leading to overestimation of the performance of the classification.

Under this perspective, we constructed two versions of enriched databases. For the first one (enriched database), the above mentioned centered images were shifted one pixel in the four basic directions (left, right, up and down). In the second case (fully enriched database), one cross of five possible positions for each eye was considered (original position, one-pixel left, right, up and down), resulting into 25 different possible pairs of eyes. The position of these pairs of eyes were then used for the production of the final centered following the above mentioned procedure for centering the images, resulting in translated, rotated and scaled images.

In a second level, we implemented a number of combinations of subspace learning techniques exploiting the PCA, LDA and DNMF algorithms and the three well known classifiers NCC, KNN and SVMs in order to examine their effectiveness in classifying the aforementioned facial expressions along with the neutral emotional state. For this purpose we conducted a five-fold cross-validation. Regarding the PCA and LDA outputs we used the Nearest Centroid algorithm, while, the SVM method was applied at the DNMF algorithm outputs.

We conducted three series of experiments. In the first one, the centered images were used to form both the training and the testing set. Secondly, the centered images were used for the training set, while the left-shifted images were used for the testing set, in order to examine the sensitivity of the performance in displacements of the bounding box. In the last series of experiments, the training was formed from the whole set of the images (both centered and shifted images), while the centered images alone constituted the testing set.

The comparative results, for the KANADE, JAFFE and BU database, are depicted in the Tables 1, 2 and 3 respectively. In the first two columns of the tables the various methods utilized are given, both for reducing the dimensionality and for classifying the samples.

KNN was used for $K = 1$ and $K = 3$. The second case is presented, due to its better results. As far as the presented method of PCA plus LDA is concerned, PCA used for maintaining the 95% of the covariance matrix energy while the LDA reduced the resulted vector to the dimension of 6. The cases of maintaining other percentages of the covariance matrix energy were tested as well, without leading to better results. Regarding the DNMF followed by SVM approach, the dimension of the feature vector was reduced from 1200 to 120 by the DNMF and then the SVM realized the classification using a RBF kernel. Other type of kernels were, also, used producing similar results.

In the third column of the tables there are the success rates, in the case of the centered images, for both the training and testing set. The next column shows the performance when misplaced images are used for the testing set (1-pixel misplacement on the horizontal axis in this case). In the fifth column, the performance of the enriched database, exploiting, merely, the translated images, is depicted. Finally in the last column, the performance of the fully enriched database is appeared, where the 25 transformed versions of the original database were used.

On one hand, it can be, easily observed, that even a slight divergence from the centered images (one pixel in the case of our experiments) lead in significant lower performance (up to 8%). On the other hand, after the enrichment with transformed images, a clear improvement in the performance is observed in the vast majority of the cases for both the two versions of the database enrichment (up to 15.9% for the enrichment with the translated images and 22.3% for the fully enriched version). Both the sensitivity in small translations of the bounding box and the robustness when enriching the training set are systematically observed in our experiments. Additionally, it was observed that the more transformations are used the greater the improvement of the accuracy becomes.

Table 1. KANADE 5-fold cross validation accuracy rates

Classifier	Approach	Centered(%)	Misplaced(%)	Enriched(%)	Fully Enriched(%)
	PCA	36.4	36.0	36.5	39.7
NC	LDA	62.5	55.0	72.4	74.9
	PCA+LDA	67.0	65.1	68.8	73.7
	PCA	39.0	39.2	39.7	38.5
KNN	LDA	63.3	55.7	71.6	75.7
	PCA+LDA	67.3	65.8	67.6	69.4
SVM	DNMF	56.4	49.4	67.6	69.2

Table 2. JAFFE 5-fold cross validation accuracy rates

Classifier	Approach	Centered(%)	Misplaced(%)	Enriched(%)	Fully Enriched(%)
	PCA	29.0	26.0	27.5	34.6
NC	LDA	53.5	45.5	51.5	62.9
	PCA+LDA	54.5	46.5	63.5	62.4
	PCA	31.5	31.0	26.0	40.0
KNN	LDA	52.5	44.5	51.5	62.0
	PCA+LDA	57.0	48.5	58.5	64.9
SVM	DNMF	41.6	34.6	57.5	63.9

Table 3. BU 5-fold cross validation accuracy rates

Classifier	Approach	Centered(%)	Misplaced(%)	Enriched(%)
	PCA	34.6	34.0	34.9
NC	LDA	56.0	54.4	62.3
	PCA+LDA	63.3	62.3	64.9
	PCA	33.1	33.0	32.7
KNN	LDA	56.6	53.7	61.3
	PCA+LDA	60.4	60.0	62.1
SVM	DNMF	55.4	53.0	61.4

5   Conclusion

Facial expressions consist an integral part of the human communication. Efficient methods for recognizing human emotions, exploiting the facial expressions, are expected to revolutionize the scientific field of human-machine interaction. Subspace learning techniques followed by well known classifiers are among the most used methods for human facial expression recognition. However, after a series of experiments we observed a great sensitivity of this kind of algorithms to geometrical translation of the images, even for the case of one pixel. Real-world applications carry an inherent difficulty regarding the precise detection of the facial characteristics' position, resulting in inaccurate image registering. The experiments, we conducted, show that the systematic enrichment of a database with geometrically transformed (translated, scaled and rotated) images results in significant improvement in the performance in the majority of the cases. By using more sophisticated transformations for enriching the initial databases, in the future, further improvement in the performance could is expected.

References

1. Ekman, P., Friesen, W.V.: Constants across cultures in the face and emotion. Journal of Personality and Social Psychology 17(2), 124–129 (1971)
2. Zeng, Z., Pantic, M., Roisman, G.I., Huang, T.S.: A survey of affect recognition methods: audio, visual and spontaneous expressions. In: ICMI 2007: Proceedings of the 9th International Conference on Multimodal Interfaces, pp. 126–133. ACM, New York (2007)

3. Jolliffe, I.: Principal Component Analysis. Springer, Heidelberg (1986)
4. Lee, D.D., Seung, H.S.: Learning the parts of objects by non-negative matrix factorization. Nature 401, 788–791 (1999)
5. Zafeiriou, S., Tefas, A., Buciu, I., Pitas, I.: Exploiting discriminant information in non negative matrix factorization with application to frontal face verification. 17(4), 395–416 (2007)
6. Belhumeur, P.N., Hespanha, J.P., Kriegman, D.J.: Eigenfaces vs. fisherfaces: Recognition using class specific linear projection. IEEE Transactions on Pattern Analysis and Machine Intelligence 19(7), 711–720 (1997)
7. Lee, D.D., Seung, H.S.: Algorithms for non-negative matrix factorization. In: NIPS, pp. 556–562 (2000)
8. Chellappa, R., Wilson, C.L., Sirohey, S.: Human and machine recognition of faces: a survey. Proceedings of the IEEE 83(5), 705–741 (1995)
9. Tefas, A., Kotropoulos, C., Pitas, I.: Using support vector machines to enhance the performance of elastic graph matching for frontal face authentication. IEEE Transactions on Pattern Analysis and Machine Intelligence 23, 735–746 (2001)
10. Yin, L., Wei, X., Sun, Y., Wang, J., Rosato, M.J.: A 3d facial expression database for facial behavior research. In: FGR 2006: Proceedings of the 7th International Conference on Automatic Face and Gesture Recognition, Washington, DC, USA, pp. 211–216. IEEE Computer Society, Los Alamitos (2006)
11. Lyons, M., Akamatsu, S., Kamachi, M., Gyoba, J.: Coding facial expressions with gabor wavelets, pp. 200–205 (1998)
12. Kanade, T., Cohn, J.F., Tian, Y.: Comprehensive database for facial expression analysis. In: Proceedings of the Fourth IEEE International Conference on Automatic Face and Gesture Recognition, Grenoble, France, pp. 46–53 (2000)

Variational Bayesian Image Super-Resolution with GPU Acceleration

Giannis Chantas

Department of Informatics and Telecommunications, TEI of Larissa,
41110 Larissa, Greece

Abstract. With the term super-resolution we refer to the problem of reconstructing an image of higher resolution than that of unregistered and degraded observations. Typically, the reconstruction is based on the inversion of the observation generation model. In this paper this problem is formulated using a variational Bayesian inference framework and an edge-preserving image prior. A novel super-resolution algorithm is proposed, which is derived using a modification of the constrained variational inference methodology which infers the posteriors of the model variables and selects automatically all the model parameters. This algorithm is very intensive computationally, thus, it is accelerated by harnessing the computational power of a graphics processor unit (GPU). Examples are presented with both synthetic and real images that demonstrate the advantages of the proposed framework as compared to other state-of-the-art methods.

Keywords: Variational Inference, Bayesian Super-Resolution, Image Prior Student's-t distribution, CUDA, GPGPU.

1 Introduction

The problem of super-resolution is defined as obtaining an image with enhanced resolution from a set of lower resolution unregistered degraded images. The super-resolution problem has a long history. In this paper we will not attempt overview it; for this purpose the interested reader is referred to [1], [2] and [3]. An important category of methodologies used for this problem formulates it as an ill posed reconstruction problem. Thus, prior information is introduced (regularization) to complement the available observations and reconstruct the super-resolved image.

One powerful stochastic methodology to apply regularized reconstruction to inverse problems is Bayesian inference [4]. The main advantage of Bayesian inference is that the unknown image is treated as a random variable and the posterior pdf given the observations is found. Thus, unlike the maximum a posteriori (MAP) estimation approach, which only provides point estimates, Bayesian inference provides variance information also about the estimate [4]. However, the application of Bayesian inference is difficult when complex models and large data sets are used. Therefore, MAP estimation has been much more popular for image super-resolution problems [3].

K. Diamantaras, W. Duch, L.S. Iliadis (Eds.): ICANN 2010, Part I, LNCS 6352, pp. 480–489, 2010.

In this work the Bayesian inference framework using the variational approximation is applied for the first time to the image super-resolution problem. In this formulation a spatially varying edge-preserving image prior is used. This prior has been used previously with success for the image restoration problem in a Bayesian inference framework [8]. Bayesian inference is easier for image restoration than for super-resolution because the imaging operator in restoration is a simple convolutional operator. In contrast, in super-resolution the imaging operator is more complex and is not convolutional [3]. Thus, for the super-resolution problem a similar in spirit prior was applied only in a MAP framework [5].

Another novel aspect of this work is the use of graphics processor unit (GPU) to speed up the proposed super-resolution algorithm for large images. Specifically, a parallel CUDA [10] implementation of the linear solver in this algorithm was used to speed up the computations required.

The rest of this paper is organized as follows. In Sect. 2 and 3 the imaging model and the proposed image prior models are presented, respectively. In Sect. 4 the variational algorithm is derived. In Sect. 5 the implementation details of the GPU linear solver used to accelerate our algorithm, and the initialization method of the proposed algorithm are presented. In Sect. 6 experiments with synthetic and real data that demonstrate the properties of our algorithm are presented. Finally, in Sect. 7 conclusions and thoughts for future research are provided.

2   Imaging Model

In what follows for simplicity we use one-dimensional notation. A linear imaging model is assumed according to which P low-resolution images (observations) $\mathbf{y}_1, \mathbf{y}_2, ..., \mathbf{y}_P$ of size $N_L \times 1$ are produced by operating on the high-resolution image $\mathbf{x}$ of size $N_H \times 1$. Thus the decimation factor d can be defined as the ratio $d = N_H/N_L$. Each observation is produced by first translating and rotating the high-resolution image, then blurring and decimating it by the factor d. Lastly, a noise vector $n_k, k = 1, ..., P$ is added at each observation. This is mathematically expressed by the following P equations:

$$\mathbf{y}_k = \mathbf{B}_k(\zeta_k)\mathbf{x} + \mathbf{n}_k = \mathbf{DHW}(\zeta_k)\mathbf{x} + \mathbf{n}_k, \ \ k = 1, ..., P \ , \tag{1}$$

where $\mathbf{B}_k = \mathbf{B}_k(\theta_k) = \mathbf{DHW}(\theta_k)$, $\mathbf{D}$ is the known decimation matrix of size $N_L \times N_H$, $\mathbf{H}$ is the square $N_H \times N_H$ known convolutional blurring matrix that is assumed circulant and $\mathbf{W}(\zeta_k)$ is the $N_H \times N_H$ geometric transformation operator that translates and rotates the image. For the $k - th$ observation, $\zeta_k = [\gamma_k, \delta_k]$ is the parameter vector that contains the unknown rotation angle γ^k and the unknown translation parameter δ_k. Lastly, n_k is the $N_H \times N_H$ noise vector that is modeled as white Gaussian with the same (unknown) precision β for each observation, i.e. $\mathbf{n}_k \sim \mathcal{N}(\mathbf{0}, \beta\mathbf{I})$, where $\mathbf{0}$ and $\mathbf{I}$ are the $N_H \times N_H$ zero and identity matrices, respectively.

Let $\mathbf{y}$ be a $PN_L \times 1$ vector, containing the P low-resolution images: $\mathbf{y} = [\mathbf{y}_1^T, \mathbf{y}_2^T, \ldots, \mathbf{y}_P^T]^T$. Using this notation, the observations are given by:

$$\mathbf{y} = \mathbf{Bx} + \mathbf{n},\tag{2}$$

where $\mathbf{n} = [\mathbf{n}_1^T, \mathbf{n}_2^T, \ldots, \mathbf{n}_P^T]^T$ and $\mathbf{B}$ is the $PN_L \times N_H$ imaging operator:

$$\mathbf{B} = [\mathbf{B}_1^T, \mathbf{B}_2^T, \ldots, \mathbf{B}_P^T]^T.$$

Lastly, in this work, to model the geometric transformation (rotation-translation) operation the Shannon (sinc) interpolator is used, which is linear and thus can be represented by the matrix $\mathbf{W}$.

3   Image Model

In what follows we introduce the image prior for the high-resolution image $\mathbf{x}$ of the imaging model described in Sect. 2. We first define K linear convolutional operators (filters) $\mathbf{Q}_1, \ldots, \mathbf{Q}_K$ of size $N_H \times N_H$. These filters are high-pass, such as first order differences in the vertical and horizontal direction. The filter outputs $\epsilon = (\epsilon_1^T, \ldots, \epsilon_K^T)^T$ are produced according to the following K equations:

$$\epsilon_l = \mathbf{Q}_l \mathbf{x}, \quad l = 1, \ldots, K.\tag{3}$$

Then, it is assumed that all $\epsilon_l(i)$ for every i are iid zero mean Student's-t distributed with parameters λ_l and ν_l:

$$p(\epsilon_l(i)) = St(0; \lambda_l, \nu_l) = \frac{\Gamma(\nu_l/2 + 1/2)}{\Gamma(\nu_l/2)} \left(\frac{\lambda_l}{\nu_l}\right)^{\nu_l/2} \left(1 + \frac{\lambda_l \epsilon_l(i)^2}{\nu_l}\right)^{-\nu_l/2 - 1/2},$$

for $l = 1, \ldots, K$, where the parameters λ_l and ν_l are different for every filter but remain the constant as the spatial location i varies. To analyze the properties of the Student's-t distribution we write it down as the integral:

$$p(\epsilon_l(i)) = \int_{a_l(i)} p(\epsilon_l(i)|a_l(i)) p(a_l(i)) da_l(i)\tag{4}$$

where $a_l(i)$'s are random variables that are iid Gamma distributed $p(a_l(i)) = Gamma(\nu_l, \nu_l)$, and $p(\epsilon_l(i)|a_l(i)) = \mathcal{N}(0, a_l(i)^{-1})$. The Student's-t distribution can be viewed as an *infinite mixture* of zero mean Gaussians [4] with different precisions. Thus, it can be heavy-tailed. Therefore, when used as a prior on the outputs of the $\mathbf{Q}_l$ high-pass filters it allows reconstructed images to have sharp edges. In contrast Gaussian based models have the tendency to smooth out edges.

4   Variational Inference

The variational methodology for Bayesian inference proposed in [8] for the imaging model in equation (2) is applicable only when the imaging operator $\mathbf{B}$ is convolutional and thus commutes with $\mathbf{Q}_l$, which is not the case for the super-resolution problem. In this section we present a modification of the variational algorithm in [8] which overcomes this difficulty, it is more general and can be applied to any linear imaging model of the form in (2).

As in [8], to perform Bayesian inference we introduce an alternative imaging model, which is derived by applying the operators $\mathbf{Q}_l$ to (2):

$$\mathbf{y} = \mathbf{B}\mathbf{Q}_l^{-1}\boldsymbol{\epsilon}_l + \mathbf{n}, \ l = 1, \ldots, K, \tag{5}$$

where we have used the relationships $\mathbf{x} = \mathbf{Q}_l^{-1}\boldsymbol{\epsilon}_l, l = 1, \ldots, K$, stemming from the definitions of the ϵ_l's in 3. Here, the key difference from [8] is that we avoided the multiplication with the operators $\mathbf{Q}_l$ but we embedded directly the relationships between the image and the filter outputs. This is the main reason for which the following derivation of the variational algorithm is novel and differs from that in [8].

With this imaging model, we work in the field of the filter outputs, and we treat $\boldsymbol{\epsilon} = (\boldsymbol{\epsilon}_1^T, \ldots, \boldsymbol{\epsilon}_K^T)^T$, where $\boldsymbol{\epsilon}_l = (\epsilon_l(1), \ldots, \epsilon_k(N_H))^T$, for $l = 1, \ldots, K$ and $\mathbf{a} = (\mathbf{a}_1, \ldots, \mathbf{a}_K)$, where $\mathbf{a}_l = (a_l(1), \ldots, a_l(N_H))$, for $l = 1, \ldots, K$, as hidden variables. Then, according to Bayesian inference we find the posterior distributions for the hidden variables and estimate the parameters $\theta = \lambda_k, \nu_k$. The marginal of the observations $p(\mathbf{y}; \theta)$, which is required to find the posteriors of the hidden variables is hard to compute [4]. More specifically, the integral

$$p(\mathbf{y}) = \int_{\boldsymbol{\epsilon},\mathbf{a}} p(\mathbf{y}, \boldsymbol{\epsilon}, \mathbf{a}) d\boldsymbol{\epsilon} d\mathbf{a} \,, p(\mathbf{y}, \boldsymbol{\epsilon}, \mathbf{a}) = p(\mathbf{y}|\boldsymbol{\epsilon})p(\boldsymbol{\epsilon}|\mathbf{a})p(\mathbf{a}) \,, \tag{6}$$

$$p(\mathbf{y}|\boldsymbol{\epsilon}) = \prod_{l=1}^{K} p(\mathbf{y}|\boldsymbol{\epsilon}_l), p(\mathbf{y}|\boldsymbol{\epsilon}_l) = N\left(\mathbf{B}\mathbf{Q}_l^{-1}\boldsymbol{\epsilon}_l, \beta\mathbf{I}\right) \,, \tag{7}$$

$$p(\boldsymbol{\epsilon}|\mathbf{a}) = \prod_{l=1}^{K}\prod_{i=1}^{N} p(\epsilon_l(i)|a_l(i)), \ p(\mathbf{a}) = \prod_{l=1}^{K}\prod_{i=1}^{N_H} p(a_l(i)) \,,$$

is intractable. Notice here that we have combined the K observation equations of (5) in one, by assuming that the data likelihood of a single observation is given by the product: $p(\mathbf{y}|\boldsymbol{\epsilon}) = \prod_{l=1}^{K} p(\mathbf{y}|\boldsymbol{\epsilon}_l)$. This idea stems from the principal of *opinion pooling* proposed in [6] that combines multiple probabilities.

The variational methodology, bypasses the difficulty of computing the integral in (6) and maximizes a *lower bound* $L(q(\boldsymbol{\epsilon}, \mathbf{a}), \theta)$ that can be found instead of the log-likelihood of the observations $\log p(y; \theta)$ [4]. This bound is obtained by subtracting from $\log p(\mathbf{y}; \theta)$ the Kullback-Leibler divergence, which is always positive, between an arbitrary $q(\boldsymbol{\epsilon}, \mathbf{a})$ and $p(\boldsymbol{\epsilon}, \mathbf{a}|\mathbf{y}; \theta)$.

When $q(\boldsymbol{\epsilon}, \mathbf{a}) = p(\boldsymbol{\epsilon}, \mathbf{a}|\mathbf{y}; \theta)$, this bound is maximized and $L(q(\boldsymbol{\epsilon}, \mathbf{a}), \theta) = \log p(\mathbf{y}; \theta)$. Because the exact posterior $p(\boldsymbol{\epsilon}, \mathbf{a}|\mathbf{y}; \theta) = \frac{p(\boldsymbol{\epsilon},\mathbf{a},\mathbf{y};\theta)}{p(\mathbf{y};\theta)}$ cannot be found we are forced to find an approximation of it. The mean field approximation is a commonly used approach to maximize the variational bound w.r.t. $q(\epsilon, \mathbf{a})$ and θ [4]. According to this approach the hidden variables are assumed to be independent, i.e. $q(\epsilon, \mathbf{a}) = q(\epsilon)q(\mathbf{a})$. Thus, next we derive the variational algorithm that maximizes the bound $L(q(\epsilon)q(\mathbf{a}), \theta)$, aiming at maximizing approximately the logarithm of the likelihood.

Unconstrained maximization of the bound $L(q(\epsilon)q(\mathbf{a}), \theta)$ is suboptimal for this formulation. Thus, we resort the modified *constrained variational* approximation, as explained above. In short, the goal is to combine all the information given by the K observation equations of the new model in (5). According to this approach, each $q(\epsilon_l)$ is constrained to have the form:

$$q(\epsilon_l) = N(\mathbf{Q}_l \mathbf{m}, \mathbf{Q}_l^T \mathbf{R} \mathbf{Q}_l), \tag{8}$$

where $\mathbf{m}$ is a $N_H \times 1$ vector, is taken as mean of the high-resolution image, and $\mathbf{R}$ the $N_H \times N_H$ its covariance matrix. Using this model the parameters $\mathbf{m}$ and $\mathbf{R}$ are learned instead of $q(\epsilon_l)$ in the framework of the proposed constrained variational methodology.

In the VE-step, the maximization of $L(q(\epsilon), q(\mathbf{a}), \theta)$ is performed with respect to $q(\mathbf{a})$, $\mathbf{m}$ and $\mathbf{R}$ keeping θ fixed, while in the VM-step, the maximization of the same quantity is performed with respect to θ keeping $q(\mathbf{a})$, $\mathbf{m}$, and $\mathbf{R}$ fixed. At the j-th iteration of the variational algorithm we have:

VE-step:

$$[\mathbf{m}^j, \mathbf{R}^j, q^j(\mathbf{a})] = \arg \max_{\mathbf{m}, \mathbf{R}, q(\mathbf{a})} L(q(\epsilon; \mathbf{m}, \mathbf{R}), q(\mathbf{a}), \theta^{j-1}) \tag{9}$$

VM-step:

$$\theta^j = \operatorname*{argmax}_{\theta} L(q^j(\epsilon; \mathbf{m}, \mathbf{R}), q^j(\mathbf{a}), \theta) \tag{10}$$

The updates for the VE-Step are:

$$q^j(\epsilon_l; \mathbf{m}, \mathbf{R}) = N(\mathbf{Q}_l \mathbf{m}^j, \mathbf{Q}_l \mathbf{R}^j \mathbf{Q}_l^T), \tag{11}$$

$$\mathbf{m}^j = \beta \mathbf{R}^j \mathbf{B}^T \mathbf{y}, \quad \mathbf{R}^j = \left(\beta \mathbf{B}^T \mathbf{B} + \frac{1}{K} \sum_{l=1}^{K} \lambda_l^{j-1} \mathbf{Q}_l^T \mathbf{A}_l^{j-1} \mathbf{Q}_l \right)^{-1}. \tag{12}$$

From the above equations it is clear that $\mathbf{m}$ merges information from all filters $\mathbf{Q}_l$ to produce the estimate of $\mathbf{m}$ which is used as the estimate of $\mathbf{x}$.

Finally, the approximate posterior of $\mathbf{a}$ in the VE-step is given by

$$q^j(\mathbf{a}) = \prod_{l=1}^{K} \prod_{i=1}^{N_H} q^j(a_l(i)),$$

$$q^j(a_l(i)) = Gamma\left(a_l(i); \frac{\nu_l^{j-1}}{2} + \frac{1}{2}, \frac{\nu_l^{j-1}}{2} + \frac{\lambda_l^{j-1}}{2} u^j(i) \right), \tag{13}$$

$$u^j(i) = (\mathbf{m}_l^j(i) + \mathbf{C}_l^j(i,i)), \mathbf{m}_l^j = \mathbf{Q}_l \mathbf{m}^j, \; \mathbf{C}_l^j = \mathbf{Q}_l \mathbf{R}^j \mathbf{Q}_l^T,$$

for $l = 1, 2, \ldots, K$, $i = 1, 2, \ldots, N_H$. Also, $\mathbf{m}_l^j(i)$ is the i-th element of $\mathbf{m}_l^j$ and $\mathbf{C}_l^j(i,i)$ is the i-th diagonal element of $\mathbf{C}_l^j$.

In the VM-step, the bound is maximized w.r.t the parameters. For λ_l we have that the update formula is

$$\lambda_l^j = \frac{N}{\sum_{i=1}^{N} < a_l(i) >_{q^j(\mathbf{a})} u^j(i)} . \tag{14}$$

Similarly, for ν_l, $l = 1, 2, \ldots, K$, we have that ν_l^j is taken as the root of the function ϕ:

$$\phi(\nu_l) = \frac{1}{N_H} \sum_{i=1}^{N_H} \log < a_l(i) >_{q^j(\mathbf{a})} - \frac{1}{N} \sum_{i=1}^{N_H} < a_l(i) >_{q^j(\mathbf{a})} + \psi \left(\frac{\nu_l^{j-1}}{2} + \frac{1}{2} \right)$$

$$- \log \left(\frac{\nu_l^{j-1}}{2} + 2 \right) - \psi \left(\frac{\nu_l}{2} \right) + \log \frac{\nu_l}{2} + 1 , \tag{15}$$

where ψ is the digamma function. We find $\phi(\nu_l^j) = 0$ numerically using the bisection method.

5 Computational Implementation

In this section we describe some of the implementation details of the variational algorithm derived in Sect. 4, given by (12), (14) and (15).

5.1 GPGPU Linear Solver

The most computationally intensive operation of our algorithm is the multiplication of the matrix $\mathbf{R}^{-1}$ (its inverse is given by (12)), which is the matrix of the linear system we aim to solve, with a vector $\mathbf{p}$. To parallelize these operations, we take advantage of the structure of $\mathbf{R}^{-1}$, which is composed by products and sums of circulant and diagonal matrices and implement them efficiently on the GPU using CUDA.

The multiplication of the diagonal matrix $\mathbf{A}_l$ with a vector, can be viewed as an element wise multiplication of two vectors and is parallelized very easily. For the implementation of this operation, each thread running on the GPU performs a multiplication of two elements.

The products of circulant matrices $\mathbf{H}$ and $\mathbf{Q}_l$ with vectors is similarly straight forward to parallelize, though it is slightly more complicated. We first note that a circulant matrix can be diagonalized in the DFT domain. We use this diagonal form and perform the operation with circulant matrices by alternating between the spatial and frequency domain.

The computation of the diagonal elements $\mathbf{C}_l^j(i,i)$ in (13) is also a very challenging computational task since the matrix $\mathbf{R}$ is of size $N_H \times N_H$ with

$N_H = 65,536$ for 256×256 high-resolution images. In this work a random sampling Monte-Carlo method is used for this computation. Due to space constraints we will not provide the details. However, generation of each sample requires the solution of the linear system $\mathbf{Rd} = \mathbf{e}$ where $\mathbf{e}$ is a random vector. The parallelization described above is used for the solution of this system. However, this computation is very expensive computationally and slows down significantly the proposed algorithm. Thus, we also propose an algorithm which avoids this computation.

5.2 Initialization

Initially, the image $\mathbf{m}$ and the noise variance β are set equal to the estimates obtained from the application of the super-resolution algorithm in [9], where a stationary simultaneously auto-regressive image prior is used. This algorithm is very efficient because it can be implemented entirely in the DFT domain.

The registration parameters for the proposed algorithm are computed by the BFGS [7] optimization by solving the following minimization problem:

$$\zeta_k^* = \arg \min_{\zeta_k} \|\|\mathbf{W}_{N_L}(\zeta_k)\mathbf{y}_k - \mathbf{y}_1\|_2^2, \ k = 1, \ldots, P \,, \tag{16}$$

where $\mathbf{W}_{N_L}(\zeta_k)$ is the low-resolution counterpart of $\mathbf{W}(\theta_k)$ of size $N_L \times N_L$. Finite differences are used to compute the gradient required by this approach.

The overall algorithm proposed can be summarized as:

1. Find the registration parameters using (16).
2. Find the initial high-resolution image $\mathbf{m}^0$ and the noise variance β^0 by using the algorithm in [9]
3. Repeat the computations in (12), (14) and (15) until convergenece.

6 Numerical Experiments

In order to test the proposed methodology, we used both artificially generated and real data. We compared the proposed algorithm with two previous state-of-the-art algorithms. The total variation (TV) regularization proposed in [13] and the non-stationary prior proposed in [5]. Both of these works deal with the super-resolution problem, however, they assume an imaging model different from (2). For a fair comparison we modify these algorithms to include the same registration model and in addition we initialize then with the same procedure described in Sect. 5. The non-stationary prior with the Maximum a Posterior (MAP) proposed in [5] and the Majorization-Minimization (MM) in [13] are abbreviate as MMTV and NSMAP, respectively. Furthermore, we use the same GPU linear solver described in Sect. 5 in order to solve the linear systems used by these algorithms to reconstruct the high-resolution image. This is straightforward because the matrices of the linear systems are of the same form with $\mathbf{R}^{-1}$. The model parameters for both algorithms were found by trial and error experiments, contrary to the proposed algorithm where the model parameters are found automatically.

In order to conduct experiments where the ground truth is known, we used synthetic data. One set of eight 128×128 low-resolution images were generated using the well-known "Cameraman" image of size 256×256 according to the imaging model given by (1), with decimation factor $d = 2$. One type of blur and three types of noise were used (resulting in three image sets): uniform point spread function (PSF) of size 5×5 and AWG noise corresponding to signal to noise ratio (SNR) $SNR = 40, 30$, and $20dB$. This metric and the MSE metric between the restored image and the original that was used to evaluate the performance of the algorithm, are defined as

$$SNR = 10 \log_{10} \frac{\|\mathbf{z}_i\|_2^2}{N_H \sigma^2} dB, \ MSE = \frac{\|\mathbf{x} - \hat{\mathbf{x}}\|_2^2}{N_H},$$

where σ^2 is the variance of the additive noise and N_H is the size of the zero mean image $\mathbf{z}_i$ and $\mathbf{x}$ and $\hat{\mathbf{x}}$ are the original and estimated images, respectively.

In Fig. 1a the low-resolution image of the experiment with uniform blur 5×5 and $SNR = 20$ is shown. In Fig. 1 we show the super-resolved images (b) with MMTV, (c) with NSMAP, (d) the herein proposed variational algorithm *without* the diagonal elements $\mathbf{C}_l^j(i, i)$ labeled as $ALG1$ and (e) the herein proposed variational algorithm *with* the diagonal elements $\mathbf{C}_l^j(i, i)$ labeled as $ALG2$.

In Table 1 we provide the MSE results for these three experiments. From these results it is clear that the proposed algorithms provides superior results as compared to MMTV and NSMAP.

Table 1. MSE's for the experiments using synthetic data

Method	$SNR = 40$	$SNR = 30$	$SNR = 20$
[13]	85	92	141
[5]	78	82	113
$ALG1$	63	72	**95**
$ALG2$	**62**	**71**	97

We also used the proposed super-resolution algorithm on a real data set that includes four low-resolution degraded images that contain both translations and rotations. One of them is shown in Fig. 2a. Each low-resolution image is of size 256×256. The $2\times$ super-resolved images obtained by (b) MMTV, (c) NSMAP and (d)-(e) the herein proposed variational algorithms are shown in Fig. 2.

We tested the proposed algorithms in terms of their speed also. The main body of the algorithms was implemented in MATLAB (R2009a). The graphics chip used is NVIDA's GTX 285, which contains 240 CUDA cores, 1GB RAM and 1.47 GHz core clock frequency. For 256×256 image, the proposed algorithm $ALG2$ with use of the GPU takes about 60' while the other three NSMAP, MMTV and *ALG1* take about 1'. This large difference is due to the computation of the diagonal elements $\mathbf{C}_l^j(i,i)$. The acheived speed up by running these algorithm on the GPU was 8-10x as compared to using a CPU (Intel Core i7, 2.47Mhz).

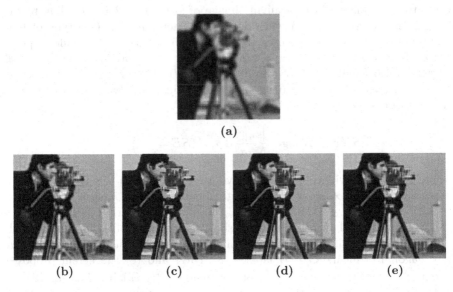

Fig. 1. (a) Low-resolution observation and 2× super-resolved images using: (b) MMTV, (c) NSMAP, (d) and (e) and the herein proposed variational algorithms *ALG1* and *ALG2*

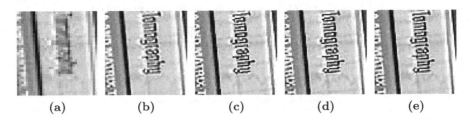

Fig. 2. (a) Low-resolution observation and 2× super-resolved images using: (b) MMTV, (c) NSMAP and the proposed (d) *ALG1* and (e) *ALG2*

7   Conclusions and Future work

We proposed a variational inference super-resolution algorithm where all the model variables and parameters are estimated automatically. We demonstrated numerical experiments that showed the superiority of the proposed methodology. Precisely, the resolution of the super-resolved images shown in Fig. 1 and 2 has greatly improved. Furthermore, the super-resolved images with the proposed algorithm have better edge structure and are visually more pleasant. Also, the MSE in Table 1 with the experiments on the artificial data the proposed algorithm to be superior to all other tested algorithms.

The GPU implementation of the linear solver achieved up to a 10x speed-up as compared to the CPU. This allowed us to estimate the diagonal elements of the inverse of matrix, which gave significant better results in terms of MSE, compared to other two state-of-the-art algorithms.

References

1. Park, S., Park, M., Kang, M.: Super-resolution Image Reconstruction: a Technical Overview. IEEE Signal Processing Magazine 20(3), 21–36 (2003)
2. Tom, B., Galatsanos, N., Katsaggelos, A.: Reconstruction of a high resolution image from multiple low resolution images. In: Chaudhuri, S. (ed.) Super-Resolution Imaging, ch. 4, pp. 71–105. Kluwer, Dordrecht (2001)
3. Katsaggelos, A.K., Molina, R., Mateos, J.: Super resolution of images and video. Synthesis Lectures on Image, Video, and Multimedia Processing, Morgan and Claypool (2007)
4. Tzikas, D., Likas, A., Galatsanos, N.: Life After the EM Algorithm: The Variational Approximation for Bayesian Inference. IEEE Signal Processing Magazine 25(6), 131–146 (2008)
5. Chantas, G., Galatsanos, N., Woods, N.: Super Resolution Based on Fast Registration and Maximum A Posteriori Reconstruction. IEEE Transactions on Image Processing 16(7), 1821–1830 (2007)
6. Genest, C., Zidek, J.V.: Combining probability distributions: A critique and an annotated bibliography. Statistical Science (1986)
7. Nash, S.G., Sofer, A.: Linear and Nonlinear Programming. McGraw Hill, New York (1996)
8. Chantas, G., Galatsanos, N.P., Likas, A., Saunders, M.: Variational Bayesian image restoration based on a product of t-distributions image prior. Transactions on Image Processing 17(10), 1795–1805 (2008)
9. Woods, N.A., Galatsanos, N.P., Katsaggeloss, A.K.: Stochastic methods for joint restoration, interpolation and registration of multiple under sampled images. Transactions on Image Processing 15(1), 201–213 (2006)
10. Keane, A.: CUDA (compute unified device architecture) (2006), http://developer.nvidia.com/object/cuda.html
11. Buatois, L., Caumon, G., Levy, B.: Concurrent Number Cruncher: An Efficient Sparse Linear Solver on the GPU. In: Perrott, R., Chapman, B.M., Subhlok, J., de Mello, R.F., Yang, L.T. (eds.) HPCC 2007. LNCS, vol. 4782, pp. 358–371. Springer, Heidelberg (2007)
12. Bolz, J., Farmer, I., Grinspun, E., Schröder, P.: Sparse Matrix Solvers on the GPU: Conjugate Gradients and Multigrid. ACM Transactions on Graphics 22(3), 917–924 (2003)
13. Galatsanos, N.: A Majorization-Minimization Approach to Total Variation Image Reconstruction of Super-Resolved Images. In: EUSIPCO 2008, Lausanne, Switzerland (2008)

A Novel Approach for Hardware Based Sound Localization

Mauricio Kugler, Takanobu Hishida, Susumu Kuroyanagi, and Akira Iwata

Department of Computer Science and Engineering
Nagoya Institute of Technology
Showa-ku, Gokiso-cho, 466-8555, Nagoya, Japan
mauricio@kugler.com, kuroyanagi.susumu@nitech.ac.jp, iwata@nitech.ac.jp

Abstract. Sound localization is an important ability intrinsic to animals, being currently explored by several researches. Even though several systems and implementations have being proposed, the majority is very complex and not suitable for embedded systems. This paper proposes a new approach for binaural sound localization and the corresponding implementation in an Field Programable Gate Array (FPGA) device. The system is based on the signal processing modules of a previously proposed sound processing system, which converts the input signal to spike trains. The time difference extraction and feature generation methods introduced in this paper create simple binary feature vectors, used as training data for a standard LVQ neural network. An output temporal layer uses the time information of the sound signals in order to reduce the misclassifications of the classifier. Preliminary experimental results show high accuracy with small logic and memory requirements.

1 Introduction

Being able to localize sound sources is a very sophisticated ability of animals. In recent years, sound localization and spacial hearing have been extensively studied. Many works aim to model biological hearing systems, while others try to reproduce their basic functionality with artificial systems. However, the development of a consistent and robust artificial hearing system remains a challenge. Nevertheless, several practical implementations have been proposed, the majority of them based on the estimation of time-delay between signals from one or more pairs of microphones.

Several authors proposed methods for time-delay estimation based on variations of the Generalized Cross-Correlation technique [1]. Although mathematically consistent and achieving good performance, these methods present complex implementations and have no relation to real biological hearing systems. More recently, several biologically inspired sound localization approaches based on spiking neural networks have emerged. These methods have the advantage of naturally dealing with temporal data and presenting a simpler implementation in hardware [2] when compared to the cross-correlation based methods.

K. Diamantaras, W. Duch, L.S. Iliadis (Eds.): ICANN 2010, Part I, LNCS 6352, pp. 490–499, 2010.
© Springer-Verlag Berlin Heidelberg 2010

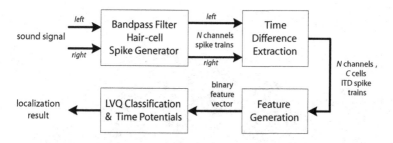

Fig. 1. Proposed sound localization system structure

Kuroyanagi and Iwata [3] proposed a spiking neural model for detecting location of a sound source based on inter-aural time difference (ITD) and inter-aural level difference (ILD). This model was further expanded through the addition of a competitive learning spiking neural network [4] in order to combine the output of ITD extractors of all frequency channels. Schauer and Paschke [5] proposed a similar structure except for the use of a Winner-Takes-All (WTA) spiking neuron structure that combines the several frequency channels outputs. Later, the model was extended to a 360° localization model by using a special microphone arrangement [6]. Schauer and Paschke also presented a partial hardware implementation of their system [7].

Due to high computational costs, sound localization systems are often implemented in hardware for real-time application, using Field Programable Gate Array (FPGA) devices. Methods such as the ones proposed in [4,5] suffer from the disadvantage of presenting a large number of critical parameters, while requiring a large FPGA area, despite of claims of implementation efficiency of spiking neural networks in digital hardware.

This paper proposes a new approach for sound localization and its corresponding hardware implementation in an FPGA device. A very robust feature generation method enables high accuracy for a predefined number of directions with an efficient implementation in hardware. The proposed method presents few parameters on the learning process, and these parameters are all non-critical.

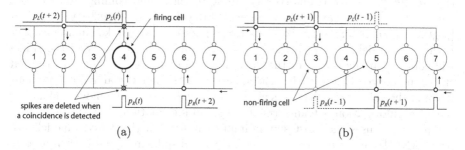

Fig. 2. Time difference extraction using modified Jeffress's model: (a) spike coincidence at $t = 0$ (b) spike removal at $t = 1$

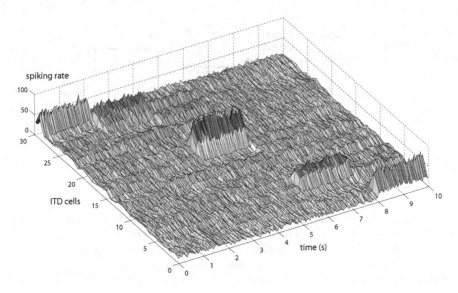

Fig. 3. ITD spike map for a segment of *noise* sound (sum of all frequency channels)

2   Binaural Sound Localization

Several researchers defend the theory that information being processed in the brain is represented by the rate of the spikes. However, temporal patterns of spikes are believed to be present in specialized organisms. The mammals hearing system is a very well known example of the timing of the spikes being used to process information [8]. The human hearing system presents a structure that maps the signal of the two ears in a spatial representation of frequency and delays of these two signals. This model was proposed by Jeffress [9] more than 60 years ago, but it still remains as the core of most of the reviewed models published afterwards. Recently, evidence of structures similar to the ones proposed by this model were found in the human brain.

The basic model proposed by Jeffress contains two antiparallel delay lines that receive the spike trains corresponding to the sound coming from the left and right ear. The delay lines are connected to coincidence detectors along their lengths, which generate a spike if its two inputs receive a spike simultaneously. If there is no delay between the two sound signals, the majority of the spikes will coincide in the center of the delay lines. For instance, as more to the left the sound source is, the earlier the spikes from the left ear arrive in the delay line and the coincidence happens closer to the right side of the model. Thus, the temporal information is transformed to spatial information.

This paper uses the most simple implementation of the Jeffress model, utilizing AND logical coincidence detectors. Spatial spike mapping is then used to generate a set of binary features, which are then to be classified into the final localization estimate.

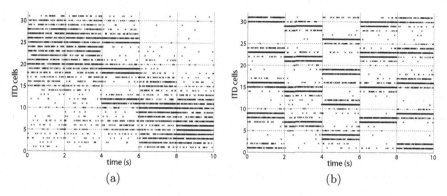

Fig. 4. Binary features for the *noise* sound signal (a) channel 5 (337 Hz) and (b) channel 12 (2.8 kHz)

3 Proposed Method

Kugler *et al.* [10,11] demonstrated a sound recognition system specifically developed for hardware implementation. This system can be divided into three main parts: signal processing, feature extraction and classification block. The signal processing block, inspired by the human hearing system, is composed by a bandpass filter bank, a hair-cell non-linear function and a spike generator. The classification consists of a Learning Vector Quantization (LVQ) neural network followed by an integration layer named *time potentials*. These modules form a robust framework for classifying real-time sound-related data, with the requirement that the generated features must be binary. The proposed system is based on the same framework, except for the time difference extraction and feature generation modules. Its main structure is shown in Figure 1.

The stereo sound signal is sampled at 48kHz, converted to single-precision floating-point representation and sent to the filter bank module, which divides it into N frequency bands. The experiments in this paper use 15 bands per channel, logarithmically spaced from 200 Hz to 7 kHz. Each bandpass filter consists of two stages of second order elliptical Infinite Impulse Response (IIR) filters. After that, the signals are applied into a non-linear hair-cell like function and their amplitude is used for controlling the period of the spike generator' output. All the spike trains $p_n(t)$ $(n = 1 \ldots N)$ become the input data of the time difference extraction module. An important difference from the system described in [10,11] is the removal of the lowpass filter after the hair-cell function. With this, the quality of the pulses generated on the ITD extractor are increased, and thus, the accuracy for high frequency sounds is improved.

The ITD extraction is performed by a Jeffress's model of C cells using simple AND logical coincidences, including the spike canceling modification proposed in [12]. For each frequency band n, the left and right channels' spikes are used as inputs in opposed sides of the extractor, and are sequentially shifted at each new sample. At a given time t, if the cth cell received spikes from both left and

494   M. Kugler et al.

right simultaneously, an output spike $q_n^c(t)$ is generated and both left and right spike is removed from the shift line. This is diagrammatically show in Figure 2.

Following the same framework as proposed in [11], the energy in each ITD cell c for each band n is determined by counting the number of spikes in a time window of length W, as shown in equation (1). Figure 3 shows the energy of ITD cells for a white noise sound, used in the experiments in Section 5. The sound changes directions every 2 seconds, from $0°$ to $180°$ in $45°$ intervals, with $C = 31$ and the window W set to 1000 samples.

$$x_n^c(t) = \sum_{i=1}^{W} q_n^c(t - i) \tag{1}$$

Even though the order of the highest firing rates may contain information about the pattern, a robust set of features can be obtained by ignoring this information and selecting the F highest features of each frequency band as follow:

$$z_n^c = \begin{cases} 1 \; if \; x_n^c \geq \max_i^F x_n^i \wedge x_n^c > 0 \\ 0 \; otherwise \end{cases} \tag{2}$$

where $\max^f$ represents the fth highest element in a vector. It is important to notice that, in case there are no spikes in a certain window, its correspondent z_n^c is not set. This is due to the fact that, in the case of very low level signals, few or no spikes are generated in the ITD extractor, sometimes for more than W samples. In this case, less than F features will contain non-null spikes counting.

Finally, the new feature vector becomes a binary vector composed of the concatenation of all the bands' vectors, $C \cdot N$ bits in total with up to $F \cdot N$ bits equal to 1. Figure 4 shows examples of the binary features for channels 5 (337 Hz) and 12 (2.8 kHz) of the *noise* sound signal.

As previously mentioned, the classification is performed by a standard LVQ neural network [13]. The learning rate α was reduced linearly along the training epochs by a β factor. The codebook vectors were initialized using the Max-Min Distance clustering algorithm [14]. As the patterns were reduced to simple binary vectors, they can be compared by Hamming distance:

$$d(\mathbf{r}, \omega) = \sum_{i=1}^{CN} |r_i - \omega_i| \tag{3}$$

where $\mathbf{r}$ represents the samples formed by all concatenated vectors and ω are the reference vectors. The elements of ω, during the training process, are converted to binary values only for distance calculation. Up to this point, the resolution of the sound localization depended on the distance of the microphones, the number of cells C in the ITD extractors and the sampling frequency. As the LVQ classifier requires a limited number of categories, a number K of directions has to be chosen as the categories of the classifier. In the experiments for this paper, five directions ($0°$, $45°$, $90°$, $135°$ and $180°$) were used. This eliminates the problem of irregular resolution of the ITD extractor, in which the cells that are closer to

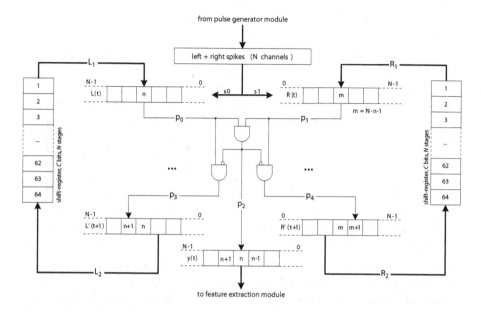

Fig. 5. Hardware implementation of the time difference extraction module

the center present higher resolution than the cells that are closer to the left and right end. Instead, the sinusoidal nature of the ITD extractor is learned by the LVQ network.

Up to the LVQ neural network block, no time information had been used for the classification. It can be assumed that the sound sources being recognized will not present instant changes in position, i.e. their approximate position will last for periods of time much larger than the size of the time window. Thus, by the use of potentials similar to the membrane potential of spiking neurons, one can remove instant errors from the LVQ neural network without modifying the training process. The time potentials are defined as:

$$u_k\left(t\right) = \begin{cases} \min\left(u_{\max}, u_k\left(t-1\right) + \gamma\right) & if \quad k = y\left(t\right) \\ \max\left(0, u_k\left(t-1\right) - 1\right) & if \quad k \neq y\left(t\right) \end{cases} \tag{4}$$

where u_k is the potential of the kth category, $y\left(t\right)$ is the output of the LVQ classifier, γ is the increment for the winner category and $u_{\max}$ is the maximal potential. Hence, the winner category at time t is the one with higher $u_k\left(t\right)$ value. It must be noted that, by setting the $u_{\max}$ parameter, the increment γ does not need to be adjusted. In the experiments mentioned in this paper, γ was fixed to 2.

4   Hardware Implementation

The circuit was implemented in an Altera Stratix II EPS260F484C4, which contains 48352 Adaptive Look-Up Tables (ALUT) and more than 2M bits of internal

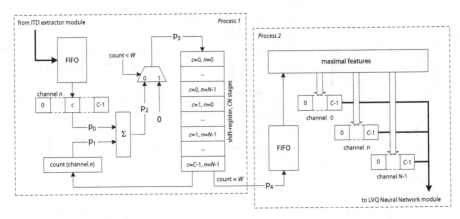

Fig. 6. Hardware implementation of the feature extraction module

memory. As mentioned before, the signal processing modules are identical to the ones used in [11], as well as the LVQ and time potential modules.

The ITD extraction module is shown in Figure 5. When the spike vector from the pulse generator is written on the input, each nth bit of the left (s_0) and right (s_1) channel is written on the respective delay line. The past bit vectors $L1$ and $R1$ are read from a circular shift-register. Every time two new bits are processed (p_0 and p_1), the circular shift-register shifts one position and the coincidences are detected by a logic structure composed of three AND gates. The signal p_2 is a simple AND of the two input bits, while p_3 and p_4 are the bits shifted for the next sample, or reset by the logic circuit if a coincidence is detected. The shifted vectors L_2 and R_2 are inputted in the respective circular shift-registers. For each processed bit, the ITD vector is written into the Feature Extraction block, shown in Figure 6.

The spike counters of the feature extraction block would require an enormous amount of logic if naively implemented. A better alternative is to keep the counting values in the internal memory. In this way, when the first of the N ITD vectors is written on the input FIFO (First In First Out) memory, each bit (p_0) is used to update the current counting (p_1). Until the samples' count is less than the window length W, the updated count values (p_2) are rewritten on the shift-register input (p_3). When a window is completed, the final countings

Table 1. FPGA resources utilization

Stratix II - EPS260F484C4				
Module	*ALUTs*	*DLRs*	*DSP Elements*	*Memory*
Signal Pre-Processing	4677 (9.67%)	4229 (8.75%)	56 (19.44%)	36171 (1.42%)
ITD Extraction	267 (0.55%)	149 (0.31%)	0 (0.00%)	780 (0.03%)
Feature Extraction	3231 (6.68%)	1174 (2.43%)	0 (0.00%)	7314 (0.29%)
LVQ Neural Network	2564 (5.30%)	518 (1.07%)	0 (0.00%)	479232 (18.84%)
Time Potentials	268 (0.55%)	43 (0.09%)	0 (0.00%)	0 (0.00%)
Total	48352	48352	288	2544192

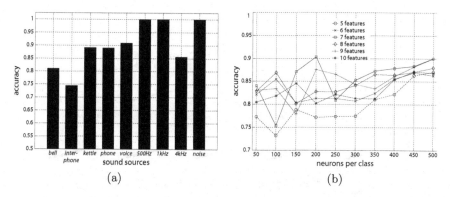

Fig. 7. Sound localization accuracy (a) for each type of sound source and (b) as a function of features number and neurons per class

are written in a second FIFO memory and zero is written onto the shift-register. In an independent process, the maximal countings are sequentially searched and set as '1' in the final feature vector.

Table 1 shows the resource utilization of the sound localization system related modules, for $N = 15$, $C = 31$ and 5 directions. The feature extraction and LVQ modules use a larger amount of data, as their interface is a single vector of $CN = 465$ bits. Also, no post-processing of the reference vectors obtained by the LVQ training was performed. Thus, several redundant vectors might exist and their removal could reduce the LVQ memory utilization significantly.

5   Experiments

Nine sound signals were used on the experiments: *alarm bell, interphone, kettle, phone ring, human voice, 500Hz, 1kHz, 4kHz* and *noise*. The database was split into training and test sets in a 2:1 rate, with a total of 178.33 s (8559 samples) for training and 89.17 s (4280 samples) for testing. The sounds were recorded using WM-E13UY omnidirectional microphones, spaced by 20 cm, at a 1 meter distance from the sound source.

The LVQ network was trained with $\alpha_0 = 0.1$, $\beta = 0.99$ and a maximum of 1000 learning epochs. Figure 7(a) shows the raw LVQ localization accuracy for the nine sounds in five used directions. From the nine sounds, seven achieved raw accuracies higher than 85%. The *bell* and the *4kHz* sounds present high frequency components and their ITD firing patterns are much more complex than the others sounds. The *interphone* sound contains large segments of very low sound levels (intervals between dings) during which the localization fails. If only the segments of true sound are considered, it performs as good as the other signals. Figure 7(b) shows the variation in total accuracy when changing the number of neurons and the number of features. As can be seen, these parameters have small influence on the accuracy and do not need to be exhaustively tuned.

Figure 8 shows the results when calculating time potentials, for a maximal potential u_{max} equal to 50. In this figure, all sounds' signals from each direction

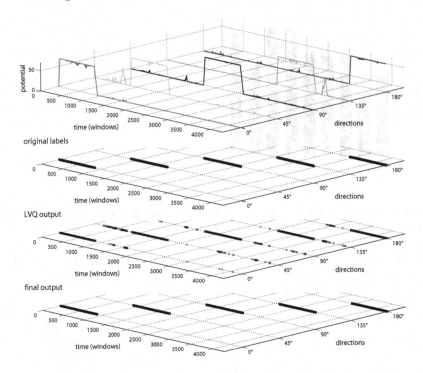

Fig. 8. Time potentials and final classification results

were concatenated, and the resulting signal processed by the localization system. All the misclassifications were eliminated, with the drawback of a small delay introduced to the response of the system.

6 Conclusions

This paper proposed a new method for implementing a sound localization system on an FPGA device. The proposed feature generation approach permits the use of a very simple classifier, a standard LVQ neural network, while an independent temporal layer eliminates most of the misclassifications. The final hardware implementation is compact and can be easily extended.

Some of the used sound signals (e.g. *bell, 4kHz*) present a high frequency spectrum that results in very complex mapping in the ITD extraction and low raw accuracy in the LVQ classifier. One of the reasons might be the fact that, as the frequencies are log-spaced, the width of the high frequency filters is larger and proportionally more spikes are generated for these channels. This, together with the fact that wavelengths shorter than the distance between the microphones generate multiple coincidences in the ITD extraction, creates very complex and noisy patterns. Preliminary experiments with gain correction in order to compensate for this difference and also with linearly spaced filters seem to resolve this problem, increasing the raw LVQ accuracy of the high frequency sounds.

Future works include experiments with a higher resolution in directions, as well as alternative methods for spike generation that are less dependent on signal amplitude. Experiments dealing with reflection and multiple sound sources are currently being planned.

References

1. Knapp, C.H., Carter, G.C.: The generalized correlation method for estimation of time delay. IEEE Transactions on Acoustics, Speech, and Signal Processing 24(4), 320–327 (1976)
2. Maass, W., Bishop, C.M.: Pulsed Neural Networks. MIT Press, Cambridge (2001)
3. Kuroyanagi, S., Iwata, A.: Auditory pulse neural network model to extract the inter-aural time and level difference for sound localization. IEICE Transactions on Information and Systems - Special Issue on Neurocomputing E77-D(4), 466–474 (1994)
4. Kuroyanagi, S., Iwata, A.: A competitive learning pulsed neural network for temporal signals. In: Lee, S.Y., Yao, X. (eds.) Proceedings of the 9th International Conference on Neural Information Processing (ICONIP 2002), Singapore, vol. 1, pp. 348–352 (November 2002)
5. Schauer, C., Paschke, P.: A spike-based model of binaural sound localization. International Journal of Neural Systems 9(5), 447–452 (1999)
6. Schauer, C., Gross, H.M.: Model and application of a binaural 360° sound localization system. In: Proceedings of the International Joint Conference on Neural Networks, vol. 2, pp. 1132–1137. IEEE Computer Society Press, Los Alamitos (July 2001)
7. Ponca, M., Schauer, C.: Fpga implementation of a spike-based sound localization system. In: Proceedings of the 5th International Conference on Artificial Neural Networks and Genetic Algorithms, Prague, pp. 22–25 (April 2001)
8. Joris, P.X., Smith, P.H., Yin, T.C.T.: Coincidence detection in the auditory system: 50 years after jeffress. Neuron 21(6), 1235–1238 (1998)
9. Jeffress, L.A.: A place theory of sound localization. Journal of Comparative and Physiological Psychology 41, 35–39 (1948)
10. Kugler, M., Iwasa, K., Benso, V.A.P., Kuroyanagi, S., Iwata, A.: A complete hardware implementation of an integrated sound localization and classification system based on spiking neural networks. In: Ishikawa, M., Doya, K., Miyamoto, H., Yamakawa, T. (eds.) ICONIP 2007, Part II. LNCS, vol. 4985, pp. 577–587. Springer, Heidelberg (2008)
11. Kugler, M., Benso, V.A.P., Kuroyanagi, S., Iwata, A.: A novel approach for hardware based sound classification. In: Köeppen, M. (ed.) ICONIP 2008. LNCS, vol. 5507, pp. 859–866. Springer, Heidelberg (2009)
12. Iwasa, K., Inoue, H., Kugler, M., Kuroyanagi, S., Iwata, A.: Separation and recognition of multiple sound source using pulsed neuron model. In: de Sá, J.M., Alexandre, L.A., Duch, W., Mandic, D.P. (eds.) ICANN 2007. LNCS, vol. 4669, pp. 748–757. Springer, Heidelberg (2007)
13. Fausett, L.: Fundamentals of Neural Networks: architectures, algorithms and applications. In: Neural Networks Based on Competition, 1st edn., Fundamentals of Neural Networks, New Jersey, pp. 156–217 (1994)
14. Friedman, M., Kandel, A.: Introduction to Pattern Recognition: statistical, structural and fuzzy logic approaches. In: Classification by Distance Functions and Clustering, 1st edn., pp. 73–77. Imperial College Press, London (1999)

Color Segmentation Using
Self-Organizing Feature Maps (SOFMs)
Defined Upon Color and Spatial Image Space

Ioannis M. Stephanakis[1], George C. Anastassopoulos[2], and Lazaros S. Iliadis[3]

[1] Hellenic Telecommunication Organization S.A. (OTE),
99 Kifissias Avenue, GR-151 24, Athens, Greece
and
Technological Educational Instutute of Pireaus,
GR-122 44, Pireaus, Greece
stephan@ote.gr
[2] Democritus University of Thrace, Medical Informatics Laboratory, GR-681 00,
Alexandroupolis, Greece
and
Hellenic Open University, Parodos Aristotelous 18, GR-262 22, Patras, Greece
anasta@med.duth.gr
[3] Democritus University of Thrace, Department of Forestry &
Management of the Environment & Natural Resources, GR-682 00
Orestiada, Thrace, Greece
liliadis@fmenr.duth.gr

Abstract. A novel approach to color image segmentation is proposed and formulated in this paper. Conventional color segmentation methods apply SOFMs – among other techniques – as a first stage clustering in hierarchical or hybrid schemes in order to achieve color reduction and enhance robustness against noise. 2-D SOFMs defined upon 3-D color space are usually employed to render the distribution of colors of an image without taking into consideration the spatial correlation of color vectors throughout various regions of the image. Clustering color vectors pertaining to segments of an image is carried out in a consequent stage via unsupervised or supervised learning. A SOFM defined upon the 2-D image plane, which is viewed as a spatial input space, as well as the output 3-D color space is proposed. Two different initialization schemes are performed, i.e. uniform distribution of the weights in 2-D input space in an ordered fashion so that information regarding local correlation of the color vectors is preserved and jointly uniform distribution of the weights in both 3-D color space and 2-D input space. A second stage of Density-Based Clustering of the nodes of the SOM (utilizing an ad hoc modification of the DBSCAN algorithm) is employed in order to facilitate the segmentation of the color image.

Keywords: Color segmentation; Self-Organizing Feature Maps (SOFM); Density-Based Spatial Clustering (DBSCAN algorithm).

K. Diamantaras, W. Duch, L.S. Iliadis (Eds.): ICANN 2010, Part I, LNCS 6352, pp. 500–510, 2010.
© Springer-Verlag Berlin Heidelberg 2010

1 Introduction

Image segmentation consists of determining K disjoint segments of an image, denoted as I, that are compact in image space, feature smooth boundaries and are homogeneous regarding color distribution within each region, i.e. a partition

$$P(I) = \{R_1, R_2, R_3, \ldots, R_K\}, \tag{1}$$

where $R_i \cap R_j = \varnothing$ with $i, j \subset [1, K]$ and $i \neq j$. Image segmentation is an essential processing step inherent in a variety of algorithms that are intended for image enhancement (in the context of acquisition of medical imagery, outdoor and vision imaging systems etc), for automatic pattern recognition (as implemented in radar and sonar systems, in medical diagnostic systems or in the context of automatic recognition of machine printed or handwritten texts), for shape recognition (as implemented in the context of robot vision and low-level vision), for coding of video sequences and still images (MPEG-4/H.264 and JPEG-2000), for multimedia retrieval in object-oriented databases (DB) and for a variety of other image processing tasks. Many segmentation methods for gray level images have been applied directly or with slight modifications to the segmentation of color images.

1.1 Approaches to Image Segmentation

Image segmentation methods for gray level and color images may be classified into the following categories:

- Histogram thresholding using two or more thresholds based on the peaks and the valleys of the global histogram of an image [1]. Histogram thresholding may be crisp or fuzzy [2], [3].
- Local filtering approaches such as the Canny edge detector [4] and similar techniques.
- Region-growing and merging techniques based on pixel classification in some feature space [5], [6].
- Deformable model region growing [7].
- Global optimization approaches based on energy functionals [8] and/or mixture models of individual component densities (usually Gaussians). These approaches employ such techniques as Bayesian/Maximum a-posteriori criteria [9], the Expectation Maximization (EM) Algorithm [10], propagating fronts/level set segmentation [11], [12] and Minimum Description Length (MDL) criteria.
- Morphological methods like watersheds, morphological image analysis [13], [14] and hybrid morphological-statistical techniques [15].
- Fuzzy/rough set methods like fuzzy clustering and others [2], [3].
- Methods based on Artificial Neural Networks (ANNs) like unsupervised learning and evolutionary/genetic algorithms [16].
- Hybrid methods that attempt to unify several of the above approaches.

Particular segmentation algorithms are, generally, not applicable to all images. Practice shows that a specific method may yield segmentation results of varying quality when applied to images with different characteristics. This implies that different algorithms are not equally suitable for a specific application. Edge detection and histogram thresholding methods work well with gray level images, but may not be suitable for color images because the color components should not be processed separately in view of their interdependence. Neighborhood-based methods such as region growing use only local information, while global methods such as feature space clustering do not take advantage of local spatial knowledge. Color Structure Code (CSC) [17] is a segmentation method that employs hierarchical region growing for color images.

Colors are perceived as combinations of the three primary colors, red (R), green (G) and blue (B). The attributes generally used to distinguish one color from another are brightness, hue and saturation. There are several standard color spaces that are widely used in image processing like RGB, CMY, HIS, YIQ and others. All systems can be calculated from the tristimuli R, G, B by appropriate transformations. However, these models are not uniform color spaces [18]. The use of a uniform color space such as $L^*u^*v^*$ or $L^*a^*b^*$ [19] is recommended for good performance in color clustering because the difference between two colors can be simply measured by their Euclidean distance. In $L^*u^*v^*$ color space, u^* and v^* represent color chromaticities and L^* the intensity.

1.2 Self-organizing Feature Maps

The Self-Organizing Feature Map (SOFM) [20] is an efficient method for cluster analysis of a high-dimensional feature space onto 2-D arrays of reference vectors. Frequently, there exists no-apriori knowledge about the distributions of the features. There are three basic steps involved in the application of the SOFM algorithm after initialization, namely, sampling, similarity matching, and updating. These three steps are repeated until the map formation is completed. The algorithm is summarized as follows:

1. *Initialization.* Choose the initial values for the weight vectors $\mathbf{w}_j(0)$, which in the proposed approach are comprised by the weights of the spatial coordinates (denoted as $\mathbf{w}_j^x(0)$) and the weights (denoted as $\mathbf{w}_j^c(0)$) of the color vectors at pixel of the image specified by the spatial coordinates. Index j equals 1,2,...,N, where N is the number of neurons in the lattice. It may be desirable to keep the magnitude of the weights small.

2. *Sampling.* Choose randomly a pair of image coordinates, $\mathbf{x} = (x_1, x_2)$, and the corresponding color of the sampled pixel, $\mathbf{v} = (L^*, u^*, v^*)$.

3. *Similarity Matching.* Find the best-matching (winning) neuron $i(\mathbf{x},\mathbf{v})$ at time t, using the minimum complex Euclidean distance:

$$i(\mathbf{x}, \mathbf{v}) = \arg \min_j (\alpha \mid \mathbf{x}(t) - \mathbf{w}_j^x(t) \mid^2 + (1-\alpha) \mid \mathbf{v}(t) - \mathbf{w}_j^c(t) \mid^2) , \qquad (2)$$

where $j = 1,2,..., N$ and $\alpha \in [0\ 1]$. For α equal to zero one gets the similarity matching criterion of the conventional SOFM algorithm whereas for α equal to one gets local mean color vectors.

4. *Updating*. Adjust the synaptic weight vectors of all neurons, using the update formula

$$\mathbf{w}_j^x(t+1) = \begin{cases} \mathbf{w}_j^x(t) + \eta_x(t)\big(\mathbf{x}(t) - \mathbf{w}_j^x(t)\big), & j \in \Lambda_{i(\mathbf{x},\mathbf{v})}(t) \\ \mathbf{w}_j^x(t), & \text{otherwise} \end{cases} \quad \text{and}$$

$$\mathbf{w}_j^c(t+1) = \begin{cases} \mathbf{w}_j^c(t) + \eta_c(t)\big(\mathbf{v}(t) - \mathbf{w}_j^c(t)\big), & j \in \Lambda_{i(\mathbf{x},\mathbf{v})}(t) \\ \mathbf{w}_j^c(t), & \text{otherwise} \end{cases}, \tag{3}$$

where $\eta_x(t)$ and $\eta_c(t)$ are the learning-rate parameters, and $\Lambda_{i(\mathbf{x},\mathbf{v})}(t)$ is the neighborhood function centered around the winning neuron $i(\mathbf{x},\mathbf{v})$; $\eta_x(t)$, $\eta_c(t)$ and $\Lambda_{i(\mathbf{x},\mathbf{v})}(t)$ are varied dynamically during learning for best results.

5. *Continuation*. Continue with step 2 until no noticeable changes in the feature map are observed.

Alternative updating rules can be used which preserve the topology of the distribution of data points in the complex color and image space by producing a graded mesh. One may apply for example visualization-induced SOM (ViSOM) [21] or other multidimensional scaling (MDS) techniques employed for structural dimensionality reduction like the ISOMAP (isometric feature mapping) algorithm [22]. Nevertheless standard SOM is used in the context of an initial attempt to segment the original image since we are interested in performing color reduction by exploiting the vector quantization properties of the SOM in color space rather than visualizing the image as a 2-D surface in a complex 5-D space.

2 Initialization and Training

Two different initialization schemes are used to assign values to the weights of the SOFM at t equal to 0. The first scheme initializes separately the spatial weights $\mathbf{w}^x$ from uniform distributions over the spatial coordinates of the image. Initial values of $\mathbf{w}^c$ are conditioned upon the initialization of $\mathbf{w}^x$. This approach suggests spatial indexing of the nodes of the network over the plane of the image and allows for skeletonization of the images should pruning of the nodes be carried out. Alternatively, $\mathbf{w}^x$ and $\mathbf{w}^c$ may by jointly initialized in a 5-D space assuming uniform distributions.

2.1 Original Images

The medical images used to apply the proposed approach to image segmentation are selected from a histological database that has been developed in the Laboratory of Histology of the Democritus University of Thrace, Greece. They represent histological intestinal sections of rats with apoptotic cells. The induction of enterocyte apoptosis is made by counting the positive TUNEL staining cells (red cells in Fig. 1). The detection of apoptotic cells is performed at a 400X magnification by the Olympus BX40 microscope, saved in JPEG format.

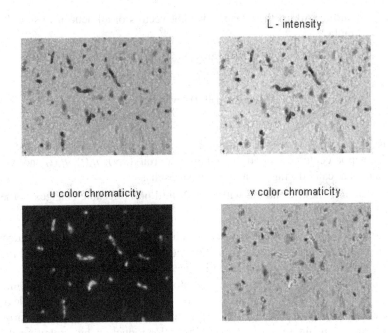

Fig. 1. Initial image and its analysis into $L^*u^*v^*$ color space

2.2 Conventional Approach Using a 2-D SOFM Defined in 3-D Color Space

The distribution of color vectors of the image in Fig. 1 in $L^*u^*v^*$ space is depicted in Fig. 2.a. A 2-D SOFM featuring 10 by 10 nodes is employed for reducing the number of colors in the test image. Conventional uniform initialization of the weight vectors in color space is employed. The resulting map after a training cycle of 100 epochs with a dynamically varying learning rate parameter is depicted in Fig. 2.b. One may easily see that it approximates reasonably well the actual distribution of color vectors.

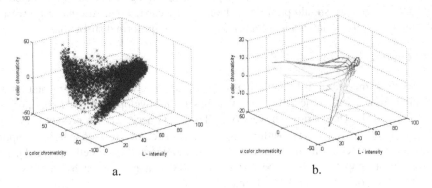

Fig. 2. Distribution of color vectors (-a-) and 2-D SOFM (-b-) after a training cycle of 100 epochs

2.3   Training a SOFM Defined Upon Color and Image Space

A 10 by 10 node SOFM initialized jointly in color and image space following a uniform distribution is used to in order to obtain spatial information. The resulting map in color space after a training cycle of 100 epochs with a dynamically varying learning rate parameter is depicted in Fig. 3.a. It resembles the map obtained for the conventional case. Spatial information is best retained when initialization is carried out on the image plane in a uniform fashion. SOFMs featuring 15 x 20 nodes are initialized in such a way and trained with learning rate parameters - $\eta_x(t)$ and $\eta_c(t)$ - equal to 0.02 for the winning neuron ($\Lambda_{i(x,y)}(t)=0$) and equal to 0.0005 for all other neurons within a neighborhood $\Lambda_{i(x,y)}(t)=1$. Several variants of training cycles of 100 epochs for different values of α in Eq. 2 are performed. The resulting maps approximate reasonably well the actual distribution of color vectors but they are slightly distorted compared with the previous obtained results. Nevertheless nearest neighbor nodes are uniformly distributed on image plane even after training.

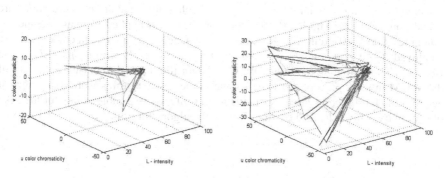

a. Uniform initial. in color and image space   b. α=0.2 (uniform initial. on image plane)

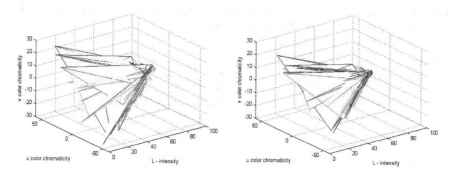

c. α=0.5 (uniform initial. on image plane)   d. α=0.8 (uniform initial. on image plane)

Fig. 3. 2-D SOFM after a training cycle of 100 epochs (uniform initialization of the weight vectors in a combined 5-D color and image space and uniform initialization of the weight vectors in 2-D image space for α=0.2, α=0.5 and α=0.8)

3   Assigning SOFM Clusters to Image Regions

3.1   The DBSCAN Algorithm

Nodes of the SOFM may be used to obtain a color reduced image after the first stage of the segmentation. Nevertheless clustering of the network nodes is necessary to determine the segments. The DBSCAN algorithm [23] and [24] is used to carry out this task. It introduces the notion of core points, directly-density-reachable points, border points and density-reachable points. The neighborhood of a given point within a radius of E_{ps} is called the E_{ps} neighborhood of this point. If the E_{ps} neighborhood of a point contains at least a minimum number of points, *MinPts*, this point is called a core point. A point p is directly density-reachable from a point q if p is within the E_{ps} neighborhood of q and q is a core point, i.e.

$$\text{dis}(p,q)<=E_{ps} \quad \text{and} \quad |\{r|\text{dis}(r,q)<=E_{ps}\}|>=MinPts \,. \tag{4}$$

Density-reachability is the transitive closure of direct density-reachability and it is an asymmetric relationship. Directly density-reachable points that are not core points are called border points. The DBSCAN algorithm has been applied to image segmentation in [25]. Two different E_{ps} distances one in image space and one in color space are employed. Core points are determined by projecting pixels within $SpatialE_{ps}$ upon $ColorE_{ps}$. The following modified DBSCAN algorithm is used to cluster the nodes of the SOFM in a consequent processing stage in the context of this work. Only nearest neighbor nodes are considered as candidates for directly-reachable points for the sake of simplicity. This reduces the complexity of the algorithm from $O(n \log n)$ to $O(n)$.

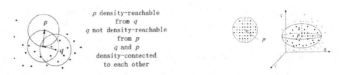

Fig. 4. Definition of the notion of density-reachability and density-connectivity and the application of the E_{ps} neighborhood in color and image spaces

```
Input:
   D={t₁,t₂,...,tₙ} // Nodes of the SOFM after training
   MinPts // Number of nearest neighbor nodes for core points
   Eps // A combination maximum distance for density measure
Output:
   K={K₁,K₂,...,Kₖ} // Set of clustered SOFM nodes
Begin algorithm:
   K=0; // Initially there are no clusters
   for i=1 to N do
     if tᵢ is not assigned to a cluster
       Following NN find X={tⱼ|tⱼ is density-reachable from tᵢ};
       if X is a valid cluster, then
         k=k+1;
         Kₖ=X;
```

3.2   Segmentation Results

One may utilize the colors corresponding to the weights of the nodes after training to substitute for color values of the pixels of the initial image, i.e. $Color \in \{Color(\mathbf{w}_1^x)\cdots Color(\mathbf{w}_j^x)\cdots Color(\mathbf{w}_N^x)\}$. This is called color reduction and it is a straightforward procedure in the case in which the SOFM is defined upon 3-D color space. Nevertheless one may devise several alternative ways to accomplish this task when spatial information is used to train the weights of the SOFM. The following relationship,

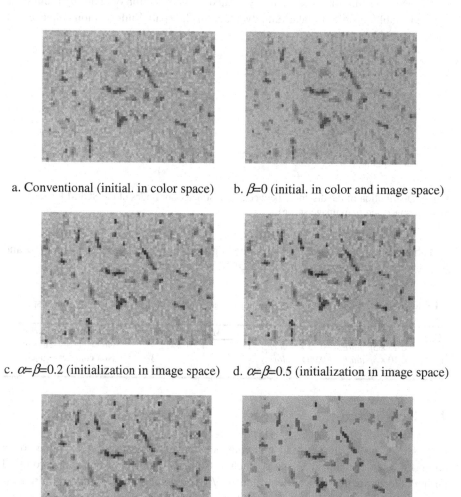

a. Conventional (initial. in color space)   b. β=0 (initial. in color and image space)

c. α=β=0.2 (initialization in image space)   d. α=β=0.5 (initialization in image space)

d. α=β=0.8 (initialization in image space) f. α=0.8 and β=1.0 (initial. in image space)

Fig. 5. Color reduction after first stage clustering

$$Color(I(\mathbf{x})) = Color(\arg \min_{j} (\beta \mid \mathbf{x} - \mathbf{w}_j^x \mid^2 + (1-\beta) \mid [L(\mathbf{x})\, u(\mathbf{x})\, v(\mathbf{x})]^{\mathrm{T}} - \mathbf{w}_j^c \mid^2)) , \qquad (5)$$

where β is equal to α in Eq. 2, yields results that are similar to results obtained for the conventional case regardless of the value of α. Values of β approaching 1 yield color reduced images with prominent image segments. Nevertheless this holds true only when the weights of the nodes of the SOFM are uniform initialized in 2-D image space (see Fig. 5). The use of a composite $ColorE_{ps}$ and $SpatialE_{ps}$ for the modified DBSCAN algorithm that is not directly related to the selection of α during training is, thus, advisable in order to take full advantage of the spatial information conveyed by the trained SOFM.

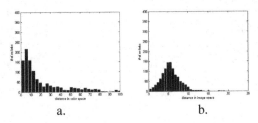

a.   b.

Fig. 6. Distribution of the distances between nearest neighbor nodes of the SOFM for α=0.5 (a. in color space and b. in image space)

Table 1 summarizes the results of the segmentation for different values of α and for various parameters of the modified DBSCAN algorithm.

Table 1. Segmentation parameters for the proposed method (uniform initial. in image space)

$\alpha=\beta$	E_{ps}	MinPts	Segments	Qualitative remarks
0.2	0.25 x $SpatialE_{ps}$ + 0.75 x $ColorE_{ps}$= 16	4	29	Non-compact segments
0.5	0.10 x $SpatialE_{ps}$ + 0.90 x $ColorE_{ps}$= 12	4	23	Non-compact segments
0.8	0.05 x $SpatialE_{ps}$ + 0.95 x $ColorE_{ps}$= 8	4	23	Compact segments

4 Discussion

Values of α less than 0.6 yield non-compact image segments whereas values of α around 0.8 yield compact image segments. Compact patches of color are produced during color reduction as well for values of β approaching 1 when uniform initialization in image space has been carried out. The DBSCAN algorithm is applied directly to the color reduced image to produce the segments in such a case. This is not possible when the weights of the nodes of the SOFM have been jointly initialized in color and image space following a uniform distribution in 5-D.

References

1. Otsu, N.: A Threshold Selection Method From Gray-Level Histograms. IEEE Trans. Syst. Man Cybernet. 9(1) (1979)
2. Kerre, E.E., Nachtegael, M. (eds.): Fuzzy Techniques in Image Processing. Series Studies in Fuzziness and Soft Computing, vol. 52. Springer, Heidelberg (2000)
3. Tizhoosh, H.R.: Fuzzy Image Processing: Introduction in Theory and Applications. Springer, Heidelberg (1997)
4. Canny, J.R.: A Computational Approach to Edge Detection. IEEE Transactions on Pattern Analysis and Machine Intelligence 8(6), 679–698 (1986)
5. Adams, R., Bischof, L.: Seeded Region Growing. IEEE Trans. Pattern Analysis and Machine Intelligence 16(6), 641–647 (1994)
6. Beveridge, J.R., et al.: Segmenting Images Using Localizing Histograms and Region Merging. Int'l J. Compt. Vision 2 (1989)
7. McInerney, T., Terzopoulos, D.: Deformable Models in Medical Image Analysis: A Survey. Medical Image Analysis 1(2), 91–108 (1996)
8. Mumford, D., Shah, J.: Optimal Approximations by Piecewise Smooth Functions and Associated Variational Problems. Comm. Pure Appl. Math. 42, 577–684 (1989)
9. Geman, S., Geman, D.: Stochastic Relaxation, Gibbs Distributions and the Bayesian Restoration of Images. IEEE Transactions on Pattern Analysis and Machine Intelligence 6, 721–741 (1984)
10. Dempster, A., Laird, N., Rubin, D.: Maximum Likelihood From Incomplete Data Via The EM Algorithm. Journal of Royal Statistical Society, Series B 39, 1–38 (1977)
11. Osher, S., Sethian, J.A.: Fronts Propagating with Curvature Dependent Speed: Algorithms Based on Hamilton-Jacobi Formulations. Journal of Computational Physics 79, 12–49 (1988)
12. Brox, T., Weickert, J.: Level Set Based Image Segmentation with Multiple Regions. In: Pattern Recognition, 415–423 (2004)
13. Vincent, L., Soille, P.: Watersheds in Digital Spaces: An Efficient Algorithm Based on Immersion Simulations. IEEE Trans. Pattern Analysis and Machine Intelligence 13(6), 583–598 (1991)
14. Serra, J.: Image Analysis and Mathematical Morphology. Academic, New York (1982)
15. Stephanakis, I.M., Anastassopoulos, G.K.: Watershed Segmentation of Medical Images With On-The-Fly Seed Generation and Region Merging. WSEAS Transactions on Information Science and Applications 1(1), 303–308 (2004)
16. Bounsaythip, C., Alander, J.T.: Genetic Algorithms in Image Processing - A Review. In: Proc. Of the 3rd Nordic Workshop on Genetic Algorithms and their Applications, Metsatalo, Univ. of Helsinki, Helsinki, Finland, pp. 173–192 (1997)
17. Sturm, P., Priese, L.: Properties of a Three-Dimensional Island Hierarchy for Segmentation of 3-D Images with the Color Structure Code. In: Van Gool, L. (ed.) DAGM 2002. LNCS, vol. 2449, pp. 274–281. Springer, Heidelberg (2002)
18. Robertson, A.R.: The CIE 1976 Color-difference Formulae. Color Research and Applications 2, 7–11 (1977)
19. Tominaga, S.: Color Classification of Natural Color Images. Color Research and Applications 17, 230–239 (1992)
20. Kohonen, T.: Self-Organizing Maps. Springer Series in Information Sciences. Springer, Berlin (1995)
21. Yin, H.: ViSOM – A Novel Method for Multivariate Data Projection and Structure Visualization. IEEE Trans. Neural Networks 13(1), 237–243 (2002)

22. Tenenbaum, J.B., de Silva, V., Langford, J.C.: A Global Geometric Framework for Nonlinear Dimensionality Reduction. Science 290, 2319–2323 (2000)
23. Ester, M., Kriegel, H.-P., Sander, J., Xu, X.: A Density-Base Algorithm for Discovering Clusters in Large Spatial Databases With Noises. In: Proceedings of the International Conference on Knowledge Discovery and Data Mining, pp. 226–231 (1996)
24. Ester, M., Kriegel, H.-P., Sander, J., Xu, X.: Clustering for Mining in Large Spatial Databases. KI-Journal 1, 18–24 (1998)
25. Ye, Q., Gao, W., Zeng, W.: Color Image Segmentation Using Density-Based Clustering. In: Proceedings ICASSP, Hong Kong, Vol.3, pp. 345–348 (2003)

Independent Component Analysis
of Multi-channel Near-Infrared Spectroscopic Signals
by Time-Delayed Decorrelation

Toshifumi Sano, Shuichi Matsuzaki, and Yasuhiro Wada

Nagaoka University of Technology,
1603-1 Kamitomioka, Nagaoka, Niigata 940-2188, Japan
tsano@stn.nagaokaut.ac.jp

Abstract. Multi-channel near-infrared spectroscopy (NIRS) is increasingly used in empirical studies monitoring human brain activity. In a recent study, an independent component analysis (ICA) technique using time-delayed decorrelation was applied to NIRS signals since those signals reflect cerebral blood flow changes caused by task-induced responses as well as various artifacts. The decorrelation technique is important in NIRS-based analyses and may facilitate accurate separation of independent signals generated by oxygenated/deoxygenated hemoglobin concentration changes. We introduce an algorithm using time-delayed correlations that enable estimation of independent components (ICs) in which the number of components is fewer than that of observed sources; the conventional approach using a larger number of components may deteriorate settling of the solution. In a simulation, the algorithm was shown capable of estimating the number of ICs of virtually observed signals set by an experimenter, with the simulation reproducing seven sources where each was a mixture of three ICs and white noises. In addition, the algorithm was introduced in an experiment using ICs of NIRS signals observed during finger-tapping movements. Experimental results showed consistency and reproducibility of the estimated ICs that are attributed to patterns in the spatial distribution and temporal structure.

Keywords: Near-infrared Spectroscopy, Independent Component Analysis, Time-delayed Decorrelation, Neuroimaging.

1 Introduction

Human brain activity has been actively measured in recent studies clarifying underlying mechanisms such as cognitive and motor-learning processes. Near-infrared spectroscopy (NIRS) is increasingly used in neuroimaging studies because of the convenience of the equipment and the decreased restriction of a subject's movement. However, NIRS analysis can be hampered by artifacts induced by various factors (e.g., periodic factors that reflect blood flow regulation and physical factors due to unsuited equipment). Therefore, many methods, including Independent Component Analysis (ICA), have been introduced to facilitate analysis of brain activity induced

K. Diamantaras, W. Duch, L.S. Iliadis (Eds.): ICANN 2010, Part I, LNCS 6352, pp. 511–520, 2010.

purely by an experimental task. Conventional ICAs, such as fast-ICA[1] and JADE[2], have been used to estimate independent components (ICs) that optimize independence of the sources as the cost function[3]. On the other hand, Statistical Parametric Mapping (SPM)[4] using the regressive approach is increasingly applied to fMRI and NIRS analyses, although whether those analyses accurately separates the source signals is still under discussion. The regressive approach can exclude a signal induced by brain activities if it is not interpreted as a selected Hemodynamic Response Function (HRF) in the model. In contrast, since ICA can directly separate observed signals, it preserves information about brain activities as long as the number of components can be estimated.

The characters of ICA highly depend on the cost function. Medvedev et al.[5] applied fast-ICA using non-Gaussianity, and Kohno et al.[6] applied ICA using time-delayed correlations to an observed signal by NIRS. Both works succeeded in estimating a heartbeat, skin blood flow and white noise as ICs to be removed. We selected time-delayed correlations as a measure of independence, since we consider that changes in NIRS signals are not represented by the linear coupling of random variables, but by a temporal fluctuation induced by a certain event. In this case, the stationary process does not exist and only the second order statistics (variance and correlation) can be treated according to the weak stationary process. However, NIRS signals have a strong temporal structure. The structure is stronger than that of a mere random variable. Conventional ICA models, except those in which ICs are extracted individually, such as fast-ICA, have assumed the number of ICs is equivalent to the number of measurement channels. However, this assumption is not always correct since the number of channels is usually set irrespective of the state of observed signals. For example, when we use a 24-channel system to measure a subject's brain activity, ICs, such as a signal evoked by blood flows and artifacts, are usually much fewer than the number of channels. In this case, even if 24 ICs are estimated, the possibility that each IC shows the true change of the cerebral blood flow and the artifacts is low. Kohno et al.[6] proposed an ICA technique designed to reduce the ICs in a way that removes signals that are considered noise or artifacts.

In the present study, we applied the ICA algorithm proposed by Kawamoto et al.[7] that is used for NIRS signal analysis. Using the algorithm, we estimated the number of ICs through time-delayed decorrelations. We confirmed whether the algorithm can accurately estimate ICs for virtually observed signals made by a simulation. Moreover, we actually conducted a finger-tapping experiment having three trials. We evaluated whether ICs estimated using this experiment data exhibit components with correlating temporal and spatial structures.

2 Materials and Method

2.1 ICA Model for Temporal Sources

ICA models can be classified into two types: one is represented by the linear coupling of independent random variables and the other by temporal signals. NIRS signals can be regarded as temporal because they are subject to the concentration changes of oxygenated and deoxygenated hemoglobin, which are presumably affected by events during experiment.

The simplest expression for the temporal structure of NIRS signals $x(t)$ is given by the time-delayed correlation, i.e.,

$$x(t) = \mathbf{A}s(t), \tag{1}$$

where A is a suitable mixture matrix and $s(t)$ is a set of source signals, such as brain activity and artifact signals. Moreover, if the separation matrix W satisfying $\mathbf{A}^{-1}=\mathbf{W}$ can be estimated, then estimated source signal $y(t)$ is obtained by

$$\mathbf{W}x(t) = y(t). \tag{2}$$

When $x(t)$ has n components and y(t) has m components, we cannot estimate the model unless $n \geq m$. Here $\mathbf{W}$ is not the square matrix, so we use the pseudo-inverse matrix for the calculation of the inverse matrix because we are handling the case of n>m. The time-delayed correlation matrix for $y(t)$ is shown by

$$\mathbf{C}_\tau^y = E\left\{ y(t)\, y(t-\tau)^T \right\}. \tag{3}$$

Because components of $y(t)$ are mutually independent signals,

$$E\left\{ y_i(t)\, y_j(t-\tau)^T \right\} = 0 \tag{4}$$

when using arbitrary $i \neq j$ and τ. Therefore, ICA using time-delayed correlations leads to an eigenvalue problem for $\mathbf{C}_\tau^y$. If time-delayed correlations are used, enough information for estimating ICs is obtained. Higher-order information is unnecessary.

2.2 Algorithm of ICA Using Time-Delayed Correlations

When S is chosen as appropriate sets of τ, the cost function is shown by

$$\begin{aligned} J_1 &= \sum_{\tau \in S}\sum_{i \neq j}\left(\mathbf{C}_\tau^y\right)_{ij}^2 \\ &= \sum_{\tau \in S}\sum_{i \neq j}\left(\mathbf{W}\mathbf{C}_\tau^x\mathbf{W}^T\right)_{ij}^2, \end{aligned} \tag{5}$$

which minimizes the off-diagonal element of $\mathbf{C}_{\tau \in S}^y$. The algorithm by Herault and Jutten[8] was advocated by Molgedey and Schuster[9] to solve J_1. Kohno et al.[6] applied this method to data observed by NIRS. However, we use the cost function for diagonalizing the proposal by Kawamoto et al.[7], which is different from J_1.

$$\sum_i \log m_{ii} \geq \log|\det\mathbf{M}|. \tag{6}$$

T. Sano, S. Matsuzaki, and Y. Wada

In Eq. (6), $\mathbf{M}$ is an arbitrary positive definite matrix and m is an element of $\mathbf{M}$. The equation only holds when $\mathbf{M}$ is a diagonal matrix. Therefore, diagonal indication of $\mathbf{M}$ can be measured by

$$F(\mathbf{M}) = \sum_i \log m_{ii} - \log|\det \mathbf{M}|.$$ (7)

When $z(t)$ is shown by

$$\mathbf{E}^T \mathbf{C}_0^x \mathbf{E} = \mathrm{diag}(d_1\ d_2 \cdots d_n) = \mathbf{D}$$
$$\mathbf{V} = \mathbf{D}^{-1/2} \mathbf{E}^T$$ (8)
$$z(t) = \mathbf{V}x(t)$$

as a white signal obtained by PCA for $x(t)$, the cost function using $F(\mathbf{W})$ becomes

$$J_2 = \frac{1}{2} \sum_{\tau \in S} F(\mathbf{W}\mathbf{C}_\tau^z \mathbf{W}^T)$$
$$= \sum_{\tau \in S} \sum_i \frac{1}{2} \log(w_i^T \mathbf{C}_\tau^z w_i) + const$$ (9)

by use of Eq. (8) because $\mathbf{W}$ is an orthogonal matrix. The inclination of J_2 is

$$\frac{\partial J_2}{\partial \mathbf{W}} = \sum_{\tau \in S} \mathbf{Q}_\tau \mathbf{W} \mathbf{C}_\tau^z.$$ (10)

However, $\mathbf{Q}_\tau$ is shown by

$$\mathbf{Q}_\tau = \mathrm{diag}(\mathbf{W}\mathbf{C}_\tau^z \mathbf{W}^T)^{-1}.$$ (11)

After each repeat, $\mathbf{W}$ should be orthogonalized. This is done by

$$\mathbf{W} \leftarrow (\mathbf{W}\mathbf{W}^T)^{-1/2} \mathbf{W},$$ (12)

using the square root of the matrix. Uniform random numbers in section (-1,1) were used for an initial value of $\mathbf{W}$. The algorithm proposed by Kawamoto et al.[7] is superior, because it is simpler than JADE[2] and is better global convergence than the algorithm by Herault and Jutten[8].

Moreover, $x(t)$ is reconstructed by

$$\dot{x}(t) = (\mathbf{W}\mathbf{D}^{-1/2}\mathbf{E}^T)^{-1} y(t) = \dot{\mathbf{A}} y(t).$$ (13)

An element of $\dot{\mathbf{A}}$ at row i column j shows a contribution from $y_j(t)$ to $x_i(t)$.

2.3 Using Virtually Observed Signals by NIRS

We generated NIRS signals that measure brain activity in a simulation to apply and consider ICA that uses time-delayed decorrelations. Only concentrations of oxygenated hemoglobin (oxyHb[mMcm]) were used in this study, though oxyHb and deoxyHb can be observed in the measurement of brain activity by NIRS because the correlation of oxyHb with the blood oxygenation level dependent (Bold) signal by fMRI is high. Buxton et al.[10] developed the model

$$h(t) = \frac{1}{k\tau_h (k-1)!} \left(\frac{t}{\tau_h} \right)^k e^{-t/\tau_h} , \qquad (14)$$

which is called the hemodynamic response function (HRF) and shows the response based on the dynamics of blood circulation. Degree k is assumed to be 3. A full width at half maximum (FWHM) is given by the expression $\tau_h = 0.242\tau_f$. Moreover, in the event-related experiment, oxyHb observed by NIRS had two signal changes identified by Kato[11]. The negative change is called the Fast Effect, with a peak about 4[s] after the event onset, while the positive change is called the Wash Out Effect, with respective peak about 20[s] after the event onset. $h_f(t)$ and h_w were generated with Eq. (14) as those changes. Figure 1(a) shows $h_f(t)$ and h_w. $g(t)$ was defined as a pseudo Meyer wave with a peak of about 0.1[Hz], also shown in Fig. 1(a).

$$g(t) = \sin\left(2\pi 0.1t + 5\cos\left(2\pi 0.03t\right)\right) \qquad (15)$$

Where $g(t)$ is an artifact signal reflecting the low frequency blood pressure weave. The problem was simplified in the simulation. The observed signal was measured by 7 channels (Fig. 1(b)). Moreover, ICs $s(t)$ signal are assumed to be only $h_f(t)$, $h_w(t)$, $g(t)$ with added white gaussian noise. Therefore, the virtually observed signal $x_{simu}(t)$ can be shown by the general ICA model with noise.

$$x_{simu}(t) = As(t) + \varepsilon . \qquad (16)$$

For $x_{simu}(t)$ to look like the actual NIRS signal, mixture matrix $\mathbf{A}$ was appropriately defined.

2.4 Finger-Tapping Experiment

The NIRS signal of finger tapping was measured in a study by Morihiro et al.[12] whereas our analysis employed only one of those subject's data. Informed consent was obtained from each subject and approved by the ethics committee of Nagaoka University of Technology. ICA using time-delayed correlations was applied in our experiment. The experimental environment is shown in Fig. 2(a). Subjects sat in a chair with their bodies held shill by a belt. Their right hands were placed on the desk and their left hands on their thighs. A x-mark, about 10[cm] in height and width, was set on a white screen. The movement was tapping of the right hand. Subjects were instructed to do a multi-finger tapping task in time with an electronic metronome at 3.00–3.17[Hz]. The multi-finger tapping task consisted of the thumb "tapping" each of the other fingers in turn. While resting, the subjects were instructed to gaze at the sign and relax. While moving, they were instructed to close their eyes. The NIRS system used in the trials (an OMM-3000 from Shimadzu Corporation, Japan) consisted of 8 near-infrared light-source probes and 8 detectors, resulting in 24 source-detector pairs. A schematic illustration of the probe placement is shown in Fig.2(b). The probes covered an area from the left primary motor cortex to the supplementary motor cortex (positioned according to the international 10/20 system for electrode placement). The sampling rate was 1/0.13[Hz]. Each trial took 60[s] (10[s]: rest; 20[s]: action; 30[s]: rest). The time for the NIRS signals to stabilize before the next trial started was about 60[s]. The subjects were informed of the start and end of the movement periods by a beep. The observed signal for three trials in the subject was assumed to be $x_a(t)$, $x_b(t)$ and $x_c(t)$ (see Fig. 4). The ICs $y_a(t)$, $y_b(t)$ and $y_c(t)$ of each trial were estimated and compared.

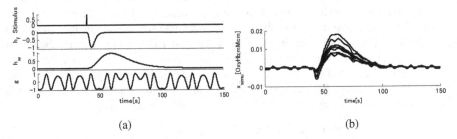

(a)   (b)

Fig. 1. Components of $s(t)$ and virtual observed signals $x_{simu}(t)$ used in a simulation. The simulation up to 150[s] is set to the sampling frequency of 10[Hz]. (a) Stimulation in the simulation began at 40[s]. $h_f(t)$ had a peak at 45[s]. h_w had a peak beginning at 45[s]. $g(t)$ was defined as a pseudo Meyer wave with a peak of about 0.1[Hz]. (b) Measured by 7 channels and assumed to be only $h_f(t)$, $h_w(t)$, $g(t)$ and white gaussian noise. $x_{simu}(t)$ is shown by Eq. (**16**).

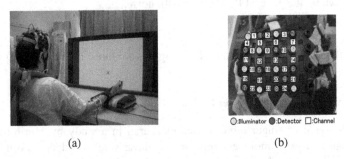

(a)   (b)

Fig. 2. Conditions in finger-tapping experiment. (a) Experimental environment. (b) Probe placement.

3   Results

3.1   Analytical Results of Using Virtually Observed Signal by NIRS

ICA using time-delayed correlations was applied to the virtually observed signals shown in Fig. 1(b). $x(t)$ has n=7 components, therefore $y(t)$ should have m=3 components. However, we show the results estimated for m=7 as well as m=3 and compared them. $\{0.1, 0.2, \cdots 50\} \in S$ is assumed because in this case time-delayed correlations were simultaneously diagonalized as $50 \geq \tau \geq 0$[s]. Each component of $y(t)$ is shown in Fig. 3(a) for m=7 and Fig. 3(b) for m=3.

In Fig. 3(a), it is estimated that each of $y(t)$ signals is considered a mixture of $s(t)$ components. In contrast, in Fig. 3(b), the temporal structure of estimated $y(t)$ looks like that of each component of $s(t)$.

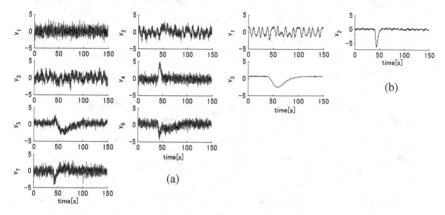

Fig. 3. Typical changes in virtual signals. Results of ICA using time-delayed correlations where (a) m=7, (b) m=3.

3.2 Analytical Results of Finger-Tapping Experiment

The results of ICA using time-delayed correlations applied to the observed signal in the tapping experiment are shown in Fig. 5. The number m of ICs of $y(t)$ must be estimated, but m is not strictly given for an actual observed signal. Here, IC $y(t)$ is estimated for the observed signal in each of three trials as m=3. $x_a(t)$ is polluted by an artifact that has a frequency of about 0.1[Hz]. However, oxyHb in all the trials tends to increase with an onset at 10[s] to an offset at 30[s] after the event. A tendency to decrease is also seen in the oxyHb in all the trials from the event offset. Next, ICs $y_a(t)$, $y_b(t)$ and $y_c(t)$ are shown in Fig. 5. They are the ICA results for $x_a(t)$, $x_b(t)$ and $x_c(t)$ respectively. $y_{a1}(t)$, $y_{b1}(t)$ and $y_{c1}(t)$ are each the first component of $y_a(t)$, $y_b(t)$ and $y_c(t)$ respectively. They each include the oxyHb change related to the experiment task. Moreover, the component of the artifact that appeared for $x_a(t)$ was calculated as $y_{a2}(t)$, and calculated to independent for $y_{a1}(t)$.

To evaluate the weight of $y_{a1}(t)$, $y_{b1}(t)$ and $y_{c1}(t)$ for $x_a(t)$, $x_b(t)$ and $x_c(t)$ respectively, each respective element $\dot{A}_{a1}$, $\dot{A}_{a2}$ and $\dot{A}_{a3}$ is shown in Fig. 6. The maps in Fig. 6 correspond to the measurement site and calculated by smoothing the element of $\dot{A}$. A large positive weight is seen in Fig. 6 in the field centered on channel 23, this is also clear from Fig. 4. Therefore, from the results of an experiment consisting of three trials of the same experiment task, an independent signal with a temporal structure related to the onset and offset of the event can be effectively estimated. We were able to confirm that the components have weight in the common field in the map between the trials.

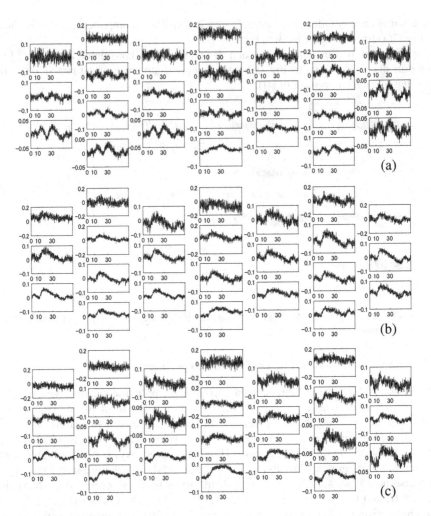

Fig. 4. Changes in oxyHb concentration (NIRS signals) in finger-tapping experiments. (a), (b) and (c) are respective measured results of $x_a(t)$, $x_b(t)$ and $x_c(t)$. Vertical axis indicates oxyHb concentration change in mmol-cm. Horizontal axis indicates time in seconds measured within sampling period of 130[ms].

4 Discussion

We discuss an appropriate setting for obtaining estimated values of components and discuss effectiveness of ICA using time-delayed correlation from the results. The setting having more independent elements than the number of observed signals deteriorates the estimation accuracy, as seen in simulation results in Fig. 3. Kohno et al. succeeded in estimating a heart beat, skin blood flow and white noise as ICs to be

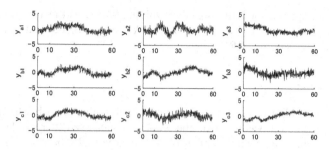

Fig. 5. Analytical results for finger-tapping experiment data by ICA. Estimation ICA for observed signal in three trials, $x_a(t)$, $x_b(t)$ and $x_c(t)$. Horizontal axis indicates time in seconds measured within sampling period of 130[ms].

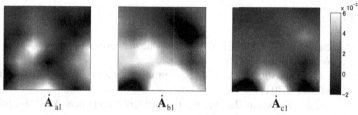

Fig. 6. Contribution from $y(t)$ to $x(t)$ represented by elements of $\mathbf{A}_{a1}$, $\mathbf{A}_{a2}$ and $\dot{\mathbf{A}}_{a3}$. Map corresponds to measurement site and calculated by smoothing the elements of $\mathbf{A}$.

removed. In the results in Fig. 3(a), independent signal y_1 mostly reflects white noise, and y_2 and y_3 reflect artifact signal g. Removing these components and recomposing then looks like deflation by PCA. However, after removing and recomposing the y_2 component that seems to contain a small amount of component $h_f(t)$, part of observed signal $h_f(t)$ is lost. Therefore, deflation by removal and recomposition of the artifact components is effective when an accurate estimation of the ICA model. As shown in Fig. 3(b), when the number of ICs is the same as the number of present signals, present signal $s(t)$ is estimated almost exactly.

Figure 5 shows the results of estimation by ICA for the observed signal in three trials $x_a(t)$, $x_b(t)$ and $x_c(t)$, where the three components that should be estimated are the ICs. $y_{a1}(t)$, $y_{b1}(t)$ and $y_{c1}(t)$ include the oxyHb change related to the experiment task. Moreover, the component of the artifact that appeared for $x_a(t)$ was calculated as $y_{a2}(t)$ and the IC was calculated as $y_{a1}(t)$. In Fig. 6, we were able to confirm that the components have weight in the common field of the map between the trials. An independent signal with a temporal structure related to the onset and offset of the movement event and related to the offset can be clearly estimated.

In summary, we defined the number of ICs as three, but we did not prove whether the setting is appropriate. However, the results for an assumption of 3 components were accurate and reproducible. In addition, this paper did not explain if the ICA method using time-delayed correlations is more effective than other methods using non-Gaussianity. As discussed by Medvedev et al.[5], since ICs by NIRS signals can be regarded as non-Gaussian signals, ICA method using non-Gaussianity was effective. Thus, like the approach by Vigário et al.[13], the approach to evaluate ICA algorithms that applied for NIRS signals involving various artifacts and brain activities is necessary; However, we show that ICA using time-delayed correlations is effective in analysis of the NIRS signal.

5 Conclusion

We used an algorithm using time-delayed correlations that was able to estimate the number of ICs when it was less than the number of observed sources. The algorithm was able to estimate a specific number of ICs for a virtually observed signal. Moreover, the algorithm could estimate the ICs of the observed signal in three actual trials in a finger-tapping experiment. The estimated ICs exhibited reproducible spatial distribution and temporal structures.

References

1. Hyvärinen, A., Oja, E.: Independent component analysis: algorithms and applications. Neural Networks 13(4-5), 411–430 (2000)
2. Cardoso, J.F., Souloumiac, A.: Blind beamforming for non Gaussian signals. IEE Proceedings-F 140, 362–370 (1993)
3. Hyvärinen, A., Karhunen, J., Oja, E.: Independent Component Analysis. John Wiley & Sons, New York (2001)
4. Ye, J.C., Tak, S., Jang, K.E., Jung, J., Jang, J.: NIRS-SPM: Statistical parametric mapping for near-infrared spectroscopy. NeuroImage 44(2), 428–447 (2009)
5. Medvedev, A.V., Kainerstorfer, J., Borisov, S.V., Barbour, R.L., VanMeter, J.: Event-related fast optical signal in a rapid object recognition task: Improving detection by the independent component analysis. Brain Research 1236, 145–158 (2008)
6. Kohno, S., Miyai, I., Seiyama, A., Oda, I., Ishikawa, A., Tsuneishi, S., Amita, T., Shimizu, K.: Removal of the skin blood flow artifact in functional near-infrared spectroscopic imaging data through independent component analysis. Journal of Biomedical Optics 12(6), 062111 (2007)
7. Kawamoto, M., Matsuoka, K., Masahiro, M.: Blind Separation of Sources Using Temporal Correlation of the Observed Signals. IEICE Transactions on Fundamentals of Electronics, Communications and Computer Sciences E80-A(4), 695–704 (1997)
8. Jutten, C., Herault, J.: Blind separation of sources, part I: An adaptive algorithm based on neuromimetic architecture. Signal Processing 24(1), 1–10 (1991)
9. Molgedey, L., Schuster, H.G.: Separation of a mixture of independent signals using time delayed correlations. Physical Review Letters 72(23), 3634–3637 (1994)
10. Buxton, R.B., Uludağ, K., Dubowitz, D.J., Liu, T.T.: Modeling the hemodynamic response to brain activation. NeuroImage 23(S1), S220–S233 (2004)
11. Kato, T.: Principle and technique of NIRS-imaging for human brain FORCE: Fast-oxygen response in capillary event. International Congress Series 1270, 85–90 (2004)
12. Morihiro, M., Tsubone, T., Wada, Y.: Relation between NIRS Signal and Motor Capability. In: Proceedings of 31st Annual International Conference of the IEEE EMBS, pp. 3991–3994 (2009)
13. Vigário, R., Jousmáki, V., Hämäläinen, M., Hari, R., Oja, E.: Independent component analysis for identification of artifacts in magnetoencephalographic recordings. In: Proceedings of 1997 Conference on Advances in Neural Information Processing Systems, vol. 10, pp. 229–235 (1998)

Micro Nucleus Detection in Human Lymphocytes Using Convolutional Neural Network

Ihor Paliy[1], Francesco Lamonaca[2], Volodymyr Turchenko[2],
Domenico Grimaldi[2], and Anatoly Sachenko[1]

[1] Research Institute of Intelligent Computer Systems, Ternopil National Economic University,
3 Peremoga Square, 46020, Ternopil, Ukraine
{ipl,as}@tneu.edu.ua
[2] Department of Electronics, Informatics and Systems, University of Calabria,
via P. Bucci 41C, 87036, Rende (CS), Italy
{flamonaca,turchenko,grimaldi}@deis.unical.it

Abstract. The application of the convolution neural network for detection of the micro nucleuses in the human lymphocyte images acquired by the image flow cytometer is considered in this paper. The existing method of detection, called IMAQ Match Pattern, is described and its limitations concerning zoom factors are analyzed. The training algorithm of the convolution neural network and the detection procedure were described. The performance of both detection methods, convolution neural network and IMAQ Match Pattern, were researched. Our results show that the convolution neural network overcomes the IMAQ Match Pattern in terms of improvement of detection rate and decreasing the numbers of false alarms.

Keywords: Micro nucleus detection, Convolutional neural network, Image processing.

1 Introduction

The recent literature has highlighted that the lymphocytes can be used as biological dosimeter in order to relive the presence and the action of carcinogenic factors [1]. In order to relieve structural chromosome aberrations [2], [3], [4], a new architecture of flow cytometer measurement device (image flow cytometer IFC) [5] able to recognize and automatically count the Micro Nucleuses (MNs) on the acquired images of human lymphocytes has been pointed out. Biology experts recommend specific criteria to identify one or more MNs in the cell [6], [7]. In particular, the condition that the MNs are in the range [1/3, 1/16] of the diameter of the associated nucleus is the fundamental constrain to perform correct detection. The assessment of this condition is absolutely necessary and permits to distinguish the MN from the remaining objects in the image.

One of the most used ways to detect the MN in real medical systems is to run the pattern matching software. Due to the overall software architecture of the IFC, the used pattern matching algorithm is the one implemented in the LabVIEW IMAQ

K. Diamantaras, W. Duch, L.S. Iliadis (Eds.): ICANN 2010, Part I, LNCS 6352, pp. 521–530, 2010.
© Springer-Verlag Berlin Heidelberg 2010

Vision [8]. It calls IMAQ Match Pattern (IMP) method. The IMP method is robust to image alterations with intensity belonging to a well defined range. However the IFC can introduce the alteration of bad exposure, out of focus and Gaussian noise. These alterations have caused doubtful detection when we use the IMP method. Therefore we have developed a preprocessing block [9], [10] able to evaluate the image quality and, on the basis of this evaluation, the image is corrected or rejected. This permits to improve the correctness of the final medical response.

Another cause of doubtful detection using IMP method is the zoom of the acquisition system. In this case our preprocessing block considers zoom as an alteration of the image that can be evaluated and corrected. It resizes the MN according to the zoom factor evaluated on the acquired image using the algorithm of digital zoom and the learning phase is repeated. This digital zoom introduces artifacts that do not permit the correct detection of the MNs. One of the possible solutions of this problem is to apply artificial neural networks (NNs) due to their good classification and detection properties based on similarity, high adaptability and fault tolerance [11]. In this case the NNs can easily analyze the similarity in zoomed and un-zoomed images, detect the MNs and avoid repeating the learning phase.

Nowadays more preferable are the appearance-based methods for object detection [12] in terms of detection validity and speed. They are based on the scanning of an input image at some scale levels by fixed-size window in order to find objects in different positions and scales. Each window is handled by a two-class (object/non-object) classifier presented by NNs [13], [14], support vector machines [15], [16], Bayesian classifiers [17], etc. After classification the detected objects are grouped and the areas with some number of multiple detections are accepted as objects of interest.

In 2001, P. Viola and M. Jones [18] presented one of the fastest appearance-based object detection approach which is able to process input image in near real-time mode. The novelty of their approach comes from the integration of a new image representation (integral image), a learning algorithm (based on AdaBoost) and a method for combining classifiers (cascade of weak classifiers). They used a set of rectangular Haar-like features instead of raw pixels information as an input for the weak classifiers. R. Lienhart [19] extended the Haar-like features set with rotated ones and S. Li et al. [20] proposed a novel learning procedure called FloatBoost. One of the highest validity is demonstrated by the object detection approach of C. Garcia and M. Delakis [14]. They used a convolutional neural network (CNN) that processes an input image in two stages: coarse and fine detection. During the coarse detection, the CNN handles an image of any size at once and detects object candidates. The same CNN is used then to verify these candidates within fine detection. The CNN may be used in more usual way by scanning an input image with fixed-size window at some scale levels. The last approach was used in this paper for detection of the MNs in zoomed and un-zoomed human lymphocyte images.

The goal of this paper is to investigate the method of C. Garcia and M. Delakis [14] for the detection of the MNs. We use the CNN because it promises to be one of the best classifiers in pattern recognition. The rest of the paper is organized as follows. First we shortly introduce the IFC image acquisition system and general LabVIEW IMP method. After the proposed CNN training algorithm and the detection procedure are presented. On the experimental stage the comparison between the LabVIEW IMP method and CNN is fulfilled.

2   IFC Image Acquisition System and LabVIEW IMP Detection Method

In this section we provide a short description of the IFC and standard LabVIEW IPM method which have been used to detect the MNs in the acquired images.

After the chemical treatment of the lymphocyte by biology expert in order to block the cytodieresis process and to mark the genetic material with the citocalasina B, the lymphocyte, in fluid suspension, is introduced on the input of the Image Flow Cytometer (Fig. 1). Then the cell reaches the *flow cell* through a system of *pump and conduct*. Then it is photographed by the image acquisition system. The picture of the cell is stored into the databases for further elaboration in order to evaluate the image quality and to detect the MNs [5].

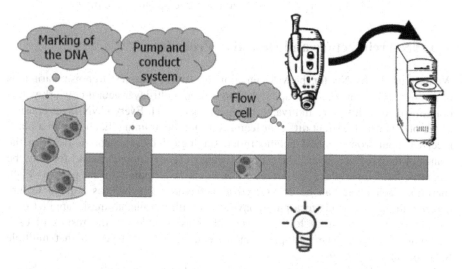

Fig. 1. A block-scheme of the operations implemented in the IFC

The image acquired by the IFC is 8 bit grayscale level. Due to the biological process applied to the lymphocytes to mark the genetic components [5], the darker levels are used to represent the nucleus and MNs, the middle levels are used to represent the cytoplasm and the lighter levels are used to represent the background. First it is defined the template to be searched. It is important to choose a template with a high contrast because the search routine does not simply try to find exact matches to the template's grayscale intensity matrix. Instances of the template can often be detected in the source image under different ambient lighting conditions and with different background information [15]. Moreover it is necessary to select only the characteristic of the template avoiding the background. In order to define the templates the following steps are performed. Once the source image has been loaded, the user defines a region of interest. This forms the search template. The next step is to train the system to recognize it, which is achieved by first defining the learn pattern parameters using IMAQ Setup Learn Pattern. This virtual instrument creates a learn pattern parameter string. These parameters specify the invariance mode to use. Three parameters must be set: (i) Shift (default), which extracts information to specify shift (position) invariant pattern matching; (ii) Rotation, which extracts information to specify rotation invariant pattern matching; (iii) All, which extracts information to specify both shift and rotation invariant pattern matching. Once the template is learned, the next step is to search for it. The virtual instrument simply constructs a match pattern parameter string based on its inputs: (i) Minimum contrast, which defines the minimum contrast you expect to find in the image. It assists the searching when the source image has lighting variances relative to the template image; (ii) Match mode, which sets the invariance mode to either shift (default) or rotation invariant; (iii) Subpixel accuracy, which sets the search routines to use interpolation to attempt searches on a subpixel level and (iv) Rotation angle ranges, which sets a part of an image that will be placed in a front of the lens with a rotation of a particular range of angles. The actual searching process is executed using the convolution of the template on the image.

3   CNN Architecture and Detection Procedure

We have used the CNN for the MN detection due to its robustness to noise, variations of position, scale, angle, and shape [14]. It is a deep multi-layer neural network with a brain-inspired architecture motivated by vision tasks [21]. Every CNN layer consists of the planes which extract different features during the training. Each unit in a plane receives input from a small neighborhood (biological local receptive field) in the planes of the previous layer. The trainable weights (convolutional mask) forming the receptive field for a plane are forced to be equal at all points in the plane (weight sharing). Each plane can be considered as a feature map that has a fixed feature detector that corresponds to a pure convolution with a trainable mask, applied over the planes in the previous layer. A trainable bias is added to the results of each convolutional mask. The multiple planes are used in each layer so that multiple features can be detected.

Y. LeCun [21] distinguishes two kinds of the layers: convolutional and subsampling, but the CNN's structure proposed by P. Simard et al. [22] joins both layers' types into one, thus decreasing the layers number and making the network faster.

The output value of a neuron with the coordinates (m,n) of p-plane and l-layer [23]

$$y_{m,n}^{l,p}(x) = F(S_{m,n}^{l,p}(x)),\qquad(1)$$

where x is an input sub-image, F is a neuron's transfer function and $S_{m,n}^{l,p}(x)$ is a neuron's weighted sum. According to the recommendation of [24] the bipolar sigmoid transfer function is used for CNN with the output interval [-1; 1]. Therefore, the last expression (1) may be represented as

$$y_{m,n}^{l,p}(x) = \frac{2}{1+\exp(-S_{m,n}^{l,p}(x))} - 1,$$

where a neuron's weighted sum is defined by expression [23]

$$S_{m,n}^{l,p}(x) = (\sum_{k=0}^{K-1}\sum_{r=0}^{R-1}\sum_{c=0}^{C-1} y_{2m+r,2n+c}^{l-1,k}(x) \times w_{r,c}^{l,p,k}) - b^{l,p},$$

where K is the input planes' number (as well as convolutional kernels), R and C are the convolutional kernel's height and width, $w_{r,c}^{l,p,k}$ is the synaptic weight with coordinates (r, c) in the convolutional kernel between k-plane of the $(l$-1)-layer and p-plane of the l-layer, $b^{l,p}$ is the neurons' threshold of the p-plane and l-layer.

The sparse structure of the CNN is used instead of the full-connected structure as well as the number of layers is decreased by performing convolution and subsampling operations in each plane simultaneously [22] (Fig. 2) in order to increase the neural network's processing speed.

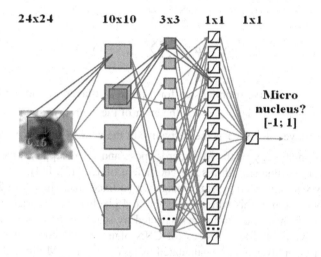

Fig. 2. CNN structure for the MN detection

We have fulfilled the process of automatic CNN structure creation depending on the following input parameters: training image size, convolutional kernel size and steps, input layer planes' number and planes' coefficient. The training image size, kernel size and steps are chosen in order to provide the integer values of planes' sizes calculated using (2) and (3), and also to achieve the output layer plane's size equal to 1x1 neurons.

$$h^{l+1} = (h^l - h_k^{l+1})/s_{k,r}^{l+1} + 1, \qquad (2)$$

$$w^{l+1} = (w^l - w_k^{l+1})/s_{k,c}^{l+1} + 1, \qquad (3)$$

where h^l and w^l are the l-layer plane's height and width, h_k^{l+1} and w_k^{l+1} are the $(l+1)$-layer convolutional kernel's height and width and $s_{k,r}^{l+1}$ and $s_{k,c}^{l+1}$ are the $(l+1)$-layer convolutional kernel's steps across rows and columns.

The planes' number for the next layer

$$p^{l+1} = p^l \times PK ,$$

where PK is the planes' coefficient.

The random-number generator is used to calculate the planes' number for each layer (except the last one). The input planes for the connections are chosen randomly too. The last plane of each layer and the output layer's plane are connected with all planes of the previous layer.

On-line gradient backpropagation algorithm with an adaptive training step [25] is used to calculate the modifications of CNN weights and biases on each training epoch

$$\Delta w_{r,c}^{l,p,k} = -\alpha^{l,p} \times \sum_{m=0}^{M-1}\sum_{n=0}^{N-1} \gamma_{m,n}^{l,p} \times F'(S_{m,n}^{l,p}) \times y_{2m+r,2n+c}^{l-1,k} ,$$

$$\Delta b^{l,p} = \alpha^{l,p} \times \sum_{m=0}^{M-1}\sum_{n=0}^{N-1} \gamma_{m,n}^{l,p} \times F'(S_{m,n}^{l,p}) ,$$

where $\alpha^{l,p}$ is the adaptive training step for p-plane of l-layer, M and N are the height and width of p-plane of l-layer, $\gamma_{m,n}^{l,p}$ is the error of the neuron with coordinates (m, n) on p-plane of l-layer, $F'(S_{m,n}^{l,p})$ is the derivative of the neuron's output value.

The detection strategy of the MNs across pose and scale supposes the gradual decrease of the input image with a scale coefficient of 1.2 [13], [14]. The detection is performed by scanning each pyramid image with a fixed size window of 24x24 pixels size. The motion step of this window is equal to 4 pixels in both horizontal and vertical directions. Each of the sub-images selected by scanning window is classified by CNN. The convolutional kernel sizes for CNN planes were chosen empirically. The plane size for each layer may be calculated using (2) and (3). Multiple detections are often happen in object detection issues. They are handled by averaging the detections with close positions and sizes. Only the objects with the multiple detections above the threshold of 2 are concerned as the MNs. This allows decreasing the number of false detections.

4   Experimental Results

For the training within both CNN and IMP approaches we have gathered 75 positive (which includes correct image of the MN) images (Fig. 3a). Also 75 negative images for training were also chosen (Fig. 3b) besides the positive images (the proportion of positive and negative images was 50% per 50%). A minimum detected MN size is equal to 24x24 pixels. The CNN's input size of 24x24 is chosen as a result of analysis of known object (face) detection methods. For example, P.Viola and M.Jones [18] used 24x24 window as an input for their face/non-face classifier, H.Rowley at el. [13] - 20x20, T.Poggio and K.Sung - 19x19, C.Garcia and M.Delakis [14] - 32x36. At the same time the selection of input image size should provide integer values for planes' sizes in all layers of CNN.

The average processing time of an input image (400x400 pixels or near 27000 windows) by CNN method is equal to 20 sec using the workstation with Dual Core Celeron E1200 1.6GHz. The 50 nucleus images were used for the testing the performance of IMP and CNN methods. Several examples of the nucleus images with detected MNs by the CNN method are presented in Fig. 4.

Fig. 3. Examples of positive (a) and negative (b) training images

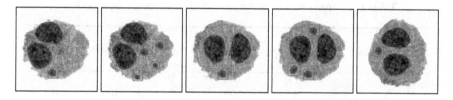

Fig. 4. The images of nucleuses with detected MNs

We present the comparison of the detection results within the CNN and IMP methods on the example of three nucleus images with different zoom factors in Table 1. We have evaluated the number of correct matches, the false positive and false negative detections. The column "# of false positive" represents the number of the detections not associated with the MN (it is known as *false alarms* in literature). The column "# of false negative" shows the number of MNs not detected by the detection algorithm. Therefore, for each image, the sum of the correct matches and the number of false negative detections must be equal to the number of MNs presented in the image. On the basis of these data we have obtained the detection or hit rate $DetectionRate = \dfrac{NumberOfMatches}{NumberOfMNs} \times 100\%$, which is specified in Table 2. Also the total number of false alarms is presented in Table 2 for both methods.

As we can see, the CNN method provides no false alarms for each zoom factor of the tested images. The number of false negative detections is much lower in comparison with the IMP method. The detection rate of 87.5% of the CNN method is much higher than 25% of detection rate of IMP method for the considered examples.

Table 1. Experimental results obtained using CNN and IMP methods

Image	Zoom factor	# of MN	CNN			IMP		
			Match	# of False Positive	# of False Negative	Match	# of False Positive	# of False Negative
image2	1,0	1	1	0	0	1	0	0
	0,5	1	1	0	0	0	0	1
	2,0	1	1	0	0	0	2	0
	3,0	1	1	0	0	0	1	0
image4	1,0	4	3	0	1	2	0	2
	0,5	4	1	0	3	0	0	4
	2,0	4	2	0	2	2	2	2
	3,0	4	3	0	1	0	2	4
image6	1,0	3	3	0	0	3	0	0
	0,5	3	3	0	0	0	0	3
	2,0	3	3	0	0	0	1	3
	3,0	3	3	0	0	0	4	3

Table 2. Comparison of detection rate and false alarms for both methods

Image	Zoom factor	CNN		IMP	
		Detection rate, %	False alarms	Detection rate, %	False alarms
image2	1,0	100	0	1	0
	0,5	100	0	0	0
	2,0	100	0	0	2
	3,0	100	0	0	1
image4	1,0	75	0	50	0
	0,5	25	0	0	0
	2,0	50	0	50	2
	3,0	100	0	0	2
image6	1,0	100	0	100	0
	0,5	100	0	0	0
	2,0	100	0	0	1
	3,0	100	0	0	4
Average detection rate		87,5		25	
Total number of false alarms		0		12	

5   Conclusions

The application of the convolution neural network for detection of the micro nucleuses in the human lymphocyte images acquired by the image flow cytometer is considered in this paper. The existing method of detection, called IMAQ Match Pattern, implemented inside of the image acquisition system is described and its limitations concerning zoom factors are analyzed. The convolution neural network is chosen to fulfill the detection due to its robustness to noise, variations of position, scale, angle, and shape. The training algorithm of the convolution neural network and the detection procedure were described. The performance of both detection methods, convolution neural network and IMAQ Match Pattern, were researched on the 50 test images of human lymphocytes and the results obtained on 12 images (3 images with different zoom factors) are presented. Experimental results show that the convolution neural network gives very promising results. It provides no false alarms for each zoom factor. The number of false negative detections is much lower in comparison with the IMP method. The detection rate of 87.5% provided by the convolution neural network is much higher than 25% of detection rate of IMAQ Match Pattern method on the considered example images.

The latest medical researches have proved that the human lymphocytes can be used as biological dosimeter in order to relive the presence and the action of carcinogenic factors. The application of the neural network approaches for this important task of detection of micro nucleuses on human lymphocyte images, in particularly convolution neural network, allows improving the correctness of the final medical response.

The application of convolution neural network for the detection of micro nucleuses under other alterations conditions, for example, bad exposure, out of focus, Gaussian noise, etc could be considered as a future line of the research. We also plan to parallelize the training and detection stages for convolutional neural network using MPI technology.

Acknowledgement

The co-author of this paper, Dr. Volodymyr Turchenko, acknowledges the financial support of his Marie Curie International Incoming Fellowship grant, Ref. Num. 221524 under the 7th European Community Framework Programme.

References

1. Coskun, M., Top, A., Orta, T.: Biological Dosimetry Following X-ray Irradiation. Turkish Journal of Medical Science 30, 563–569 (2000)
2. Cram, L.S., Martin, J.C., Steinkamp, J.A., Yoshida, T.M., Buican, T.N., Marosiorone, B.L., Jett, J.H., Salzman, G., Sklar, L.: New Flow Cytometric Capabilities at the National Flow Cytometry Resource. Proc. of IEEE 80(6), 912–917 (1992)
3. Liu, Y., Fisher, A.C.: Human Erythrocyte Sizing and Deformability Study by Laser Flow Cytometer. In: Proc. of Ann. Int. Conf. of the IEEE Eng. in Medicine and Biology Society, vol. 1, pp. 324–325 (1992)
4. Maguire, D., King, G.B., Kelley, S., Durack, G., Robinson, J.P.: Computer-Assisted Diagnosis of Hematological Malignancies Using a Pattern Representation of Flow Cytometry Data. In: Proc. of 12th South. Biom. Eng. Conf., vol. 1, pp. 153–155 (1993)
5. Abate, G.F., Bavaro, F., Castello, G., Daponte, P., Grimaldi, D., Guglielmelli, G., Martinelli, F.U., Mauro, U., Moisa, S., Napolitano, M., Rapuano, S., Scerbo, P.: Tomography System to Acquire 3D Images of Cells in Laminar Flow: Hardware Architecture. In: Proc. Intern. Workshop on Medical Measurement and Applications MeMea 2006, Italy, pp. 68–73 (2006)

6. Grimaldi, D., Lamonaca, F.: Reduction of Doubtful Detection of Micro-nucleus in Human Lymphocyte. Int. J. Advan. Media and Comm. 3(1/2), 80–94 (2009)

7. Balestrieri, E., Grimaldi, D., Lamonaca, F., Rapuano, S.: Image Flow Cytometer. In: Murkopadhyay, S.C., Lay, E.A. (eds.) Adv. in Biomed. Sens., Meas., Instrum. and Syst. LNEE, vol. 55, pp. 210–239 (2010)

8. Relf, C.G.: Image Acquisition and Processing with LabVIEW, pp. 164–168. CRC Press, Boca Raton (2004)

9. Carnì, D.L., Grimaldi, D., Lamonaca, F.: Image Pre-processing for Micro Nucleuses Detection in Lymphocyte. Intern. Sci. J. of Computing 4(3), 63–69 (2005)

10. Carnì, D.L., Grimaldi, D., Lamonaca, F.: Pre-Processing Correction for Micro Nucleus Image Detection Affected by Contemporaneous Alterations. IEEE Transaction on I&M 56(4), 1202–1211 (2007)

11. Haykin, S.: Neural Networks and Learning Machines, 3rd edn. Prentice Hall, Englewood Cliffs (2008)

12. Yang, M.: Recent Advances in Face Detection. In: IEEE ICPR 2004, Tutorial, Cambridge, UK, 93 (2004)

13. Rowley, H., Baluja, S., Kanade, T.: Neural Network-based Face Detection. IEEE Trans. on Patt. Anal. and Mach. Intellig. 20, 22–88 (1998)

14. Garcia, C., Delakis, M.: Convolution Face Finder: A Neural Architecture for Fast and Robust Face Detection. IEEE Trans. on Pat. Anal. and Mach. Intellig. 26(11), 1408–1423 (2004)

15. Romdhani, S., Torr, P., Schlkopf, B., Blake, A.: Computationally Efficient Face Detection. In: Proceedings of ICCV, vol. 1, pp. 695–700 (2001)

16. Heisele, B., Serre, T., Prentice, S., Poggio, T.: Hierarchical Classification and Feature Reduction for Fast Face Detection with Support Vector Machines. Pattern Recognition 36(9), 2007–2017 (2003)

17. Schneiderman, H., Kanade, T.: Probabilistic Modeling of Local Appearance and Spatial Relationships for Object Recognition. In: Proc. IEEE Conf. Comp. Vision and Patt. Recog. pp. 45–51 (1998)

18. Viola, P., Jones, M.: Robust Real-Time Face Detection. Int. J. of Comp. Vis. 57(2), 137–154 (2004)

19. Lienhart, R., Maydt, J.: An Extended Set of Haar-like Features for Rapid Object Detection. In: Proc. of IEEE Inter. Conf. on Image Proc. vol. 1, pp. 900–903 (2002)

20. Li, S., Zhang, Z.: FloatBoost Learning and Statistical Face Detection. IEEE Trans. on Patt. Analys. and Mach. Intellig. 26(9), 1112–1123 (2004)

21. LeCun, Y., Bottou, L., Bengio, Y.: Gradient-Based Learning Applied to Document Recognition. Intellig. Sign. Proc., 306–351, IEEE Press (2001)

22. Simard, P., Steinkraus, D., Platt, J.: Best Practices for Convolutional Neural Networks Applied to Visual Document Analysis. In: 7th Intern. Conf. on Document Analys. and Recogn., vol. 2, p. 958 (2003)

23. Paliy, I.: Human Face Detection Methods Using a Combined Cascade of Classifiers, Inter. J. of Computing 7(1), 114–125 (2004) (in Ukrainian)

24. Wasserman, A.: Neural Computing: Theory and Practice, vol. 230. Van Nostrand Reinhold, New York (1989)

25. Golovko, V., Galushkin, A.: Neural Networks: Training, Models and Applications. Radiotechnika, Moscow, 256 (2001) (in Russian)

Region Matching Techniques for Spatial Bag of Visual Words Based Image Category Recognition

Ville Viitaniemi and Jorma Laaksonen

Aalto University School of Science and Technology
P.O. Box 15400, FI-00076 Aalto, Finland
{ville.viitaniemi,jorma.laaksonen}@tkk.fi

Abstract. Histograms of local features—bags of visual words (BoV)—have proven to be powerful representations in image categorisation and object detection. The BoV representations have usefully been extended in spatial dimension by taking the features' spatial distribution into account. In this paper we describe region matching strategies to be used in conjunction with such extensions. Of these, the rigid region matching is most commonly used. Here we present an alternative based on the Integrated Region Matching (IRM) technique, loosening the constraint of geometrical rigidity of the images. After having described the techniques, we evaluate them in image category detection experiments that utilise 5000 photographic images taken from the PASCAL VOC Challenge 2007 benchmark. Experiments show that for many image categories, the rigid region matching performs slightly better. However, for some categories IRM matching is significantly more accurate an alternative. As a consequence, on average we did not observe a significant difference. The best results were obtained by combining the two schemes.

1 Introduction

Large quantities of digital image and video material are continuously produced in the world of today. Lots of useful information could potentially be extracted by analysis of such material, but the data volumes involved make manual analysis unappealing in most cases. Automatic methods for analysis of the visual content can hugely extend the range of applications where content analysis becomes worthwhile.

Large variety of visual content analysis tasks—e.g. automatic image annotation, semantic multimedia search, object detection and visual mobile robot navigation—can be phrased as visual category detection problems. In the experiments of this paper, we limit ourselves to still photographic images, although similar methods can be applied also for analysis of video content. In supervised image category detection the goal is to predict whether a novel test image belongs to a category defined by a training set of positive and negative example

K. Diamantaras, W. Duch, L.S. Iliadis (Eds.): ICANN 2010, Part I, LNCS 6352, pp. 531–540, 2010.
© Springer-Verlag Berlin Heidelberg 2010

images. The categories can correspond, for example, to the presence or absence of a certain object, such as a dog. In order to automatically perform a visual category detection task, one must use a representation for the properties that can be extracted automatically from the images.

Histograms of local features have proven to be powerful image representations in category detection. Consequently their use has lately become commonplace in image content analysis tasks (e.g. [1,2]). This paradigm is also known by the name Bag of Visual Words (BoV) in analogy with the successful Bag of Words paradigm in text retrieval. In this analogue, images correspond to documents and different local descriptor values to words.

In its basic form the BoV approach does not take into account the local features' spatial distribution within images. However, many image categories are such that spatial structure could be useful in their detection. A common extension to BoV is to partition all the images geometrically with the same tiling pattern. Each part is then described with a separate histogram and the image dissimilarity is formulated as the sum of the dissimilarities of corresponding tiles. This often used matching scheme (subsequently denoted as rigid matching) seems to assume the image categories to be sensitive to the overall ordering of objects that the images contain. For example, an image with a car on the left side and a motorbike on the right side would be considered very different from images where the ordering is opposite. It would seem that such requirement of rigidity of image layout is too strict in many object recognition and scene analysis tasks. In practice many categories are, for example, completely invariant to left-right mirroring of the images.

In this paper we present an alternative to the rigid matching scheme, namely a matching scheme based on Integrated Region Matching (IRM), which has originally been proposed for matching automatically segmented images [3]. In IRM, the image segments, or the geometric tiles, can be completely freely permuted. Although using IRM for category detection is not a completely novel idea, the image segment features used in the original publication were very primitive in comparison with the local feature histograms that represent the state of the art in visual content analysis nowadays. It is therefore of interest to experimentally compare the two region matching strategies when region descriptions themselves are of comparable top quality. In this paper, we perform such comparisons using images and categories of the popular PASCAL VOC 2007 object recognition benchmark. Using this experimental setup, we investigate several issues related to region matching, including fusion of the matching strategies.

The rest of this paper is organised as follows. In Section 2 we delineate the processing stages in a BoV visual category detection system and describe our implementation of those stages. Section 3 discusses spatial BoV extensions, including region matching. In Section 4 we define the experimental task and procedures that we subsequently use in Section 5 for experimentally comparing region matching techniques. Finally, in Section 6 conclusions from the experiments are presented.

2 Bag of Visual Words (BoV) Framework for Image Category Recognition

2.1 System Architecture

The use of local image feature histograms for supervised image classification and characterisation can be divided into four steps:

Step 1. Selecting image locations of interest. This can be implemented e.g. by interest point detection or regular dense sampling of locations.

Step 2. Describing each location with suitable visual descriptors (e.g. SIFT [4]).

Step 3. Characterising the distribution of the descriptors within each image with a histogram.

Step 4. Using the histograms as feature vectors of the images in a supervised vector space algorithm, such as the support vector machine (SVM).

2.2 Our BoV Implementation

In the first step of our implementation of the BoV pipeline, interest points are detected from each image with a Harris-Laplace detector [5] that outputs around 1200 interest points per image on average with the images used in the current experiments. In Step 2 the image area around each interest point is individually described with a 128-dimensional SIFT descriptor [4], a widely-used and rather well-performing descriptor. In Step 3 each image is described by forming a histogram of the SIFT descriptors. We determine the histogram bins by clustering a sample of the interest point SIFT descriptors (20 per image) with the Linde-Buzo-Gray (LBG) algorithm. In the current experiments, we set the histogram size to be 2048 bins. In our earlier experiments [6] we have found such codebooks to perform reasonably well while the computational cost associated with the clustering still remains manageable.

A clustering tree structure is used in order to facilitate fast approximate nearest neighbour search and thus reasonably fast histogram generation. In the histogram generation phase, we employ the soft histogram technique [7] that has been observed to provide a significant performance gain. Strictly speaking, due to softness the obtained image descriptors are no longer exactly histograms but can still be used as the feature vector for an image exactly the same way in final fourth BoV step, where the soft histograms of both training and test images are fed into a probabilistic supervised classifier algorithm. For this purpose, we employ weighted C-SVC variant of the SVM algorithm combined with probability estimation stage, as implemented in the version 2.84 of the software package LIBSVM [8]. As the kernel function g we use the exponential function

$$g(i,j) = \exp\left(-\gamma d(i,j)\right) \qquad (1)$$

of the distance $d(i,j)$ between images i and j. In Section 3.2 we describe such distance functions. Details of the SVM classification stage can be found in [9].

3   Spatial Extensions to BoV

3.1   Partitioning Images with Tiling Masks

In the basic BoV method, the image-wide distribution of values of interest point descriptors is described by means of a single histogram. Every interest point has exactly equal contribution to the histogram, regardless of its spatial location. However, in practical category detection tasks, exploiting spatial information has proven to be useful. To this end, the BoV model can be extended by partitioning several sub-images with geometric masks. In the experiments of this paper, we consider partitioning the image area with a 2×2, 3×3, 4×4, 5×5 and 6×6 rectangular grids.

Instead of crisp tiling masks, one can also consider the technique of spatially soft tiling, which we proposed in [10]. There the tile borders are made fuzzy, so that interest points near the tile boundary contribute to the histograms of not only one but several tiles. The soft tiling can be presented with spatially varying tile membership masks. In the experiments we have normalised the memberships of each image pixel to sum to one. Figure 1 shows 2×2 and 4×4 tiling patterns and some of the corresponding membership masks for spatially soft tiling. The dark areas correspond to large membership degrees.

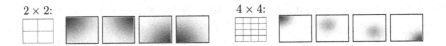

2 × 2:   4 × 4:

Fig. 1. 2×2 and 4×4 hard tiling masks and some of the corresponding membership masks for spatially soft tiling

3.2   Image Tile Matching

When the image area has been partitioned with a tiling mask into N tiles, one obtains several histograms $H_{i1}, H_{i2}, \ldots, H_{iN}$ for each image i. One has to the decide, how to define the similarity of or distance between two images i and j in terms of the histograms. A traditional approach is to first compare histograms of spatially corresponding tiles and then sum the distances over all the tiles:

$$d_{\mathrm{R}}(i, j) = \sum_{n=1}^{N} d_{\chi^2}(H_{in}, H_{jn}). \tag{2}$$

The χ^2 distance d_{χ^2} between M-dimensional vectors $\mathbf{x}$ and $\mathbf{x}'$ is given by

$$d_{\chi^2}(\mathbf{x}, \mathbf{x}') = \sum_{m=1}^{M} \frac{(x_m - x'_m)^2}{x_m + x'_m}. \tag{3}$$

We denote this matching scheme as *rigid* matching of regions as each tile of image i has only one possible corresponding tile—the tile in exactly the same geometric location.

Another alternative that we consider is a region matching scheme that is adapted from Integrated Region Matching (IRM) [3]. Originally the regions for IRM were result of an unsupervised segmentation step, but in this paper we use the geometrically determined image tiles instead. Whereas the rigid region matching is one extreme in terms of rigidity constraint, the IRM scheme represents the other extreme where no geometric constraints are imposed to regulate which tiles can correspond to each other, as long as each tile in image i corresponds to exactly one tile in image j. In the IRM scheme, the distance between the images i and j is given by

$$d_{\text{IRM}}(i,j) = \min_{\mathbf{S}} \sum_{k=1}^{N} \sum_{l=1}^{N} s_{kl} d_{\chi^2}(H_{ik}, H_{jl}) \tag{4}$$

where the matrix $\mathbf{S} = \{s_{kl}\}$ describes the correspondence of regions of the images. The matrix is subject to constraints

$$s_{kl} \geq 0 \ \forall k,l \qquad \sum_{k=1}^{N} s_{kl} \leq w_{jl} \ \forall l \qquad \sum_{l=1}^{N} s_{kl} \leq w_{ik} \ \forall k \tag{5}$$

with w_{ik} being the weight or importance of the k:th tile in the image i. Here we set all $w_{ik} = 1$, so that the constraints translates precisely to requiring that each tile in image i corresponds to exactly one tile in image j.

Evaluating d_{IRM} between a pair of images requires one to find the optimal $\mathbf{S}$ for that pair. In [3], a heuristic greedy algorithm called "most similar highest priority" (MSHP) is proposed for approximately searching the optimal alignment. In that algorithm, one continuously looks for the best-matching pairs of regions. Those regions are then marked as corresponding and the involved regions are no longer considered as candidates to match any other region. An alternative to this greedy algorithm is the exact solution of the problem, which actually is a transportation problem. Rather efficient algorithms exist for finding the solution. In the experiments of this paper we consider the algorithm described in [11], implemented by the authors of [12] for evaluating earth mover's distances (EMD).

In addition to rigid and IRM matching schemes, we consider also combining the two schemes. Our first combination method alternative is forming a linear combination of the distances:

$$d_{\text{C}}(i,j) = \lambda \frac{d_{\text{R}}(i,j)}{\bar{d}_{\text{R}}} + (1 - \lambda) \frac{d_{\text{IRM}}(i,j)}{\bar{d}_{\text{IRM}}}. \tag{6}$$

Here $\bar{d}_{\text{R}}$ and $\bar{d}_{\text{IRM}}$ are empirical average values of the distance measures. In the second alternative we first perform image analysis separately on basis of both rigid and IRM matching. Then we combine the results using Bayesian Logistic Regression (BBR) [13].

4   Experimental Task and Procedures

In the experiments we consider the supervised image category detection problem. Specifically, we measure the performance of several algorithmic variants for the task using images and categories defined in the PASCAL NoE Visual Object Classes (VOC) Challenge 2007 collection [14]. In the collection there are altogether 9963 photographic images of natural scenes. In the experiments we use the half of them (5011 images) denoted "trainval" by the challenge organisers. Each of the images contains at least one occurrence of the predefined 20 object classes, including e.g. several types of vehicles, animals and furniture.

In the experiments the 5011 images are partitioned approximately equally into training and test sets. Every experiment is performed separately for each of the 20 object classes. The category detection accuracy is measured in terms of non-interpolated average precision (AP). The AP values were averaged over the 20 object classes resulting in mean average precision (MAP) values. To obtain more reliable results, the MAP values are further averaged over six different train/test partitionings. The average MAP values tabulated in the result tables have 95% confidence intervals of order 0.01 in all the experiments.

5   Experiments and Results

5.1   Comparison of Region Matching Schemes

In our first set of experiments, we compare the effectiveness of rigid and IRM region matching schemes in our category detection tasks. The experiments are repeated for a number of different individual tiling masks. Figure 2 shows the results of the comparison. The rightmost set of bars in the images corresponds to the fusion of tiling masks, where the category detection is performed first separately on basis of each tiling mask and then the results are fused using the BBR fusion technique.

We can make several observations from the figures. First of all, on average the rigid matching scheme (white bars) works slightly better than exactly optimised IRM matching (grey bars). The MSHP algorithm for calculating IRM distances produces clearly inferior performance. This is somewhat surprising, as the correlation between the two distance measures is empirically observed to be almost perfect and the distance values differ only by a few percents on average. Possibly the numerically small errors that the greedy MSHP approach makes in the relative ordering of similar images are of large importance when detecting image categories.

By comparing the subfigures 2a and 2b we notice that the individual soft tilings generally give better performance than corresponding hard tilings. We notice that the performance of individual hard tilings starts to degrade as the tiling mask becomes finer. With soft tilings, this is not so strongly the case, but the performance first improves and then saturates. The fusion of different tilings is essential for good performance in case of hard tilings. The mask fusion still helps somewhat in the soft tiling case, but is not that essential. Similar kinds

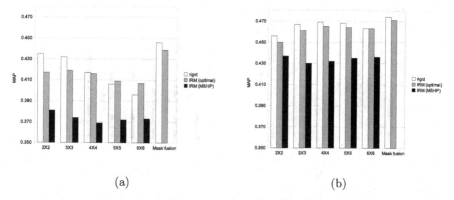

(a)   (b)

Fig. 2. Performance comparison of region matching schemes when either (a) hard, or (b) soft assignment of interest points to tiles is employed

of observations were made in [10] for the rigid matching scheme and now we can confirm that they hold also for IRM matching. Altogether, the soft tiling technique seems to be compatible with IRM matching.

5.2   Combining Region Matching Schemes

Figure 3 shows the result of combining the rigid and IRM region matching schemes with the linear combination and BBR techniques. We see that combining the region matching schemes results in somewhat better performance than either the rigid or IRM matching alone. We notice that in case of soft tilings, fusion of tilings is no longer better than the best individual tilings (5×5 and 6×6). For these results, we have set the parameter λ in Eq. 6 to value 0.5. A fixed value for all cases is naturally somewhat suboptimal, but this value seems to be a rather safe choice, as was observed in an experiment where we scanned a range of values for λ (results not shown here due to lack of space).

5.3   Class-Wise Results

Class-wise breakdown of the category detection results might be interesting as it seems plausible to think that different image categories could be different in the respect how rigid their spatial structure is. Identifying such differences might give insight to the role of region matching in visual category detection. In the results of our experiments, there indeed seems to be a category ("bus"), for which IRM matching tends to work quite much better than the rigid matching. Also a few other classes show similar tendency, although less strongly.

However, the statistical fluctuations between the six sets of trials are strong. It is therefore challenging to obtain reliable object class specific results. In the MAP values some of the variation tends to average out. In order to be able to identify systematic class-specific patterns, we try to maximise the number of trials whose outcomes can be considered as i.i.d. random variables. To this

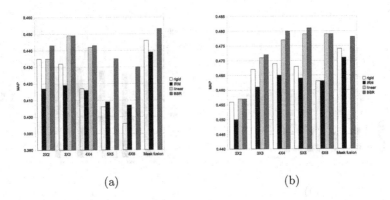

(a)   (b)

Fig. 3. Comparing the performance of rigid and IRM matching (white and black bars) to the fusion of the matching techniques in the case of either hard (a) or soft (b) spatial tiling

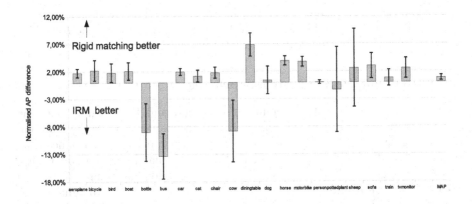

Fig. 4. Category-wise comparison of rigid and IRM region matching when soft spatial tile assignment is employed

end, we combine together the results obtained by the four different rectangular tiling masks. Combined with the six partitionings of the data, this results in 24 different experimental conditions. For each condition, we perform the experiment using both rigid and IRM region matching and subtract the AP results. We assume the AP differences come from the same normal distribution. Repeating this analysis for each class, we can assess whether the mean of the distribution deviates significantly from zero, and to which direction, i.e. whether rigid region matching is significantly better than IRM or vice versa.

Figure 4 shows the results of the category-wise analysis for the case of spatially soft tiling. For hard tiling, the results are very similar. In the figures, the thick bars represent average performances across all the rectangular tiling patterns. The error bars indicate 95% confidence intervals. The relative AP differences have been normalised to the performance level of 2 × 2 hard tiling employing rigid region matching. The analysis is indeed able to confirm the existence of systematic differences between image categories. For a couple of image categories ("bottle","bus" and "cow") IRM matching consistently works significantly better than rigid matching. There is a larger number of image categories for which rigid matching works consistently better, but the differences between the matching methods are smaller for those categories. The rightmost bar (MAP) in the figures confirms the impression that on average, rigid region matching may work slightly better than IRM matching, but the difference is not practically significant.

6   Conclusions

In this paper, we have described two different region matching schemes to be used in a BoV image category detection system: traditionally employed rigid region matching and an alternative scheme based on Integrated Region Matching (IRM). We also discussed implementation details related to IRM.

In the experiments, the rigid and IRM region matching schemes showed only insignificant performance difference on average. However, for many image categories, rigid matching works somewhat better. This is balanced by the observation that for a smaller set of image categories, IRM matching produces notably better detection accuracy. We obtain our best results by combining the rigid and IRM region matching schemes. We could not observe significant difference between the two investigated fusion methods: linear combination of image distances and late fusion by BBR. When evaluating the IRM distance, the MSHP heuristic proposed earlier [3] is not accurate enough for image category detection. Instead, the distances have to be evaluated exactly. This is despite the fact that the heuristic distances differ only slightly from the true distances on average.

Spatially soft tiling seems to be compatible with IRM matching as well as rigid region matching. We observe our best performance when tiling is performed by the 5×5 soft tiling mask, and rigid and IRM region matching are combined. In particular, accuracy is not improved over this single-mask result by multimask fusion. This is somewhat different from [10], where multi-mask fusion was observed to be slightly advantageous when rigid matching was used. In the case of hard spatial masks, multi-mask fusion is more important, both here and in the experiments of [10].

The investigated region matching schemes represent two extremes in terms of geometrical rigidity required from the matched images. It is somewhat surprising that the rigid region matching scheme works as well as it does. Certainly the image categories of the current experiments are invariant to some geometric image transforms. One explanation could be that in our experiments there are enough training images so that it is effectively possible to enumerate all the possible geometric configurations in the training material. If this was the case, one would expect IRM matching to perform relatively better as the number of training images is decreased. However, this seemed not to be the case when we performed such preliminary experiments. Apparently the complete geometric invariance of IRM is thus excessive. One would probably benefit from a region matching scheme that allows for some more transformations than the rigid matching, but would still not completely abandon rigidness as IRM matching does. Designing such a matching scheme is a possible direction for future research.

References

1. Sivic, J., Zisserman, A.: Video Google: A text retrieval approach to object matching in videos. In: Proc. of ICCV 2003, vol. 2, pp. 1470–1477 (October 2003)
2. Zhang, J., Marszałek, M., Lazebnik, S., Schmid, C.: Local features and kernels for classification of texture and object categories: a comprehensive study. International Journal of Computer Vision 73(2), 213–238 (2007)
3. Wang, J.Z., Liu, J., Wiederhold, G.: SIMPLIcity: Semantics-sensitive integrated matching for picture libraries. IEEE Transactions on Pattern Analysis and Machine Intelligence 23(9), 947–963 (2001)
4. Lowe, D.G.: Distinctive image features from scale-invariant keypoints. International Journal of Computer Vision 60(2), 91–110 (2004)
5. Mikolajcyk, K., Schmid, C.: Scale and affine point invariant interest point detectors. International Journal of Computer Vision 60(1), 68–86 (2004)
6. Viitaniemi, V., Laaksonen, J.: Experiments on selection of codebooks for local image feature histograms. In: Sebillo, M., Vitiello, G., Schaefer, G. (eds.) VISUAL 2008. LNCS, vol. 5188, pp. 126–137. Springer, Heidelberg (2008)
7. van Gemert, J.C., Veenman, C.J., Smeulders, A.W.M., Geusebroek, J.M.: Visual word ambiguity. IEEE Transactions on Pattern Analysis and Machine Intelligence (2010)
8. Chang, C.-C., Lin, C.-J.: LIBSVM: a library for support vector machines (2001), Software available at http://www.csie.ntu.edu.tw/~cjlin/libsvm
9. Viitaniemi, V., Laaksonen, J.: Improving the accuracy of global feature fusion based image categorisation. In: Falcidieno, B., Spagnuolo, M., Avrithis, Y., Kompatsiaris, I., Buitelaar, P. (eds.) SAMT 2007. LNCS, vol. 4816, pp. 1–14. Springer, Heidelberg (2007)
10. Viitaniemi, V., Laaksonen, J.: Spatial extensions to bag of visual words. In: Proceedings of ACM International Conference on Image and Video Retrieval (CIVR 2009), Fira, Greece (July 2009)
11. Hillier, F.S., Lieberman, G.J.: Introduction to Mathematical Programming. McGraw-Hill, New York (1990)
12. Rubner, Y., Tomasi, C., Guibas, L.J.: A metric for distributions with applications to image databases. In: Proc. of IEEE International Conference on Computer Vision, India, pp. 59–66 (January 1998), Code available on-line at http://www.cs.duke.edu/~tomasi/emd.htm
13. Genkin, A., Lewis, D.D., Madigan, D.: BBR: Bayesian logistic regression software (2005), Software available at http://www.stat.rutgers.edu/~madigan/BBR/
14. Everingham, M., Van Gool, L., Williams, C.K.I., Winn, J., Zisserman, A.: The PASCAL Visual Object Classes Challenge 2007 (VOC 2007) Results (2007), http://www.pascal-network.org/challenges/VOC/voc2007/workshop/index.html

Application of K-Means and MLP in the Automation of Matching of 2DE Gel Images

Dalius Matuzevičius, Artūras Serackis, and Dalius Navakauskas

Vilnius Gediminas Technical University,
Department of Electronic Systems,
Naugarduko st. 41, Vilnius, LT-03227, Lithuania

Abstract. Critical information that is related to vital processes of the cell can be revealed comparing several two-dimensional electrophoresis (2DE) gel images. Through up to 10 000 protein spots may appear in inevitably noisy gel thus 2DE gel image comparison and analysis protocols usually involve the work of experts. In this paper we demonstrate how the problem of automation of 2DE gel image matching can be gradually solved by the use of artificial neural networks. We report on the development of feature set, built from various distance measures, selected and grounded by the application of self-organizing feature map and confirmed by expert decisions. We suggest and experimentally confirm the use of k-means clustering for the pre-classification of 2DE gel image into segments of interest that about twice speed-up the comparison procedure. We develop original Multilayer Perceptron based classifier for 2DE gel image matching that employs the selected feature set. By experimentation with the synthetic, semi-synthetic and natural 2DE images we show its superiority against the single distance metric based classifiers.

1 Introduction

The discovery of clinical biomarkers, identification of prognostic and diagnostic markers makes possible to understand the human disease and its treatment better. The two-dimensional electrophoresis (2DE) is the tool for achieving this for the modifications that cannot be predicted by the analysis of genome sequences [5,7]. Through up to 10 000 protein spots may appear in the gel, the comparison of two 2DE gels is very complicated and time consuming. To speed up this process, the automatic pre-analysis of 2DE gel images needs to be implemented. Comparison of 2DE gels reveals the critical information about differences in protein samples, related to the vital processes of the cell [1]. In order to find differences, correct matches of protein spots between the examined 2DE gel pairs needs to be found, i.e., gels must be aligned. Existing gel image registration methods are feature (landmark) based, image intensity based, or hybrid [12].

Feature based image registration methods [6] are of low computational cost and of high distinctiveness. They operate on features that are extracted from protein spots: spot positions, intensities, areas, appearance. To this group belong the following methods: point pattern matching, point matching based on

K. Diamantaras, W. Duch, L.S. Iliadis (Eds.): ICANN 2010, Part I, LNCS 6352, pp. 541–550, 2010.

graphs [4], spot position descriptors, Delaunay triangulation [9]. The main disadvantage of feature based image registration methods is the fact that protein spots must be detected before their matching procedure. Comparison of several 2DE gel images highly depends on the spot extraction results so failing in a first stage brings feature matching problems. 2DE gel images without process noise can be pre-processed without problems however most gels are produced according to 2DE protocols that are fine-tuned for ongoing specific experiment. Thus during the pilot experiments formed 2DE gel images are far from the ideal and all methods presented in publications and commercially available software fail or do not present satisfactory results. The process noise manifests as: highly merged protein spots (separation problems) [10]; varying background, streaks, leftovers, saturated spots (sample preparation protocol variations); oversaturated spots (silver staining of highly abundant proteins) [11].

Intensity based image registration methods exploit computational power of modern computers. They are based on the maximization of similarity or minimization of the distance between regions of images [8]. Usually correlation coefficient-based [8,13] or mutual information-based [8] registration methods are used. Image intensity based registration methods do not require feature extraction so they do not inherit false feature extraction errors. However image intensity based registration methods are not satisfactory robust against geometric and large intensity distortions usually present in 2DE gels. Other disadvantages of them are: computational complexity, low distinctiveness and low capture range.

Hybrid image registration approaches exploit both intensity and feature information, thus the erroneous feature extraction still influences performance of 2DE gel image alignment. One possible solution is to develop based on image intensities distance measure that is sensitive to the characteristic protein spot patterns. So, in Sect. 2 we present tests of distance measures and select the promising ones. In order to speed-up a pair-wise comparison in Sect. 3 we suggest and experimentally confirm the use of k-means clustering for 2DE gel image segments pre-classification. Section 4 presents the development of Multilayer Perceptron based detector, that unifies all our propositions and by pair-wise determination of 2DE gel image segments correspondence allows alignment of gel images under registration.

2   Development of Feature Set

Various metrics are used to compare 2DE gels. In the following we: outline the selected for evaluation distance measures, present the development of gel image sets, and report on evaluation of distance measures by SOM and by experts.

2.1   Selected Distance Measures for Initial Evaluation

Distance between image samples x and y is denoted by $d(x, y)$. In general, distance on N is a function $d : N \times N \to \mathbb{R}$, where N is a set, and for any $x, y \in N$ holds: $d(x, y) \geqq 0$; $d(x, y) = d(y, x)$; $d(x, x) = 0$. We aim to determine how well each distance measure represents the dissimilarity of two 2DE gel images.

Table 1. Distance measures selected for comparison

Distance measure	$d(x,y)$	Alternatives	
Squared Euclidean	$\sum_i (x_i - y_i)^2$	–	(1)
Cosine	$1 - \dfrac{\sum_i x_i y_i}{\sqrt{\sum_i x_i x_i} \cdot \sqrt{\sum_i y_i y_i}}$	–	(2)
Pearson correlation	$1 - \dfrac{\sum_i (x_i - \bar{x})(y_i - \bar{y})}{\sqrt{(\sum_i (x_i - \bar{x})^2)(\sum_i (y_i - \bar{y})^2)}}$	–	(3)
Spearman's rank correlation	$\dfrac{6 \cdot \sum_{i=1}^{n} (\text{rank}(x_i) - \text{rank}(y_i))^2}{n(n^2 - 1)}$	–	(4)
Chebyshev	$\max_i |x_i - y_i|$	–	(5)
Histogram intersection	$1 - \sum_i \min(p_i(x), p_i(y))$	$1 - \sum_i \min(\hat{x}_i, \hat{y}_i)$	(6a,b)
Jeffrey divergence	$\sum_i p_i(x) \ln \dfrac{2 \cdot p_i(x)}{p_i(x) + p_i(y)} +$ $\sum_i p_i(y) \ln \dfrac{2 \cdot p_i(y)}{p_i(x) + p_i(y)}$	$\sum_i \hat{x}_i \ln \dfrac{2 \cdot \hat{x}_i}{\hat{x}_i + \hat{y}_i} +$ $\sum_i \hat{y}_i \ln \dfrac{2 \cdot \hat{y}_i}{\hat{x}_i + \hat{y}_i}$	(7a,b)
Bhattacharyya (Hellinger)	$\sqrt{1 - \sum_i \sqrt{p_i(x) p_i(y)}}$	$\sqrt{1 - \sum_i \sqrt{\hat{x}_i \hat{y}_i}}$	(8a,b)
χ^2	$\sum_i \dfrac{(p_i(x) - p_i(y))^2}{2 \cdot (p_i(x) + p_i(y))}$	$\sum_i \dfrac{(\hat{x}_i - \hat{y}_i)^2}{2 \cdot (\hat{x}_i + \hat{y}_i)}$	(9a,b)
Normalized mutual information	$\dfrac{1}{2}\left(1 - \dfrac{H(x) + H(y)}{H(x,y)}\right)$	–	(10)

Here: rank($\cdot$) – position of the data after sorting in ascending order;
  $p(x), p(y)$ – probability density functions of discrete random variables x and y;
  $\sum_i p_i(x) = 1$; $\sum_i p_i(y) = 1$; $\sum_i \hat{x}_i = 1$; $\sum_i \hat{y}_i = 1$; $\bar{x} = \frac{1}{n}\sum_i x_i$; $\bar{y} = \frac{1}{n}\sum_i y_i$;
  $H(x), H(y)$ – marginal entropies; $H(x,y)$ – joint entropy;
  $H(\cdot) = -\sum_i p_i(\cdot) \ln p_i(\cdot)$; $H(x,y) = -\sum_i \sum_j p_{ij}(x,y) \ln p_{ij}(x,y)$.

Distance measures selected for the comparison are summarized in Table 1. Distances in (1)–(5) and their alternatives in (6b–9b) are computed directly on 2DE gel image pixels so they concern spatial properties of image structure. Distances in (6a–9a) and (10) are information-theoretic measures computed on probabilistic distributions.

2.2   Creation of Image Sets for Evaluation

Distance measure must respond to features that are specific for images under registration so it could facilitate comparison accuracy. If a set of images that are sorted by their monotonically changing true similarity could be available, then measured dissimilarity should increase when the first image is compared with all the subsequent ones. However it is impossible to sort natural 2DE gel images as similarity measure tools do not exist. Thus synthetic and semi-synthetic sorted image sets that represent the essential 2DE gel image features were developed.

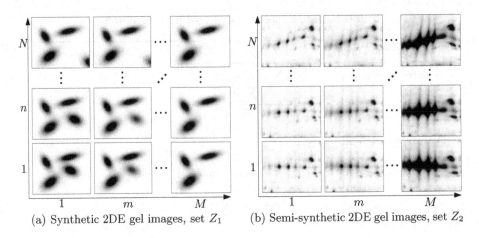

(a) Synthetic 2DE gel images, set Z_1 (b) Semi-synthetic 2DE gel images, set Z_2

Fig. 1. Illustrations of created image sets

Synthetic image set Z_1. Parametric 2D Gaussian model was used to generate synthetic protein spot patterns. This model is fully capable to represent regular protein spots. 2D Gaussian function to model one protein spot is given by:

$$z(n,m) = A(m) \cdot \exp\left(-\frac{i_R^2(n)}{2\sigma_i^2}\right) \cdot \exp\left(-\frac{j_R^2(n)}{2\sigma_j^2}\right) , \qquad (11)$$

here $i_R(n) = \cos(\alpha)(i - i_0(n)) + \sin(\alpha)(j - j_0(n))$; $j_R(n) = -\sin(\alpha)(i - i_0(n)) + \cos(\alpha)(j - j_0(n))$; α – rotation angle in radians; (i_0, j_0) – centre of the function; A – height of the peak; σ_i, σ_j – widths in vertical and horizontal directions.

An image set Z_1 of size $N \times M = 25 \times 25$ was produced by monotonically changing a pair of parameters $\{n, m\}$ that define the particular synthetic image. These are the parameters of the Gaussian function: centre coordinates $(i_0(n), j_0(n))$ and amplitude $A(m)$. Other parameters of the Gaussian function are constant for the same image set but differ between the sets. Thus, synthetic 2DE gel images differ in position and size of one spot. At the same time, few synthetic spots are added in all images (for illustration see Fig. 1(a)).

Semi-synthetic image set Z_2. Spatial and geometrical variations from natural 2DE gel images were used to generate semi-synthetic images. Having corresponding image areas x and y from different 2DE gels, we generated intermediate images by *morphing* from one image to another. Morphing consists of warping and cross-fading procedures. Manipulating these processes independently, i.e., gradually changing warping parameters and generating linear combinations of original images, we generated a set Z_2 of similar to Z_1 size (cf. Fig. 1(b)).

Having two of the same size sample images x and y' (y' being a variant of y registered on x) collected from original registered 2DE gel images, *cross-fading* is achieved through linear combination of those images:

$$Z(1,m) = x\frac{M-m}{M-1} + y'\frac{m-1}{M-1} . \qquad (12)$$

Here M – preferred number of images, counting original and generated images ($M = 25$); $m = \{1 : M\}$ – image cross-fading index; $Z(1,1) = x$; $Z(1,M) = y'$.

Geometrical distortions are modelled by extracting match vectors (mapping image $f : y \rightarrow y'$) from images x and y. Each cross-faded image $Z(1,m)$ is monotonically *warped* onto image $Z(N,M) = y$ in equal 25 steps ($n = \{2 : N\}$ – image warping index), by *thin-plate spline* transformation:

$$f(n,m) = a_1(n) + a_i(n)i + a_j(n)j + \sum_{p=1}^{k} w_p(n)U\left(\parallel (i_p, j_p) - (i,j) \parallel\right) . \quad (13)$$

2.3 Evaluation of Distance Measures

Let us recall that the purpose of the following tests is to select a group of distance measures that must represent similarity of 2DE gel images under the registration. For a comparison and selection of distance measures seven independent tests were performed and their ranked results are summarized in Table 2. By rank equal to 1 we indicate the best result in a group (row of table), higher rank values indicate worse results (rank equal to 14 beeing the worst result).

During the comparison of distance measures three factors were taken under the consideration: a) time needed to compute value of particular distance measure (1st row of Table 2); b) results of Self-Organizing feature Map (SOM) classifiers (2–6 rows); c) results of classification by experts (7th row). In order to have more general view of SOM applicability, we performed five tests utilising one, two, or three distance measures (indicated by 1DM, 2DM, or 3DM, correspondingly) calculated on synthetic, semi-synthetic or both image data sets (indicated by Z_1, Z_2, or Z_*, correspondingly).

Input for SOM classifiers consisted of the selected type(-s) of distance(-s) between image $Z(1,1)$ and the rest images, i.e., $d(Z(1,1), Z(n,m))$, where $n = \{1 : N\}$, $m = \{1 : M\}$. All SOMs were tested for the task of classification into 3 classes. As distances $d(Z(1,1), Z(1,1))$ (self similarity) and $d(Z(1,1), Z(\{1 : N\}, M))$ are the largest ones, preferred classification of SOM into three classes should be such that images appearing near $Z(1,1)$ in the set were assigned to the

Table 2. Raking of 2DE gel image sets pairwise comparison results

Comparison way	Distance measure, $d(x,y)$													
---	(1)	(2)	**(3)**	(4)	(5)	(6a)	**(6b)**	(7a)	(7b)	(8a)	(8b)	(9a)	**(9b)**	(10)
Processing time	4	6	**7**	14	1	11	**3**	10	8	12	5	9	**2**	13
SOM/1DM/Z_1	8	6	**1**	5	3	13	**2**	11	9	10	13	14	**4**	7
SOM/1DM/Z_2	7	6	**1**	4	2	10	**3**	12	9	11	14	13	**5**	8
SOM/1DM/Z_*	8	7	**1**	5	2	13	**3**	10	6	11	12	14	**4**	9
SOM/2DM/Z_*	8	7	**1**	5	2	13	**3**	10	6	11	12	14	**4**	9
SOM/3DM/Z_*	6	2	**1**	4	3	9	**5**	12	8	13	14	11	**7**	10
Expert/1DM/Z_N	8	2	**1**	4	9	10	**3**	13	6	14	11	12	**5**	7

same class, images near $Z(N, M)$ were assigned to the other marginal class and the middle part of data set appeared in the third class. During the tests we were seeking for classifications that are topologically similar to the preferred. The number of correct classifications of given image sets using each one of distance measures were counted and represented as ranks in 2–6 rows of Table 2.

For expert classification dataset Z_N was collected taking parts of natural 2DE gel images that should be registered. Image samples were taken at expert-defined control point positions. Control points (landmarks) show positions of corresponding areas of 2DE gel images with the same proteins. During the test we calculated the number of times the use of distance measure allows correct matching in a Z_N set and represented as ranks in 7 row of Table 2.

After assessing all tests results, a group of three distance measures (in Table 2 marked in bold): Pearson correlation distance (3), Histogram intersection computed on normalized image pixel values (6b), and χ^2-distance on normalized pixel values (9b), were selected for the further development. Spearman's rank correlation (4) and Chebyshev (5) distance measures produced competitive results, however were not selected either because of the slow speed or the lack of relevance to what a human expert would use.

3   Automation of Selection of Segments of Interest

Nevertheless that 2DE gels possibly may have thousands of protein spots, not all image area needs (in cases of artifacts even is prohibited) to be used for matching. In the following we propose k-means clustering for the initial pre-classification of 2DE gel image into segments of interest and report on evaluation of pre-classification results.

3.1   k-means Clustering for Pre-Classification of Image Segments

The parametric k-means clustering is selected for the classification of 2DE gel images. The algorithm partitions image samples into two subsets C_1 and C_2 (the first defining segments of interest) by minimising the sum-of-squares of the distance between feature vector, representing image segment, and geometric centroid of the data points in the feature subset.

Feature vectors for pre-classification are calculated based on rectangular non-intersecting segments taken on a regular basis from natural 2DE gel image. In total six features are taken into account: mean intensity, intensity median, intensity variance, intensity standard deviation, skewness (the asymmetry measure) and Kurtosis (the peakedness of pixel intensity distribution). All statistical estimates are computed along protein molecular mass (MM) axis.

3.2   Evaluation of Pre-classification Results

The use of feature vectors for pre-classification prevents image segments with noise peaks passing into subset C_1. Such drawback has classification methods that analyse the pixel intensity range in each segment (compare images in Fig. 2).

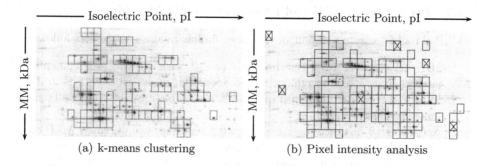

(a) k-means clustering   (b) Pixel intensity analysis

Fig. 2. Illustration of pre-classification results using different algorithms. Selected segments are enclosed in boxes; noisy segments are additionally crossed.

To ascertain the suitability of pre-classified samples for 2DE gel image matching an experimental investigation is performed on a natural 2DE gel images. Three distance measures (1),(3) and (5) are selected for the experiment (see Table 1). Each distance measure gives one or several extremum points during image sample matching. The global minima in distance measure means the highest match in the search space. For the same image sample the position of global minima may vary for the different distance measures. The standard deviation of all highest match points for each image sample are calculated along isoelectric point and along molecular mass axes. For the optimal image matching, the standard deviation for each sample should vanish to zero. Total of 1025 image samples from C_1 and C_2 subsets were analysed. Using three selected measures, the mean standard deviation of the highest match points for the C_1 subset is equal to 4.01 along isoelectric point axis and 4.36 along molecular mass axis. For the subset C_2 the mean value of standard deviation is equal to 8.49 and 12.45, respectively. The mismatch for subset C_1 is 2–3 times less than for subset C_2.

To evaluate the influence of additional measures, used for image sample matching, three additional distance measures: (6a), (8a), (10), were added to the experiment. The mean standard deviation of highest match points for the subset C_1 using six distance metrics increases to 8.78 along isoelectric point axis and 13.44 along molecular mass axis. For the subset C_2 the mean value of standard deviation increases to 11.16 and 16.17, respectively. These experiments shows, that pre-classification of image samples increases the accuracy of image matching, which also depends on the number of distance measures used.

4   Automatic Matching of 2DE Gel Images

2DE gel images under registration needs to be aligned by the use of landmarks. In the following we: outline automatic matching procedure, that uses Multilayer Perceptron (MLP) for a landmark detection; present the development of MLP detector; by experimentation with synthetic, semi-synthetic and natural 2DE images show its superiority against the single distance metric based classifiers.

4.1   Procedure of 2DE Gel Image Automatic Matching

MLP classifier selects one pair of the most similar image segments as follow:

1. 2DE gel segment from one image is paired with all selected segments of interest in a second image (extracted according to description in Sect. 3).
2. In Sect. 2 grounded three distance measures are computed between all paired image segments.
3. According to distance measures, segment pairs are compared by MLP classifier and one pair is selected as containing the most similar images.
4. Selected segment pair is marked as corresponding regions in two gel images and is used as control point for 2DE gel image registration.

4.2   Development of MLP Based Classifier

Structure of MLP was constrained by the available dataset. Supervised learning requires target vectors, and it was possible to provide only information about relative distances between image pairs – not absolute values $d(x, y_1)$ and $d(x, y_2)$ but which one of them is smaller. Distances $d(x, y_1)$ and $d(x, y_2)$ are presented to MLP as inputs. If the first distance is smaller (x segment is more similar to y_1 than to y_2), then MLP output value should be "1" (value "-1" – otherwise).

All MLP training samples were collected from three sources – synthetic, semi-synthetic and natural image sets (Z_1, Z_2, Z_N, correspondingly). Such combination of samples allows to cover a wider range of variations in gel images. Training samples from Z_N set were composed according to matched regions by an expert.

Let us by x_m and y_m denote image regions ($m = 1, \ldots, M$) by the expert taken from two natural 2DE gel images X and Y and marked as corresponding. Then $d(x_m, y_m)$ are distances between corresponding image areas. Distances between all mismatching areas $x_m \neq y_i$ we denote by $d(x_m, y_i)$, here $i = 1, \ldots, i_{\max}$ and $i_{\max}$ is a number of all image Y areas selected using procedure proposed in Sect. 3. Similarly, distances between all mismatching areas $y_m \neq x_j$ we denote by $d(y_m, x_j)$, here $j = 1, \ldots, j_{\max}$ and $j_{\max}$ is a number of all image X areas selected using proposed procedure.

MLP training set is composed as follows: a) for all training samples $S_{mi1} = \{d(x_m, y_m), d(x_m, y_i)\}$ and $S_{mi3} = \{d(y_m, x_m), d(y_m, x_i)\}$ target value $T_{mi1} = 1$ is assigned; b) for all training samples $S_{mi2} = \{d(x_m, y_i), d(x_m, y_m)\}$ and $S_{mi4} = \{d(y_m, x_i), d(y_m, x_m)\}$ target value $T_{mi2} = -1$ is assigned.

Considered four core structures of MLP are presented in Fig. 3. Blocks in diagrams denote the layers of neurons. Layer I represents triplet of inputs where features from each pair of segments under comparison are fed. H_1, H_2, H_3 represent hidden layers of selectable $\{5; 10; 15; 20; 30; 40\}$ size. O represent a single output, where the final decision about similarity is computed. Transfer functions of neurons in H_1 layer are Log-Sigmoid (LS), in H_3 layer are Tan-Sigmoid (TS), while in H_2 layer they can be Log-Sigmoid or Tan-Sigmoid. MLP-A–MLP-C type structures are partitioned into two parallel, symmetrical and same size branches of layers, while MLP-D type – reasambles traditional MLP structure.

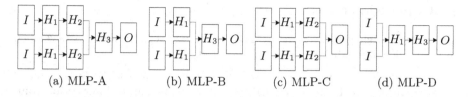

(a) MLP-A   (b) MLP-B   (c) MLP-C   (d) MLP-D

Fig. 3. Generalized pictorial representation of considered core MLP structures

All possible specific MLP structures were tested on 57 380 images randomly partitioned for training (60 %), validation (20 %) and testing (20 %) purposes. Each MLP was initialized using Nguyen-Widrow rule and trained by Levenberg-Marquard algorithm. Used training parameters: maximum number of epochs – 100; performance goal – 0; maximum validation failures – 5; minimum performance gradient – 10^{-10}; $\mu_{init} = 0.001$; $\mu_{dec} = 0.1$; $\mu_{inc} = 10$; $\mu_{max} = 10^{10}$. Best MLPs from each group were selected: MLP-A – 3-5(LS)-5(TS)-30(TS)-1; MLP-B – 3-40(LS)-15(TS)-1; MLP-C – 3-30(LS)-5(TS)-1; MLP-D – 3-30(LS)-10(TS)-1. They were used in the follwing natural 2DE gel image matching experiments.

4.3   Results of Automatic Matching of Natural 2DE Gel Images

Testing 2DE image sets for matching experiments were collected in the same way as during the collection of training set from the natural images. There were used images from three biochemical experimental groups where proteins from the specific cells were analysed: HL-60 cells, Human heart conduction system cells and Mesenchymal stem cells. From the first group of images testing set of 186,992 image samples was generated; from the second – 76,722 image samples; and from the third – 101,007 image samples.

Summarized results of the use of single distance measure classifiers and previously found the best MLPs from each four core structures are presented in Table 3. Results are shown in percentage of successful similarity comparisons from each test group. The best achieved results outlined in bold font. Comparative testing results show that MLP structures with separated symmetric input layers have advantages at similarity comparison of image regions. These structures firstly allow to make a separated fusion of distance measures of image pairs and decision about most similar pair is made in the terminal part of the network.

Table 3. Percentages of succesful natural 2DE gel image similarity comparisons

Origin of 2DE gel sets	Single feature classifier			Multilayer Perceptron			
	(3)	(6b)	(9b)	A	B	C	D
HL-60 cells	99.965	99.985	99.987	99.983	**99.990**	99.961	99.973
Human heart cells	98.915	99.014	98.811	99.363	**99.589**	99.159	99.253
Mesenchymal stem cells	99.919	99.864	99.868	99.959	**99.974**	99.930	99.954

5 Conclusions

Automatic matching procedure for 2DE gel image registration was developed
and the following main outcomes can be listed:

1. From considered and investigated 14 distance measures, the feature set of
   three measures: Pearson correlation distance, Histogram intersection computed on normalized image pixel values, and χ^2-distance on normalized pixel
   values, was shown representing well similarities in 2DE gel images.
2. k-means clustering for pre-classification of 2DE gel image into segments of
   interest that about twice speed-up the comparison procedure was proposed.
3. Multilayer Perceptron detector for 2DE gel image registration was proposed,
   and with the found the best structure outperformed sigle distance measure
   based classifiers in the test with three natural 2DE gel image sets.

References

1. Daszykowski, M., Stanimirova, I., Bodzon-Kulakowska, A., Silberring, J., Lubec,
   G., Walczak, B.: Start-To-End Processing of Two-Dimensional Gel Electrophoretic
   Images. Journal of Chromatography A. Data Analysis in Chromatography 1-
   2(1158), 306–317 (2007)
2. Fung, G.: A Comprehensive Overview of Basic Clustering algorithms. Technical
   Report, University of Winsconsin, Madison (2001)
3. Kohonen, T.: Self-organized formation of topologically correct feature maps. Biological Cybernetics 43, 53–69 (1982)
4. Lin, D.-T.: Autonomous sub-image matching for two-dimensional electrophoresis gels using MaxRST algorithm. Image Vis. Comput. (2010),
   doi:10.1016/j.imavis.2010.01.004
5. Lopez, J., Bermudez-Crespo, J.: Possibilities of two-dimensional gel electrophoresis
   in the understanding of human disease. Current Proteomics 4(4), 187–197 (2007)
6. Matuzevičius, D., Navakauskas, D.: Feature selection for segmentation of 2-D electrophoresis gel images. In: Proc. of the 11th Int. Biennial BEC, pp. 341–344 (2008)
7. Matuzevičius, D., Žurauskas, E., Navakauskienė, R., Navakauskas, D.: Improved
   proteomic characterization of human myocardium and heart conduction system by
   computational methods. Biologija 4(54), 283–289 (2008)
8. Penney, G.P., Weese, J., Little, J.A., Desmedt, P., Hill, D.L.G., Hawkes, D.J.: A
   Comparison of Similarity Measures for use in 2D-3D Medical Image Registration.
   IEEE Transactions on Medical Imaging 17(4), 586–595 (1998)
9. Rohr, K., Cathier, P., Worz, S.: Elastic Registration of Electrophoresis Images using
   Intensity Information and Point Landmarks. Pattern Recognition 5(37), 1035–1048
   (2004)
10. Serackis, A., Navakauskas, D.: Reconstruction of Overlapped Protein Spots Using
    RBF Networks. Electronics and Electrical Engineering 1(81), 83–88 (2008)
11. Serackis, A., Navakauskas, D.: Treatment of Over-Saturated Protein Spots in Two-
    Dimensional Electrophoresis Gel Images. Informatica 21(3), 307–322 (2010)
12. Shi, G., Jiang, T., Zhu, W., Liu, B., Zhao, H.: Alignment of Two-Dimensional Elec-
    trophoresis Gels. Biochemical and Biophysical Research Communications 2(357),
    427–432 (2007)
13. Veeser, S., Dunn, M.J., Yang, G.Z.: Multiresolution image registration for two-
    dimensional gel electrophoresis. Proteomics 1(7), 856–870 (2001)

Robust Workflow Recognition Using Holistic Features and Outlier-Tolerant Fused Hidden Markov Models

Athanasios Voulodimos[1], Helmut Grabner[2], Dimitrios Kosmopoulos[3],
Luc Van Gool[2,4], and Theodora Varvarigou[1]

[1] School of Electrical & Computer Engineering,
National Technical University of Athens, Greece
{thanos,dora}@telecom.ntua.gr
[2] Computer Vision Laboratory, ETH Zurich, Switzerland
{grabner,vangool}@vision.ee.ethz.ch
[3] Institute of Informatics and Telecommunications, N.C.S.R. Demokritos, Greece
dkosmo@iit.demokritos.gr
[4] ESAT-PSI/IBBT, K.U. Leuven, Belgium
luc.vangool@esat.kuleuven.be

Abstract. Monitoring real world environments such as industrial scenes is a challenging task due to heavy occlusions, resemblance of different processes, frequent illumination changes, etc. We propose a robust framework for recognizing workflows in such complex environments, boasting a threefold contribution: Firstly, we employ a novel holistic scene descriptor to efficiently and robustly model complex scenes, thus bypassing the very challenging tasks of target recognition and tracking. Secondly, we handle the problem of limited visibility and occlusions by exploiting redundancies through the use of merged information from multiple cameras. Finally, we use the multivariate Student-t distribution as the observation likelihood of the employed Hidden Markov Models, in order to further enhance robustness. We evaluate the performance of the examined approaches under real-life visual behavior understanding scenarios and we compare and discuss the obtained results.

Keywords: Robust workflow recognition, Hidden Markov Models, classifier grids, multi-camera fusion.

1 Introduction

Event understanding in video sequences is a research field rapidly gaining momentum over the last few years. This is mainly due to its fundamental applications in automated video indexing, virtual reality, human-computer interaction, assistive living and smart monitoring. Especially throughout the last years we have seen an increasing need for assisting and extending the capabilities of human operators in remotely monitored large and complex spaces such as public areas, airports, railway stations, parking lots, industrial plants, etc.

K. Diamantaras, W. Duch, L.S. Iliadis (Eds.): ICANN 2010, Part I, LNCS 6352, pp. 551–560, 2010.
© Springer-Verlag Berlin Heidelberg 2010

Task #1

Task #5

Occlusions,
abnormalities,
difficulties

Fig. 1. Sequences from the dataset. The relatively low resolution and the several occlusions and self occlusions make very difficult the task of tracking thus necessitating holistic features and a robust model to recognize workflows. The first two rows depict two different tasks that would be difficult to distinguish even for the human eye; the third row shows some example frames of occlusions, outliers, and other challenges faced in this industrial dataset.

Focusing on industrial scenes, the serious visibility problems, the heavy occlusions, along with the high diversity, complexity or sometimes resemblance of the behaviors and events taking place, make workflow recognition extremely challenging. In this paper the case study is an assembly line of an automobile manufacturer, where several different tasks are performed, and a sequence of specific tasks forms a workflow. The goal of recognizing these tasks (classes) and workflows is even more difficult to achieve when taking into consideration the high intraclass and low interclass variance, as shown in Fig. 1. Typical methods tend to fail in such environments, since they rely on object detection and tracking, which are rarely successful under such circumstances. To overcome the aforementioned problems, we propose a robust framework for workflow recognition that contributes to the solution in the three following ways:

- We propose new holistic features, which can be efficiently computed, do not rely on target detection and tracking and can be used to model complex scenes, thus resulting in robust input.
- In addition, we include redundant data by using multiple cameras in order to provide wider scene coverage, solve occlusions and improve accuracy. This is achieved by fusing time series of the above mentioned holistic image features, which is, according to our knowledge, a novel approach.
- Moreover, we scrutinize the effectiveness of the multivariate Student-t distribution, instead of the Gaussian, as the observation likelihood of the employed

Hidden Markov Models (HMMs), so as to solve the problem of outliers and further enhance the robustness of the model.

The rest of this work is organized as follows. In Sec. 2 we briefly survey the related work. Sec. 3,4 and 5 describe details of our approach, with respect to efficiency and robustness respectively. In Sec. 6 we verify our methods experimentally on a real-world dataset from an assembly line of an automobile industry. Finally, Sec. 7 concludes the paper.

2   Related Work

The field of behavior and workflow recognition has attracted the interest of many researchers. Holistic methods, which define features at the pixel level and try to identify patterns of activity using them directly, can bypass the challenging processes of detection and tracking. Such methods may use pixel or pixel group features such as color, texture or gradient, see e.g. [1] (histograms of spatiotemporal gradients), [2] (spatiotemporal patches). Of particular interest due to efficiency and representation of motion are approaches such as [3], which introduced Motion Energy Images (MEIs) and Motion History Images (MHIs), and [4], where Motion History Volumes are extracted from multiple cameras. Pixel Change History is used in [5] to represent each target separately after frame differencing. What is needed to model complex scenes is a representation that will be able to operate in any adverse condition effected by occlusions, illumination changes or abrupt motion.

As far as multiple cameras are concerned, to our knowledge no previous work has investigated fusion of holistic time series. The works on multicamera behavior recognition that have been reported so far try to solve the problem of position or posture extraction in 3D or on ground coordinates (e.g. [6,7]). However, camera calibration or homography estimation is required and in most cases there is still dependency on tracking or on extraction of foreground objects and their position, which can be easily corrupted by illumniation changes and occlusions.

Concerning the classification part, a very popular approach is HMMs ([8], [9], [10]) due to the fact that they can efficiently model stochastic time series at various time scales. Several fusion schemes using HMMs have been presented, which were typically used for fusing heterogeneous feature streams such as audio-visual systems, but can be applied to streams of holistic features from multiple cameras as well. Such examples are the early fusion, the synchronous HMMs [11], the parallel HMMs [12] and the multistream HMMs [13]. The reliability of each stream has been expressed by introducing stream-wise factors in the total likelihood estimation as in the case of parallel, synchronous or multistream HMMs.

3   Robust Scene Representation

Classifier grids were initially introduced to perform background modeling [14]. In this approach, an input image I_t is spatially (location and scale) sampled with a fixed highly overlapping grid. For each grid element i, an adaptive classifier C_i is created. These classifiers can now be used in a static camera setting in order to aggregate scene and location specific information. Classifier grids have been successfully used for pedestrian detection, e.g. [15]. Experiments show that very good detection results can be achieved compared with the sliding window technique, which uses a fixed pre-trained classifier which scans the whole image.

In our work, we propose to use the output of the classifier grid as scene descriptor. In other words, the local classifiers can be seen as features which extract "high level" information from each image. Hence, our proposed approach analyses time series, and afterwards all classifier responses are concatenated into one vector. These vectors observed over time t define finally the *grid time matrix*. The principle is depicted in Fig. 2.

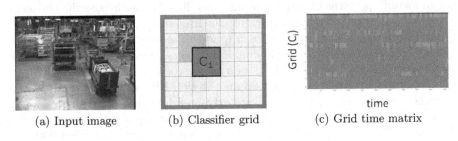

(a) Input image   (b) Classifier grid   (c) Grid time matrix

Fig. 2. Grid time matrix composition: An input image (a) is analyzed by a highly overlapping grid of classifiers (b). Classifier responses are concatenated over time and used as holistic image description.

4   Multi-view Learning

The goal of automatic behavior recognition may be viewed as the recovery of a specific learned behavior (class or visual task) from the sequence of observations O. Each camera frame is associated with one observation vector and the observations from all cameras have to be combined in a fusion framework to exploit complementarity of the different views. The sequence of observations from each camera composes a separate camera-specific information stream, which can be modelled by a camera-specific HMM.

The HMM framework entails a Markov chain comprising a number of N states, with each state being coupled with an observation emission distribution. An HMM defines a set of initial probabilities $\{\pi_k\}_{k=1}^{N}$ for each state, and a matrix A of transition probabilities between the states; each state is associated with a number of (emitted) observations O (input vectors). Gaussian mixture models are typically used for modeling the observation emission densities of the HMM hidden states. Given a learned HMM, probability assignment for an observation sequence is performed.

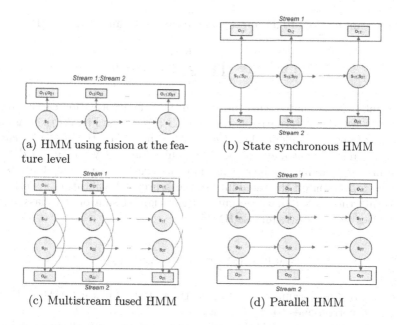

(a) HMM using fusion at the feature level

(b) State synchronous HMM

(c) Multistream fused HMM

(d) Parallel HMM

Fig. 3. Various fusion schemes using the HMM framework for two streams

In a multicamera setup each sensor stream can be used to generate a stream of observations. The ultimate goal of multicamera fusion is to achieve behavior recognition results better than the results that we could attain by using the information obtained by the individual data streams (stemming from different cameras) independently from each other. We will examine in the following some representative approaches, which can support scalable behavior recognition with several overlapping cameras.

Among existing approaches *Feature fusion* is the simplest; it assumes that the observation streams are synchronous. The related architecture is displayed in Fig. 3(a). For streams from C cameras and respective observations at time t given by $o_{1t}, ..., o_{Ct}$, the proposed scheme defines the full observation vector as a simple concatenation of the individual observations: $o_t = \{o_{ct}\}_{c=1}^{C}$. Then, the observation emission probability of the state $s_t = i$ of the fused model, when considered as a k-component mixture model, yields:

$$P(o_t|s_t = i) = \sum_{k=1}^{K} w_{ik} P(o_t|\theta_{ik}) \qquad (1)$$

where w_{ik} denotes the weights of the mixtures and θ_{ik} the parameters of the kth component density of the ith state.

In the *state-synchronous multistream HMM* (see Fig. 3(b)) the streams are assumed to be synchronized. Each stream is modelled using an individual HMM; the postulated streamwise HMMs share the same state dynamics. Then, the likelihood for one observation is given by the product of the observation likelihood of each stream c raised to an appropriate positive stream weight r_c [11]:

$$P(o_t|s_t = i) = \prod_{c=1..C} [\sum_{k=1}^{K} w_{ik}P(o_{ct}|\theta_{ik})]^{r_c} \qquad (2)$$

The weight r_c is associated with the reliability of the information carried by the cth stream. Another alternative is the *parallel HMM* (see Fig. 3(c)); it assumes that the streams are independent from each other. This HMM model can be applied to cameras that may not be synchronized and may operate at different acquisition rates. Similar to the synchronous case, each stream c may have its own weight r_c depending on the reliability of the source. Classification is performed by selecting the class $\hat{l}$ that maximizes the weighted sum of the classification probabilities from the streamwise HMMs:

$$\hat{l} = \underset{l}{\mathrm{argmax}}([\sum_{c=1}^{C} r_c log P(o_1...o_T|\lambda_{cl})]) \qquad (3)$$

where λ_{cl} are the parameters of the postulated streamwise HMM of the cth stream that corresponds to the lth class.

The *multistream fused HMM* is another promising method for modeling of multistream data [13] (see Fig. 3(d)) with several desirable features: (i) it is appropriate for both synchronous and asynchronous camera networks; (ii) it has simple and fast training and inference algorithms; (iii) if one of the component HMMs fails, the remaining HMMs can still work properly; and (iv) it retains the crucial information about the interdependencies between the multiple data streams Similar to the case of parallel HMMs, the class that maximizes the weighted sum of the log-likelihoods over the streamwise models is the winner.

5 Robustness to Outliers

Outliers are expected to appear in model training and test data sets obtained from realistic monitoring applications due to illumination changes, unexpected occlusions, unexpected task variations etc, and may seriously corrupt training results. Here we propose the integration of the Student-t distribution in our fusion models, in order to address the problem.

The probability density function (pdf) of a Student-t distribution with mean vector μ, positive definite inner product matrix Σ, and ν degrees of freedom is given by:

$$t(x_t; \mu, \Sigma, \nu) = \frac{\Gamma\left(\frac{\nu+p}{2}\right)|\Sigma|^{-\frac{1}{2}}(\pi\nu)^{-\frac{p}{2}}}{\Gamma\left(\frac{\nu}{2}\right)\{1 + d(x_t, \mu; \Sigma)/\nu\}^{\frac{\nu+p}{2}}} \qquad (4)$$

where $\Gamma(.)$ denotes the gamma function and d the Mahalanobis distance. The heavier tails of the Student-t distribution compared to the Gaussian ensure higher tolerance to outliers. The Gaussian distribution is actually a special case of the Student-t for $\nu \to \infty$. Recently, it has been shown that the adoption of the multivariate Student-t distribution in the observation models allows for the efficient handling of outliers in the context of the HMM framework without compromising overall efficiency [16]. Based on that we propose the following adaptations in the above fusion schemes: For the feature fusion, synchronous, parallel and multistream models we use the Student-t pdf as predictive function for the streamwise models. We use a modified EM training algorithm and solve numerically to obtain ν. For the interstream fusion model we employ a mixture of Student-t functions to increase robustness.

6   Experiments

We experimentally verified the applicability of the described methods. For this purpose, we have acquired very challenging videos from the production line of a major automobile manufacturer[1]. Two synchronized, partially overlapping views are used. Challenges include occlusions, similar colors of the individual people clothing and the background, and real-working conditions, such as shaking cameras and sparks.

Experimental setup. The production cycle on the production line included tasks of picking several parts from racks and placing them on a designated cell some meters away, where welding took place. Each of the above tasks was regarded as a class of behavioral patterns that had to be recognized. A specific sequence of those tasks constitutes a workflow. The information acquired from this procedure can be used for the extraction of production statistics or anomaly detection. The workspace configuration and the cameras' positioning is given in Fig. 4. The behaviors we are aiming to model in the examined application are briefly the following:

1. A worker picks part #1 from rack #1 and places it on the welding cell.
2. Two workers pick part #2a from rack #2 and place it on the welding cell.
3. Two workers pick part #2b from rack #3 and place it on the welding cell.
4. A worker picks parts #3a, #3b from rack #4 and places them on the cell.
5. A worker picks part #4 from rack #1 and places it on the welding cell.
6. Two workers pick part #5 from rack #5 and place it on the welding cell.
7. Welding: two workers grab the welding tools and weld the parts together.

For our experiments, we have used 20 segmented sequences representing full assembly cycles, each one containing each of the seven behaviors/tasks. The total number of frames was approximately 80,000. The videos were shot by two PTZ cameras at an approximate framerate of 25 fps and at a resolution of 704×576. The annotation of these frames has been done manually. For more dependable results, in our experiments we used cross-validation, by repeating the employed training algorithms several times, where in each repetition all scenarios are considered except for one used for testing (leave-one-out cross-validation).

---

[1] We are currently investigating legal issues of making the dataset publically available.

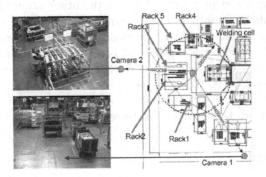

Fig. 4. Depiction of workcell along with the position of the cameras and racks #1-5

Representation and feature extraction. We created a classifier regular grid with overlap 0.5 (50%). Each frame was eventually represented by a 42-dimensional feature vector. For learning and adapting the classifiers we have used a simple motion based heuristic. Each local classifier learns a simple background model [17]. As classification function, the amount of moving pixels, i.e. the difference between the current image and the background model, is used. For each stream corresponding to a different viewpoint we have selected a region of interest, to which the classifier grids have been applied, as the activity taking place in the remaining area of the frame is noise.

Learning. We trained our models using the EM algorithm. We used the typical HMM model for the individual streams as well as feature fusion, synchronous, parallel and multistream HMMs. We experimented with the Gaussian observation model as well as with the multivariate Student-t model. We used three-state HMMs with a single mixture component per state to model each of the seven tasks described above, which is a good trade-off between performance and efficiency. For the mixture model representing the interstream interactions in the context of the multistream HMM we use mixture models of two component distributions.

Results. The obtained results of the experiments are shown in Fig. 5. It becomes obvious that the sequences of our features and the respective HMMs represent quite well the assembly process. Information fusion seems to provide significant added value when implemented in the form of the multistream fused HMM, and about similar accuracy when using parallel HMMs. However, the accuracy deteriorates significantly when using simple feature level fusion or state-synchronous HMMs, reflecting the known restrictions of these approaches.

The confusion matrices in Fig. 6 show the percentage of successful and unsuccessful task recognitions averaged across all classes (tasks). A look at the matrices would justify the complementarity between the two camera streams due to the different viewpoints. Camera 1 performs well for task number 2 and 7

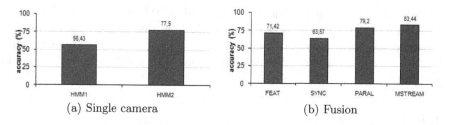

(a) Single camera   (b) Fusion

Fig. 5. Success rates obtained using Student-t distribution and (i) individual HMM for camera 1 (HMM1); (ii) individual HMM for camera 2 (HMM2); (iii) feature-level fusion (FEAT); (iii) state-synchronous HMMs (SYNC); (iv) parallel HMMs (PARAL) and (v) multistream fused HMMs (MSTREAM)

(a) Camera 1 (HMM1)

Recognized As

Is	1	2	3	4	5	6	7
1	0.10	0	0.10	0.30	0.30	0.05	0.15
2	0	0.85	0.10	0.05	0	0	0
3	0	0	0.80	0.05	0.05	0.10	0
4	0.05	0	0.10	0.80	0.05	0	0
5	0	0	0.05	0.60	0.15	0.05	0.15
6	0.05	0	0.50	0.20	0.15	0.05	0.05
7	0	0	0	0	0	0	1.00

(b) Camera 2 (HMM2)

Recognized As

Is	1	2	3	4	5	6	7
1	0.95	0	0	0	0.05	0	0
2	0.45	0.05	0	0	0.45	0	0.05
3	0	0	1.00	0	0	0	0
4	0.05	0	0	0.95	0	0	0
5	0.20	0	0	0	0.75	0.05	0
6	0	0	0	0.05	0	0.95	0
7	0.90	0	0	0.05	0	0	0.05

(c) Multistream fusion

Recognized As

Is	1	2	3	4	5	6	7
1	0.80	0	0	0	0.10	0	0.10
2	0.10	0.75	0	0	0.10	0	0.05
3	0	0	0.90	0	0.05	0.05	0
4	0.05	0	0.05	0.85	0	0.05	0
5	0.05	0	0.05	0.20	0.60	0	0.10
6	0	0	0.05	0.05	0	0.85	0.05
7	0.05	0	0	0	0	0	0.95

Fig. 6. Confusion matrices for individual tasks

while camera 2 performs better for the rest. For example, camera 1's viewpoint is such, that discerning task 1 from task 5 is extremely difficult - even for a human - hence the low success rates in these particular tasks; on the contrary, camera 2's viewpoint is much better for viewing tasks 1 and 5 and therefore allows for a significantly higher performance, which can be confirmed by noticing the confusion matrices. This complementarity of the two streams results in the improvement of the accuracy by the streams' fusion when the latter is implemented as a multistream fused HMM. Finally, the employment of the Student-t distribution as observation likelihood of the employed HMM provides additional improvement from 81.43% (Gaussian) to 83.44% (Student-t) in recognition rates.

7   Conclusion

It has been shown that a fused holistic scene representation, which uses a grid time matrix, is very well suited for monitoring and classifying well structured processes such as the production tasks in an assembly line. Using the proposed holistic features to bypass the challenging tasks of detection and tracking, which are usually unsuccessful in such environments, leads to a rather satisfactory representation. Furthermore, exploiting redundancies by fusing time series from multiple cameras using the multistream fused HMMs results in higher recognition rates than those achieved when employing one single camera. Finally, employing an outlier-tolerant observation model based on the Student-t multivariate distribution instead of the Gaussian further enhances accuracy and robustness.

References

1. Zelnik-Manor, L.: Statistical analysis of dynamic actions. IEEE Trans. Pattern Anal. Mach. Intell. 28(9), 1530–1535 (2006)
2. Laptev, I., Pe'rez, P.: Retrieving actions in movies. In: Proc. Int. Conf. Comp. Vis. (ICCV 2007), Rio de Janeiro, Brazil, pp. 1–8 (October 2007)
3. Bobick, A.F., Davis, J.W.: The recognition of human movement using temporal templates. IEEE Trans. Pattern Anal. Mach. Intell. 23(3), 257–267 (2001)
4. Weinland, D., Ronfard, R., Boyer, E.: Free viewpoint action recognition using motion history volumes. Comput. Vis. Image Underst. 104(2), 249–257 (2006)
5. Xiang, T., Gong, S.: Beyond tracking: modelling activity and understanding behaviour. International Journal of Computer Vision 67, 21–51 (2006)
6. Antonakaki, P., Kosmopoulos, D., Perantonis, S.: Detecting abnormal human behaviour using multiple cameras. Signal Processing 89(9), 1723–1738 (2009)
7. Lao, W., Han, J., de With, P.H.N.: Automatic video-based human motion analyzer for consumer surveillance system. IEEE Trans. on Consumer Electronics 55(2), 591–598 (2009)
8. Bregler, C., Malik, J.: Learning appearance based models: Mixtures of second moment experts. In: Mozer, M.C., Jordan, M.I., Petsche, T. (eds.) Advances in Neural Information Processing Systems, vol. 9, p. 845. The MIT Press, Cambridge (1997)
9. Ivanov, Y.A., Bobick, A.F.: Recognition of visual activities and interactions by stochastic parsing. IEEE Trans. Pattern Anal. Mach. Intell. 22(8), 852–872 (2000)
10. Bashir, F.I., Qu, W., Khokhar, A.A., Schonfeld, D.: Hmm-based motion recognition system using segmented pca. In: ICIP, vol. 3, pp. 1288–1291 (2005)
11. Dupont, S., Luettin, J.: Audio-visual speech modeling for continuous speech recognition. IEEE Transactions on Multimedia 2(3), 141–151 (2000)
12. Vogler, C., Metaxas, D.: Parallel hidden markov models for american sign language recognition, pp. 116–122 (1999)
13. Zeng, Z., Tu, J., Pianfetti, B., Huang, T.: Audiovisual affective expression recognition through multistream fused hmm. IEEE Trans. Mult. 10(4), 570–577 (2008)
14. Grabner, H., Bischof, H.: On-line boosting and vision. In: Proc. CVPR, vol. 1, pp. 260–267 (2006)
15. Stalder, S., Grabner, H., van Gool, L.: Exploring context to learn scene specific object detectors. In: Proc. PETS (2009)
16. Chatzis, S., Kosmopoulos, D., Varvarigou, T.: Robust sequential data modeling using an outlier tolerant hidden markov model. IEEE Transactions on Pattern Analysis and Machine Intelligence 31(9), 1657–1669 (2009)
17. Stauffer, C., Grimson, W.: Adaptive background mixture models for real-time tracking. In: Proc. CVPR, vol. 2, pp. 246–252 (1999)

A Neural Approach to Image Thresholding

Ahmed A. Othman* and Hamid R. Tizhoosh**

a4abdelr@uwaterloo.ca
tizhoosh@uwaterloo.ca

Abstract. Image thresholding (as the simplest form of segmentation) is a very challenging task because of the differences in the characteristics of different images such that different thresholds may be tried to obtain maximum segmentation accuracy. In this paper, a supervised neural network is used to "dynamically" threshold images by assigning a suitable threshold to each image. The network is trained using a set of simple features extracted from medical images randomly selected form a sample set and then tested using the remaining medical images. The results are compared with the Otsu algorithm and the active shape models (ASM) approach.

1 Introduction

Image thresholding can be viewed as the simplest technique for image segmentation since it separates an object from its background (bivalent pixel classification). However, because of the differences in the properties of the images, by using any thresholding algorithm we may achieve accurate segmentation for some images and low accuracy for others. Therefore, the threshold may always need to be altered in order to receive higher segmentation accuracies. A "dynamic" approach is more flexible in adjusting the threshold for each image. In this paper, a neural network is used to segment images by assigning a different threshold to different images according to the inherent features.

There exist a vast number of methods to threshold gray-level images [1]. The Otsu method uses the image histogram to assign a threshold to the image [2]. It divides the image into two different classes of gray levels and assigns a threshold to the image where the variance of these two level is minimal. It is difficult to provide an in-depth review of all neural approaches to image segmentation. Suchendra et al. [3] discuss the advantages of a hierarchical self-organizing neural network for image segmentation over the traditional (single-layer) self-organizing feature neural network. Mohamed N. Ahmed et al. [4] present a two-stage neural network for volume segmentation of medical images. Other neural approaches can be found in[5–8]. In other group of segmentation techniques, Cootes et al. [9] proposed a new statistical technique termed active shape models (ASM), which iteratively adapt to refine estimates of the pose, scale and shape of models of image objects. They propose a method to generate a model of shape and appearance of 2D images objects.

---

* Ahmed A. Othman is a PhD candidate at the Department of Systems Design Engineering, University of Waterloo, Ontario, Canada
** Hamid R. Tizhoosh is a faculty member at the Department of Systems Design Engineering, University of Waterloo, Ontario, Canada

K. Diamantaras, W. Duch, L.S. Iliadis (Eds.): ICANN 2010, Part I, LNCS 6352, pp. 561–564, 2010.
© Springer-Verlag Berlin Heidelberg 2010

2   Proposed Approach

The proposed algorithm uses a trained neural network to segment the images directly by generating the threshold; the neural network estimates the suitable threshold based on the image characteristics. This technique starts with extracting features from a set of randomly selected images with known optimal thresholds (e.g. through trial-and-error manual segmentation, or via brute force). These optimal thresholds which are used to train the neural network are generated by adjusting the Otsu threshold (the Otsu method delivers the initial guess and then the proposed approach finds the best threshold by trying the neighboring values). The proposed technique uses the test images along with their optimal thresholds to train a backpropagation neural network. After being trained, the neural network is used to segment a set of new images. The average accuracies are calculated for each segmented image by comparing it with its gold standard image generated via applying the optimal threshold.

Feature Extraction – The proposed technique starts with extracting a set of features from every image and uses these features to assign best thresholds to different images. We use several sub-images constructed around multiple points in every image as different seeds such that every sample image can be used multiple times. In order to obtain an initial seed point we can ask an expert user to click inside the region of interest, here the algorithm starts to operate internally and divide the image from this point into four sub-images and the features of these four sub-images are calculated. The algorithm continues and randomly selects n points (e.g. $n = 20$ points for each image) within the region of interest and for every point the process is repeated as the image is divided into four sub-images and the features for each sub image are calculated. The valid points inside the region of interest are known during the training since gold standard images are available. As we have multiple seed points inside every image, every point divides the image in four sub-images if we draw a vertical and a horizontal line going through that point. So, for every image we will have $4n$ sub-images (e.g. 80 for $n = 20$). Moreover, for each sub-image, the optimal threshold is calculated in order to be used for supervised learning. We use simple features that can be calculated fast: 1) the mean gray level μ_{S_i} for each sub-image S_i. The average gray level of a sub-image is indication of its darkness/brightness, 2) the standard deviation σ_{S_i} for each sub-image S_i. The intensity variation captured by the standard deviation quantifies our confidence in darkness/brightness of the sub-image, 3) the distance $d_{S_i} = \max_i S_i - \min_i S_i$ between the maximum and the minimum of each sub-image. This distance provides additional information to distinguish between different variation levels captured by standard deviation. For $n = 20$, 4 sub-images (created for each seed point) and $F = 3$ features, we will have $n \times F \times 4 = 240$ features from every image.

Training the neural network – A feed-forward backpropagation neural network is used to learn the set of sample images. The network consists of one input layer with nodes as many as we have seed points and one hidden layer with 40 nodes and the output layer with one output (=the estimated threshold). For every training set, five different sample images are randomly selected from a larger database to train the neural network. The optimal thresholds for these five images are assigned as the target of the neural network. The network is trained using Matlab *trainrp* function with desired error set to 0.00001 to be achieved within maximum 50000 epochs.

Testing the neural network – In this step any new image is processed by a detection algorithm which calculates the position of the first seed point inside the region of interest. This point is calculated by tracing a 10×10 mask over the image and calculating the sum and the standard deviation of every mask and the correlation between the mask and its neighbors. For our images, the region of interest has the lowest graylevel and so it always has the minmum standard deviation and the minimum sum. Moreover, to be sure that the minimum sum and the minimum standard deviation are indeed from inside the region of interest, the correlation coefficients between each 10×10 mask and its preceding mask and its following mask are calculated. The algorithm takes this point and divides the image into four sub-images and calculates the features for every sub-image. We test 1) $\mathrm{NN_{AVER}}$: Taking the average of thresholds $T_1, \cdots, T_4$ assigned by the neural network to each sub-image: $T^* = \frac{1}{4} \sum_i T_i$, and 2) $\mathrm{NN_{INTER}}$: Interpolating the thresholds $T_1, \cdots, T_4$ assigned by the neural network to each sub-image: $\mathbf{T}^* : \mathbf{T}_{2 \times 2} \to \mathbf{T}_{M \times N}$ (from 4 thresholds we generate a threshold for each pixel in an $M \times N$ image).

3   Experiments and Results

A set of 20 medical images are used to train and test the proposed technique. We randomly select five of the images as a training set and the remaining 15 images are used for testing. This process is repeated 4 times to generate different training sets and investigate the generalization ability of the network. The purpose of this experiment is to compare the results from the proposed technique with average thresholds ($\mathrm{NN_{AVER}}$) and interpolating thresholds ($\mathrm{NN_{INTER}}$) with the results by Otsu segmentation technique and active shape models (ASM) via accuracy calculation using the gold standard images to verify the improvement (Figure 1). The following metrics have been employed: 1) the average segmentation accuracy J is calculated using the area overlap (also called Jaccard Index): $J(A, B) = \frac{|A \cap B|}{|A \cup B|}$ where A is the binary image and B is the gold standard image, 2) the standard deviation σ of the average of accuracy, and 3) the confidence interval (CI) of J. The Table 1 summarizes the results of the four training sets.

Fig. 1. Sample result (from left to right): original image, Otsu, ASM, $\mathrm{NN_{AVER}}$, $\mathrm{NN_{INTER}}$, and the gold standard image

Table 1 shows a summary of the results of the four training sets. Generally, it is obvious that the proposed algorithm in both approaches has the highest average segmentation accuracy, the lowest standard deviation and the shortest confidence intervals over the Otsu and ASM algorithms, which means that the proposed system has more

Table 1. Summary of the results for the Jaccard Index J, σ and 95%-confidence interval CI of J

Method	First Training set			Second Training set			Third Training Set			Fourth Training Set		
	J	CI	σ	J	CI	σ	J	CI	σ	J	CI	σ
Otsu	73%	63%-83%	18%	73%	63%-83%	18%	75%	64%-85%	19%	72%	59%-84%	22%
ASM	75%	68%-83%	13%	74%	67%-82%	13%	75%	67%-82%	13%	76%	69%-82%	12%
NN$_{INTER}$	83%	77%-88%	9%	83%	78%-88%	8%	83%	79%-90%	9%	81%	78%-88%	14%
NN$_{AVER}$	82%	75%-88%	12%	80%	74%-86%	10%	84%	77%-89%	10%	82%	75%-88%	11%

accurate and more consistent results. For example, in the first training set, the average accuracy of the proposed system using average threshold raised from 73% (Otsu) and 75% ASM to 82% and to 83% with interpolation. Moreover, the confidence interval of the proposed system using average thresholds is pushed higher from 63%–83% (Otsu) and 68%–83% (ASM) to 75%–88% and to 77%–88% using interpolation of the thresholds which means that the proposed system is more consistent.

4   Conclusions

Intelligent segmentation by training a neural network to generate the threshold for unseen images seems to be a viable alternative. This process extracts features from each image by dividing it into several sub images. The extracted features are then used to train a feed-forward backpropagation neural network along with their optimal thresholds as target values of the network. The neural network could provide a threshold for new images resulting in higher accuracies compared to another intelligent technique (ASM) and a "static" technique such as Otsu method.

References

1. Sezgin, B.S.: Survey over image thresholding techniques and quantitative performance evaluation. J. Electronic Imaging 13, 146–165 (2004)
2. Otsu.: A threshold selection method from gray-level histograms. IEEE Trans., 62–66 (1979)
3. Bhandarkar, S.M., Koh, J., Suk, M.: A hierarchical neural network and its application to image segmentation. In: IMACS, pp. 337–355 (1996)
4. Ahmed, A.F.: Two-stage neural network for volume segmentation of medical images. PRL 18, 1143–1151 (1997)
5. Chang, P.C.: medical image segmentation using a contextual-constraint-based Hopfield neural cube. Image and Vision Computing 19, 669–678 (2001)
6. Kurugollu, F., Sankur, B., Harmanci, A.E.: Image segmentation by relaxation using constraint satisfaction neural network. Image and Vision Computing 20, 483–497 (2002)
7. Nuneza, J.L.: Astronomical image segmentation by self-organizing neural networks and wavelets. N.Ns. 16, 411–417 (2003)
8. Kurnaz, M.N., Dokur, Z., Ölmez, T.: An incremental neural network for tissue segmentation in ultrasound images. CMPB 85, 187–195 (2007)
9. Cootes, Hill, A., Taylor, C.J., Haslam, J.: The use of active shape models for locating structure in medical images. Image and Vision Computing 12, 355–366 (1994)

Bubbles Detection on Sea Surface Images

Carlos M. Travieso, Miguel A. Ferrer, and Jesús B. Alonso

Signals and Communications Department,
Institute for Technological Development and Innovation in Communications
University of Las Palmas de Gran Canaria, Spain
Campus de Tafira, Edificio de Telecomunicación, E-35017 Las Palmas de Gran Canaria
{ctravieso,mferrer,jalonso}@dsc.ulpgc.es
http://www.gpds.ulpgc.es

Abstract. In this work a novel system for sea surface images pre-processing and processing has been developed in order to detect bubbles on the sea surface. This application is fundamental to verify radiometer satellite systems which are used to the study of the floor humidity and the sea salinity. 160 images of 8 kinds of salinity have been processed, 20 per class. Two main steps have been implemented; the first step is the image pre-processing and enhancing, in order to improve the bubbles detection. The second step is the segmentation and the bubbles detection. A combination system has been used in order to improve the final result, getting a recognition rate of 95.43%.

Keywords: Bubble Detection, Image Processing, Pattern Recognition.

1 Introduction

The weather and nature disaster prediction depends on the availability of global and periodicity information from humidity and sea salinity on their superficial layers. Therefore, in 1999, European Space Agency (ESA) approved the SMOS mission (Soil Moisture and Ocean Salinity), whose objectives were the study of the floor humidity and the sea salinity on the oceanic surface, doing use of the radiometer in the L-band [1][2]. The goal was to improve the emissivity models of the sea surface, including the effects of the rain and the surf which had not been considerate before [3]. Therefore, the goal of this present work is to isolate the sea surf of the images and the bubbles of the surface layer, applying image processing techniques and image analysis, in order to find the kind of salinity from bubbles and surf patterns.

2 Database Used

The studied salinities were 0 psu, 5 psu, 10 psu, 15 psu, 20 psu, 25 psu, 30 psu and 34 psu, where psu stands for "practical salinity unit". These images were recorded with a video-camera, multisession and with different videos for session. From video were extracted frames each 3 seconds, storing each image on gray-scale, with 8 bits and a resolution of 640x480 pixels with 160 images, 20 per class. This quality is chosen in order to have initial resolution for the bubbles detection.

K. Diamantaras, W. Duch, L.S. Iliadis (Eds.): ICANN 2010, Part I, LNCS 6352, pp. 565–568, 2010.
© Springer-Verlag Berlin Heidelberg 2010

3 Image Pre-processing

The first step of the final proposed system is to detect the different layers of the sea-images and the bubbles shape detection, but it is a hard and strong task due to low contrast and the similarity between classes. Therefore, it is required an image pre-processing in order to increase the contrast, in particular, between the different layers and the variability in the same layer.

The borders appear enhanced because it has been found the subtraction between an image with smooth borders (filtering image) and another image with strong borders. If the difference found between both images is mayor or minor, the enhancement will be mayor or minor in order to increase the dynamic range of the interesting zone. The applied function responses to (2) [5]:

$$g(x, y) = k_1 \frac{M}{\sigma(x, y)} [f(x, y) - m(x, y)] + k_2 m(x, y) \tag{1}$$

where, $k_1 \cdot \dfrac{M}{\sigma(x, y)}$ is the gain factor used to enhance the image contrast, and $k_2.m(x,y)$

is a factor to restore the medium intensity image level ($m(i,j)$ and $\sigma(i,j)$ are the average and standard deviation intensity levels of a centered window in the pixel (x,y)).

This image pre-processing has modified the contrast and the dynamic range and does easier the following tasks, because we will work in spatial domain for the features extraction.

4 Image Pre-processing

In this section, the segmentation of the different layers and the bubbles detection are implemented thanks to the choice of the best empirically threshold in each step.

Method 1. It was applied eight convolution masks, one per each angle, 0°, 45°, 90°, 135°, 180°, 225°, 270° and 315°, on the enhanced image. The enhanced image contains much information in its different layers, but the present work only needs the surf layer. Besides, many pixels have been detected as edges, but they are not. In order to solve those problems, this work only uses the surf layer, and it is fixed a certain threshold, whose value is chosen empirically from the gray levels of each image, in order to eliminate the mayor quantity of false edges. Only those pixels whose level of intensity surpasses the threshold value will be considerate as edge.

Sometimes, the edges of diverse bubbles appear united formed a unique object. It is applied mathematical morphology, in order to separate them. Fig. 5 shows the edges from the both methods and its logic combination.

Method 2. This method treats to find the edge based on the different gray levels which belong to the bubbles and the gray levels of the rest of pixels of the surf layer. The surf layer is divided in diverse regions applying the segmentation with multilevel threshold, and finally, the image is binarized, getting the bubbles edges.

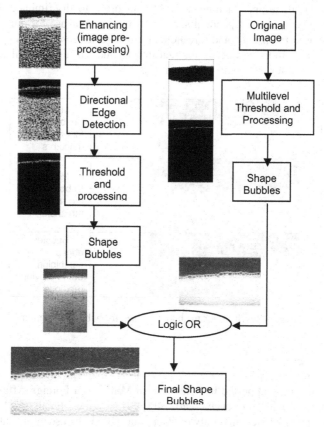

Fig. 1. Schedule of segmentation and bubbles detection

Combination system: evaluation. In order to justify the use of both methods in the process of bubbles detection, it is shown an example, seeing the detection of both methods, and after logic combination, the detection of the most bubbles. The method 1 does not detect certain bubbles of small size. On the other hand, method 2 detects some bubbles with more precision, different bubbles from bubbles detection of method 1. Combining both methods is achieved a better approximation.

Once the main process in this work (pre-processing and segmentation image) has been done, to finalize, it has been used a Support Vector Machine (SVM) [6] to verify how the proposed method works, in supervised classification and using features from bubbles edges and other parameters. Each experiment has been done 5 times. The recognition rate is $95.43 \pm 0.3\%$, using 50% of our database for training process.

This experiment is the indicator of a good result of the proposed method, that it is the most important issue in this work.

5 Conclusions

In this present work has been shown the automated image pre-processing and processing for the bubbles detection. The measure of quality has been implemented with supervised classification, reaching a 95.43% in order to discriminate the different kinds of salinity; using independent samples from our database for our experimental setting. The use of constants and thresholds is a particular case for this application, in the next future; authors will check the real images and will use general expression or automatic method for calculating those values.

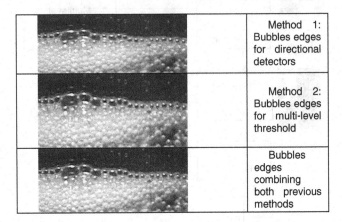

Fig. 2. Result of our method proposed for bubbles detection.

Acknowledgment

This work has been supported by The Spanish Ministry of Foreign Affairs under the research project with reference "D/027406/09". Authors thank to Prof. Adriano Camps from Polytechnic University of Catalonia (UPC), the use of his database.

References

1. Camps, Vall-llosera, M., Villarin, R., Reul, N., Chapron, B., Corbella, I., Duffo, N., Torres, F., Miranda, J.J., Sabia, R., Monerris, A., Rodríguez, R.: The Emissivity of Foam-Covered Water Surface at L-Band: Theorical Modeling and Experimental Results From the Frog 2003 Field Experiment. IEEE Transactions on Geoscience and Remote Sensing 43(5), 925–937 (2005)
2. Villarino, R., Camps, A., Vall-llosera, M., Miranda, J., Arenas, J.: Sea Foam Effects on the Brightness Temperature at L-Band. In: International Geoscience and Remote Sensing Symposium IGARSS 2003, pp. 3076–3078 (July 2003)
3. Villarino, R.M.: Empirical Determination of the Sea Surface Emissivity at L-Band: A contribution to ESA's SMOS Earth Explorer Mission, PhD Document, Polytechnic University of Catalonia, Spain (June 2004)
4. Gonzalez, R.C., Wood, R.E.: Digital Image Processing. Addison-Wesley, Reading (2002)
5. Sonka, M., Hlavac, V., Boyle, R.: Image Processing, Analysis and Machine Vision. Thomson Engineering (2007)
6. Steinwart, I., Christmann, A.: Support Vector Machines. Springer, New York (2008)

No-Reference Video Quality Assessment Design Framework Based on Modular Neural Networks

Dragan D. Kukolj, Maja Pokrić, Vladimir M. Zlokolica,
Jovana Filipović, and Miodrag Temerinac

Faculty of Technical Sciences, University of Novi Sad, Trg Dositeja Obradovića 6,
21000 Novi Sad, Serbia
{Dragan.Kukolj,Maja.Pokric,Vladimir.Zlokolica,
Jovana.Filipovic,Miodrag.Temerinac}@rt-rk.com

Abstract. This paper presents a novel no-reference video quality assessment (VQA) model which is based on non-linear statistical modeling. In devised non-linear VQA model, an ensemble of neural networks is introduced, where each neural network is allocated to the specific group of video content and features based on artifacts. The algorithm is specifically trained to enable adaptability to video content by taking into account the visual perception and the most representative set of objective measures. The model verification and the performance testing is done on various MPEG-2 video coded sequences in SD format at different bit-rates taking into account different artifacts. The results demonstrate performance improvements in comparison to the state-of-the-art non-reference video quality assessment in terms of the statistical measures.

Keywords: Video quality assessment, modular neural networks, data clustering.

1 Introduction

In recent years there has been an increased development of media networks for various applications, the video being one of the most important and demanding media. Since the perceived quality of the video for the end-user is an important issue, a necessity has arisen for constant video quality monitoring in different applications, such as mobile telephony, internet and TV broadcast. Digital video signal is compressed prior its transmission to the end-user in order to reduce the bandwidth requirements. Depending on the network bandwidth and the end-user application, different video formats at different resolution, are compressed at different bit rates. Depending on the compression rate and the content characteristics, the artifacts are more or less noticeable, and may significantly influence the viewer subjective impression of the video quality. In this paper we consider the following video artifacts related to broadcasting coded video signals: (i) blocking, (ii) blurring, (iii) ringing, and (iv) motion related.

In recent past, a number of algorithms were proposed for the estimation of coded video artifacts (some of them given in references [1]-[5]). In order to develop a true video quality assessment model a set of objective measures for defined type of

K. Diamantaras, W. Duch, L.S. Iliadis (Eds.): ICANN 2010, Part I, LNCS 6352, pp. 569–574, 2010.
© Springer-Verlag Berlin Heidelberg 2010

artifacts and video content have to be combined and validated with the results of visual perception tests (i.e. subjective assessment). Subjective video quality assessment includes a panel of people estimating the visual quality of displayed video using the values on a predefined scale. In proposed scheme, the score is obtained from the tests performed according to ITU-R BT.500-10 recommendations using Double-Stimulus Impairment Scale (DSIS) method in which random pairs of original and impaired sequences are presented to the viewer [6]. The mean opinion score (MOS) is then obtained by averaging all scores.

In this paper we present a practical way to devise a single visual perception-based video quality assessment model through use of neural networks [7], [8]. The model derivation is based on a statistical evaluation of a set of considered objective measures in conjunction with the subjective video quality assessment which incorporates modular neural network (MNN) scheme with video content based artifact clustering.

2 VQA Framework Description

In the proposed video quality assessment model two main stages can be distinguished: (i) VQA model design phase and (ii) VQA exploitation phase. The VQA model design model phase relates to the construction of the VQA model based on training on test video sequences and their corresponding subjective quality assessments. This is essentially enabled by a "learning-system" capability of the proposed modular neural network scheme. The exploitation VQA phase, on the other hand, is intended for a real-time processing of video streams, not know a priori.

The general block-scheme of the proposed framework for the video quality assessment system design phase is shown in Fig. 1.

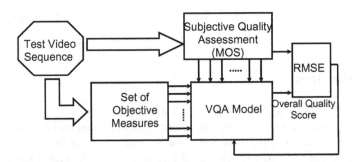

Fig. 1. General block scheme of the VQA training model

As shown in Fig. 1 the idea is to derive a non-linear VQA model based on the training test video sequences objective and subjective descriptors. The derived model represents the least difference between the desired MOS and determined combination of selected objective measures (estimated MOS). The proposed VQA model is trained until the difference between the overall quality score (OQS) and MOS is minimized.

The model design phase can be roughly divided into three sequential stages in the following order (see Fig. 2): (i) feature selection, (ii) feature based clustering and (iii) VQA model training based on modular neural network (MNN) scheme.

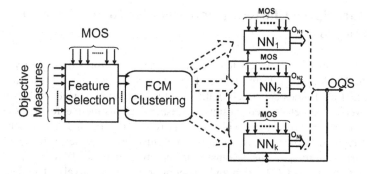

Fig. 2. Detailed scheme of the VQA design phase

From Fig. 2 it can be seen that firstly the objective quality measures are combined with subjective quality measures (MOS) in order to reduce the set of objective measures. The feature space reduction is performed by unsupervised clustering algorithm. The resulting data clusters contain the data samples which are the most similar but at the same time sufficiently different from data belonging to different clusters. The main principle of the no-reference VQA model derivation is based on a model training phase using a modular structure of non-linear MOS estimators. In the past complex problem decomposition into a number of sub-tasks such as modules and ensembles had been addressed [9]. In VQA framework, the modular NN (MNN) scheme is adopted comprising a number of modules each being represented by a multilayer perceptron NN. In addition, to increase accuracy and robustness the "bias-variance decomposition" principle is incorporated in the MNN modeling [10].

VQA exploitation phase is effectively VQA implementation stage at which a video quality is estimated automatically, in a real-time, without the necessity for subjective quality assessment. In this phase, clustering is not necessary and only the level of a cluster membership is determined based on the distance of a data sample from the corresponding cluster centers. The estimated MOS (i.e. video quality score) is computed as a weighted averaging of outputs of individual NN.

3   The Selection of the Objective Quality Measures

In the proposed framework we have included 29 objective measures (some given in [1]-[5]) that mainly describe video artifacts present in the video sequences coded according to MPEG-2 standard. The input feature space at the starting stage contains 29 features (measures) with various degrees of the contribution to the overall video quality. The selection is performed by taking the five most representative features with the highest correlation to the MOS. The selection of the dominant features is based on feature vector statistical analysis and its correspondence to the MOS, through the implementation of NN prediction models using forward selection approach and a RMSE as ranking criteria of the selection process. In the feature selection scheme, we have chosen the non-linear model for mapping the objective measures to MOS in the form of multilayer perceptrons (MLPs) NNs [11].

4   Feature Space Clustering and Modular Neural Network Framework

The selected set of five video features is further used for video quality modeling within the VQA system design phase. The features are computed for all training se-quences and all frames separately with feature data samples grouped in appropriate data clusters. The determined clusters correspond to distinctive feature space areas reflecting different artifact-free video content (e.g. temporal and spatial activity) and different types of video coding artifacts. The clustering is done in the selected five-dimensional feature space using clustering methods such as: (i) K-means (KM) and (ii) fuzzy C-means (FCM), crisp and fuzzy approach respectively. The data clusters are utilized for definition of the MNN scheme, whereby each NN is assigned to the particular data cluster (see Fig. 2).

5   Algorithm Verification and Experimental Results

In our experiments we have used a set of 9 sequences in SD format available from the Video Quality Experts Group (http://www.its.bldrdoc.gov/vqeg/). The MPEG-2 com-pression scheme was used and degradation introduced at five different levels at fol-lowing bit rates: 0.5, 1, 2, 3, and 4 Mbps. The sequences were used for the VQA train-ing and testing applying cross-validation procedure for model verification.

The forward selection approach used for the feature selection has found the follow-ing five most relevant features: blocking occurrence [5], global motion detection [1], zero-crossing rate [3], blocking [3] and HVS variance [2]. For the evaluation of the proposed MNN based VQA algorithm, we have used the video sequences which were not used for the algorithm design procedure, within the cross-validation test scheme. Namely, this scenario assumes that all samples from the test sequence (used for the evaluation) are completely excluded from the MNN training (VQA design phase) and represents completely unknown video sequence.

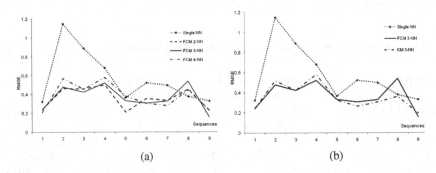

(a)   (b)

Fig. 3. (a) Cross-validation accuracy of MOS estimation on 9 SD sequences with FCM based MNN structures (b) Cross-validation accuracy of MOS estimation on nine SD sequences with FCM selected MNN structure with 3 NNs and k-means selected MNN structure with 3 NNs

For the MNN structure combined with the clustering, we have evaluated MNN structures based on FCM clustering with two, three and four NN, and additional case with the single NN. From the evaluation tests for these 4 examined configurations with 5 inputs with selected features, the following results were obtained in terms of the averaged RMSE across all 9 SD sequences: (i) single NN: 0.57, (ii) the MNN with two NN: 0.37, (iii) MNN with three NN: 0.36, (iv) MNN with four NN: 0.384 (see Fig. 3a). Fig. 3a shows a significant increase of the estimated MOS accuracy (in respect to "true" MOS) in case of FCM based MNN configuration with 2 and 3 NN in comparison to the single NN scheme. Apart from the sequence 8, for which the estimated MOS using the single NN configuration is better, for all other cases the MNN structure is obviously superior, as expected. The results do not show significant influence of the number of NNs variation on the estimated MOS accuracy, which renders additional analysis. The Fig. 3b illustrates the cross-validation accuracy of the estimated MOS, which shows that the performance between the KM clustering and the FCM clustering approach is very small (in terms of the average RMSE 0.357 and 0.359 for the (i) and (ii), respectively) with the FCM performing slightly better, hence being incorporated into the VQA framework.

The results of nine-fold cross-validated MOS estimation of the proposed MNN structure of VQA framework are shown in Fig. 4, along with the single NN solution, Wang *et al.* VQA algorithm of [4] and the "true" MOS.

The number of hidden neurons in the all NNs neural networks was set to 12. The results shown represent the estimated MOS for 9 sequences with 5 degradation levels, giving thus in total 9 x 5 = 45 points. Each point on the plot represents the median of the quality estimates across all evaluated frames for the corresponding sequence. As can be seen from the figure, both the single NN and MNN approach achieve better performance results than Z-score of Wang *et al.* [4], where (for a fair comparison) the parameters of the Z-score were tuned and adopted to all the SD sequence frames.

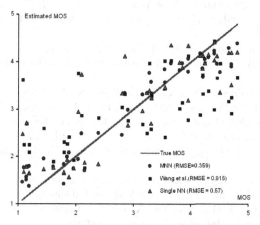

Fig. 4. Estimated MOS vs true MOS

Additionally, in terms of the average RMSE (ARMSE), the Z-score [4] has shown to be of significantly lower accuracy (ARMSE=0.915) then both NN based approaches, the MNN and the single NN, with ARMSEs 0.359 and 0.57, respectively.

Moreover, by comparing the single NN and the MNN VQA frameworks it is apparent that the accuracy of the estimated MOS using MNN is higher for each analyzed sequence.

6 Conclusions

In the proposed VQA framework, we have introduced a novel scheme for selecting the most relevant video features out of a larger feature set, which are further used for the design of the content-driven MNN structure scheme. The proposed MNN structure, within the VQA model, is based on the selected features space clustering which enables training of separate models related to the corresponding video content and the MOS. The proposed VQA framework for video coding applications which includes five selected features, three clusters and MNN structure with three NN, has been found to be superior in terms of RMSE to the compared VQA method of [3] and the VQA framework with the single NN.

References

1. Wolf, S., Pinson, M.: Video Quality Measurement Techniques. In NTIA Report 02-392 (2002)
2. Babu, R.V., Perkis, A.: An HVS-based no-reference Perceptual Quality Assessment of JPEG Coded Images Using Neural Networks. In: IEEE Int. Conference on Image Processing, vol. 1, pp. 433–436 (2005)
3. Wang, Z., Sheikh, H.R., Bovik, A.C.: No-reference Perceptual Quality Assessment of JPEG Compressed Images. In: IEEE International Conference on Image Processing, vol. 1, pp. 477–480 (2002)
4. Gillespie, W., Nguyen, T.: Classification of Video Sequences in MPEG Domain. In: Signal Processing for Telecomm. and Multimedia, ch. 6, vol. 27, pp. 71–86 (2005)
5. Quicker, U.N: PQM Block Artifact Detection Method. MICRONAS Intership Report (2008)
6. ITU-R Recommendation BT.500-11: Methodology for the Subjective Assessment of the Quality of Television Pictures. In: International Telecommunication Union, Geneva, Switzerland (2002)
7. Pokric, M., Kukolj, D., Pap, I., Lukic, N., Teslic, N., Temerinac, M., Marceta, Z., Zlokolica, V.: Video Quality Assessment on CELL. In: 4th International Workshop on Video Processing and Quality Metrics for Consumer Electronics, Scottsdale, USA (2009)
8. Zlokolica, V., Kukolj, D., Pokric, M., Lukic, N., Temerinac, M.: Content-Oriented Based No-Reference Video Quality Assessment for Broadcast. NEM Summit, Saint-Malo, France (2009)
9. Dietterich, T.G.: Ensemble Methods in Machine Learning. In: Kittler, J., Roli, F. (eds.) MCS 2000. LNCS, vol. 1857, pp. 1–15. Springer, Heidelberg (2000)
10. Brown, G., Wyatt, J., Harris, R., Yao, X.: Diversity Creation Methods: A Survey and Categorization. Journal of Information Fusion 6(1) (2005)
11. Haykin, S.: Neural Networks: A Comprehensive Foundation. Macmillan, NY (1994)

Removing an Object from Video Sequence Algorithm Implemented on Analog CNN and DSP Microprocessors

Emel Arslan[1] and Sabri Arik[2]

[1] Istanbul University Research and Application Center for Computer Sciences,
Istanbul, Turkey
[2] Istanbul University Department of Computer Engineering,
Istanbul, Turkey
{earslan,ariks}@istanbul.edu.tr

Abstract. CNN Universal Machine which contains Digital Signal Processor (DSP) in addition to ACE16k which is the hardware verification of Cellular Neural Networks are used increasingly in image processing applications with their advanced computational features. In this study, an removing an object from video sequence algorithm on a Bi-i Cellular Vision System which is a CNN Universal Machine was applied and the running times of both processors were evaluated.

Keywords: Image processing, Cellular Neural Networks, Digital Signal Processor, ACE16k, Bi-i Cellular Vision System, CNN Universal Machine.

1 Introduction

The Cellular Neural Network (CNN) theory suggested in 1988 is an analog, non-linear neural network model performing real-time operations [1]. CNNs have advanced features for image processing. Therefore, CNN Universal Machine the architecture of which consists of Analogical Cellular Engines (ACE4k, ACE16k etc.) which tare the hardware realization of the CNN are very suitable for image processing applications with their advanced computational features [2]-[3]. The Bi-i Cellular Vision System which is a CNN Universal Machine can be defined as a compact, standalone and intelligent camera capable of real time operations at very high speed. The B-i Cellular Vision System has high resolution sensors and two inter-communicating processors, namely a CNN processor (ACE16k) and a Digital Signal Processor (DSP) [4].

The processing of moving images attract increasingly more attention and the fields of application of processing of moving images expand further every day. In this study, we will discuss the Removing an Object from Video Sequence Algorithm (ROVSA). This algorithm has been applied by using the both the analog processing feature (ACE16k) and digital processing feature (DSP) of Bi-i Cellular Vision System, and the results have been compared.

K. Diamantaras, W. Duch, L.S. Iliadis (Eds.): ICANN 2010, Part I, LNCS 6352, pp. 575–580, 2010.
© Springer-Verlag Berlin Heidelberg 2010

2 CNN Architecture and Bi-i Cellular Vision System

2.1 Architecture and of the Cellular Neural Networks

Each cell of a 4x4 CNN is represented by a square and shown in Figure 1.

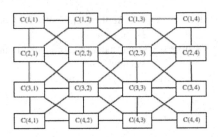

Fig. 1. A 4x4 cell two-dimensional CNN

In this CNN architecture, each cell is linked only to its neighbors.

Let us assume a CNN with MxN cells arranged in M rows and N columns, the cell in row i column j is shown as $C(i,j)$[1]. r-neighborhood of a $C(i,j)$cell is defined as follows provided that r is a positive value:

$$N_r(i,j) = \left\{ C(k,l) \left| \max_{1 \le k \le M, 1 \le l \le N} \{ |k-i|, |l-j| \} \le r \right. \right\} \tag{1}$$

2.2 CNN Universal Machine

The hardware verification of CNN is easier compared to the Artifical Neural Networks as there is only connection between the neighbor cells and the cell structure. Analogical Cellular Engines (ACE4k, ACE16k etc. [5]) are based on CNN Universal Machine architecture. CNN Universal Machine architecture has been called by Roska and Chua as analogical computation since it can perform analog array operations and logical operations together [2].

2.3 ACE16k Processor

ACE16k, is a CNN based processor of CNN Universal Machine which can perform analog operations. ACE16k which is used to perform various image processing operations contain low resolution (128 x 128) CMOS gray level image sensor and analog processor arrays. This processor array is much faster (30000 frames per second) than the conventional processors in image processing applications since it can processes the whole image in parallel.

2.4 Bi-i Cellular Vision System

The Bi-i Cellular Vision System which contains two different processors, a CNN based ACE16k and a DSP that can be defined as a compact, standalone and intelligent camera capable of real time operations at very high speed [4]. The images are stored in local memories with the help of two different sensors as a (1280x1024) color CMOS sensor, and a (128x128) ACE16K sensor.

2.5 Bi-i Programming

CNN Universal Machine has two different programming methods. One of them is AMC (Analogical Macro Code) language which is a conventional Bi-i programming method. The codes written in AMC language are converted to binary basis and run on Bi-i. Another method is the Bi-i (Software Development Kit - SDK) which is used to develop more complex applications. Bi-i SDK, consists of the C++ programming library which is a group used to develop applications. These libraries can also used for the Digital Signal Processor (DSP) with the development unit Code Composer Studio and they contain many functions to control the whole ACE16k circuit [6].

3 Removing an Object from Video Sequence Algorithm

An algorithm determining certain objects and their features in moving images by using Bi-i Cellular Vision System and removing the objects with pre-defined characteristics from the moving image has been developed. The block diagram of this algorithm is shown in Figure 2.

When applying this algorithm, first, the features of the object desired to be deleted from the moving image is entered into the system. Then, a frame is loaded to the system as input from the moving image to be processes to identify the objects contained and their features. The features of an object obtained is compared to the features of the object introduced to the system. The matching objects are extracted from that frame. When this operation is applied to all frames of the moving image, a new moving image not containing the specified object is obtained as the output.

As it can be seen in Figure 2, currently processed frame first passes through a Low Pass Filter to eliminate the noise and a gray level mage is obtained [7]. Then, this gray level image is subject to a thresholding operation by using ConvLAMtoLLM function on ACE16k, and a binary image is obtained an intermediary value. The binary image obtained is subjected to set of morphological operations for better identification of the objects contained.

In this algorithm, we created a Negation function that negates binary objects and used Opening8, HoleFiller, Dilate8 functions in Instant Vision Signal and Image Processing Library. Opening8 function was applied to eliminate the small objects which are considered as noise in the moving image. HoleFiller function was used to fill the holes on the objects in order to identify them better, and finally, a dilation was applied with Dilate8 function [8].

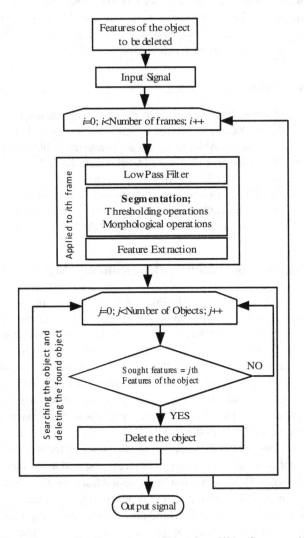

Fig. 2. Block diagram of an Removing an Object from Video Sequence Algorithm

Following the morphological operations, the Feature Extraction processed in Instant Vision Signal and Image Processing Library were applied to find the number and features of the objects in the binary moving image. Feature Extraction converts the visual information of a binary image into numeric values. It is based on indexing the array of connected in the image and then identifying some features of each (area, boundary values, extremes, orientation, center etc.) [6].

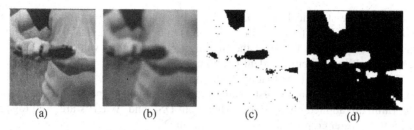

(a)   (b)   (c)   (d)

Fig. 3. (a) Original image (b) Image filtered through a low pass filter (c) Unmatched image (d) Image after morphological processing

In this study, some features as Bounding Box, Extremes, Eccentricity, Diameter, Orientation, Extent and Center are used to identify an object [6].

After the algorithm identifies features of the object in the frame, a set of functions, first, compare the object whose features have been identified to the features of the object. When there is a match, it executes the related function to delete the object from the frame taking into consideration the color features of the sought object.

After each frame of the moving image is processed according to that algorithm, a moving object in which the specified object does not exist is obtained as the output.

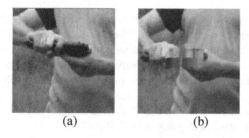

(a)   (b)

Fig. 4. (a) Original Moving Image (b) Output Moving Image

4   Experimental Results

Functions coded again in C++ were used to identify the distribution of the features used in the application referred to in section 3, and some statistical information was obtained, such as the maximum, minimum and average values of such features. Some of the statistical values obtained as a result of these functions are presented in Table 1.

Table 1. Statistics of certain features of the object

Feature	Min.	Max.	Average
Area	229	1546	733.93
Eccentricity	0.50	0.99	0.96
Diameter	17.08	44.37	30.31
Orientation	0.01	179.99	92.88
Extent	0.32	0.87	0.66
Center x value	17.42	108.23	60.98
Center y value	12.58	76.70	48.36

All of these statistical information have been computed by processing the whole moving image (1394 frames). Since the object does not have exactly the same shape and position in every frame of the moving image, average values were used to describe the object to facilitate identification.

Table 2 shows the time that application runs on DSP only and with both DSP and ACE16k. Although only thresholding and morphological operations portions of the algorithm are applied on ACE16k, when both DSP and ACE16k are used together, it is 25491μs faster compared to running only on DSP.

Table 2. Running times of the algorithm

Operation	DSP	DSP+ACE16k
Segmentation	41285 μs	15794 μs (ACE16k)
Feature Extraction	519107μs	519107 μs (DSP)
Find and delete the object	59826 μs	59826 μs (DSP)
TOTAL	620218 μs	594727 μs

5 Conclusion

In this study, the removing an object from video sequence algorithm developed by using Cellular Vision System was used. The segmentation step of algorithm consisting of thresholding and morphological operations was performed on ACE16k while all other steps such as identifying the features of the object, finding the object and extracting it from the image was executed on DSP, and as a result a moving object in which the specified object does not exist was obtained.

The results presented that when the algorithm is executed by using both DSP and ACE16k, it is much faster than using only DSP.

References

1. Chua, L.O., Yang, L.: Cellular neural networks: Theory and applications. IEEE Trans. on CAS 35(10), 1257–1290 (1988)
2. Roska, T., Chua, L.O.: The CNN universal machine: an analogic array computer. IEEE Trans. on CAS-I 40(3), 163–173 (1993)
3. Roska, T., Rodriguez-Vazquez, A.: Towards visual microprocessors. Proceedings of the IEEE 90(7), 1244–1257 (2002)
4. Zarandy, A., Rekeczky, C.: Bi-i: a standalone ultra high speed cellular vision system. IEEE Circuit and Systems Magazine 5(2), 36–45 (2005)
5. Vazquez, A.R., Cembrano, G.L., Carranza, L., Moreno, E.R., Galan, R.C., Garrido, F.J., Castro, R.D., Meana, S.E.: ACE16k: the third generation of mixed-signal SIMDCNN ACE chips toward VSoCs. IEEE Trans. CAS-I 51(5), 85–863 (2004)
6. http://www.analogic-computers.com/Support
7. Acharya, T., Ray, A.K.: Image Processing: Principles and Applications. Wiley and Sons, Chichester (2005)
8. Gonzales, C., Woods, R.E.: Digital Image Processing. Prentice Hall, New Jersey (2002)

Author Index